CW01024417

Cultural Expression in the Old Kingdom Elite Tomb

Sasha Verma

Archaeopress Egyptology 1

Archaeopress
Gordon House
276 Banbury Road
Oxford OX2 7ED

www.archaeopress.com

ISBN 978 1 905739 78 3

Printed in England by CMP (UK) Ltd

This book is available direct from Archaeopress or from our website www.archaeopress.com

Dedicated to my Grandmother Bhagwati Debi

"The day will come that he must pass through the wall of oblivion and he wants to leave a scratch on the wall – Kilroy was here – that someone a hundred or a thousand years later will see"

W. Faulkner

Contents

Acknowledgements

This work is the revised version of my doctoral dissertation for the Department of Egyptology at Leiden University. During the course of my research I was fortunate to have as my mentors a great number of scholars, and I am much indebted to them for their time, interest, and encouragement in the ongoing research in my topic. I wish to acknowledge my debt of gratitude to all of them specifically to Professor Loprieno and Dr. A. Gnirs (University of Basle) who were instrumental in getting me to get an appreciation of the ancient Egyptian language.

To my co-supervisor Dr. René van Walsem I owe a debt of gratitude for his constant and unflagging support. I particularly thank him for enduring numerous hours of discussions and for the ensuing guidance plus inspiration, which encompassed every stage of this book's development. He was instrumental in opening up my mind to a whole new way of looking at funerary culture.

I would also like to thank my supervisor Professor Olaf Kaper for his insightful and constructive comments during the final stages of the dissertation. A thank you also to my "neighbor "Professor Bourghouts (we shared the same space at the Netherlands Institute of Near Eastern Studies), who was a source I could always turn to when I became lost in the finesses of the Egyptian language and religion: challenging discussions from which I profited greatly.

I was also fortunate to have been able to spend time at New York University at the Institute of Fine Arts, and I thank Professor Ann Macy Roth for this. Thank you to Professor Ron Leprohon (University of Toronto) too for granting me the space and resources to put the finishing touches to the final phase of this book's production.

Special thanks go to John Walker for his cooperation and friendship for having taken time from his own busy schedule to read the entire manuscript before publication, and the many hours he spent on the phone discussing contentious points. Thanks also to Amanda Wagner of Toronto University's Technical Section for final help in solving formatting difficulties.

Last but not least I would like to thank my wife Elsbeth for her patience and understanding: without her support it would not have been possible to undertake and complete this book.

Abbreviations

AA	American Anthropologist
ÄA	Ägyptologische Abhandungen
ANOC	Abydos North Offering Chapel
AnzÖAW	Anzeiger der Österreichischen Akademie der Wissenschaften in Wien
ASAE	Annales du Service des Antiquités d'Egypte, Cairo
AV	Archäologische Veröffentlichung, Deutsches Archäologische Institut
BACE	The Bulletin of the Australian Centre for Egyptology
BAR	British Archaeological Reports
BMA	The Brooklyn Museum Annual, Brooklyn
BSEG	Bulletin de la Société d'Egyptologie de Genève
CA	Current Anthropology
DE	Discussions in Egyptology
EA	Egyptian Archaeology
GM	Göttinger Miszellen: Beiträge zur Ägyptologischen Diskussion, Göttingen
BIFAO	Bulletin de l'Institut francais d'archéologie orientale, Cairo
JANES	Journal of the Ancient Near East Society of Columbia University, New York
JAOS	Journal of the American Oriental Society
JAR	Journal of Archaeological Research
JARCE	Journal of the American Research Centre in Egypt
JEA	Journal of Egyptian Archaeology, London
JESHO	Journal of the Economic and Social History of the Orient
JFA	Journal of Field Archaeology
JMFA	Journal of the Museum of Fine Arts, Boston
JNES	Journal of Near Eastern Studies, Chicago
JSA	Journal of Social Archaeology
LA	Lingua Aegyptica
LÄ	Lexikon der Ägyptologie
LP	Linguistics and Philosophy
MÄS	Münchner Ägyptologische Studien
MDAIK	Mitteilung des Deutschen Archäologischen Instituts Abteilung Kairo, Mainz
MIO	Mitteilung des Instituts für Orientforschung, Berlin
MMA	The Metropolitan Museum of Art, Dept. of Egyptian Art, New York
MMJ	Metropolitan Museum Journal, New York
NAR	Norwegian Archaeological Review
OEAE	Oxford Encyclopedia of Ancient Egypt
PB	Psychological Bulletin
PM	Porter and Moss, Oxford
PDS	Psychology and Developing Societies
RAIN	Royal Anthropological Institute Newsletter
RdE	Revue d'Ègyptologie, Paris and Cairo
SAK	Studien zur Altägyptischen Kultur, Hamburg
SAOC	Studies in Ancient Oriental Civilizations, Chicago
SÖAW	Sitzungsberichte der Akademie der Wissenschaften in Wien
WA	World Archaeology
WZKM	Wiener Zeitschrift für die Kunde des Morgenlandes, Wien
ZÄS	Zeitschrift für ägyptische Sprache und Altertumskunde, Leipzig and Berlin

Explanation of Signs

[ ]   Damaged text partly restored

…   Indicates the omission of non-essential material

( )   Non-original text added as an explanatory addition to translations

(?)   Uncertain rendering of words/phrases

< >   Material enclosed was omitted by error from original text

Chapter 1: Introductory Remarks

Scholars have given different meaning to the motifs found in the Old Kingdom elite tombs. Addressing this problem means finding a common thread that runs right through all these tombs, a task not made easy by the numerous extant interpretations.

This common thread if it is to apply universally, will also have to be an aspect, which is a raison d'être of these tombs, i.e. a funerary culture based in the preservation of memory. The purpose of the following study is to determine the extent to which identity, individuality, ideology, memory, and change, are aspects of elite funerary culture, and are reflected in the iconography of Dynasties 4, 5 and 6 elite tombs, especially in relation to context, content, and culture and their intrinsic tendency for change. These are termed the 'cultural generics' (generics for short) and will be shown to be the main aspects of funerary art. The search for these generics involves going back in time, such that the connection between the manifestation of culture and the underlying funerary beliefs, symbols, and society, is established as a starting position.

Ancient Egyptian Funerary Culture as expressed in Tomb Design and Tomb Decoration

This is a book about the material and immaterial culture left behind by the ancient Egyptian elite in their tombs starting some 5000 years ago. The book intends to understand this culture reflecting the "intention" of the ancient Egyptians. All these "intentions" are now inaccessible to us, a paradox indeed. A start to solving this paradox is to consider how other Egyptologists have understood tomb culture over the past century. Two main clusters of thought dominate the history of this topic, the literal and/or the symbolic meaning:

Literal: This is based on what is directly seen and is a popular approach for the modern world. One looks at the ancient monuments, hieroglyphs, tomb decoration and any available texts in terms of our own modern conceptions. This amounts to a closed rigid system of analysis based on the obvious and the logical, and does not even refer to observed changes in the iconography.

Symbolic: The symbolic meaning of the funerary culture encompasses the ancient Egyptians' ideas about (1) the meaning of life in this and the next world and (2) metaphysical perfection. Here one tries to conjecture from concepts (e.g. 'known' religious ideas) to derive the symbolic meaning behind a particular motif, ancient monument, text, etc., and this has its own peculiar difficulties, chief of them being the accusation of a subjective bias.

Of course one can argue for a third mid-way course somewhere between the literal and the symbolic meaning; i.e. an attempt to study the evidence in its reality and to search for common, universal factors which may be present and which may aid understanding. This approach has been used. Many Egyptologists oscillate between the literal and the symbolic, attempting what is an either/or approach, simultaneously ignoring the inherent contrasting complexity underpinning any general principles, which may be there.

Some background information and examination is necessary before the general principles can be derived, which may form the central basis for any understanding of the iconography of funerary culture. The start involved asking: How to explain the state of interrelatedness of cultural elements based on a CONSISTENT pattern of values, which are evident in tombs?

One is immediately faced with the problem that there was no such thing as a 'consistent pattern of values', that these values are always and forever in a state of flux. Indeed no two tombs have exactly the same iconography. This fact, although questioned many times, has never been adequately explained. The question then becomes:

1. How to explain the state of interrelatedness of cultural elements based on a DIFFERING pattern of values, which appear to be consistent?
2. How to explain the state of interrelatedness of cultural elements based on a differing pattern of values that are changing?

In order to do so, one has to visualize all the elements that could conceivably form part of a funerary culture. In the funerary cultural context of tomb decoration and construction, one has to think in terms of totalities and then to typify these into relevant sub-categories. The following scheme is proposed where the eight totalities involved are:

1. The human elements as the patron.
2. The necropolis as a sacred landmark having ideological meaning.
3. The gravesite as a particular entity.
4. The location of the materials to be used.
5. The actual materials used.
6. Quarrying methods.
7. The method of transport to the gravesite.
8. The inanimate totality of the value systems behind the construction and decoration as expressed in the entire tomb (decoration plus texts).

Categorization of each of these above totalities in the context of tomb building/decoration gives the following sub-categories:

- Human: King, officials (priests, scribes), craftsmen, and the others.
- Necropolis: Giza, Saqqara, Abusir, Dashur, etc.
- Gravesite: Pyramid, mastaba, and tombs, which are rock-cut.
- Material location: Upper and Lower Egypt, the Eastern and Western desert, and outside Egypt, e.g. colonized parts of Nubia.
- Materials used: Sand, gravel, timber, unbaked brick and various types of stone.
- Quarrying: Depended on type - for soft stone like limestone, mainly open cut methods; for hard stone, mainly pounding in open trenches, were used.
- Transport methods: Humans (i.e. 'others'), donkeys, oxen plus sledges, and boats.
- Value Systems: Belief in gods, magic, *M3't*'s efficacy, and the king's supremacy, collaboration, and kinship.

From the various tombs and texts of the Old Kingdom, it becomes clear that the stimulus for all or some of the above-mentioned activities, could include a range of possibilities, depending on the control aspirations of those in power, artistic/scribal capabilities, and access to raw materials/tools, age and status of the 'tomb owner', etc.

Tomb construction could take a number of years and it is assumed to have started at an early stage of the official's career. The successful completion of such a large project over this long period obviously required extensive co-ordination between the participants, and the integration of value systems. When an order for the construction and decoration of a tomb is given, this will then of necessity, include a chain of decisions on the entirety of the eight totalities and their constituent sub-categories interacting at different levels. This could be something along the following lines:

When one contracts to build/decorate a tomb, one sets in motion a whole social process which influences the outcome, as values (economic/social) are added stage by stage through the social and economic network. Borrowing from economics, this accretion of values will result in increasing efficiency (if the number of mastabas and royal pyramids in the Old Kingdom are any guide) and increasing returns for all participants (if the increasing levels of hierarchy as evidenced in the titles are a guide) - the so-called multiplier and recycling effect.

These effects arise regardless of the resources used (whether goods, precious commodities, or information -such as accrued knowledge), and consequently stimulate further cultural development. Of course in this context, the time-scale between stimulus and development can vary from years to centuries.

We have extremely limited knowledge of the actual type of interaction between the eight totalities and their sub-categories. However this is not a limiting factor because the significant issue is that once a certain stimulus produces a certain response, which is accepted as worthy, it becomes a learnt experience. To build the perfect pyramid, the angle of inclination, etc. had to be exact, otherwise it was not a pyramid; for the tomb owner to become a 'venerated' one, definite rituals had to be performed, and so on. This development is now accepted as following normal evolutionary principles; stressing the accumulation of only those rules, traits, etc. which have been a proven success based on a sort of learning by experience. This is called adaptive change because it depends on the accumulation and building up of successful past patterns (contrast this with natural change, e.g. biological decay and death, which is the outcome of entropy). The advantage of this type of adaptive change is that one does not have to have it hardwired into oneself; by combining relevant tested rules to any new situation, one can take appropriate action, without any other direction. In due course these patterns of behaviour will then build up to strengthen those attributes/traits/ideas, which can be and are critical for cultural progress but remain subject to subtle change.

Consider the following evolutionary changes which are evidence of the above processes and seen in both royal and elite tombs:

Royal burials:

Dynasties 1 and 2	Pit tombs →Tombs accessed by staircase → Mastaba
Dynasty 3	Step pyramid
Dynasty 4 to MK	Perfect geometric pyramids (Very few exceptions)
NK	Deep rock cut tombs
TIP and Late Period	Burial within temple enclosures

Elite burials:

In a parallel development, beginning in Dynasty 4, the use of stone is extended to the construction of elite tombs, partly grouped into cemeteries around the pharaoh's pyramid, as in the Giza necropolis. These structures also known as mastabas, continue to be used by the elite down to the Middle Kingdom, along with the rock cut tombs all along the Nile valley, the rock cut tombs of Aswan and those at Thebes during the New Kingdom.

Concurrent with the above progress, there are other developments including:

- Emerging State as a central entity.
- Organizational functions/abilities of the bureaucrats' religious/funerary/official roles.
- Craftsmen's abilities (e.g. working of various materials) and their efficient co-operation.

These developments also result in the crucial underpinning of the funerary culture in the form of memory, both private and collective.

- We can therefore propose that central to the development of any society and its culture is the fact that this is always the accumulated contribution of individuals over time, and that such development incorporates memory.

Humans may muddle through the present but their hopes and fears about their future existence, is quite a different proposition. It is especially so, when the whole belief system (as is the case with ancient Egypt) is built on an endless life in the hereafter, of which there is no actual information[1] for the non-royals of the Old Kingdom. Therefore the most important problem concerns the future: how to get around the fact of natural death. The way the ancient Egyptians did this would largely depend upon their expectations, strategies, and interrelationships of the individuals and the cultural value system. This is where identity, individuality, and ideology start to play a role. Because we are dealing with individual non-linear behaviour, obviously there is no certainty of prediction. Indeed as more interactions take place, the transformations among the participants, the goods, and the services will become increasingly complex. Complexity will result in behavioural differences needing explanation. One explanation is to describe the changed behaviour as individualistic and the fact of change as subject to the concepts of entropy and related complexity.

This enables one to be aware of the range of possibilities and consequences of behaviour at a given time and place, applicable in both the living and the funerary context.

An outline was envisaged of all (animate and inanimate) components in funerary culture and an analysis of their interdependencies, etc., and this identified four components that are 'Generic' general principles i.e. Identity, Individuality, Ideology, and Memory; and the process of human behavior that lead to: Change and Cultural Transmission.

This analysis will involve additional thought patterns and academic disciplines, than previously employed by most Egyptologists, who tended to pay lip service to:

- The idea of constant change.
- The need for a selective weighting of observed changes.
- Identifying the agents involved as precursors of various possibilities.
- Recognizing the agents' involved as subject to complexity, change, and evolving newer forms

rather than as merely describable and discrete elements.

Firstly it is accepted that Egyptologists generally have to deal with an enormous expanse of time. Correlating all aspects of change pertaining to a topic then becomes a sheer impossibility, especially in view of the differing amounts of evidence that are available over the different periods. Secondly issues dealing with society as they occur and change over time, is complex and if we have to wait for all aspects to be finalized before publication, very few new ideas would be born, but this does not mean that new ideas should not be put forward based on the available evidence. An extremely good example of this approach is Antonio Loprieno's groundbreaking study on reinterpreting what is sacred in Egyptian culture.[2]

A cursory glance at the vast amount of material culture left behind will make the above comments obvious. There must have been involved a vast number of interactions among the population. This must of necessity have included the transfer of matter, energy, and information, which in turn would have caused the ancient Egyptian to anticipate and refine the consequences of their actions.

The resultant trend would be towards increasing sophistication and functionality, indeed towards more complexity. Accordingly a concept of permanent equilibrium and stability is far off the mark, and has never existed in Egyptian society and culture (although this appears to be so) nor for that matter can ever exist in any institution, whose essence is its ability to adapt to learnt changes. The model "GRM" below shows possible influences on and interactions within generics.[3]

The model's applicability is universal, and there is not a single branch of the hard or so-called soft sciences, in which it cannot provide useful analogies.[4] Physics and behavioural sciences are well founded but mainstream Egyptologists do not greet interdisciplinary approaches warmly, although they may be aware of the limitations of continuing with their old methods.

Generics Reactions Model ('GRM')

Before applying it to Egyptology a brief recapitulation of the ideas behind each circle in the GRM is necessary.[5]

---

[1] From the MK non-royals wrote the Coffin Texts on the interiors of wooden coffins in use. Another funerary composition of the MK was the Book of Two Ways, which depicted a map of the hereafter, accompanied by a vignette. However, during the NK the best known and most widely used is the Book of the Dead, which is richly illustrated with vignettes. Further developments are seen in the later compositions, which portray the image of the hereafter as a subterranean world, and a nocturnal solar journey.

[2] Loprieno, *La Pensée et L'Écriture, Pour une Analyse Sémiotique de la Culture Égyptiene*, 13-50.
[3] The scheme was inspired by and adapted from Holland, *Hidden Order: How Adaptation Builds Complexity* and Kiel, *Chaos Theory in the Social Sciences*. Also see the application of these ideas by Lehner, "Fractal House of Pharaoh: Ancient Egypt as a Complex Adaptive System, a Trial Formulation", in *Dynamics in Human and Primate Societies*, Eds. T. A. Kohler and G. J. Gumerman, 275-353.
[4] Byers, *The Blind Spot: Science and the Crisis of Uncertainty*, 69-90. He gives examples of the ambiguity in the various sciences.
[5] I have postponed a full discussion of entropy, chaos, and complexity till later so as not to overcomplicate a subject, which needs to be discussed separately. For full details see pages 27-32.

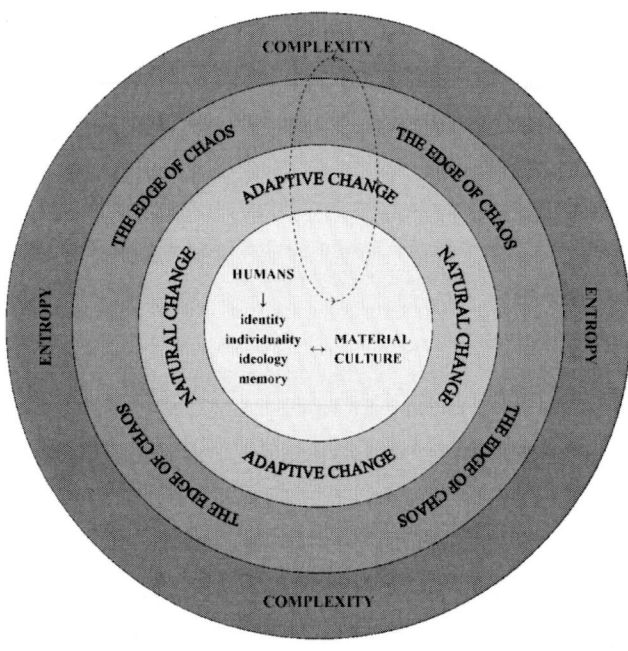

GENERICS REACTIONS MODEL ('GRM')

The starting point in any process, which results in a transition from one phase to another, is the circle titled **'The Edge of Chaos'**. This is the part where things/ideas exist in a transitional phase. This apparent instability is not a drawback, because they (things/ideas) are stable enough to receive and store information yet temporary unstable enough to transmit it. Thus they have the ability to perform complex computations, which may transform things/ideas from being in a transitional phase into higher levels of organization, assuming the right conditions. "Everything is connected, and often with incredible sensitivity".[6] The way information gets into the things/ideas is by the process of repeated learning and application of useful rules through evolutionary processes (Complexity). Entropy on the other hand ensures change, in that the unavoidable dissipation of energy will help to destroy the things/ideas partly. Therefore the way to ensure stability is by the constant input of relevant energy. These processes are encountered in the extreme outer circle titled **'Complexity/Entropy'**.

At the same time the learning process will give rise to Adaptive Change such that worthy rules are strengthened to even more worthy ones, which tend to be more differentiated (complex) than the previous ones, thus conferring on the system the ability to respond to challenges.

Natural Change refers to things/ideas which phase out because they have not been validated enough by the learnt rules, as well as the absence of new energy. The circle titled **'Adaptive/Natural Change'** refers to these processes.

The innermost circle titled **'Humans/Material'** includes the generics, and play a crucial part in the transmission of patterns of traits, which lead to cultural transmission. Cultural transmission is a process by which information (values, knowledge, and practices in the form of cultural traits) is acquired and passed on from individual to individual irrespective of any family relationship.[7] Being cultural, this must be acquired by way of social learning (i.e. learning through interaction with other individuals and not self-learning). This contrasts with the biological transmission of genetic material, which is from parent to offspring only. It is precisely this cultural information, which in ancient Egypt provided the standards for action and ruled their everyday lives.

For our purposes one can propose a scheme as follows:

- The unit of cultural transmission can be termed a cultural trait.
- The social aspects of transmission between individuals can represent the actual pathway it takes, directly or indirectly.
- The area of influence of these cultural traits can be determined by the relevant location(s) and time/period(s) under investigation.

Cultural transmission can take place through many channels and can include oral or written instruction, material artifacts, as well as imitation and emulation. In general there are three forms of persistent cultural transmission: vertical, horizontal, and oblique via parents, one's peers, and social institutions.[8] In addition transmission can also happen from outside one's own culture and, can be the result of less intended activities.

(Note: the constituents of the innermost circle are not fixed and can be adapted to fit any of the other sciences).

Let us now apply these concepts and processes to the building/decoration of a tomb in ancient Egypt:

1. The mere idea to build or decorate a tomb exists in the first place in the mind of the 'tomb owner' (his Intentions). Since these have not yet materialized, they are in a transitional form and thus present in the circle titled 'the Edge of Chaos'.
2. The 'tomb owner' and craftsmen benefit from the information flow contained in the circle 'Complexity and Entropy' which ensures that the tomb is built in more or less keeping with previously exploited rules and belief systems. The information flow would also point to the amount of energy input required in terms of resources and manpower to build a particular type of tomb.
3. The above-mentioned transitional ideas would be further subject to any adaptation constraints which might crop up in terms of location, materials,

---

[6] Waldrop, *Complexity: The Emerging Science at the Edge of Order and Chaos,* 66.

[7] Boyd and Richerson, *Culture and the Evolutionary Process,* 2- 4.
[8] Schönpflug, "*Introduction to Cultural Transmission*", 1-8.

decorative elements, value systems, and so on. These processes, which consist of validating and recognizing tested and new rules, would be augmented by previously learnt rules. This would ensure production according to general principles, which have widespread use both in practical terms and conceptuality and result in creative transformations. These come under the circle titled 'Adaptive/Natural Change'.

4. The effect of all of the above ongoing processes on and in the 'tomb owner' would result in a particular way of showing his 'Identity', and 'Individuality',

5. which would have to be in approximate keeping with the prevalent 'Ideology' (belief systems).

6. The end result of processes 1 - 4 would be an example of material culture and it does not matter whether it is the building of a tomb, decoration within a tomb, grave goods, etc. because the processes above would be the same.

7. In due course, without the necessary energy input (i.e. maintenance), the reverse energy outflow 'Entropy' would mean a return to 'the Edge of Chaos' and the cycle would be repeated albeit with DIFFERENT INPUTS and a CHANGED OUTPUT.

Accordingly this book is an investigation of certain distinct and perhaps universally applicable[9] aspects of elite funerary culture (generics), which can be gleaned from a reading of the elite tombs of Dynasties 4, 5 and 6 in the Memphite region, primarily those in Giza, Abusir, Saqqara, and Dahshur, and the lesser necropolises of Abu Roash, Heliopolis, and Maidum.

The goal is to identify and analyze those aspects of funerary culture, which are inherent in tomb art. By focusing on the formal and thematic aspects of the elite tombs' iconography (involving as they do society, religion and the individual dimension and applying these to the selected motifs)[10], it is hoped to reveal two interrelated elements:

1. Core traditional culture and the integrative value systems of Old Kingdom Egyptian society.
2. Appearance of bonding/adaptive elements therein, which I term the 'generics', i.e. Identity, Individuality, Ideology, and Remembrance,

The way these are depicted in the selected iconography of the Old Kingdom tombs will, it is hoped, also open a window into the mind-set of the ancient Egyptian. One is well aware that due to the restricted nature of this research other periods are not within its scope, but that does not mean that one is taking a synchronic approach only. It is argued that within a limited time span but at different times, one can still study what happened within a particular social context and at a particular time, provided one pays due attention to time and change as limiting factors. Like all systems culture has the characteristic, that changes in one part of the system will create changes in other parts of the system.[11] This means that a host of factors can be involved in the understanding of social groupings in society. Culture in its processes and occurrences is thus to be understood as a symbolic phenomenon continuously changing and underscoring a communicative function. It also signifies that because culture cannot be seen as an entity, one will be concerned with its socially layered manifestations as evidenced in the different behavioural traits.[12] One way of extracting culturally significant meaning is from the grave goods (of whatever kind including iconography), because these goods must have played a part in the culture of that particular society at that specific time, otherwise they would not be present at a time when the cultural life of the deceased had 'ceased' to exist. However culture is not something that is static and its categories of significances are being continually refined such that it is extremely difficult to put any boundaries around culture specific concepts.[13] Therefore when grave goods are understood to represent a concept of cultural signification, these may refer to the ideal rather than reality. In order to overcome this objection, change will also be considered as part of the evolution of culturally significant meaning. When determining the beliefs and attitudes of the ancient Egyptians towards an activity/object, it is assumed that the Egyptians' attitudes changed between Dynasties. In Dynasties 5 and 6 we shall observe the development of an elite class within Egyptian society, with new forms of ideology, identity and even individuality, i.e. the generics. The tomb motifs indicate that these generics would have been influential factors, leading to changes, which resulted in a more sophisticated elite class and structured society.

The majority of the work on elite tombs has been of a descriptive nature calling attention to among other things:

- Architectural developments.
- Relating certain material artifacts to chronological dating and some details of iconography.

---

[9] Universal as applied in this study is restricted to meaning a pattern or mode of behaviour which is widespread.

[10] The selected motifs and related inscriptional texts are as follows: Carrying-chair, Taking Account (Document Presentation), and Mourning. Wherever these are referred to by plate/fig. number and/or tomb owner's name, then this refers to the plate/fig. number in the the relevant publication. Further rather than use the words "themes" and "sub-themes", which could result in a misunderstanding because these could mean either a specific theme for each tomb or a single decorative theme, I have used the words "motif" and "sub-motif" because I think these are less confusing.

[11] Rappaport, "Ritual, Sanctity and Cybernetics", *AA*, (73), 59. While this article focuses specifically on the relationships of ritual form and performance, nevertheless his approach highlights the way ritual behaviour makes social communication between individuals, a reliable indicator of the reciprocal relationships between them.

[12] Matsumoto, *Culture and Psychology*, 24-26. He gives a useful definition of culture - "a dynamic system of rules, explicit and implicit, established by groups in order to ensure their survival, involving attitudes, values, beliefs, norms, and behaviours, shared by a group, but harbored differently by each specific unit within the group, communicated across generations, relatively stable but with the potential to change across time".

[13] Hodder, *Reading the past*, 24-25. He states that it is incorrect to take a passive view of society, which disregards the cultural context so central to ideology and ideological functions.

- Describing, and interpreting the wall decorations.

Because of the impossibility of getting to grips with how the ancient Egyptians may be understood, and the emphasis on a narrow philological approach, the result has been a variety of piecemeal approaches and differing, frequently confusing interpretations.

As a starting point it must be admitted that this type of research has been useful in highlighting the problematic character of the interior tomb decoration. However, because its roots were seeped in philology and western logic, it failed to take into account the cultural generics adequately.

A metamorphosis started in the late 90's when Egyptologists sought a new alliance with the hard sciences, and it is ironic that Egyptology aligned itself with the classical mathematics of 'causality' at the same time that the mathematicians/physicists were embracing 'uncertainty' and 'complexity' theories. At best this new inclination was lukewarm - too many vested interests were afraid to think outside the box. In their narrow circles they deluded themselves by supporting each other despite the fact that Egyptology was becoming a marginal discipline. As Lord Keynes said in another but equally relevant context "The difficulty lies, not in the new ideas, but in escaping from the old ones, which ramify, for those brought up as most of us have been, into every corner of our minds."[14]

A survey of the main research yields the following grouping:

Group 1 attempts to explain the decoration both as symbol and reality simultaneously. Unfortunately this group's conclusions have no objectively verifiable methodological basis, as exemplified by Junker "Alles ist Wirklichkeit und Sinnbild zugleich".[15] While the idea is understandable, it is just a starting point.

Group 2 attempts to connect the decoration to the earthly, and the life in the hereafter of the tomb owner.[16] However because they go further and try to give meaning to the decorations using the two forms of 'life', their interpretations are varied because these include concepts, which are not verifiable. This is the largest group by far and includes:

U. Langner: representation of the tomb owner's life in the hereafter.[17]

J. H. Taylor: the wall decorations reflect the earthly life of the deceased and not the afterlife.[18]
A. O. Bolshakov: the Old Kingdom representations "are essentially realistic, only scenes of real life are shown, nothing transcendental brought forward".[19]
H. Altenmüller: "Es sind Bilder, die in ihrer Gesamtheit jene Verrichtung darstellen, die für die Versorgung des Menschen in der grossen Gemeinschaft des altägyptischen Staates von Bedeutung sind und von denen der Verstorbene auch für seinen Totenkult profitierte".[20]
C. Barocas: The tomb was built and decorated because of a fear of the dead, still recognizing the desire for a good life in the hereafter.[21]
S. Morenz: The decorations are a recording of the tomb owner's lifetime activities which he wished to continue in his afterlife.[22]
H. Groenewegen-Frankfort: Biographical memoir of the tomb owner's life on earth.[23]
P. Montet: Aimed at giving the spectator a vision of the everlasting world.[24]

Group 3 explains the decoration as a means of the sympathetic magic that they were supposed to be imbued with, and the reproduction of the mortuary cult.

R. K. Ritner: Visualized images constitute magical reinforcements.[25]
E. el-Metwally: "Die Dekoration der altägyptischen Privatgräber von Anfang an" bildet "eine Wiedergabe des Totenkultes".[26]

Group 4 attempts to use the decoration in terms of orientation, placement, and chronological development, with a view to the dating of the tombs. This is exemplified by the approaches of *Harpur*[27] and *Cherpion*.[28]

Group 5 suggests a method based on linguistic and semiotics research. It avoids any interpretation until analyzed with the logic and objectivity of funerary-religious language game theory, when it opens the way for a more logical and objective approach, e.g. *van Walsem*.[29]

---

[14] Keynes, "Preface" *The General Theory of Employment, Interest and Money.*
[15] Junker, *Giza*, vol. 5, 73.
[16] It is acknowledged that in the OK, the tomb owner is never shown as dead. Nevertheless, because the word "deceased" and "tomb owner" are explicit in the mortuary context, they should be understood as identical wherever they appear in this book. Further while the majority of tomb owners are male, some females also have tombs and the use of the word 'he' should not detract from this issue.
[17] Langner, *Forschungsarbeiten zur frühen Kultur der Menschheit*, 313.
[18] Taylor, *Death and the afterlife in Ancient Egypt*, 150.
[19] Bolshakov, "The Old Kingdom Representations of Funeral Procession", *GM* (121), 31.
[20] Altenmüller, "Lebenszeit und Unsterblichkeit in den Darstellungen der Gräber des Alten Reiches", in *5000 Jahre Ägypten*, eds. J. Assmann and G. Burkhard, 79.
[21] Barocas, "La décoration des chapelles funéraires égyptiennes", in *La mort, les morts dans les sociétés anciennes*, eds. G. Gnoli and J. P. Vernant, 430.
[22] Morenz, *Ägyptische Religion,* 212.
[23] Frankfort, *Arrest and movement,* 34.
[24] Montet, *Eternal Egypt*, 179.
[25] Ritner, "Magic in the afterlife", in *OEAA,* vol. 2, 333. Also see Simpson, ed., *The Literature of Ancient Egypt*, 165, l. 39-40. The Teaching for King Merikare: "He has ordained for them magic, as weapons to fend off the impact of what may come to pass". (*ḥsf-ꜥ n ḫprjjt*)
[26] Metwally, *Entwicklung der Grabdekoration in den Altägyptischen Privatgräbern*, 165.
[27] Harpur and Scremin, *Decoration in Egyptian tombs of the Old Kingdom.*
[28] Cherpion, *Mastabas et hypogées d'Ancien Empire.*
[29] Walsem, *Iconography of Old Kingdom elite tombs*, 101.

These studies have been important in laying some of the groundwork; however existing research does not sufficiently explore the affiliation of the iconography and its association to its creators in socio-cultural and art-historical aspects. Indeed there are no studies which I am aware of that have systematically related tombs to dynasties and to regions, to illustrate aspects which have general application in the cultural sense. The dominant philological and archaeological bias is now generally accepted as the theoretical basis of all Egyptological studies. When texts exist and a linguistic translation approximates the meaning, all the other aspects such as archeological context, material, size, and shape are treated as largely irrelevant. The philological/visual culture divide persists. The result is that content is emphasized, but the connections to the cultural processes behind the production of the artifacts are forgotten. These are left to lie in a vague area. This is not to deny the immensely useful contributions of both philologists and archaeologists but one has to take an additional bolder step, which I propose to do in this book. By concentrating on the cultural generics I hope to bridge the perceived gap.

At present there are very few current books dealing specifically with the said cultural aspects like those by Erman, Evers, Von Bissing, and Schäfer (see Bibliography).

The older site reports, e.g. Petrie, Reisner, Junker, Hassan (see Bibliography), try in varying degrees to include aspects of cultural significance. Because this is not conceived of within an overall framework but as an adjunct, it does not provide a concentrated focus and is of limited use.

Some modern site reports, e.g. those that are part of the *Australian Centre for Egyptology,* have understood this problem of too little focus on the cultural/historical aspects of Egyptian elite tombs, and have started to look at this area.[30]

The position in this book subscribes to the view that any attempt at understanding ancient Egyptian funerary culture must go beyond peripheral attempts at interpreting social organization. Material culture should not exclusively be a descriptive list of artifacts or interpretation arising out of ideas about their possible functions, or be based solely on a study of the textual material. In order to understand material culture, one must search for those concepts, which are generic in the nature of the society under investigation, as well as quite possibly being part and parcel of every major past and existing society with similar funerary underpinnings. Further the impact of other disciplines like the hard sciences should also be called into aid.[31] This central premise is based on the belief that "the ultimate purpose of studying Egyptian art just as with archaeology and philology, is to increase our understanding of the culture that produced it".[32]

In fulfilling the task of finding these generics, a conceptual as well as a methodological framework is required. The conceptual framework recognizes that a prerequisite for the development of knowledge is an a priori identification followed by classification, which gives meaningful cultural significance to man's existence. In all cultures this is an ongoing perpetual process and in the case of the Old Kingdom can be witnessed through, among other ways, the media of elite tomb iconography. Further, societies which lay a great emphasis on life after death like the ancient Egyptians will need to perpetuate cults of memory. This will result in the development of belief systems, which being abstract have to be given a material manifestation, in order to be successfully transmitted within society.

The explanation for the world that one lives in is predicated on such a system of beliefs, and because these beliefs, if they are to have any effect at all, have to be communicated, a need for the means to do so arises. The means are varied, but all can be treated as symbols, which convey beliefs. These can be of various kinds, but the ones that are of interest at first are the ones that can be recovered archaeologically in elite tombs: reliefs including wall painting, stelae, inscriptions, and anything of a tangible nature.

These needs arise pursuant to the need for communication and commemoration. Societal behaviour will be affected by both these symbols, those that relate to activities which are of everyday occurrence, as well as to those of a 'metaphysical' nature, e.g. funerary beliefs, both of which indicate an accepted way of doing things as practiced by certain segments of society, in this case the elite. Consider the progression and connection between symbols and society. The examples given below go back to the beginning of Egyptian history, and are found in the Pre-dynastic gravesites of the Badarian ca. 4500-3800 BC, and the following Naqada l, ll, and lll periods ca. 3850 – 3300 BC.

Cemetery T at Nagada excavated by Petrie containing 2043 burials (excluding the adjacent area of Ballas), is one such example,[33] which exhibits a variety of material symbols.

The decorated tomb 100 at Hierakonpolis is another example of a large brick lined pre-dynastic tomb with wall paintings[34] and may have been the tomb of a pre-dynastic king.[35]

[30] Kanawati, *The Rock Tombs of El-Hawawish.*
[31] Germer, "Problems of Science in Egyptology", *In Science in Egyptology,* ed. A. R. David, 521-525.
[32] Russmann, "The State of Egyptology at the end of the second Millennium", in *Egyptology at the dawn of the twenty-first century: proceedings of the Eighth International Congress of Egyptologists,* (2), eds. Z. A. Hawass and L. P. Brock, 26.
[33] Petrie and Quibell, *Naqada and Ballas,* pl. 1A (map showing the number of burials). The undisturbed cemetery T5 contained a variety of grave goods totaling 42 pots, 5 vessels of stone, ornamental beads made of precious metals and stone like gold, lapis lazuli, and carnelian. Cemetery T also contained three large brick lined chambers (T15, T20 and T23). All these grave goods can be said to be symbols of a kind.
[34] Case and Payne, "Tomb 100: The Decorated Tomb at Hierakonpolis", *JEA,* (48), 11-16.
[35] Kemp, "Photographs of the Decorated Tomb at Hierakonpolis", *JEA,* (59), 28.

The internment of the body is itself the development of a belief that it has to be preserved. Initially to seal off the smell of a decaying corpse but in time this rationale became subsumed under the concept of commemoration (dismemberment at least from Naqada 1C onwards makes multiple arenas of commemoration possible), and mummification, which became the standard funerary treatment for elite bodies through the dynastic period and into Roman times. This is a progression from the pre-dynastic funerary beliefs, which possibly led to the development of mummification.[36] Mummification became common practice during the Old Kingdom among members of the royal family and the elite, the earliest evidence being the viscera of Queen Hetepheres found in her canopic box.[37] Just like tomb iconography mummification was meant to preserve the 'youthful appearance' of the tomb owner as someone who would live in the hereafter in a high status.[38] This process transformed the body into an image and then stands for a symbol. The explanation of this symbol is provided by the initial belief (since at least Dynasty 1) that the body had to be preserved so that through it, the owner's 'K3' or spirit could emerge from the burial chamber to partake of the food offerings. Later from the New Kingdom onwards the reasons for body preservation also include its recognition by the 'b', the psychic forces of the deceased depicted as a bird with a human head.[39] This very fact would then point to the reality that both the levels of expenditure as well as the practice of formal burial, were in themselves progressive socially determining symbols.[40]

Bodies without any grave goods have also been found in mass graves, and this should not detract from the body being used as a symbol. All it shows is that these 'others' of society (i.e. the non-elite) did not even have a burial, and is suggestive of the fact that levels of hierarchy were well developed at this stage.

- The vast majority of the bodies found by Petrie at Naqada are placed with head to the South and facing West. While we do not have any texts from this period, the symbolism asserts that the ancient Egyptians understood their place in relation to the points of the compass and of the West being a place of the dead.[41]

- Monumental graves were necessary for the well being of the tomb owner in the afterlife, and as a place where the living could perform the necessary rituals,[42] emulating to some extent the interplay of text, image, and architecture, which is evident from a study of the royal graves.[43] If this hereafter is modeled on similar concepts as pertaining to the now, then it is reasonable to expect to find in the graves the very elements which were essential to the tomb owner in this life on earth, and which he thought would be essential to him in the hereafter. The symbols could represent tangible objects, as well as the abstract sentiments found in the literature, which would underpin its communal/state integrating function. If certain goods occur frequently they are likely to be indispensable, and accordingly imply cultural importance in view of their repeated presence, their ostensible use, as well as the class of people assisting in this process. In this view all the biological, psychological, and social processes even though they may appear to be discrete, should be seen as symbolizing different aspects of the human being. Seen in this light it becomes obvious that the different symbols represent our personal and collective identities. The way we transmit these memories to others is a way how humans make themselves, i.e. it is a study of what we are and how we want to be understood by other humans. In addition, the tomb and its contents reflect a continuing cultural discourse, which would have had some influence on the understanding of the tomb for all sections of the society.[44] Textual evidence of this cultural discourse in the Old Kingdom is sparse and restricted to the king (the Pyramid Texts). From the First Intermediary Period (FIP) onwards it was extended in the Coffin Texts to include the elite and the non-elite of which there is evidence.[45] The real value of this approach of equating symbols with cultural significance will depend on the cumulative effect of the analyses of the underlying themes and their application to certain selected motifs which forms the contents of the case studies in Part 2.

Significantly this evidence, judging from the brick lined chambers, and the variety of grave goods found (e.g. foodstuffs, body ornaments, cosmetic palettes, jewellery, tools, flint, knives, ceramics, and stone vessels), implies

---

[36] Mond and Myers, *Cemeteries of Armant I*, 12. Here two burials were found covered with animal skins and others covered in reed matting. Similar observations by Petrie, "Diospolis Parva", 1901: 35, who writes that evidence was found at the cemetery at Semaineh where the burials show that limbs were disarticulated, covered in bark and then rejoined. It would appear, that the advancement of a belief in total protection of the body led to another way of preserving it, namely mummification.

[37] Lucas and Harris, *Ancient Egyptian Materials*, 271.

[38] David, "Mummification", in *OEAA*, vol. 2, 439-44.

[39] D'Auria, Lacovara, and Roehrig, *Mummies and Magic*, 29. Although the relationship between the ba and the body is known from the FIP (Simpson, ed. *The Literature of Ancient Egypt*, 157, l. 52-53), no depiction of the Ba exists prior to the NK.

[40] Baines and Lacovara., "Burial and the dead in ancient Egyptian society: respect, formalism, neglect", *JSA*, (2), 9.

[41] Bard, "Analysis of the Predynastic Cemeteries of Nagada and Armant",

Ph.D. Dissertation, University of Toronto, 143.

[42] Lukes, "Political Ritual and Social Integration", *Sociology*, (9), 291. He defines ritual as a "rule governed activity of a symbolic character which draws the attention of its participants to objects of thought and feeling which they hold to be of special significance".

[43] Brinks, *Die Entwicklung der königlichen Grabanlagen des Alten Reiches, HÄB*, (10), 157-58.

[44] Kemp, *Ancient Egypt: Anatomy of a Civilization*, 1-5.

[45] Baines, "Communication and Display", *Antiquity*, (63), 476. This is not meant to imply a sequential encroachment of the royal powers by the non-royals but simply a pointer to change as a continuous phenomenon, and to the implication that the non-royals probably had knowledge of the cultural discourse, although the evidence for this may now be lost or is at best circumstantial.

that the preservation of the body in a specially prepared place, and the inclusion of specific grave goods in the burials, reflected a belief in their usefulness following death. It is further a pointer to the slowly emerging status of certain tomb owners by grounding them in a shared understanding of an entire way of life, as opposed to the non-elite.

One may argue that some of these examples are of the functional kind, but evidence from five burials at Abadiyeh where jars with scarab beetles were found,[46] would point to the symbolism behind the placement of grave goods (i.e. beliefs which are expressed as material symbols and which existed since pre-dynastic times). This is of added significance especially in light of the beetles' relationship with the sun god and immortality, albeit in later times.[47] While the primary evidence is from Upper Egypt, it is evidence of a trend towards increasing disparity in burial form and content between the elite and the non-elite. They are the visible expression of complex concepts and relationships,[48] which pre-existed in the Old Kingdom and which, with increasing societal complexity, had the additional purpose of the creation and maintenance of both individual identity and intra/interregional relationships.

The focus of this study will not be on style in art but in the way the iconography can be used to deal with the tomb as a system of transferring knowledge, tradition, and communication (read information) between the living and the dead based on communal values and belief systems during the Old Kingdom.

We can never know the exact intention of the ancient protagonists and advancements in understanding will therefore depend upon the accumulation of facts and ideas, their order, and in the way these are interpreted and analyzed.

This book is in two Parts:

Part 1 addresses and expands on the important concepts of the generics and shows that these have existed since the pre-dynastic times right up to our own. In order to do so it will cut across the underlying nature of Egyptian society and culture during the relevant periods, including the questions of: how, and by whom, were the ideas, skills, and beliefs of the ancient Egyptian transferred and communicated into the content of the iconography? Considering the fact that ancient Egypt had no modern means of transport/communications, state power and control over the population could only be accomplished by the use of legitimated ideology, and accepted beliefs, which transcended the everyday. The interconnection of nearly every aspect of society in this process means that

the process had to be simplified, and easily understandable by all, if absolute transmission was to be achieved.

The methodology will also impose a theoretical framework of linguistics and radical pragmatism that relates both to the symbols, the pattern of evidence and changes to this as proposed both by Wittgenstein[49] and Van Walsem.[50] It also take into account the "intellectual aesthetic" which these reliefs must reflect.[51] While this book is primarily about funerary culture, nevertheless an attempt is made to bring in contemporary examples, which add a flavour of reality.

Part 2 analyzes three case studies of Old Kingdom elite tomb iconography, for evidence confirming the generics. It applies the conceptual framework to the chosen individual motifs and their constituent iconographic examples in depth and extends their implications, sometimes utilizing statistical analysis. The goal is twofold:

1. To apply the identified generic aspects in the selected motifs and textual material of the known elite tombs, keeping in mind how the extant social conditions accompanied or facilitated the creation of iconography.
2. To identify the ways the protagonists broadcasted the ideas contained in the generics.

This will establish any corresponding patterns, which may exist. By identifying common features that expose the cultural generics, wide spread aspects of cultural significance can be isolated. Possibly it might also assist in the understanding of other ancient mortuary cultures, which like the ancient Egyptian were based on remembrance, and mortuary art.

The iconographical drawings/figures that form part of Part 2's case studies appear in Appendix "I", where reference to tomb names mentioned in the motifs chosen for analysis in this book can also be found. For ease of reference these are also included in Appendices A, B, C, and D.

[46] Petrie, *Diospolis Parva: The Cemeteries of Abadiyeh and Hu*, 33.

[47] The god Khepry is depicted with a beetle in place of a head and the word means "he who is coming into being", understood as the morning manifestation of the sun god.

[48] Bard, *An introduction to the archaeology of ancient Egypt*, 4.

[49] Wittgenstein, *Philosophical Investigations*, § 83-87.

[50] Walsem, *Iconography of Old Kingdom elite tombs*, 17-65. Based on previous work "The Interpretation of Iconographic Programmes in Old Kingdom Elite Tombs of the Memphite Area. Methodological and Theoretical (Re) Considerations", ed. C. J. Eyre, Orientalia Lovaniessia Anatecta.

[51] Kemp, *Ancient Egypt: Anatomy of a Civilization* 72. See pages 135-137 for examples.

Chapter 2: Methodology and Research Assumptions

This section, primarily addresses issues of methodology. The chapter examines the emic and etic approaches to an understanding of the types of meaning which lie in the iconography of the Old Kingdom. The stage is then set to provide a comprehensive approach to the ideas behind the methodological considerations of Wittgenstein and Van Walsem.

Wittgenstein acknowledges the problems of intention and proposes the concept of language games as a way of understanding meaning in a particular context. Van Walsem agrees with this approach but he concentrates on the problems of the literal/ symbolic meaning of an artifact, and proposes a purely objective approach questioning whether there is a single central meaning to Old Kingdom elite iconography. The approach here follows both the above but extends it by taking into account common suppositions, which man shares as set out in the research assumptions.

2.1 Methodology

In considering elite tomb iconography, one is faced with the problem that the mental processes by which the ancient Egyptians collectively and over time endeavored to construct an accurate and reliable consistent symbol of their world, are now lost. Because one lives in another era, with different cultural, social, economic, psychological, and religious values, one may fail to understand the meaning and relevance of these principles. In this case categorization of the constituent parts that is part of the heritage of Western logic will not provide a solution, because clear boundaries or common properties are just not there. In other words, categories can have extendable boundaries.[52]

The modern difficulty in understanding tomb iconography could also have something to do with the fact that the starting point is often Eurocentric (under the aegis of modern art history), rather than in the context in which they were created, and meant to be viewed. It is therefore no surprise that different Egyptologists, applying what they think are the appropriate criterion, have come up with different results for the same object (see Introductory Remarks). This has led researchers in this field to comment that it is an understatement to say that there are still problems concerning the interpretation of the iconography of the Old Kingdom elite tombs, including rock cut tombs.[53]

The act of interpretation may involve several ways of translation because Egyptian culture is not based on Western logic. The problem is that "in Egyptian thought, two fundamentally different formulations are evidently not mutually exclusive but complementary" … "the pairs do not cancel each other out; they complement each other. A given *x* can be both *a* and not *a; tertium non datur* the law of the excluded middle does not apply".[54] Hornung expands this further by describing it as a "many valued

logic", "logic of complementarity" something, which in the face of alternative affirmations can have concurrent legitimacy. However, he also concludes "so long as the intellectual basis of a many sided logic remains uncertain, we can only indicate possibilities, not definite solutions",[55] leading one to suppose that the "many valued logic" approach may have its limitations.[56]

Van Walsem expands the "many valued logic" idea one step further. In his book on the methodological analysis of Old Kingdom elite tombs, he opens up the problems in present day approaches and suggests alternatives.[57] According to him, deciphering the meaning of elite tomb decorations is dominated by the problems of deciding whether: these scenes are literal (Sehbild) or symbolic (Sinnbild), or are these scenes magical ways of continuing life in the hereafter, or are they a copy of the tomb owner's earthly existence? In other words, can something exist simultaneously in both states - the literal and the symbolic?

In line with this difficulty, another researcher asks, "When common objects acquire a symbolic meaning, how can we know whether it applies in all contexts",[58] is there one meaning for all times and contexts?

One solution is to try to distinguish between intention and symbolic meaning. The only thing certain about intention is the resultant material object - if an object or a painting is repeatedly reproduced in a certain manner during a certain time frame, then it must imply intention.

[52] Lakoff, *Women, Fire and Dangerous Things,* 16.

[53] Baines, "Forerunners of Narrative Biographies", 34-37. He shows how the Dynasty 4 chapel of Metjen can be interpreted in different ways. For another example of possible different interpretations of the Benben stone, and the temple, see Kemp, *Ancient Egypt: Anatomy of a Civilization* 139-40 and 57.

[54] Hornung, *Conceptions of God in ancient Egypt,* 239-40.

[55] Ibid. 242.

[56] Baines, "Interpretations of religion: logic, discourse, rationality", *GM,* (76), 26-32. Essentially his critique of Hornung is based on three arguments which all have their underpinning in Western logic: (1) Similar logic in order to be applied to various branches of learning, has to be comparable on a theoretical and logical level. (2) It is inappropriate to seek a parallel concept of Western logic in Egypt. (3) Difficulties also arise because there are no meta-levels of complexity which were used by the Egyptians in their modes of explanation. From a practical viewpoint Hornung's approach has much to offer and is in my opinion in keeping with the "multiplicity of approaches" view formulated by Frankfort decades earlier in *Ancient Egyptian Religion*, 3-4.

[57] Walsem, *Iconography of Old Kingdom elite tombs,* 67-91.

[58] Robins, "Problems in interpreting Egyptian art", *DE,* (17), 53.

As for symbolic meaning it has its own baggage of difficulties. It is difficult to know with any certainty because motifs may not be sufficiently distinguishable from one another, the act of transmission may imply a meaning different from its original meaning, and the differentiation between symbols may change over time as a matter of use, and habit. Ultimately all symbolic meaning is socially constructed.[59]

Van Walsem asserts that funerary art and architecture are multifunctional, e.g. in accessible structures, in the cult practices, and in the varying motifs of tomb art, which all vary in the context of different socio-economic, religious, political and social dimensions. This leads him to ask: whether one should be searching for a *single* correct interpretation at all? In the same way as Wittgenstein proposes that games do not have a single, well-defined collection of common properties. Cricket and football for example both involve competition, strategy, and skill but even though they are different, they are still games.

To clarify these issues, Van Walsem formulates certain fundamental theoretical considerations:[60]

- A tomb is an artifact, defined as any object with attributes of human origin.
- A tomb is a part of human material culture in the shape of fossilized behaviour, which reflects the interaction of man's involvement with life and death.
- Life and death are not homogenous issues but complex and will depend on the person's *Weltanschauung* (philosophy of life).

Because life and death are not identical issues, their representation will differ and he groups the motifs into three categories:

1. Material reality as experienced by the individual.
2. Immaterial reality which he subdivides into mental/metaphorical/abstract constructs that are not 'sensorially observable', and those that are observable but may have an ideological bias.
3. Mixture of both material and immaterial, e.g. ideological scenes, which can straddle both areas.

The above considerations can be illustrated by the example of the ostrich feather as understood in ancient Egypt. This can refer to:

1. Abstract phenomena like justice, and divine power.
2. Actual circumstances such as the pattern of social life, which presents itself in an intellectual/ emotional/behavioural aspect.
3. A supposed living goddess *M3ᶜt*, the ostrich feather in Egyptian iconography being a symbol for all these.

The problem then is: how and to which of the above groups, one should allocate the motifs and sub-motifs of an Old Kingdom tomb? One way is to use the textual inscriptions.

Whether an ostrich feather means justice, the divine power of the goddess (*M3ᶜt*) or indeed herself, may well depend on the text and its context and as Baines points out "the study of texts can involve at least as many obstacles to understanding 'from the inside' as the analysis of representations".[61] If one follows this path it is soon realized that subtleness of hierarchical language becomes all-important because reality is complex, describing it becomes even more complex. Therefore the use to which language is put will also be complex and contentious.

Another way is to search for patterns that may exist in the iconography and present a statistical survey keeping in mind the limitations of applying mathematical analysis to incomplete populations.

Wittgenstein in Philosophical Investigations[62] suggested another way of understanding concepts, which are at the heart of all cultures. He suggests that language is an indefinite set of social activities, each serving a different purpose, which he called a "language game". He proposed that depending on the context, we can use different language games to understand a concept bearing in mind that conceptual categories do not have clear boundaries, and are not fixed. However categories could be united by family resemblances, in which case these resemblances can be used as a starting point. Take the example of a chair that can be a chair one sits on, a chair in which one is carried, a chair which is a throne, etc. So the category of chair can be given precise boundaries but the concept of chair is itself not limited in any of these ways; rather it is open to both limitations and extensions depending on one's purpose.

Words similarly are fluid, and can mean very different things in different circumstances. There is no permanently existing conceptual structure underlying the meaning of a word, because one can use a word to mean potentially anything depending on the context. The problem is that because we learn to play these language games by training since childhood, we employ language in an unreflecting manner and are prone to use one simplified version. Because this use does not generally take into account the various nuances of the spoken and written language, it increases confusion. He therefore suggested that understanding could only be achieved by the use of the appropriate language game for that particular context. However these language games have a deeper cultural significance in that the way humans interact in the language games they play, always refers indirectly to concepts of dominance, reciprocity, and sharing.

---

[59] Mitchell, *Iconology*, 65-71. Also see Goodman, *Languages of art*, 226.
[60] Walsem, *Iconography of Old Kingdom elite tombs*, 33-39.

[61] Baines, *Fecundity figures*, 2.
[62] Wittgenstein, *Philosophical Investigations* § 7, 64-68, 83, and 154.

Van Walsem agrees and suggests that we can only speak about life through the means of different language games, each with its own rules, starting points and aims, which together with the particular context in which it is used, can give us but one interpretation for each language game.[63] Pictures similarly like words are fluid, and can mean very different things in different circumstances. This can depend upon one's network of associations, the type of actions, and the type of participants. The emphasis then is upon how language is used in light of the knowledge, and expectations of the conversant.[64] Consequently, there are many meanings, depending on which language game is employed. However, this should not be understood to mean that symbolic meaning does not exist, or that anything goes, but that in the study of ancient objects, one must keep in mind that there was "involved a very deliberate process of selection and modification in order to create a set, a vocabulary of ideal types possessing internal consistency. This … gave scope to an endless (and for us bewildering) recombination of elements which lay at the heart of the constant invention of tradition".[65]

The application of the above ideas to the Egyptian iconography would imply that the ancient elite Egyptians had little trouble in coming to grips with the various shades of meaning. Their cultural underpinnings would have made many things clear to them that are obscure to us, because of what is termed their emic position. By this is meant that an important element in understanding the archeological record is to take into account: ancient values, people's perception of themselves as well as the world around them.[66]

In contrast today's observers of the past, take on an extra-cultural or etic position when confronted with alien material, which is seen by chance or deliberately (the terminology was developed by Lee-Pike[67] out of the linguistic terms *phonetic* and *phonemic*). One cannot have a similarity of *Weltanschauung* with our ancient fellowman. We are thus forced to generate a language game, which *we* understand and through which *we* try to make this alien material understandable to others. In attempting this, we rely on a rationalization of our experience of objects, which leads us to try to develop an explanation and then of course we run into the difficulty that things do not follow a linear path and that a single language game does not and cannot explain such a complex object like Old Kingdom tomb iconography. Such experience can however be part of a way one views Egyptian iconography in that the very attempt leads to a grouping and further analysis. In any case one will never be sure that one can understand the mindset of the Egyptian: this is and will remain the current

problem. Because of this, the iconography of the Old Kingdom elite tombs is complex and any study of these must be approached pluralistically, i.e. include as many branches of science and humanities as necessary.

The core of Van Walsem's methodology thus follows that of Wittgenstein, in that because of the complexity of existence, different language games are potentially present simultaneously in an Old Kingdom elite tomb, and therefore there is no certainty that there exists an absolute single core meaning.[68] Categories thus become movable and understanding is better obtainable through a gradient of observations in a particular environment.

However, while I agree with this hypothesis, I take a slightly different approach which does not *completely* discount the suppositions of the ancient Egyptians as they might have understood their world, because we too, "the way we understand the world is through our interactions with it".[69] Consider a modern educated person: to him first order scientific enquiry only considers logic. However there are times when we have to enquire into the suppositions as a way of thinking about the world, where the old remains, but is carried into the new. This consideration of suppositions then becomes a way of revealing features of structure and meaning out of the complexity of the Egyptian material based on experience. Equally if one accepts that most action depends upon prior thought and that this is a human trait, then in understanding the actions of the ancient Egyptians, it would be constructive to take into consideration what the others' suppositions might have been. In doing this we might find that there are certain concepts/ideas/suppos-itions which we all share, so that it is quite possible for a person who lived some 5000 years ago to have had some of the same thought patterns conducive to action as a person who lives today, but cannot be explained in logical terms.

Consider an encounter with an object like a piece of clay with a hole in the centre. From this simple artifact we can start to ask many questions (language games): what activities were entailed in its production, in what context does it appear, who were the people, the way they thought when they embarked on these activities, and perhaps any similarities to today etc.?

While aware of the dangers of basing any understanding of Egyptian artifacts on the basis of modern motivations and ideas, nevertheless if we were to stop, and only look at the logical facts, completely discounting all suppositions that could have been a basis for the action, the discussion would be weakened. In particular it would tend to imply that Egyptian art was an inert, stagnant, and fixed system. The archaeological record shows that this is not so, and that it had within itself the ability to adapt to changing circumstances. This book maintains with Van Walsem, his

---

[63] Walsem, *Iconography of Old Kingdom elite tombs,* 68-69.
[64] Nunberg, "The non-uniqueness of semantic solutions: Polysemy", *LP* (3), 143-84.
[65] Kemp, *Ancient Egypt: Anatomy of a Civilization,* 154.
[66] Melas, "Etics, emics and empathy in archaeological theory", in *The Meaning of Things: material culture and symbolic expression,* ed. I. Hodder, 138-42.
[67] Lee-Pike, *Language in relation to a unified theory of the structure of human behavior,* 37.

[68] Walsem, "The Struggle Against Chaos as a "Strange Attractor" in Ancient Egyptian Culture", 321-22. Also see Walsem, *Iconography of Old Kingdom elite tombs,* 86-88 and 98.
[69] Lakoff and Johnson, *Metaphors we live by,* 194.

opposition to the idea that we can get entry into an artistic work, merely by engaging with artistic intention.

A similar problem can be found in relation to textual data. Words in themselves as well as the way they are arranged convey information. This information may be literal or may overflow with hidden suppositions; the spectrum is unlimited when applied to abstract ideas. Any meaning will then depend upon a prior understanding and the way the sentence or text is structured. Consequently it is not only in the individual image and the hidden suppositions, where culturally significant information is found, but also in the way similar depictions are structured in similar period graves, such that 'related elements' form a meaningful pattern probably because of the same artist or workshops being involved. These patterns and the underlying suppositions will change over time as generations invent their own programmes, as can be observed in the elite tombs during Dynasties 4, 5, and 6.

The reason why significant transitions (change), albeit mostly seen when occurring across a time frame are observed in objects/signs/symbols/humans, etc. will be found in 'chaos theory'.[70] This theory's essential element is one that embraces change as an element of newness - constant decay followed by constant renewal through related events. Chaos theory studies behaviour in deterministic systems where the behaviour exhibited is both complicated and unpredictable. This is because extremely small variations in initial conditions can lead to unexpected results. In the ancient Egyptian context, it can be used as an analogy of how the Egyptians visualized the problem of change out of chaos. One version has it that at first there were only disordered primeval waters in which the creator god floated, without consciousness. The creator god then came into being of himself on a mound of earth and arose out of these waters, his first act being to bring an ordered world into existence through an act of masturbation.[71] Through this single act were born male and female deities, who in turn sexually interacted and produced another pair and so on. Similarly the rising and the setting of the sun was explained in terms of the sky goddess swallowing the sun god every evening, which in the act of being swallowed, impregnated her and was reborn again (a new sun) the following morning.[72] Comparable analogies of change can be used to explain the transitions in social complexity and cultural adjustments observed in the iconography, text, images, and architecture of the Old Kingdom mastabas.

The term 'constant renewal through related elements' requires clarification for which Quantum Physics affords us invaluable insight: just as an element can exist as a discrete known particle with specific properties and boundaries, it can also exist as a wave.[73]

At one level the related elements consist of the individual tomb owner as a unique person, who is physically present, and has boundaries. At another level related elements are something indefinable, what ontologists term the infinity in us, similar to 'the water that keeps the boat afloat'. Whilst I do not wish to imply that the ancient Egyptians had any understanding of Quantum Physics, yet by drawing this analogy from the modern world, attention is drawn to the two sides of a human being, which can exist at different levels. One as a distinct being, and the other that has no material being, in that he has a multi-leveled, multi-systemic social functioning, e.g. a person's 'base' function is active when mentioned during a meeting even though he himself may be absent. Both of these are involved in society, play an essential role in the formation of what we term a family, clan, tribe, community, or society, and ultimately socially constructed meaning.[74]

Could this then not have been the case with the Egyptians too? In trying to understand the self and its relational connectedness to others, they too felt the difference between a personal identity (like a particle), and a far-reaching social identity (which could be like a wave). Because this was something which was not tangible yet was not transient, they had to find a way to concretize it, if for no other reason than the egotistical one of cultural memory and eternal life in the hereafter. They did this through tomb art, ritual, and liturgy. They left evidence of this for posterity on the walls of their tombs, in a manner in which it is equally possible to understand the phenomenon of existential change both at the particle and the wave levels. However, the ancient Egyptians of the earlier period never characterized their thought patterns in a definite and concrete manner. This is why we moderns have such difficulty in understanding the relevance of mortuary art. If the above is correct, then this could form part of the starting process for trying to understand iconography. This does not mean that we are free to create meaning as we think fit, but that there are limits, which cannot be identified in advance.

Accordingly the methodology followed here will depend on the application initially of the language game. Like all languages it will need a vocabulary and rules of grammar.

The vocabulary is depicted in all the symbols that go into the making of the final product, i.e. tomb decoration. This could range from the material setting to the metaphysical religious ideas and to the dimensions that were relevant to the users and makers of the artifacts.

---

[70] Strictly speaking the term is 'the science of chaos' because it is not a theory in the Newtonian sense. For a fuller explanation of chaos theory see pages 28.

[71] Faulkner, *The Ancient Egyptian Pyramid Texts*, §1248-49. For a later version of this story, see Faulkner, "The Bremner-Rhind Papyrus-IV", *JEA*, (24), 41-53.

[72] Traunecker, *The gods of Egypt*, 71-72.

[73] Hornung, *Conceptions of God in ancient Egypt*, 241. Also see Walsem, "The Struggle Against Chaos as a "Strange Attractor" in Ancient Egyptian Culture", 321-23 and 33-34, and Walsem, *Iconography of Old Kingdom elite tombs*, 86-87.

[74] I am fully aware that cultural concepts cannot be simply extrapolated. from Quantum Physic's mathematical models. However, I see no detriment in using concepts from other disciplines, which may give us a clearer understanding.

As for the rules of the game (the grammar), these will emerge from the patterns that exist in and between the symbols, how and in what context they interact with each other, and how they change within a time frame, according to the ideological basis.

Being predominantly regulated by social practices, these rules do not have the certainty of mathematics like word order in a language, but may possess both an element of the empirical as well as the ideological. One way for these rules to be made visible could be by looking at distinctions which the ancient Egyptians made in similar tomb motifs and which are now visible. By doing so, it is hoped to distill those elements, which are evident in all mortuary art based on commemoration, which are termed the generics. In addition their application to funerary art will provide an understanding of individual and social practices within a given time frame in the context of funerary art. Further and crucially, it is hoped that such a study will also point to the continuum of complex cultural change, a perspective that emphasizes both the immediate as well as the continuity over time. Thus the study of Egyptian funerary art will be taken out of its exclusive cocoon and made to have significance to our contemporary world.

2.2 Research Assumptions

1. In Old Kingdom Egypt, hierarchical control was a central feature of its society[75] but this does not mean that horizontal differences within groups such as kinship can be ignored. The main instigators of change were most probably those who were at the higher levels of society.
2. Change will deliberately occur, only if the members of that society can be controlled. However where this is not the case, change is due to the incorporation of new facts and relations and then a good deal of change is accidental.
3. The more humans that are under the control of a person with power and status (the tomb owner and his heir being one such example), the higher the probability of the change being executed and documented. Thus the question of power, consent and coercion are the central points in this relationship between the dominant group and the others in the way class realities are lived.[76] These may be evidenced as part of a material artifact and the more times that a similar type of change is documented and executed, the higher the probability that this change will become socially accepted and highly regarded. After a time, the particular change is no longer experienced as such, but the recent change is accepted and recorded as the new 'convention'. Change is generally more rapid in the material aspects of culture because it is easier for an artisan to change the style of a material object than for society to change its culture. In contrast, change is slower to occur in language, religion, social customs, moral order, and institutional organizations; because these are the outcome of long evolutionary processes and the sheer time scale causes apparent inertia to exist. Additionally, as the outcomes become culturally embedded, they develop increasing acceptability and may become even more resistant to change. Accordingly, it is assumed that in case of funerary culture, changes may be caused by any or all of the following:

- Conscious decision of the tomb owner prior to death.
- Conscious decision by the progeny and/or other relatives after the tomb owner's death.
- Artistic freedom to a limited extent.
- Economic factors, i.e. access to or control of resources.

1. Given that Egyptian society was divided into different levels, the modes of pictorial and written representation reflect not only this division of society but also the differential abilities of the tomb owners to acquire these resources. The resulting iconography could then be seen as a possible indicator of the competitive nature of Egyptian society as well as a propensity to exhibit those modes of representation which were accepted as being at the top of the cultural apex.[77]
2. Mortuary differentiation is a function of increasing societal complexity.[78]
3. Linear change never occurs in any culture because the underlying factors are complex and will contradict.[79]
4. In all societies people build long-term, interdependent relationships, which produce feelings of attachment. Termination of these relationships following death results in some form of emotional distress in any society.[80]

[75] Wilkinson, "Social Stratification", *OEAA*, vol. 3, 301-05.
[76] Crehan, *Gramsci, Culture and Anthropology,* 98-105.
[77] Baines, "Forerunners of Narrative Biographies", 24-25.
[78] O'Shea, *Mortuary Variability*, 21.
[79] Seidlmayer, "Die Ikonographie des Todes", in *Social Aspects of Funerary Culture in the Egyptian Old and Middle Kingdoms*, ed. H. Willems, 205-06.
[80] Averill, "Grief: its nature and significance", *PB*, (70), 721-28.

Chapter 3: The Search for the Generics in the Material Aspects

This chapter brings together all the material features, which are tangible and affect the primary nature of the accessible working material, the elite tomb, and its contents. The aim is to assess how material features including location, shape, size, main architectural progression, and spatial context influenced the elite tomb's iconography. Each person has an individualized image of his world because his image is the product of among other things, his physical and social environment. In addition the role that the main actors, the tomb owner, and the anonymous artist played in this context and their interaction is examined for its communicative value and as pointers to the generics. These actors appear in this section even though it is realized that any effect that they have on the iconography, is a result of their ideas that are intangible.

3.1 The Physical Setting

All civilizations have roots in their physical environment because they need a place in which to proliferate. Space gives them the place, which they can call their own, and time gives them the period in which to develop their collective memories, an idea refined by the Egyptologist Assmann in his study of Culture and Memory.[81] The end result is the development of a landscape combining a common perception of history as well as ideology in which one would wish to be buried; a desire reinforced by continual subsequent use.

A glance at any satellite image of Egypt shows its unique position, isolated by the Sahara and the Sinai and watered by the Nile; a self-contained area. However, this should not be understood to mean that there was no alien cultural cross-pollination, or that this was the sole cause of the development of a unique civilzation. It is now widely accepted that Egypt had parallel social developments to those that had already started in the Mesopotamian region in 4000BC, where the introduction of writing and the first state formation are evidenced.

The studies done by Hoffman[82] among others, confirm that Egypt was a stratified society before 3000BC, and therefore it would be naive to assume that Egypt lived in isolation and developed its own pristine form of self-contained culture irrespective of it's geographic destiny.

It is highly probable that trade with the outer regions such as the Mediterranean, Palestine, Mesopotamia, Nubia, and Libya as well as local conflicts among fortified cities, (as seen on the Libyan palette) may also have been crucial influencing factors in this development.

The Nile provided not only a means of transport and communication but ensured all agricultural fertility. In addition the climatic shift to a dry arid type assisted in the preservation of the many artifacts, which are present. The cyclic phenomena of the inundation and drying up of the Nile, as well as the eternal question of birth and death in all spheres, must have powerfully influenced every aspect of Egyptian life, including the type of society and the material record left behind.

Surprisingly there are not many known records of water management in ancient Egypt. However, it is clear that they must have had regulated the flow of the Nile seasonally, because their collective existence without the annual inundation is an impossibility. The organization of the flood plains and its control raises complex questions about the reach of central authority versus local village organization, and the extent to which it was the dominating factor in the rise and maintenance of its culture for some 3000 years.[83] Its importance cannot be doubted, because of the tracts of arable land shown being used for a variety of agricultural purposes in the elite tombs (a good example being that of the Dynasty 5 matsaba of Neferherenptah at Saqqara). Further examples are seen in the OK Tomb of the Two Brothers where the caption in a farming scene is said to take place in the plot of land *šd(w)t* and *š* (basin) of the estate. In the tomb of Hapdjefay (Dynasty 12) reference is made to what has been given "See I have endowed you with fields, with people, with flocks, with basins (*š*)...[84]".

Land thus was an extremely important element in the provisioning and construction of the tomb, as well as for one's existence. Indeed this is what is implied by the term *imakhu* meaning one who is provided for. While initially this took the form of a gift from royal property as seen in the Offering Formula, from Dynasty 4 onwards it could take the form of an endowment of an estate comprising land, people, cattle, and equipment. These lands were assigned to officials of high rank, and were meant primarily for use towards his funerary estate. Another way of obtaining an interest in land was by way of reversion; by which the income received from royal cults, temples, or even other tombs could be redirected for use in some other tomb, creating a sort of sharing of the revenue. Private individuals could own arable land at all periods of ancient

---

[81] Assmann, *Das kulturelle Gedächtnis*. 34-38. Collective memories refer to a group's association with the past, communicated verbally and/or in writing (narrative), as well as symbols (e.g. monuments, art, and rituals). Both narrative and symbol are crucial indicators of the group's values and belief systems, and their complex of hidden ideas.

[82] Hoffman, *Egypt before the Pharaohs*. London: ARK Paperbacks, 1979. See also Bard, "An Analysis of the Pre-dynastic Cemeteries of Naqada and Armant in Terms of Social Differentiation: The Origin of the State in Pre-Dynastic Egypt" Ph.D. diss., University of Toronto, 1987.

[83] Park, "Early Trends toward Class Stratification: Chaos, Common Property, and Flood Recession Agriculture", *AA*, vol. 94, 90-117.

[84] Eyre, "The Water Regime for Orchards and Plantations in Pharaonic Egypt", *JEA*, (80), 57-80. For a review of flood irrigation and basins in ancient Egypt, see Willcocks, *Egyptian Irrigation*", 37-57.

Egyptian history; provided this property was passed in joint possession to the eldest son, with the proviso that it could never be alienated in any form whatsoever. The earliest record of such a transaction is that from the Dynasty 4 tomb of *Mtn*.[85] However, if the Wilbour Papyrus 1142 BC (which is a survey of lands belonging to temples, institutions, and some private land) can be seen as somewhat indicative of lands held (e.g. the size of agricultural lands held, the varieties of crop grown and the basis of assessment of lands to which they had rights), then we can also get a glimpse into the social composition of the lands, the relationship of title to lands held, as well as the interconnections that must have existed between the religious and the secular institutions including the royal cult institutions.[86] These associations point to the existence of complex systems and to different ways of looking at ancient Egyptian society, especially in the way in which the qualitative differences in lands held could ultimately result in stratification of society, and lead to a certain type of structure of the Egyptian State.

Set apart on a plateau at the entrance to the Delta region, where the Nile flows northwards to join with the Mediterranean Sea, are the great cemeteries of the elite located near the old capital of Memphis. These tombs followed the pattern set by the royals, and as these moved from Saqqara to Medum, and then to Dahshur, Giza, Abu Roash, Abusir and back to Saqqara again, so did the elite who wished to be buried near the king.[87] The majority of the elite tombs and their iconography are located in this unique setting, in an environment of monumental pyramids and a desert area bordered by steep slopes of limestone cliffs (limestone being the predominant stone found in this area).

These monuments of the past and their contents, such as elaborate tombs and temples, serve as the ground material for examining past social relationships because they function as statements to social authority and prestige in "culturally and historically situated social action".[88]

3.2 The Elite

The term elite as it is used here, relates to any Egyptian who was important enough to acquire a monumental tomb building, such a tomb being a privilege reserved for the highest class.[89] These persons constituted "the cultural and the administrative and executive core of a society".[90] Such a person would fulfill as a minimum the following criteria:

- Be part of a select and restricted group of people having titles.
- Be buried in a distinctive place with distinctive architecture.
- Be directly or indirectly chosen by the king and/or his closest advisors.
- Have "the production and consumption of aesthetic items" under his control through which he can benefit.[91]
- Being accepted as deserving of reverence and following.

This should not be understood as the elite being a homogenous group[92] because the whole communal system depended upon what Kemp calls "family ties and a network of patronage and obligation",[93] the very existence of which implies some form of opposition within the prevalent society. As Goody suggests: "Culture does not simply consist of inbuilt tendencies or customary (traditional) procedures of a socialized kind, but includes a kernel of doubt, its own critique of itself that may lead to the adoption of opposed forms of behaviour",[94] and of course be the harbinger of change.

3.3 The Elite Tomb

The establishment of a monumental tomb was an act requiring the expenditure of both intellectual and material property. The tomb representations show the grave as a place where the tomb owner intends to start a new life 'in the hereafter',[95] similar in munificence to that of his previous life.

---

[85] Baer, "The Low Price of Land in Ancient Egypt", *JARCE*, (1), 25.

[86] Katary, *Land Tenure in the Ramesside Period*, 1-24 and 265. Even though her evidence is mainly from the Wilbour Papyrus, which only deals with 4.6% of the arable land, nevertheless it gives a good idea of the type of social analysis that may be performed, because it includes lands held by both religious and secular institutions, and private lands held as part of the domain.

[87] Kemp, "Old Kingdom" in *Ancient Egypt – A Social History*, 86.

[88] Nielson, *Memory Work*, 208.

[89] Mariette and Maspero, *Les mastabas de l'ancien empire*. They found a mass burial field of the poor in Saqqara. The bodies were a metre below the surface. Present were small bowls and food rests for the deceased to use in the hereafter. So we have to deduce that building a tomb superstructure was not a commonplace occurence.

[90] Baines and Yoffee, "Order, legitimacy, and wealth: setting the terms", in *Order, legitimacy and wealth in ancient states*, eds. Richards and van Buren, 16. This article is a flow-on of the earlier article, which appeared in 1998 (see following footnote).

[91] Baines and Yoffee, "Order, legitimacy and wealth in ancient Egypt and Mesopotamia", in *The Archaic State: A Comparative Perspective*, eds. G. M. Feinman and J. Marcus, 235. High Culture is defined as "the production and consumption of aesthetic items under the control, and for the benefit, of the inner elite". They include under the term aesthetic items a wide range of items and traditional ways of life, e.g. visual art, musical performance, garments, high quality food and drink, and hunting.

[92] For a survey of the hierarchical structure within the elite see: Endesfelder, "Formierung der Klassengesellschaft", in *Probleme der frühen Gesellschafsentwicklung im Alten Ägypten*, ed. J. Hallof, 33-37.

[93] Kemp, *Ancient Egypt: Anatomy of a Civilization*, 282. While this appears in the chapter entitled 'New Kingdom Egypt', the quotation itself refers to the "earlier periods". Also see Eyre, "Work and the Organization of Work in the Old Kingdom", in *Labor in the Ancient Near East*, ed. M. A. Powell 40. While he views the assertions of the officials emphasizing the performance of their public duties, as "over-formalized", nevertheless he concludes that "the general picture is likely to be correct, of patronage and provision working downwards through society from the king, in return for labour and service working up from the lowest peasant". Each member of the household was thus dependent on the favour of the patron, who himself was equally dependent for his provisions on the king.

[94] Goody, *Representations and contradictions*, 257. Also see Baines, "Forerunners of Narrative Biographies", 24. Similarly in Kemp, *Ancient Egypt: Anatomy of a Civilization*, 111.

[95] While some of the iconographical scenes can probably be related to some form of similar life in the hereafter, nevertheless this is not a foregone conclusion. The funerary process scene can certainly not be put in this category, because no tomb owner would want to die a second time,

Mastaba: Prior to ca. 2700 BC the mastaba[96] was the architectural form used for both royal and private elite individuals and the division of the tomb into a sub- and a super-structure is well established.[97] The development of the mastaba for private elite individuals emphasizes three key points:[98]

1. Its architectural origins in the Neolithic burial mound.
2. Its occurrence in the isolated areas reserved for expressions of monumental elaboration.
3. Its role as one of the earliest expressions of monumentality, which functions to spread elite awareness among the non-elite.

The elite tomb as characterized by a mastaba has the following specific architectural features including:

- A sub-structure containing a burial chamber with access via a stairway, then a slope and later by a shaft.
- A super-structure built over the burial chamber. It was made of mud-brick or stone, with paneling or smooth limestone casing. The super-structure could have an inaccessible room, where the statue(s) of the tomb owner and members of his family were placed, called the serdab (Arabic for "cellar").
- A chapel where offerings were made and funerary services performed and where a stela or false door could be located.[99] The chapel was built either beside or into the super-structure.

It is outside the scope of this study to go into the details of the architectural development of the elite tomb; suffice it to say that in the period that this study is concerned with, the elite tomb had already undergone considerable progress as seen in the stone built elite tombs which replaced the primarily mud-brick ones of Dynasty 3.[100] What started out as an effort primarily to imitate earthly estates and mansions in Dynasties 1 and 2,[101] now increasingly

becomes in addition, an obsession with the security of life in the hereafter.

For our purposes and from Dynasty 4 onwards, the mastaba represents a special class of tomb meant exclusively for the elite[102] developed to satisfy certain tomb functions, namely as a:

- Place where the body is contained and protected, realized by the burial chamber, the shaft and later the sloping passage.
- Marker for the memory of the person, realized by the inscriptions of names and titles of the tomb owner, the addresses to the living, display of royal favour and social virtues of charity and justice, and the demonstration of their wealth and power.
- Place where service to the dead is performed, realized initially by the outside niche, then by the inside false-door in the above ground chapel, and by the development of an independent repertoire of forms and representations on the surrounding walls.
- Interface between this world and the next, realized in the refinement of the false door in the cult chapel of the Western wall of the super-structure.

Some of these functions are common to most funerary cultures, whilst others are specifically Egyptian in nature especially the cult and the memory function which show considerable development in their forms, texts and representations.[103]

One consequence of this development was the enhancement of the chapel, because of its role as the primary place of ritual transformation. The Egyptian architect achieved this refinement by three modifications to the interior and from the evidence it would appear that all were used,[104] namely:

1. Add externally to the existing elite tomb core as in tomb G2110 (Nefer) at Giza.[105]
2. Eliminate part of the elite tomb core and build onto and into it as in tomb G2155 (Kaninisut)[106] and G4970 (Nesut-nefer) at Giza.[107]
3. Build a chapel inside the core of the elite tomb as in tomb G1225 (Nefret-iabet) at Giza[108] and tomb G4000 (Hemiunu).[109]

These ideas are not new and many examples in the cemeteries at Giza, Maidum, Dahshur, and Saqqara are known.

---

nor for that matter the ploughing scene - the intention by the elite to do agricultural labour was never envisaged during the Old Kingdom.

[96] Shaw and Nicholson, *The British Museum Dictionary of Ancient Egypt*, 192. Also see Brinks, "Mastaba", *LÄ*, vol. 3, 1214-31. Also see Schulz and Seidel, eds., *Egypt: The World of the Pharaohs*, 30. Seidlmayer notes here that in Dynasty 1, the royal tombs at Abydos had no monumental superstructure but only a covering of sand held by brick walls which surrrounded the tomb.

[97] Reisner, *The development of the Egyptian tomb down to the accession of Cheops*, 14.

[98] Renfrew, "Beyond a subsistence economy," in *Reconstructing Complex Societies*, ed. C. B. Moore, 69-96.

[99] Wiebach, *Die ägyptische Scheintür*, 198.

[100] Garstang, *Mahâsna and Bêt Khallâf*, 9. Also see Barta, "The Transitional Type of Tomb at Saqqara North and Abusir South", in *Texte und Denkmäler des Ägyptischen Alten Reiches*, ed. Seidlmayer, 69-87. Thus tomb development is not to be understood as sequential, and stone lined chapels did not instigate stone mastabas. The evidence would point to a sort of transitory tomb, where the burial chamber is approached by a deep shaft which opens in the middle of the tomb, vertical shafts becoming exclusive during the reign of Senefru at Maidum and Dahshur. For an architectural based analysis, see Fritz, *Typologie der Mastabagräber des Alten Reiches*, 48-81.

[101] Gardiner, *The attitude of the ancient Egyptians to death and the dead*, 10. Also see Jánosi, *Die Gräberwelt der Pyramidenzeit*, 3-32.

[102] Seidlmayer, „Funerärer Aufwand und soziale Ungleichheit", *GM*, (104), 47.

[103] Harpur and Scremin, *Decoration in Egyptian tombs of the Old Kingdom*. Also see Alexanian, "Tomb and Social Status", in *The Old Kingdom Art and Archaeology*, ed. Barta, 1-8.

[104] Jánosi, *Giza in der vierten Dynastie*, 154-203 and 275-296.

[105] Junker, *Giza*, vol. 6, fig. 3.

[106] Junker, *Giza*, vol. 2, fig. 12.

[107] Junker, *Giza*, vol. 3, fig. 26.

[108] Reisner, *Giza Necropolis*, vol. 1, fig. 229.

[109] Junker, *Giza*, vol. 1, fig. 18.

What is new in Dynasty 5 is the predominance of an elite tomb type in which the cult chamber and the offering stela take their place inside the kern of the elite tomb, with a corresponding expansion in the type of scenes depicted. A high proportion of Dynasty 5 elite tombs also have a serdab, a feature that was already in evidence since its introduction in tomb FS3073 of Khabausokar and his wife Hathor-nefer-hetep during the reign of Djoser.[110]

The reliefs and inscriptions, which are elaborated in Dynasty 5 elite tombs, are already seen in their most important, albeit not in so extensive forms in the Dynasty 4 tombs of Nefermaat, Atet, Rahotep, and Neferet at Maidum and Akhtihetep and Metjen at Saqqara.[111]

Rock Cut Tombs[112]

These were developed primarily because of geological[113] as well as economical considerations.[114] Early rock cut tombs are found in the neglected quarries at Giza and Saqqara,[115] and in areas less suited for building an elite type of tomb such as the cliffs of Middle and Upper Egypt (e.g. Deshasha, Zawiet el-Maytin, Sheikh Said, Meir, Deir-el-Gebrawi, El-Hawawish, Salamuni, El-Khokha, and Quibbet-el-Hawa[116]).

Their main feature is that they do not have a significant super-structure,[117] the chapel being cut parallel to the cliff into the rock from which a shaft leads to the burial chamber, but have significantly large wall surfaces and thus allows for an expansion of the types of scenes.[118]

In contrast, the cruciform chapels at Saqqara and Maidum, and the L-shaped chapels at Giza were not highly suited to the expansion of scenes of daily life because of their smaller wall surfaces.

3.4 Tomb Architecture, Decoration, and Cultural Affiliation

Elite tombs were called *is*.[119] They were unique and visible, and attested to the tomb owner's ability to command a labour force, and having vicarious access to natural resources.[120] Elite burials were finely and richly decorated e.g. foreign goods such as cedar for their coffins and other costly materials for their grave goods. These goods were primarily procured for and used by the king. The private person's dependency on royal craftsmen was unavoidable, because it was only they, who could provide the highest quality of workmanship. If we couple these material requirements with the religious beliefs, which required an elaborate burial for a good afterlife, an additional source of kingly power becomes self-evident. In addition, the presence of the obligatory *ḥtp-di-nswt*[121] formula publicized the fact that the king as the representative on earth of the divine legitimized the tomb owner.

The tomb owner thus had the indirect approval of the divine too.[122]

Since the kings had monumental tombs, which at the least represented power, the elite by also building monumental tombs became an extension of this power of the king and the central government, of which he as a member of the elite was an integral part. The indirect cultural effect was to glorify and consolidate the power of the official and the divinity of the king.

The architectural forms of elite tombs are thus no accident; just like the temple for the gods,[123] and the 'palace' for the king, they are there to create a perfect inhabitable world for the elite. A world, which in its representations distances itself from the reality, and produces its own kind of truth of what should be, in contrast to what is, because what is can never be perfect or absolute. Indeed this is also relayed in the ancient Egyptian's view of the cosmos during this period. The tomb is a replica of this world model, through its architecture, paintings, reliefs, and grave goods; it reproduces an illusion of a unified reality of life. The totality of these is made to function for the use of the tomb owner in his afterlife by the process of the cultic rituals, and the concept of sympathetic magic. The artist and the tomb owner are fused into one unified endeavour, that of the literal visualization of activities in this world as well as having a communicative function which could be of symbolic value for all who visit the tomb.

During the Old Kingdom and up to the Middle Kingdom, the mastaba appears as a place where the tomb owner is the

[110] Brovarski, „Serdab," *LÄ*, vol. 5, 875.

[111] Harpur and Scremin, *The tombs of Nefermaat and Rahotep at Maidum*, 55-119. Also see Junker, *Giza* vol. 2, 18-21. In these bird netting, fishing, hunting, slaughtering, agricultural pursuits, manufacturing and offerings by personified estates, attendants and followers are already depicted.

[112] Reisner, *Giza Necropolis*, vol. 1, 219-47. Also see Stevenson-Smith, *A History of Egyptian Sculpture and Painting in the Old Kingdom*, 166. Both date the earliest rock cut tombs to the reign of Menkaure. However evidence now points to the reign of Khafre as being the earliest for such tombs, based on the finds of his sons and queens who are buried in rock cut tombs. For fuller details, see Jánosi, *Giza in der vierten Dynastie*, 296-429.

[113] Giedion, *The Eternal Present*, 403.

[114] Private communication by Kanawati (Macquarie University) that certain rock cut tombs, e.g. Kai-Khent, Irukaptah and Min-Ankh, mimic mastabas in certain architectural features. A link to expenditure and extent of the rock-cut tomb should always be kept in mind.

[115] Reisner, *A History of the Giza Necropolis*, 219-20. Also see Jánosi, *Giza in der vierten Dynastie*, 296-429.

[116] Brunner, *Die Anlagen der Ägyptischen Felsengräber bis zum Mittleren Reich*, 14-25.

[117] Dodson, *Egyptian Rock-Cut Tombs*, 7-11.

[118] Harpur and Scremin, *Decoration in Egyptian tombs of the Old Kingdom*, 104-06.

[119] Walsem, *Iconography of Old Kingdom elite tombs*, 17-19.

[120] Mohr, *The Mastaba of Hetep-Her-Akhti*, 34.

[121] This formula appears for the first time in the tomb of Rahotep (Dynasty 4). Also see Lapp, *Die Opferformel des Alten Reiches*, 30-38.

[122] Junker, *Giza* vol. 2, 43-45.

[123] Baines, "Temple Symbolism", *RAIN*, (15), 10-15. While no Old Kingdom palaces have been found, it would be naïve to believe that the head of the power base would not have allocated himself and his cohorts a specially designated place.

recipient of veneration and worship, because everything revolves around him: the chief character. Totally missing from the elite tomb in terms of iconography is any depiction of any deity (apart from that sanctioned hieroglyphically in the *ḥtp-di-nswt* formula).[124] This is even more surprising when these formulae voice the desire to enjoy the divine presence in the hereafter so frequently. Admittedly this desire is an indirect inference from the formulae that invoke Osiris, Wepwawet or Anubis. The latter two can be conceived of as identical gods, because of their similar features, and by the fact that the epithets *nb t3 ḏsr* (lord of the sacred land i.e. read cemetery) can be applied to either of them. Wepwawet means 'the one who opens the ways' and is a reminder of his function; that of guiding the newly deceased over the unknown paths crossing the desert to the kingdom of Osiris, and of making sure that the deceased is protected from adversaries as well as from any obstacles/difficulties. The relationship between all the funerary gods is a fluid one and admittedly there are subtle differences in the way their names are invoked.[125] Wepwawet was a pointer to ideology (vindication against enemies) and Anubis was mainly associated with the cultic purpose of embalming. However, in the context of this study it is the desire to be with 'a god' after death, unobstructed in any way, which is a logical but not a clear-cut inference.[126]

Other aspects such as the belief in a self-attainable afterlife may have played a role in the elaboration of themes and in the formation of an independent elite persona, which are pronounced and discernible in the court cemeteries.[127] However, it is only at the end of the Old Kingdom that the sort of afterlife in which the king participates in the eternal life of Osiris (as seen in some of the Pyramid Texts), is available to all. They too can now be identified with Osiris as "the Osiris N".[128]

Thus the elite tomb is not only defined by its plans and architectural subdivisions but more importantly by the events and the rituals that took place inside and around it and that may be depicted, which give the tomb its meaning.[129]

Every mastaba from the purely architectural evidence can be viewed as the representation of the desire of a tomb owner for equivalent life in the hereafter.[130] They are the outcome of beliefs shared within a society whose intention was realized in the physical act of building a tomb and the decoration of the interior, developed in the socio-cultural and the physical context of Egypt. The increase in the type and number of wall scenes is related primarily to the spatial development of the elite tomb.[131] All levels of society can now be reached: both as an expression of status during the life of the tomb owner, and as a source of commemoration and possible competition for his peers on his death. Architecture thus performs an ideological function by linking rulers and the elite through the stonework and monumentality to their forefathers, and expressly linking them (at least as far as the kings are concerned) to the cosmos.

3.5 The Artist

All decoration in a tomb required the abilities of a craftsman experienced in the techniques of drawing/painting/sculpting and since he is a vital element in this process, his role cannot be ignored.

The role of the 'artist' can be comprehended as an anonymous enabler and purveyor of accurate representation; he thus assumes a central albeit undefined position in the realization of the tomb owner's posthumous existence/state of being. The system of representation was influenced by a convention as to how the visual depiction had to be executed. The artist was there to ensure that what was depicted was recognizable, and was repeated, such that reality was codified by integrating function and position into a single motif.[132]

As far as the individual artists more correctly the 'dependent specialists'[133] are concerned, there is not much evidence as to their identity.[134]

[124] Sørenson, "Divine Access: The so-called democratization of Egyptian funerary literature as a socio-cultural process," in *The Religion of the Ancient Egyptians*, ed. G. Englund, 112-13. This is in contrast to the New Kingdom, where the tomb owner is depicted adoring and communicating with the gods in scenes reminiscent of a temple like character (where the king is shown in temples, adoring/communicating with the gods). At Thebes and Saqqara, the main deities shown in the eighteenth dynasty tombs are Osiris, Re-Harakhte, and Hathor as a cow; thus strengthening the argument that adaptive change and consequent development are crucial for the understanding of funerary iconography. Also see Kampp-Seyfried, "The Theban Necropolis: An overview", in *The Theban Necropolis*, eds. N. Strudwick, and J. H. Taylor, 2-10.
[125] DuQuesne, *The Jackal Divinities of Egypt*, 437-40.
[126] Lapp, *Die Opferformel des Alten Reiches* 56-58 and 85. In the offering formula one of the requests has been interpreted as a wish – may he (the deceased) be accompanied by his KA to the pure place and his arm be grasped by the great god. Another frequent request is for the deceased to be able to travel along the roads of the beautiful West. This has been interpreted literally. However, the crucial point is that the West is a synonym for the place where the gods of the dead reside, and where the deceased now hopes to go. It is in this sense that I have used the desire to be with a god. The specific god's name is uncertain but from Dynasty 5 onwards it is Osiris.
[127] Alexanian, "Social Dimensions of Old Kingdom Mastaba Architecture", in *Eighth International Congress of Egyptologists*, vol. 2, ed. Z. Hawass and L. P. Brock, 88-96.
[128] Taylor, Death and the Afterlife in Ancient Egypt, 27-31.

[129] Suaad, *Space Kinship and Gender*, Ph.D. Dissertation, University of Edinburgh. "… Space acquires meaning through the patterns of events observed…"
[130] Jánosi, *Die Gräberwelt der Pyramidenzeit*, 3. "Der vielfältige Inhalt und die besondere Ausstattung vieler Gräber zeugen von der Jahrtausende währenden, ungebrochenen Vorstellung an ein Leben nach dem Tod".
[131] Smith, *A History of Egyptian Sculpture and Painting in the Old Kingdom*, 167.
[132] Junge, "Vom Sinn der Ägyptischen Kunst", in *5000 Jahre Ägypten*, eds. J. Assmann and G. Burkhart, 43-60. For an account by an ancient artist on his abilities and his training see Barta, *Das Selbsterzeugnis eines altägyptischen Künstlers*, *MÄS*, (22), 138-41. .. "I am a craftsman successful in his craft, through that which he knows…I know the movement of a figure, the stride of a woman, how one looks at another, how to make frightened the face, the poise of the arm of him who harpoons the hippopotamus, and the pace of the runner…".
[133] Trigger, *Early Civilizations*, 57-59. For a general survey of craftsmen, see Valbelle, "Craftsmen", in *The Egyptians*, ed. S. Donadoni, 31-59.
[134] For one example of a named artist from Dynasty 6 see Borchardt, *Denkmäler des Alten Reiches*, 94, no. 1418. "… his trusted man, his beloved, the assistant sculptor of the palace, Iren-Akhti", offering his

Working under the patronage and control of the king had the effect that they could aspire to unprecedented levels of refinement and sophistication, and develop a unified style, which shows the hallmarks of durability and consistency. As all elite art appears to be produced by artisans associated with the royal court in the Old Kingdom Memphite region, a uniform style in the principles of register composition as well as the rendering of the human form is evident. It is seen in its most easily recognizable form emphasizing certain universally known aspects of the body. Human faces, lower torso, legs and feet are shown in profile; eyes and shoulders frontally, and the big toes are on the same side, as well as in the scaling of the protagonist and the depiction of women, invariably with either one or both breasts exposed.[135]

However, there are glimpses, which reveal, that even though they were not part of the established instigators of change (i.e. had very little or no power), they still could reveal their creative ego to the extent allowed by the accepted ideas of decorum[136] and requirements of the mortuary cult.[137] A very good example[138] is the way the artist in the tomb of Ty has shown the various herdsmen in a presenting the scroll motif. Not only does he depict the partial baldness, the nudity, and the various types of kilts worn but he also depicts this in opposition to a standardized man wearing a short wig and short kilt.

The captions in the sub-motifs of Dynasties 5 and 6, also betray creative logic on the part of the artist in making understandable the funny side and toil which must have been part of the everyday life of the non-elite for "sie sind ein merkwürdiges Zeugnis dafür, wie der alte Künstler selbst seine Bilder auffasste[139]".

Corrections by Egyptian artists also provide proof that they had judgments of their own, notwithstanding that they were dependent specialists.[140] The tomb artist is like the modern theatre director producing Shakespeare according to the original script without any improvisation: in such a script none of the living actors expresses any individual personality. The actor is secondary to the role model of the part: in that his lines, his clothes, body language, and mannerisms define the role. Similarly the

tomb artist depicted the formula symbols associated with the role model for a member of the elite, not the actual tomb owner himself. That is why so many paintings/reliefs of different tomb owners have so many similarities. Of course it is accepted that there are some reliefs[141] that try to portray an actual individual, but even these were subject to strict artistic conventions. While an Egyptian artist is seldom seen as signing his work in the modern sense,[142] nevertheless from his titles it is recognized that he was an honoured member of society.

Consider the example of Imhotep the great architect of Djoser who had one title that of "royal carpenter and mason and an "opener of stone",[143] which can relate to his expertise in the design and construction of the Step Pyramid. He also had at the same time other high-sounding titles like "Seal Bearer of the King of Lower Egypt, Administrator of the Great Mansion and Chief of Seers".[144] During the New Kingdom he is remembered for being a wise man and not just for his artistry in building the Step Pyramid.[145] However as far as the archeological record is concerned, his (Imhotep) craftsmanship, artistry, skill, etc. are seen nowhere other than in the Step Pyramid. Apart from a fragment of a statue with his name and sparse indirect references, now at the museum at Saqqara, he could for all intents not have existed.

Because of the formally conceived ideology of Egyptian kingship, any major changes in tradition or innovation in art form could not be attributed to the work of one individual. Therefore the absence of signed pieces means that one will never know the real contribution to advancement, by any particular person. Modern celebrity implications of automatically correlating name and fame with apparent skill would appear to have no place in ancient Egypt, at least during the lifetime of the individual.

We do not know the extent to which the artist's innate desire to produce art, which he wished to create, was realized. The artist's choice of attributes was therefore limited to what was the essential categorization of the thing, person, activity, and the material with which he had to work. Whatever he created had to have permanence not only in the sense of being physically permanent but in the sense of being based on a permanent and recognized Egyptian concept of the ideal, and so the necessity to name individual artists became irrelevant- he remained nameless.[146]

Indeed from as early as the Narmer palette, the tendency in Egyptian art is to inform, and so there is no attempt to convey

lord three geese.

[135] Schäfer, *Principles of Egyptian Art*, 91. Schäfer's solution was in proposing the absence of foreshortening and perspective. This is found in many cultures, accordingly the intellectual basis of Egyptian representation is a mystery.

[136] Baines, "Communication and Display", 471-82. Also see Baines, *Visual and Written Culture in Ancient Egypt* 14-21 and 304. This contains his latest thoughts on decorum. He has expanded the concept considerably from simply the juxtaposition of power relations and the sacred character of knowledge, to include inaccessible features of lived practice; acknowledging that decorum is not a single determining factor.

[137] Bolshakov, "The Ideology of the Old Kingdom Portrait", *GM*, (117/118), 89-142. He refers to among others: the depiction of the chief sculptor Niankhptah shown having a drink in a papyrus boat in the tomb of Ptahhotep at Saqqara.

[138] Wild, *Le Tombeau de Ti*, vol. 3, pl. 167.

[139] Erman, *Reden, Rufe, und Lieder auf Gräberbildern des Alten Reiches*, 4.

[140] Smith, *A History of Egyptian Sculpture and Painting in the Old Kingdom*, 252. Also see Junker, *Giza*, vol. 3, 203.

[141] Mostly from Dynasty 4: see Smith, *A History of Egyptian Sculpture and Painting in the Old Kingdom* pl. 6, 7, 8 and 9.

[142] A single leaf of a carved wooden panel from the tomb of Kaemkhaset (Dynasty 5) now in the Cairo Museum, identifies the sculptor's name as Itw. Author's personal observation.

[143] Firth, Quibell, and Lauer, *Excavations at Saqqara*, pl.58.

[144] Helck, "Titel und Titularen", *LÄ*, vol. 6, 597. It is accepted that one could have many titles and that this did not mean that these actually were one's official duties or work because many of them were purely honorific.

[145] Breasted, *A History of Egypt*, 113. "In priestly wisdom, in magic ... in medicine, in architecture ... his name was never forgotten".

[146] Hermann, "Zur Anonymität der ägyptischen Kunst", *MDAIK*, (6), 157.

an aspect from any one angle, idealization is pervasive, things are represented as they should be and not as they are. This relative idealization explains why throughout the pharaonic period Egyptian art remained distinctive, and can always be recognized as something Egyptian.

Funerary art was religiously inspired, and had to conform to the dictates of decorum, and could also be an element that explains the striving for excellence on the part of the artist. The evidence for this comes from the so-called Memphite Theology, which purports to describe how the deity Ptah (also a patron of artisans and builders) created the gods:

> "He settled their offerings, he established their shrines, he made their bodies according to their wishes. Thus the gods entered into their bodies, of every wood, every stone, every clay everything that grows upon him in which they came to be".[147]

This could help to explain why artists were not individually honoured in the modern sense, because the attainment of excellence by any craftsman may have been ultimately understood to be a product of divine inspiration.

However, since it is known that there was profit oriented economic exchange in ancient Egypt,[148] this explanation would seem incomplete. The modern view is to consider the artist just like any other worker, whose technical expertise could win him a slightly privileged position thus explaining the few instances in which he is identified by name.[149]

Workshop scenes from non-royal Old Kingdom tombs depict artists and craftsmen working together in numerous pursuits.[150] It can therefore be assumed that Egyptian artists saw themselves as part of a tradition, in which people who had specialized in drawing, painting, and hieroglyphic skills, etc. all collaborated jointly in the manufacture of particular goods desired by the patron. For the most part therefore, one does not see much evidence of artistic individualism. Occasionally however an Egyptian artist allowed himself a flicker of individuality and to these one will turn when discussing the specified tombs.

Since most Egyptian art had social, religious, and political meanings;[151] the fulfilling of these meanings meant that he would have had to combine the intentions of the patron, the prevalent value systems and the accepted way of doing

FIG. 1: SHEIKH EL-BELED IN THE EGYPTIAN MUSEUM, CAIRO CG 34

things, and yet produce an entity that was a combination of all these. An art object thus becomes a symbol, which the artist had encrypted, because he *was* astute enough to select only those attributes which society considered ideal and essential "for the correct identification of the culturally defined category represented by the figure".[152] The quality of what skilled craftsmen created also reflected the support by the patron because of the nature of what Barry Kemp calls a "court culture".[153] The more input and investments that were provided by the patron, the more chances that the development of artist skills would reach a higher level of perfection. His hands were however relatively tied by the demands of decorum,[154] the actual material with which he had to work, as well as the power at the court in Memphis. However within the broad rules of artistic convention, there was some room for variation,[155] e.g. the reserve heads from Giza,[156] the statue of Rahotep and his wife Nofret from Maidum,[157] the statue of Hemiunu from Giza,[158] the scribal statue of Kai from Saqqara,[159] the bust of prince Ankhhaf,[160] and a statue of a man described as 'Sheikh el-Beled'.[161]

147 Sethe, *Dramatische Texte zu altägyptischen Mysterienspielen*, 68. For translation, see Lichtheim, *Ancient Egyptian Literature*, vol. 1, 55. The dating of this text by Lichtheim to the OK has been questioned, it is now believed to be a pious text of the Late Period, see Junge, "Zur Fehldatierung des. sog. Denkmals memphitischer Theologie", *MDAIK*, (29), 195-204.

148 Warburton, *Macroeconomics from the Beginning*, Civilisations du Proche-Orient, 116 and 28.

149 As illustrated by the artist named Niankhptah in Harpur, "The Chapel of Ptahhotep", pl. 211 and the eldest brother named Ihhi in Duell, "The mastaba of Mereruka", vol. l, pl. 43.

150 Kanawati, *The Teti Cemetery at Saqqara*, vol. 2, pl. 40. Examples of this cooperative tradition are seen far into the NK. Also see Dunham et al., *The mastaba of Queen Mersyankh III*, Fig. 5, and Wild, *Le Tombeau de Ti*, vol. 3, pl. 173.

151 Kemp, *Ancient Egypt: Anatomy of a Civilization* 135-37.

152 Weeks, "Art , Word, and the Egyptian World View", in *Egyptology and the Social Sciences*, ed. K. Weeks, 65.

153 Ibid. 112.

154 Baines, "Communication and Display", 474-75. Also see Baines, *Visual and Written Culture in Ancient Egypt*, 14-30, where he expands on his original concept of decorum.

155 Wilson, "The Artist of the Egyptian Old Kingdom", *JNES*, (6), 231-49. For extensive examples, also see Bolshakov "The Ideology of the Old Kingdom Portrait", 89-142.

156 Smith, *A History of Egyptian Sculpture and Painting in the Old Kingdom*, pls. 7-9.

157 Ibid. pl. 6 (c).

158 Ibid. pl. 6 (d).

159 Ibid. pl. 18 (a).

160 Ibid. pl. 15 (a).

161 Saleh and Sourouzian, *The Egyptian Museum Cairo: Official Catalogue*, CG 34.

Chapter 4: The Search for the Generics in the Immaterial Aspects

The previous chapter was concerned with the identification of material influences on the development of the elite tomb and its iconography.

In contrast, this chapter explores all those influences, which are not explicit in the archaeological record, but concern the inner rationalizations of Egyptian society, and which may be the justification for the way the material record was fashioned. The range of immaterial factors that might have been involved, are explored in this chapter because these provide the primary reference points and give meaning to acts which can otherwise be routine, ordinary or not even understandable.

4.1 Organizational and Behavioural Aspects of Egyptian Society

The Old Kingdom is characterized by a society, which is hierarchical and status based, characterized by rapid change, and social as well as economic development.[162] Kanawati views the early Old Kingdom administration as one that was centralized, where officials who lived in, and were buried in Memphis administered the provinces.[163] One knows very little of the social organization that existed up to the early part of Dynasty 4 and it is impossible to tell how united and national the ruling elite was. Even when officials at Memphis held titles of provincial authority, it is difficult to infer whether this was a statement about underlying political unity, or just a declaration of local connections. The material evidence from the earlier cemeteries at Tarkhan, Saqqara, and Helwan point to a stratified society indicated by certain graves having a separate burial chamber and cult place.[164]

Prior to Dynasty 4 absolute power is seen in the king. However, by the end of Dynasty 4, growing complexity of society and the cumulative effects of increasing expectations in the elite of upward mobility in this world, and of direct access to god in the next, results in a change in the organization and behaviour of elite society marked by:

- Changes in the spatial dimensions of the elite tomb.
- Development of various genres of representational motifs and elaboration of sub-motifs.
- Progression in the biographical inscriptions from a concentration on the grave, to a career type

enumeration and finally to that of an individual in his own right, stressing his claim to a moral stature.
- Mechanisms that allowed for households to expand into larger entities.

Change then is to be understood more than just simple adjustments to climate or patterns of dominance as exhibited in grave architecture and must include the changing perceptions of the socio-economic structure, and the relations between the crown and the elite, and within the households of the elite.[165] While the elite tombs yield some idea of daily life in OK society, the royal tombs are completely silent in this regard.

In the tomb of Nikanswt (Dynasty 5), his tomb chapel depicts what can be described as important members of his extended household; these include: "Two overseers of property … in overall charge … supported by eleven 'scribes'. A 'director of the workforce'… two 'directors of the dining hall', two 'overseers of linen', a 'seal bearer', three butchers, two bakers, one cook, and five butlers … and twelve "*K3*-priests/servants" … Another fifteen men … are without an indication of their profession.[166]" Further evidence of the varied nature of society can be seen from the cache discovered by Winlock in the MK tomb of Meketre, which include models of houses, boats, granaries, and human /animal figurines, etc. Especially in relation to the granary which was the main treasure of an Egyptian estate, he writes: "The personnel needed to run this granary numbered at least sixteen men … who are obviously the minimum in an establishment of this size[167]". Again from the Hekanakhte letters we learn that although his home was at Nebesit, he had a variety of moderate landholdings some distance away from his home. Reference in his letters is also made to the fourteen people in his household, who include his eldest son and houschold, plus Hekanakht's other dependents. These people are in his description completely under his control:

---

[162] Strudwick, *The Administration of Egypt in the Old Kingdom. The Highest Titles and their Holders*, 320-321 and 338-339. There is growing penetration of the state (in early Dynasty 5, kings' sons apparently ceased to hold functional office). The trend is towards bureaucratically defined power structures, and expansion of the role of the state. Also see Kanawati, *Governmental Reforms in the Old Kingdom*, which mainly deals with the situation from Dynasty 6 onwards.

[163] Kanawati, *Governmental Reforms in the Old Kingdom*, 1-2. Also see Müller-Wollermann, *Krisenfaktoren im Ägyptischen Staat des ausgehenden Alten Reichs* Ph.D. Dissertation, Eberhard-Karls Universität Tübingen, 80.

[164] Petrie, *Tarkhan II*, pl.14. See Emery, *Archaic Egypt*, pls. 8 and 9. Also see Köhler, "Seven Years of Excavations at Helwan in Egypt", *BACE*, (15), 84. Further see Jánosi, *Die Gräberwelt der Pyramidenzeit* 3-32.

[165] The term household is extended to mean more than just one family and covers families living in a large socioeconomic unit. These may include persons in different levels of authority as well as the resources under their command. This could be the structure that existed in ancient Egypt.

[166] Malek and Foreman, *In the Shadow of the Pyramids*, 93.

[167] Winlock, *Models of daily Life in Ancient Egypt*, 26. See also his plates 1-53, and pages 71-80, for general remarks on the models he found.

THE SEARCH FOR THE GENERICS IN THE IMMATERIAL ASPECTS

"the entire household is like [my] children and everything is mine".[168]

In addition from at least early Dynasty 4 (the tomb of Nefermaat at Maidum), we see the train of offering bearers, each of which represents a personification of a (*niwt*), and (*hwt*), bearing offerings to the (*pr ḏt*).

The offering bearers point to the existence of large estates of land, and the other dependents point to the complex web of interrelationships that must have existed within the extended household and the outside. Accordingly it can be asserted that the household unit points to complexity, ranging from simple provision to expansion into greater estates, and ultimately into the State.[169] As Eyre observes "the key social unit was not the individual but a larger family grouping, whose head needed to ... promote the socially necessary family solidarity, to make social alliances, especially through marriages, and to ensure provision for individual family members".[170] These family relationships by necessity extended beyond the immediate blood relationships.

For the individual elite member of society, the closeness to the king in status when alive and nearness to him when dead, are the most important determining factors. The resulting structure of society is pyramidal with the king at the apex assisted by the royal family and literate officials and at the bottom the masses of illiterate others.[171] We have scant evidence of the social position of the non-elite, but from the little we have (i.e. the fact that estates of cults and tomb endowments belonged to the deceased tomb-owner and so were not able to be alienable by the living), it is clear that they were not treated as separate items of property to be bought and sold as a commodity. However, this structure is fluid because society as observed in this period of ancient Egypt is still in the stages of being formed. It is neither a loose aggregate of people because hierarchy is evident, nor is it a totally structured society because of the absence of intertwined parts, which make up a well thought-out and carefully planned whole.

Consider the structure of an ancient Egyptian village during this period. It is well known that the ancient Egyptian villages produced a wide range of handicrafts, and that local trade was exclusively based on an exchange of surplus products.[172] Even though these villages were self-sufficient, they were not characterized by the belief that all inhabitants should have equal social, economic, and 'political rights', as the evidence from the earlier cemeteries

of Naga-ed-Deir clearly demonstrate.[173] Inequalities therefore must have not only been approved but actively maintained, but the degrees of inequality among the non-elite which a well-knitted society would show are absent. Evidence points to there being important non-royal people and that kinship was the basis of the elite.[174] Accordingly by the end of Dynasty 4 Egyptian society can be understood as a community tending towards increasing hierarchy, and complexity. The king is absolutely established as a god on earth, and a cornerstone of national unity.[175] As Wilson notes,[176] the written language of Old Kingdom Egypt has no words for "government", "state", "nation", as impersonal terms conceived apart from the pharaoh, and the nearest approximation is in the word *nswt*,[177] which refers to the religious-ideological nature of kingship rather than to the organization of society as such. Although the origins of the state are unclear,[178] Wilson continues that the "theory of government was that the king was everywhere and did everything, a large proportion of the officials who acted for him carried titles expressing their direct responsibility to him". Particularly in the Old Kingdom, inscriptions suggest that the pharaohs personally ensured the consolidation of royal power, by the elimination of all independent discourse and the defense of the frontiers as a fulfillment of their duty to the gods. There is evidence from certain rituals, which express this permanency of the institution of the king, his right to power as well as his role in the maintenance of order, e.g.

1. the "circuit of the wall" a ceremony performed during his coronation emphasizing the symbolic appropriation of territory,
2. the ritual of opening the canal as depicted on the Scorpion mace head indicating the renewal of living things - similar to what Osiris was supposed to do,
3. the depiction of the king smiting his enemies indicating victory over chaos,

The instructions given by Pharaoh Wahkare Khety III (ca. 2070-2040 BC) to his son Merikare are also illuminating in this regard.[179]

Royal power over the masses was exercised through a hierarchical bureaucratic structure in which all officials were ultimately subject to royal authority. One of the duties

---

[168] Baer, "An Eleventh Dynasty Farmer's Letters to his Family", *JAOS*, (83), 1-19.
[169] Weber, *Economy and Society*, 105-133. His patrimonial regime is of value as to a possible method of emergence of the Egyptian State; although his views on Egypt are now outdated.
[170] Eyre, "Feudal Tenure and Absentee Landlords", in *Grund und Boden in Altägypten*, ed., S. Allam, 113.
[171] Wilkinson, "Social Stratification", 302.
[172] Erman, *Life in Ancient Egypt*, 494-97. Also see Wengrow, *The archaeology of early Egypt*, 72-98.

[173] Reisner et al., *The early dynastic cemeteries of Naga-ed-Dêr*. See also Petrie and Griffith, *The Royal Tombs of the Earliest Dynasties, Part II*, especially p. 8 and 12. (The tombs of Djer and Khasekhemwy at Umm el-Qa'ab, Abydos are among the earliest examples of class and status hierarchy).
[174] Helck, "Die soziale Schichtung des ägyptischen Volkes im 3. und 2. Jahrtausend v. Christus", *JESHO*, (2), 5-16. The important non-royals are Imhotep and Hesyre of Dynasty 3 and Metjen and Pehernefer of early Dynasty 4. Also see Campagno, "Kinship and the emergence of the ancient Egyptian State", *BACE*, (11), 39.
[175] Janssen, "The Early State in Egypt", in *The Early State*, eds. H. Claessen and P. Skalnik, 213-14.
[176] Wilson, *The Burden of Egypt*, 79.
[177] *Wörterbuch der Ägyptischen Sprache*, II, 332-333.
[178] For a helpful survey of the literature on this subject, see Endesfelder, "Formierung der Klassengesellschaft", esp. 6-9.
[179] Simpson, ed., *The Literature of Ancient Egypt*, 152-65.

of bureaucracy was to collect taxes from the peasantry, these being levied on grain, animals, and handicrafts. Corvée labour was required for state projects and thus supported both the state and the elite who had control of this.[180] Because the Egyptian kings had at their disposal exclusive access to scarce resources and craftsmen skills, as well as a monopoly on all foreign trade, the elite were forced to turn to royalty to access these goods, both for their intrinsic value and as a sign of royal favour. It was this that resulted in the substantial increase in royal power as well as those of his elite in the early Old Kingdom.

In addition there is a resultant increase in state wealth because of trade with nearby countries as well as the exploitation of Nubia and Sinai for their mineral resources. Side by side follows the development of the administration and technical know-how, especially in regard to royal funerary complexes. The application of organizational and technical skills results in the construction of the first full stone building - the Step Pyramid of Djoser at Saqqara. Further experimentation follows in early Dynasty 4 in the building of the pyramids at Medum, Dashur, and Giza.

The elite too progress to a tomb super-structure made of stone, but from a cultural point of view what is more salient is the nature of the elite tomb inscriptions. In the early part of this period the stress is on the nature of the grave and who made it.[181] However, in early Dynasty 5, the emphasis is on aligning oneself as closely as theoretically possible to the king,[182] because it is only through this organizational structure that one could advance (until the end of Dynasty 4, major officials tend to be close relatives of the king).

In late Dynasty 5 and continuing into the FIP a radical and subtle change in the perception of kingship is witnessed.[183] The king is no longer quite as supreme, as he was when he was first designated "son of Ra". The close hold on power that he had until Dynasty 4 in the institution of the delegate princes/family is now replaced by the substitution of career officials, who in Dynasty 6 became prominent enough to establish their own areas of authority.[184] Side by side is the developing role of the priests, who as servants of Ra assume growing importance in the capital.[185]

Another tendency is for the rise of officials, who serve in the palace and in the estate of a deceased king and thus are exempt from all imposts.[186] With the passage of time these officials look to the mortuary benefices entrusted to them as an inheritable right and an inalienable possession. This group of officials is designated ḥnti-š and occurs for the first time in Dynasty 5 indicated by persons such as the vizier Mereruka and the nomarch Sabni.[187]

The characteristic from Dynasty 5 onwards is the desire to free oneself and with it the awakening of a sense of individuality.[188] This is observed among other things in texts, which reveal the personal intervention of the tomb owner in helping the disadvantaged.[189]

Egyptian society became one based on institutionalized inequalities, because humans will always pursue their own meaningful interests, whether it is in the acquisition of new arable land, in gaining the favour of a higher individual, or simply by the denial of or limiting the amount of information flow. Each person being dependent on the next higher up, right up to the king, excessively determines Egyptian society in this period. Add to this the competition that existed between the households themselves, then a picture of the nascent existence of inequality emerges. Both the biographies of Weni the Elder and that of Harkhuf are instructive in this regard.[190] In both of them the protagonists stress that not only did they do everything that the king wanted but that these happened within a specified period, thus suggesting the ruthless nature of competitive power strategies, and what would be required to attain bigger favours and with it the extension of their own household. Bureaucratic hierarchy was the order of the day and there must have been endless layers of officials each trying to be a part of managing the state's business, if the range of titles is anything to go by. The Egyptians accepted the status quo because of their fundamental belief that order had to be maintained, and that this was a divine pre-requirement to

---

[180] Brewer and Teeter, *Egypt and the Egyptians*, 95.
[181] Sethe, *Urkunden des Alten Reiches*, 8, l. 14-17. "His eldest son Tjenti is he who made this when he was buried in the beautiful West, according to what he (the father) had ordered when he was alive and on his two feet".
[182] Ibid. 51-53. The phrase "esteemed by the king more than any other servant" appears six times including numerous references to closeness to the king.
[183] Lichtheim, Ancient Egyptian Literature, vol. I, 89. " I nourished Imyotru in years of misery". It is precisely in statements like this, which one would expect to be the prerogative of the king, that we see a dilution of his powers.
[184] Müller-Wollermann, *Krisenfaktoren im Ägyptischen Staat des ausgehenden Alten Reichs* 73-75, and 130-34. She considers the social structure in the Old Kingdom to be an example of Weber's 'Patrimonialbürokratie', with similarities to the patterns found in an extended household.
[185] Baer, *Rank and title in the Old Kingdom,* 245-47 and 50. This is not denying the presence of other local gods which existed by ca. 3100 B.C., e.g. Seth at Naqada, Horus at Hierakonpolis, Neith at Sais, Min at Koptos, Wepawawet at Abydos, etc. However, the culmination of battles and

alliances which resulted in a unified state also demanded the transition to a cosmic god, and Ra the primaeval sun god at Heliopolis grows in stature. For further details regarding the early devlopment of religion, see Hassan, "Primeval Goddess to Divine King", in *The Followers of Horus*, eds. R. Friedman and B. Adams, 307-321.
[186] Baud, "La date d'apparition des xnti-s", *IFAO*, (96), 13-49.
[187] Helck, *Untersuchungen zu den Beamtentiteln des Ägyptischen Alten Reiches*, 107-108. Both Baer and Helck agree with this dating. However Roth in *A Cemetery of Palace Attendants,* 43, seems to advocate an earlier date following the dating of the tombs in the cluster in the Western Cemetery at Giza.
[188] The previously held view of a 'decentralization leading to democratization of the afterlife' (Wlson: *The Burden of Egypt*, 87) has been called into question. Whilst I agree that this term is ill conceived, and it could be replaced by a better term (e.g. societal evolution), he has done a service to Egyptology by pointing to a significant factor involving the historical processes of change. We still have to explain the causes and the relationship between the observed evidence and the changes in the behaviour of the individual elite, e.g. in their autobiographical inscriptions, in the architecture of their tombs, and in the increasing stratification of titularies and official rankings especially in Dynasties 5 and 6. Accordingly, whatever name we decide to give to these historical processes and their observed effects in society, they still are cogent evidence of change and expansion of the body politic, which is undeniable.
[189] A survey of these can be seen in Gnirs, "Die ägyptische Autobiographie", in *Ancient Egyptian Literature,* ed. Loprieno, 191-241.
[190] Simpson, ed., *The Literature of Ancient Egypt*, 404 - 410.

a happy existence (although this must have been restricted to the happy few). Hence, it has been suggested that all intellectual enquiry was restricted to those whose interest it served, namely both the secular and religious elite, with consequential effect on the material traces left behind.[191]

State and religion were one and the same and there was social stability before its eventual decline. This can be the only inference, because the monuments and the refinements in art produced during this period could not have been achieved without an appearance of stability and unity among the inhabitants of Egypt at this time.

Another aspect of the structure of Old Kingdom society was that the elite bureaucrats were generalists with wide areas of control over the population group that they were responsible for. This was the norm in most ancient societies until the modern spread of education enabled non-elite individuals to acquire these skills and gradually displace the previous nepotism.[192]

Bureaucrats held office initially by accident of birth but by Dynasty 5 by appointment. In this context, since writing/reading was an elite activity, only an elite class could engage in bureaucracy. The social relationships which were the outcome of the above, were not an abstract concept, they were based on relational connections between the people, the place and on the divine principle of *M3ʿt*.

As already stated, in the Old Kingdom behaviour was dominated by social relationships based on give-and-take around the central foundation of absolute kingly power, and the principle of *M3ʿt*.

Even though the evidence at our disposal does not indicate direct participation by ordinary Egyptians in temple based practiced religion, it has been shown that private religion existed, but very few traces of it have been preserved.[193] The evidence implies at the very least that the "pre-formal mud-brick temple" was a focus of local religious and cultural activity,[194] that pious foundations, and the practice of cult-magic also co-exist and therefore the word 'religion' should not be restricted to official state religion but should mean to include all human behaviour vis-à-vis the invisible.[195] A separation between the official and the private categories of practiced religion is not sustainable. It can be argued that the pious foundations relate primarily to economic wealth redistribution, and to a lesser degree

private religion and behaviour. Nevertheless the 'filter through' effect of the building projects of both the royals and the elite, connected as these were to a form of religion, which ensured the perpetual maintenance of the cults for gods, kings, and the elite private person, may have induced a variety of attitudes according to the situation of the individual. The ambivalence between official religion, self-interest, personal religion, and cult-magic cannot be ignored, and must have had some effect on the behaviour and the religiousness of the ancient Egyptian. Such attitudes were in the main to the benefit of the ruling elite because it reflected a society that was marked by extreme disparity in economic and social standing, further aggravated by the elite having the monopoly over rule making. This is particularly so in archaic societies when in due time the split in kinship between ruler and followers accompany social stratification and a changing ideology.[196]

Even in today's largely secular societies, this concept may not seem so alien. For many years, a Protestant establishment in Ireland behaved in a manner which can only be described as being systematic defamatory towards Catholicism and the largely Roman Catholic population. While it goes without saying that there are differences between Northern Ireland and Egypt with regard to religion practiced/understood and the structure of their societies, nevertheless it cannot be denied that religion has the power to influence behaviour in a population. Often the state is jealous of this power that a rival mass organization might wield, how else can one explain the persecution of spiritual movements, e.g. Falun Gong in modern China?

Unfortunately as already stated, the non-elite members have left very little by way of archaeological material, but this does not mean that they had no part in the construction/decoration of the elite tomb beyond merely implementing orders. Their political influence was exceptionally limited. Nevertheless the continued consumption of great quantities of the products of craftsmanship in building and in the decoration of tombs, could probably only be sustained, because the elite recognized particular rights and duties associated of being in their position. These come under the heading of *M3ʿt* as opposed to *jzft* and *grg*[197] (i.e. the rise of ideas of kindness and related social expediency), and because they (both the elite and the non-elite) believed in the nature of divine kingship.[198] Further,

[191] Helck, "Die soziale Schichtung des ägyptischen Volkes im 3. und 2. Jahrtausend v. Christus", 17-21.

[192] Thompson, *Economic and Social History of the Middle Ages*, vol. II, 752-53. (A medieval parallel would be the influence of the English Lords of the Manor, who had a virtual monopoly of most state and legal powers in feudal England).

[193] Baines, "Practical Religion and Piety", *JEA*, (73), 79-98.

[194] Kemp, *Ancient Egypt: Anatomy of a Civilization*, 111-135.

[195] Trigger et al., *A Social History*, 85, and 105-107. Also see Kemp, "How Religious were the Ancient Egyptians", in *CLJ*, (5), 25-54. As regards the role of cult-magic see Dunand and Zivie-Coche, *Gods and Men in Egypt*, 122-128. We learn that God "has ordained for them magic, as weapons to fend off the impact of what may come to pass", see also Simpson, ed., The *Literature of Ancient Egypt*, l. 139, 165.

[196] Earle, *How Chiefs Come to Power*, 6.

[197] Simpson, ed., *The Literature of Ancient Egypt,* 132, line 6.5. "Great is Ma'at, and its foundation is firmly established; It has not been shaken since the time of Osiris". Also see Sethe, *Urkunden des Alten Reiches*, vol. l, 198f. "I have come down from my town, I have descended from my nome, having done justice (Ma'at) for its lord, having contented him with what he loves: I spoke truly (Maa), I did justice (Ma'at)...I rescued the weak from one stronger than he as much as I could; I gave bread to the hungry, clothes to the naked..."

[198] Faulkner, *The Ancient Egyptian Pyramid Texts*, § 134-193. Here the supremacy of the king as a god from Unas to Pepy ll is asserted. Although these utterances are part of the Pyramid Texts and therefore restricted to the king, these texts as opposed to the physical artefact had a much earlier pedigree before their introduction to the tomb, thus implying that the elite had knowledge of these. See Allen, "Funerary Texts and their Meaning", in "*Mummies and Magic*", eds. S. D'Auria etal. 39.
A clearer picture of the king's relationship with the gods Osiris, Seth and

because increases in population occurred slowly,[199] the nature of Old Kingdom society must have been one that was grouped, and to some extent interlocking. This was an additional factor why manpower, skill, and resources to a project could be easily secured[200] such that monumentality and artistic refinements assume a particular role in social relations.

These behavioural attitudes could have helped to give the elite a sense of who they were, and to the non-elite the meaning of their interdependent existence. This book will show that this connection between the tomb owner and the community was an essential element in an approach that affected their everyday life and the accepted methods of its expression in the tombs. A behavioural principle that might also have been operative was the notion of kindness, a further refinement to the meaning of *M3ʿt*, which may have provided additional solidarity for the communities. In his writings on Egypt, Diodorus Siculus remarks that:

> "… among the Egyptians, the punishments of the wicked and the rewards of the good are not mythological ideas, but visible facts, and both sorts of people are reminded of their responsibilities every day; and in this way is wrought the greatest and most profitable reformation of man's character".[201]

Lichtheim aptly points out "what matters is that the inherent moral values … were respected not only by officials … but by society at large".[202]

The 'political' ethos of the times as evidenced in the biographical inscriptions may have also been the acknowledgement of vulnerability that made them generous, and not just compassionate.

Goedicke published a stela, which is claimed to be from the West field at Giza. While the top is entirely missing, that which remains tells us that due to an official becoming sick, the king granted him the use of a carrying-chair as follows:

"Now when he was ailing, His Majesty caused that a carrying-chair be brought to him from the Residence … and His Majesty caused (a guard of) young men from the Residence be made for him to enter the Residence with him".[203]

Another similar inscription is seen on the entrance jamb of Hetepherniptah:

> "the king caused that he be made comfortable in a carrying-chair and that young recruits carry him in it following the king".[204]

A further similar example is that in the biographical inscription of Washptah where the king orders a carrying-chair for a sick official as well as a group of young men to carry it.[205]

Again in early Dynasty 5, the inscription of Rawer a high palace official and 'šem-priest, narrates how his leg was touched during the taking of the prow rope during the divine barque ceremony[206] by the *ames*-sceptre of the king. Thanks to the intervention of the king, this did not have any magical or other consequences for Rawer in this or the next life.[207]

These incidents emphasize that the king presumably cared for his elite. The reliance on *M3ʿt* in daily life is therefore obvious at least as far as the king and the elite are concerned, even though the question as to the intention of the biographer can never be ascertained, and the tension between self-propaganda and human compassion will remain a mystery.

However, as regards the non-elite it may have been different in the degree to which it was practiced. The 'Tale of the Eloquent Peasant' from the Middle Kingdom, is an example which defines the constructs and thought processes of Egyptian society: namely the limits of socially defined boundaries and a collective identity based on the concept of *M3ʿt*, which embodies among other things the fulfillment of hierarchical expectations, as well as correct social behaviour. When the peasant says:

"Speak Ma'at! Perform Ma'at! For it is great, it is exalted, it is enduring, its integrity is evident, and it will cause (you) to attain the state of veneration",[208] he is expressing what was in reality "an assertion of conscience as an influential force",[209] that righteousness is the precursor to being remembered.

It was part of the understood system that a better life for the individual could only be had when the community as a whole had a better life. It should be stressed that the notions of religion, which instilled the belief that through certain forms of behaviour like kindness, one transforms oneself, promoted this concept. The resultant ethical foundation

---

Horus, can be got if these utterances are read in conjunction with the 31 drawings depicted in the Ramesseum Dramatic Papyrus. See Sethe, *Dramatische Texte zu altägyptischen Mysterienspielen*, 245-258.

[199] Kemp, *Ancient Egypt: Anatomy of a Civilization*, 11.

[200] Weeks, "Preliminary report on the first two seasons at Hierkonpolis. Part II", *JARCE*, (9), 29-33.

[201] Diodorus, *Diodorus On Egypt*, 122. Although he was a contemporary of Caesar, this quotation casts a historical light on what someone living at a much later period than the OK, understood to be the character of the ancient Egyptians, which is a pointer to rights and duties as practiced; indeed the essence of Ma'at.

[202] Lichtheim, *Ancient Egyptian Autobiographies*, 6.

[203] H. Goedicke, "A Fragment of a Biographical Inscription of the Old Kingdom", *JEA*, (45), figs. 1 and 2 and p. 8-9.

[204] Sethe, *Urkunden des Alten Reiches*, vol. I, 231, l. 14-15. The hieroglyph before the carrying chair symbol is to be recorded as *s im3* (to make well disposed) and not *s bnr*. This is clearly denoted by the variant of the sign (M1-Gardiner List). Now listed as M1++ in Borghouts, *Egyptian*, 80.

[205] Sethe, *Urkunden des Alten Reiche*, vol. I, 43, l. 15-19.

[206] "Ceremony" as used in this book, means an act conducted elaborately in accordance with prescribed religious and social procedures, which serve to reinforce and renew the event, i.e. this could relate to any prescribed procedure enacted in accordance with the rules of an established written or unwritten code, which express social relationships.

[207] Strudwick, *Texts from the Pyramid Age*, 305.

[208] Simpson, ed., *The Literature of Ancient Egypt*, 320.

[209] Breasted, *The Dawn of Conscience*, 123.

is that the only viable life is the collaborative life with other people, especially illustrated in the biographical inscriptions. However the biographies go beyond this and in so far as they are a narrative about the past, they also have a historical perspective.

Assmann sums this up as follows: "Diese biographische Grabinschriften sind echte End-Texte, sie blicken vom anderen Ufer der imaginativüberschrittenen Todesschwelle her auf das als abgeschlossenes Ganzen vor Augen liegende Leben zurück. ... Daher ist die Grabbiographie in Ägypten die einzige Form, die narrative in die Vergangenheit zurückgreift und in diesem Sinne als 'Geschichtsschreibung' eingestuft werden kann".[210]

If this was then the general modus Vivendi, why did the Old Kingdom decline?

Different views have been proposed as to the ultimate decline of the Old Kingdom, the focus being on the "disintegration of central authority and the rise of the semi-autonomous families in the provinces"[211] but there is no single reason for the decline.[212] All one can say from the inscriptional and archaeological evidence from the FIP is that the masses of 'others' at the base of the organizational pyramid, also try to participate in this unwinding of the strict bonds, and in so doing accelerate the final demise of the Old Kingdom.[213] This implies that change took place and to the issue of the underlying theoretical explanations we shall now turn.

4.2 Entropy, 'Chaos Theory', and Complexity as an Explanation of Cultural Change

Considering the apparent consistency of Egyptian art, change in the form of entropy,[214] chaos and complexity, might seem a strange theme at first glance. The following series of ideas attempts to explain these concepts in a non-mathematical way.

Entropy is a term originally used to define aspects of thermodynamics. The common understanding of the word refers to the growing internal disorder of organized systems by the spreading out of energy from within closed systems. From being just a concept of physics (usually applied to changes in the two forms of energy transfer, i.e. work and heat in closed systems which can be quantitatively measured), entropy's qualitative aspect can be used to make constructs in the cultural realm easier to explain. Just like we use abstract numbers in mathematics to understand, say the speed of a car, we can use entropy to explain and understand how and why cultural change occurs. Simply put for order to exist and be maintained, more energy input

and information is required (e.g. building a shack, a house, a palace, a pyramid, etc.), because in the natural state, energy tends to spread out and revert to disorder. Consider the following example:

Consider a bucket of 10 bricks numbered one to ten and all aligned in numerical order. We pick up the bucket and dump the contents onto the ground. The result will be a random assortment of brick locations and the final position of the bricks will be accidental. What is important to understand is that whatever order is left after throwing the bricks, it is less than the order present beforehand. Similarly in daily life there are numerous processes in which order spontaneously decreases; a cup of tea cools down when left on its own, a house not maintained becomes uninhabitable, etc. Coming back to my example maintaining an ordered, aligned brick stack will require someone to apply work or energy, and to stay stacked, additional energy will be required in the system, because over time, these stacked bricks will revert to a lower state of energy and higher disorder (for example because of decay in organic matter, environmental conditions, etc.). This inevitable *decrease in order* is also called the *increase in entropy*, which in mathematical terms equates to the amount of disorder in a system, i.e. closed systems are characterized by the spontaneous loss of order e.g. structure.

It is essential to realize that entropy explains both:

- the localization of energy, which results in creating something and,
- dissipation of energy, i.e. the breaking of rules, and the disruption of order.

In this sense entropy becomes the synonym of change, leading to unpredictable results. One aspect of entropy, after all, is nothing but the constant departure from systems, the leaving behind of conventions, and the destruction of stereotypes. This is the reason why entropy has a lot in common with cultural perfection in the form of art and related cultural deviance. In the vocabulary of thermodynamics, entropy means 'expansion' through the spreading out of energy. In the cultural sense this could be caused by any of the following:

1. A lack of Personal Alignment: between the stated values of individuals and their behaviors, this leads to a lack of trust.
2. A lack of Structural Alignment: between the stated values of the organization and the behaviors of the organization, e.g. when the organization does not live up to its stated values leading to cynicism.
3. A lack of Values Alignment: between the personal values of individuals and the collective values of the group, this leads to a lack of coherence exemplified by fragmentation.

All these conditions in society lead to a lowering of energy input and a decrease in the capacity for collective action. This will then result in some form of a society/culture,

[210] Assmann, "Denkformen des Endes der Altägyptischen Welt" in *Das Ende: Figuren einer Denkform*, ed. K. Stierle and R. Warning, 19.

[211] Baer, *Rank and title in the Old Kingdom*, 1.

[212] Tainter, *The Collapse of Complex Societies*, 47-48.

[213] Müller-Wollermann, *Krisenfaktoren im Ägyptischen Staat des ausgehenden Alten Reichs*, 116-25.

[214] Walsem, "The Struggle Against Chaos as a "Strange Attractor" in Ancient Egyptian Culture", 318-22.

which is different to the previous one, with correspondingly changed flows and types of information.

Consider every piece of art displayed whether in a gallery or in the iconography of ancient Egyptian tombs. These will ultimately change to some newer form if the process of cultural transmission (of social orientations, knowledge, skills, behaviours, belief systems, etc.) and the expansion of communication/understanding about the aspects of reality, are not done/accepted, and maintained. In this way artistic creativity (read iconography) fills the world (and it does not matter whether it is the ancient or the modern world) with an understanding of reality. However, when a new form of reality is depicted there will be an energy flow to the newer form and energy depletion in the older form that existed. Entropy is thus used to explain the constant change that tomb art was subject to, irrespective of any idiosyncratic behaviour of the individual tomb owner. It is also important to note that living systems, of which culture is one example, are not exactly in the nature of closed systems. They have an openness and freedom of their own, especially human beings and societies who make up the culture. They always endeavour to transform as much energy as possible into their way of life. The more the energy which is used to either maintain or develop newness, the more the probability of increasing structural complexity and differentiation of functions. These transformations (in either abstract or material constructs) will result in perceived change, a process that is characterized by energy being localized (maintained), in contrast to perceived decay when energy is not localized. This would then also explain the apparent contradiction of why if order deteriorates over time as the Second Law of Thermodynamics states, then why do things become more complex as they grow.

Chaos theory has been used in many inter-disciplinary studies. At the start it is useful to reiterate that entropy is a measure of disorderliness in a system and this is the realm of the science of thermodynamics. Chaotic behaviour does not rest on quantum mechanics.

In a scientific context, the word "chaos" has a slightly different meaning than it does in its general usage as a state of confusion. Chaos, in *chaos theory*, refers to an apparent lack of order in a system that nevertheless obeys particular laws or rules. It is based on two main pillars:

- the idea that complex systems rely upon an underlying order, and that
- very small events can cause very complex and unexpected behaviors. This latter idea is known as sensitive dependence on initial conditions, a circumstance discovered by Edward Lorenz with respect to weather patterns (who is generally credited as the first experimenter in the area of chaos) in the early 1960's.

Chaos theory is identical with dynamical instability, and refers to an inherent lack of predictability in some physical systems, and is concerned with the study of behaviour in a nonlinear closed system. This behaviour is unlike that of Newtonian physics, which is stable and predictable. Chaos theory is thus the study of complicated and unpredictable behaviour. It is unpredictable because uncertainty in a system's initial state grows exponentially over time (sensitive dependence on initial conditions). An example is the weather: if snowfall is quantified for long periods we get an average mean (cycle), but if the time frame is divided into smaller units something peculiar happens, the sub means (sub cycles) do not trend towards the overall long term mean. This chaotic quality can show up any time, and the period/amplitude of the sub cycles becomes unpredictable, and is then termed chaotic. Knowing the long term range does not allow us to predict any given future snowfall level other than to say it can be expected to be within the range. This then means that a given set of conditions (e.g. averages, means, etc.) are not a reliable basis for predicting future conditions, although the basics of the determinants are correct.

When nonlinear behaviour is plotted graphically an array of geometric patterns result. This geometric pattern is known as 'fractals' and is seen as unusual computer generated visual images. These images show a certain order known as a 'strange attractor'. Strange attractors are unique because one does not know exactly where on the system they are. Again two points on the attractor, which are near each other at one time, may appear arbitrarily apart at other times. Strange attractors are also unique because the motion of the system never repeats itself, and therefore averages or means cannot be used to cater for any infrequent deviations (chaotic behavior of complex systems).

However, systems, which are outside the physical sciences, are much harder to control, quantitative/ graphical methods cannot be applied so easily, and resort must be made to metaphors.

In this book the social dynamics apparent in tomb iconography are the result of the interactions between the individual, the group, and the environment. The complexity of human interactions, which makes up the different social dynamics means that there exists instability, uncertainty, and nonlinearity within it as to a particular future predictability. It is precisely this, which makes for chaotic behaviour, and chaos theory shows a way of understanding how systems can function in a wide state of (dis) equilibrium: "a science of process rather than state, of becoming rather than being".[215]

In a socio-cultural sense the protagonists in any culture appear as part of the world they have helped to collaboratively construct, i.e. there is a continuing process of interaction between knowledge and human values. Because these values may be different at different times, they will result in changed formulations/constructions, i.e.

---

[215] Gleick, *Chaos: Making a New Science,* 5.

new ideas will arise because of the inherent uncertainty of human discourse.

Accordingly rather than look for a unique objective description, we would be better served by looking at the complementary ways of parallel construction. And because these constructions do not arise from a linear based pattern of thinking but are non-linear and pluralistic, we gain a better understanding of the multifaceted nature and manifestations of (past) worlds by adopting a bottom up approach.

Consider the application of the above theoretical considerations to ancient Egypt: it would imply that we can say with certainty that the Nile floods regularly, but that the amount of water flow cannot be predetermined. In order to gain a better understanding, we could begin by looking at the patterns of land distribution, and say flood irrigation which would involve the individual, the group and the environment, because it is precisely their interactions which will have a decisive influence on the amount of water flow. Similarly we can say that the elite priests had access to restricted knowledge but we cannot predict with any certainty to whom and to what extent this would be transmitted, nor the final outcome of any such transfer on Egypt's material artifacts and language. However, by looking at the interfaces between the methods of competition and cooperation, resulting patterns of behavior between the various stakeholders might be exposed through which we might get a better understanding, of how Egyptian society developed and evolved.

Accordingly uncertainty, indeterminacy, and chaos are the prerequisites for progressive adaptation, survival and change in complex systems, in which knowledge is to be seen as a kind of dialogue with nature, in which we are both actors and spectators, with many voices. Because of the many interactions between the many and the varieties of questions that may be involved, there is no one unique language by which knowledge is to be defined. Indeed as Prigigone argues: "the various possible languages, the different points of view about the system are complementary; they all deal with the same reality, but they cannot be reduced to one single description. This irreducible plurality of perspectives on the same reality expresses the impossibility of discovering a comprehensive perspective from which the whole reality is simultaneously visible".[216] A pluralistic view of reality is therefore not only desirable but also essential for understanding complex phenomenon.

Fruitful applications have been achieved using chaos theory as a source of metaphors, explaining how change happens, and its possible effects in subjects ranging from economics to theology.[217]

While metaphors and their uses themselves can be subject to criticism, at the very least their use in explaining things, which are complex, adds authority to their use.

Complexity is about the intricate informational exchanges, which result from a large number of sub-systems interacting according to simple rules, and how this information is built up into newer rules and incorporated into newer systems. As Gleick puts it: "One has to look for scaling structures - how do big details relate to little details. You look at … structure in which the complexity has come about by a persistent process".[218] In the case of ancient Egypt this concept of complexity could lead to many questions such as: the nature of its society, and the triggers that led to its periodic disintegration and subsequent survival, what was the nature of the individual household, and the underlying processes that enabled cooperation between households, how and to what extent was the economy regulated by the nobility, and what were the interrelationships between the master and his relatives, and other dependents', etc.?

An example shall make this clear:

Let us consider information as the precondition of knowledge in the Old Kingdom. If information is power, then its existence does not mean that it will equally flow to everybody within that society, nor does it guarantee standard quality. Initially information would have only moved among the restricted routes between the king and his elite. Eventually with the expansion of the population, there would be a corresponding increase in the quantity/quality of information and because of existential pressures will result in more complex information flow between within the people of the household and other groups. One upshot of this leakage in Old Kingdom terms is that the limits of power become better understood in the population (undermining/consolidating the supremacy of the king); while another one could be the enrichment of the collective knowledge available to the others (increased levels of officialdom), etc. What then was the exclusive preserve of the few is now available to some extent to the 'others'. In any case the outcome of this increased supply of information will induce diversity of opinion. Thus a constant struggle is guaranteed between the information rich elite and the information poor 'others'. This in time will become one driver of change leading to either adaptation or destruction of a previous state of affairs. It would also imply that one factor in the development of a hierarchical society could be differential access to information; imposed through individualized risk management strategies, which may be chaotic, and which when institutionalized are reflected in the nature of society as a hierarchical stratified one (the king, the elite, and the others).

---

[216] Prigogine and Stengers, *La Nouvelle Alliance*, 313. The essential point to note is that we cannot sidestep reference to the role played by the actors in constructing their concept of reality, and of man's relationship with nature as a process of understanding, and modification. See also Order out of Chaos, 292 (for their view on pluralistic reality).

[217] Roe, "Chaos and Evolution in Law and Economics", *HLR*, (109), 641-648.
[218] Gleick, *Chaos*, 186.

In the context of the Old Kingdom, the 'others' (the great majority), had no choice, having little education and no access to educated feedback/discussion, because dominance and hierarchy characterized the information environment. However, as soon as there is a leakage, there is a drip effect from the elite to the others, and this should not be underrated. Yes, this is a slow process with the information undergoing "systemic change" as it moves "from top to bottom".[219] The concentration from complex and abstract concepts, which the elite had access to, becomes "the more obviously recognizable objects of immediate experience as family, job, and immediate associates" of the others.[220] Information's inherent property that of a precursor of change through adaptation will thus in due time, cause a change at the individual and the community level.

In this book, it is accepted that there are differences between the concepts of entropy, chaos, and complexity. Nevertheless it is suggested that these concepts be thought of as part of a complementary way of looking at how random behaviour operates as a catalyst for change and evolution of society. Consequently and this needs to be clearly understood all of the concepts (entropy, chaos theory, complexity) are heavily interrelated.

The way that the information, which is a constituent of the above concepts is relayed, could be via symbols, and can be related to all aspects of the individual or the society at a particular time. In ancient Egypt this can refer to changes in the iconography, material objects, religious ideas, language, architectural adaptations, etc. It is therefore clear that change is endemic in our material world, and that in order to prevent, delay, or introduce change, one has to expend energy. In the case of the Old Kingdom, the changes are the results of inter alia an obsession with denying death's effective power. This means that the tomb and its contents contextualize the needs of the tomb owner in a similar way to that when he was alive, sustenance being the common element. Similarly too in his transformed state, the needs of shelter and food predominate. How these were met is a theme that leads to different ways of doing things and could be the result of diverse factors and influences. Insofar that these differences are evidenced in the elite tombs, they are again pointers to the concepts of entropy/chaos/complexity which resulted in change, and are therefore ultimate measures of informational complexity. These are the subjects of this section.

Every culture is confronted with issues concerning how to provide for and/or dispose of its dead. The function of bodily protection may also be seen as a symbol of communicating rank, class, and wealth. The extent to which it does so will also indicate that particular culture's role in the creation and maintenance of social memory. In ancient Egypt these issues were very conspicuous, because the hereafter was

more or less regarded as an extension of everyday life at least as far as the elite are concerned, with the caveat that this was never understood as the never-ending repetition of *this* life. The Egyptians were well aware: of the destruction of the body; that promised cultic services with time might be forgotten or just not be forthcoming; and that graves could be desecrated. The proof for this can be found in the 'reserve heads',[221] the models of food found in the mastabas, the effective imagery on the mastaba walls including the various threat formulae, and the preservation of the body, all of which are evident in the Old Kingdom. They attest to the fact that the energy used to circumvent the above-mentioned contingencies was devoted primarily to providing:[222]

1. The necessary conditions so that the individual tomb owner could be guaranteed sustenance for life in the hereafter.
2. Proof of the fact that the burial was in conformity with religious practices and the social status of the tomb owner.
3. Evidence in permanent form of the relationships between the living and the tomb owner in a cultural context, i.e. relating to the cultural generics.
4. Similarly to the expenditure of energy to sustain everyday life, energy was expended to ensure life in the hereafter.

The Egyptians attitude towards death was expressed in two ways:

1. Denying death's effective power:

   By using mummification techniques, disguising the smell of decay with the use of palm wine or perfume, and using indirect ways to express the notion of being dead, such as:
   "Going out from the house of the estate to the beautiful West",223 "May the Desert extend her arms to you",224 etc.
   Providing the deceased with food, drink, and requisite equipment and thus enabling them a successful journey into the netherworld.[225]
   Writing letters to dead relatives which belief, implies that the 'dead' were considered capable of delivering the asked for benefit, i.e. 'alive and connected'.

2. Keeping alive the memory of the tomb owner:

   By erecting monuments in stone, developing stelae, images/statues in tomb iconography, inscriptional devices, e.g. biographies and the seeking of ritual

---

[219] Converse, "The Nature of Belief Systems in Mass Publics", In *Ideology and Discontent*, ed. D. Apter, 213.
[220] Ibid.
[221] For an interesting variation in the function of reserve heads see Nuzzolo, "The 'Reserve Heads': some remarks on their function and meaning", in *Old Kingdom, New Perspectives*, ed. N and H. Strudwick, 215.
[222] Taylor, *Death and the afterlife in Ancient Egypt*, 10-45.
[223] Kanawati, *The Teti Cemetery at Saqqara: the Tomb of Ankhmahor*, pls. 56 and 57 (A).
[224] Lüddeckens, "Untersuchungenüber religiösen Gehalt", *MDAIK* (11), 25.
[225] Taylor, *Death and the afterlife in Ancient Egypt,* 13 and 46.

sustenance from passersby (probably as insurance against possible neglect by the descendants), visiting cemeteries, and taking part in commemoration rites on feast days beliefs concerning death, and memory were continually reworked.[226]

The elite tomb owner to establish and maintain his status and power by way of the mortuary cult used all of these devices.

Death was not feared as would seem from the repeated desire to travel the beautiful roads of the West. Zandee has shown that it was always regarded in a negative sense; his evidence relies mainly on the Pyramid Texts and the later Coffin Texts.[227] However, numerous references of a more positive kind are also found in the Coffin Texts,[228] and spell 20[229] has been chosen as representative of the expectations towards death. Spell 20 is as follows and even though it refers to Geb, the idea can easily be understood if the idea of an all providing deity in the hereafter is accepted, all one has to do is to insert the name of Osiris instead:

> "Geb will open for you your blind eyes; He has straightened for you your contracted knees. There will be given to you your heart of your mother, your heart of your body, your ba which [was] on the ground, Bread for your body, Water for your throat, and sweet air for your nostrils".

It is accepted that while this cannot be relied upon as direct evidence for Old Kingdom non-royal beliefs, but it can be relied upon as confirming the Egyptian belief in an evolving truth. Because the archaeological material of the early dynasties is dominated by funerary material, and the only textual evidence (the Pyramid Texts) are funerary in context, and relate to the king, it is suggested that Spell 20 can be treated as a possible indicator of complex beliefs relating to death, imprecise as it is. Moreover, it is now well established that the Pyramid Texts already existed for a century or more before their introduction as physical artifacts in the pyramid of Unas, and were *known* by the elite.[230] Further that both the Pyramid and the Coffin Texts share quite a body of material; this of course is not to say that they are exactly similar, but that the differences may be attributed to traditions of display and that of ceremonial recitation during the funeral ceremony.[231] Accordingly to deny any cultural connection with the Coffin/Pyramid Texts would be misleading, when what is being referred to, i.e. the attitude towards death, is one of the central tenets of material evidence.

Death was thought of as a future extension of a 'life' where interdependence, communication and re-incorporation in the social network, were as essential as it had been on earth[232] and not seen as an abrupt end to living. This concern for future existence required the same demands as life on earth, namely material requirements, e.g. food, clothing, housing, and immaterial requirements such as social intercourse resulting in the perpetuation of social status in the memory of the community.[233] One consequence of this was the prerequisite that the elite Egyptian build a tomb for himself and his wife.

> "Make good your dwelling in the graveyard, make worthy your station in the West … The House of death is for life".[234]

A way of satisfying both of these requirements was the building of a monumental tomb with iconography. Kanawati asserts this could have only taken place when one had the necessary resources, which would normally be at the height of one's career.[235] However there is evidence that there need be no relation between the dates of construction and decoration, as seen from the texts in the tomb of Senedjemib-Inti at Giza, where it took the son fifteen months to complete the tomb of his father, who must have started rather late in his career to plan for his tomb.[236] Although the number of similar sources is scarce, it cannot be doubted that the building of a massive structure as a mastaba required serious finances, and to this extent supports Kanawati's assertion.

---

[226] Verhoeven, "The Mortuary Cult in Ancient Egypt", in *The World of the Pharaohs*, ed. R. Schulz and M. Seidel, 481. Also see Junker, *Giza*, vol. 2, 60-62. For further details of appeals to the living, mortuary feasts, and the mortuary cult, see *LÄ*, vol. 1, 293-299, vol. 6, 645-647, and 659-676 respectively.

[227] Zandee, *Death as an Enemy, according to ancient Egyptian conceptions*, 10-16.

[228] Coffin texts are a collection of mortuary texts sometimes including parts of the Pyramid Texts, inscribed on the wooden coffins of non-royal but elite individuals, and emerge during the FIP (ca. 2200-2040 B.C.). The use of coffin texts here is one way of contrasting the developing and different attitudes towards death, but does not imply a "democratization" of funerary beliefs.

[229] Faulkner, *The Ancient Egyptian Coffin Texts*, vol. 1, 11.

[230] Breasted, *Development of Religion and Thought in Ancient Egypt*, 272. He implies that the Pyramid Texts are "identical in function but evidently more suited to the needs of the common mortal". Even if it is accepted that these texts were for use by the king, evidence as to the knowledge of the contents, was surely known to the priests/elite as demonstrated in the various tombs. The tomb owner Ty, says: "es werden mir alle herrlichen, verklärenden Riten ausgeführt, die einem Gutgegestellten (durch die Dienstleistung des Vorlesepriesters) ausgeführt zu werden

pflegen", *Urkunden des Alten Reiches*, vol. I, 174, l. 15-16 and Edel "Untersuchungen zur Phraseologie der ägyptischen Inschriften des Alten Reiches", vol. I, 66-67. Another example is from the provinces, where the tomb owner Ibi says, "Ich kenne jeden geheimen Zauber des Hofes, namentlich jedes Gehei[mnis], wodur[ch] man verklärt wird in der Nekropole", *Urkunden des Alten Reiches*, vol. I, 143, 2-3 and Edel "Untersuchungen zur Phraseologie", 23). Numerous other examples exist in other tombs, e.g. that of Hezi, Nekhbu, Nimaatre, Nihetepptah, Ankhmahor, etc. Restricted knowledge and the ritual performance to become an 'Akh' was therefore also known to non-royal persons.

[231] Jürgens, *Grundlinien*, 85-86. "Aber es gibt doch auch eine ganze Reihe von Sargtexten, die sich weder inhaltlich noch hinsichtlich ihrer Textgattungen wesentlich von den Pyramidentexten unterscheiden".

[232] Assmann, "Todesbefallenheit im Alten Ägypten, in *Tod, Jenseits und Identität*", ed. J. Assmann and R. Trauzettel, 243, and 47-48. Connectivity and conviviality were the 'Grundwerte' of existence in ancient Egypt.

[233] The means by which social intercourse is evidenced, are the letters to the dead, appeals to the living (OK), and votive offerings (from the MK), which imply connectivity between the living and the dead.

[234] Lichtheim, *Ancient Egyptian Literature*, vol. 1, 58.

[235] Kanawati, "The Living and the Dead in Old Kingdom Tomb Scenes", *SAK* (9), 214.

[236] Sethe, *Urkunden des Alten Reiches*, 65, l. 5-8.

Subsumed in the term the elite tomb, is the fact that these tombs are and cannot but be the products of a joint effort.

On the one hand the tomb owner and his authority, playing as they do a central part in the construction of the tomb, indirectly express his identity as well as convey his expectations as to its eventual functionality.

On the other hand is the consequential connection and adaptation with the tomb owner's external social and physical environment, including those who actually built the tomb (especially the super-structure) and in the shared circumstances surrounding its production.

Certain choices had to be made incorporating numerous elements, e.g.

- The use of the desert plateau or cliff.
- The use of different types of local and other stone and the methods of transport of the raw material.
- The assemblage of skilled craftsmen and artisans.
- The size of the super-structure and inner room segmentation.
- The type of medium used, i.e. sunken or raised relief, or painting over a coating of plaster.
- The composition and execution of the iconographic programme.
- The choice of endowment.
- The development of an administration for organizing all of the above.

The culture of Old Kingdom tomb building thus became an element of structure integrated into the nature of society and its religious beliefs, as well as the system of administration, which were all part of Egyptian society. The needs of the tomb owner and the actions of the craftsmen, both of which are interdependent, then serve to introduce change in this structure.[237] Thus all aspects of a tomb have a socio-cultural context including the decoration. This association of the elements of collaboration and skill calls attention to all the people who participated in the tomb's creation: the patron, the craftsmen, and maybe the king (e.g. in the case of the tomb of Senedjemib-Inti).[238] The fact that their actions were dependent and not isolated can be an actual source of understanding of cultural, historical and social processes impacting upon society. The implications of these were transmitted via the contents and placement of the tomb decoration. Patterns of social behaviour however, do not always lead to logical analysis, and as a source for the understanding of social significance, raise questions of intention as well as the "forces that constrain, delimit, and direct potential intentions"[239] to which there is no definite answer. As Kemp quite rightly asserts, "continuity of forms" can mask "changes in meaning and practice".[240]

The way the iconographic programme was broadcast can be observed in the tomb owner's or his progeny's choice of the artist for which there is little evidence and the content of the tomb decorations for which there is a lot more evidence. The iconography then is the medium through which the tomb owner not only relays the identity of his person, the social institution to which he belonged, as well as the ideology of the particular component of his class, but also the fact that this was a community effort. According to Binford,[241] this social phenomenon is symbolized in two ways:

1. " … by the social persona of the deceased which is a composite of the social identities maintained in life and recognized as appropriate for consideration after death".
2. " … the composition and the size of the social group which has status responsibilities to the deceased".

Additionally the size of the tomb super-structure and chapel give important clues.[242]

It is clear then, that social group and social persona are important elements in any analysis of the way the elite might be represented.

Where instances of change become noticeable, these may result in the revelation of the processes, which relate the elite and their iconography to the environment and any ideological and social factors. In addition, iconography because of its extensive use and permanent presence in elite tombs, highlights the interrelations of the elite and the 'others' and their interface between culture and environment in producing the material products, which are the object of this book's case studies.

Egyptian cultural institutions appear for the most part to be static, however they really are not, because the nature of change was disguised under the façade of conservatism and by the fact that change appears to be slow and in phases as seen in numerous examples.[243] This fundamental relationship has been stated as follows:

"What historical archeology teaches us is that common sense is culturally relative, that in the past people have done things and behaved in ways that to us might seem almost irrational, but that to them may not have been, and that the phenomenon of cultural change is far more complex and imponderable than we might suspect, were we to rely only on the detailing of it by prehistorians".[244]

---

[237] Giddens, *The Constitution of Society,* 2.

[238] Sethe, *Urkunden des Alten Reiches*, 65, l. 1-10

[239] David, "Intentionality, Agency, and an Archaeology of Choice", *CAJ*, (14), 70.

[240] Kemp, *Ancient Egypt: Anatomy of a Civilization* 107, esp. 4-5.

[241] Binford, "Mortuary practices", in *Approaches to the social dimensions of mortuary practices*, ed. J. A. Brown, 17.

[242] James and Apted, *The Mastaba of Khentika called Ikhekhi*, 14-15. They suggest that the original chapel built was extended after Khentika's promotion to vizier.

[243] Kemp, *Ancient Egypt: Anatomy of a Civilization*, 371-72. For a useful discussion, also see Baines, "Ancient Egyptian Concepts and uses of the past", in *Who needs the past? Indigenous Values and Archaeology*, ed. R. Layton, 131-49.

[244] Deetz, *In small things forgotten*, 23.

4.3 Transmission of Culture and Evolution of Meaning

This section will be concerned with ways in which material culture was involved in the transmission of memory. Additionally it will aim to highlight the use of such knowledge and interactions to interpret facets of Old Kingdom society, especially the ways that the people, the king, the divine and objects combined in the construction and transmission of social memory and culture.

Transmission of cultural ideas can involve a variety of ways and people and is relatively stable over time. In the Old Kingdom, because of the nature of kinship relations, and the supreme nature of the office of kingship, the numbers of people involved in the transmission of meaning are numerous, as evidenced in the elite tombs decoration. Just how successful they were in transmitting their ideas, is seen by the later foreign rulers of Egypt who took on the related myths and symbols of divine kingship.

The mediums used for the evolution of meaning, e.g. orality, writing, iconography (painting, sunk and high relief), are associated with the development of and the combination of symbols as ways of structuring a type of reality. One aim is both to communicate and to educate, but in view of the illiterate condition of the masses, the fulfillment of these objectives remains an open question. However, an unquestionable aim was provision for their lives in the hereafter, but equally the representations give a definite conception of the world they lived in, and provide a record for the future.

The ancient Egyptians as has been observed in the previous section were well aware of the natural phenomena of change: sunrise and sunset, harvest period and inundation, etc. In their everyday lives too, the technological advances in developed methods of stone working and the related rise in food production must have led to some degree of change. These changes were either understandable or were coped with. However, in terms of the iconography there arose a problem, precisely because they attempted to portray the ideal and not the actual.

How, asks Baines can one depict something, which is continually subject to the processes of change, and is there something like an ideal form, which never changes? He suggests an answer: they 'solved' these problems through the canon of proportion, determination of picture content, standardization of the hieroglyphic script, and the concept of decorum. This is why funerary art appears fixed and static. In fact as we shall see: adaptation and innovation within the bounds of decorum, was a continuing process. The knowledge required for addressing this problem, was available in the Old Kingdom albeit restricted to the elite, e.g. religious texts with knowledge of their context, which possibly replaced what was an earlier oral tradition,[245] which should not be looked upon as something of an

oddity, because as Stephen Quirke remarks, "Words have meaning and life not as the atomized automata of dictionary definitions, but within the flow of the living language of human language-users with all their varying competencies and pressures. The resonance of a word in every new context draws on all the other occasions it has been used before, in the consciousness and sub-consciousness of the speaker/writer".[246] Written records of course help to freeze a version at any stage in the transmission, but in their absence, as in the early history of Egypt, we are forced to rely on other evidence, which while not having the standard quality nevertheless is equally salient.

Additionally expressions of culture are relatively stable over time unlike a fad or a fashion. This however is only a partial answer, for within these processes, which are of an adaptive nature, is the fact that matter, energy, and information is being moved in complex ways. In fact multiple factors may have affected the iconography including variation in the prevailing norms and in the cosmological aspects, and in traditions respecting what could be displayed and what could be actually used in the funerary context.

Both the tomb owner and the wider community must have participated in the transmission of cultural traits: the resultant tomb iconography being one confirmation thereof. Iconography would then identify and give a definite form to the beliefs of cultural importance of all parties concerned, i.e. the tomb owner, his family, wider society and the king. Because of the nature of society with its masses of others, the elite as representatives of the king had to ensure by their own constancy, that there was a stable and visible specifically prescribed style, pose, and inscription.

However, we can never know the relation between displayed images and the meanings to which they were connected in the mind and memory of the ancient Egyptian, since there can be no ongoing perception of this process of change, because this process obliterates itself in passing.[247]

However, the recognizable details of prescribed style, etc. and their patterns provide a guide for ideological and social information of at least the elite members of society. They further show how 'high culture', could have expanded at the expense of other local traditions. Baines and Yoffee think that cultural change and its transmission depend upon who has power, how it is got, on whom the power is exerted, how it is exercised, and the institutionalization of the people's acceptance of this power. They argue that this can only take place when the surplus produced by the community is used to create value laden stylistic

---

[245] Baines, "Restricted knowledge, hierarchy, and decorum: modern perceptions and ancient institutions", *JARCE*, (27), 22.

[246] Quirke, *Egyptian Literature: questions and readings,* 38.
[247] Jakobson and Bogatrev, "Le folklore, forme spécifique de la création", in *Questions de poétique*, ed. R. Jakobson, 59-72. They describe how oral transmission from generation to generation is successively altered, yet this process is seldom noticed. It is just like the small changes that we do not daily see in ourselves. It is only when comparing an old photograph that we finally realize that – yes change has taken place.

works.[248] In the case of Old Kingdom Egypt, the elite used the surplus to produce what is termed 'high culture' as a means of control and change.

It is equally true that cultural motifs arise out of the needs that a particular individual/society seeks to accomplish. The motifs that are created take into account both the long established authoritative tradition and any prohibitions. A comparison of the numerous similarities in the work processes seen in the tomb of Aba (Dynasty 6), and that of Ibi (ca. Dynasty 26) evidences the similarities of tradition[249] that must have existed despite the intervening years. The transmission[250] of these cultural traits could be by any means:

- Spreading by word of mouth from generation to generation.[251]
- Developing and perpetuating it in the immaterial form of 'cultural memory'.
- Using particular modes of transmission, which occupy a certain status in tradition, e.g. the cultic use of the false door, autobiographical inscriptions, letters to the dead, etc.
- Expressing the instinctive love of form and drawing which may be a particular artistic bent.
- Reproducing and recollecting past practices including copying errors in the transmission of literature; motives for which are now lost to us.

The aim of transmission was to communicate knowledge. Whether this knowledge was true, false, or indeterminate is immaterial for this discussion. The primary concern was that of concretizing both tradition and the abstract ideas behind it. As far as we are concerned this transmission had two consequences:[252]

- It enabled a clearer perception of the world for all concerned.
- It formed a record for posterity, and because of its permanent status, was responsible for the widespread belief in these perceptions.

Implicit in the above is the fact that whilst the materialization of ideas into ideology can take place in a variety of ways, this was, in ancient civilizations, always the responsibility of that section of the polity, which had the power to enforce its ideas, as well as the resources at its command with which to do so. In ancient Egypt initially this was the king revealed in his aspects of human, god, and royal office.[253] His role as transmitter was crucial because only he was the instigator of aggression, the cause of victory, the creator of agricultural land and the intermediary to the gods.[254] The elite and the priests acted as 'adjuncts' to the king and thus legitimized their maintenance of community order, their supply to the necessary religious foundations, and their tomb decoration to the extent allowed by lived practice.

While it is accepted that the elite art produced was subject to royal material, labour and ideological considerations, the consequences of satisfying increasing social needs of the upper classes, must have led to new ways of doing things, which may have resulted in less restraint, although keeping within the bounds of tradition. The iconography as will be seen in the chosen motifs in Part 2, is the culmination of a complex maze of influences which include to varying degrees: the desire of the tomb owner and his family, the aspiration and technical expertise of the craftsman, and the prevailing religious beliefs of a particular period. Accordingly one must avoid too narrow a focus, especially when one is aware that Egyptian art is the product of material and immaterial idioms. The ancient Egyptian had a strong sense for the continuity of tradition and it is to be assumed that with the development of writing[255] and pictorial representation, an instrument of permanent transmission was developed. However, it is quite possible that an oral tradition existed prior to this method of transmission[256] and that what we see as evidence of written transmission pre-existed in a form which is now lost. The scribe as the central character in this endeavor and as part of a group, which included the elite, no doubt ensured that by looking back at the 'first time' *sp tpy* (a mythical time before history when creator gods ruled Egypt), and by constantly referring back to this

---

[248] Baines and Yoffee, "Order, legitimacy and wealth in ancient Egypt and Mesopotamia", 235-37. Also see Baines and Yoffee, "Order, legitimacy, and wealth: setting the terms", 13. However, their view on the dominance of high culture as a transmitter is not entirely complete. It has been noted that too little attention has been given to communicative aspects between the elite and other lower groups, which may have resulted in shifting access to resources over time. See Richards and Van Buren, *Order, legitimacy, and wealth in ancient states,* 9-10.

[249] Davies, *The rock tombs of Deir el Gebrâwi*, vol. 1, pls. XIII-XVI. Compare with Kuhlmann and Schenkel, *Das Grab des Ibi, Obergutsverwalters der Gottesgemahlin des Amun,* taf. 30.

[250] *Webster's New Third International Dictionary*. The verb transmit means "to cause to go or to be conveyed to another person or place", being derived from the latin verb 'transmittere'. It is used here in this sense.

[251] Kuhlmann and Schenkel, *Das Grab des Ibi,* 72. Inscribed as part of an appeal to the living, are words which imply orality, writing, repetition as methods of transmission: "(namentlich) das, was ihr auf leeren Papyrus schreiben wollt, damit ein Mund dem anderen den Ausspruch (weiter) gibt - wenn (es) (schon) auf dem (ehemals leeren) Papyrus zerstört ist, (namentlich) das, was man dort fand - zur Leitung in späterer Zeit".

[252] Baines, *Visual and Written Culture in Ancient Egypt* 146-78. He traces the connections between the different modes of transmission across Egyptian history.

[253] O'Connor and Silverman, *Ancient Egyptian kingship*, 56. Also see Assmann, "State and Religion in the New Kingdom", in *Religion and philosophy in ancient Egypt*, ed. W. K. Simpson, 58.

[254] Some early examples illustrating the central focus of ideology on the king, include the Cities Palette in the Cairo Museum (bull as king? destroying walled enclosures?), Scorpion Macehead in the Ashmolean Museum E. 3632 (king creating agricultural land) and the Narmer Palette in the Cairo Museum (king with deities). While the symbols for these may not seem to us moderns as an efficient way of doing things, nevertheless in the context of the age and the technical wherewithal then, they are without parallel in their symbolic effect. The chronology of early state formation is still not complete. For a comprehensive review see Wilkinson, *State formation in Egypt*. For convenient chronological tables, see Wengrow, *The archaeology of early Egypt,* 272-76.

[255] Baines, *Visual and Written Culture in Ancient Egypt*, 156-61. He surveys the development of writing and notes that the written tradition across Egyptian history, can only be understood by setting it in its living oral context. However he does not expand on how this tradition is to be accessed.

[256] Baines, "Modelling Sources, Processes, and Locations of Early Mortuary Texts", in *Textes des Pyramides et Textes des Sarcophages*, eds. S. Bickel and B. Matthieu, 23.

concept, he ensured that cultural tradition was recorded, communicated and maintained albeit subject to gradual change. Accordingly the imagery left in the mastabas not only reflects the social, religious, and cultural setting but also is a source of knowledge of the senders and receivers as well as the evolving meaning.

While the meaning of tangible symbols can be understood as concepts, there is no clear and unambiguous explanation of abstract concepts such as god, love, sexuality, the hereafter, etc. One has to wait till a later period for the full extent of the depiction of the hereafter, which can be observed from the Coffin Texts on Middle Kingdom coffins, and in some cases can be traced back to the Pyramid Texts of the Old Kingdom.[257] This implies that just because we cannot find something in the material objects left behind, we must be wary of categorical denial of the ideas ever having existed.

It seems that the Egyptians tried to explain their abstract concepts by attempting to make them into something real and tangible, which could be understood and transmitted by living human beings. Many obvious aspects of everyday life are symbolized in the wall paintings. However abstract ideas behind these symbols, e.g. of the hereafter (an important part of funerary culture) can only be indirectly inferred from the inscriptions (as developed and inscribed later, in the Coffin Texts on Middle Kingdom coffins, with a fullest version in the New Kingdom Book of the Dead).

Transmission of culture in the form of symbols has the advantage that it can be applied across society and only those values that are shared and understood will form part of this durable transmission.

In ancient Egypt, this would mean that certain but not all symbols would have to be 'understood' by all social strata, both the literate elite and the illiterate others. While the elite would be no strangers to the hidden meanings behind the symbols, the illiterate too could be assumed to have some rudimentary understanding, because the materialized concepts in the representations are to some extent anchored in their real world, of which they had knowledge. This understanding by all strata of society would be further enhanced by the fact that the symbols could be seen, touched, subject to magical manipulation, and perhaps felt psychologically, a routine in almost all developed cultures.

Another way of understanding the transmission of symbolic meaning is to take the emphasis off the material object and to transfer it to the act of its formation. Focusing on the rules for its production, leads to an understanding of both the object in its context and the processes that went into its formation. These would then generally be in keeping with the traditions that are the fundamental framework of a society. Thus, if objects are produced according to certain accepted rules, which are the traditions of a society, then these objects must of necessity, become pointers to the culture of a society at the time of its production. Because of the constant interaction between individual actions and the context under which the individual acts, the rules by which objects are created, modified, and destroyed undergo change. The result may be a different object but with the same function, and this would then point backwards to times when meaningful cultural change occurred in the first place. This process of constant addition, subtraction, modification is not restricted but applies to societies generally and is known as structuration.[258] Because of these changes, one never quite returns to the original starting point. It is because layers upon layers of different ideas come to be added or subtracted to form current meaning that it becomes so immensely difficult, and time-consuming to try to peel off these layers. Discovering intention in the evolution of meaning will therefore always be a problem, because intention encompasses both a state of mind and a state of action, the latter is manifest while the former can never be so and this is why it is so difficult to uncover.[259]

4.4 Necessity for Decoration

This section deals with the causes for the initial introduction of representations, the motivation for this form of expression and some of the underlying factors in their continuing development.

The development of images is intimately tied to the nature of the ancient Egyptian society, and the multi-faceted nature of royal, and kinship relationships reflecting the differences between royal and private representations.

The primary means for the elites to display their presence and influence initially, was through stelae, and then in the expanding iconography in the mastabas. There is no one reason why the representations develop as they do, and restrictive access to language, religious beliefs, and tradition might have played a role. However with time, delineation between text and image was understood by the ancient Egyptians and sometimes used deliberately to shape or enhance the message.

Representational expansion in private tombs can be viewed as an important indication of the evolution of meaning in religious ideas. Consider the Instructions of Hardedef:

"Equip your house in the necropolis and make excellent your place in the West. Accept (this maxim), for death is bitter for us.

Accept (this maxim), for life is exalted for us. The house of death is for life".[260]

[257] Silverman, "Textual Criticism in the Coffin Texts", in *Religion and Philosophy in Ancient Egypt*, ed. W. K. Simpson, 30.

[258] Sperber, *Rethinking Symbolism*, Introduction, X.

[259] Bratman, *Intention, plans, and practical reason*, 23-27.

[260] Simpson, ed. *The Literature of Ancient Egypt*, 128. Also see Assmann, *Death and Salvation in Ancient Egypt*, 16-18. He considers the production of a counter world with counter images as an effort to counteract death, and one factor in the generation of ancient Egyptian culture.

Here he is implying that while death is inevitable, yet it can be contained. The very act of creating something of a permanent nature, (like the tomb and its decorations) contrasts with the impermanent nature of life and creates a counter world in the here and now, and thus somehow mitigates the horrors of death.

Decoration could also be connected with the development of individuality in the official; when one considers that it is only when the elite's role as a delegate on behalf of the king starts to weaken, that the official feels stronger and can depict various parts of his earthly office/life. A brief chronological survey is instructive, and would indicate the main trends as follows:[261]

The first three dynasties are characterized by evidence of inscriptional material in the form of short titles and names, (it is only from Dynasty 4 that one finds fuller sentences in the elite tombs). The stress in this inscriptional material is mainly that of an administrative nature documenting the rights and demands of the tomb owner. With very few exceptions, they deal mainly with his property, official contracts and endowments, gifts from the king, threat formulae against grave despoilers, payment to craftsmen for building the grave, and texts relating to their closeness to the king.[262] In contrast, the cultic demands of the tomb owner during this period are of a predominantly religious nature and require a different type of emphasis. Cultic rituals and their depiction require a compositional force which can only be adequately represented when all the actors are shown performing the rites because a picture is more direct. Since at least late Dynasty 2 and continuing till early Dynasty 3, the predominant depictions in private tombs is that of stelae showing the tomb owner before his offering table,[263] with inscriptions describing the nature and quantity of the memorial offerings.

Dynasty 4 results in important changes and these are not uniform as the various necropolises evidence. At Maidum, private tombs show in addition to the offering table scene a wide genre of representations seen in the early Dynasty 4 graves of Nefermaat and his wife Atet, Rahotep and his wife Nefert and Metjen at Saqqara. At Giza from the time of Khufu ca. 2604-2581 BC, representations disappear from most private graves apart from the offering table and associated offering lists. The dependency on the king is in stark relief to the earlier period graves at Maidum.

Late Dynasty 4 to early Dynasty 5 represents a fundamental shift and the East wall is predominantly used for the expansion of scenes which are usually seen outside the royal mortuary temples such as the bringing of the offerings, representation of domain offering bearers,

slaughtering, presenting the scroll, and boats over the entrance as see in the tomb of Meryib.[264]

Late Dynasty 5 private graves result in more varieties of non-cultic (earthly) scenes. This development is to be seen side by side with the institution and the development of the career official.

The central role of the cult in Egyptian life and the intimate association between writing and cult is well established since pre-dynastic times. However, this does not mean that all sections of the elite had total and unhindered access to all forms and types of media that were being used for representational purposes. This is notwithstanding the fact, that there existed similarities between the royal and private representations at Maidum, and those in Senefru's valley temple of the Bent Pyramid.

The evidence as already indicated suggests that the elite had restricted access to the language used in the Pyramid Texts, and that the development of the spoken and the written language proceeded at different speeds.[265] Further religious knowledge at an official level was not available to all, but only to the higher echelons of the elite.[266] Additionally, the existence of a distinction between display and performed ritual between the king and the elite, could help explain some of the disparity shown in the existing decoration of the king vs. the elite.

Underlying all of this would have been the general nature of the force of decorum, and its regulation of what could be represented. It is quite probable that some, or all, or a certain mixture of the above elements played different roles, at differing times and places, in the development of the iconography in the elite tombs.

While these factors may explain why cultic representations arose in the earlier part of Egyptian history, they do not answer the question of why 'daily life scenes' continued to exist till the end of pharaonic period; at a time when language was fully developed and access was widespread across the various layers of society.[267] Consider for example the fact that hymns to the sun coexist with vignettes in the New Kingdom.

Again take the depiction of hunting in the desert scene in the grave of Raemkai at Saqqara (end Dynasty 5). The representations here act as determinatives: *tsm* is written above a pair of dogs, *ghs* is written above a pair of gazelles, *nw* is written above that of a hunter, and *ni3* is written above a pair of ibexes. In fact the whole scene is described by the words *sph ni3 in nw* "catching an ibex by a hunter" which

---

[261] For fuller details see Smith, *A History of Egyptian Sculpture and Painting in the Old Kingdom*, 144-213.
[262] Helck, "Zur Frage der Entstehung der ägyptischen Literatur", *WZKM*, (63/64), 6-26.
[263] Gardiner, "An Archaic Funerary Stele", *JEA*, 256-260. One of the earliest rounded top stela depictions of the 'Offering table scene' probably representing a king's daughter. Also see Köhler and Jones, *Helwan II*, 122-203.

[264] Lepsius, *Denkmäler aus Ägypten und Äthiopien*, vol. III, pls. 19-22.
[265] Westendorf, "Die Anfänge der altägyptischen Hieroglyphen", in *Frühe Schriftzeugnisse der Menschheit*, 56-57.
[266] Spalinger, "The Limitations of Formal Ancient Egyptian Religion", *JNES*, (57), 241-60. "For earlier periods, there is little documentation of just how involved the populace may have been with their cults".
[267] For a diagrammatic representation of the development of the Egyptian language, see Schenkel, *Tübinger Einführung in die klassisch-ägyptische Sprache und Schrift*, 21.

is written above the hunter shown lassoing the ibex.[268] The animals and the hunter are depicted with no determinatives indicating that the development of language and text was beginning to reach a certain stage of maturity. This raises complicated issues of language development and is outside the scope of this study, but it does point out that no matter how developed and understood language becomes, the need for representations never disappears.

An additional element in the expansion of iconography could be its use in reinforcing and consolidating an existing ideology without the spectator realizing that this was happening (a particularly useful functionality where mass illiteracy exists). A medieval example is the depiction of heaven and hell at the entrance of many Spanish cathedrals, when the church controlled the use of the Latin language. Even if one did not understand the language, the picture itself was a direct method of maintaining the awe of the people and the ascendancy of the church, because it was direct and well understood with no need for explanation. A similar interpretation could very well apply to and be one of the driving forces behind the representations found in the elite tombs and it is difficult to agree on the division between RES SACRAE and *RES RELIGIOSAE* (which if it existed was probably restricted to the elite).

Another instigator could have been the belief in an afterlife, which required for its functioning a sure provisioning of food, representations of which could be made to come alive through the nature of 'sympathetic magic'. The K^c or life force of the tomb owner had to be sustained by a sure provision of food, an element that is well established in the Pyramid Texts,[269] and in the early grave goods from pre-dynastic gravesites.

> "O King, raise yourself, receive your head, gather your bones together, shake off your dust, and sit on your iron throne, so that you may eat the foreleg, devour the haunch, and partake of your rib-joints in the sky in company with the gods"[270] and such like.

This is also the attested relationship with the simple and humble food offering, the material remains of which have been found as early as the pre-dynastic times at El Omari, Tasa, and Badari (food rests, stone and clay vessels, linen, and fur)[271].

In order to supply the tomb owner with the wished for necessities, it is obvious that these had to be produced, transported to the tomb and accepted by the recipient. The archeological record of Dynasties 1, 2, and early 3

lists evidence of an ample supply of actual grave goods.[272] However, by the end of Dynasty 3 there is a marked diminution, and the models,[273] wall-representations, and texts[274] replace the actual grave goods.

It may be that in an era of relatively limited food supply and production, its very unpredictability and unavailability in perpetuity, would support the belief that the sculpted and/or painted scenes could be brought back to life, and could be partaken through some means, e.g. through the Opening of the Mouth and Eyes ritual (*wp.t-r3*).[275] This ritual would ensure that the K^c of the tomb owner would not go without, in the event the descendants or the appointees under the endowment, failed to make the regular offerings of food and drink. The genius of the ancient Egyptian was to create a controlling link between a given human and the depiction of things:

> "durch den Glauben an die magische Kraft des Wortes kann der Besitz von Gütern schon durch die blosse Niederschrift ihrer Namen garantiert werden".[276]

Accordingly images of people, places, things, and inscriptions in tombs could supposedly be made to come to life should the occasion warrant, to aid and provide for the tomb owner in his life in the hereafter.

By converting the imagined into representation, the everlasting provisioning of the tomb owner in all its forms in the hereafter, becomes one catalyst for tomb painting and relief and consequently provides a focus on the generics including memory. Figures and names could not only have visual qualities but also possess the same qualities as living beings – useful or dangerous.[277] However, it must be noted that this sympathetic magical religious function has its limitations, because it has never been clearly specified in the texts. In any case it is a historical fact that the Egyptians had developed images as far back as the late Paleolithic/early Neolithic period,[278] when religious beliefs were relatively undeveloped but must have been present. Therefore reading magic in every image can result in serious errors, because there is no emic proof for this concept. Therefore the way to understanding the initial attempts at funerary layout and imagery is to

[268] Hayes, *The scepter of Egypt,* vol. 1, 99.
[269] These are the oldest known body of mortuary texts found on the inner chamber walls of the pyramid of the last king of Dynasty 5, Unas ca. 2490-2460 B.C., and the kings and some queens of Dynasty 6.
[270] Faulkner, *The Ancient Egyptian Pyramid Texts*, § 736, § 859, § 1882. Admittedly these were meant for the king but in some way they must also relate to wishes, which the earlier Egyptians must also have had, if the food rests discovered are to have any behavioural significance.
[271] Hendrickx and Vermeersch, "Prehistory", in *The Oxford History of Ancient Egypt*, ed. I. Shaw, 36-43.

[272] Emery, *A funerary repast in an Egyptian tomb of the Archaic period*, 1 and 6-7.
[273] Ikram, "Portions of an Old Kingdom offering list reified", in *The Old Kingdom Art and Archaeology*, 167-73. The Czech Institute of Egyptology displayed these models in a special room in the Cairo Museum opened in April 2008, at which the author was a guest.
[274] Köhler, "Ursprung einer langen Tradition", in *Grab und Totenkult im Alten Ägypten.*, ed. H. Guksch, E. Hoffmann, and M. Bommas, 14-18. Also see Köhler and Jones, *Helwan II*, 56-77.
[275] For details of this ritual, see Otto, *Das ägyptische Mundöffnungsritual*, 6-8. The reconstructed model is from the New Kingdom, although its antecedents go as far back as Dynasty 1.
[276] Bonnet, *Reallexikon der Ägyptischen Religionsgeschichte*, 553.
[277] Ibid. 119.
[278] Davis, "The Earliest Art in the Nile Valley", in *Origin and Early Development of Food-Producing Cultures in North-Eastern Africa*, ed. L. Krzyzaniak and M. Kobusiewicz, 82. He identifies two rock drawing stations: SJE 382c and 382d, as the oldest recorded, showing geometric designs and game as well as human figures.

adopt a polysemic approach,[279] where function can be but one element. It is not my intention to give it the aura of empirical objectivity, for even though a function may be a reason, why does it cause and motivate something into being accepted as normal social behaviour in the first place? Certainly it may still have (a) potential function(s) over and beyond that.

Consider the concept of funerary iconography in general: this may tell us something about the social habitat of the tomb owner but may also additionally indicate ideas relating to prevailing religious beliefs, levels of hierarchy and status, technical know-how, subsisting aesthetic skills, and be of a didactic nature. However, not all of these ideas will always be present in the iconography of a tomb, and even if they are, the displayed artistic/literary work may still be incomplete because not all parts of the social and personal relations are necessarily depicted. The evidence therefore points to differing and non-linear expansion. One may even answer the question posed regarding the necessity for decoration, simply by concluding that it arose because there was an audience.

Accordingly in order to highlight generic aspects of cultural significance, it will be necessary to deconstruct the motifs to ascertain their contents in terms of their communications, commemorative, and manifestations of social order aspects, keeping in mind that it is the experiences of real life that form the medium through which all this is expressed. It is all part of the human condition. This will be undertaken in Part 2 of this book.

4.5 Symbols

By symbols is meant – either a sign whose link to its referent is entirely arbitrary, or a sign where the link while having some non-arbitrary component,[280] depends for understanding upon convention, such as justice symbolized by a blindfolded woman holding balanced scales. In either sense it has a communicative function shared and understood by other members of society.

The ideas enumerated and developed in the works of Wittgenstein and lately by Van Walsem are useful when considering symbols. Because symbols are related to a thing or an idea, they get their meanings via equivalences to the things/ideas concerned, and thus help one to understand the external reality.

Communicative aspects of culture in the Old Kingdom primarily used visual methods, shown by the intimate connection between the hieroglyphic script and representation. The tomb then becomes a composite of signal emitting elements in the form of symbols, to which the rules of semiotics can apply. The consequence is that the description of the function and conditions under which

an artifact's communicative aspects are to be understood, become pointers to the generics. Symbols thus can result in the communication of cultural aspects (information).

Consider the example of the hieroglyph for 'mother' and for 'death' transcribed as *mwt*. As early as the predynastic period one encounters figures of authority with the headdress of a vulture and a snake (the Two Ladies Nekhbet and Wadjet). In the Pyramid texts we also find the word for mother written with the vulture hieroglyph (G15). It (the headdress) is also seen on many goddesses during the Old Kingdom. From Dynasty 5 onwards it begins to be depicted on the forehead of queens as an insignum of royalty, equating goddesses with queens, i.e. a symbol of motherhood easily understood by all, without any further explanation.

Even though the word *mwt* can mean both mother and death as shown below, these are two different words, because the consonantal writing of these words hides their vocalization for us. The way death was written was to show either the determinative of a prostrate man, or one lying on a bed, but never a vulture:

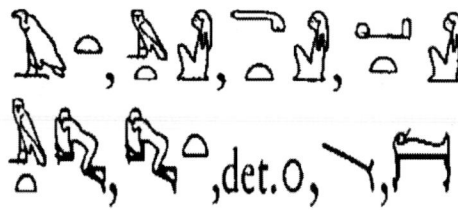

The idea of a vulture as a scavenger on carrion which must have been known to the Egyptians is lost, as the evidence only points to the selected meaning, one symbolic of motherhood, eliteness, and femininity. A further change occurs during the Amarna period, when the vulture is erased from the name of the goddess Mut and from the word for 'mother' such that any connections with something distasteful or death are removed.

Accordingly one can expand the term symbol to mean:

> "… any structure of signification in which a direct, primary, literal meaning designates, in addition, another meaning which is indirect, secondary, and figurative and which can be apprehended through the first".[281]

Concepts and ideas as has already been stated may be represented by well-known symbols capable of definition and meaning, and these existed in ancient Egypt at least from the pre-dynastic times if not earlier. Equally, symbols and their meaning may vary with context and in relation to different persons, because "meanings are not inherently ambiguous, but become so as the same, or different, "knower's" engage with the Sign … again and

---

[279] Evans, *A glossary of cognitive linguistics*, 163. Refers to something which exhibits multiple distinct yet related meanings.
[280] Peirce, "The icon, index, and symbol", in *Collected Papers of Charles Sanders Peirce*, eds. C. Hartshorne and P. Weiss, 156-73.

[281] Ricoeur, The Conflict of Interpretations, in *Essays in Hermeneutics*, ed. D. Ihde, 12-13.

again in different contexts".[282] That the individual units of each motif or sub-motif in tomb iconography may have a symbolic value in themselves, regardless of their being part of a cultural whole, cannot be denied. It is accepted that symbols can have many meanings[283] and because it is a culturally assigned phenomenon having multiple levels of meaning, it becomes a "slippery term especially when applied to images".[284]

In contrast Freud's insistence on limiting the value of symbols ("the language of symbolism knows no grammar"[285]) to the temporality of the physical mind and body of the individual imposes an artificial boundary. It cannot be used to explain how meaning is transferred in society over time, when it shows up in the continuing culture, and its symbolic forms. For this to happen we must accept that symbolic and cultural frameworks proceed together in transferring meaning, i.e. communicating. Symbols can then have various functions being used as a means of:

- Providing communication and transferring meaning.
- Standing for concepts.
- Making visible that which is invisible.
- Explaining contradictions.
- Producing a certain form of action and reaction.

Archaeologists often rely on both textual and non-textual objects to give clues about the past. Such objects may have obvious functional purposes but may also symbolize issues of far greater importance, e.g. the best preserved remnants often belonged to a society's elite members, whose possessions may have indicated status, rather than their routine functions. Pure functionality can be easier to assess than symbolic attributes, which are more difficult to detach from the researcher's own subjective perceptions. One should be concerned that one's own background attitudes will alter one's perception and thus the understanding of past cultures' symbols. For example, contemporary culture apparently places more emphasis on efficiency than on preserving traditions, therefore a modern person runs the danger of either over-playing functional efficiency or the role of tradition in compensation for modern values.

The effort to extract the maximum symbolic evidence from artifacts with minimal contamination by the observers' own preconceptions has generated interest in the following academic fields that study symbols.

Semiotics

In its broadest sense semiotics involves the study not only of what we refer to as "signs" in everyday speech,

but anything that stands "for something else".[286] In this sense signs may take the form of words, images, sounds, gestures and objects. Semiotics is thus concerned with meaning making and representation in many forms. The spoken and written words and pictures are signs of both the object itself and the meaning(s) attached to the sign.[287] The co-founders of Semiotics are Ferdinand de Saussure[288] and C. S. Peirce[289] who followed Locke and understood semiotics as the formal doctrine of signs.[290] Applying semiotics to the representations found in the elite tombs of the Old Kingdom results in the following understanding:

- The generation of meaning in symbols can be influenced by concepts such as decorum and is a cultural phenomenon.
- The repertoire of symbols represents various levels of communication.
- Cultural conventions, e.g. the canon of proportions as well as religious factors underscore the connotative aspects of symbols, both in their combined and individual forms.
- The result is that symbols regulated by the canon of proportions and influenced by decorum and religious factors ensure that both what is represented and its context yield an adequate understanding of the world of the deities, the world of mankind, as well as their necessary interconnections.

Accordingly there are related elements, which combine to portray and to yield meaning. The resultant meaning is a blend of the accrued beliefs and the ensuing actions. The material objects then encompass both the immaterial and material aspects of culture and give rise to forms of communication. Because of the emphasis which may be put on all or selective parts of the related elements that combine to portray the communicative aspect in the representations, the message can present itself to society at different levels.

This selection will also result in the application of a particular language game and a specific understanding of reality which may or may not be true, and that is why symbols and their meanings are subject to differing interpretations. However this may be the communicative feature of all symbols cannot be denied as shown in Table 1.

[282] Preucel and Bauer, "Archaeological Pragmatics", in *NAR*, (34), 93.
[283] Fitzenreiter, "Grabdekoration und die Interpretation Funerärer Rituale im Alten Reich", in *Social Aspects of Funerary Culture in the Egyptian Old and Middle Kingdoms*, ed. H. Willems, 78-79.
[284] Gombrich, *Symbolic Images*, 2.
[285] Freud, *The standard edition of the complete psychological works of Sigmund Freud*, ed. J. Strachey, vol. 14, 212.
[286] Eco, *A theory of semiotics*, 8.
[287] Ibid. 9-14, 85-86, and 165-67.
[288] Saussure et al., *Course in general linguistics*, 15. They state, "It is possible to conceive of a science which studies the role of signs as part of social life", which he termed semiology. Semiotics is now recognised as a synonym for semiology.
[289] C. S. Peirce, *Collected Papers*, 5. 484. Peirce extended Saussure's definition by not demanding that a sign be intentionally released or be artificially produced. His understanding of semiotics as "an action" involving "a cooperation of three subjects, such as a sign, its object and its interpretant" is more practical.
[290] Locke, Berkeley, and Hume, *A letter concerning toleration; The second treatise of government; An essay concerning human understanding*, (IV), 21. 4.

TABLE 1

> **Semiotic Components applied to**
> **the Egyptian Decorative Programme**
> The cosmos
> World of deities
> World of mankind
> The particular society
> Human beings
>
> ↓
>
> Chain of events, resulting in the
> communicative aspects of culture
>
> ↑
>
> The elite tomb resulting from an interaction
> of the particular concepts encompassing:
> Receiver (tomb owner)
> Sender (all others)
> Geographical setting
> Architecture
> Medium used
> Symbols used in the motifs/sub-motifs, inscriptions,
> Context of representations,
> Functionality of representations

Modern refinements to the theory of semiotics have resulted in theories of:

Structuralism: attempts to create structures of signs, such that individual systems can be deduced in a variety of cultures and was made popular by Claude Lévi-Strauss[291] in the field of Anthropology. Structure refers to and means the traditions that provide a framework for a society.

Neo-Structuralism: was a result of Edmund Leach's dissatisfaction with popular Structuralism, which he believed overlooked the complexity of such systems due to other factors. Leach modified Structuralism with the politics of kinship, to create Neo-Structuralism, which recognizes a less static significance of symbols.[292] Giddens[293] who included in addition the traditions and the concept of agency later refined this further. By agency he means the creativity of the people constituting a particular society that has an impact on the maintenance and transformation of the structure of that society.

Such theories have been stretched beyond their original roles, and then have been criticized for not being panaceas for unrelated problems. However whilst these theories certainly were not tailor-made for archaeological use, they still have relevance, including in the archaeological analysis of ideology, identity, individuality, and components of memory.

Consider ideology: for people living inside a reality dominated by an ideology, this ideology may seem the natural order of things. However, for an outsider, e.g. a modern archaeologist, this ideology is just one method among many for relating to existence, i.e. ideology is a method for symbolizing reality (or forces acting upon reality). If ideology can be treated as a symbol, then it can also be subjected to some of the tools of semiotics.

Consider social identity: this can be distinguished as the individual's social position. This role is determined by the rigid expectations of members of the host society, even though these expectations are not totally rigid over time, possibly because the underlying ideology changes. Therefore in assessing roles, it is useful to examine the attitudes and values that determine social significance, e.g. wealth, power, education, and the distribution of roles that can also be ascertained through symbols.

Regardless of an individual's inherent character, abilities, etc., the requirements associated with her/his identity or role will alter the individual's and the society's perception of that individual. For example, a tomb owner may have been selfish, arrogant, and cruel but if this is not what the society thought of what an elite person was, then irrespective of actuality, he will not be recorded in deprecating terms. Perception being influenced by the general characteristics expected of this role. For the purposes of this study, the development of the theory of Symbolism/Semiotics need not be further explored.

What is vital to realize is that these theoretical studies led to the realization that "the whole of social life could be viewed as a sign process or as a system of semiotic systems"[294] The consensus now is that:

- Symbols have to be discussed not in isolation but in the total social context.
- The product and the process whereby a symbol is generated are equally important.
- The nature of the symbol is not arbitrary and only appears to be so if detached from the world around it, i.e. taken out of context.

So how do these theoretical abstractions work in practice?

Let us assume that both hieroglyphs and material objects (and this includes wall paintings, reliefs, statuary, grave goods, and non-funerary objects of all kinds) are:

1. Symbols of a kind.
2. Hide within them an immense variety of cultural meaning, depending upon other objects with which they may have been associated, or how they were used within a specific time frame.

---

[291] Duke, *Issues in sociological theory*, 23-40.
[292] Leach, *Culture and Communication*.
[293] Giddens, *Central Problems in Social Theory*.

---

[294] Eco, "Social Life as a sign system", in *Structuralism*, ed. D. Robey, 61.

If these assumptions are correct, then one is forced to explain why and how exactly symbols operate? The varied functions of symbols have already been alluded to and it now remains to answer this question.

In order to understand how symbols operate in so far that they may represent changing concepts, one has to search for either texts, or historical circumstances that show us that change has taken place. The meaning of symbols changes over time. Because change means a new way of doing things, it also implies that there was a choice made to do something in that particular way, i.e. conscious decision to do things differently which may reveal a change in values/beliefs. It may also reveal individuality because implicit in the choice must be intention, a desire to know what one is doing, and the desire to understand why one is acting as one is. It is acknowledged that things may also change due to a misunderstanding of the past, because innovative tools may have unintended consequences, or for more obscure reasons. Because of their subjective nature, these causes of change are not archaeologically verifiable. However this may be the repeated appearance of a specific type of sub-motif, or types of object, or relief in the archeological record is a pointer of the impulses that create cultural significance, which because they are preserved, are capable of retrieval, and have communicative and chronological value.

Like all cultural behaviour, the behaviour that results in the production of tomb iconography as a certain set of patterns and sequences of events, or detail, is influenced both by the inherent meaning of the symbols and the rules that dictate how these are to be placed relative to each other. Symbols follow codes and patterns. They are like words in a sentence and can only be understood if they are arranged following strict rules that follow societies' understanding of their original meaning.

Just like temples can be understood "as symbols, guarantors, and participants in Egyptian civilization"[295] the elite tomb too has a common progenitor in symbols as illustrated in the science of Semiotics, and just like temples, the elite tomb too, can be regarded as a single complete object, and as a combination of communicating elements. It can then be considered as capable of relaying many meanings depending on who is asking the question, and how it is framed. Consider the following, and you will immediately realize that just thinking of the elite tomb while considering its position in ancient Egyptian culture, you can come up with the diverse understandings it could represent,[296] i.e. as a symbol of:

- Social integration, exemplified by being part of a network of social relationships with others in the necropolis, and with his town/household

- A place where one could connect with the dead
- A polytheistic religion exemplified in the funerary sphere (by the placement of the deceased in the coffin, this being akin to being placed in the womb of Nut, the goddess of the sky and the giver of life; after which the deceased is revived in the same way as the sun, so that he may live in the company of all gods)
- The desire for continuity
- Sympathetic magic as it relates to whatever is portrayed in the tomb in whatever form becoming real
- A place where ethical ideas could be communicated and learnt
- Hope

Regarding the rules which symbols follow, consider the placement of the various human figures in an ancient Egyptian wall painting. One is immediately struck by the fact that the spatial configurations are an important factor. Their positions directly in front of or behind the tomb owner, in separate registers or sub-registers, all characterize their relationship with their master, as well as between themselves, as one of control and direction.

Therefore any depiction is the result of a deliberate putting together of symbols, a unique event that had a real function at the time of its creation, and was capable of transmitting meaning.

The consequences of social discourse ensured that any find must have had acting upon it diverse conditions, some results of which would be passed on and become the accepted norm, while others would be rejected. Each archaeological find therefore becomes an expression of past conditions that led to its creation. However there are phenomena which are not directly observable and in considering the diverse phenomena which act upon iconography, one is constantly faced with information that is latent in any explanation of the finds. Some of this hidden information affecting the find may be vague and abstract e.g. religious dogma, and intention, and therefore difficult to clarify with full assurance, because intentionality is a conceptual space that both separates and links function and praxis (as socially embedded individual action.[297]

Fitzenreiter suggests a way out of this dilemma, which is to consider the hidden information as proceeding along a continuum.[298] As he writes, there is no 'religion' in itself, but only the constant reconstitution of religiosity by means of religious practice; no mortuary beliefs, but only the constant revision of funerary concepts in the framework of funerary actions; no abstract decorative program for funerary complexes, but only the concrete expressions of some of the possible repertoires of motifs. While this is an extremely useful description of the continuousness

---

[295] Baines, "Temples as symbols, guarantors, and participants in Egyptian civilization", in *The Temple in Ancient Egypt*, ed. S. Quirke, 223-26.
[296] These understandings are not new; Assmann has expounded these in detail: see *Death and Salvation in Ancient Egypt,* and *Theologie und Weisheit im alten Ägypten.*

[297] Russel, "Can Archaeology Recover Past Intentions?", *CAJ,* (14), 64.
[298] Fitzenreiter, "Raumkonzept und Bildprogrammen in dekorierten Grabanlagen im Alten Reich", in *Dekorierte Grabanlagen im Alten Reich*, eds., M. Fitzenreiter and M. Herb, 62.

of culture, it does not explain why culture occurs in the first place, its transmission, and changes over time. Van Walsem (personal communication) suggests that every new generation has and wants to define and assert its position with respect to the previous one, and so symbols are given different significances over time. Since these attributes are mostly but not necessarily realized over a considerable time span, their importance appears only after full realization, which may be some many generations away. It is almost as if this is a 'biological evolutionary necessity'

Fitzenreiter has also suggested, that since each manifestation ("Erscheinung" - as part of the decoration) is the result of concrete actions, the key to its interpretation, finally lies in tracing back all the conditions that limit its meaning and purpose, or more simply in its function.[299]

However can we speak of *a function* and how did it change over time? How can one decipher this? Can one link those who created the find to those who used it and how much control did they have over its use? Did the "Erscheinung" have any essential meaning (if there was one)? While these are important questions, they do not yield straightforward or definite answers.

Consider the false door, a symbol which is present in nearly every Old Kingdom tomb and which has been interpreted by various Egyptologists as having different and complementary functions,[300] thereby implying the multi-dimensionality of symbols. Because any artifact or depiction has the potential to have different kinds of functions, e.g. funerary, cultic, symbolic, or aesthetic, analyzing these functions, and how those various functions are stressed, may tell us something about the culture of the period.

Consider the clothes worn by the tomb owner and/or his servants. One can analyze these as a fundamental human activity of a practical kind: clothes being used to protect the body and tools to produce these clothes. We know however that this is not accurate, the very varieties of clothing, and the context of their usage, indicates that clothes were not just a mere byproduct of human endeavor since they were also crucial in the creation and maintenance of social life. Significantly clothing has both a general, and a specific symbolic function. It may also serve all of the social, moral, communicative, aesthetic, or nationalistic roles and thus serve to reinforce in the wearer his/her part in society. Therefore, not taking into account the facts of change over time, in response to, or along with other aspects of societal change with regard to any data of tomb iconography, will give rise to problems.

Consider the wall representations in the elite chapel. Text and image in both mastabas and rock cut tombs cover the interior walls and are usually divided into separate registers - a feature which is common to most iconography of the Old Kingdom,[301] and whose use is attested since the early dynastic year tags.[302] Whatever its function, even in incompletely decorated tomb chapels, text and image adhere to the pattern of register divisions leaving out the area underneath - the dado, which varies from about 30 cm. to over a metre from the floor. The symbol of the register divisions is immediately an indication of tomb art, and it elicits a call for questioning their meaning.

Underlying the various choices regarding the type of symbol is the a priori fact, that for any civilization, there is the basic need to classify both the physical and the abstract elements of its environment, this being essential for a systematic and collective understanding. Week's suggestion that the representations depict "the way in which the Egyptians viewed and categorized their world",[303] explains the need for classification as directly essential for the propagation of culture; the paintings, reliefs and inscriptions in elite tombs being one such method. The frequent recurrence of a motif or clusters of motif types that are similar in various tombs, signals at the very least, an engagement with an idea to which meaning must be attributed. The more similar types of motifs/texts there are, the more it serves to strengthen our understanding, because repetition reinforces both the ascribed meaning[304] as well as the associated symbols. All mastabas of the Old Kingdom have a false door with related ritual scenes; however no two mastabas have exactly similar motifs. Why? One answer is that the furnishing of the other areas of a tomb (excluding the offering motif on the false door in the West wall) was a relatively undifferentiated act; every tomb owner could therefore select those scenes that he thought were effective for his particular position and self-presentation.

In the tombs we find a plethora of titles indicating various positions that the tomb owner occupied. If the motifs understood as symbols were in any way associated with the titles, this would result in a wide array of motifs. This is in direct contrast to the actual evidence, where there are a maximum of 17 main motifs estimated from a survey of 237 published decorated tombs.[305] Accordingly the

[301] I am aware that this is not true of OK provincial art in all cases as seen at Qubbet-el-Hawa, where the decoration is carved/painted on sections of a wall or pillar, leaving a great section of the wall surface in a rough state. Only those parts of the walls which were intended to receive an image were smoothed. This results in a series of panel type pictures which do not conform to the traditional Memphite design. Numerous examples exist, e.g. the tombs of Mekhu, (QH 25), Sabni I, (QH 26), and Sobekhetep, (QH 90).

[302] Petrie and Griffith, *The Royal Tombs of The First Dynasty, Part I*, pl. 15. It depicts the sed festival run in three separate registers.

[303] Weeks, "Art , Word, and the Egyptian World View", in *Egyptology and the Social Sciences*, ed. K. Weeks, 60. Also see Hornung, *Ideas into Image*, 34, who says: "The Egyptian used the power of image as a means of describing and constructing their world".

[304] Barthes, "Theory of the Text", in *Untying the Text*, ed. R. Young, 33-35.

[305] Walsem, *Leiden MastaBase*, which is a CD-ROM available from the

[299] Ibid., 63 "Da aber jede Erscheinung Ergebnis von konkreten Handlungen ist, liegt der Schlüssel der Interpretation letztendlich wieder in der Zurückführung aller Rahmen-bedingungen auf deren Sinn und Zweck - vereinfacht in der Funktion".

[300] Wiebach, *Die ägyptische Scheintür*, 63. Also see Wiebach, "False Door", *OEAE*, vol. 1, 498-501.

question of what prevented massive proliferation of motifs must be addressed. It could be any combination of things, e.g. ideology, decorum, religious beliefs, restrictions of having to choose from sources which had already been established and represented in the past (eclectic archaism):[306] all or any of which would have limited the expression of individual concepts. However Egyptian innovation was not entirely restricted as is demonstrated by the proliferation of the many sub-motifs,[307] e.g. in the Leiden MastaBase, common motifs like "Fishing and Fowling" have 25 sub-motifs. These sub-motifs are a reminder of the many and simple experiences of daily life, which because these were the products of everyday experience, are easily copied, developed, and understood. Inscriptions were also used in a similar way. Take for example the ubiquitous offering formula[308] that accompanies the representations of food and drink and other items, which could be activated to supply the tomb owner in perpetuity. Here the power of the spoken/recited and written word (hieroglyphic symbol) was assembled to feed the physical body of the tomb owner, in much the same way as were the 'appeals to the living' found inscribed on tomb doors and walls. Even though there are no funerary texts akin to the Pyramid/Coffin texts in the elite tombs of the Old Kingdom, nevertheless since the middle of Dynasty 5 a reference to a god starts appearing in the offering formula. In the tomb of Ptahshepses "*ḥtp di wsir*" is "an offering which Osiris gives",[309] and by Dynasty 6, the offering formula is extended to include another god Khentimentiu 'foremost of the Westerners'.[310] Because the tomb owner is associated with the offering formula in his tomb, to the divine, this could be one reason why a deity is never represented in non-royal Old Kingdom iconography. However, this goes against the fact that royal funerary iconography does depict gods. A better explanation would lie in stressing that the needs of the king and all others had to be differentiated according to decorum, and that the change in Dynasty 5 is an indicator of modification of the traditional offering formula, because social boundaries were becoming permeable!

This partial answer could be attributable to the relaxation of decorum demarcations in the context of self-presentation. Because the desire for self-knowledge and self-understanding increases by Dynasty 5, so too do desires to know what one is doing and to understand the reasons why one does something. The enquiry of what sort of an after-life a non-royal would have, is no longer dependent on a myth (dependency on the king) which increasingly starts to weaken, but is finally accepted as something which one

is himself capable of fashioning, e.g. as the biography of Simut-Kyky (18th Dynasty) so clearly demonstrates, being centred on his relationship to the goddess Mut.[311] Witness too the multitude of answers proposed by the different contemporary religions of the world, which reinforce this sentiment of god available to all.

The sender, the receiver, and the medium all acted in unison to transmit and communicate knowledge (information), which had the end effect of creating and perpetually maintaining *Mꜣꜥt*. The result as this example shows is that in the Egyptian language, idea and word become increasingly intertwined in the creation of symbols.

With time certain iconographic motifs become fixed in meaning in the form and way they might be represented. These then become well-known timeless icons and because their meaning and context of action is unequivocal, they perform a useful function: that of the representation itself and presenting the narrative behind it,[312] to the literate and illiterate.[313] We do not know the actual literacy rates, an estimate of between 1% and 10% has been proposed,[314] but this is based on very limited available evidence. These low levels can be accounted for by the fact that scribal training was a long process. Written Egyptian was presumably based on an elegant version of the language spoken at court, which would be immediately understandable by all elite individuals, irrespective of any regional differences. In any case accessibility by the elite few (males) to hieroglyphs would imply that it was restricted both in its use and function. However, the question as to what part literacy played in the life of the non-literate person/female still remains unanswered. While its limited nature is not to be denied, yet it seems unduly restrictive to imply that elite women in general were not literate, the evidence sparse as it is does not follow.[315]

As far as kings were concerned, they were most probably able to read and write.[316]

Accordingly while the hieroglyphic script was not available to all Egyptians, these glyphs were constantly repeated, and the symbols would have come to represent a meaning which was commonly understood. Assmann writes in this context that while "Only a few knew how

publisher: Uitgeverij Peeters / Leuven.

[306] Russmann, "Aspects of Egyptian Art: Archaism", in *Eternal Egypt*, 40-44.

[307] "Sub-motif" means scenes which denote a specific type of activity, e.g. fishing is a general activity but fishing with a clap net, hook or seine is a specific way of fishing, which would be a sub-motif under the motif of fishing.

[308] For a philological survey see Lapp, *Die Opferformel des Alten Reiches*. The tomb of Metjen is the earliest example of the offering formula at Saqqara. See Lepsius, *Denkmäler aus Ägypten und Äthiopien* Bl. 4.

[309] Strudwick, *Texts from the Pyramid Age*, 303-305.

[310] Mariette, *Mastabas*, 149, 259.

[311] Kitchen, *Ramesside Inscriptions, Translated and Annotated, Translations*, vol. 3, 246, Simut-Kyky says, "Whoever takes Mut as a protector, how happy is his lifetime…Whoever takes Mut as protector, <he> comes forth…favoured…No god shall overthrow him, as one who knows not death…I entrust myself to Mut…that she may decree for me the West at old age. [I] being [free from? d] read of the king".

[312] Smith, *A History of Egyptian Sculpture and Painting in the Old Kingdom* 212. It is acknowledged that narrative depictions are a rarity in the Old Kingdom, therefore the siege scenes in Kaem-heset and Yenti (if these are considered to be true narratives) will need to be reassessed.

[313] Bryan, "The Disjunction of Text and Image in Egyptian Art", 166-67.

[314] Lesko, "Literacy", *OEAE*, (2), 297-99. Also see Baines and Eyre, "Four Notes on Literacy", *GM*, (61), 65. For a useful discussion see Velde, "Scribes and literacy in ancient Egypt", in *Scripta Signa Vocis*, eds. H. l. J. Vanstiphout, et al., 253-64.

[315] Robins, *Women in Ancient Egypt*, 111-14. Also see Piacentini, "Scribes", *OEAE*, (3), 187-91.

[316] Baines, *Visual and Written Culture in Ancient Egypt*, 78.

to write, but what "writing" was, was hidden from no Egyptian ... its influence was all encompassing ... and all that was connected with it".[317]

The offering formula, the appeals to the living that were addressed to all; both literate and illiterate confirm a commonly understood meaning. Equally on the many feast days, sections of society must have seen and maybe talked about these inscriptions (stories repeated are like epidemics and spread from mouth to mouth).

These would then come to have some meaning, even to those members of the society who were female, too young, craftsmen and artisans, and even the masses of the illiterate others.[318]

To this effect it could well be that all symbols did not have to be explicit, as the following examples will show:

- Consider the example of the 'smiting of the enemy' motif. Since pre-dynastic times it is an example of a symbol with well-known meaning, and is depicted on the Narmer palette. Irrespective of whether or not it was a real event, crucially in time, it became a recognized pharaonic emblem,[319] and one that needed no explicit translation, demonstrating for all in no uncertain terms the king's power.
- In the royal decrees, which appear on a stela at the gateway to the temple of Min at Coptos, the hieroglyph for *nswt-bity* occurs before nearly every cartouche.[320] In addition the Horus with a double crown is apparent in the first vertical line on a large scale in the right hand column, sometimes with a record of the sealing and the date beneath it.[321] The origin of this title is obscure but is attested since Dynasty 1 as the embodiment of "der unveränderlichen Institution des Königsamtes".[322] However, the etymological foundations of both signs together are still unanswered (recent suggestions from the Hamito-Semitic language have been taken to imply the meaning of *bit* as that of a "big strong man",[323] interestingly the '*n*' of the title only appears from Dynasty 3 onwards) and the exact meaning is still unclear. In an explanation as to why this was not done at the end of Dynasty 1 when the title first

appears, Kahl validates the hypothesis that symbols could be both explicit and implicit. He states: "Hier scheint die häufige schriftliche Wiedergabe dieser Königsbezeichnung eine Rolle zu spielen, die bereits zu einer fest eingeprägten Gruppen- oder Wortschreibung geführt hatte, deren Aufgabe auch einen Verlust ihrer identifizierenden Funktion bedeutet hätte. Das königstheologisch so bedeutsame Wort *nsw* hätte vom Schreiber wie vom Leser erst wieder neu erkannt werden müssen. Dieses Phänomen ... oftmals weniger von ihrer "linguistischen Angemessenheit" als vielmehr von ausserlinguistischen Faktoren ... abhängt".[324]

- Similarly even though the king is referred to as a perfect god (*ntr nfr*), he is still not regarded as a deity, and it is likely that the divinity of the king was a problem for the Egyptians.[325] This is seen in the title 'Horus in the palace' which appears as early as Dynasty 4 on a statue of Khafre. He is designated as one who is both under the protection of the sky god Horus while at the same time he is a subordinate of the sun god, because one of his titles is the 'son of Ra'. Without going into the semantic problems that arise from the difference between the office of kingship and that of the individual king himself,[326] the masses must have understood that both symbols stood for something royal and authoritative, because of their consistent placement before the name of the king even prior to the Old Kingdom.[327]
- Consider again the *heb sed* festival which celebrated the continuing rule of the king; a symbolic representation of which is seen on an alabaster vase found in the funerary complex of Djoser (Dynasty 3).[328] It shows a man carrying the sockel of the *heb sed* pavilion in his outstretched arms. If the man is understood as the god of millions (*ḥḥ*) then its symbolic meaning could be that it portrays the wish of the king to have many such festivals. Additionally it could also be understood as divine legitimation for the king. Whether this interplay between material object and hieroglyphs was known, cannot now be ascertained, but it is certainly a possibility that the ancient Egyptians were aware of this; especially in view of the numerous references of this festival going back as early as Dynasty 1 (king Den).
- A further instance which shows the continuing nature of the above process how symbols and meaning keep on being developed and understood, is from the Middle Kingdom stela of Senwosret III, Year 16, set up in the fortress at Semna. In line 8 is the hieroglyph that may represent in the widest

---

[317] Assmann, *Death and Salvation in Ancient Egypt,* 411.

[318] Goldwasser, *From Icon to Metaphor,* 33. "It seems that categoric definition and differentiation play a most important cognitive role within the script system, as well as in the maintaining of the control by the leading group (read elite) over the conceptual system of the reader and to a certain extent, also that of the non-literate beholder".

[319] Wildung, "Erschlagen der Feinde", *LÄ,* (2), 15. For later period references see the monumental depiction on the 1st. pylon at Medinet Habu (Ramses III) and the 7th. pylon at Karnak (Thutmoses III) of the smiting of the enemy motif.

[320] Goedicke, *Königliche Dokumente aus dem Alten Reich,* ÄA (14), 17, 23, 39, 56, 81, 89, 121, 28, 45, 49, 57, 79, 87, 201, 09, and 17.

[321] Ibid. 56, 145, 57, 79, 87, 209, and 17.

[322] Martin-Pardey, *Das Haus des Königs 'pr-niswt',* 271. For a critical analysis of other views see p. 282-285.

[323] Schneider, "Zur Etymologie der Bezeichnung König von Ober- und Unterägypten", *ZÄS,* (120), 181.

[324] Kahl, "*nsw und bit*: Die Anfänge", 310.

[325] Hornung, *Conceptions of God in ancient Egypt,* 141-42.

[326] Windus-Staginsky, *Der ägyptische König im Alten Reich,* 241-49 for a review.

[327] Schlögl, *Das Alte Ägypten,* 73-74. Here material examples from Dynasties I and II are given.

[328] Saleh and Sourouzian, The Egyptian Museum Catalogue, pl.19. For more examples see Morenz, *Sinn und Spiel der Zeichen.*

sense a female organ (uterus).[329] In the context of the stela (war and victory against the wretched Kush), this is understood to be a synonym for cowards, and further on only the hieroglyph for *ḥm* translated as "retreat is vile, he who is driven from his boundary is a back tracker (coward)"[330] appears. So it may have been understood by those who could read the stela as a synonym for cowardice, and not necessarily male, and similarly by those who could not, as the equivalent of female or servant like, a meaning that could have been passed on by word of mouth.

• This mode of understanding can also be found in the New Kingdom temples.[331] On certain feast days the masses were allowed into the outer courtyard, which was situated just behind the pylon walls of the temple precinct. On many of the courtyard walls and columns there is a depiction of the *rekhyt* bird on a neb sign, followed by a five-pointed star. Although the masses were illiterate, they understood this sign as meaning a place where they could stand and participate in the festivities.[332] Similarly at the rear of temples there are chapels, which have carved on them: the ear of the god. This was a place where the common man could address his prayers to the gods. In this case the symbol is not quite as cryptic as the *rekhyt* bird but its meaning was unambiguous. The said hieroglyphs may or may not have been a mystery to the people who visited the temple. However, they were well known symbols of a clear authoritative public character. Thus they required no further explanation as to the intention of the message being broadcasted.

If this analysis is correct, then it could well be that in ancient Egypt, all representations were in some form – symbols, which did not have to be explicit, or to be read, or to be recited, or even to be understood in context of the accompanying text, because they would have been 'generically' understood, something that is lost to us today.

As Assmann has pointed out "Icons could at anytime be developed into stories and stories could at any time be condensed into icons".[333] Different iconography could then be the result of not only the individuality of the tomb owner, but also the subtle pressure of the cultural development at a particular time. Thus the visual image goes beyond the verbal message in presenting something, parts of which

may be pre-recognized and generally understood and needed no further explanation.

Finally did symbols have a function over and above that of the literal meaning? My answer is yes – the creation of symbols could have been underpinned by an understanding of their didactic function: that of instructing the visitors in the meaning of the funerary offering ceremonies, for artistic emulation,[334] and for reinforcing the belief that commemoration would result in a personal benefit. The ancient Egyptians chose to do this by means of symbols including iconography in any of its forms, because transmission of the meaning both symbolic and literal could take place at different levels to all concerned, and thus have the broadest possible target and consequential support.

Symbols arose because the Egyptians understood the benefits of minimalisation, they mutated because of a possible disjoint between experience and expectations, and they were useful precisely because they increased order.

As all of the data from the selected motifs, is to be understood as composed of symbols, it is essential to have an idea of what symbols are and how they may operate, and the approaches used to discover their meaning at any level, hence the somewhat detailed framework presented above.

4.6 Art of Remembrance: Memory and its Components

The concept of remembrance requires for its maintenance the presence of some kind of reminders, without which there would be no need for markers of any kind. Markers assist in the maintenance of cultural memory. The reasons are quite complex ranging from religious fervor to megalomania and need not detain us. In the Old Kingdom, cultural memory was an essential cornerstone of the physical and social aspirations of the tomb owner. The Egyptians ensured the continuance of cultural memory by the use of markers as follows:

• The elite depict their status, actions, titles, and names in a manner which stereotyped the elite as one class, whose main occupation it would seem, was the saying and doing of *Mȝˁt* and thus be worthy of remembrance.

• Through a combination of inscriptions, which advertise their identity and contain material inducements, apotropaic curses/benefits and such like.

• The building of an elite tomb itself required a lot of financial and material backing over an extended period of the lifetime of the tomb owner. This great effort to create a "system of notation in service

---

[329] Obsomer, *Les Campagnes de Sésostris dans Hérodote,* 182. The female organ is to be understood as the *ḥm* sign (Gardiner sign list N41/42), although the two occurences of *ḥm* in line 8, the first with no determinative and the second with a dripping phallus can hardly be read as "cowardly". It appears that the notion of 'coward' is of a later date, given by Herodotus, who probably got it from a priest. Also see Obsomer's explanation, 51-52.

[330] Parkinson, *Voices from Ancient Egypt,* 45. Indeed all it is, is an expression of what Kissinger would say 'realpolitik', a legitimized act of aggression against the Nubians who must be eradicated.

[331] Wilkinson, *The complete temples of ancient Egypt,* 71.

[332] Ibid. 99.

[333] Assmann, *The Search for God in Ancient Egypt,* 112.

[334] Wildung, "Besucherinschriften", *LÄ,* vol. 1, 766-67. "Durch das Lebenshaus erhielten die Bildhauer...Auskunftüber die Inschriften und Dekorationen, die sie anzubringen hatten". Also see Weber, *Beiträge zur Kenntnis des Schrift- und Buchwesens der alten Ägypter,* 11.

of memory"[335] points to a common basis for funerary art, because "all culture is a struggle with oblivion".[336]

Herodotus begins his '*Histories*', which were written sometime before 425 BC, and testify to the value of the preservation of memory, by a statement explaining its purpose. The purpose is to prevent the traces of human events from being erased by time, and to preserve the fame of the important and remarkable achievements produced by both the Greeks and the non-Greeks.[337]

Inherent in this statement are three ideas: that memory is fragile, that without memory we cannot live and that it has to be preserved.[338] Accordingly in pursuing the question of how memory was preserved, one has to include indications of how the social structure was preserved, thus forcing us to rely on the material objects and the related cultural concepts and the influence if any, that the humans involved may have had.

From the archaeological evidence and the previous discussion of symbols, it would appear that:

- The creation of iconography was not a random but a deliberate act. This deliberate act emphasizes both communication and the need for being remembered.
- Where rare motifs are present, an explanation outside the recognized value of symbols has to be sought.

Repeated motifs in the iconography may be considered symbols/codes, which act as markers for complex concepts and which belong to the cultural domain of a society. Judging from the tomb art left behind, the ancient Egyptians must have been aware of the above, when they converted the preservation of memory into a visible art form. The hierarchical system as it existed meant only a few had the means to ensure that they would maintain their social awareness, and be remembered. For as long as someone is remembered, he still is somebody special.

Tomb art may also reflect the fact that humans when alive form bonds of attachment, the disruption of which through death, leads to the desire for remembrance - the simple burial mound being the first external evidence of this fact.

By making others think of them through their depictions/ monuments, the elite eradicated the risk of their own social oblivion. They did this by ensuring that there co-existed a widespread willingness to cooperate by those left behind, endowments being one material inducement thereof.

Assmann has stressed the desire to be remembered as the "principle that we owe the institution of the monumental Egyptian grave and with it not only thousands and tens of thousands of the most magnificent iconography, sculptures, and buildings, but also hundreds of important biographical inscriptions. In them the owner of the grave gives accounts for his life to posterity".[339]

While this is certainly true, it disparages other equally relevant aspects, i.e. satisfaction of having achieved those acts for which the actor wants to be remembered, the desire to be boastful, the sense of history and moral discourse, which an elite person might have entertained. One can suppose that this discourse did not start and end with the mortuary inscriptions/representations, and that the awareness of a living audience long after the death of the tomb owner must have played a significant part in the formulation of these scenes.[340]

While it may be that the sheer status of being a tomb owner automatically warranted that he be commemorated, it must be equally accepted that all strata of society subscribed to the belief in an afterlife. This is evidenced since pre-dynastic times in the fundamental necessity for the dead to be supplied with all his requirements, because he continued to exist in some form.

Remembrance thus played a very central and cultural role in the life of an elite Egyptian. This leads to the following questions:

1. What role did the tomb owner play in perpetuating his memory?
2. How would his memory be preserved?
3. What would be worthy of remembrance?

Tomb owner's Role

All tomb decoration is different. This therefore suggests that the individual tomb owner or his trustee(s) chose certain pictorial content for his/their own reasons in addition to satisfying the mortuary ritual and decorum requirements. The use of different content can be correlated to the desire of the tomb owner to create a tomb different from others, because he wanted to make sure that not only would he be remembered, but also that he would be remembered as a unique individual. This then leads to the need to record both individuality and personal/social identity in the tomb decoration. Consequently the tomb owner asserts his individuality, and identity, causing changes to:

---

[335] Assmann, *Religion and Cultural Memory*, 87. This ensures that any symbols can be referred to in the future, which is essential in a memory-based culture like that of ancient Egypt.

[336] Ibid. 81. The construction of a national identity is only possible when groups share the memory of what has been. This process has to be continually worked at.

[337] Herodotus, *The Histories*, ed. J. M. Marincola, 3.

[338] Mendelsohn, *The English Auden*. A similar longing would appear to be widespread in modern humans too because "And none will hear the postman's knock, without a quickening of the heart. For who can bear to feel himself forgotten".

[339] Assmann, *Religion and Cultural memory*, 90. Also see Assmann, *Stein und Zeit,* 172. My translation: "For the dead live on in memory and not in the grave, which is only an outer signpost of this social continuity and as such is a social phenomenon".

[340] Antonio Loprieno has pointed out to me that the development of a fictional discourse is better seen as a continuous phenomenon linked to the development of individual consciousness, which of course is part memory and part remembrance.

- Place of burial.
- The external approach to the tomb.
- Number of rooms in the tomb.
- Content of the tomb inscriptions and pictorial representations.
- Distribution of decorative programme in the rooms of the super-structure but very rarely in the burial chamber.
- Type of medium used, e.g. sunken, raised relief or painting.

The changes made to the above elements, can be seen when one compares the decorative content and style of the internal chapel walls and the tombs of Rahotep, Seshathotep, Seshemnefer 3, Hetep-her-akhti, Mereruka, Kagemni and Ty spanning across Dynasties 4, 5 and 6.

However, in pursuing his goals of eternal commem-oration, the tomb owner's dependence on other people suggests a certain commonality of goals between the wider community and the tomb owner, and thus is a pointer to the importance of agency, both present and future. In this context "agency" is to be understood as "events of which an individual is the perpetrator" and "whatever happened would not have happened if that individual had not intervened". The stress here is neither on whatever intention people may have had, nor to the consequences of their action/s, but "to their capability of doing those things in the first place (which is why agency implies power)".[341]

The ancient Egyptians must have been aware not only of the obvious physicality of the monuments, but of their implications. Being involved in their production, they must have realized that the monuments themselves would broadcast at the very least, a relationship of informed knowledge and resulting meaningful actions. Of course the depth of understanding would vary with the individual concerned but as already indicated some objects need little or no explanatory memoranda. It is suggested that the mastaba with its interior iconography (at least that part which was obvious) was one such and could be 'understood' by all.

Consider further the rights and duties imposed by the system of endowments, as an example of the idea of mutual exchange between the tomb owner and the living. This social relationship could not have been a nominal one, because it existed in different forms right through the pharaonic period, one in which both parties were forced to think of the other through kinship and exchange commitments.[342] These commonalities of goals and the effect of the interdependencies of the wider community and the tomb owner, raises the question about whether this was peculiar to ancient Egyptian society. Indeed, in all societies, which are dependent upon each other,

have religious homogeneity, and live within a specified territory; the correlation between the individual and the commonality of societal goals is more evident, and ancient Egypt is a prime example of this interaction.

Memory Preservation

The iconography and textual evidence tend to support the assumption of mutual commitments. In ancient Egypt in matters of life and death, what one did for one's parents or master, was later done for one's progeny. In any community including the Egyptian, the technique of social discourse is one means, whereby the above interdependencies, would have been worked out. Take for example writing and depiction. Both these artistic forms not only describe a particular reality, but recreate and fix knowledge about a place and time. At the same time these elaborate the various kinds of political and cultural powers that may underpin the material object. The writings and depictions thus create traditions, which involve all aspects of social reality: the tomb owner, the craftsmen, and the lived practice.

Further, because we can only witness communally,[343] it follows that the places of commemoration: the elite tombs together with the visual and written word - become a kind of public memory - a type of trace that would act against forgetfulness. Articulation allows one to share objective memory, although this sharing doesn't make it social. Thus we define both our personal and collective memories in the way we structure and transmit these. "Social memory is a source of knowledge. This means that it does more than provide a set of categories through which … a group experiences its surroundings; it also provides the group with material for continuous reflection".[344] Its importance is that while it (social memory) may be inaccurate or selective, it can at the same time be exact, because the people have found it to be socially relevant. Thus the issue of the accurateness of memory is sterile, as memory cannot be studied without its social context.

The etymology of the word 'monument' comes from the Latin word 'môneo' meaning both 'to remind' as well as 'to warn'. This refers to something that is present in the sense that it is physically there but it also warns of something that is now absent and should be remembered.[345]

In ancient Egyptian culture, this aspect of remembrance can be inferred as far back as the Narmer palette. One may conclude among other things, that the deposition/creation of this palette was a guarantee of cultural survival, which served to remind the beholders of the present state of affairs, and to warn against forgetting them. As an expression of collective experience, it may have given

---

[341] Giddens, *The Constitution of Society*, 9. In this formulation, he restricts agency to humans only, and impliedly differentiates between the capability to act, the intention to act, and the results thereof.
[342] Kemp, *Ancient Egypt: Anatomy of a Civilization,* 166-71. Also see Goedicke, *Die privaten Rechtsinschriften aus dem Alten Reich*, 190-214.

[343] Halbwachs, *The Collective Memory*, 44-49 and 77-78. He maintains correctly that social groups construct their own images by establishing an agreed version of past events. He further emphasizes that these versions are established by communication, and that even private memory contains much that is social in origin.
[344] Fentress and Wickham, *Social Memory*, 26.
[345] For "môneo" see *Latin Dictionary*, ed. C. T. Lewis, 1161.

to the ancient beholders a sense of the past. The codes which are being developed at this early stage as observed on the palette will in time serve to transform individual memory into collective history through the institution of the monumental grave, both royal and elite.

Preservation of Intrinsic Excellence

As already indicated in the Old Kingdom, there are two main avenues of memory preservation in the tomb, that from the inscriptions and that from mortuary art. The ethical considerations in private and public dealings as enumerated therein can be collectively signified as actions of preserving intrinsic excellence.

Public documents

Royal decrees and documents of the elite exist during the Old Kingdom[346] their main purpose being utilitarian historical records. The royal documents are found inscribed on durable material, mostly accessible to all, and have the advantage of being enforceable and therefore are authoritative statements, of what the king expected one to do, e.g. "It was the Majesty of Userkaf who commanded the performance of the priestly service for Hathor, mistress of Rainet … it is my children who are to perform priestly service for Hathor, mistress of Rainet … after I have passed to the perfect West…".[347] Insofar as this was a cultic ritual performance this is a delegation of powers, and it implies that the person who performs the actions is maintaining the structure of society. Importantly this delegation could be treated as inheritable property, able to be passed on to one's children; thus continuing and maintaining the ideological base of the king's powers, and its reflection in the powers of the elite.

In contrast, the documents of the elite do not have the same enforceability, although their performance has the same effects upon society, but because these are more concerned with ownership and property rights, a more useful picture of society is obtained. The elite authors are forced to distinguish rights and obligations and thus between members of their community. The point to note is that the initial cause was one of administrative needs as the property documents of *Mṯn*, what is generally considered to be one of the oldest such documents testifies.[348]

However the concern here is with that part of the inscriptional evidence found in the elite tombs that highlight the interactive nature of social dependency, kinship, and religious beliefs, of which the biographical inscriptions, the appeals to the living, the threat formulae, and the letters to the dead, are major elements.[349] It is

interesting to note that there is no evidence of royal biography akin to the elite biography during the OK.

Biographical Inscriptions

The biographical inscriptions start to appear for the first time during the late Fourth or early Fifth Dynasty developing from extended title strings,[350] and in their developed forms from the reign of Neferirkare Kakai (early Dynasty 5) they become prominent features of the elite tombs at Giza, and extend into Dynasty 6 at Saqqara.[351]

In the OK these inscriptions in hieroglyphs are restricted to the walls of the elite tombs, and in the FIP they can be also seen on stelae. In the NK this genre expands into statues set in temples, tombs and on stela, and in the Ptolemaic period extends to the coffins. Being found within the funerary context they have generally been attributed an equivalent role. In particular these biographies emphasize the activities of the tomb owner, his relationship to the king, what he did for the common man and in a way legitimize the rule of the king. The texts' main purpose is to transmit the way officials should act and how the individual should respond to the ideological expectations of society.[352] The biographical inscriptions from the Old Kingdom reflect these tensions between social expectations, what Loprieno calls '*topos*', and individual reactions to them what he terms '*mimesis*'.[353] The inscriptions do not refer to a specific time, but suggest how the moral qualities continue to play a role even after death, in that good deeds while alive will result in a good life in the hereafter.

Although there are many examples available, I shall restrict these to three types which span the main contents of these inscriptions indicating: (1) the importance of the concept of the ethical person, (2) relationship to the king and (3) career progression of the tomb owner. In all of these, there is the central element of social relationships, which run like a golden thread right across the ideas of the cultural generics. In that these are personalized vis-à-vis the king and society in general, they assist in reconstructions of the period, and are pointers to the aspects of cultural significance namely identity, individuality and ideology and more specifically to early signs of the bit-by-bit developing consciousness in the elite. At first these are articulated in the third-person, possibly because of the absolute power of the king. However, in the tomb of Senedjemib these are partly in the first- and partly in the third person but they appear to be recorded after the tomb

---

[346] Goedicke, *Die privaten Rechtsinschriften aus dem Alten Reich*. For royal documents see Goedicke, *Königliche Dokumente aus dem Alten Reich*.

[347] Sethe, *Urkunden des Alten Reiches*, 25, l. 4-6 and 26, l. 14-16.

[348] Goedicke, *Die privaten Rechtsinschriften aus dem Alten Reich* 5-20 and Taf. Ia, Ib and II.

[349] While the technical meaning of the definition of biography and autobiography listed by Kloth are important, there are problems relating

to issues of authorship and the reducing of biographical texts to types. These are outside the scope of this work. See Kloth, "Beobachtungen zu den biographischen Inschriften des Alten Reiches", *SAK*, (25), 193-194. Also see Baines, "Forerunners of Narrative Biographies", 37. As such I prefer the term "biography" and not "autobiography" to texts referred to in the biographical inscriptions.

[350] Baud, "The birth of Biography in Ancient Egypt, in *Texte und Denkmäler des Ägyptischen Alten Reiches*, ed. S. J. Seidlmayer, 93-96.

[351] Kloth, *Die Autobiographischen Inschriften des ägyptischen Alten Reiches*, 222-23.

[352] Loprieno, *Ancient Egyptian literature,* 10-13.

[353] Ibid. 46.

owner's death.[354] It is instructive to view these so-called biographical inscriptions as incentives to the general practice of ethics in an interrelated community, bearing in mind the benefits of a favorable posthumous judgement,[355] as well as the desire to be in favour with the king and society at large during their lives.[356]

The examples given below have been selected because they are typical and representative of this form of literary discourse and appear frequently:

1. The biography of Methethi (reign of Teti to Pepy I) is on the left façade and the left entrance jamb of his tomb.357

    The left façade (Toronto, Royal Ontario Museum 953.116.1) reads:

    > "I did not allow them to see any unkindness, from their youth till they joined the ground in the beautiful West. [I was beloved of] everyone. I have done nothing that could anger anyone since my birth, for I am considerate when speaking of all the king's works I have done".

    The left Entrance Jamb (Kansas City, Nelson-Atkins Museum 52-7/1) reads:
    > "I was honoured by men; I was beloved of the multitude. As for all who saw me anywhere ('a blessed soul and beloved man is coming', they said of me in every place)".

2. Another more extensive description is from the tomb of Qar at Edfu.[358] It reads:

    > "I have given bread to the hungry and clothes to the naked whom I found in this nome. I have given jars of milk and measured out Upper Egyptian barley from my estate for the hungry man whom I found in this nome. As for every man I found in this nome with a grain debt to someone else against him, it is I, who repaid it to the creditor out of my estate. It is I, who buried everyone belonging to this nome who had no son with garments out of my goods …. I have protected the poor man from one powerful than he. I have judged between two litigants that they might be satisfied. I am one loved by his father, praised by his mother, whom his brethren love".

3. A contrasting example is that from the biography of Weni from Abydos (whose career spanned the reigns of Teti, Pepy I, and Merenre I). The interesting part of his biography (apart from its rhythmic structure, the first line is always the same while the second line alters), is the way he justifies why he should be provided with the various funerary accessories. Because he was "excellent, was rooted in his heart (the king's) and his heart (again the king's) was for me". He insists that he was the sole person for whom the king did this favour, because "never before had the like been done for any servant", and again "never before had anyone like me heard the secrets of the royal harem".[359] It may also be that the promotion of Weni of 'apparently' low background to a commander of royal servants and bodyguard (ḫnty-š pr-ꜥꜣ) is a sign of how the relations between the crown and the elite were exercised. It was a way in which royal control could be implemented over areas of government that had expanded vastly. One of Weni's titles was that of overseer of Upper Egypt (imy-rꜣ šmꜥ), a title of which he was the earliest holder in the provinces.[360] Considering that this title existed parallel to that of the vizier, it is probable that this too was an attempt by the crown to deal with the tensions between centralized control and the expanding state organization. This fact emphasizes once again the processes of change that were ongoing during the Old Kingdom.

4. Similarly texts in the tomb of Sabbw a high priest at Memphis, read:[361]

    > "Never had the like been done for any servant like me by any sovereign, because His Majesty (always) loved me more than any servant of his for my doing of that which he praises every day, because my reverence was in his heart, I being competent in the presence of His Majesty (and) finding a solution to every problem of the Residence, so that I was respected by His Majesty".

    The question of broad social responsibility so evident in Methethi's biography is not manifest here, the emphasis being on the fulfillment of the duty towards the king and the resulting esteem.

5. From the false door of Ptahshepses from Saqqara (early to middle Dynasty 5):

    This inscription lists his career, which spans the reigns of Menkaure (infant), Shepeskaf (youth), Userkaf (marriage to eldest royal daughter Khammat) and Sahure (great controller of craftsmen, and guard).[362] Surprisingly his other extensive titles, which appear on the architrave, are not specifically mentioned, the stress being on his importance to the king, and Ptahshepses taking part in royal ceremonies.

[354] Brovarski, *The Senedjemib Complex,* (1), 89-110.

[355] Sethe, *Urkunden des Alten Reiches,* 123, l. 2. "I desired that it be well with me in the presence of the Great God".

[356] Ibid. 47, l. 1-4. "I am one beloved of his father, praised of his mother, honoured by his companions, loved by his brothers, whom his servants loved", "I am one who was loved by all people... I did what men praise".

[357] Kaplony, *Studien zum Grab des Methethi,* 31-34. Also see Strudwick, *Texts from the Pyramid Age,* 298-99.

[358] Sethe, *Urkunden des Alten Reiches,* 254, 13-17 and 55, 1-3 and 6-7.

[359] Strudwick, *Texts from the Pyramid Age,* 352-53.

[360] Kanawati, *Governmental Reforms in the Old Kingdom,* 54.

[361] Sethe, *Urkunden des Alten Reiches,* 83, l. 17 and p. 84, l. 1-6.

[362] Strudwick, *Texts from the Pyramid Age,* 304-05.

The biography of Weni has already been mentioned; its interest now lies at the point when he describes how he was promoted above others.[363] It reads:

> "His Majesty made me Sole Companion and Overseer of the *ḫnty-š* (palace attendants) of the palace after four Overseers of the *ḫnty-š* of the palace, who were there, had been demoted in my favour".

Personal relationship with the king was far more valuable as an indicator of social identity, because it was only the king, who could make the type of life worth remembering possible. In addition, because the king was supposed to be immortal (Your name which is on earth lives, your name which is on earth lasts. You will not disappear nor will you be destroyed in all eternity);[364] high favour from the king deeming the tomb owner worthy had the effect of 'immortalizing' his identity, and may even have been more important than the inscribing of titles.

Just like relief carving or painting was a representation of the tomb owner suitable for commemoration, the biography too was a portrait, a form of self-presentation albeit a very idealistic one, which had a similar goal as that of reliefs, namely to eternalize that what had to be said. "Der vergängliche Augenblick des Ereignisses ist wertlos; nur das, was in Stein "bleibt" (*mn*), ist Denkmal (*mnw*) und damit "vorhanden".[365]

Being an epitaph meant for eternity, it could not but express praise: the tomb owner impliedly is a 'miracle of human perfection in his dealings with men and gods', (i.e. they clearly do not match historical reality, are fictional) but this would be to take a sceptical attitude, one that does not take into account his world view. When one considers that the elite in their self-presentation, deal with connections which arise from service to the king, maintenance of cultic activities, and generally care for people who are in need; the complexity of the acts binding both religious and ethical behavior become all the more apparent. In the FIP a change is reflected in the way that the self is viewed, resulting in the development of self understanding, reaching its classical height in the MK. Finally in the NK there is in addition an emphasis on expressions of service to the gods and extreme loyalty to the king; what Gnirs terms as an indication of increased competition for visibility among the elite.[366] A good example is found in the stela of Userhat (Dynasty 18), it reads:

> "… The lord of the two lands knew me, and I was greatly esteemed in his heart … in the seclusion of his palace, so that he exalted me above the courtiers and I mixed (with) the great ones of the palace. My lord was pleased with my solutions, ignoring ones from those greater than me. Hidden things of the heart were told to me while I was in the place of silence … I was one who caused the cult statues to rest in their shrines perpetually … being the one charged with sailing the king in his barque; I was in its prow, one who trod upon the place of electrum in order to report on the state of the Two Lands".[367]

One way of having a balanced approach would be to look at these writings not simply as portraits in self-promotion, but as an inspiration to the living. They serve to remind them of what matters most, e.g. by emphasizing that one's positive acts are divinely sanctioned, praised by king and loved by his community, and lead ultimately to a state of worthiness (*im3ḫw*),[368] they serve to inspire them to emulate the best qualities of the deceased. The wordings of these biographies signify that the successful fulfillment of one's duty towards the king, family and fellow humans, depends upon the ethical and intrudes into every facet of everyday behaviour. It becomes therefore an essential part of the ideal Egyptian role model.[369]

Implicit in the self-laudatory phrases of the biographies are the concepts of authority, protection and the maintenance of *M3ꜥt*. The tomb owner recites his actions "I brought the boatless to land, I was one who buried him who did not have a son", "I was one who made for them the plan … not one thereof plundered sandals from the wayfarer, not one thereof took bread from any city, not one thereof took any goat from any people …", and numerous other phrases signifying help towards the needy and helpless, and his own moral worthiness.[370] In these instances he is implying in part that he is going beyond the needs of his immediate family, and trying to look after the needs of the wider community of which he is an integral part. Thinking and acting properly becomes a relationship of giving, which power forms an important part of Egyptian social relationships.

These statements are not restricted to the Old Kingdom and can be traced further to the Middle[371] and New Kingdom too,[372] the moral obligation stresses the 'thou shall' culture of action and giving.

---

363 Sethe, *Urkunden des Alten Reiches,* 100, l. 7-8.
364 Faulkner, *The Ancient Egyptian Pyramid Texts,* § 764.
365 Helck ", Zur Frage der Entstehung der ägyptischen Literatur", 8.
366 Gnirs, "Die ägyptische Autobiographie", in *Ancient Egyptian Literature,* 233. She believes that this led to a new "confessional" form of biography through which a person could be transformed by the king into elite, much in the same way that the gods did in the Ramesside period. If this is correct, then it is again a pointer to the importance of the cultural generics.

367 Stela number 19b is in the Rijksmuseum van Oudheden at Leiden, see picture on page 61.
368 Sethe, *Urkunden des Alten Reiches,* 222. l, 3-7. Worthiness (*im3ḫw*) is to be understood as one who is assured of a place in social memory.
369 Lichtheim, *Ancient Egyptian Literature,* vol. I, 58-76. As evident in the writings of Hardjedef, Kagemni, and Ptahhotep.
370 For a detailed list of such phrases, see Kloth, *Die Autobiographischen Inschriften des ägyptischen Alten Reiches,* 77-107.
371 Lange and Schäfer, *Grab- und Denksteine des Mittleren Reichs,* no. 20001(b) lines 3 ff. "I did not take the daughter of a man, I did not take his field...I provided Gebelein with food in its worst years...I served my senior lord and I served my junior lord, and no misfortune came over me".
372 G. Lefebvre, *Historie des grands prêtres d'Amon de Karnak,* 132. For translation see Kitchen, *Ramesside Inscriptions, Translated and Annotated, Translations,* vol. 3, 214. The biographical inscription concerns Bakenkhons, the High Priest of Amun during the New Kingdom (reign of Ramses II) who dedicated two block statues at Karnak: one is in

At another level similar inscriptions could also indicate a grab for power in so far that the distribution and storage of resources was a prerogative of the king illustrated by the inscriptions of the FIP nomarch Ankhtifi of Moalla. We may conclude that the elite are searching for another situation beyond survival to that of immortality. Furthermore their (nomarchial biographies) effect on royal inscriptions should not be underestimated, as this may well be the inspiration for detailed royal narrative, which begins to appear following the turmoil of the FIP.

Dying, death and burial are then to be understood in a wider sense extending to and including socially dependent persons. In this way the biographical inscriptions open a window on society in general and who the others were.[373] These others are to be included because only by including all members, could one keep the social community intact. It is common to help others who are close to one, but in the biographical inscriptions, we see that the elite go beyond this to provide for others. This is vaguely similar to the examples of royal concern, examples of which were given earlier.

Further the inclusion of non-elite in elite tomb representations is itself an indication of this aspect and suggestive of the constant focus on the maintenance of the physical and social structure, and clustered nature of the Egyptian world. Apart from their own name and titles which are obviously obligatory, the elite's use of the representations is such as to impose a different vocabulary: they try to show both their own point of view, e.g. in the splendour of their lives, while at the same time imaginatively identifying with the 'common pain', by including the others in the iconography. One could postulate that biographical excerpts are all examples of the point of being human, i.e. to spend one's life upholding the principles of social justice. In a state of relative dependency such as we find in the Old Kingdom, this ideal could have been the glue that held it together for as long as it did. Although the result was the favouring of a minority, yet it activated the collective consciousness through *M3ˁt*, which provided another way of "colonizing the future".[374] By the communicative interplay present in the 'ideal-biography', it showed that the poor were essential elements of society not to be forgotten, and this acted as a spur to the "discourse of

inequality and power".[375] While the requirements of food and drink are important and thus found in every tomb, there seems to be an imperative to include other factors which point to elements of social concern albeit with self-interest at heart. Another way of looking at these is to accept the premise that the inscriptions do not match reality.

However, if the biographical inscriptions are read in the manner I have suggested, then it becomes clear that the elite were aware of the cultural and social dynamics that existed in society, of the dangers of a rising opposition, and the need for some sort of control. Thus the seemingly dry ritualistic statements inscribed - no longer merely describe *M3ˁt*; they are 'creating' it too, i.e. words are their weapons. Communication then becomes an independent and effective tool for influencing the others and hidden behind the inscriptions is their policy explanation.

The elite eventually become masterful at delivering outcomes through words (their well being in posterity), as much as by deeds (what they say they did for the deserving). Indeed what is most striking is that the elite reframe public discourse about society not so much by what they say about it, but by what they implicitly persuade the others to assume. The key point is this: what underpins society is an intangible issue of community trust in the elite.

Thus they create a regime in which all participants knowingly or not, are compelled by what is a series of 'inscriptions'. Even if this sounds irritatingly abstract to Egyptologists it has two practical consequences.

- First, it suggests that the modern day researcher needs to spend more time reflecting on the implicit 'social contract' and cultural messages in all inscriptions.
- Second, it is no longer appropriate just to think of the narrator only in the ritualistic context. One also needs to think of the narrator as someone who was a 'masterful story teller and cultural analyst', one who could read social sentiments, shape norms, (re) create trust, and most importantly, for a community where inequality was a given fact, to persuade all to think in a manner that suited his goals, without the others even noticing them.

This may have generated thoughtful reflections of the present and historical past, and be the precursor of the biography.

Threat Formulae, Appeals to the Living and Letters to the Dead

Threat Formulae

In order to keep the commemorative aspect working posthumously, the tomb owner had to rely on the living

---

the Cairo Museum and the other in the Staatliche Sammlung Ägyptischer Kunst in Munich. The theme of the Munich statue is a list of offices held and his resposibility for the temple staff, he says "I will inform you of my character when (I) was upon earth, in every office that I exercised since my birth…I was a good father to my personnel, bringing up their young people, giving a (helping) hand <to> who(ever) was needy, sustaining who(ever) was in need, and performing benefactions in the temple…I am a truly decent man, useful to his god…". For further New Kingdom examples see Rickal, "*Les épithètes dans les autobiographies de particuliers du Nouvel Empire égyptien*", Ph.D. dissertation, Université de Paris IV-Sorbonne, 2005.

[373] Franke, "Arme und Geringe im Alten Reich Altägyptens", *ZÄS*, (133), 120. Franke draws attention to the levels of power and the levels of dependency that existed in ancient Egypt. In doing this, he points to the existence of members of society who were not part of the community. In the biographical inscriptions they are specifically referred to as the afflicted (*m3r*), poor (*šw3*), and nomadic (*šm3*) and they are said to be deserving of protection.

[374] Giddens, *Modernity and Self-Identity*, 75.

[375] Richards and Van Buren, *Order, legitimacy, and wealth in ancient states*, 11.

for survival in the beyond, for only thus could he ensure that he had conquered mortality. This he could only do by stimulating the living through rewards, apotropaic benefits, and/or threats.

A word of caution is in order here: the tendency to separate the religious from the secular particularly when treating threat texts is one of the main causes of misunderstanding. That the Egyptians never imposed this false dichotomy is self-evident in their use of metaphoric and divine language.[376] The texts must therefore be understood as relating to both the earthly sphere as well as the divine. It was of little consequence to the ancient Egyptian whether the tomb threats were meant to be enacted during the life of the individual, because meaning to them was not an either or situation, but one in which if consequences' were not effectual in this world they would certainly happen in the next. Of course there were threats, which could be exercised in this world, namely death by fire, denial of a burial, etc.; but those threats, which are ambiguous, pose a problem in that they invoke multiple realms and polyvalent meaning. Baines hits the nail on the head when he writes: "For the actors that world is real, even if its status may be less straight-forward than that of the human world.[377]"

The category of Egyptian literature, which deals with threats and blessings, has the following characteristics:[378]

- A method of communication between the dead and the living.
- The tomb owner is the alleged sender.
- All other living individuals are the recipients.
- They contain an implied threat and a corresponding benefit.
- They appear on the usual monumental forms e.g. stelae, offering tables, tomb walls, coffins and so forth but are also seen in the later periods on temple walls, as well as on papyri and wooden amulets.
- Their usefulness depends on society's belief in superhuman powers and not in the existing legal institutions.

The fact that only a small minority was literate should not be taken as an indication of the limited reach of these formulaic inscriptions. The common masses would have been exposed to the funerary services and equipment, and were at times part of the cultic services as $K3$ priests (Hekanakht for example was most probably illiterate and was a $K3$ priest of the vizier Ipy, Dynasty 11).[379] This contact was not just a physical one, but one which must have also entailed some sort of cognition of the norms and values based on their 'worldview' which was built around

the socio-ethical aspects encompassing social order, truth, and justice. This then could explain why the suppositions of the common masses even if illiterate were complex. This would also imply that even when they could not read or write they had a basic understanding of what blessings and curses meant, because they believed in the power of the word, whose guarantors were the gods.[380] This belief was reinforced by the idea that the efficiency of connective justice went "well beyond the sphere of legal institutions into the sphere of divine maintenance of cosmic order".[381]

At the other end of the scale one has to reconcile this lofty ideal with the fact of increasing degradation of tombs in Dynasties 5 and 6. This was a problem that required a solution, one such being the inscription of curses, threats and apotropaic benefits.[382]

Appeals to the living

These start to emerge at the beginning of Dynasty 5[383] and are an interesting example of evolving thought patterns between the dead and the living. They were a significant element of the tomb decoration programme in addition to biographical inscriptions, and were inscribed in places that could gain the attention of passers-by: for example, the tomb wall at the entrance, or on the false door, and in later periods also came to be inscribed on stela and generally on the rear of statues.[384]

While in the beginning a certain element of compulsion is detected in the appeals, from the Middle Kingdom onwards mere recitation was all that was required. Further and importantly, the passages indicate that these were not only meant for people that the tomb-owner knew, but for general dissemination, and all people who made an offering and/or read the texts would have his support.

Three examples from the many should hopefully suffice to follow the thought patterns of the ancient Egyptians:

1. Cairo text of Nekhebu from Giza (JE 44608), the reign of Pepy I.

   "O you who live on earth and who shall pass by this tomb, do you desire that the king favour you and that you be *imakhu* in the sight of the Great

---

[376] In Papyrus Hermitage 116A verso, from lines 47-50 and 110, it is clear that punishment against the rebels is to be meted out by the king if he is to retain his throne, but in both cases the language refers to divine retribution.

[377] Baines, "Egyptian Myth and Discourse", *JNES*, (50), 86.

[378] Nordh, *Aspects of Ancient Egyptian Curses and Blessings*, 2-5. See also Morschauser, *Threat-Forumlae in Ancient Egypt*, 20.

[379] James, *Pharaoh's people:scenes from life in Imperial Egypt*, 167. Also see James and Gunn, *The Hekanakhte papers*, 1-2.

[380] Boochs, "Religiöse Strafen" in *Religion und Philosophie im Alten Ägypten*, 62.

[381] Assmann, "When Justice fails", *JEA*, (78), 151.

[382] Simpson, *Mastabas of the Western Cemetry (Part 1)*, vol. 4, fig. 15. Note the specific nature of the curse in the tomb of Tjetu Kanesut: "As to any man who will take or tear out a stone or brick from this tomb, [I] will be judged with [him] in the court of the great gods, [I] shall put an end to him on account of it for the living ones who are upon earth to see". The threat in the tomb of Kagemni adds in addition a specific threat to "any person who shall enter this tomb of mine in an impure state, I shall wring his neck like that of a goose" for which see Edel, "Inschriften des Alten Reichs", 213.

[383] Bommas, "The mechanics of social connections between the living and the dead in ancient Egypt", in *Living through the Dead: Burial and Communication in the Classical World*, 166.

[384] Müller, *LÄ*, vol. 1, 293-299.

God? Then you shall say "a thousand of bread and
a thousand of beer for Nekhebu, the *imakhu*
You shall not destroy anything in this tomb....
With regard to any man who shall destroy anything
in this tomb, I shall be judged with them by the
Great God".[385]

2. Lintel, left-hand side, text of Bia, from Saqqara.

"With regard to any man ...
and who shall pass by this tomb and who shall read
the (inscription on) this doorway, I shall be his
support in the court of the Great God"[386]

3. At the other extreme from the Middle Kingdom,
the   threat becomes a humble request to the scribe
just to read the offering formula aloud to the people,
or to all passers-by just to recite the formula as
seen in the following inscription from the stela of
Nebipusenwosret, reign of Amenemhat lll.[387]

"Every scribe who shall read aloud (the text) and all
people who shall listen".
(This is) "breath of the mouth, excellent for the
noble dead. It is no weight on your shoulders".[388]

The reasoning is persuasive for all visitors to the chapel,
in that recitation of the funerary formulae costs nothing,
neither effort nor weariness[389]

Another interesting part about these appeals is not the
exaggerated amounts of food, threats, or benefits but the
fact that both the priest's offering ritual and the visitor's
offering of food have a great communal significance in
terms of commemoration. The performance of these actions
requested by the tomb owner presupposes a community, in
which co-operation and communication are an essential
element in the achievement of social goals, indirectly
reflecting these as matters of cultural significance.

For the givers the act was important, because this was the
creation and the maintenance of the concept of *M3ʿt* on
which his future after-life could depend.

For the receiver the act was an indication that he had
not been forgotten in the memory of future generations;
that the protection of his self-interests in the hereafter
were assured, thus again alluding to aspects of cultural
significance.

Letters to the Dead

This medium was another vehicle, which echo the mindset of the living towards that of the dead in contrast to the
appeals to the living, which are from the dead to the living.
They are to be found on pottery vessels, papyrus, and linen
deposited as offerings to the tomb-owner.[390] These were
then put on the offering table which is found in front of the
false door; the idea being that when the tomb-owner came
back to partake of the offerings, he would read the letter and
act as requested. In their content they generally parallel the
appeals and threats, in containing the obligatory elements
of a perceived problem, a request, and the promise of a
reward to the deceased addressee.

These letters serve to remind one that the living recognized
the dead, as possessors of special power (*ʿkh-iker*, the life
force of the able spirit of the *K3*) and that ancestor worship
may have been an informal practice.[391] These letters also
point to the reciprocal duty towards the living; while the
deceased could not come down in person, yet he could be
effective in lending support for the resolution of certain
family problems (childbirth, inheritance, and sickness).
The letters also display the prevailing mindset; that this
world and the next were not disconnected, and that the
dead continued to be part of the living society.[392]

These letters therefore represent an indirect method of
remembrance; in the same way as the cults of the dead
were a means for communicating with and remembering
the deified dead which grew up around the tombs in the
Old Kingdom, e.g. Hardjedef,[393] and Kagemni[394] at Giza
and Saqqara and Heqaib at Aswan.[395]

The need to be in touch by the living and the dead
is recognized, dependency in certain instances is
acknowledged, and memory is preserved.

As these letters follow a similar pattern with minor
variations, I shall restrict myself to one letter, which is
dated to between Dynasties 6 and 11. It reads:

"... Behold now there is brought (to you) this vessel
in respect of which your mother is to make litigation
... that you should support her. Cause now that there

---

[385] Strudwick, *Texts from the Pyramid Age,* 268.
[386] Ibid. 269.
[387] The belief that the spoken word was more effective than the written
word, resulted out of the desire for certainty for their posthumous welfare.
For evidence see the stela of Sebekhotep in Brunner, *Hieroglyphische
Chrestomathie*, Tafel 11 and that of Neferniy in *Cataloghi dei musei e
gallerie d'Italia*, 2590.
[388] Simpson, *The Terrace of the great God at Abydos*, ANOC 11.1, CG
20 017. Such phrases from the Middle Kingdom and later have been
collected by Spiegelberg, "Eine Formel der Grabsteine", *ZÄS*, (45), 67-
71.
[389] Vernus, "La formule 'Le souffle de la bouche' au Moyen
Empire", *RdE*, (28), 142-43.

[390] Gardiner and Sethe, *Egyptian letters to the dead.*
[391] Fitzenreiter, "Zum Ahnenkult in Ägypten", *GM*, (143), 51-56. The
connection of the living to the dead evidenced in the letters to the dead,
is not an act of veneration. The leap to ancestor worship happens later
on, as evidenced in the akh-iker stelae, an example of which is in the
Petrie Museum UC 14228. Also see a fragment of an Old Kingdom
letter to the dead at the British Museum (BM EA 10901), where akh-
iker is mentioned, for which reference I thank Dr. R. J. Demarée (Leiden
University).
[392] Hafemann, "Feinde und Ahnen-Briefe an Tote als Mittel der
Feindbekämpfung", in *Feinde und Aufrührer*, ed. H. Felber, 162-63.
[393] Junker, *Giza*, vol. 7, 26-27.
[394] Firth and Gunn, *Teti Pyramid Cemetries 1*, 1-30. Also see Goedicke,
"Ein Verehrer des weisen Djedefhor aus dem späten Alten Reich", *ASAE*,
(55), 49-55.
[395] Habachi, *Elephantine IV. The Sanctuary of Heqaib*, 2 vols., *AV*, (33),
19-21. For general details see Meulenaere, "Verehrung verstorbener
Privatleute", *LÄ*, vol. 6, 973-974.

be born to me a healthy male child ... as for the two serving- maids who have caused Seny to be afflicted, (namely) Nefertjentet and Itjai, confound (?) them, and destroy for me every affliction which is (directed) against my wife for you know that I have need thereof (?). Destroy it utterly ... the Great God shall be glad over you; he shall give you pure bread with his two hands".[396]

A compilation across periods can be found in "Letters from Ancient Egypt".[397]

The Protagonist Remembered

All the components in the mastaba from architecture to decoration to inscriptions work together towards a goal that is both functional and communicative. The goal in the context of funerary culture is connected to an individual elite identity manifested in title and name, which shares in the prevailing ideology, and perhaps individuality.

Titles

The depiction of official titles was an important theme in the elite's self-presentation because it showed both their importance and proximity to the king as well as an indication of royal favour.[398] By titles is meant an indication of "a specific office, function, or dignity".[399] However, it is questionable whether these titles represent true functions, or are significant pointers of status, or even correspond to the terminology of desirable qualities, because "the Old Kingdom is notoriously imprecise in the qualifications of very important titles".[400] Opinion is divided on whether the titles in a tomb represent "in all probability the accumulation of a lifetime",[401] or whether they represent those that the tomb owner had at the time of the construction of the tomb, or those which he specifically wished to display.

In the elite tomb one is usually faced by the names and titles of the tomb owner and in addition his imposing figures as a way of distinguishing and remembering who he was.[402]

As far back as at least Dynasty 3, the administration of the state demanded that it be compartmentalized into five main departments: scribal administration, granaries, the treasury, public works, and the judiciary. Strudwick has selected a representative title for each of these departments: *imy-r sš ꜥ-nswt, imy-r šnwt (y), imi-r pr (wy)-ḥd, imy-r kȝt*

nbt nt nswt, and *imy-r ḥwt-wrt*.[403] While the titles of the elite include in the main, reference to these departments, it must be noted that Strudwick does not specify whether these are the only departments or that these are the highest possible titles in each department during the Old Kingdom. However his selection has the merit that the departments represent a broad array of the important functions of the Old Kingdom administration. An overseer of these departments would certainly belong to the elite element of Egyptian society.

As already stated the elite tombs present a wide variety of titles,[404] some being official, others being merely conventional. Over time, the number of titles held, makes it impossible to use these predominantly as a signpost of nobility. Furthermore the titles are not arranged chronologically but according to ranking conventions, which may vary according to the nature of specialized duties, main functions, territory, particular area of competence, a specialized department, etc.[405] It would seem that variations in the age of the tomb owner do not have any effect upon the titles, e.g. as in the early Dynasty 3 tomb of Hesyre, and it probably reflects a separation of duties (cultic vs. administrative). Titles then arose out of an administrative necessity[406] but in time become a sort of identity card without any narrative function. The vizier for example, always held the title of "overseer of works" but it was also granted to any official in charge of a building project and each called himself an overseer of works. Still other titles such as "hereditary prince and count", "seal bearer of the king of Lower Egypt", did not imply any special function but conferred high rank on the bearer.

Again in a predominantly agricultural society like Egypt, the annual assessment of harvest and supervision of the granaries must have been of especial importance. The agricultural department was divided into two sections dealing with crops and livestock and one must assume that within each section, there must have been a vast number of administrators. The plethora of titles is therefore not surprising. Even so titles such as the "overseer of granaries" and "chief stewards of kings", who handled his vast personal estates, must have been of major importance. Perhaps a constructive way is to view titles according to their type: bureaucratic, priestly, geographical, epithet, and royal based, focusing on their nature rather than on the implied function. No clear demarcation is possible between honorific and official titles at any period. Many titles, which may have begun as official titles, evolve in due course to become purely honorific. Similarly honorific titles may also refer to official work of a totally different

[396] Gardiner, "A New Letter to the Dead", *JEA* (16), 19.
[397] Wente and Meltzer, *Letters from Ancient Egypt*, 210-20. Also see O'Donoghue, "The 'Letters to the Dead' and Ancient Egyptian Religion", *BACE*, (10), 87-104.
[398] Baer, *Rank and title in the Old Kingdom*, 6.
[399] Ibid. 4.
[400] Strudwick, *The Administration of Egypt in the Old Kingdom*, 322.
[401] Baer, *Rank and title in the Old Kingdom*, 35.
[402] An exception is in some boat representations when the tomb owner is depicted on the same scale as the others, e.g. in the tomb of Ty, an indication of possible individuality in another motif.

[403] Strudwick, *The Administration of Egypt in the Old Kingdom*, 175.
[404] Jones, *An Index of Ancient Egyptian Titles, Epithets and Phrases of the Old Kingdom, BAR*, (Series 866). Kanefer son of Senefru (Dynasty 4) held 47 titles.
[405] Baer, *Rank and title in the Old Kingdom*, 9-41. He cites multiple variations of conventions especially from mid- Dynasty 5 onwards.
[406] The admiministrative core can be identified in the tomb of Nikaankh, where the priests are named with their monthly service duties related to the land and this is not an isolated example. See Sethe, *Urkunden des Alten Reiches*, 25f.

nature.[407] Attempts have been made to identify patterns in the placements of elite tombs ranked according to title but with so many imponderables; this task is still in its infancy.[408]

Titles are important in this study only in so far as they relate to ideas of status and rank superiority and thus as a pointer of social significance. Additionally the titles were instrumental in making clear (both to the visitor and the returning *K3*) the tomb owner's distinctive identity and any claims to power.

From the Middle kingdom the wives of the elite were termed merely *nb.t pr* 'mistress of the house' although there are cases where women also use an exclusive title such as "sole companion".[409] In contrast to elite women we have very little evidence of the social or economic status of non-elite women.

Name

In a sense the Egyptians were no different to modern man; we too have graveyards with named family crypts, headstones, and named urns. However, whereas names matter less to modern man, considering the ease with which names can be changed (with major exceptions like with proprietary rights), to the ancient Egyptian, *rn* (name) was an essential part of being. Combined with the other elements of *ḥꜥ* (body), *K3* (life-force or double, necessary for restoring his social status, which had been destroyed by death), *šwt* (shadow), and *B3* (that part of his physical sphere which included his ability to take on different forms), they were necessary for his postmortem existence.[410] Names and titles then are an embodiment of the tomb owner's identity, and as Fitzenreiter remarks: "Erst durch die Namengebung wird das Neugeborene offiziell anerkannt und ist neben seiner biologischen Existenz auch als sozial existent in die Gesellschaft integriert".[411]

The name is 'a rigid designator'.[412] Consider silver with the atomic number 47. It is a metal having a lustrous appearance and the highest thermal conductivity of all metals; therefore silver rigidly designates the element with the atomic number 47. Anything else is not silver even though it may look like it e.g. platinum.

The name of the tomb owners is similarly a rigid designator of a particular individual. It is mentioned several times from the entrance door to the innermost parts of the chapel on the false door, it also appears in inscriptions, which

relate to his biography as well in appeals to the living,[413] and in every possible part of the interior decoration. These rigid designations supplement the actual depiction of the tomb owner and shape a complete identity kit of how the elite tomb owner wished to be represented. Whether sitting in front of the offering table, sitting in a carrying-chair, in his striding pose, in a hunting scene or viewing the presentations, his name is typified and this is what serves to distinguish him forever. "Der aufgeschriebene Name stellt die Verbindung zwischen Dargestelltem und Darstellung her; er ist gewissermassen der Zauberzwang, der die Lebenskraft (*KA*) des Dargestellten in die Statue zwingt".[414]

Even if no name were to be seen, one would still be able to recognize the tomb owner from his pose and size. However, it should be noted that the pose and size of the principal character in a particular tomb, is no more than an obvious symbol of that character being a successful member of the elite class, rather than portraying a specific tomb owner.

In Egyptian religion, the name indicates three essentials:[415]

1. Boundary denoting the individual sphere of the person.
2. Power associated with good and evil
3. Insurance of eternal life, which only the elite could have.

In life it is easy to be denoted by a name but in death one has to ensure that it will be pronounced and thereby remembered. The name is thus a symbol of what is to be commemorated "he whose name is pronounced lives on"[416] and therefore the preservation of the memory of a name is paramount.

Most ancient Egyptian names that one encounters have some form of association with the world of myth and gods. Names can be looked on as 'word games' subject to the same sort of manipulation that the symbols (including myths and gods) they were associated with. Just like the same sun god could be named Khepri in the morning, Ra at noon and Atum in the evening,[417] the name could also mean different things. In understanding the concept of a name we must not lose sight of the way it was used, in ensuring that it became among other things, an indispensable element for the continuation of life after death. Thus the Egyptian

[407] Baer, *Rank and title in the Old Kingdom*, 231-39.
[408] Roth, "The Organization of Royal Cemeteries at Saqqara", *JARCE*, (25), 201-14.
[409] Robins, "Women", *OEAE*, (3), 512-514. For a cross-cultural comparative study see Walthall, *Servants of the Dynasty: Palace Women in World History*. She edits 15 articles on woman's roles in royal courts, illustrating how they served as mothers, wives, concubines, entertainers, officials and servants.
[410] Allen, *Middle Egyptian*, 79-81.
[411] Fitzenreiter, "Grabdekoration und die Interpretation Funerärer Rituale im Alten Reich", 70.
[412] Kripke, *Naming and Necessity*, 3-4, and 77.

[413] Vernus, "Name", *LÄ*, vol. 4, 320-23. Also see Johnson, "What's in a Name", *LA*, (9), 143-52.
Also see Breasted, *Ancient Records of Egypt*, vol. 1, 131 and 58. He warns that one should be aware that the Egyptians were fond of giving similar names to brothers and sisters, which could lead to the erroneous belief that the name was of no consequence.
[414] Helck, "Zur Frage der Entstehung der ägyptischen Literatur", 7-8.
[415] Doxey, "Names", *OEAE*, vol. 2, 490.
[416] Otto, *Die biographischen Inschriften der ägyptischen Spätzeit*, 62. For a general review of the importance of the survival of the name, see 58-65.
[417] Morenz, *Egyptian Religion*, 145.

was very serious about leaving his name on monuments through which association he hoped to live permanently.[418]

Whether or not the monument belonged to him was unimportant, what was essential to him was that a social system of memory and specific identity existed in the concept of a monument, because a monument only makes sense in a system where social memory is commemorated.[419] Wengrow sums this up clearly "in attaching growing numbers of people to particular places, and in reproducing these attachments over generations, the urbanization of the dead may have been more important than the urbanization of the living, the density of social memory more vital than the massing of private "dwellings".[420] Although the foregoing statement was made in the context of the development of Egypt as a whole, it nevertheless points to how the concept of a widely understandable elite identity, and ideology may have developed and been maintained.

However, it is a fact that certain graves were usurped and this was not restricted to any class/period, for even Ramses II is famously known for his usurpations. While for the normal person this could be because of the scarcity of burial space, this could hardly apply to a king and in the ethical context demands an explanation. Interestingly usurpation, when it is pictured, is of the *name*, because it is the identity and memory which is being destroyed and not the representation itself, which is an idealized fiction. In the tomb of Hetep-her-akhti an indirect reminder of this is seen on his tomb entrance, he says that he built his tomb in a pure place where there was no previous grave, thus respecting the name, and property rights of every dead.[421] This statement was inscribed possibly due to the fact that tomb robbery and destruction were self-evident elsewhere.[422] The phenomenon of usurpation is probably due to human nature because at all times and in all societies, some people care, and respect, but others are indifferent and insensitive. Kemp would classify this as perversity. He expands on this by asking why this sort of behaviour arises and his answer is that:

> "whilst one direction of human endeavor is towards inhabiting a stable system … it stands constantly in a tension with jagged moments or long nurtured schemes of rejection … everything provokes its opposite; everything needs its opposite in order to survive".[423]

4.7 Religious Concepts

Egypt had many gods, and its polytheistic nature (illustrated by the existence of many gods and their functions in the cosmic correlations), gave it the flexibility to combine different forms of gods/beliefs.[424] You will not see any aspects of exclusivity or intangibility, which are the preserve of the book religions (i.e. Judaism, Christianity, and Islam). You will not even see any definition of god. As Assmann writes: "There was no explicit and coherent explanation of Egyptian theology on the metalevel of theoretical discourse … any more than there were theoretical explanations in other areas, such as grammar, rhetoric, or histiography".[425] Accordingly there is no systematically ordered set of beliefs, and any understanding of their basic beliefs has to be by inference from the authoritative texts (e.g. Pyramid Texts, Coffin Texts, and Book of the Dead). However, what you will observe from the authoritative texts is the varied ways in which religious gods and concepts were combined, altered, omitted and reunited to support the central concept of order, as is evident from the many inscriptions found in the funerary context. Indeed it is because the Egyptians had so many gods that it enabled them to work towards a realization of competing truths; something that was essential for the subsequent development of its culture. Goebs rightly observes that while one function of these texts was to achieve the deceased's transfiguration, "… an even wider usage cannot be ruled out. Within the material presented in the Pyramid and Coffin Texts we are looking at an enormous fund of religious and often mythical associations filling a variety of (cultic) contexts".[426] Interpretations as applied by the priestly elite in certain religious documents may also be of assistance in understanding what they meant by certain expressions. Indeed in this context one must admit that while the past sources of religious belief are not amenable to strict logic, yet "records of these sources are not formulae. They elicit in us an intuitive response which pierces beyond dogma".[427] Considering that there were no written laws, as we know that existed in the OK, the 'theory' of a general concept that encompassed the social obligations and duties of the populace, would imply an unprecedented order of complexity in the established relationships within society. Religious concepts can then be viewed as the cement upon which the solidarity of Egyptian society was achieved.

The focus here however will be on those religious ideas, which were essential to solving the elite's problems concerning the continuation of life in the hereafter, and of social existence in the world of the living. These are the three ideas of *B3, K3* and *M3ʿt*. In ancient Egyptian religion these integral elements must be incorporated into any analysis that purports to show the individual as a vital part of society, and culturally significant. In the maxims of Ptahhotep it is said

---

[418] Assmann, *Stein und Zeit*, 139.

[419] Assmann, *Tod und Jenseits im Alten Ägypten,* 70. In relation to his father Ramses I, Sethos says: "Mein Herz sorgt sich um meinen wahren Vater, indem ich wie Horus bin, zur Seite seines Vaters und des Namens meines Erzeugers gedenke, (denn) an dem Ort, an dem man eines Namens Millionen Male gedenkt, vernachlässigt man nicht ihren (der Toten) Zustand".

[420] Wengrow, *The archaeology of early Egypt,* 83.

[421] Mohr, *The Mastaba of Hetep-Her-Akhti.*

[422] Peden, *Egyptian Historical Inscriptions of the Twentieth Dynasty,* 225-279.

[423] Kemp, *Ancient Egypt: Anatomy of a Civilization,* 5.

[424] Faulkner, *Ancient Egyptian Book of the Dead*, 84. "… I am Horus the Elder on the Day of Accession, I am Anubis of Sepa, I am the Lord of All, I am Osiris…" (Spell 69).

[425] Assmann, *The Search for God in Ancient Egypt,* 9.

[426] Goebs, "The Cannibal Spell: Continuity and Change in the Pyramid Text and Coffin Text and Versions", *IFAO*, (139), 143.

[427] Whitehead, *Religion in the Making*, 144.

"That man will endure who is meticulous in uprightness".[428]

Implied in this statement are the concepts of who is to be remembered (*B3/K3*) and why he is to be remembered (because he is upright, i.e. he has said and done *M3ˁt*). The tomb owner who is thus identified is rewarded with eternal life in the hereafter and with remembrance in the society, which he has left.

Memory is then to be understood as an effort by the Egyptians to explain their hierarchical world and its problems and in so doing point to the significance and existence of the generics. The motifs not only served a decorative purpose but were concepts which embodied the tradition of Egyptian cultural beliefs. Being cultural they were never static; they were modified by being supplanted with new ideas and by being extended and standardized that conformed best with the needs of the society at that time as well as the principal religious ideas.

B3 and K3

Both of these concepts cannot have an afterlife if the previous life has not been in conformity with *M3ˁt*. The simplest way of understanding them is to think of an individual as having two areas: the physical and the social. The *K3* is the avenue by which the social sphere of the deceased is restored; is static and not able to move between the two realms of this world and the next; and for my purpose the more important element of the two. In contrast the *B3*, represents the 'physical' sphere of the person,[429] which is able to move between the two relams of the living and the dead, and is depicted in the iconography as a bird with a human head. This differentiation of both the *K3* and the *B3* are alluded to in Papyrus Westcar.[430]

However, it is not clear why this should be so. If *M3ˁt* as a socially practiced concept is the basis for the afterlife of the *B3* it seems to me that it is extremely difficult to separate the two spheres of the physical and the social. Both *B3/K3* exist during life, and both are part of the individual in the community. As such from the point of view of the society at large this differentiation is blurred. However, from a strict religious view point the separation between the physical and the social sphere may be used to show the difference between *B3* and the *K3*. This is an artificial construct because the *B3*, is related to the person himself as part of the community and not separate from it. In this sense both are important elements of memory.

The hieroglyph for *K3* is depicted as a pair of arms stretching upwards and refers to a gesture meaning a mutual embrace. It is found in both the Pyramid and Coffin Texts, and continues to be seen across the pharaonic period, and still to date is a matter of some debate.[431] The concept defies any one single meaning, because it is a concept that is used by the gods, the king and humans, and accordingly has different levels of understanding. As far as the human is concerned it is said to be the interface between the dead and the living, between the individual and society and between the father and the son, which continues even after death.[432] The role of the *K3* in defining a person as having many aspects at the spiritual, social, and material level is now well recognized.[433]

The *K3* is one's "hyper-physical vital force"[434] during life, and necessary for transformation as a transfigured deceased (*3ḫ*) afterward. According to ancient belief, the god Khnum manufactured each person's *K3* and although made at the same time as the physical body, it had no separate existence until the time came "to go to one's *K3*" meaning the time of physical death.[435] At the time of physical death the *K3* is no longer active; it becomes so after the Opening of the Mouth and Eyes ritual, and is then of use in the afterlife, and in this funerary context describes the transfigured deceased.[436] In this way the former living being and the spirit jointly continue to live in the monumental tomb just like they had lived when the tomb owner was alive on this earth.[437]

Accordingly in his dead state (after having been subjected to the Opening of the Mouth and Eyes ritual) the tomb owner could enjoy all his faculties as when he was alive. This included the ability to partake of food, to be sustained by the food offerings received or depicted in the representations, and inscriptions in his tomb. The *K3*'s importance lies in the fact that for the deceased to be able to partake of the offerings, the *K3* had to inhabit a recognizable statue or depiction of the deceased, and so the *K3* came to represent a guarantee of his survival and eternal life. Even a cursory look at the names from the early dynastic periods onwards, indicates the importance that '*K3*' played in the composition of the name.[438]

Equally the offering formula on the false door of the chapel - a prayer requesting that offerings be given to the deceased, mostly end with the hope that the offerings provided are 'for the *K3* of N'; sometimes this is extended to "may his *K3*

[428] Simpson, ed., *The Literature of Ancient Egypt*, 138, l. 10.3.

[429] Lopreino, *Topos und Mimesis*, 91-93. Though the *B3* survives death, it is independent of social bonds, unlike the *K3*. Also see Žabkar, *A Study of the Ba Concept in Ancient Egyptian Texts, SAOC*, (34), 3.

[430] Simpson, ed., *The Literature of the Ancient Egyptians*, 19, l. 7. 23-26. "May your *K3* contend with your enemy, and may your *B3* learn the ways leading to the Portal of the One Who Clothes the Weary One".

[431] Borioni, *Das Ka aus religionswissenschaftlicher Sicht*, 64-74. He provides a helpful review of the different understandings of the *K3*.

[432] Loprieno, "Drei Leben nach dem Tod", in *Grab und Totenkult im Alten Ägypten*, eds. H. Guksch, E. Hoffmann, and M. Bommas, 203-06.

[433] Kaplony, "Ka", *LÄ*, vol. 3, 275-82.

[434] Morenz, *Egyptian Religion*, 170. Bonnet in "*Religionsgeschichte*", 357-63, translated it similarly to Morenz as "Lebenskraft". Kaplony *LÄ* III, 275 translated it as "Macht im Leben". This 'vital force' could differ in strength among individuals or in the same individual. cf. Bolshakov, *JMFA*, vol. 3, 5-14.

[435] Assmann, *Tod und Jenseits im Alten Ägypten*, 62, 131, 34.

[436] Englund, *Akh, une notion religieuse.* 108-109, 158, 192.

[437] Ibid. 135.

[438] Ranke, *Die ägyptischen Personennamen*, vol. I (esp. Chapter 2). Also see pls. 26.60 (11), 31.5, and 11.16 (1) in Petrie and Griffith, *The Royal Tombs of the Earliest Dynasties, Part I and II*. Also evident in royal names of Dynasties 4, 5 and 6, e.g. Menkaure, Shepeskaf, Djedkare, Userkaf and Neferirkare.

dwell in the presence of the king";[439] which again refers to his memory, and to the memorial offerings for that person. In any event the offering formula always connects with food and so the connection between survival and memory is explicit. Just like the body cannot survive without food, the spirit too needs food to be sustained eternally. This idea helps to reinforce the *K3*'s commemorative role, the concept of the *K3* as the "animating force",[440] that part which belonged to the social sphere of the person and has to be revitalized, (such that when he became a transfigured person; the body and its constituents which had been disorganized by death could be brought to a new merger with each other, thus restoring his previous status and dignity). The *K3* then plays a significant commemorative role, it is the memory of a person and in this role it brings into focus all the implications of the cultural generics.

Underpinning *M3ˤt*

This section continues and expands on what has already been stated in relation to *M3ˤt* under the behavioural aspects of Egyptian society. What follows illustrates how *M3ˤt* was part of the religious belief, its relation to the monumental tomb, and its role in ensuring commemoration and consequently social connectivity.

Although this concept of doing the right thing (*M3ˤt*) is well known ("Die Ma'at ist das Gute, und das Gute ist das, was geliebt, gewünscht, und gewollt wird"[441]), there are no explicit philosophically precise statements about *M3ˤt* itself. What we have is a variety of direct and indirect references in the five groups of writing: wisdom literature, non-royal tomb chapel biographies, funerary literature, liturgical solar texts, and kingship texts.[442] The ancient Egyptians seem to have had a habit of not expounding fundamental values and the way they were implemented at a practical level within society. Consider their explanation about the creation of humans which is equally obscure even though it was a most serious subject that formed the basis of the very structure of Egyptian society.[443]

Sometime during 3100BC with the union of Lower and Upper Egypt progress is seen in many areas of human knowledge including that of state and religion; "in this period we are watching the higher aspects of an evolutionary process which cannot be observed at so early a stage elsewhere in the career of man. We are contemplating the emergence of a sense of moral responsibility…".[444]

M3ˤt is thus the 'ideological mother' of the Egyptian state, being the daughter of the creator god Ra, identified with cosmic order, and thus present from the beginning as a fundamental part of the cosmos.[445] Textual evidence of its great antiquity is also confirmed in the maxims of Ptahhotep, it says: "Great is *M3ˤt* and its foundation is firmly established. It has not been shaken since the time of Osiris, (here the reference is to the first appearance of the rising sun - (*sp-tpy*)). And he who violates the laws must be punished".[446] *M3ˤt* is thus a standard of divine origin, which has a mandatory sanction to be followed by society, for king and commoner alike.[447]

Accordingly, the cultural unity of Egypt depended among other things on a complex of fundamental values, which were sanctioned by the deities, and which underlay the major patterns of everyday thought and behaviour. This ethos acts jointly with the quasi-divine role of the pharaoh, to produce an unquestionable moral system. One does *M3ˤt* because it is what the king wills; and the king does *M3ˤt* because it is what the gods will. This union between a way of thinking (*M3ˤt* as the intermediary between god and men, governing the behavior of society, which on earth is regulated by the king), and the coercive power of the king combine to define and refine all those significant factors which form the backbone of this society. These hold the community, parts of art, religion, and justice together.

Because this was such a deep-rooted principle, (having royal and divine antecedents) it becomes indisputable, and because everyone was supposed to practice it, it needs no overt explanation.

It is interesting to note that since Dynasty 4 the king's name expresses a committemnt to *M3ˤt*. King Senefru is named "*Nb M3ˤt*" (possessor of *M3ˤt*), Userkaf is named "*Ir M3ˤt*" (he who does *M3ˤt*) and this phenomenon continues into the Ramessid period when the king's titularies include *M3ˤt* as the ideal manifestation of kingship.

In any event this concept of *M3ˤt* is archeologically noticeable: in the monumental royal architecture (mortuary temples), monumental elite tombs, the Pyramid Texts (in spell 319b, the king Unas is represented as a bringer and doer of *M3ˤt*). This theme albeit confined to speaking and doing *M3ˤt* continues in the non-royal funerary inscriptions, the iconography, and a few papyri.

At one level it can be visualized as an eminent symbol for Egypt, representing "in the minds of the Old Kingdom thinkers a term expressing a sense of the national order, the moral order of the nation…"[448] At another level it contains

---

[439] Strudwick, *Texts from the Pyramid Age*, 219.
[440] Gordon, "The ka as an animating force", *JARCE*, (32), 185-96.
[441] Assmann, *Ma'at: Gerechtigkeit und Unsterblichkeit im Alten Ägypten*, 108.
[442] Ibid. 50.
[443] Parkinson, *Poetry and Culture in the Middle Kingdom*, 169-74. He relates the implementation of MAat in the Tale of the Eloquent Peasant as a practical example of the thinking within society. The peasant is only able to reconcile social injustice and the ideal, by coming to terms with what should be, and what is reality. This example forcefully exposes the critical role of the nature of MAat. It would be naive to dismiss this tale just because it is from the Middle Kingdom, because equivalent instances of injustice are a common feature of developing societies today, where the rule of law is still in its infancy.

[444] Breasted, *The Dawn of Conscience*, 123.
[445] In this regard see Coffin Texts ll, 32b-33a [chapter 80].
[446] Simpson, ed., *The Literature of Ancient Egypt*, 132, l. 6.5
[447] Faulkner, *The Ancient Egyptian Pyramid Texts*, § 386.
[448] Breasted, *The Dawn of Conscience*, 143.

within it the germ of the idea that of undiluted power and indirect social control.

In concrete terms, to the ancient Egyptian *M3ˁt* was what held the universe, the natural world, the state, and the individual together? Helck interprets the hieroglyph for *M3ˁt* as a base of the world and human life.[449]

In addition it indirectly serves to highlight two attributes symbolized in the monumental grave: that of achievement of success in this life and survival in the memory of posterity, "zum einen als äusseres Zeichen des Lebenserfolgs und zum anderen als Aussenhalt der sozialen Erinnerung und Zeichen diesseitiger Fortdauer".[450]

In practical terms there is awareness that while violence and injustice cannot be eliminated, they can be tamed by the state (read king through his elite officials). The Pyramid Texts assert the cosmic role of the king and in the ritual where he raises *M3ˁt*, he is symbolizing that everything in the world is in its proper order.[451]

Consequently by Dynasty 5 Old Kingdom society was based on a concept of what is known as "vertical solidarity".[452] This refers to achievement of social cohesion that is vertical, directed from the king and elite down to the masses of others that need or desire protection. To live according to *M3ˁt* becomes a guiding principle. *M3ˁt* serves to assure all of the right way of doing justice, righteousness, solidarity, and the resultant benefits of this social intercourse. There are numerous instances[453] of biographies beginning with the following combination of phrases, which assume a set of values that reflect the norms of society, and the example here is from the tomb of Neferseshemre at Saqqara in the reign of Teti:

> "I came forth from my town, I went down into the afterlife; I carried ou   t *M3ˁt* for her Lord; I satisfied him with regard to that which he loves; I spoke *M3ˁt*, I carried out *M3ˁt*".[454]

The 'lord' in the above sentence refers to the king, and is a direct indication of the good behaviour expected by the king, in return for the memorial offerings. The implication is that *M3ˁt* represents the truth of what was being said and the fairness of what was done. This is why such clauses are common in the OK biographies, because they establish the connection between the religious principle of *M3ˁt* and

the monumental grave[455] especially in the references by the tomb owner to:

- Building the grave where there was no other.
- Destroying no other graves in the process of building a grave.
- Plundering no other grave for stone and materials.
- Paying the craftsmen who built the grave.[456]
- Respecting the graves of others who had gone to their Ka's- meaning the previous dead.
- Carrying out *M3ˁt*.

The link between *M3ˁt*, memory, and society thus comes to the fore and is one based on the idea that *M3ˁt* was a normative fact of man's integration in society, and that there were many ways of showing one's responsibility for *M3ˁt*, as the biographies testify. Further the monumental tomb and its contents indicate to society that the particular owner is one who is to be remembered, because he has fulfilled his ethical duty and therefore is worthy of remembrance and thus provides the means by which social connectivity prevails.[457]

The emphasis on the personal quality of the individual so predominant in the inscriptions thus reinforced his social identity and individuality, which ultimately called for commemoration, an act which would not only keep the cosmos in order but keep *M3ˁt* functioning for all time. These examples and their literal connection might seem exaggerated, but they do point to the ideal notion of a person, who would be acknowledged, remembered, and venerated. Even if the phrases are general and if the events described did not actually take place, even if the phraseology is about the effective (*mnḫ*) and excellent (*iḳr*) practice of official careers, or from evidence that is entirely from the world of the literate, and even if it has nothing to do with charity or compassion,[458] they are still important. The importance of these inscriptions and the underlying religious ideals lies in the fact that they are there at all. They point to the deep-rooted dependent nature of the then prevailing societal attitudes towards the formation and preservation of memory, which is the foundation of all iconography based on a funerary culture and the underlying generics. How far down did these ideals filter, and why they appeared, and to what extent the surviving record represents society practicing them as a whole are difficult questions to answer with certainty. However, if the craftsmanship of the elite tombs and the effort put by them in their interior decoration is anything to go by, then the answer is obvious.

[449] Helck, "Ma'at", *LÄ*, vol. 3, 1110.
[450] Assmann, *Ma'at: Gerechtigkeit und Unsterblichkeit im Alten Ägypten*, 36.
[451] Faulkner, *The Ancient Egyptian Pyramid Texts,* § 1775. "The sky is at peace, the earth is in joy, for they have heard that the King will set right [in place of wrong]".
[452] Assmann, *Ma'at:Gerechtigkeit und Unsterblichkeit im Alten Ägypten*, 248. Some sort of horizontal solidarity must have existed between the elite because their basic interests (e.g. control of the others and resources) were similar.
[453] Kloth, *Die Autobiographischen Inschriften des ägyptischen Alten Reiches,* 54-128.
[454] Strudwick, *Texts from the Pyramid Age*, 224.

[455] Ibid. Texts no. 202, 10, 16, 20, 23, and 24.
[456] Simpson, "*Topographical Notes on Giza Mastabas*", 494-95. He notes the similarities in the texts. In the tomb of Nimaatre, it says "as for his tomb, all the craftsmen who made it, he gave them a very great payment so that they thanked all the gods for him". Hetep-her-akhty's mastaba now at the Leiden Museum, reads "people built this for me upon bread, upon beer, upon clothing, upon oil and upon barley in very great quantities". A similar expression can be found in the tombs of Ankhmare (G7837+7843) and Nefer-Khuwi (G2098).
[457] For a contrasting view see Fox, "World Order and Ma'at", *JANES*, (23), 37-48.
[458] Franke, "Arme und Geringe im Alten Reich Altägyptens", *ZÄS*, (133), 112.

Prevailing social concerns must have impinged on the elite and the other people constituting Egyptian society. While *M3ʿt* might have been a word used by the elite, surely it is incredulous to argue that doing what was right was not in the vocabulary or the mindset of the masses especially in the developmental phases of this culture.

Against the above argument that *M3ʿt* as an ethical concept was widespread and practiced in Egyptian society, one can argue that these so-called good works did not put rich and poor on an equal basis, because the elite continued to have lavish tombs and funerary practices. They were a mere subterfuge by the tomb owner to avoid having to face any accusations of impropriety in the hereafter. Equally one could also argue that the paintings and reliefs because of their artistic merit were sufficient in themselves for commemoration, and no other underlying idea was necessary. Reducing arguments thus to a one-dimensional purely tentative prescription, and excluding the full range of historical developments is an incorrect, and wrong approach, and will not be pursued.

We must not forget that ancient Egypt, like all societies, had contradictions between the ideal and the practice. Why should this universal phenomenon of inherent contradictions preclude candid commitment to a moral standard? It is suggested that an attempt should be made (difficult as it is) to visualize this concept through the eyes of the ancient believers, accepting that what is written was how it was meant to exist. For the ancient Egyptians the structure of their world as they knew it then, its abundance and its natural order, were not just modes of thought but the uncircumventable products of creation as related in the creation mythology. The world in their view was not just created anew but was the continuation of the original primeval matter. *M3ʿt* the principle of eternal order that should govern the world is together with the god Shu, one of the predestined and primary cosmological powers, which existed since creation[459] and an undisputed fact.

The biographical inscriptions contain ideas about success in this world and the next. They can also be viewed as a sort of critical didactic discourse, because they have a message for the viewer, which in turn serves to underpin what must never be forgotten. The message may have been one such: in death, those who were highly thought of because they had observed *M3ʿt* joined the community of the blessed dead, and would be forever remembered in communal memory.[460] In contrast for those who did not practice *M3ʿt,* the results would be a tragic eternal death. Consider the hieroglyphic words *ntt* and *iwtt,*[461] the former means "that what is" and the latter means "that what is not", and therefore cannot exist, may be seen as indirect markers of

this social process of being part of, or permanently cast off from an ordered community.[462]

The reality of *M3ʿt* is clearly shown by a comparison with the way it was understood at a time of change in the FIP. During the dying days of the Old Kingdom, the first thing to suffer was the ideological basis of the king's power. Side by side is observed the emphasis by the elite protagonists as they attempt single handedly to better the living conditions, to avert famine and violence, to build new temples and places of offering in their nome, e.g. as known from the tomb of Itibi (Dynasty 10-11).[463] Another well-known example is from the tomb of Ankhtifi (Dynasty 11) at Moalla, who states:

> "I am the champion who has no peer, who spoke out when the nobles were silent … I am the van of men, the rear of men, for my like has not been, will not be, my like was not born, will not be born. I have surpassed the deeds of my forbears, and my successors will not reach me in anything that I have done for the next million years … and as for anyone on whom I placed my hand, no misfortune ever came to him".[464] He also points to his efforts to build a better community, and states further, "I made a man embrace the slayer of his father … I would not permit the heat of discord".

Of course this is to be seen in the context of instability but it does reflect more than a moral concern, because for the first time we see that it reflects the belief that one can build a moral community. A new attitude is also obvious in that personal success is no longer measured by the close connection with the institution of kingship but alone on one's own political power;[465] a harbinger of times when individuality is in the ascendant.

The doing of *M3ʿt* then points to action leading to independent development of the self, to being commemorated irrespective of dependency on the king, examples of which can be seen in the other FIP 'autobiographies' such as that of Kheti 1, Men-ankh-paep (Mni), Iti, etc.

However, the issues of reconciling the possible divergence between individual and collective memories and of judging whether the individual and collective authorship is historically accurate cannot be verified.

How then should one assess their social significance?

One suggestion would be, not to think of inscriptions of the biographies as a store of images, and their constitutive

[459] Assmann, *Theologie und* Frömmigkeit, 209. Also see Tobin, *Theological Principles of Egyptian Religion*, 200-205.
[460] Assmann, *Stein und Zeit*, 159.
[461] Hannig, *Die Sprache der Pharaonen*, vol. 1, 37 (welche nicht ist) and 440 (das was ist).

[462] Assmann, "Schrift, Tod und Identität", in *Schrift und Gedächtnis*, eds. A. u. J. Assmann and C. Hardmeier, 67.
[463] W. Schenkel, *Memphis, Herakleopolis, Theben. Die epigraphischen Zeugnisse der 7.-11. Dynastie Ägyptens*, 74-81.
[464] Lichtheim, *Ancient Egyptian Autobiogrpahies*, 25-26. For full text see Schenkel, *Memphis, Herakleopolis, Theben. Die epigraphischen Zeugnisse der 7.-11. Dynastie Ägyptens,* 45-57.
[465] Gnirs, "Die ägyptische Autobiographie", in *Ancient Egyptian Literature*, 224.

meaning. If one were to consider remembrance as the process of production and transmission, then the above issues would be peripheral because the focus would be more on the society and the means by which remembrance is evoked, rather than their interpretation. This is not to argue that interpretation is wrong per se. However, if the first step in understanding Egyptian art is to analyze the characteristics of the people for whom it was produced, the composition of the society that produced it, and the social discourse that led to its proliferation; then this would imply a shift in focus primarily to that of a mode of behaviour adding up to the cultural generics, and secondarily on meaning and interpretation.

The conclusion though cannot be denied, that the preservation of the social structure and its affiliated memorial function in the iconography, ensured for the elite, the prospect of mitigating death and perpetuating the tomb as a symbol of elite distinctiveness, with all its consequential connotations. These *Grundgedanken* are certainly evidenced in every period of ancient Egyptian history (although there is a discernible change in the relationship and the organization of *M3ˁt* between the self, the king, and the gods during the OK, MK, and Rammesid periods[466]). The inference that 'all' the members of the community are together, whether in this world or the next and so the rigors of death have been modified, is however, unchanged. Admittedly these are indirect inferences, and arise because "the sources for investigating practical religion and morality are sparse and indirect",[467] but this should not be an excuse for ignoring their force on the culture of ancient Egypt.

Private elite tombs thus existed within a well defined and ordered memorial functional system, of which as already stated, religious concepts, cult and endowment practices, inscriptions, and decorum were integral parts. By focusing on the interpretation of the representations in terms of social memory, which is a cultural aspect, one can identify strategies by which material culture was employed to commemorate the dead in ancient Egypt.

The theoretical basis for *M3ˁt* as already stated was most likely established prior to the establishment of the Old Kingdom. What was perfected in the OK was the moral imperative: that because *M3ˁt* had a divine basis ordained by the king, it was to be understood as something different to evil, falsehood, and wrong doing. The sanction of not doing *M3ˁt* on both the personal and social level was being condemned to being dead forever. Only by practicing it could one become a worthy soul capable of being remembered on a permanent basis and thus realize eternal life.

STELA OF USERHAT (19B) AT RIJKSMUSEUM VAN OUDHEDEN AT LEIDEN

I would go even further and posit that commemoration should be viewed as a widespread consequence of people living together in certain relationships, and although the ancient Egyptian evidence is of a purely funerary nature, it should not be restricted to the funerary theme alone. Present societies would do well to put this universal ideal into practice for "the Egyptian ideal of *M3ˁt* (truth, justice, and order) was not only the principle of social but also of temporal connectivity, of permanence, endurance, and remembrance, of the continuity of the past and future".[468]

---

[466] Assmann, *Theologie und Weisheit im alten Ägypten,* 45-53. In the aftermath of the Amarna period the elite increasingly depend upon the divine, although formally the idea of divine kingship continues till the end of pharaonic times.

[467] Baines, "Society, Morality, and Religious practice", in *Religion in Ancient Egypt*, ed. B. E. Shafer, 131.

[468] Assmann, *Death and Salvation in Ancient Egypt,* 55.

Chapter 5: Characterizing the Generics

The evidence of the existence of the generics has been construed over a certain time frame. Difficulties exist with the combining of material and context, distortions caused by the nature of the archaeological record, and the influence of the changing nature of lived practice. Nevertheless by including both the influences of the material and the immaterial nature of ancient Egyptian culture, it has been possible to identify those concepts of cultural significance which were essential for the Old Kingdom elite in their own right, as being fundamental to the concept of a funerary culture based on the preservation of individual and collective memory. These were common to all elite tombs and are part of what I term the 'generics'. They refer to the intuitive concepts of identity, individuality, and ideology. Remembrance and change, which play a significant part in their constitution and evolution, have been discussed previously.

The goal of this chapter then is to explain the remaining generics both theoretically and practically, i.e. in terms of their relationship to either the existing world or a possible world and to their real and implied detection in Egyptian artifacts.

Previous chapters have examined most of the necessary ingredients that could possibly be involved in the demarcation of aspects of cultural significance, which could have widespread application. At the end of the preceding examination it had become apparent that connected with the perpetuation of memory and associated change, there was a clear and consistent pointer to certain widespread cultural aspects. These were referred to as constituting support for the cultural generics, i.e. identity, individuality, and ideology. These are what were termed the generics, and while not formally expressed, nevertheless are implicit in the iconography of the Old Kingdom, and shall be analyzed in Part 2.

However before doing so, it would be worthwhile to consider the theoretical basis of these generics. In attempting this, difficulties and distortions that may be apparent in the archaeological record due to accidents of preservation, as well as influences of religious and other beliefs, must be kept in mind.

A precise definition of these generics shall not be attempted, because going down this path would lead to a lessening of exploration; making the definitions either so short as to be unacceptable, or so long as to be totally incomprehensible. Take for example the definition of ideology as:

> "a set of closely related beliefs or ideas or even attitudes, characteristic of a group or community".[469]

On the surface this appears as a logical and concise definition. On scrutiny however, one begins to wonder what is meant by beliefs and ideas and how can these be established? A similar epistemological difficulty confronts one with the concepts of identity and individuality; both pertain to the self, but what is the self? The controversial natures of these abstract/psychological deliberations are outside the scope of this study.[470]

However a clarification of the uniqueness of each of these aspects (identity, ideology, and individuality) is still necessary, because of the considerable divergence of views in the sociological literature as to the ideas and effects on the individual, and the group, and their interactions as they relate to material culture.

The ideas that affect the individual and the group interactively give rise to those cultural aspects which are referred to as the generics, and which are expressed in different ways in the iconography.

5.1 Identity

Identity is explored in the context of the tomb owner's personal and socio-cultural environment. In particular it is the latter context, which awakens identity aspirations, because it intimately connects the individual and the community together in a wide range of life processes. These aspirations can be explicitly and implicitly observed in the material artifacts of funerary culture and are illustrated in the numerous examples found in the elite tombs.

The concept of identity has been traditionally approached in two ways as:

1. The sum of abstract qualities, which are connected to the individual,[471] which has its basis in both psychology, and behavioural sciences.
2. The particular outcome of interaction and positioning in different social and cultural contexts[472] having its basis in sociology.

Both of these approaches envisage a particular pre-existing notion of the individual and this presupposition is not questioned. A major concern is to determine the origin of identity. This is not something, which we can take on

---

[469] Palmenatz, *Ideology*, 15.

[470] For different views see Russell, *Authority and the Individual*. Also see Dumont, *Homo Hierarchicus*.

[471] Mauss, *Sociology and Psychology*, 29-31. He indicates the self as the site where the organic, psychological, and social converge, as characterizing the interrelated human condition. Also see Marcia, "The ego identity status approach to ego identity", in *Ego Identity*, ed. J. E. Marcia, 3-21.

[472] Shotter, "Becoming Someone: Identity and Belonging", in *Discourse and lifespan identity*, ed. J. F. Nussbaum and N. Coupland, 5-27.

or discard at our whim, because it is fundamental to both approaches to identity. In ancient Egypt, whether you were a vizier, a landowner, a high priest, or a normal scribe, one was associated with a certain image because of one's participation in a range of cultural practices. The outcome of this involvement resulted in one being addressed and accepted as a person of a particular kind. In this context identity in the main can be imagined as a sort of exclusivity, as an attachment to a specific position. Both the personal and social identity of the tomb owner, because they relate to different aspects of the self, is represented in elite tomb iconography.

Webster's Third New International Dictionary offers a Latin root for identity – *identitas* from *idem* meaning 'the same'.[473] Identity thus could refer to:

- Sameness of objects, as in A1 is identical to A2 but not to B2; and the consistency or continuity over time; that is the basis for establishing the definiteness and distinctiveness of something.

At the most fundamental level this would therefore require a comparison of similarities and differences, which is a behavioural activity.

In this study the fact is stressed that the tomb complex served to highlight four levels of the tomb owner's identity at:

1. *The individual's personal level*: concerning his striking physical traits, and unique desires.
2. *The family level*: concerning his responsibility for and towards his family.
3. *The communal level*: concerning his responsibility and those normative wishes, which he shared as part of various communities including as a 'citizen' of Egypt.
4. *The political level*: concerning what was 'politically' expected of him, as part of an elite segment of society as a valid justification for obligations and privileges held.

All these levels involve a contradiction, which comes about from the dichotomy of a certain amount of mutual inclusiveness as well as individual distinctiveness. Even when the protagonist was not a living member, the funeral programme would reflect the past identity of the individual. The treatment accorded to him would not only be consistent with the status of the particular person's social position, but would reflect the political and social aspirations of the 'pecking order' to which he belonged. The nature of that particular society and maybe the wishes of his progeny would also be an element of the extent and nature of the funeral practices, which would be appropriate.[474]

In contrast to personal identity, social identity has been described as "that part of an individual self-concept which derives from his knowledge of his membership in a social group (or groups) together with the values and emotional significance attached to that membership".[475] As a concept it does not explain how to measure emotional significance, nor does it define the number of groups an individual must belong to. The starting point then is again the individual. Because the group is composed of individuals each of whom have diverse personalities, social identity transcends the individual. It has as its raison d'être all those recognized and accepted shared values, in the formation of which most individuals have very little input. It is these shared and connected values, which define oneself as part of a certain group.[476] Social identity refers to ways in which individuals and collectives interact, which then results in the creation and maintenance of the norms and values of society.[477] For example, one defines oneself as Dutch because one accepts and recognizes the commonality of values, which are part of the collective norm of being a member of the Dutch community. These have evolved over years and over which one has very little, if any influence. One's acceptance into the community is a reflection of one's accepting, following, and projecting one's social identity in terms of the prevailing patterns of normative social behaviour for a person in a particular social position.[478] However in the sharing of common cultural norms there is an effective crossing over of group specific boundaries[479] and ultimately in a Dutch social identity.

In ancient Egypt the crossing over of cultural traits between the South and the North has been suggested by Kaiser[480] which may have resulted in the formation of a unified Egyptian culture/state as seen in the decoration of the Narmer palette, the ceremonial knives, and combs.

It is clear that in contrast, one has far greater influence as regards one's personal identity.

That social identity by stressing the group does so at the expense of the individual, is evident, but it is equally true that groups and inter-group relations play a significant role in one's self definition, and that social identity sustains belief structures.

Long before the royal cult was established, the belief in human survival beyond the grave (as evidenced by an ample supply of grave goods) is well attested in the

---

473 *Webster's New Third International Dictionary: Unabridged*, 1123.
474 O'Shea, *Mortuary Variability*, 32-39.
475 Taifel, "Social Categorization, Social Identity and Social Comparison", in *Differentiation between Social Groups*, ed. H. Taifel, 61-76.
476 Assmann, "Todesbefallenheit im Alten Ägypten", 231.
477 Díaz-Andreu et al., *The Archaeology of Identity*, 1-12.
478 I am not referring to the sort of ethnic identity, which can only be perceived on the basis of cultural differences and/or common descent but to the sort of 'ethnic identity', which is an aspect of relationship and not a property of a specific group. A modern illustration is the case of the 'migrating countries' e.g. Australia/Canada, which represent a cross-section of the world's cultures, resulting in layers of identities beneath a state imposed one.
479 Emberling, "Ethnicity in complex societies," *JAR*, (4), 295-340.
480 Kaiser, "Trial and Error", *GM*, (149), 5-14.

prehistoric cemeteries.[481] It is also evidenced later in the Pyramid Texts:

"...your bones shall not perish, your flesh shall not sicken,[482]

"...receive your water, gather together your bones, stand on your feet, raise yourself to this bread of yours, that you may be effective thereby, that you may be powerful thereby, and that you may give some to him who is in your presence".[483]

"...cast off your bonds, throw off the sand which is on your face...".[484]

"...you have your milk which is in the [breast] of your mother Isis...".[485]

These are parts of spells indicating a belief in life after death, and encompass all the types of identity, which I proposed, other than the political one, because politics as understood today, did not exist then. For this we have to turn to indirect inferences, expressions of political ideology as delegates of the king, and on the emergence of the self-conscious person reflecting his ideology in the biographical texts.[486]

The transmission of the concept of a social identity involves to some extent also the transmission of political ideology because it is through this means that an ordered society and identity can be maintained. The king's main political aims were that of maintaining order within Egypt and that of protecting its borders. One way in which this is reflected is in the different names of the king.[487] Prior to Dynasty 4 these names echo the political reality of the times as follows:

The Horus name is the oldest royal name encompassing the god of kingship in the person who resides in the palace.

The "two ladies" name incorporates the cobra goddess and the vulture goddess, necessary for the protection of Lower and Upper Egypt respectively.

The "Golden Horus" name probably had some connection to the sun and the sky stressing the connections of the king to these elements.

The *nswt bity* is one of the two names, which appear within a cartouche symbolizing the fact that the king rules over everything. It identifies the person who resides in the palace as the ruler of Lower and Upper Egypt.

The beginning of a political ideology is to be seen in the act of assuming in addition to the above four names, that of "son of Ra" which Djedefre does in Dynasty 4. What might appear at first glance a mere chronological assimilation of names was in reality a chronological assimilation of political power? At one stroke all the gods and their cults are linked to the person of the king. As the highest priest he is responsible for the well being of the gods, a consequence of which is the flow- on effect to society as a whole. The price for this is an eternal ideological dependency of all the people on the king as consisting of a particular version of the office of kingship – that accepted by the gods. By mid-Dynasty 5 this political ideology is exemplified by Nuiserre taking on the title of 'lord of the two lands' (*nb t3wy*), which in fact becomes the social identity of future kings. All and everything on earth belongs to the king and the only way to prosper is to ally oneself as close to him as possible.

The elite in taking over delegated powers from the king then implicitly take on a particular social identity, and role, reinforcing their eliteness. In addition they are responsible for maintaining and propagating his political ideology. Because the effective exercise of political power depends largely upon economic control, the elite's social identity then reflects political ideology, the seeds of which were sown in the earlier periods. This is evidenced in their various titles appearing prior to Dynasty 4 as seen in the seal impressions, e.g. incorporating executive power,[488] leader of escorts,[489] leader of officials,[490] administration of royal revenue,[491] and in the funerary cult.[492]

Indeed as far back as King Den persons were designated as royal seal bearers (*ḫtmw-bity*).[493] Therefore the person who carried the royal seal was also the agent of the king and the *ḫtmw-bity* / *nswt* must have exercised symbolic as well as executive authority.

Embedded in this is the fact that the materialization of ideas into ideology was the responsibility of two sections of the polity whose social identity is well established: the king and the elite as far as the maintenance of a community order was concerned, and the priests whose main task was to supply the religious underpinning.

The tendency for the lower echelons to follow the beliefs of the higher ones is well known.[494] Consider the fact that the

[481] Bard, "The Egyptian Predynastic", *JFA*, (21/3), 265-88. Also see Midant-Reynes, *The Prehistory of Egypt,* 100-66.

[482] Faulkner, *The Ancient Egyptian Pyramid Texts*, § 725.

[483] Ibid. § 858.

[484] Ibid. § 1878.

[485] Ibid. § 1883.

[486] Assmann, "Sepulkrale Selbstthematisierung im Alten Ägypten", in *Selbstthematisierung und Selbstzeugnis: Bekenntnis und Geständnis*, ed. A. Hahn and V. Kapp, 213-21.

[487] For details of the development of the different names see Kahl, "*nsw und bit*: Die Anfänge", 307-351.

[488] Kaplony, *Die Inschriften der ägyptischen Frühzeit*, vol. I, ÄA, 23. For the seal impressions indicating power see Kaplony, *Die Inschriften der ägyptischen Frühzeit*, vol. III, ÄA, figs. 298-300. For a general survey of early administration see Wilkinson, *Early Dynastic Egypt*, 109-49, esp. 28-33.

[489] Kaplony, *Die Inschriften der ägyptischen Frühzeit*, vol. III, fig. 872.

[490] Ibid. figs. 267 and 769.

[491] Ibid. figs. 214, 29 and 862.

[492] Ibid. figs. 368-70.

[493] Emery, et al., *Excavations at Saqqara*, vol. III, pl. 81.37.

[494] Platvoet and Toorn, *Pluralism and Identity,* 42-45. Also see Converse, "The Nature of Belief Systems in Mass Publics", 206-261. Although his essay is concerned with political systems, the proposition that individuals follow over time beliefs of others, especially those who possess more information, cannot be denied.

Pyramid Texts were most probably compiled from earlier sources, and were the result of different traditions acting upon them, which must have been known to some of the elite.[495] The development of the non-royal mortuary ritual in line with that reserved for the royals would then seem natural; particularly in view of the fact that both textual and pictorial forms of mortuary discourse have a common final aim; that of a social identity of an (*3ḥ*)Akh. Usually there are no Old Kingdom burial chambers inscribed with continuous texts, however pictorial and textual descriptions of offerings are found in a few tombs.[496] The implication that the non-royal elite would also like to be transformed into a blessed dead (*s3ḥ.w*) with a view to being admitted into the society of the gods, does not seem far-fetched. The elite would then continue to live with the social identity, which they possessed when alive, and in their desired social sphere in the netherworld. All that the elite had to do was to ensure that what was described both in painting/relief and text was a reconfirmation of his social identity when alive. This is exactly what we find in Dynasties 5 and 6, when the elite state in their chapel inscriptions that they have personal knowledge by which one becomes an *3ḥ*, and the appropriate rituals that ensure him to become one such.

> "And I know everything by which an Akh who is passed to the necropolis as one venerated of the great god by the king becomes an Akh. And I know everything by which he ascends to the great god".[497]

As Assmann points out, personal identity is for the Egyptian, a function of social integration and approval and a human being is a person only within the limits of the image, which the (significant) others hold of him.[498]

Social identity is thus primarily constituted through discourse, language, society, and the regulating symbols. Since this is itself subject to varying nuances, the concept of social identity is contextual and therefore relational.

Zijlmans and Van Kooij claim that because identity is unique, it cannot be used as a concept for comparative research.[499] However they only consider a person's distinctive individual identity. They neglect social identity, which is bestowed by society on the individual based on his/her interaction with society, which may change over time and not be just self-generated. Different subjects including people, are unique but this should not inhibit classifying, comparing and/or researching them, etc. It

is restrictive to only consider one immediately apparent notion of identity and deny the implications of wider definition and related analysis.

5.2 Individuality

The development of individuality is one process that parallels the slackening of the bonds between the supreme, the senior, the junior, and the dispossessed in Old Kingdom Egypt. It is the outcome of the continuous struggle for betterment in mankind in both the material and the spiritual sense, which is a universal phenomenon. Limited archaeological data means that its evidence in elite tomb iconography is manifested as an atypical form of behaviour. This behaviour is a psychological phenomenon in so far as it relates to activities/outcomes of certain personality traits, and strictly speaking does not become an immediate part of culture. However when these traits become assimilated into being beliefs, system of rules and finally shared behaviour across society and time, they then become part of culture, and must be included in any study of cultural expression. Indeed it is the product of, social, geographical, and historical contexts; and while it may be superficially easy to detect, it is extremely difficult to distinguish between true innovation, and what appears as changes in ongoing practices. Moreover the fact that data availability varies between the periods requires us to draw assumptions when trying to link data between periods.

A model is developed such that accidental-erroneous/negligent acts, which would introduce noise, could be discounted, and individuality would be made visible as a special form of behaviour; yet separate from that which happens only once.

The very existence of a community is predicated on the existence of the individual and the collective group. In order to generate individuality and consequently a certain identity, we have to have a group or at least other individuals on whom the 'distinguishing behaviour' can be projected. Otherwise it would be meaningless as projection on to, and acceptance by the group is an essential requirement. Earlier ideas were marked by the assumption that individuality is the result of a fundamental conflict between the individual and the group, hence the need for its resolution by an absolute sovereign, an idea that can be traced back to Thomas Hobbes.[500] This assumption of conflict is now open to question, "Society and the individual are not antagonists".[501] As this book is not about political conflict, it will only examine this concept's unique characteristics that are relevant for the analysis of the motifs in elite tomb decoration.

Any reference to the tomb owner as an individual implies that he is the central player in the context of his particular tomb. It is obvious that human beings are characterized by individual differences, and that no two are 100% similar.

---

[495] Taylor, *Death and the afterlife in Ancient Egypt*, 193-200.
[496] James and Apted, *The Mastaba of Khentika called Ikhekhi*, pls. 34-38.
[497] Myśliwiec et al., *Saqqara 1: The Tomb of Merefnebef*, 73-74. Other examples from Dynasties 5 and 6 can also be seen in the tombs of Ty, Ibi, Nimaatre, Ankhmahor, Mereruka, etc.
[498] Assmann, "Persönlichkeitsbegriff und -bewusstsein", *LÄ*, vol. 4, 963-78. It seems that Assmann is fusing the concepts of personal and social identities, which I think are two related, yet separate issues.
[499] Zijlmans and Kooij, *Site-seeing: places in culture, time and space*, 6. Their idea has its origins in a book by J. Z. Smith, "To Take Place", 35, where he talks about 'absolute uniqueness'. However, even if something is unique, it still has relative comparable features, and so the assertions of Zijlmans/Kooij are open to question.

[500] Hobbes, *Leviathan*, 98-102.
[501] Benedict, *Patterns of culture*, 251-53. "...no civilization has in it any element which in the last analysis is not the contribution of an individual".

This is evident when one projects one's differences to other humans, for it is then that one begins to realize oneself as a certain type of person. This self-differentiation may be the result of inter alia: desires of self-esteem enhancement, achievement of positive respect, competition, greed, or just simple reduction of uncertainty.

Therefore, individuality in order to be comprehensible must be expressed as a certain type of behaviour. This behaviour manifests itself in the way one tries to define oneself that accentuates the uniqueness of the self vis-à-vis the differences from others, in the stress that one places on certain ideas or objects, in craving after social approval, in interpersonal relationships or indeed any action that may be personally gratifying. The outcome of these social processes becomes the wanting to achieve a particular presentation of the self, and hence the notion of individuality which may result in a distinct identity. Individuality then is not a fixed idea in one's head; rather it is the manner that one wants to appear to society in a particular context; which may manifest itself in various ways and times.

In a study of modern individuality and the group, certain characteristics were documented.[502] To the extent that this was a contemporary study of modern man, not all of its conclusions can be applied to ancient man, but key facts emerge which follow through irrespective of time. These indicate that individuality is a constantly changing phenomenon, being constantly restructured by the action of both personal and social identity in a classic struggle to find out who we are, and what we are. The following is a summary of the relevant applicable characteristics of individuality mentioned in that study:

1. Individuality is a highly variable form of behaviour and perception differing among fellow humans as well as across particular situations.
2. It is a product of societal and psychological forces.
3. There exist certain interdependencies between identity, individuality, and ideology.

In their application, which is universal, the above characteristics could apply to the ancient Egyptian elite tomb owner too. He too wanted to appear to his fellow humans in a certain way, and this is evident from the fact that there is no one set type of iconography with no differentiation whatsoever.

So does this mean that all tombs show individuality? To answer this question we must delve into the reasons why individuality would arise in a state, which at least in the beginning consisted of subservient family members whose desire to conform could be reasonably assumed.

Prior to Dynasty 3 there was a distinct division between the institution of dominant quasi-divine kingship and the related subservient kinship. It is when the emphasis changes from the dominant divine nature of kingship to a more human actuality, that the kinsmen develop ideas about their own individuality. This is seen in the art of the late Dynasty 4 mastabas and onwards.[503] Apart from a loosening of the bonds of king and kin that this implies, there is evidence that from middle Dynasty 5 onwards, a new class of officials arose who did not live in the capital, but locally administered the various outlying provinces.[504] The result was the gradual rise of an upper class that was wealthy, independent, and could afford and wanted to project a form of behaviour, and perception different from their fellow humans across particular situations. Related with this, there is evidence of religious change in the prominence of Ra, reflected in the sun temples as well as in the first great upswing in the worship of Osiris. One consequence of this is to free the deceased from reliance for his material needs in posterity from the living king, but to the king of the dead who now was Osiris.[505] The deceased also come increasingly to depend on the living kinsmen for his needs in the hereafter, as the biographical inscriptions evidence.

These changes were gradual, but they could well be the triggers that ultimately provided the elite with their own innate sense of worth articulated as individuality, and which was ultimately expressed in their tomb art (also evident in the provincial tombs).[506]

However, as regards the others, the reality was that in the Old Kingdom, the masses of individuals were coerced to follow the normative beliefs of the king and his elite in all areas. Thus as far as the masses were concerned this constraint must have had important limitations on the

---

[502] Turner, et al., "Expressing and Experiencing Individuality and the Group", in *Individuality and the Group*, ed. T. Postmes and J. Jetten, 16-17.

[503] Stevenson-Smith, *A History of Egyptian Sculpture and Painting in the Old Kingdom,* 157-75 and 85-91. Prior to Dynasty 5, evidence of the way an elite should be represented, is evident in the ideal of sheer perfection plus individual differences in physicality, and relates to the understanding of the elite by the elite. From Dynasty 5 onwards, the tendency is to have a less differentiated view, one in which the representation of an elite tends towards that which is understood by all. However the idea behind the ideal as such, does not change (the desire to overcome death and to continue to exist in an undying environment in the hereafter). All that changes, is in the representation, which goes from being a specific realistic one as in Dynasty 4, to a general, non-specific one, in which the individual is recognized not in a specific sense but as an individual as such. This then becomes the norm and is evidenced in the ensuing periods. This tendency may have been accelerated by 'the increasing number of men who were able to climb the Egyptian equivalent of the corporate ladder' during Dynasties 5 through 6: one element of which success, was the ability to have a tomb and related iconography (See Russmann, *Egyptian Sculpture*, 27-41 esp. 30).

[504] Altenmüller, "Old Kingdom", *OEAE*, vol. 2, 597.

[505] M. Smith, "Democratization of the Afterlife", in UCLA Encyclopedia of Egyptology, 1-15. See http://escholarship.org/uc/item/70g428wj. He gives evidence of non-royal individual access to royal ritual utterances and asserts that democratization is in reality just a consolidation of a practice already evident in the tomb of Metjen (Dynasty 4). However his stress on time frames and dating criteria whilst important, tend to obscure the fact that change is endemic all the time, even when one cannot date it.

[506] Edel, *Die Felsengräber der Qubbet el Hawa bei Assuan, 2 Abt: Die althieratischen Topfaufschriften. 1.Bd. Die Topfaufschriften aus den Grabungsjahren 1960-1963 und 1965. 2.Teil: Text,* 94-107. Many of the tombs at Qubbet-el-Hawa, evidence a tradition of inscribing the offering vessels, such that they identify the food being offered as well as the individual responsible for the offering. This is unique and serves to identify the people concerned, their connection and support of each other.

range of options available for expressing individuality within their cultural context.

What is discernible from the tomb art may point to stimuli other than causative (i.e. our perception of events in a cause-and-effect relation), and by implication to other aspects of the person. A general and a specific example are illustrative:

Prior to Dynasty 5 slaughtering scenes are a common feature of entrance thicknesses in the Old Kingdom tombs at Giza, Saqqara, and Abusir but after mid-Dynasty 5 slaughtering becomes regularly positioned on the West wall.[507]

Iymery depicts his father Shepseskafankh, in presumably HIS carrying-chair in HIS tomb something which is counter intuitive to the centrality of the tomb owner.

The issues as to why a particular form of individuality was expressed by the elite and their recognition as such are difficult. Although tomb art is geared towards a particular individual, it rarely shows him as one such, rather he is always part of the elite, the group of officials of the king. The representations follow clear rules, as to the type of scenes and the way they are depicted. The rules impose a system of graded ranks through size differentiation (hierarchy), a spotlighting system which ensures that the tomb owner is always at the centre of attention, and a system of spatial organization by registers as a way of delimiting and describing a particular theme. One can also argue that ancient Egypt was a collectivist society (the means of production being controlled by the king as personification of the Egyptian State) and as such, individuality was not as preeminent a 'virtue' as in modern Anglo-Saxon countries and Europe.

However, our experience of objects must also play a role here and must provide a further basis for understanding, something that goes beyond mere physical presence and spatial orientation. As far as the predetermined system is concerned, it implies at the very least social acquiescence and cultural coherence, and more importantly the apparent absence of individuality. However, as soon as we mix life experience and religious ideas into the equation, the presence of individuality raises its head. Because life experience in each individual is a unique journey, this could well be the reason why 'individualistic' traits are not obvious and apparent, and are seen with difficulty.

The tomb owner is always represented in three forms, as:

1. The recipient of a sacrificial offering.
2. A landowner viewing his estates and in action scenes.
3. A member of the elite or as the king's official, enjoying the life of plenty in the company of his family and non-family.

In these forms the tomb owner's status and identity are fixed. As a loyal courtier, successful and respected member of society, provider of the community, upholder of right order, caring landowner, talented scribe, brave soldier, loving husband and father, etc. All these characteristics represent the essentials; every tomb owner would wish for the ideal of a successful person as sanctioned.[508]

Where glimpses of any sentiment of individuality are revealed in the iconography/texts of the tomb owner, these are subsidiary aspects but the sentiments are there nevertheless, tearing aside the veil of conformity so typical of Egyptian art as seen in the following examples.

Consider and compare the slaughtering motif in the tombs of Ty,[509] Mereruka,[510] and Ptahhotep.[511]

Ty's tomb has a full 'narrative' sequence all in one register, showing:

- Lassoing of the bull with erect penis.
- Pinning the bull to the ground.
- Sharpening of the butchering knife.
- Taking out the heart of the beast.
- Holding a bowl for the blood of the animal by a man described as a butcher, followed by another person sharpening a knife.
- Hacking off the foreleg.

In total there are 13 participating persons. It is as if a series of film slides are being shown in sequence.

In contrast, in the slaughtering scene in Mereruka's tomb, there is the sense of rush and urgency. Here there are 2 registers with 16 butchers all busy with carving up the four bulls, which are already pinned to the ground. One of the participants is shown with a foreleg ready to carry it to the offering chamber. Accordingly one is left with just the essentials, there is no rhythm, and the whole register seems to be asymmetric.

In the two scenes in Ptahhotep's tomb (West and North walls) the standard slaughtering motifs of knives, butchers, animals, and short captions are depicted. However on the North Wall there is also depicted what Harpur calls "a procedure without parallel in butchery scenes of the Old Kingdom",[512] which I understand to indicate a motif which is not seen elsewhere. Here the fifth man who is holding the haunch of a slaughtered ibex, extends his hand to a man in a pointed kilt (the physician, Irenakhet, whose title is Overseer of the wab- priests of the palace), saying

---

[507] Harpur and Scremin, *Decoration in Egyptian tombs of the Old Kingdom*, 56-57.

[508] A good illustration of these is to be found in the multi-roomed chapels of the officials of Teti (but they are not restricted to them). The only exception is the reference to a brave soldier, which appears only in two tombs: that of Yenti at Deshahsheh and Kaem-heset at Saqqara (see Stevenson Smith, "*A History of Egyptian Sculpture and Painting in the Old Kingdom*", 212).

[509] Épron et al., *Le Tombeau de Ti*, vol. I, pls. XIII-XV.

[510] Duell, *The Mastaba of Mereruka*, vol. I, pl. 54.

[511] Quibell et al., *The Ramesseum and The Tomb of Ptah-hetep*, pls. XXXIV, XXXVI.

[512] Harpur and Scremin, *The Chapel of Ptahotep*, 279.

"examine this blood". The physician grasps the butcher's forearm and replies "it is pure".[513]

In all of the above three scenes, the function of the slaughtering is clearly not an issue, and its stages are well documented.[514] However the scenes also include variables which while not being an essential element of the motif (e.g. erect penis), add to it a distinctive character. Perhaps in depicting the normal and the understandable, there was an element of individuality, which while not going beyond the bounds of what was allowed, yet tried to show a distinctive and individual quirk, which could be distinguished as an example of individualistic behaviour. The examining of the blood certainly points in this direction.

Another example is from the rock cut tomb G7721 of Kaherptah that possesses 29 freestanding statues, the most in any Old Kingdom tomb.[515] The almost total exclusion here of any other form of art, is evidence of a sort of personality that was willing to depart from the common standards, and express his desire to create something different from his peers.

Another example is from the tomb of Nefermaat and Atet at Medum (Dynasty 4), where the tomb owner is himself seen snaring birds. This is in itself an unusual depiction because it is usually the servants of the tomb owner who do the provisioning. What makes it even more interesting is the size of the tomb owner, the number of birds in the net as well as the size of the inscriptions, all of which point to something that is not quite in keeping with accepted practice. Other clap-net scenes in this tomb show the sons of the tomb owner and unnamed persons engaging a clap-net too, but these do not have the same number of birds, the size of the participants is smaller and the inscriptions are nowhere as large.

Again the depiction of Sekerkhabau,[516] Rahotep,[517] and Wepemnefret[518] with a mustache is a depiction of the elite that is prevalent in Dynasties 3 and 4, and which is probably a "Bildnis nach dem Leben"[519] but after this period is extremely rare.

These examples indicate that perhaps the Egyptian did think of his person in an instinctive way, and perhaps this is a possible common human trait. He may have also understood the Egyptian conception of life and death, and its traditional portrayal. However, in due course, time and the conditions of his life affected a process in which he went beyond that of accepted normative selection to that of private natural selection. It is this, particularly in the context of the individual scenes to be described in Part 2, which yield glimpses of the private and related expressions of difference and individuality.

So how can one describe something as individual when one cannot get inside the ancient Egyptian mind i.e. how can one decide if the object was not the result of an oddity, fluke, or accident? How are we then to understand the aspect and/or character of individuality, which Nefermaat and the other previous examples, sought to convey?

To answer these questions the following scheme is proposed; individuality must be divided into the following two groups:

1. Type 'A': individuality characterized by behaviour that spreads across a time frame and eventually destroys itself by replacement.
2. Type 'B': individuality characterized by behaviour that is aberrant, not followed across a time frame, and is restricted to one or a few individuals, e.g. painting the seasons as in the tombs of Mereruka and Khnetika.[520]

As previously stated, for individuality to exist as a behavioural pattern it had to be in a particular context. Accordingly donning a red peaked hat in the Netherlands Institute for Near Eastern Studies library for example, would qualify in the first instance as an expression of type 'B' individuality. However for this behaviour to be truly individualistic in the type 'A' sense, and to eliminate any noise, which may be the result of error/negligence, it will have to be carried across a time frame and become an acceptable norm in its own right in a similar context. Admittedly the question of a time frame is an artificial construct, its use being to distinguish between intentional, and that which is unintentional behaviour. If we accept that repetition of something is an indication of intention calling for no objective quantification of time, because for it to occur some sort of time-period is an a priori. This is crucial if all difference is not to be understood as an instance of individuality. It is only, when the manifested behaviour transcends from being merely idiosyncratic to that which is ubiquitous, and accepted in society, that one can refer to it as an example of individualistic behaviour. Of course when this happens and all of Leiden University students start to wear a red peaked hat in the library, it can no longer be classified as individuality, but it is a confirmation of

---

[513] Montet, *Les scènes de la vie privée dans les tombeaux égyptiens de l'Ancien Empire,* 158.

[514] Eggebrecht, *Schlachtungsbräuche im Alten Ägypten und ihre Wiedergabe im Flachbild bis zum Ende des Mittleren Reiches*, 53-57. Also see Ikram, *Choice Cuts: Meat Production in Ancient Egypt*, Ph. D. Dissertation, University of Cambridge, 44-54 and 145-82.

[515] Kendall, "An unusual Rock-Cut Tomb at Giza", in *Studies in Ancient Egypt, the Aegean and the Sudan*, ed. W. K. Simpson and W. M. Davis, 104-14. In comparison the tomb of Debehen (Dynasty 4) at Giza has 13 engaged statues, the tomb of Qar and Idu has 7 statues, the tomb of Djedi has 11 standing statues, in Irukptah there are 14 statues, and in the tomb of Queen Meresankh lll there are 20 statues (14 being standing females and 6 being seated miniature scribes).

[516] Murray, *Saqqara Mastabas*, vol. 1, pl. I.

[517] Harpur and Scremin, *The tombs of Nefermaat and Rahotep at Maidum,* 136, fig. 19.

[518] Russmann, "Aspects of Egyptian Art: Two-dimensional Representation", in *Eternal Egypt*, 29, fig. 15.

[519] Junker, "Das Lebenswahre Bildnis in der Rundplastik des Alten Reiches", *AnzÖAW*, (19), 401-06. Few cases of men with mustaches were depicted in Dynasties 4 to 5.

[520] Duell, *The Mastaba of Mereruka*, vol. I, pl. 7. Also see James and Apted, *The Mastaba of Khentika called Ikhekhi*, pl. X.

what was *ONCE* individualistic behaviour in the more meaningful type 'A' sense.

Understood as providing a guideline in the sense of a criterion and not as an exclusive definition, this approach has merit, because not only will it point to change, but possibly how, when, and what change became accepted in society. This will also assist in recognizing that everything novel is not individualistic, and that everything, which appears individualistic now, was probably part of the way of doing things in the past.

If one applies this logic to the examples already given, it will be seen that the behaviour of Nefermaat, and Kaherptah, the examining of blood in the tomb of Ptahhotep all fall into the definition of type 'B' individualistic behaviour, because their behaviour in that context was not followed across a time frame. Numerous other examples in this category can be cited, most well known among these are the reserve heads, the statue known as Sheikh-el-beled, the bust of Ankh-haf, the Louvre scribe and the statue of Hemiunu.[521]

However, the behaviour of Sekerkhabau, Rahotep and Wepemnofret in depicting themselves with a mustache, the slaughtering scenes in the tombs of Ty, and Mereruka are possible examples of type 'A' individualistic behaviour, because it is carried through in different periods including any fine distinctions. While this time distinction may seem arbitrary, its justification lies in the fact that it at least forces us to concentenrate on real individualistic behaviour, that which was followed across time rather on one which was temporary and aberrant.

A few more examples will make this line of reasoning clearer of trying to equate the first instance of change as an example of type 'A' individuality which because of the scarcity of archeological remains may never be known and of the dangers of accepting all change as individualistic.

In the period PRIOR to the reign of Khufu examples of interior decorated chambers with offering lists exist only at Maidum.[522] Under Khufu the quantity of decoration in tombs is curtailed, and is substituted by the slab stelae, which now are placed outside the tomb,[523] which contains no interior chapels or decoration. These funeral stelae are found encased in the brickwork of the mastabas.[524] Theories

of royal intolerance and a scarcity of craftsmen as these would have been otherwise occupied in the building of the pyramids have been proposed.[525] The stelae thus serve the functions of identity, cult, and memory, because depicted on all of them is the funerary repast motif, offering lists and identifying inscriptions.

However it is the element of behavioural choice by the individual tomb owner not to follow the anterior examples at Maidum, where there already existed decorated interior chambers with offering lists; and to depict a single object which was both an elite type of burial equipment, and which served his essential needs, that is relevant to the issue of individuality. As already stated the single slab stelae contained all the necessary elements essential for a continuing life of the tomb owner in the memories of those left behind, and in the hereafter while at the same time in keeping with decorum.

By Dynasty 5, there is evidence of the stela moving from the exterior to the interior of the tomb.[526] It is when the stela moves inside the tomb, predominantly in Dynasty 5, that a separation of the cultic, the memorial, and the identity functions is realized; and then the slab stelae disappear altogether. The cultic function becomes confined mainly to the false door and the Western wall; while the identity/memorial function is seen in the expanding iconography, e.g. in the representation of the tomb owner, in the variation in his attire and adornment and in the way he displays his wealth, power, and access to royal favour and of course the biographical inscriptions.[527] Admittedly this separation would lend itself to more choices, which are manifested as different individualistic behaviours, and this is exactly what is observed in the tomb decoration. What begins as an act of individualistic behaviour sows the seeds of its own destruction when it is copied and followed by the many and when society and its beliefs become more refined. We may never know who started this form of behaviour because of the lack of evidence but the search for it can be informative.

Again in the Old Kingdom the statue of the tomb owner is hidden in the serdab, in line with one function of the mastaba, which is to conceal and protect, and he is able to partake of the offerings in total privacy.

However from the Middle kingdom, the mastaba is no longer the predominant form of burial but the rock-tomb

---

[521] Smith, *A History of Egyptian Sculpture and Painting in the Old Kingdom,* pl. 6(d), 7-9, 14-15, and 18 (aandc). Some modern scholars would attribute their presence to some form of religious beliefs connected with the solar cult, but this opinion is not adopted in this book.

[522] Petrie, *Medum* , pl. 9-28.

[523] Smith, *A History of Egyptian Sculpture and Painting in the Old Kingdom* , 159. Examples of slab stelae are found in the nucleus cemeteries G1200, G2100, and G4000. The stelae are set in exterior chapels of mud brick, which surrounds the recess on the south side of the East face of the mastaba, e.g. Setji-hekenet (G1227) / Cairo JE 37.726. Fifteen such stelae are known. For details see Reisner, *A History of the Giza Necropolis,* Appendices A, C, D. See mastabas numbered G1201, 1203, 1205, 1207, 1223, 1225, 1227, 1235, 2120, 4140, 4840. Also see tombs numbered G2135, 4150, and 4860 plus fragment in Junker, *Giza* pl. 8, 26, and 38b.

[524] Junker, *Giza*, vol. 1, 26.

[525] Manuelian, „The Problem of the Giza Slab Stelae," in *Stationen: Beiträge zur Kulturgeschichte,* eds. H. Guksch and D. Polz, 115-134. Also see Manuelian, *Slab Stelae of the Giza Necropolis,* 133-139. The evidence for this behaviour is from the mastabas at the Western side of the Great Pyramid and most likely points to a purposeful and intentionally chosen form of tomb decoration resulting from supply scarcity.

[526] Jánosi, "The tomb of officials", in *Egyptian Art in the Age of the Pyramids,* eds. J. P. O'Neill, 31. For more details, also see Jánosi, *Giza in der vierten Dynastie. Die Baugeschichte und Belegung einer Nekropole des Alten Reiches, Band I,* 275-296.

[527] Harpur and Scremin, *Decoration in Egyptian tombs of the Old Kingdom.* The authors detail the chronological development of Old Kingdom elite tombs and their internal decoration.

and the concealment function becomes redundant. The statue moves to the open part of the cult chamber and is able to take part in the cultic rituals. This (making visible and placing the statue in the open cult chamber) is not a random act but one that was deliberately chosen. The tomb owner can now not only be directly related with the food offerings but can be part of all the rituals/ceremonies depicted on the adjoining walls in line with the formation and refinement of cultural memory; the generics of which are identity, individuality and ideology and which become increasingly important.

Changes in emphasis in textual inscriptions are another example. Consider the appeals to the living and their eventual subtle changes. From mid-Dynasty 5 these start of as a request of worship for the benefit of the deceased, in due course an additional request to visitors to purify themselves before entry into the tomb is added, and soon thereafter we see the addition of prohibitive spells and threats plus humble requests.[528] In the tomb of Ankhmahor Dynasty 6, we see the appeal being extended specifically to the 80 men including the embꜥlmers and administrators of the necropolis, with a request to place the lid securely on its mother (read sarcophagus).[529] A similar request is also seen in the tomb of Khentika.

We are thus faced with changes in the architecture, the iconography, the function of the tomb, as well as the textual representations, which may or may not have been followed across time. Taken as one of a kind they may appear as idiosyncratic type 'B' individualistic behaviour, as an indication of change at a certain time. However taken in the context of development of ideas across a time frame, the changes when and where these first occur, are relevant to what I would refer to as type 'A' individualistic behaviour. If these can be followed over time then not only will they serve to provide an insight into the development of society and religion, but will serve to pinpoint the cultural generics. What is important to note, is that change as expressed by behaviour may be synonymous with individuality, but it does not have to be so. Actions, which denote change, can only be truly individualistic in the narrow sense of the term if imitated and accepted across a time frame. The question of time frame will depend on the requirements of the research in question and cannot be pre-ordained.

Of course one can argue that there are grades of individuality that change takes place along a continuum, but this would open up the question of quantifying something that we can only detect but analyze with great difficulty due to the absence of objectively verifiable causality. Therefore individuality can exist in both type 'A' and type 'B' forms

of behaviour, the emphasis on either of which will, as already indicated depend on the research demands.

All cultures indicate in some manner changes in their society.[530] When this individualistic behaviour becomes a widespread phenomenon especially in a particular context, and can be traced in the iconography, it becomes a valuable avenue for detecting alteration in behavioural patterns.

The constraints of this study mean that one can only trace this for the Old Kingdom, for the selected motifs in the case studies, and within the limits of the archaeological evidence.

5.3 Ideology

Ideology is the science of ideas usually confined within a socio-political and economic context. It is primarily concerned with the need to address certain existing belief systems in society and it functions in reinforcing, elevating or relegating, existing ideologies.

In ancient Egypt social inequality may have been the reason why a particular ideology arose in the first place.

Ideology in ancient Egypt functioned as a disguise for the elite's competition for power in areas which mattered to it: the social and the religious. It is in these areas that the elite constructed or invented belief systems that enhanced their position at the expense of the others (control and dominance). Ideology thus served to ease tensions within the dominant group by concentrating the focus of attention on the subordinate group.

For the newer and complex expressions of ideologies to succeed they had to be accepted by the others resulting in defining and sharing of some fundamental values.

The ideology in the OK, as it appears to an outsider belies this tension; it is splendid, all are in agreement with certain beliefs and practices, while the fact of legitimation, reinforcement, and control is successfully hidden from the others. In this context, the warning by Thucydides in his 'History of the Peloponnesian War' (an eyewitness account of the war between Sparta and Athens) as it unfolded, and, significantly, about the behaviour of the people as the long war dragged on, is constructive. He comments that we must always be aware that the witnesses to the individual events do not describe the same event in a similar way.[531] Ideology just like the writing of history is also subject to the diverse influences of the witnesses at our disposal. This difficulty is compounded in the case of the ancient

---

[528] Sainte Fare Garnot, *L'appel aux vivants dans les textes funéraires égyptiens des origines à la fin de l'Ancien Empire*, 1-7 emphasises the way the appeals are structured across the various time periods. Detailed examples are cited throughout the book across the time period of the Old Kingdom.

[529] Badawy, *The Tomb of Nyhetep-ptah at Giza and the Tomb of Ankhmahor at Saqqara*, 15.

[530] Aruz, ed., *Art of the First Cities, MMA*, 148. Here she (Jean M. Evans) traces the development of the standing figure in Mari culture in Mesopotamia. Mesopotamia has been chosen as an illustration because the appearance of new motifs in Egyptian Art ca. 3000 B.C. had direct antecedents in archaic Susa and the Uruk culture that was prevalent in Mesopotamia. Also see Kemp, *Ancient Egypt: Anatomy of a Civilization*, 5-6 and 150-160.

[531] Thucydides, *History of the Peloponnesian War*, vol. 1, 39.

Egyptian elite because of the limited ways of estimating their historical veracity.

The past reverberates with the fact that ideology is necessary to cultural and political progress, which requires action, but at the other extreme it also points to the fact that ideology is a system of ideas. It is the ways, in which people organize, characterize, and interpret their world and ideas (each individual's cognitive world) that they appear to give universal, everlasting, unquestionable qualities to ideology for it is "the residual condensate".[532]

From the evidence it would appear that the issue of central importance to the Egyptian state (read king) was to propagate those ideas which could satisfy his wants and those near to him, as well as to create new goals which could be of benefit primarily to him, and then to all. His actions are related to that what the gods desire him to do now and in the future, so that he can act pre-emptively to counter any threat of disorder. In so far as his actions are divinely sanctioned, he and his inscriptions are exempt from most ethical considerations.[533]

These concepts would then ultimately result in an ideology consisting of common beliefs, and common values. As a result individual beliefs will generally overlap greatly with those of their fellow humans.

The king gave effect to the above by the fiction that only through him (read the omnipotence of the king), could primeval chaos be averted. The propagation of this ideology, its effect on the population and its targets, meant that ONLY by preservation of this natural order could this be achieved. Its propagation was so successful that it lasted throughout Egyptian history and was extremely resistant to change.

Ideology as it appears in the iconography of the elite follows a somewhat similar pattern, and is concerned with two main themes that of indicating domination and that of implying a sense of shared ideals.

In this context one has to consider three key concepts from mortuary analysis, which are crucial to the understanding of the actors and their relationships that lead to the development of ideological thought.[534] These are:

- Social identity: by which is meant a social position or title.
- Identity relationship: by which is meant the rights and duties by which two or more social identities are connected.
- Social person: by which is meant the sum total of an individual's identities (personal and social).

While no natural reason exists as to why attitudes should vary as regards particular 'social identities', nevertheless it is precisely these attitudes, which point to inequality, to a relationship of hierarchy, to status and rank distribution encompassed within ideology. It may be that wealth, power, literacy, or whatever might be considered as socially significant are the external factors which go into the making of such attitudes. The way these factors act upon the others is by frequent repetition of ideas, about values, which determine what, is or is not socially significant, irrespective of its truth. This is the process of operational culture, and once roles are accepted, given, or inherited, they have to be maintained. In ancient Egypt they were maintained by the imposition of a mystifying quality of kingship – the son of Ra.

Consider 'the teaching of Khety' where one is exhorted to be a scribe as follows: "But if you know writings, all will be well for you, more so than with these professions I have shown you. Look at them, at their wretchedness".[535] This is a prime example where ideology abducts the natural and replaces it with an ideal, confuses the use with its value and shrouds all scribes in 'mystical' wellness.

Ideology of Domination

Imposed systems of ideas, which involve a role of domination (i.e. the desire to control, to compel actions, and to determine fate), was of great significance in the Egyptian concept and indeed generally to the workings of all societies. However, if one is to dominate on the strength of a particular system of ideas, then he must be more titled, more powerful, more learned, have more possessions, or whatever is necessary to achieve the desirable effect. This is because people everywhere seem to drive satisfaction from associating with or ideas of the elite group/s and Egyptian society was no different.

Ideology then is a part of human interactions that allows among other things for the control of people.[536] This social power is used to manage and manipulate the labour and other activities of the general population, such that the dominant individual or group is able to obtain certain benefit.[537] This is an argument for unequal access to social and material resources, at the expense of other members of society. Obviously this leaves unanswered the question as to why people accept the legitimacy of values (read ideology), which do not benefit them. It has been suggested that acceptance implies that there must have been some form of negotiation, struggle, and/or complicity between all parts of the polity, although the participants may have had unequal resources.[538] As regards ancient Egypt this is difficult to ascertain directly. Indirectly however the evidence points to the role played by ideology as a creative

[532] Barthes and Balzac, *S/Z*, 98.
[533] Baines, "Ancient Egyptian Concepts and uses of the past", 131-149.
[534] Saxe, *Social dimensions of mortuary practices,* Ph.D. Dissertation, University of Michigan, 1970, 4-7.

[535] Parkinson, "The Teaching of Khety", in *The Tale of Sinuhe and other Ancient Egyptian Poems*, 275-279.
[536] Carlton, *Ideology and Social Order*, 23-39.
[537] Marrais, Castillo, and Earle, "Ideology, materialisation and power strategies", *CA,* (37/1), 15-31.
[538] Mann, *The Sources of Social Power*, 2-3.

one, which produced a unified state under as already stated the pretext of an omnipotent king. He was considered the representative of the divine on earth, and the only means by which disorder could be turned into order,[539] which on modern logical grounds would be termed nonsense, and one that misrepresented reality, and in that way added to the control exerted over the masses of other human beings.[540]

If we were to look for explicit words denoting ideology in Egypt, we will not find them. The only early hint comes from the Early Dynastic period in the concept of the 'two lands' characteristic of the ideological basis of Dynastic Egypt.

What is evident is the fact that through the coming together (by war or otherwise) a single political state arose in the Nile Valley. It may well be, that the development of a stable state required this fact to be permanently impressed on all: that two major parts of the land had been brought under one control. Egyptian ideology can be then seen as a response to this fundamental idea, which had as its goal among other things, the expression of unity and stability brought about by an omnipotent king. Available records at least from Dynasty 3 onwards, point to accomplished developments in art and architecture, both of which are the consequences of a stable and united society. Thus society came to be held together by an artificial ideology of Egyptian kingship, in the interest of which all were expected to subordinate their desires. The role of the king is explicitly stated as follows and while this is from the New Kingdom, the same sentiments are to be found in "The Teachings of Merikare" a late Old Kingdom text; he (the king) was placed on earth:

> "… for ever and ever, judging humanity and propitiating the gods, and setting order in place of disorder. He gives offering to the gods and mortuary offerings to the spirits (the blessed dead)".[541]

This ideology of "one single, indivisible theopolitical unity"[542] stressed domination. Initially it was the king versus the rest; later with the rise of the career bureaucrat, it becomes that of the king and the elite versus the rest, what I have called the 'others'. Official ideology however at the beginning of Dynasty 3 at least, reflected royal ideology and the position of the 'others' was of very little consequence but should not be dismissed entirely.

Accordingly the ideology underlining the iconography of the Old Kingdom: that of a society with wealth and status differentiation can best be understood by referring to the central focus on the king and his office of kingship. The king is shown triumphing over enemies; he has power to repel chaos and guarantee order, he is "an intermediate between" the people "and the deities",[543] and he is always accepted into the hereafter by the gods, no matter what the actual state of affairs might have been. The king and the gods have a reciprocal relationship; he (the king) ensures their existence through offerings and the building of temples, they (the gods) in return grant him total power over all in his dominion.[544] It would appear that the king in this period combined in himself all the ritual, political power and legitimacy what Assmann terms an "identitäre Theokratie",[545] his all-powerfulness would seem was the glue that held society together, something which gradually changes between the highpoint of the Old Kingdom and the beginning of the Ramessid period, but that is another story.

The resultant basic premise suggests that every Egyptian was bound to his place in the divine order, without being deprived of all his rights under the umbrella of a supreme king with divine affiliations.

This concept that all Egyptians had a degree of equity that could NOT be infringed upon is supported by the archaeological record which yields numerous scenes of status and rank differentiation, implying a certain awareness of one's place in the system and what was the right order of things. How far this was reality, is quite another question, if we are to go by the number of times (nine) and the eloquence required by the eloquent peasant in order to attain justice.[546]

In the Old Kingdom the social group is well defined archaeologically as consisting of the king at the apex followed by his secular and sacral elite, and then the others. Interaction between these groups did take place and it would do well to keep in mind Seidlmayer's suggestion that:

> "Der Blick auf die kleinen Leute und auf das archäologische Material hilft die Uniformiesierung dieser kulturellen Normvorstellungen zu durchschauen und das Vielerlei der gelebten Wirklichkeit anzuerkenen".[547]

---

[539] Faulkner, *The Ancient Egyptian Pyramid Texts*, § 265. Unas arrives in heaven after "having set right [Ma'at] in the place of wrong [Isfet]".

[540] Bloch, "Property and the end of affinity", in *African Studies Association Studies*, ed. M. Bloch, 5-28.

[541] Assmann, "State and Religion in the New Kingdom", 58. Also see Simpson, ed., *The Literature of Ancient Egypt*, 158, l. 65, 63, l. 15, 64, l. 30, 65, l. 35. The respective lines found in the Teaching for King Merikare are: "Replenish the offerings, multiply the sacrificial loaves, Increase the daily offerings", "And God has made him pre-eminent over the land among countless others, The Kingship is an excellent office", "Shepherd the people, the cattle of the God", "For them He has made rulers from the egg, Leaders to raise up the backs of the weak". Also see Bonhême, "Kingship", *OEAE*, vol. 2, 238-45.

[542] Assmann, "State and Religion in the New Kingdom", 58.

[543] Silverman, "The Nature of Egyptian Kingship", in *Ancient Egyptian Kingship*, ed. D. O'Connor and D. Silverman, 67.

[544] Sethe, *Urkunden des Alten Reiches,* vol. I, 153-54ff. For an example of offerings being shared by the gods and the king in the temple, see Stadelmann, "Die Wiedererlebung religiösen Gedankenguts des Alten Reiches in der Architektur des Totentempels Sethos' I. in Qurna", in *Structure and Significance*, ed. P. Jánosi, 489.

[545] Assmann, *Stein und Zeit*, 244-245. In modern terms this is best summed up in *Troilus and Cressida*, 1, iii, 164; where Shakespeare's Ulysses puts this point with theatrical force, "Take but degree away, Untune that string, Hark what discord follows".

[546] Simpson, ed., *The Literature of Ancient Egypt*, 29-44.

[547] Seidlmayer, "Vom Sterben der Kleinen Leute", in *Grab und Totenkult im Alten Ägypten*, ed. H. Guksch, E. Hoffmann, and M. Bommas, 60-74.

Be that as it may, the relationship between the classes most probably was one as follows:

Domination by the king in all aspects at least until the end of Dynasty 4, and reciprocal arrangements between the king and his elite,[548] so as to justify his aims and policies, and to affirm and condition everybody into believing a particular version of reality. Consequently there is a sort of sharing process between the elite and the rest resulting from "a keen awareness of kinship" and a "sense of mutual obligation"[549] something which was probably done out of socio-political necessity, rather than altruism. This ideology was maintained by developing and refining the concepts of religion and mortuary culture as expressions found in the tomb, as a source of art, literature, social memory, and didactic discourse. As Assman says, religion and politics were "aspects or dimensions of one single, indivisible theological unity"[550] and as such the boundaries are not easily discernible.

For this ideology to succeed as long as the Old Kingdom did, there had to be a stable agricultural system, capable of producing more than necessity required. Notwithstanding this material requirement, there also had to be an interconnected communication between various parts of the polity.

If we are to understand the iconography as one aspect of this ideology of domination, then the symbols of this ideological discourse are well documented: in the Pyramid Texts, the monumental graves, the sun temples in Dynasty 5, the iconography, and inscriptions.

The Old Kingdom lasted some 500 years, therefore one can assume that the people of this time consented in, believed in, or at the very least begrudgingly accepted the prevalent ideology.

In Old Kingdom Egypt there were probably no alternatives other than accepting the articulated values of the king and his elite, and that acceptance or consent to the values of the dominant class, was a given "which is quite different from belief in the legitimacy of those values".[551]

Williamson has this to say about ideology:

"A central part of ideology is the constant reproduction of ideas which are denied a historical beginning or end, which are used or referred to because they already exist in society and continue to exist in society, because they are used and referred to and which therefore take on the nature of a timeless, synchronic structure, out of history although this structure as a whole does exist in history. It only seems timeless i.e. inevitable, natural, from the inside: obviously an ideology can never admit that it began because this would remove its inevitability. Thus, although systems of knowledge do have a beginning and an ending and a place in historical developments, their internal workings must be purely structural and self-perpetuating not from any movement onwards, but from a process of translation and re-translation between systems."[552]

Ideology as characterized above relates to the way it is used to achieve certain goals, and that the way it is packaged is crucial to its transmission and maintenance.

Kemp takes a different approach and is more concerned with how ideology arises in what he calls the invention of tradition. To him it is in the pursuit of a balancing act between past and future that ideology arises. He says, "At the heart of a cultural tradition is a trade-off between respect for past achievements and the accommodation of fertile and creative minds that look for something new. Ancient Egypt provides an early case history of the dynamics of the Great Tradition of culture: how it arose and was maintained as a living system, how it expanded at the expense of local traditions, and how it achieved this difficult balance between past and present".[553]

Ideology of Shared Fundamental Values

Another way of thinking about ideology is to avoid any question of domination or conflict and treat it as value neutral: simply stating that ideology relates to the system of values and interests that are fundamental to a society and shared by all members.[554] This would mean that the Egyptian state was a tight organization under the supreme authority of the pharaoh who shared a common economic interest with the elite and the rest of society.[555]

Both of these versions have merit: the first version serving to uncover how a dominant class uses ideology, while the latter highlights the reason for social cohesion and integration, (ultimately self-interest).

Because both versions do give an indirect indication as to how the forms of ideology, be it institutional or individual, were created, transmitted, accepted, and reproduced and because both are present in Old Kingdom Egypt, I propose that their joint use as characteristics of ideology

---

[548] G. Jéquier, *Le monument funéraire de Pepi II*, vol. 2, *Fouilles à Saqqarah*, pls. 48, 57, and 59. This is as far as I am aware the only iconographic example of the dialogue between the king and his councillors. They are portrayed as a corporate body of four different groups and one can suppose that these men represented the central administrative system - a depiction which one would expect to find in a royal tomb.

[549] Lloyd, "Psychology and Society in the Ancient Egyptian Cult of the Dead", in *Religion and Philosophy in Ancient Egypt*, ed. W. K. Simpson, 120.

[550] Assmann, "State and Religion in the New Kingdom", 56.

[551] Merquior, *The Veil and the Mask,* 11-14. Followed by Thompson: *Studies in the Theory of Ideology*, 63, who says: "Consent may be given to a dominant value system but this does not mean they accept them as legitimate".

[552] Williamson, *Decoding Advertisements,* 99.

[553] Kemp, *Ancient Egypt: Anatomy of a Civilization,* 160.

[554] Bell, *Ritual Theory, Ritual Practice,* 187-189.

[555] I use the term "economic" in a restricted sense, to refer specifically to the manner of the production and distribution of goods in ancient Egyptian society, albeit without the use of money as a medium of exchange.

have merit, and should be considered when analyzing the iconography.

Practice of Ideology in the Old Kingdom

The Egyptians during the Old Kingdom did not opt to change their society to any meaningful extent. The effect was that the initial ideology continued to have both a legitimating and reinforcing role right through this period. This in fact aided the realization of the normative goals of the king and his elite, to the end of the dynastic period.

The ways that ideology was used in its legitimating and reinforcing role to justify, mystify and manipulate, is shown in the use by the elite of inscriptions. If we accept that these inscriptions are a part of the shifting function of texts as they pass from one social stage to another, then we must also accept that they are a constructed medium of communication and therefore a cultural construct. The understanding of statements such as:

"never before had the like been done for any servant of his, for I was excellent in the heart of His Majesty",[556] becomes a reflection on the generics. In this statement alone we can discern all the generics: the identity of the phraseologist, the nature of the statement indicating a certain amount of individuality, the fact that both these aspects correlate to the ideology of the elite person as someone worthy of such an accolade pointing indirectly to the value of *M3ʿt* and one worthy to be remembered.

Ideology is thus eternalized into the service of the elite by the forms expressed in tomb iconography, as well as in later forms of literature. In a way similar to the instances when the king, because of his identification with Horus, becomes empowered, the elite in their identification with someone, who the king thinks highly of (the ideal), become empowered in the eyes of the others. Ideology thus plays an identical legitimating, mystifying, and empowering role for the elite, as it did for the king.

An example from a later period because it is well documented is equally instructive about this particular role of ideology. When Hatshepsut depicts the story of her divine birth, the truth of her femininity is hidden as against that of a usual male pharaoh. When she implies that she was directed by the god Amun to wage war, the truth about expansionism and economic goals as fundamental to her kingship are hidden, because the directions of Amun are self-sufficient and do not warrant any further discussion, thus adding a convenient veneer of divine respectability and rationality.[557]

One effect is to depict at least on the outer surface, a fixed continuous proof, that the right order is being maintained, and that the ideal of the self-made and self-reliant ethical man is paramount (outer surface, because this is but one part of the story). If the images selected by the officials are but reflections of choice (which is a possibility), then it must also be accepted that they imply a value judgement. The question of what a person is or what he wants to be can then be seen as role assuming, and not necessarily one of domination and deceit. However this may be, at the very least this implies that the past had an ideological value worth repeating and preserving. It is this retrospective orientation of learning for the future from the past, which was an important attribute of Old, Kingdom ideology; seen very clearly in the writings at the end of the Old Kingdom,[558] when Egyptian society and culture start to disintegrate.

There is of course a danger here. It lies in the fact that just like the written word, the depicted word, and painting, might equally be incomplete, it may be selective, or it may be a portrayal of past events, which never occurred in the present but which were portrayed. For example the depiction of an identical Libyan campaign appears in the mortuary temples of Sahure, Userkaf, and Pepy ll, and later Taharqa in Nubia, which is not evidenced, from the archaeological record. As Helck warns

"Damit wird der Wert vieler historischer Darstellungen suspekt und der Kreis unserer Geschichtsquellen stark eingeschränkt".[559]

In the context of the tomb, the satisfaction of needs in the hereafter is the generator of ideological thought, which when combined with religion serves to sustain the placement needs of the elite. The placement needs could have been any or all of the following:

- The body had to be protected.
- Various funerary rituals had to be performed to enable the tomb owner a secure access in the hereafter.
- The people, places, and things depicted on the walls of the tomb had to become 'real' and meet the tomb owner's physical and social needs, through the process of sympathetic magic. This belief in magic can be indirectly inferred from the spells that the herdsman utter for a safe crossing of the waterways often depicted in the mastabas,[560] and in the use of amulets[561] and spells against snake and scorpion bites etc.[562] which although they appear in

[556] Simpson, ed., *The Literature of Ancient Egypt* 403. (Weni the Elder).
[557] Lacau and Chevrier, *Une chapelle d'Hatshepsout à Karnak*, vol. I, 105-14. "This [land] which I opened for you, you are the king who utters words against his enemies. Your knife is the servant of the hot flame and its heat is there to burn those who rebel in the land...that your terror may seize that which acts as a crime and those who plan rebellion...you will subdue chaos, you will cut off the arm of civil war...". Also see Tyldesley, *Hatchepsut: the female pharaoh*, 69-74 and 141-143.

[558] Simpson, ed., *The Literature of Ancient Egypt,* 216-220. The Prophecies of Neferty are one such example.
[559] Helck, *Geschichte des Alten Ägypten*, 65.
[560] Kanawati, *The Teti Cemetery at Saqqara: the Tomb of Ankhmahor,* pl.37 (a). "May you be watchful against that aquatic which is in the water. May these not go to that aquatic and may he be blind-of-head. May you be watchful against him, greatly". For further examples see Duell, *The Mastaba of Mereruka*, vol. I, pl. 21, also see Wild, *Ty,* vol. II, fig. 124.
[561] Andrews, "Amulets", *OEAE*, vol. l, 77-78.
[562] Leitz, "Die Schlangensprüche in den Pyramidentexten", *Orientalia* 65, 381-427.

the Pyramid texts (PT 230 etc.) imply a belief in some supernatural power.

The tomb owner's name, titles, status, and the society of which he was a part had to be broadcast and celebrated.

The hierarchy and decorum of the social order would be maintained in what was displayed and how the actors were placed on the tomb walls.

The tomb owner had to be transformed and recognized as a 'blessed dead', as one having both the right to have a tomb, as well as a guaranteed association with the king, the gods (Osiris, Anubis, and Geb) and the other inhabitants of the hereafter.

The tomb owner would also have a special and independent place of existence, just as he had when he was alive in a town and a Nome.

The ideas inherent in the above list of placement needs, which were once the paramount desire of the elite, in time, become an aim for all the masses, such that all concept of an externally forced ideology is lost and these needs become the 'attainable' norm of the later accepted ideology.

All Old Kingdom ideology whether it is personal, communal, religious or of a political nature, can be associated with any or all of the above mentioned placement needs, examples of which can be found in one form or the other in most Egyptological literature/iconography. These requirements must have influenced the elite in the way they created and manipulated the varying religious and political ideas and must have had a far-reaching affect on the others too.

Consider the funerary inscriptions in the tombs of Akhmahor, Djaty, Ipy, Mehu, Mereruka, Ptahhotep, Senedjemib-Inti and Hermeru. In these tombs, the tomb owners are identified in the funerary rites as those who will be guided to the necropolis, to the "beautiful West" and transported in a boat even though there is never any mention made of whether or not they are deserving of this honour.

> "… to traverse the paths of the revered in great peace, and finally to ascend to the mountain heights of the necropolis (similar to the mythical royal funerary procession to the sun god)".[563]

The implications however, of a certain type of conduct and resulting fulfillment are clear. They seem to be available for all who act similarly, although it is patently obvious that only a few could afford a tomb, or aspire to such high office. Yet, it is part of accepted ideology right throughout the dynastic period.

Similarly the tomb as attested in the offering formula,[564] advertises to the living, the fact that the occupant's right to a tomb is condoned both by the king (a living god) and

some of the other gods (Osiris/Anubis/Wepwawet).[565] That every elite tomb depicts such a formula should not be seen to diminish its value, for it is evidence that it has now become a socially recognized fact. It stands out like a symbol of having achieved all that was desirable during the Old Kingdom: the fact that one had served the king diligently and loyally, that one was respected and beloved of one's family and by one's fellow humans and therefore deserving of a tomb. The inscriptions are also a pointer to the facts that order, truth, and legitimacy have not only been achieved but also officially accepted by the king and gods as achieved.

> "I have come from my town, come up from my Nome and been buried in this my tomb,"[566] and "burial at the end of a very old age, near the great god, lord of burial as one *imȝḫw* with the king".[567]

Where it was not possible to be buried near the royal cemetery, the sentiments of wanting to be are still evident.[568]

The cult for the gods, the king, and the dead, thus all combine to play a central role in the cultural and social life of the individual/community and influence the development of a certain form of ideology.

The king is an earthly representative of god and his officials act on his behalf, those who question this state of affairs are the king's enemies, and by implication gods' enemies and their destruction is thus a sacred act.

After death, the non-royal who had achieved the *imȝḫw* status could depend both on the great god for authority and redress[569] and on his fellow humans for keeping his memory and all the other culturally significant aspects termed generics alive.

The entire elite tomb culture was based on this ideological assumption because it became an accepted fact that:

> "A man will survive after death, His deeds will be set out beside him as (his) reward, and existence in the beyond is for eternity".[570]

---

[565] It is clear that in the Old Kingdom offering formula, both the king and the gods, are responsible for fulfilling the wishes of the tomb owner. The question of the evolution of this formula in the Middle Kingdom into something in which only the gods are responsible for, has been questioned on grammatical grounds (the plurality of gods being introduced by a single masculine suffix *di=f*)? See in this regard the argument by Willems, "Food for the dead," in *Pap Uit Lemen Potten*, ed. W. H. van Soldt, 98-108.

[566] Sethe, *Urkunden des Alten Reiches*, 57, l. 11-12.

[567] Hassan, *Excavations at Giza*, vol. IX, 23. This is part of the offering formula.

[568] Sethe, *Urkunden des Alten Reiches*, 118, l. 14-16. The expressed sentiment is clear: "Though I have made this tomb in Abydos, it is one *imȝḫw* with the incarnation of the dual king Neferkare, alive forever and with the incarnation of the dual king Meryra and the dual king Merenra".

[569] Faulkner, *The Ancient Egyptian Pyramid Texts*, § 399. The king being described as the lord of judgemnt in the hereafter.

[570] Simpson, ed., *The Literature of Ancient Egypt*, 157, l. 55.

---

[563] Kees, *Totenglauben und Jenseitsvorstellungen der alten Ägypter*, 108-109.

[564] Goedicke, *Die privaten Rechtsinschriften aus dem Alten Reich*, 37.

Chapter 6: Criteria for the Selected Motifs

Part 1 abstained from extensive discussions of the attributes of the individual motifs found in the elite tombs in Dynasties 5 and 6, because the objective was to establish an understanding of whether generic (i.e. common) values of iconography existed and could apply to funerary art. The present section deals with the criteria for the selection of the motifs to be analyzed in Part 2.

6.1 The Selection Bias

The West wall of the cult chapel is now accepted as being primarily concerned with the ritualistic function involving the hereafter;[571] therefore the selection will be from the other walls, and focus on their composition, placement, and communicative nature. The idea is to show that the culturally generic aspects of identity, individuality, ideology, memory, and change in the iconography of the Memphite tombs of the elite officials are an all-encompassing broad phenomenon, despite the stylistic uniformity that Memphite artists strove towards.

It is accepted that both the secular and the sacred aspects exist in some form together and to confine oneself only to one of these aspects, would be too simplistic an approach because:

- It ignores the fact that scenes which appear secular at one level (e.g. the physical act of dragging a statue may at a higher level be ritual e.g. the censing of the statue in these dragging scenes). Even at its most basic level that of grave goods, which although made in this world, could ostensibly be understood to have a putative use in the hereafter. This dichotomy of reality is endemic throughout ancient Egyptian iconography.
- It ignores the religious context in which the ancient Egyptians lived.

These all-important religious activities are often shown in the form of rituals, which follow a set, repeated, sometimes rehearsed pattern (dominated by customs, conventions, traditions, taboos linked to decorum) in which the participants play relatively fixed roles. Such rituals allow little scope for an individual person to vary the ritual, because the rituals are "patterns of thought that attribute to phenomena supra-sensible qualities which … are not derived from observation".[572] On the other hand the rituals demanded that the dead be represented (e.g. in the form of visible icons), be treated with respect and understood as distinct individuals, a corollary of which was that the dead persisted in collective memory. Once it is realized, that the concept of memory is the foundation of all funerary art, it follows that the workings of this idea play a crucial role, indeed is one of the key ingredients of the generics.

Secular activities being less subject to religious restrictions allow the individual more scope to do things in his own way, and thus to express his particular self. It becomes obvious that the expressing of the self will also involve the individual in all those common values, which are called 'generic'. One cannot deny that the individual's activities in real life might also have had a religious foundation, but because this is not directly observable in the iconography of Old Kingdom elite tombs, they cannot be pursued in detail.

The tomb owner is the central figure, therefore his involvement either directly or indirectly with people and things, results in his personal differentiation.[573] This is an archeological fact, the consequence of being part of a community. This would also suggest some correlation between the esteem, which was given to him during his life, and that, which was given to him in his tomb, again pointing to the existence of generics in the tomb and its contents.

Having established in Part 1 that certain common values are found in all funerary art it is now proposed to select the motifs, and see the extent of their application in the activities of the tomb owner and how these can be made visible.

Numerous motifs could be chosen to show commemoration; demonstrating identity, individuality, and ideology as different, culturally significant aspects. It is acknowledged that unbiased representative selection is crucial yet difficult. If one looks closely at all non-ritual scenes, it becomes obvious that they all contain some form or other of generic values. Equally, it is clear that the motifs selected must cut across a cross section of the known representations, such that they include the tomb owner during the different parts of his life. The selected motifs then should include the following abstract/iconological themes:

1. The social rank of the tomb owner and the number and composition of persons having duty relationships towards him across a time frame.
2. Active/Passive participation by the tomb owner in a communal act.
3. Participation by members of his family, kin, and community in pursuance of commemoration.
4. Inclusion of many varieties of elevated status goods made in this world but also required in the hereafter.

---

[571] Junker, *Giza* vol. 3, 103. Also see Bonnet, *Reallexikon*, 867.

[572] Gluckman, "Les Rites de Passage", in *Essays on the ritual of social relations*, ed. M. Gluckman and C. D. Forde, 22. Also see James, *The ceremonial animal*, 107.

[573] Lepsius, *Denkmäler aus Ägypten und Äthiopien*, pls. 3, 25, 44, 69, 86 and 89.

5. Indications of perceived idioms of identity, ideology, and individuality (directly or indirectly) existing as part of funerary art.

In line with the above guidelines, the selected iconographic motifs including related inscriptional texts are:

- Carrying-chair scene.
- Taking Account scene.
- Mourning as part of the funeral processes scene.

As with everything connected with Egyptology, there will always be exceptions, and it may well be that the choice of motifs will be subject to objections, all the more so when the material is incomplete or missing. However this is no excuse for avoiding an attempt to understand the causes of the conception, creation, and cultural impact of the iconography. If at a later date certain causal concepts need to be amended, this should not be seen in a negative light, because the very attempt can be illuminating, as knowledge usually grows in small increments.

Importantly the above-mentioned motifs also represent the full length of a life; they being clear illustrations of the continuing emphasis on the generics across a given life span. Additionally in the selected motifs it was felt that the processes and outcomes seemed to unfold faster and therefore easier to comprehend.

The method in this book will be to use a multi-pronged approach basing it on the macro analysis of the widespread 'socially engineered' (the generics) indications that directly affected ancient Egypt (the subject of Part I of this study). The consequences of these generics, intended and otherwise as depicted in the selected iconography (the subject of Part 2), then enable one to move down and dig deeper to uncover facts and reliable data that support, or refute, the big picture analysis. Each of the scenes will at first be deconstructed in detail, and then contextualized to highlight the cultural significance of the parties/objects/inscriptions; finally generic (common patterns) will be identified.

For ease of reference each of the tomb names in the motifs selected are included in Appendices A, B, C, and D and also appear in appendix 'I' giving full details of the relevant line drawings and plates. These are numbered as follows:

- Carrying-chair   'A'   1-37
- Empty chairs and fragment 'B'   38-43
- Taking Account   'C'   44-81
- Mourning   'D'   82-84

Chapter 7: The Carrying-Chair

Compared to today's society, our grandparents had a different mindset, e.g. attitudes and perceptions about morals, obligations, class, etc. The ancient Egyptians probably had an even more different mindset: such that whilst a modern person might be able to translate the Egyptians' words and actions accurately, the perception, and meaning of both of these may differ. Consider the carrying-chair motif, which for the ancient Egyptians could mean a number of things: representing status probably being a common understanding. However status can cover a wide variety of areas, e.g. those associated with age (e.g. village elders' experience, health), kinship structure as in feudal aristocracies, and wealth as within social classes.

For arguments sake let us begin as a starting point with the following non-controversial propositions:

- That the number of carrying-chair motifs is but a minor selection of that which may have existed.
- The carrying-chair was a scarce and valuable resource.
- As wood rots easily we do not have any existing actual carrying-chair.

Because funerary expenditure was one prime concern of the elite's existence and because this was not equal, the possession of an independent means of transport meant a higher level of status, wealth, and comfort. The depiction of such an object would therefore imply an equivalent association in the afterlife.

One can therefore conclude with a high degree of probability, that the possession of a carrying-chair was an elite attribute. The detailed analysis of the carrying-chair motif and its components attempts to attain some precision in dealing with such and related concepts, when assessing the role of the generics in Egyptian art and society.

7.1 General Characteristics

The motif of the carrying-chair and its occupant are found among the reliefs in the mastabas of the elite of the Old Kingdom as given in Appendix 'A'.[574] There seems to be no difference in the names 'palanquin', 'carrying-chair', 'litter', and 'sedan', these words are to be considered as synonymous and will be so used.

The oldest depiction of a possible carrying-chair is that seen in the Pre-dynastic period that represented on the Narmer/Scorpion mace head.[575] Motifs depicting the palanquin appear as early as Dynasty 4 (in the tomb of Nefermaat in Maidum) and it subsequently becomes part of the funerary tomb decoration, being depicted on the mastaba walls of the elite in Dynasty 5 and 6 of the Old Kingdom.

Consequently there is a huge gap in our knowledge between the earliest appearance of this motif and that depicted in Nefermaat.

The earliest attested word, which could refer to the description of a royal carrying-chair; *wṯs* is seen in the offering list of the tomb of Nefer-hetep-Hathor in Dynasty 3, indicated by the determinative of the carrying-chair.[576] The word *wṯs* however has an earlier etymology. It has the meaning of lift or raise, both in the physical sense as well

as symbolically.[577] From Dynasty 5 onwards these chairs are also called *ḥwdt / ḥwdw* in the non-royal arena.[578] The Wörterbuch lists another word *rpwt*[579] meaning palanquin but this is now considered a nisbe form meaning "she of the palanquin" and refers to the image of the person inside the palanquin, rather than the palanquin itself.[580]

Junker points to another association; that of an Old Kingdom title *wrꜥy*, attested in the tomb of Seneb, and which could be taken to mean either one who belongs to the carrying-chair, or one who has the right to be carried in a carrying-chair.[581] This meaning of the title is now open to question.[582] However if Junker is correct, then the connection with the title could allude to either being rich, having connection to someone rich, or having a social identity which goes with being transported in a carrying-chair; in all cases a sign of distinction. Since Seneb had titles associated with the carrying-chair such as 'great one of the carrying-chair', it is no coincidence that the carrying-chair scene is so prominently depicted in his tomb.

The carrying-chair from Dynasty 4 onwards comes in various shapes and designs, sometimes just an adapted chair to sit on, and at other times complete with arms, backrest, and floor to squat on with a roof for protection

---

[574] A detailed list of all related motifs appears in Appendix 'A' of the list of tombs.

[575] Quibell and Green, *Hierakonpolis*, vol. 2, pls. 26 B/C. Original in the Ashmolean Museum, Oxford, E3631. For a detailed line drawing of the Scorpion and Narmer Maceheads, see Smith, *A History of Egyptian Sculpture and Painting in the Old Kingdom*, 113-15.

[576] Murray, *Saqqara Mastabas* pl. II.

[577] For numerous examples of usage see Hannig, Ägyptisches Wörterbuch I, 387.

[578] Ibid. 933.

[579] Erman, Grapow, and Reineke, *Wörterbuch der ägyptischen Sprache*, II, 414, 12A.

[580] Ward, "Lexicographical miscellanies", *SAK*, (5), 268.

[581] Junker, *Giza*, vol. 3, 211. Also see Jones, *An Index of Ancient Egyptian Titles, Epithets and Phrases of the Old Kingdom*, 383-84.

[582] Rössler-Köhler, "Sänfte", *LÄ*, vol. 5, 338.

against the sun.[583] It is evidenced in all periods,[584] although its use after the Middle Kingdom is restricted to gods and royalty. By the end of the Hyksos period[585] the war-chariot and horse become familiar to elite Egyptians, accordingly the carrying-chair motif disappears from elite tombs entirely.

Its importance as a sign of elite display of wealth and rank can best be understood and established by looking at two elite Old Kingdom tombs albeit from Deir el-Gebrawi those of Aba and Zau.[586] In the tomb of Aba part of the carrying-chair motif depicts two sunshade carriers (pl. 8). The other part (pl. 10), from which plate 8 is severed but to which it belongs (because of the equivalence of the gap between the northern and southern part of the wall they are on), depicts the [carrying-chair] headed by a person described as an "overseer of … who is in the heart of his master". He is followed by 6 male singers clapping their hands, and by a group of dancers in special headgear of a red ball attached to a tress. The next registers represent a funeral scene, which Davies describes as "the honours paid to the prince when carried to his tours of inspection, and the last honours paid to his body as he as borne to his tomb would seem very closely allied in the Egyptian mind".[587]

In the tomb of Zau we have a full depiction of a carrying-chair motif with 4 sunshade carriers and the tomb owner sitting under an elaborately decorated canopy. Preceding him are 12 females representing his estates (incidentally this is the same number and type as in Aba plate 7). Underneath the palanquin is a complete version of the carrying-chair song. "Better is it when full, than when it is empty".[588]

If one were to place the scenes side by side, the gaps in each can be filled. It becomes apparent that one is dealing with a ceremony (a formal occasion) of the highest importance in the personal and social life of the tomb owner, one that has important cultural ramifications because it is a way of inferring and embracing social rank by individuals and the community.

In the iconography there are also depictions of empty carrying-chairs being carried as in the tombs of Mereruka,[589] Waatetkhethor,[590] Ptahshepses,[591] Seshathetep,[592] and Ty.[593]

These examples denote ownership/access to elevated status goods, pointing to status and accordingly contribute to the extension of the debate on the relationship of the tomb owner and the others, and the way these others played a meaningful role in relaying his identity as seen in the genre of a carrying-chair motif.

The issue whether these represent furniture without any context is irrelevant-because all grave goods have a locational context, i.e. they are found in the context of the monumental grave. Admittedly in the contemporary world an empty inexpensive car by itself would convey limited meaning, e.g. as a means of transport or if it was an expensive car, access to a valuable resource as well. However it cannot be denied that if found in the garage of a mansion or a palace, it has by this association a meaning even when not occupied. Indeed, even an empty car itself in such a context conveys some information on its owner's cultural embeddedness.

In keeping with the view that the deciding factors context, place plus usage are to some extent present; depictions of empty carrying-chairs will be referred to but only so far as they point to access to scarce resources.

Fragmented motifs, which have been described as belonging to a carrying-chair scene, will not be included in this study, because these are so fragmented that it is impossible to come to any definite conclusions.[594] However it may well be that future research could uncover lost fragments, and to cover such eventualities, brief details of these fragments will be found in "Appendix B Carrying-Chair Fragments and Empty Chairs".

One secondary purpose of the carrying-chair is that of being part of the offering list (as already indicated), evidenced as early as Dynasty 3 in the offering list in the tomb of Nefer-hetep Hathor (in Dynasty 3 the offering list usually contained the possessions of the deceased).[595] Its main function was that of transport because this is evident, but its association with that of attested persons of high social rank meant that the depiction of a trip in the carrying-chair became itself a symbol of high social rank and importance.[596] It may have been undertaken for a wide variety of purposes. This could include an inspection of the estates, an excursion to get some rest and recreation, official business, to inspect the craftsmen working on his tomb,[597] to make payment to those craftsmen working on his tomb[598] or it may even represent an imaginary journey overland into the "beautiful West".[599] The journey to the

---

[583] Vandier, *Manuel d'archéologie égyptienne*, vol. 4, 330.

[584] Ibid. 351-363.

[585] K. Sethe, *Urkunden der 18. Dynastie*, vol. IV, 3, l. 6. In the autobiography of Admiral Amosis, the king used a war-chariot against the Hyksos at Avaris. Accordingly the chariot and horse are known since the end of the Hyksos period.

[586] Davies, *The rock tombs of Deir el Gebrâwi*, vol. I and II. This scene was chosen because it is one of the most detailed and complete.

[587] Ibid. vol. I, pls. 8 and 10 and p. 15.

[588] Ibid. vol. II, pl. 8 and p. 11-12.

[589] Duell, *The Mastaba of Mereruka*, vol. 1, pl. 14. Also see Dunham et al., *The Mastaba of Meresankh lll*, fig. 5, showing the making of a carrying-chair similar to the Hetepheres type.

[590] Kanawati, Mereruka: the tomb of Waatetkhethor, part 2, pl. 57A.

[591] Verner, *Abusir-1: the mastaba of Ptahshepses*, pl. 10.

[592] Junker, *Giza*, vol. 2, fig. 31.

[593] Épron et al., *Le Tombeau de Ti* vol. 1, pl. 17.

[594] See fragment marked unknown in Appendix B where empty chairs** and this fragment* is listed.

[595] Barta, *Die altägyptische Opferliste, MÄS,* (3), 33. In contrast: in Dynasty 4, the amount of food in the offering lists as a proportion of the other items increases, and in Dynasty 5, the list is entirely made up of food; furniture and other items are not mentioned in the lists.

[596] Goedicke, "A Fragment of a Biographical Inscription of the Old Kingdom", 9.

[597] Junker, *Giza*, vol. 11, 250.

[598] Roth, "The practical economies of tomb building in the Old Kingdom", 232-234 and 238.

[599] Borchardt, *Denkmäler des Alten Reiches* vol. 1, pl. 1536. In the

west is a symbol of being dead, and this would then be an example of metonymy. From Dynasty 4 onwards, its use as a method of transport both for official and private purposes is well attested.[600] In so far as it was used for official purposes, one might expect it to be gifted by the king but evidence on this is sparse.[601]

The iconography reveals that the carrying-chair involves an object, which is used to transport a person of rank, the carrying of which is done predominantly by other human beings and in a few cases by animals.[602] A significant fact is that of being carried above the heads of the surrounding people. It would seem that being depicted above the common masses and in a SITTING POSITION was more prestigious, than shown standing or being placed beneath or at par with them. This would seem to be the evidence from the conventions of hierarchy in tomb decoration where the tomb owner is always at a symbolical higher level, as well as from some inscriptions. In the Instructions of Ptahhotep it is said

"If you are in the antechamber, stand and sit as fits your rank, which was assigned you on the first day".[603]

This theme is continued in the New Kingdom Instructions of Any

"Do not sit, when another is standing, One who is older than you, Or greater than you in his rank".[604]

Therefore a carrying-chair motif should contain:

- An object within which one can be transported.
- Person(s) who are carried.
- Persons who do the carrying.
- Appurtenances of rank, wealth, and power associated with the carried person/s.
- The symbolic attributes of the carried person could also be reflected in his carriers.
- Other evidence of material wealth and power.
- Indications of a journey, which, if it were to the west would have religious implications or in the case of travelling to give thanks to the craftsmen, be of a secular nature.

7. 2 Distinctive Characteristics

Material

One has to assume that the carrying-chair was mainly made of wood. The only textual reference is an indirect one from the Westcar papyrus, in which the king's son Hardedef is ordered by the king to fetch the magician Dedi, who is transported in a carrying-chair of ebony, the poles of which are made of *sesnedjem* wood and sheathed in gold (leaf).[605] Newberry in the tomb of Dejuhtynakht at el-Bersheh points out a similar type of carrying-chair. He points to the fact that the white and black colours used on the carrying-chair "point to the combination of ivory and ebony, which are so often mentioned in Egyptian texts as the most luxurious materials for furniture".[606] Another far later reference is from a verse in the Old Testament in which King Solomon is said to have made for himself a carrying-chair of cedar from Lebanon, having uprights of silver, a headrest of gold, seat of purple stuff and lined with leather.[607]

It is known that Egypt was very deficient in wood and that very little local wood could be used for carpentry.[608] Indigenous wood consisted mainly of willow (*Salix subserta*), tamarisk (*Tamarix nilotica*), oil producing trees such as acacia (*Acacia nilotica*), moringa (*Moringa peregrina*), and palm trees, mainly the dom-palm (*Hyphaene thebaica*) and the date palm (*Phoenix dactylifera*). The timber of the date palm trunks is useless for building or large furniture because of its fibrous wood. The other local timbers could be used for boxes and coffins but because of its short planks, it was quite inappropriate for larger furniture like a carrying-chair. Appropriate wood thus had to be imported and evidence exists of this from Dynasty 1 right through to the end of the Old Kingdom.[609] *Cedar* from Lebanon, *Ash* from Syria and ebony from tropical Africa and Punt (Somalia?) were imported, indicating in addition that such wood was a valuable commodity and a scarce resource. Exactly what type of wood was used is now not verifiable. The tools required for the manufacture of the wooden furniture are evidenced as far back as early Dynasty 1; copper tools were in existence then, including

---

tomb of Ipy, the deceased wishes to attain the mountain heights of the necropolis by land and the carriers sing a song, which has the following refrain: "Better that the sedan chair (with the deceased) be occupied, than that it be empty".

[600] Épron et al., *Le Tombeau de Ti*, pl. XVI. Also Blackman and Apted, *The rock tombs of Meir*, vol. 5, pl. XXXI, and Hassan, *Excavations at Giza 1930-1931*, vol. II, fig. 240.

[601] Sethe, *Urkunden des Alten Reiches*, 43, 16f. Also see Kaplony, "Eine neue Weisheitslehre aus dem Alten Reich", *Orientalia* (37), 344. "Als Mittler zwischen König und Volk wird er mit einer Sänfte belohnt im Auftrag des Königs...". This would imply that the gift of a carrying-chair was also a symbol of recognition, bestowed by the highest authority in the land for esteemed work.

[602] See Appendix "A" for a complete list.

[603] Lichtheim, *Ancient Egyptian Literature*, vol. I, 67. Similarly in PT § 490 (Faulkner, "The Ancient Egyptian Pyramid Texts", Unas says "I am the [steward] of the gods. I sit before him [the sungod])". This suggests that architecture (the antechamber) could have subtle cultural meaning at an early stage in the development of Egyptian society and that a code of social behaviour was already in existence.

[604] Lichtheim, *Ancient Egyptian Literature*, vol. 2, 139.

[605] Simpson, ed., *The Literature of Ancient Egypt* 19, 7. 10. Compare the carrying-chair in the tomb of Hetepheres, which was also gilded.

[606] Newberry, Fraser, and Griffith, *El Bersheh*, vol. 1, 30.

[607] Mueller, Sakenfeld, and Suggs, *The Oxford Study Bible,* Song of Songs, verse 3:9.

[608] Lucas and Harris, *Ancient Egyptian Materials and Industries*, 429. Also see Nicholson and Shaw, *Ancient Egyptian Materials and Technology*, 334.

[609] Lebanese timber is evidenced in many Dynasty 1 tombs, in the Dynasty 2 tomb of Khaskhemui, and from the Palermo Stone where it says that Senefru (Dynasty 4) sent 40 ships to acquire cedar from Lebanon. For the evidence from (Dynasty 6- Pepy 1), see Eaton-Krauss, "Fragment of Egyptian Jar Lid", in *Ebla to Damascus: Art and Archaeology of Ancient Syria*, ed. H. Weiss, 170.

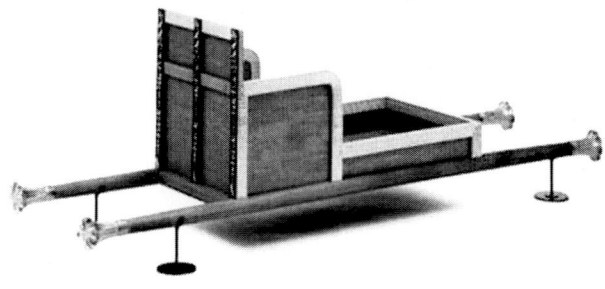

FIG. 2: RECONSTRUCTION OF THE CARRYING-CHAIR OF QUEEN HETEPHERES L: MUSEUM OF FINE ARTS, BOSTON. 38.874

the saw, the mallet and chisel for cutting mortise holes, plus the adze for shaping and smoothing wood.[610]

Carpentry was indeed far advanced as seen in the existence of a vast quantity of carpentry tools found in tomb 3471 at Saqqara, as well as the existence of the jointing, specifically the mortise and tenon joint, which replaced thonging.[611]

Unfortunately no elite carrying-chair has to date been discovered apart from a royal carrying-chair.

A questionable reconstruction of this royal carrying-chair (the only one physically available) is that of Hetepheres: one is on display in the Cairo Museum and the other at the Museum of Fine Arts in Boston. Both reproductions indicate that the chair is very short in length. Because the officials of the king were all males, and this was for a female, means that it cannot be taken as a representational prototype[612] for elite royal kinsmen. Thus any deduction from measurements as to general size, embellishments if any, consequential figuring of the actual number of porters required for its cartage, would be incorrect. However the fact of its preservation, and the bits of gilded decoration found, would indicate at the very least that it was made from hard wood and precious metals were used in its decoration, i.e. an elevated status good. The seats in both reproductions use some sort of wooden plank; however evidence suggests that this is not quite correct. The carrying-chair may have had seats, which were made from papyrus twine similar to present day caning - this seems to be the inference from the archaeological finds by Petrie in Tarkhan.[613]

Canopy

As there is no way of determining the exact dimensions of a regular carrying-chair, the main difference between the iconographic depictions seems to arise from the presence, or absence of a canopy.

The function of the canopy as a protection from the fierce Egyptian sun is an obvious inference, and one would expect to find the canopy in all such chairs, but this is not so. In view of the conservative nature of Egyptian society, it is also surprising to find a wide variation in the type and shape of these canopies. Furthermore, even if it is present, one sometimes also sees sunshade and fan carriers. A definite typology of canopies does not exist and while Vandier has tried to order these on the basis of function,[614] his method of ordering is unsatisfactory because it is more appropriate to use a geometrical type; doing which would eliminate the problem of change in usage which could distort the typology, and which additionally is objective.

The easiest discernible way of identifying them (canopies) is to address their shapes, into five (mainly geometrical) types[615] as follows:

1. Arched - built with an arched roof having a vault.
2. Curved - with no line having a straight part.
3. Square - having four equal sides forming four right angles.
4. Trapezoidal - having four sides, two of which are parallel.
5. Decorated - with wood cut indentations similar to a *kheker* pattern.

From the evidence it would seem that the canopy can be thought of either as a fixture or as a temporary awning made of lighter materials, which could be assembled as and when the occasion demanded. In the tomb of Ipy, two men are holding up the canopy from poles which are carved in the shape of a blunt bulb end, over which light material in this case decorated, is suspended.[616] Where, one does find evidence of some sort of a more durable fixed span, it is by indirect inference only, that of a monkey shown clambering down the canopy as in the Middle Kingdom tomb of Pepyankh.[617] None of the Old Kingdom carrying-chair scenes at Giza and Saqqara depicts a monkey climbing the canopy. Whether the canopy was a permanent fixture or not, is therefore still an open question. For purely functional reasons, it had to be made of light material otherwise it would be top heavy and subject to sway, and thus become unstable. In this connection mention must be made of a scene albeit in a provincial tomb of the Old Kingdom, where the canopy is so elaborately decorated that it conveys the impression of a very substantial affair.

---

[610] Emery, *Archaic Egypt*, 216-222.
[611] Emery, *Excavations at Saqqara*, vol. I, 19.
[612] Dimensions provided by the Metropolitan Museum at Boston are: Length of carrying poles = 207.5cm; Seat back = 52cm; Seat = 53.5cm. This means the available length for the carrying pole after deducting the seat area, is only 51cm. at either end, not leaving room for many porters! Reisner questioned the reconstruction on two grounds: that it was based on a depiction from the tomb of Queen Meresankh lll; and that the reconstructors did not make due allowance for the fact that wood may have shrunk over time.
[613] Petrie, Wainwright, and Gardiner, *Tarkhan 1 and Memphis V*, 9-12 and 23. Petrie notes the frequent use of baskets for coffins, for the laying of the body on a tray made of reeds, large branches being used for the roofing of a coffin, and the use of various types of webbing for beds.

[614] Vandier, *Manuel d'archéologie égyptienne*, vol. 4, 339-341. He tries to bring some order into the debate.
[615] For the tombs in which they occur, see Chart 1.
[616] Also shown in the tombs of: Niankhkhnum and Khnumhotep (fig, 60), Ptahhotep ll, Perneb, Itisen, Iymery, Ipy, Seshemnefer.
[617] Blackman and Apted, *The rock tombs of Meir*, vol. V, pl. 31.

Chart 1: Canopy Type

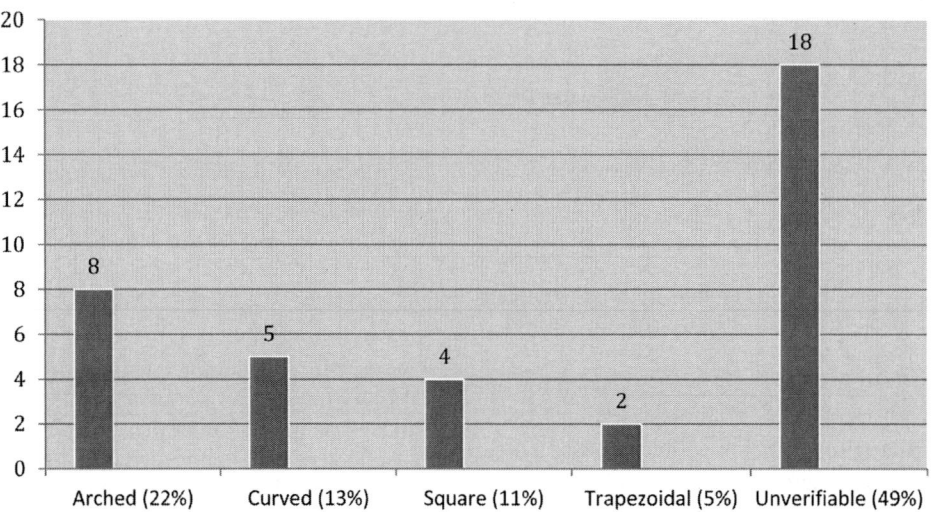

It supports the weight of monkeys shown clambering on to its roof and it certainly looks top heavy.[618] It may be that here we are noticing the extension of material goods in symbolic form as an indication of status and high culture, no matter how impracticable it might have been.

More than 50% of all carrying-chairs are shown to have some sort of canopy. This result could be even higher (60%) if the carrying-chairs in the tombs of Kagemni, Senedjem-ib-inti, and Ptahshepses are included (unfortunately these only suggest a canopy because of their structure but do not depict one as such). The rest of the scenes with carrying-chairs because of their poor state of preservation (those marked unverifiable), do not depict a canopy. Since more than half the scenes do have one, it may be that a canopy is part of the carrying chair. Moreover the type of canopy, because it is visibly striking, can have an ulterior visible effect, which could also result in the reinforcement of status and cultural embeddedness.

Chart 1 indicates the types of canopies seen in the population of tombs being investigated, and as represented by their geometrical shapes. While it is obvious from the chart that no apparent pattern favouring a particular type can be deduced, nevertheless it must be pointed out that since it was not possible to conclusively decide their shape in 49% of the cases, this statement must be treated with some caution.[619]

7. 3 Porters

A carrying-chair implies by its name that it is being carried and the mode of carrying is in most cases through

human agency, and in only three cases the use of donkeys is attested.[620] The humans are termed the porters. They are important because they are coupled to a set of values that in ancient Egypt must have paralleled or imitated those of their superiors and their attributes will now be discussed.

Headdress

Short curled hair is attested as early as Dynasty 2.[621] It would seem that by early Dynasty 4, short hair was the common form for all classes.[622] This plus the fact that short hair could be depicted in a way that looks like a 'wig', leads to difficulties. Invariably, the determination of whether or not the short crop of hair is a short 'wig' or just the normal style of hair, poses a problem, and no criterion has been found for deciding one way or another. There is "little evidence for the use of false hair in the Old Kingdom"[623] but this should not be taken to mean that there is no evidence.

The available archaeological record illustrates a broad range. The royal statuary of the head of Menkaure depicts him with short-cropped hair indicated by irregular striations, which do not extend to the back of the head and to the side burns.[624]

[618] Kanawati, *The Rock Tombs of El-Hawawish,* vol. I, fig. 13 and vol. II, fig. 21.

[619] Arched in the 8 tombs of: Ankhmare, Itisen, Kaemnofret, Khnumenti, Perneb, Ptahhotep ll, Sabw and Seshemnefer.
Trapezoidal in 2 tombs of: Ipy and Meryteti (pl. 47).
Curved in 5 tombs of: Iymery, Niankhkhnum (pl. 60), Seankhuiptah, Seshemnefer-Tjetti, and Hesi.
Square in 4 tombs of: Methethi, Nimaatre, Nefer-Khuwi and Qar.
Decorated in 2 tombs of: Ipy and Meryteti (pl. 47) which are also both trapezoidal in shape.
Unverifiable in 18 tombs of: Ankhmahor, Khnumhotep (pl. 61), Hetepniptah, Idu, Inisnfrw-ishtf, Kagemni, Mereruka (pls. 153b and 158), Merwtetiseneb, Niakauisesi, Nefermaat, Pepydjedi, Ptahshepses, Rashepses, Senedjemib-Inti, Seneb, Ty, Waatetkhethor and a fragment

from an unknown owner, in Leiden MastaBase no. 008a.

[620] In the tombs of: Khuwer, Niankhkhnum (pl. 42) and Khnumhotep (pl. 43).

[621] Quibell, *Excavations at Saqqara (1912-1914),* pl. XXVIII, 1.

[622] Lepsius, *Denkmäler aus Ägypten und Äthiopien,* pls. 8b and 11. Also see Smith, *A History of Egyptian Sculpture and Painting in the Old Kingdom,* pl.40a and 42c.

[623] Fletcher, "Hair", in *Ancient Egyptian Materials and Technology,* ed. P. T. Nicholson and I. Shaw, 496. Also see Shaw and Nicholson, *The British Museum Dictionary of Ancient Egypt,* 134.

[624] UC 14282 at the Petrie Museum of Egyptian Archaeology, is a

FIG. 3: HEAD OF MENKAURE IN THE
MUSEUM OF FINE ARTS BOSTON. 09.203

The non-royal statue of Senefru-nefer the overseer of palace singers is informative. He wears no 'wig' but his short hair is depicted by an incision marking the hairline, which is then the only indication of short hair being shown.

On the occasions that "wigs"[625] were worn by the elite and/or their personnel they two versions were in use: a short version consisting of curls overlapping each other, and a longer version covering the nape of the neck.[626] The porters appear with 'headgear' of a short, tight fitting, curled 'wig', which in some representations covers the ears, while in others the ears are exposed. This is in natural contrast to the "unkempt, balding, and sometimes graying natural hair of the non-elite labourer…".[627]

As the visual image is an important social reflection of the tomb owner, it would be inappropriate for even his servants to be improperly attired. This may be an explanation of why the short 'wig' is always shown, even though the everyday pattern was short-cropped hair. It is also probable that another reason for "wigs" "was to keep parasites at bay while allowing for the indulgence of hairstyles".[628] In line with the projection of identity, and a certain elite ideology, there is never any occasion when a porter is displayed without either a close fitting or with a small curls type of short 'wig'. Generally from evidence at Deir el-Bahri of a 'wig' workshop (there is no evidence of a similar 'wig' workshop from the Old Kingdom), it is now certain that the material used in the manufacture of "wigs" was human

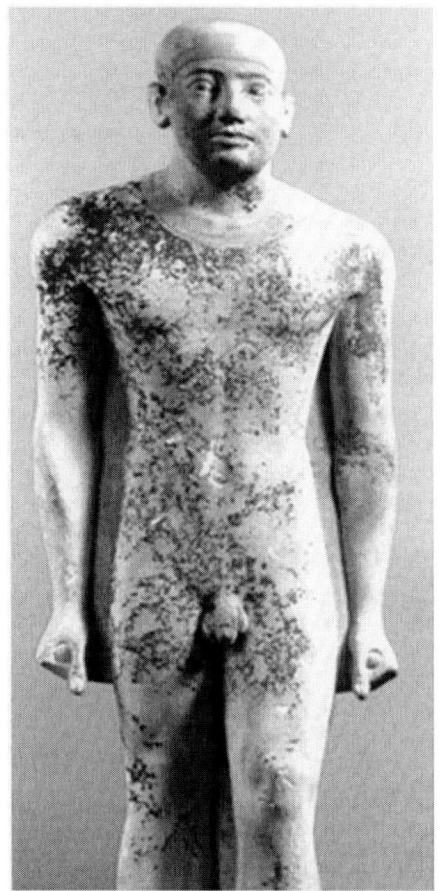

FIG. 4: SNEFRU-NEFER. KUNSTHISTORISCHES
MUSEUM, VIENNA ÄS 7506

hair.[629] This probably was the case in the Old Kingdom too because hair and its depiction in most societies has some meaning. Just like clothing is a normal feature in all members of society, being used to protect and enhance attributes of the human physique; likewise the exposed hair too can become a way of indicating differentiation, and it may be that the headgear of the porters is evidence of some of this encoding.

Attire: The majority of the porters are dressed in what is a strip of cloth covering the loins with a sheath in front. The nearest hieroglyphic word for an unworked piece of cloth is *dȝiw* but whether this was a loincloth is unclear.[630] The loincloth has been described as a simple linen triangle with strings at two corners, which were tied around the waist. The free pointed end of the triangular cloth was then draped down the back, pulled through the legs, and tucked in at the front. "Cloth loincloths were used by most of the population of Egypt for virtually all of the Pharaonic period".[631] Men engaged in strenuous activities usually wear it, e.g. agricultural workers[632] and this is a pointer to its generally non-elite status.

---

fragment of the head of Neferefre (Dynasty 5). It shows him wearing a tight fitting "skull cap" with striations very similar to Menkaure which certainly indicate hair.
[625] On hair and wigs generally, see Nicholson and Shaw, *Ancient Egyptian Materials and Technology*, 495-501.
[626] Lepsius, *Denkmäler aus Ägypten und Äthiopien,* pls. 21 and 74 (c) for an example of each type.
[627] Robins, "Hair and the Construction of Identity in Ancient Egypt", *JARCE,* (XXXVI), 63.
[628] Fletcher, "A Tale of Hair, Wigs and Lice", *EA,* (5), 32.

---

[629] Ibid.: 33.
[630] Erman, Grapow, and Reineke, *Wörterbuch der ägyptischen Sprache*, V, 417, 3. This word is fully written as ⌣ 𓏭𓅓𓏛𓏤 or in its abbreviated version, also appears in the Old Kingdom biography of Weni, and in Papyrus Westcar (Blackman, 9, 17, 26-10).
[631] Vogelsang-Eastwood, *Pharaonic Egyptian Clothing*, 10.
[632] Vandier, *Manuel d'archéologie égyptienne*, vol. 6, 55-56.

CHART 2: PORTER ATTIRE

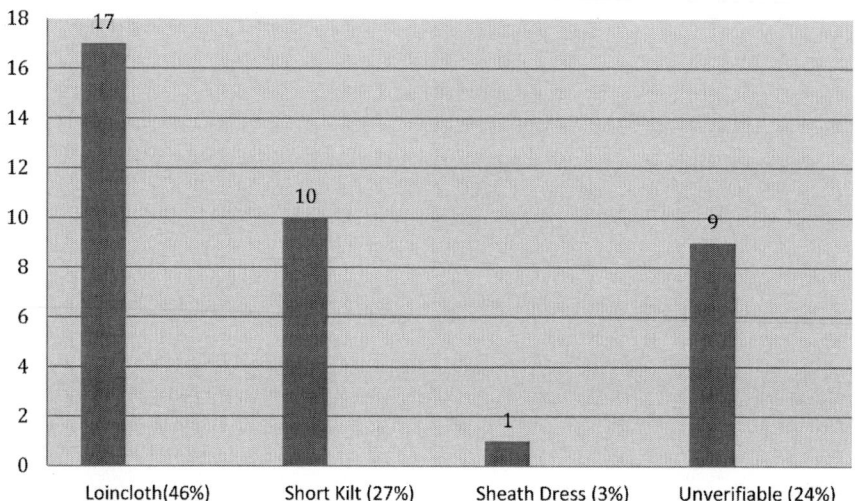

There are 17 tombs showing porters wearing this type of garment[633] and porters wearing short kilts are depicted in 10 tombs.[634] There are 9 tombs in which the porter's attire is unverifiable, and there is 1 case of porters wearing a sheath dress, that in the tomb of Waatetkhethor.

All these tombs however, are dated to Dynasty 6. Could it then be that one is witnessing in this attire the increasing tendency in the elite of showing their own importance and a diminution on the dependency on the king? Or could it be that these are indications of individuality?

However, no porters are shown wearing pointed kilts, which are reserved for the elite. It is of interest to note that the loincloth is also seen on the porters in the carrying-chair scenes at Deshasha, Meir, Deir el-Gebrawi, and el-Hawawish.[635]

While the loincloth is never seen on the elite in the Old Kingdom, yet its appearance on the standard-bearers in front of the vizier on Narmer's palette would not entirely rule this out. By Dynasty 4 the evidence indicates that it is the type of clothing worn by those of a lower socio-economic status.

As mentioned the porters are also shown dressed in the short kilt. This is attested from pre-dynastic times since the Scorpion mace head. The short kilt is a garment worn by men and covers parts of the lower body. Variations of this garment are observed in the iconography, e.g. in length and way of presentation: pleated, flapped, short, pointed, below knee length, etc.[636] depending on the status of the person and the context in which it is worn.

The porters when wearing the short kilt, are always shown wearing the plain variety as in the tomb of Seneb, where they are also identified by name as Shedji and Perw respectively.[637] As the majority of tombs show the porters in the loincloth, this would seem to be the preferred choice. Carrying a heavy wooden chair with the added weight of the tomb owner and moving in a specific direction in a specific manner is not an easy task, and this may have something to do with the type of sparse clothing worn by the porters. In keeping with the rules of lived practice (decorum), the porters are never shown entirely devoid of any clothing covering the lower extremities.

Chart 2 summarizes these findings.

Porter Count

The presence of the number of other personnel (they are present in nearly all motifs, for example offering bearers) is an indication of the social status of the tomb owner because this indicates the number of people having social obligations vis-à-vis the deceased. If this is correct then one would also have to concur, that the depiction of porters in all carrying-chair motifs, is likewise an indication of status even if they are only wearing loincloths.

Admittedly they are an essential element, for even where the carrying-chair is shown empty but being carried, it is on the shoulders of porters as in Mereruka,[638] where the

---

[633] Loin cloths in the 17 tombs of : Ankhmare, Inisnfrw-ishtef, Ipy, Itisen, Iymery, Khnumenti, Mereruka (fragment), Nefer-Khuwi, Niankhkhnum (Fig. 60), Nikawissi, Nimaatre, Ptahshepses, Sabw, Seankhuiptah, Senedjemib-Inti, Tjeti, and Ty.

[634] Short kilts in the 10 tombs of: Hesi, Kagemni, Mereruka (pl. 158), Meryteti (pls. 47 and 48), Hetepniptah, Pathhotep, Qar, Seneb, Seshemnefer and Nefermaat.

Porters' attire unverifiable in the 9 tombs of: Ankhmahor, Idu, Kaemnofret, Khnumhotep, Methethi, Merwtetiseneb, Pepydjedi, Perneb, and Rashepses.

[635] See Kanawati, "Deshasha", 48; Blackman, "Meir", vol. 5, pl. XXXI; Davies, "Deir el Gebrawi", vol. 2, pl. VIII; and Kanawati, "el-Hawawish", vol. 1 and 2, pls. 13 and 21 respectively.

[636] Staehelin, Untersuchungen zur ägyptischen Tracht im Alten Reich, MÄS, (8), 253-57. Also see Vogelsang-Eastwood, Pharaonic Egyptian Clothing, 53-71. For a review of clothing across the periods, see Bonnet, Die ägyptische Tracht bis zum Ende des Neuen Reiches, 1-73.

[637] Junker, Giza, vol. 5, fig. 20.

[638] Duell, The Mastaba of Mereruka, vol. 1, pl. 14.

CHART 3: TOTAL PORTER COUNT

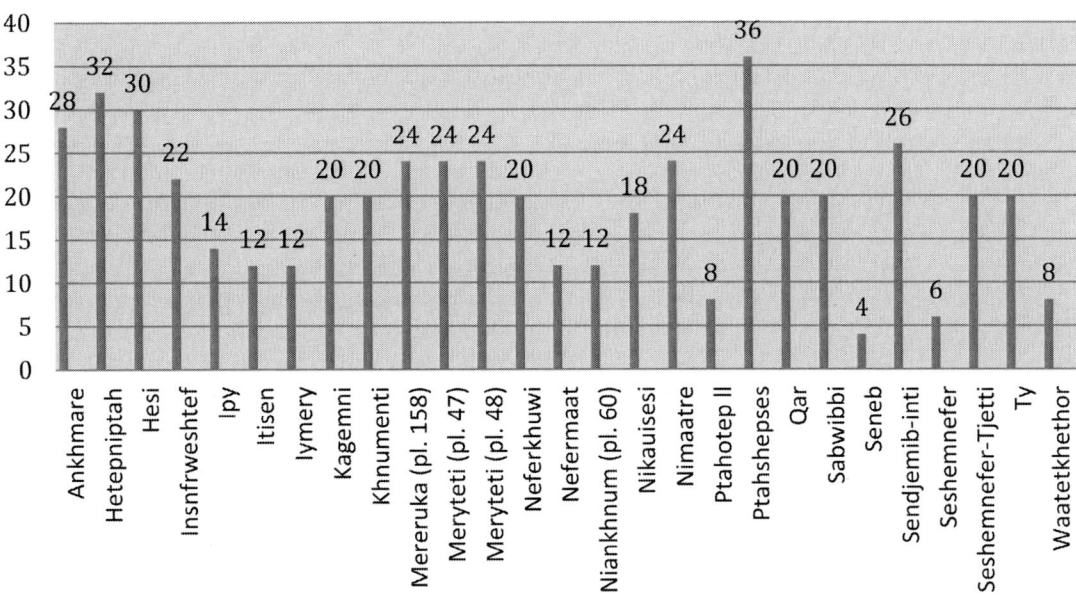

carrying-chair is being carried away from Mereruka and his wife who are shown viewing this action. However when a carrying-chair is being presented to the tomb owner it is never carried on the shoulders and the presenters are never attired in a loincloth. In the tombs of Seshathetep[639] and Ty[640] this is the case and can be explained as the offering of an elevated status good to people of high rank. This is observed from their accompanying titles and attire, e.g. the Elder of the House, Meni in the motif in Seshathetep and Sealer, Inspector of Sealers, and Funerary priest in the tomb of Ty. Indeed the representation here goes further, because when combined with all the other appurtenances connected with the carrying-chair, a picture is evoked not in terms of its functionality but in terms of the type of grave goods commanded by the elite, and thus reveals cultural embeddedness.

The numbers of porters vary from scene to scene; there is no hard and fixed rule as to the number employed. Presumably this would depend upon the type of chair, the weight of the carried person, and possibly limited by the surface area of the wall, which was available for its depiction. Equally one should realize that for reasons of displaying individuality/ideology the number of porters depicted could be exaggerated.

The actual number has posed a problem for some researchers; however there should be no problem in counting the total number of porters in a scene, provided one observes the scene from the angle of what is depicted, and what is physically possible.

The carrying-chair has to be in a balanced state in order for it to be transported in a fitting manner. Depending on the

position of the seat relative to the carrying poles, the center of gravity will shift from the middle, to the front, or rear, depending upon the weight load.

The obvious fact that there have to be two carrying poles, on either side of the base of the chair is self-explanatory.

These being the minimum requirements it follows that the porters who are shown in profile, have to be duplicated, or shown to appear duplicated in a similar manner.

To do otherwise in the supposed name of objectivity and scientific detachment, in that one is forced to count only what is actually depicted, is an impossible myth, and this book will follow the above method. In this respect Petrie, Junker, and Brovarski are correct in their method of counting of the porters[641] the count being multiplied by 2 even when only one line of them is shown.

Using this method results in a total number of 12 porters for the oldest extant carrying-chair motif that in the early Dynasty 4 tomb of Nefermaat at Medum.

Application of this method to all carrying-chair scenes reveals two particulars:

- The average number of porters in all carrying-chair motifs, in which there are porters, is about 20. The only written evidence that we have on the number of porters is from the tomb of Washptah (early Dynasty 5) - for whom the king allocated ten porters[642] and if this refers to only one part of the palanquin, then the total number would neatly add up to the postulated average. However if this refers

[639] Junker, *Giza*, vol. 2, fig. 31. The bearers of the carrying-chair wear a flapped short skirt.
[640] Épron et al., *Le Tombeau de Ti,* vol.I, pl. 17.

[641] Petrie, *Medum,* 26. Also see Junker, *Giza*, vol. 5, 83 and Brovarski, "*The Senedjemib Complex*", 120.
[642] Sethe, *Urkunden des Alten Reiches,* 41, l. 18-19.

to the actual total number, which as it was a gift from king Sahure could be considered ideal, then the average number postulated is in excess, and it maybe that the excess number shown includes reserve porters which could be required for a long journey.

- The total numbers of porters range from as low as four to as high as thirty-six as per chart 3.

The porter count could not be verified in ten tombs. Seven of these are much damaged and/or are in a fragmentary state while three tombs show carrying by donkeys and have not been included.[643]

Finally, the legs of the porters are always shown moving in unison and harmony; random foot movement is never depicted; befitting a formal occasion.

The numbers of porters and their portrayed movement is an attribute, which plays a role in the self-presentation of the tomb owner, and thus has an important bearing on the perception of his cultural significance.

Chart 3 is a summary of the total porter count in the tombs where they can be verified. The numbers above the tomb owner's name refer to the actual number of porters present but NOT the number of tombs. The total population of N = 37 includes 10 tombs in which the porter count could not be verified plus tombs with cartage on donkeys and thus are excluded.

Distribution of Porters

The placement of porters has primarily to do with the Egyptian's notion of comfortable and stable transport and indirectly with the status of the tomb owner.

In twelve tombs there are an equal number of porters in the front and the rear and this coincides with the postulated criterion of practicality for counting the porters.[644] In twenty-one tombs[645] it was not possible to segregate the front and the rear number conclusively; for reasons of compositional balance, no delineation between front and rear was noticeable, or where they may be part of a fragment, or the available evidence was only textual.

In two tombs the number of porters in the front exceeds the number at the rear[646] and in two other tombs porters at the rear exceeds those in the front.[647]

Chart 4 summarizes the distribution of porters.

Tempting, as it is to explain these unequal numbers as indicating that the weight has been reallocated and so deserves more carrying power and therefore more porters, will not do. It fails to explain the fact that the carrying pole is never shown as of unequal lengths, which would be the case if unequal number of porters were the norm. In any case porter placement is a function of available gripping place as the reproduction of the carrying-chair of Hetepheres evidences; both the poles are 207.5-cms in length. If for arguments sake, all carrying-chairs were equivalent in design to the Hetepheres reproduction, then the gripping place available means that the number of porters should be equal both in front and rear. If this is not so then it is a physical impracticality to have any porter under the carrying chair, because there is no place to grip, he would indeed be carrying the weight on his head and hands. The base of the chair and the pole are constructed to allow for a grip either by allowing for vertical or horizontal spaces between the pole and the seat (as observed in the tombs of Ipy, Khnumenti, Seshemnefer, and Niankhkhnum-fig. 60). Another method yielding identical results would be to allow for metal loops away from the seat base through which the carrying pole could be threaded (as seen in the tomb of Ty). In both instances a space is created which can be used for the purpose of gripping and cartage.

Further, 33% of the carrying-chair motifs present a balanced composition, with equal numbers of porters in the front and rear. In these motifs all the porters are shown bearing the pole.

Where there is a discrepancy between the front and rear porters, this is due to either:

- The scene being part of a fragment and so one cannot conclusively count the number of porters present.[648]
- The base of the carrying-chair covers practically the full length of the carrying pole such that there is no necessity to keep this part of the motif balanced, by equal number of porters in front and rear. The focus is on the person being carried and the carrying-chair.[649]
- The base of the carrying-chair is also part of the base of the register line and the focus is on the tomb owner.[650] The procession of carrying porters forms part of the next register, whose focus is on the number of people in the procession, and not

[643] In the 7 tombs of: Ankhmahor, Idu, Kaemnofret, Methethi, Merwtetiseneb, Perneb, and Seankhuiptah. The cartage by donkeys appears in Khuwer's tomb and the tombs of Niankhkhnum and Khnumhotep (fig. 42 and 43), which for the carrying-chair motif are to be considered as two tombs although they are in a joint tomb.

[644] In the 12 tombs of: Ankhmare, Iymery, Itisen, Mereruka (pl. 158), Meryteti (pl. 48), Nefermaat (equal front and rear numbers assumed), Niankhkhnum (pl. 60), Nimaatre, Sabw, Seneb, Ty, and Waatetkhethor.

[645] Unverifiable in the tombs of: Ankhmahor (F), Inisnfrw-ishtef, Ipy, Idu, Kagemni, Kaemnofret, Khnumenti, LMP 008a (F), Mereruka (F) pl.153b)), Methethi (F), Nefer-Khuwi (F), Merutetiseneb (F), Meryteti (pl. 47), Pepydjedi (T), Perneb (F), Ptahhotep ll, Rashepses (F), Seankhuiptah, Seshemnefer, Seshemnefer-Tjeti (F), and Hesi. "(F)" indicates a fragment and "(T)" indicates textual evidence only.

[646] In the 2 tombs of: Hetepniptah and Nikauisesi.

[647] In the 2 tombs of: Qar, and Seshemnefer-Tjeti.

[648] In the 2 tombs of: Sakhwptah and Ankhmahor.

[649] Niankkhnum's carrying-chair covers nearly the length of the pole.

[650] Meryteti (pl. 47). Compare this with Meryteti (pl. 48), where the porters are clearly displayed on either side of the pole.

CHART 4: DISTRIBUTION OF PORTERS

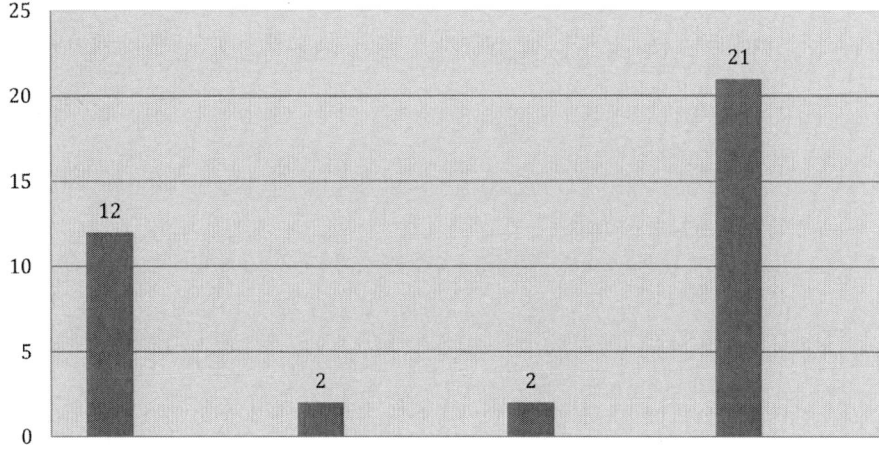

necessarily only on the porters. It therefore becomes unnecessary to balance the number of porters.

- Another reason for a different number of porters at the front and the rear may be related to the sizes of the porters. A short man would carry a lesser load if placed between two tall men. If the men are lined up in order of height (which appears to be the case as observed), the focus shifts from height to brute strength and there will be less men required at the bigger/stronger men's end of the poles. This could be one explanation for the unequal number shown and would explain all cases. However, even if the artist was aware of this, such unaesthetic deviations are never shown, as these would deviate from the essential elements of the scene, and be against decorum.
- Another equally convincing reason may be that travel over some distance required reserve porters, who while shown 'carrying', were in fact reserves, and this could be the cause for the unequal number of porters per side. Unlike the previous reasoning this would not work against decorum and is the preferred explanation.

Carrying Method

Before discussing the carrying method the issue of the relationship between the carried and the carriers needs to be addressed because it gives a vital clue to cultural significances. The question is what is this hierarchical relationship between the carried and the carriers based upon?

It is known that the public carrying of the living or dead king, was an indication of the political and social power structure that was incorporated in his office. The king when alive and dead must have been carried on something, because he could not be touched (the Rawer Incident see page 26). This carrying then raises two issues:

1. The decorum related one of being carried in a suitable manner.
2. The symbolic related one, of this being an additional interpretation of political power.

The use of the carrying-chair and its being part of royal and elite furniture is well evidenced. The material evidence ranges over a wide period of the Old Kingdom. From the Dynasty 3 offering list of Nefer-hetep-Hathor (see page 79), to the actual find from the Dynasty 4 tomb of Hetepheres (see page 81), and the numerous Dynasty 5 biographical inscriptions displaying the king's concern for an official making clear that the chair brought from the residence was to carry a person aloft (see page 26).

However these inscriptions do not say anything about the political power, which is symbolic of the image behind the carrying-chair. For this we have to turn to the Pyramid texts, where the king is carried and lifted into the barque of Sokar with all his powers intact and thus we have the first hint of any symbolic significance.[651] Another clue is from the New Kingdom sarcophagus of King Merenptah, which attests to his power, and the way it is supposedly shown:

"I carry you, you being on my back (wṯs=i sꜥḥ=k ꜥwi=i ḥr=k) and the Ennead carrying you in a carrying-chair (rmntw psḏt ḥr-spꜣ)".[652]

A vague hint to the hierarchical relationship between the carried and the porters is also given in the porter's song in the tomb of Ipy where they implore a god as follows: "O Sokar, who is on the sand come and protect N".

[651] Faulkner, *The Ancient Egyptian Pyramid Texts,* § 1823, 24, 26 and 27.
[652] Assmann, "Die Inschrift auf dem äusseren Sarkophagdeckel des Merenptah", *MDAIK,* (28), 48 and 56. This is a New Kingdom example and so while care has to be taken in extrapolating backwards into the Old Kingdom and to non-royals, yet the symbolic significance is clear.

CHART 5: CARRYING METHOD

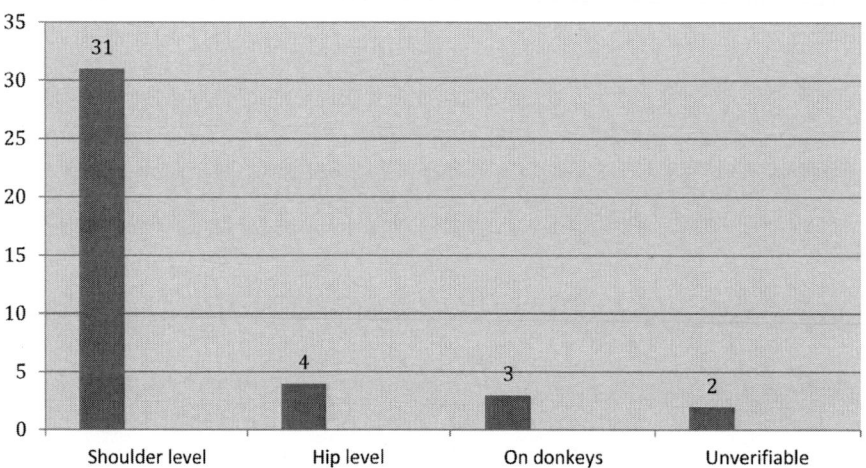

DUPLICATION: THE TOTAL NUMBER EXCEEDS 37 BY 3 BECAUSE MERERUKA AND MERYTETI OCCUR IN BOTH SHOULDER AND HIP LEVEL METHODS AND NIANKKHNUM OCCURS IN BOTH SHOULDER LEVEL AND CARRIAGE BY DONKEY METHODS; THEREFORE COLUMN FIGURES SHOULD NOT BE ADDED UP.

Admittedly there are differences in the exercise of royal and private symbols of authority, and between cultic and daily life actions, but the similarities cannot be ignored. It is suggested that similar to the display of social and political power, which was present in the carriage of a 'living' king,[653] the elite in pursuance of a particular social identity and maybe ideology, utilize the carrying-chair as one way in which to project its and their own importance. In the elite this is evidenced to the extent allowed by decorum, which results in them being depicted as being carried aloft on human hands, carrying instruments of power – the *sḫm* sceptre, and an appeal to a god Sokar for protection. Even though there are very few examples[654] of displaying the sceptre, nevertheless it depicts power and control; that is similar in meaning to when the living king is seen carrying it, albeit as a delegate of that power. The actual representation is to being lifted up and being carried, whereas its symbolic reference is to power. However in the context of the carrying-chair motif, the literal and the symbolic melt into each other, such that the difference between their daily life and cultic usage is difficult to determine. Accordingly these actions that of being carried and that of carrying the sceptre (or the baton and rod which appear in the majority of carrying-chair motifs) become powerful symbols in their own right. Thus 'Sehbild and Sinnbild' are combined, political power and the social/ cultural structure obviously fuse into each other, and meaning is created self evident to all, of status constituting elements (the identity of eliteness and the implication of power and control).

Three methods of carrying are known during the Old Kingdom:

1. At the porter's hip level, as depicted in the tombs of Nefermaat, Meryteti (pl. 48), Mereruka (pl. 158), and Waatetkhethor. The empty carrying chairs as part of the offerings are excluded although these are shown being carried at hip level in the tombs of Ty (pl. 17 (third section), Ptahshepses pl. 10, Mereruka pl. 14, and Waatetkhethor pl. 57a.
2. At the shoulder level which is the norm for all of the other carrying-chair motifs.[655]
3. Carried on a chair strapped between a pair of donkeys.

Method 1 is represented initially in Dynasty 4 (Nefermaat), and thereafter in Dynasty 6 in the combined tomb of Mereruka/Meryteti/Waatetkhethor of the Old Kingdom; it is restricted to these four known tombs only. The majority of the other known tombs show method 2 and only three tombs[656] indicate method 3.

Two other tombs are excluded: the tomb of Rashepses (textual description only) and that of Pepydjedi[657] as unverifiable. The carrying methods are shown chart 5, with the clear preponderance of evidence in favour of the shoulder level method.

[653] Rössler-Köhler, "Sänfte", *LÄ*, vol. 5, 334-39.
[654] In the tombs of: Ptahhotep (pl. 39), and Seshemnefer (fig. 3).
[655] In the 31tombs of: Ankhmahor, Ankhmare, Niankhkhnum (pl. 60), Hesi, Idu*, Inisnfrw-ishtef, Ipy, Itisen, Iymery, Kagemni, Kaemnofret, Khnumenti, Mereruka (pl. 153b), Meryteti (pl. 47), Methethi*, Merwtetiseneb, Nefer-Khuwi, Nikauissi, Nimaatre, Hetepniptah, Perneb*, Pathhotep II, Ptahshepses, Qar, Sabw, Seankhuiptah, Seneb, Senedjemib-inti, Seshemnefer, Seshemnefer-Tjeti and Ty (pl. 16).
*The three tombs marked with an asterisk, are open to question but because of the size of their chairs, the chairs shown are assumed to have been carried at shoulder level and therefore are included in the shoulder level method in Chart 5.
[656] In the 3 tombs of: Khuwer, Niankhkhnum (pl. 42), Khnumhotep (pl. 43).
[657] In the 2 tombs of: Pepydjedi, and Rashepses, also see Mariette and Maspero, *Les mastabas de l'Ancien Empire,* 401-02.

In the iconography sometimes both hands are shown being used to carry and sometimes only one and sometimes the carriers are inside the carrying pole and sometimes outside the carrying pole. Is there an explanation for this?

Approximately 90% of modern humans are right handed. Let us assume for our purposes that the majority of Egyptians were right handed too.[658]

Directionally left or right movement can be accomplished by the use of the correct arm and hand with the body outside/inside the pole. The pole would give stability of direction and vision could be ascertained by a simple vertical movement of the neck or a downward glance at the feet of the person in front. This implies that the porters are probably experienced at following the man in front, but this argument could be fallacious if experience is something that we can assume, but not decide on objectively.

In any event any carrying by being inside/outside the pole and carrying with the wrong arm would have a disastrous effect. Accordingly from the view of the observer, the correct and practical way of depicting the carrying in profile, would be any of the following, using either of the hands:

1. For movements from left to right: view would be that of either right hand, right shoulder and head inside pole or right hand, right shoulder and head outside pole.
2. For movements from right to left: view would be that of either left hand, left shoulder, head outside pole or left hand, left shoulder and head inside pole.
3. Any other combination would be impracticable and undignified.

As the porters are shown to be of similar height this attribute has been excluded from consideration.

Consider the four scenes of carrying in the tombs of Mereruka (pl. 158), Meryteti (pl. 48), his mother Waatetkhethor (pl. 69), and Nefermaat. The method of carrying with both hands at hip level and with the carriers inside the pole does indicate stability. However the base of the massive chair directly obstructs the line of the rear carriers and even though the right position and arms are being used, the iconography shown is impractical. Because these are the only scenes known occurring in the same tomb complex and belonging to the same family (Mereruka) and period (Dynasty VI), (except Nefermaat) they can be explained away as examples of individuality or even archaism.

The majority of the carrying-chair motifs however, depict carriage on the shoulders. Since this motif is shown in profile as is usual in Egyptian art, it follows that it very much depends which direction of movement is being shown. Depending on this, the correct combination of arms, shoulders, and placement of the carrying pole will be required. The essential point and one on which no importance has been attached in the literature, is the position of the head with respect to the carrying pole which also allows one to deduce the carrying shoulder. The hands, shoulder, and carrying pole are always aligned whereas the head can be inside or outside the pole depending upon which hand is used as well as the direction. The position of the head with respect to the carrying pole should provide additional stability in the direction of the movement and if correctly aligned will provide for freedom of movement of the head with little possibility of heads and arms being engaged in contorted positions, unthinkable in formal/ceremonial occasions.

A closer analysis will reveal that while this may have been the case in practice it was not always depicted correctly in the iconography.

Regarding the methods of carrying there are 21 tombs, which correlate to the fact that the porters are both outside the carrying pole, and are carrying on the correct shoulder and arm.[659] The fact that sometimes we see both arms being used is immaterial, if the correct shoulder and arm are also in operation. In early or middle Dynasty 5 there is no evidence of incorrect depictions. There are 6 correct depictions, which occur in early Dynasty 6,[660] and one[661] in late Dynasty 5 or early 6.

Three tombs depict an incorrect method.[662] It is interesting to note that most of the incorrect depictions occur in periods from late Dynasty 5 onwards and never earlier.

As already mentioned the main attribute of correctness is not some arbitrary distinction, but the fact that a carried object has to move in a certain predetermined direction in a proper manner, such that operatives are able to utilize their visual capacity fully and the profile view represents these attributes. The way the artist has chosen to depict the carrying-chair motif gives rise to the following issues:

- Certain representations show evidence of image super imposition (see Fig. 5) to create an affected sense of duplication.[663] The depiction in some tombs of a double set of porters (which was the reality depicted in those tombs) results in the compression of the carrying-chair motif. The carrying pole is

---

[658] Mandal and Dutta, "Left handedness: Facts and Figures across Cultures", *PDS*, (13/2), 173. "About 90% of the population exhibit directionally consistent right handed preference for most unimanual activities and for activities which matter in terms of consequences, the right hand is chosen".

[659] In the 21 tombs of: Ankhmare, Hetepniptah, Khnumenti, Kagemni, Ipy, Iymery, Mereruka (pl. 153b and 158), Meryteti (pl. 47), Niankhkhnum (pl. 60), Nimaatre, Nefer-Khuwi, Ptahhotep II, Ptahshepses, Sabw, Seankhuiptah, Senedjemib-inti, Seneb, Seshemnefer, Seshemnefer-Tjeti, Ty (pl. 16) and Hesi. For comments in this regard, see Junker, *Giza* vol. XI, 253-54.
[660] Mereruka, Kagemni, Seankhuiptah, Nikauissi, Khnumenti, and Hesi.
[661] Seshemnefer.
[662] In the 3 tombs of: Inisnfrw-ishtef, Itisen, and Nikauisesi.
[663] Kaplony, *Studien zum Grab des Methethi,* 23, also see Figures list no. 5.

FIG. 5: (TORONTO MUSEUM NO.3) TOMB OF METHETHI SHOWING (SUPERIMPOSITION) OVERLAPPING EFFECT ON A HERD OF DONKEYS (5 DONKEYS/7 EARS/8 LEGS).

CHART 6 : ACCURACY OF DEPICTION OF CARRYING BY PORTERS

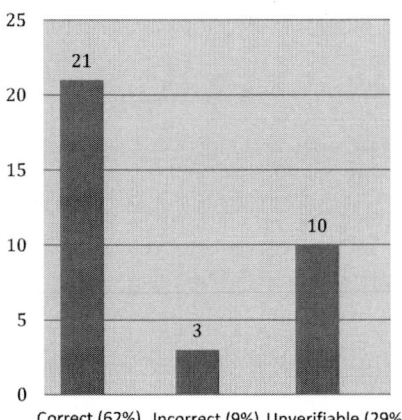

Correct (62%) Incorrect (9%) Unverifiable (29%)

THREE TOMBS CONTAIN DEPICTIONS OF CARRYING ON A DONKEY AND THESE HAVE BEEN EXCLUDED.

shown being shared by both groups of porters, e.g. in the tombs of Khnumenti, Kagemni, Mereruka (pls. 14, 53b and 158), Meryteti (pl. 48) and Seshemnefer, which enhances the reality of the picture because it shows at a glance that there were two sets of porters without the use of additional wall space.

- Again in some of these motifs the rear porter's view appears to be totally impaired by the back/base of the carrying-chair especially those showing the palanquin being carried at hip level (Nefermaat, Waatetkhethor, Meryteti (pl. 48), and Mereruka (pl. 158). However there are other representations showing the shoulder carrying method where the rear porter's vision is also shown as 'if impaired' (e.g. in the tombs of Ty (pl. 16), Ankhmare, Niankhkhnum (pl. 60), Nimaatre, Senedjemib-Inti, Seshemnefer-Tjeti, Itisen and Qar. This would imply that the artist was not aware of or incorrectly depicted, what was a most important signal of cultural embeddedness for the elite tomb owner, which is highly unlikely to be the case. A suggested explanation, which would result in zero impairment of vision, would be to observe the porters as though they are on the sides of the palanquin, which occupies a space in the middle. This is noticeable in the eight tombs cited above and shows the artists understanding and solution to the complex problem of depicting in profile view, something of a three dimensional nature.
- Another method of solving this problem has been to show the porters directly underneath the base of the carrying-chair such that the base appears elevated and centered, while the porters appear on its side, resulting in unimpaired vision (e.g. in the tombs of Ipy, Kagemni, Meryteti (pl. 47), Ptahhotep II, Seankhuiptah, Khnumenti and Hesi). Depicting porters underneath the base of the carrying-chair

implies that there is unimpaired vision and draws attention to the prominence of what is above. In the tomb of Seneb, the porters are not shown underneath the carrying-chair, yet the effect is to enhance the image of the tomb owner, and to divert the spectator away from the fact that he was a dwarf, resulting in both aesthetic and cultural significance.

- Finally in ten tombs[664] the representations are so damaged or non-existent as to give no hint as to the porter's method of carrying and these have been excluded from the summarizing chart. Chart 6 shows that the majority (62%) of the motifs showing the carrying of the palanquin were in fact represented correctly.

Hands as Indicators of Cultural Embeddedness

An interesting phenomenon in the iconography is the use to which the hands of the porters are put. While the majority of representations show cartage of the palanquin by both hands,[665] when only one hand is used, the free hand is:

- Hanging empty by the side
- Carrying a short baton
- Carrying a rolled cloth

---

[664] In the 10 tombs of: Ankhmahor, Idu, Kaemnofret, Khnumhotep, Methethi, Merwtetiseneb, Pepydjedi, Perneb, Qar, and Rashepses.

[665] Hanging empty by side in 4 tombs of: Itisen, Niankhkhnum (Fig. 60), Nimaatre and Sabw.
Carrying short baton in 4 tombs of: Inisnfrw-ishteff [R], Kagemni [R], Mereruka (pl.53b) [R], and Seshemnefer [R].
Carrying rolled cloth in the tomb of: Meryteti (pl. 47).
Both hands carrying in the 21 tombs of: Ankhmare, Hesi*, Ipy, Iymery, Khnumenti, Mereruka (pl.158), Meryteti (pl. 48), Nefer-Khuwi, Nefermaat, Nikauisesi, Hetepniptah, Ptahhotep II, Ptahshepses, Qar, Seankhuiptah, Seneb, Senedjemib-inti, Seshemnefer-Tjeti, Ty, Waatetkhethor (pl. 69) and Waatetkhethor (pl. 57a).
Unverifiable in 9 tombs of: Ankhmahor, Idu, Kaemnofret, Khuwer, Merwtetiseneb, Methethi, Pepydjedi, Perneb, and Rashepses.
[R] = right hand and [L] = left hand. * = exception explained in the text.

CHART 7: USE OF PORTERS' HANDS

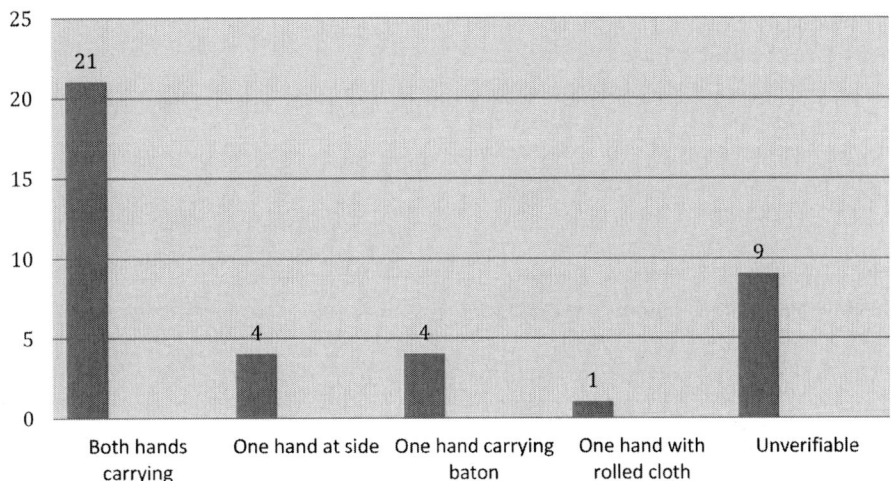

DUPLICATION OCCURS ACROSS THE TOMBS, E.G. WAATETKHETHOR HAS TWO PLATES (PL. 57A AND 69) DEPICTING CARRYING WITH BOTH HANDS; THEREFORE THE NUMBERS SHOULD NOT BE ADDED UP. THEY REFER TO THE CASES AND NOT TO THE NUMBER OF TOMBS.

The instances in which the free hand is carrying anything are few in comparison, and indeed the implication of any cultural significance behind this may be questioned, if the only goal was the secure transport of the tomb owner. Apart from sometimes a baton[666] and in one instance a rolled cloth[667] by each porter, there is no evidence of the porters carrying any other status goods.

However, whenever they carry anything in addition to the carrying-chair, the right hand is the one always used. That the baton is a status good can be inferred from the tomb of Seshemnefer, where the porters carry batons with bulbous ends, which at first glance look very much like that of a *sḫm* sceptre (but which may have been just a short club with a bulge at its end). In the context of the representation, it is quite clear that it is not a sceptre because it would detract from the tomb owner, who is himself carrying a *sḫm* sceptre as well as a large staff with a bulbous end. This motif is part of the false door and rituality may be at play here.

The need for sticks and batons however needs an explanation. It either had a functional use, i.e. the necessity of making a way through crowded paths and/or a means of signaling to the troupe of porters (this may be the implication of the baton being carried by the second leading carrier as in the tomb of Hesi). Another use would be a sort of livery (a uniform worn by servants in a non-military context), attesting to the owner's wealth and social standing, e.g. in the tombs of Inisnfrw-ishtef, Kagemni, Mereruka, and Seshemnefer. If this is so, this still leaves open the question why it is not shown in all tombs. Are these cases then to be understood as attempts at change that did not take on, i.e. instances of aberrant behaviour, which did not take on (individuality described in the broader type 'B' sense, see page 68)?

These questions and their implications cannot be proven overwhelmingly as the tomb of Mereruka would indicate. Here we have two motifs (excluding pl.14 which depicts an empty carrying-chair), each of which has different significances as follows:

- In Mereruka pl. 158 he is shown being carried on a carrying-chair, yet the porters are not shown holding any status goods.
- In the fragmentary scene in pl. 53b showing the cartage of a palanquin by porters, they are shown with batons.

Therefore both the functional and the status enhancing explanations given are open to doubt, if one tomb is enough evidence to go by. However it must be conceded that the emphasis on details underlies the fact that the tomb owner is being carried by other humans in a manner which highlights him as a member of an exclusive variety or at least someone who the community thinks needs this special care, underpin the elite status and consequent cultural embeddedness.

Chart 7 is a summary of the data.

7.4 The Other Escorts

Frequently together with the porters, five other types of escorts are present:

1. Sunshade and Fan Carriers
2. Dwarves
3. Animals
4. Supervisor(s)
5. Subsidiary Attendants carrying Tomb owner's belongings

---

[666] Inisnfrw-ishtef, Kagemni, Mereruka and Seshemnefer.
[667] Meryteti (pl. 47).

Sunshade and Fan Carriers

These escorts are connected with the same utilitarian purpose as the canopy, (i.e. protection of the carrying-chair occupant from the heat and flies), however they are being treated separately like all 'the other escorts' because it was thought that analyzing each element of the scene might throw some more light on their cultural interdependencies.

These carriers are additional to and separate in function from the porters, their main function being to enhance the state of ease and enjoyment of the journey for the tomb owner.

The common sunshade in the Old Kingdom tombs is composed of a rectangular piece of material spread over diagonal struts with another rectangular fringe on the side. It was carried on a long pole which is shown either touching the middle of the diagonal struts or shown as nding at the bottom edge of the rectangular top, each example illustrated in the tomb of Nimaatre and Seankhuiptah respectively. The term for the sunshade is *sb3* and the bearers are designated as *ḥryw sb3w* referred to as a title in the tomb of Nimaatre[668] as in fig. 6.

Indeed in the tomb of Seneb,[669] the sunshade carrier wearing a short kilt is even identified as a person named Hetes, a remarkable co-incident for a supposedly lowly job. It may well be questioned, why any additional contraptions (sunshades) were needed, when the canopy was present. This is all the more evident in the tomb of Ipy, which depicts 5 persons carrying three large sunshades both behind and in front of the carrying-chair, and a depiction in the tomb of Seankhuiptah with at least three sunshades.

One obvious answer would be to look at functionality keeping in mind the geographical position of Egypt near the equator. The rays of the sun will be at an angle in the morning and late afternoon, while they will be practically perpendicular nearing midday and so travelling during these periods would require an adjustable shade cloth. Of course the sun cannot be both behind and in front of the carrying-chair at the same time, i.e. the portrayal of many sunshade carriers adds to the argument that the representation depicts social status and to a lesser extent the actual reality. Therefore sunshades help to project and broadcast a signal about the importance of the human so accompanied. The attire of the sunshade carrier has some relation to the identity and status of the person for whom he carries the sunshade too. An example from the tomb of Mereruka[670] is instructive. In plate 167, Mereruka with his mother Nedjetempet and wife Waatetkhethor are depicted viewing agricultural activities. A man behind them in a pointed kilt is shown carrying a sunshade. Additionally as part of the agricultural activities scene (plate 168) another man is carrying a sunshade but this time for some officials

FIG. 6: TOMB OF NIMAATRE

and not Mereruka. The interesting point is that this man (holding a sunshade for officials) is shown wearing only an apron with his penis and scrotum in full view. While this is only a single example, yet it is a pointer to the levels of depicted hierarchy and their ultimate connection with the generics.

Indeed in the Narmer mace head, 2 sunshade carriers are seen just behind the person described as a *ṯ* [*3ty*] and they are wearing a short kilt just like the *ṯ* [*3ty*].

Another possible reason for sunshades could be a requirement of the tomb owner. He desired that when alighting at some point or other from the carrying-chair that sunshades be present for his comfort and status enhancing attributes.

As we do not have any knowledge of the health of particular tomb owners, one cannot comment on this aspect, which may also influence the use of this type of shade.

The sunshades carriers are depicted in 11 tombs.[671] The majority of these are dated to Dynasty 6 with only the tomb of Senedjemib-Inti dated to late Dynasty 5 (V.8 M-L).

Although the fan is depicted in only 4 carrying chair motifs; that in the late Dynasty 5 tombs of Khuwer, and Ty, and in the early Dynasty 6 tombs of Waatetkhethor and Hesi; its use in the iconography is seen much earlier as in the Dynasty 4 mastaba of Neb-em-akhet. The types shown being carried by female bearers are both the lotus type and the flap-fan.[672] Another type made of palm fronds is also known. Their appearance, unlike the sunshade that may appear at the front and rear of the procession, is always at the rear of the procession, and never in the front. That all these types were

---

[668] Hassan, *Excavations at Giza,* vol. II, fig. 240. Figures list no. 6.
[669] Junker, *Giza,* vol. 5, fig. 20.
[670] Duell, *The Mastaba of Mereruka,* vol. 2, pl. 167 and 68.

[671] In the tombs of: Ankhmahor (R1), Hesi (FRM3), Ipy (FR5), Inisnfrw-ishtef (R1), Kagemni (FR2), Merwtetiseneb (F1), Seankhuiptah (FR2), Senedjemib-inti (F1), Seshemnefer-Tjeti (R1), Seneb (F1), and Waatetkhethor (R1).
In the brackets: the alphabetical abbreviation denotes the placement of the sunshades. (F = Front, R = Rear, FR = Front/Rear, FRM = Front/Rear/Middle. The numbers denote their occurrence in that tomb.
[672] S. Hassan, *Excavations at Giza,* vol. IV, fig. 82, p. 143-144.

elite status goods can be inferred from their appearance in the Dynasty 4 mastaba of Queen Meresankh III, where all three types occur in the northern and southern entrance jambs, shown being carried by her female servants.[673]

Even if their exchange worth was modest and well within the means of the others, yet their appearance as part of a ceremonial scene would indicate that their importance lay in the depiction of their functionality, being publicly shown for performance by another person for the benefit of the tomb owner.

In the motif where the tomb owner is depicted being carried in a chair hung between two donkeys, e.g. in the tomb of Khuwer, a male person carrying a frond type of fan is shown behind the tomb owner.[674] The only other depiction of a palm frond type of fan is in the tomb of Hesi, where an attendant on a separate sub-register immediately behind the carrying-chair is depicted with one.[675] The presence of this type of fan may have something to do with the incidence of flies and such like or equally it may indicate an element of individuality. Of course this does not explain why the other two similar scenes (being carried in a chair hung between two donkeys) in the joint tomb of Niankhkhnum and Khnumhotep (pl. 42 and 43), do not depict a fan bearer.

Two other tombs depict a lotus type fan: that of Waatetkhethor where a female identified as an overseer of linen is seen holding a lotus fan and walking behind the carrying-chair, and in that of Ty, where two men in short kilts who are part of the carrying-chair processional train, are each depicted carrying a lotus fan.

As these are the only 4 tombs with such a representation, it would appear at first glance that the fan did not take on as a regular part of the carrying-chair motif. However this could be equally said about the sandal bearers, who appear

CHART 8: RATIO OF FAN AND SUNSHADE CARRIERS

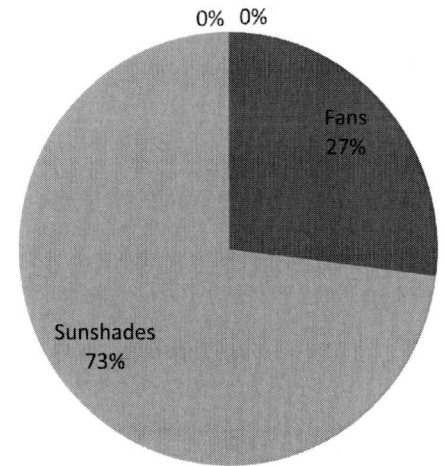

in only 8 carrying-chair motifs,[676] yet their importance as an elevated status good is well known[677] (indicated by significant precedents, e.g. Narmer palette and Mace head). It is suggested that a similar attitude should be taken towards the fan-carrying sub-motif because it appears in the royal tomb of Meresankh III, and therefore its importance should not be underrated. The sunshades seem to be more popular as per Pie Chart 8 and Chart 9 below in comparing the ratio of sunshades and fans including their placement in the carrying-chair scene. However, note this is based on a total population of 15 only.

Pie chart 8 shows the ratio of cases of sunshade and fan carriers of the (15) total cases found.

Chart 9 gives their frequency and placement in the carrying-chair motif, but note that the numbers above the columns do NOT depict the number of carriers.

CHART 9: SUNSHADE AND FAN CARRIER PLACEMENT

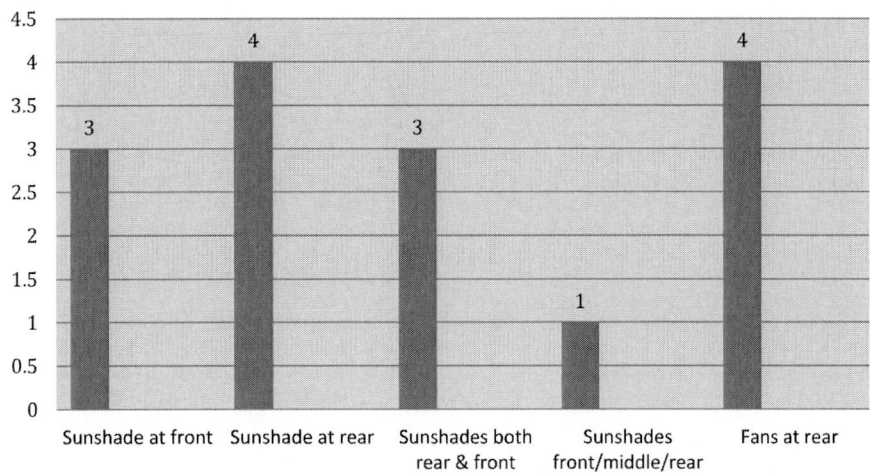

---

[673] Dunham et al., *The Mastaba of Queen Mersyankh III,* pl. 3 (a and b).
[674] Hassan, *Excavations at Giza,* vol. V, fig. 104, p. 245.
[675] Kanawati, *The Teti Cemetery at Saqqara,* vol. 5, pl. 55.

[676] In the tombs of: Ankhmare, Khnumhotep (pl. 43), Hesi, Iymery, Khnumentii, Niankhkhnum (pl. 42), Ptahshepses and Ty.
[677] The sandal carrier initially was the prerogative of a specific person, who was exposed to the personal belongings of the king. See Staehelin, *Untersuchungen zur ägyptischen Tracht im Alten Reich* 94-100, esp. 97.

Dwarves

As early as Dynasty 1, the canon of bodily proportions appears to be established in Egypt, e.g. as seen in the Narmer Palette. The body is divided to fit grids which fit the idealized image of the human body, and "as a standardization of the natural proportions of the body these ratios constitute in themselves a system of human proportions, an elementary canon, which was fully established at the beginning of dynastic times when the artistic traditions of Egypt were inaugurated".[678] Following these iconographic conventions, the dwarf is standardized in a way that represents him as such but does away with the ugliest aspects of the deformity, even though the dwarf is shown with a large head, a long trunk, and shorter limbs. The earliest depiction is in 2 stelae of dwarfs, found in the surrounding chambers of the tomb of the Dynasty 1 king Semerkhet, "which show the dwarf type clearly".[679] In most cases he is also shown wearing a kilt but can also appear naked.[680] At times in the iconography, it is difficult to distinguish between a boy and a dwarf especially when the boy is clothed and does not have a youth lock.[681] Be that as it may, the dwarf is a popular feature as evidenced in the twenty-two reliefs in various motifs in which dwarfs are shown tendering pet animals.[682] There are several theories as to the popularity of dwarfs in the social life of Egypt.[683] However it is suggested that the popularity of the dwarf in Old Kingdom iconography can best be understood by relating it to some form of superstition that could be related to the disproportions of the body.

Since the Middle Kingdom, but truly popular by the New Kingdom is the deformed god Bes. There are however no attested depictions of Bes in the Old Kingdom,[684] depictions of deities in this period being a rarity. Accordingly it is difficult to justify this as a reason for the dwarf's popularity in the Old Kingdom.

In these motifs the dwarf is seen in a range of social positions, including as an eminent person close to the king as in Seneb.[685] Two textual inscriptions both from Dynasties 6 also indicate the earliest attested term of *dng* referring to that of a small man. Other Egyptian words for small men are also known like *d3g*,[686] *nmw*, and *ḥwꜥ*.[687] It would seem that being small qualified him for ritual performances in the dances of the god *ib3w nṯr*.[688] The evidence from the titles on the statues of dwarfs found in the Old Kingdom, and the representations on the walls of the mastabas distinguishing them from others of lower rank, indicate that they were personalities[689] in their own right, and had a high socio-economic status. Nevertheless the impression from their placements in the iconography often underlines their function as a human pet, because they are depicted as an attendant bearing personal attire, as a tenderer of animals, and as an entertainer (dancer, musician, or singer).[690] In the Middle Kingdom a change occurs and the dwarf comes to be associated with sexuality and fertility.[691]

Even when they occupy a secondary role, their status is enhanced by them being placed as close as possible to the tomb owner.

In the carrying-chair scenes, the dwarfs are either shown immediately behind the tomb owner, underneath his carrying-chair, on a separate register below the carrying-chair and even on a sub-register of their own.[692] This is the only case when variations in scale do not reflect the importance of the personages (excluding the tomb owner) in Egyptian art. The dwarf is recognised and accepted as a personage in his own right and is distinguished as such, e.g. by being named.[693]

In these positions, he is usually, but not always associated with leading either a dog and/or a monkey on a leash. This should not be taken as a menial task because the animals were usually the favourite pets of the tomb owner and possibly his family, accordingly it can be argued that looking after status enhancing 'animals' was indeed a privilege.

---

[678] Iversen, "The Canonical Tradition", in *The Legacy of Egypt*, ed. J. R. Harris, 58. See Schäfer, *Principles of Egyptian Art*, 326-34. Also see Robins, *Proportion and Style in Ancient Egyptian Art*, 64-69. She builds on and refines the Canon and Proportions in Egyptian Art as proposed by Iversen, and her critique is to be found on pages 38-61.

[679] Petrie and Griffith, *The Royal Tombs of The First Dynasty, Part I*, pl. 35, numbers 36 and 37. In addition they indicate that two dwarf skeletons were also found in the adjoining chambers "L" and "M" of the king's tomb.

[680] As in the tomb of: "*Nianchchnum and Chnumhotep*", pl. 60. Another earlier example is from Dunham and Simpson "*Merysankh III*", 1974: fig. 8, where a naked female dwarf is depicted.

[681] Lepsius, *Denkmäler aus Ägypten und Äthiopien*, pl. 36c.

[682] On favourite pets, see Brunner-Traut, "Lieblingstier", in *LÄ*, vol. 3, 1054-56.

[683] Dasen, *Dwarfs in Ancient Egypt and Greece*, 89.

[684] Borchardt, *Das Grabdenkmal des Königs Sáhu-re*, pl. 22, d, 9 for Bes-like features. For a description see the accompanying volume marked 'Text', 38-39.

[685] Dasen, *Dwarfs in Ancient Egypt and Greece*, 127. Seneb has 20 titles inscribed on his false door, among them - Overseer of the dwarfs in charge of linen, Great one of the litter, Overseer of the crew of *kz* ships, and Overseer of the *iwhw*. In another example from the tomb of Ty, a dwarf named Pepy is leading pet animals and is designated as Overseer

of the *iwHw* (the precise meaning of this title is not known but it could have something to do with animal tendering).

[686] Hannig, *Grosses Handwörterbuch*, 970.

[687] Hannig, *Ägyptisches Wörterbuch I*, 631 and 788 respectively.

[688] Faulkner, *The Ancient Egyptian Pyramid Texts*, p. 191, § 1189. "I am that pygmy of 'the dances of god' who diverts the god in front of his great throne".

[689] Hawass, "The Statue of the dwarf Perniakhw, recently discovered at Giza", *MDAIK*, (47), 160.

[690] Dasen, *Dwarfs in Ancient Egypt and Greece*, 109-34. Also see Junker, *Giza*, vol. 5, 8-11.

[691] Dasen, *Dwarfs in Ancient Egypt and Greece*, 140-42.

[692] Behind the tomb owner in the 3 tombs of: Ankhmahor, Kaemneferet, and Khnumeti.
Underneath the carrying-chair in the 6 tombs of: Ankhmare, Niankhkhnum (pl. 60), Mereruka (pl. 158), Nikawissi, Seshemnefer-Tjeti, and Waatetkhethor.
Separate register below the carrying-chair in 2 tombs of: Kagemni, and Meryteti (pl.47). On a sub-register in the tomb of: Itisen.

[693] Altenmüller and Moussa, *Das Grab des Nianchchnum und Chnumhotep, AV*, (21), 129, where the dwarf is named *Ḳd(w)n.s.*

In 12 carrying-chair motifs, dwarfs are present; 8 depict a dwarf leading an animal,[694] and 4 not leading an animal.[695]

Sometimes the dwarfs carry a small stick shaped like a spatula, which looks large in comparison to their physique, as in Mereruka. At other times, dwarfs escorting animals are shown carrying a large brachiomorphic shaped baton. In the tomb of Ty,[696] the 'dwarf' is one named Pepy, and is shown wielding a brachiomorphic stick, which is proportional to his size,[697] similar to the depiction in the tomb of Kaemnofret.[698] Carrying a stick in Egyptian art is normally surrounded with some sort of status and authority. While it may be that the physical stature of the dwarf required him to carry a stick, especially when tendering animals, nevertheless sticks themselves in Egyptian Art usually indicate a symbol of authority, and thus reflect the status of the person having such a symbol.

Four motifs provide further support for a personality of the dwarf. These motifs show the escorter as an adult man.[699] In four of these motifs, men in pointed kilts are doing the tendering of animals,[700] itself a symbol of status, and in the tomb of Ipy he even carries a rod of authority in his left hand. Dwarfs may appear either leading the procession as in the tomb of Ipy, or following it as in the tomb of Sabw. Usually they appear in the middle of the porters and so appear to divide the porters into two groups. Where this could not be accommodated, the procession train being presumably too long, the animal tenderer appears in another register as in the tomb of Itisen. One inference from this could be that the tendering of pet animals was an important task and one, which was worthy of being shown in an elite tomb.

Accordingly at least in this respect in the Old Kingdom, the dwarf was on a social par with other 'normal' human beings. Confirming this observation are 3 depictions of young boys performing the escorting roles,[701] if one is to accept the scene in Hetepniptah as one of this type. In another depiction a boy is pictured directly under the palanquin carrying a bag on his left shoulder with a basket in his right hand.[702] There is also one scene, in which part of the foot and the curved back of a hunchback is shown leading a monkey.[703]

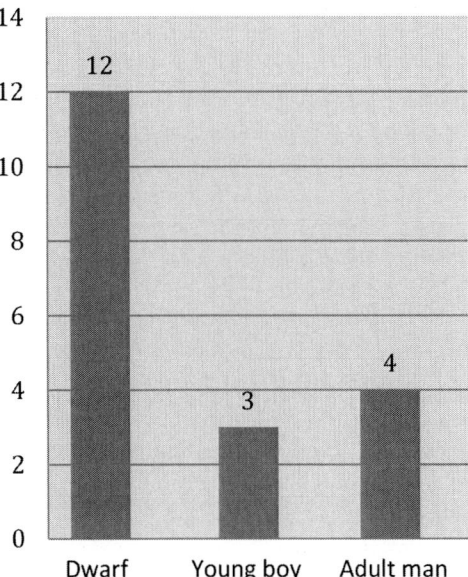

18 TOMBS OUT OF THE TOTAL POPULATION OF 37 (I.E. 49%) HAVE NO ANIMALS BEING ACTIVELY LED.

The life of dwarfs who were not part of an elite's retinue is not known, but it can be presumed that as they were a rarity, they had value, and that they would very likely have been part of an elite's status enhancing entourage, if the biography of Harkhuf, and the reference in the Pyramid texts (§1189) are any indications.[704] The equation of rarity and value was recognized early as observed in the entrance ramp to the tomb of Semerkhet, which was found saturated with perfumed oil to a depth of three feet. Petrie in his excavation report writes:

"Here the space was filled to three feet deep with sand saturated with ointment … hundredweights of it must have been poured out here" and that after nearly 5000 years the scent was "so strong … that it could be smelt over the entire tomb".[705]

This abundant use of rare products (oil being an imported luxury) and the corresponding elevation of status in its conspicuous use by royalty were it would appear, not lost on the elite. The dwarf in elite tombs may therefore represent both these aspirations. His use in the iconography may be likened to the use in modern state funerals of carrying the treasured possessions of the deceased in the cortège. See Chart 10 shows the presence of dwarfs and other escorts.

---

[694] In the 8 tombs of: Ankhmare, Ankhmahor, Kagemni, Kaemnofret, Mereruka (pl. 158), Nikauisesi, Seshemnefer-tjetti, and Waatetkhethor.
[695] In the 4 tombs of: Itisen, Khnumenti, Meryteti (pl. 47), and Niankhkhnum (pl. 60).
[696] Wild, *Le Tombeau de Ti: La Chapelle*, vol. II, pl. CXXVI. Although this example is not from a carrying-chair motif, nevertheless it is a scene in which a dwarf is shown escorting a monkey in the genre of a scene, which shows the retinue of an elite tomb owner.
[697] Épron et al., *Le Tombeau de Ti*, vol. I, pl. XVI.
[698] Simpson and Chapman, *The offering chapel of Kayemnofret*, fig. 17 (b), E. The South Wall.
[699] Adult men in the tombs of: Ankhmare, Hesi, and Itisen (here three men, each lead 2 dogs, a monkey and a baboon) and Sabw.
[700] In the tombs of: Ankhmare, Ipy, Itisen, and Sabw.
[701] In the 3 tombs of: Hetepniptah, Nefer-Khuwi and Ty (boy/dwarf is shown in a pointed kilt).
[702] In the tomb of: Nimaatre.
[703] In the tomb of: Waatetkhethor.

[704] Lichtheim, *Ancient Egyptian Literature*, vol. I, 27. "Hurry and bring with you this pigmy [dng] whom you brought from the land of the horizon-dwellers, live, hale, and healthy, for the dances of the god, to gladden the heart, to delight the heart of King Neferkare, who [may he] live[s] forever".
[705] Petrie and Griffith, *The Royal Tombs of The First Dynasty, Part I*, 14.

Animals

There are two types of animals found in the carrying-chair scenes: the dog - *ṯzm* and the monkey - *ky*[706]

Since pre-dynastic times, the dog appears on White Cross-lined pottery[707] and ivories[708] and later on in palettes as part of the hunting scene. Without going into detailed zoology, the dogs as seen on the various palettes,[709] fall into two defined categories: dogs with floppy rounded ears and a long, bushy, hanging tail, and dogs with pointed ears and a short curly tail. The former may be related to the hyena and belong to the species of

Lycaon Pictus. Their placement on the outer edges of the palettes, have lead researchers to suggest their role as keepers of order, and controller of things disorderly,[710] what Kemp calls the "containment of unrule in the universe",[711] possibly an ideological symbol in the early formation of the state.

The other type of species is the domesticated Egyptian dog, referred to as the *ṯzm*.

With the emergence of the ideology of the supreme king, representations of the *Lycaon Pictus* disappear, as the preservation of order over disorder is now the sole prerogative of the pharaoh.

The domesticated dog however continues in the representations, and one of the motifs in which he frequently appears, is that of the carrying-chair.

The existence of dogs in a human environment, where dogs are not used as food, makes a statement about their usefulness (hunting, companionship, guard-duties, etc.) in that society, as witnessed by the existence of a number of pre-dynastic animal burials.[712] Additionally because all the dogs in the carrying-chair motif have a collar, sometimes in addition a buckle, and a leash, the fact of differentiation of this breed, would imply social importance in that it is a pointer to a scarce resource, and one that has to be well looked after. Furthermore they are usually, but not always, tended to by humans who have a special status, e.g. dwarfs, and adults. The dogs also are near the tomb owner and have pride of place and are shown both free and being led, which hints at their domesticated nature.

These representations of dogs invoke various ideas as to their functionality and cultural symbolism: of hunting, of the breeding of specialized species, of forms of non-human companionship, of display of power and control over a non-human species etc., they also in addition point to access to areas of society and 'products', not readily available. By depicting these 'products' in the elite tombs, in the context of nearness to the tomb owner, they also become valuable pointers to a certain status, and to the fact of social inequality.

It may be that the dog's status as an elite symbol was a reflection from an earlier pre-dynastic period, when as part of royal iconography lions and dogs are equated as belonging to the royal domain.[713]

Moreover, since the connection of royalty and lions is unequivocal even before Dynasty 1 (Hunters palette), what we may be witnessing in these carrying-chair scenes is the encroachment by the elite on privileged symbols of strength and loyalty, which were at one time the domain of the chief/ruler, represented by the dog.

It would therefore seem that the dog was a preferred animal, and in this context the elite took on the habit of having pet dogs following the royal example (the king probably had dogs in daily attendance, both as guard dogs as well as hunting companions).

Probably symptomatic of the attitude of the Egyptian towards pet dogs, is a Middle Kingdom official who describes himself as "a dog that sleeps in the tent, a dog of the couch whom his mistress loves".[714]

The affection shown to pet dogs is also evidenced in the recorded names of dogs in the archeological finds, totaling some eighty. These names are not only terms of endearment e.g. (Abutiu), but refer to characteristics, which these dogs must have displayed, e.g. (Good Herdsman, Reliable, Brave One, North Wind, and Antelope). In the tomb of Nikauisesi all the three dogs under the carrying-chair are identified and named (Bai, Baq, and Idji).[715] Some were also buried in an appropriate manner; being provided with individual inscribed coffins and stelae.[716]

Deification of dogs is another type of evidence proving the importance of this animal. Three deities are known from very early on in the canine form: Wepwawet: the opener of the ways, Khentamentiu: foremost of the westerners, and Anubis: god of cemeteries and embalming.[717] All of them relate in some way to the hereafter and clearly point to

---

[706] Faulkner, *A concise dictionary of Middle Egyptian*, 308 and 285 respectively.

[707] Payne, *Catalogue of the Predynastic Egyptian collection in the Ashmolean Museum*, 422-24. In contrast to the African hunting dog, Lycaon Pictus has floppy ears and a long hanging tail.

[708] Gebel Tarif handle, Cairo Museum CG 14285 and the Davis comb, Metropolitan Museum, New York. 30. 8. 224. Also see Quibell, Green, and Petrie, *Hierakonpolis*, vol. l, pl. 12. no. 7.

[709] For a list of the palettes, see Fischer, "A fragment of Late Predynastic Egyptian relief from the Eastern Delta", *Artibus Asiae*, (21), 65.

[710] Baines, "Symbolic roles of canine figures on early monuments", *Archeo-Nil*, (3), 59.

[711] Kemp, *Ancient Egypt: Anatomy of a Civilization*, 92-98.

[712] Boessneck, *Die Tierwelt des alten Ägypten*, 23.

[713] Quibell, Green, and Petrie, *Hierakonpolis*, vol. 1, pl. 19. no. 6. and Quibell and Green, *Hierakonpolis*, vol. 2. pl. 66.

[714] Lange and Schäfer, *Grab-und Denksteine des Mittleren Reichs*, no. 20506, b, line 2ff.

[715] Kanawati, *The Teti Cemetery at Saqqara: The Tomb of Nikauisesi*, vol. 6, 44.

[716] Reisner, "The Dog which was honored by the King of Upper and Lower Egypt", *BMA*, (XXXIV), no. 204.

[717] Hart, *The Routledge dictionary of Egyptian gods and goddesses*. Also see DuQuesne, *The Jackal Divinities of Egypt*.

the dog having a preferred status, which the tomb owner aggregates for himself in the carrying-chair motifs, such that his desired elite image is broadcast and maintained.

Another animal seen in the carrying-chair motif is the monkey. Perhaps due to their playful nature, all monkeys in the procession train are depicted being led on a leash; there being one exception, in the tomb of Waatetkhethor. Here the monkey walks between two dogs. It may also be that apart from their other qualities, the dogs were also trained to keep the monkey in line.

It is clear that the dog was more popular than the monkey not because he appears in sixteen depictions as compared to the monkey's twelve[718] but because the scenes in which the dogs appear, depict them not only singly but also in multiples, on a leash or without, always with a flamboyant collar and sometimes named. The monkey in contrast always appears singly, apart from one exception,[719] is always on a leash or controlled by leading dogs and never named or especially collared; only a simple round band is apparent and no specific monkey burials are evident. An example from the tomb of Nikauisesi makes the distinction clear; here a monkey sitting on the head of the dwarf is shown together with three dogs and while the dogs (Bai, Baq, and Idji) and the dwarf (Iri) are all named, the monkey is not.

In an unusual scene in the tomb of Sabw, two young dogs,[720] and two monkeys are depicted being led by an adult holding a basket and a brush in the other hand. The puppies are however shown farthest away from the viewer; the focus seems to be on the monkeys, which is strange.

Another exceptional scene is that in the tomb of Hetepniptah, where the monkey is given favored status, being shown nearer to his master than the dog.

An analysis of the scenes indicates that there are ten scenes depicting both dogs and monkeys,[721] and six scenes, which depict dogs only.[722] Only two representations depict just a monkey; however both of these are fragments and thus are questionable.[723]

Chart 11 relates the motif with the animals.

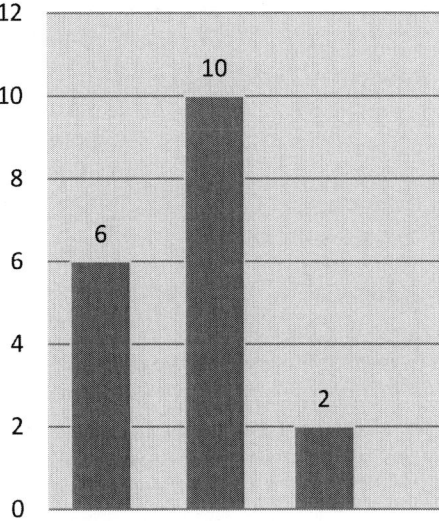

CHART 11: ANIMAL PLACEMENT

19 TOMBS (51%) OF THE TOTAL POPULATION OF 37 HAVE NO ANIMALS DEPICTED. THE ABOVE FIGURES DO NOT RELATE TO THE NUMBER OF INDIVIDUAL ANIMALS, BUT THE TOMBS IN WHICH THEY ARE DEPICTED.

All the monkeys are of the slender variety of the species *Cercopitheci*. One example of a baboon of the species *Papio Cynocephalus* being led by an adult is seen in the tomb of Itisen.

Considering their lower status, because they are never depicted on their own, or with an elaborate collar, or buried appropriately, their depiction in the carrying-chair motif can be seen as part of motif development. Another possible explanation may be that the monkeys' representation indicates the individuality of the tomb owner. The reality of his life and relationships is being used for the development of certain motifs and certain sub-motifs as a starting point for the development of an image, which encompasses complex ideas of the totality of the tomb owners reach in all earthly domains.

The monkey is clearly a pet animal, was imported, was more difficult to control 'en masse' and so has some rarity value. If however one takes into consideration ALL the scenes of the many monkeys shown on the sailing ship motifs, then this fact, together with it's purely domestic use and uncontrollability, would probably relate to a diminished value as compared to the dog.

The inclusion of the baboon in the carrying-chair motif is probably to its association with Thoth, who by Dynasty 1, is depicted as a baboon in a sitting posture. However this would then mean that there would be more baboons shown as compared to monkeys but there is ONLY 1 instance of a baboon being depicted.[724]

---

[718] Dogs in the tombs of: Ankhmare (1), Hesi (4), Ipy (1), Itisen (2), Imyery (1), Kagemni (2), Mereruka [pl. 158] (3), Nefer-Khuwi (2), Nikauisesi (3), Niankhkhnum [pl. 58] (1), Hetepniptah (1), Sabw (2), Senedjemib-inti (1), Seshemnefer-Tjeti (1), Ty (1) and Waatetkhethor (3). The dog count is indicated by the number between the rounded brackets. The monkeys are depicted in the tombs of: Ankhmahor, Ankhmare, Itisen, Kagemni, Kaemnofret, Mereruka [pl. 158], Nikauisesi, Hetepniptah, Sabw, Seshemnefer-Tjeti, Ty, and Waatetkhethor.
[719] In the tomb of Sabw, a pair of monkeys are shown being led.
[720] Houlihan, *The Animal World of the Pharaohs*, 76-77. A round head and pendant ears are the signs of a young dog and these are also seen in the tomb of Sabw.
[721] In the 10 tombs of: Ankhmare, Itisen, Hetepniptah, Kagemni, Mereruka (pl.158), Nikauisesi, Sabw, Seshemnefer-Tjeti, Ty and Waatetkhethor.
[722] In the 6 tombs of: Ipy, Iymery, Nefer-Khuwi, Niankhkhnum (pl. 58) Senedjemib-Inti and Hesi.
[723] In the 2 tombs of: Kaemnofret and Ankhmahor (fragment).

---

[724] In the tomb of Itisen, the procession of animals is being led by two dogs, followed by a monkey and then a baboon.

The placement of the animals also reveals that most of the time the animals are placed underneath the carrying-chair, there being twelve examples of dogs[725] and eight examples of monkeys[726] plus a sole example of a baboon in the procession.[727] Apart from providing an aesthetically pleasing view, it serves to show the dominance and control of the tomb owner and thus his social prestige.

In two cases the dogs are depicted behind the procession and in three cases the monkeys[728] are behind. As an artistic ploy it is understandable and in keeping with the focus on the occupant of the palanquin. However in three cases,[729] the animals (two cases of dogs and one of a monkey) are placed in front of the tomb owner, which is unusual in that it would detract from the status of the owner. However the cases can be explained. In all these cases, the way the picture is composed reveals that the artist understood the needs of decorum. The composition in the tomb of Ankhmare shows a man with a pointed kilt holding a graceful monkey on a separate sub-register, which appears to be in front of the procession. The most probable explanation for this is the lack of space in depicting a full processional train, and it may well be that this is part of the rear procession. Validating this is the sandal bearer who is shown immediately above in a separate sub-register (usually they are shown walking behind the procession). In any event even if this was an error, which is highly doubtful, it is somewhat corrected by showing the dignity of the man (leading the monkey), who wears a pointed kilt, while at the same time doing a gesture of reverence.

In the tomb of Niankhkhnum, a man in a pointed kilt identified as [ḥm kꜣ iri ꜥnwt ḥ [nw] – funerary priest and manicurist Khenu is leading the pet dog who is both elaborately collared and named ḥknn. In the tomb of Ipy, the dog is also part of the front procession, bounded on either side by the imposing figures of two men holding rods of authority, and does not detract from the main actor. It is this single factor, which is elementary in deciding questions of decorum in the foregoing three unusual representations. However in no carrying-chair motif are the animals placed above the tomb owner.

Charts 12 (I) and (II) indicate that the placement of animals underneath the carrying-chair was the usual practice, and that decorum required that no animals be placed in a position that would detract from the social position of the tomb owner. Specifically this chart focuses only on the placement of the animals' vis-à-vis the tomb owner, and is

CHART 12 (I): DOG PLACEMENT

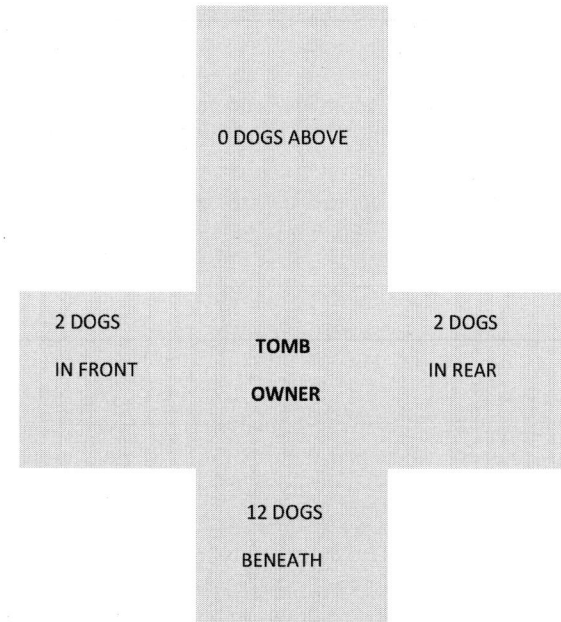

CHART 12 (II): MONKEY PLACEMENT

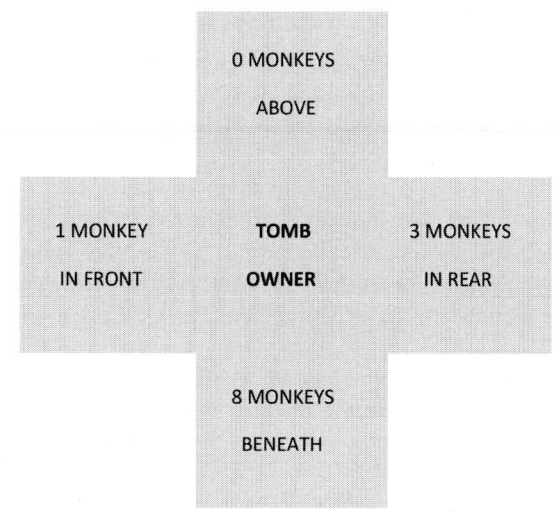

THE NUMBERS ABOVE REFER TO THE NUMBER OF CASES, WHERE THE ANIMALS HAVE A SPECIFIC POSITION RELATIVE TO THE TOMB OWNER BUT NOT TO THE NUMBER OF ACTUAL ANIMALS IN EACH TOMB.

CHARTS 12 (I) AND (II) SHOW ANIMAL PLACEMENT FROM 18 TOMBS (I.E. IN 49% OF THE TOTAL 37 TOMBS EXAMINED)

not to be understood as showing the number of individual animals.

Supervisor(s)

This section will describe all the people, who do not carry the palanquin nor escort animals but are seen in the vicinity of the carrying-chair as part of the procession, or in front of an animal on which there is a palanquin. For ease of reference, these are men known from the literature as 1) supervisors or 2) coordinators; however, the distinction is purely arbitrary as no exact functional difference is attested. Their apparel does not usually differ much from

---

[725] In the 12 tombs of: Ankhmare, Hetepniptah, Itisen, Iymery, Kagemni, Mereruka (pl. 158), Nikauisesi, Nefer-Khuwi, Senedjemib-Inti, Seshemnefer-Tjeti, Ty, and Watethathor.

[726] In the 8 tombs of: Itisen, Kagemni, Mereruka (Fig. 158), Hetepniptah, Nikauisesi, Seshemnefer-Tjeti, Ty, and Waatetkhethor.

[727] In the tomb of: Itisen.

[728] The dogs are so shown in the tombs of: Hesi and Sabw, and the monkeys are so depicted in the tombs of: Ankhmahor, Kaemnofret, and Sabw.

[729] In the 3 tombs of: Ankhmare (monkey), Ipy, and Niankhkhnum (dog) (pl. 60).

that of the porters. However the type of kilt being worn in four carrying-chair scenes may infer a higher status.[730]

The supervisors are shown either in the front, at the rear or both at the front and rear of the procession; an exception being that in the tomb of Kagemni, where the supervisor carrying a rope sling on his right shoulder is represented in the middle of the two groups of porters.[731] Supervisors are depicted in a variety of ways:

1. With one arm lightly resting on the carrying pole, and the other arm holding a rope sling, a staff, or a piece of cloth.
2. As the lead man appropriately dressed and carrying a rod of authority.
3. Immediately behind the palanquin with one arm resting on the back of the chair.

The distinguishing feature would seem to be, that while he may have an arm on the carrying pole, he is never shown doing any actual carrying. It is admitted that persons depicted as such in the representations may also have other functions. However, it is well known that persons with authority are required for directional movement involving many persons; a modern day example would be the role of the major domus in military parades.

Supervisors are frequently described in the iconography as having special status, e.g. the inscription in the tomb of Ptahshepses, where the supervisor is addressed as the "favoured one"- ḥr: ḥr(y) ḥs(wt) translated as "he who is under the favour". This caption is addressed to the man who is depicted as holding the rope sling. His ostensible function was to 'lead' the porters, ensure that the correct pace was set, and supervise the journey as befitted the customary requirements of the elite, which both included comfort and a dignified pace. If some twenty porters are moving in uncoordinated and different rhythms, the palanquin will shake incessantly and the journey will be an uncomfortable one for all parties concerned.

Whether the supervisor was one of the porters who had been given a supervisory role, e.g. foreman, is difficult to say from the iconography. Certainly from the inscription and depiction in the tomb of Ptahshepses, he probably was one of them because he is shown wearing the same type of clothing (loincloth). However he could be manifesting any of the following:

- Providing a comfortable journey for the tomb owner.[732]
- Showing his master that the favour he had been given as head of the procession was indeed earned by enduring the taunts of the other porters.[733]

- Using the sling for signaling as well as maybe enforcing discipline[734] and forcing a path, in much the same way as the porters with batons could do through the crowded narrow ways, (however, apart from the punishment scenes there are no scenes which show the function of these batons).
- Most depictions of supervisors show them wearing a pointed kilt but there are a few in which he appears in a short kilt. However in three representations he is shown wearing the same attire as the porters, namely a loincloth. These are in 3 important tombs, that of Mereruka (pl. 53b), Seshemnefer-Tjetti, and Ptahshepses, which are in Saqqara, Giza, and Abu-Sir respectively, and which date from late Dynasty 5 to mid-Dynasty 6; no explanation as to why this occurs can be made.

Supervisors are present in at least 16 representations (43%) of the known tombs.[735] In most of the motifs they carry a sling but they may also carry a stick/rod.

If one accepts that the controlling person may also be represented in sub-registers then this number would increase. Of course it may well be that the lead porter was also the co-coordinator as depicted in the tomb of Seankhuiptah; in which case the value of the term 'supervisor' might be somewhat diminished but not the implications for social status vis- à- vis the tomb owner.

Subsidiary Attendants Carrying Tomb owner's Belongings

Subsidiary attendants are shown carrying various belongings, presumably of the tomb owner as part of the procession, who may wear distinctive apparel. They may be depicted under the carrying-chair (both in front of and behind) or near it in a sub-register, and may be specifically identified and described. The men may appear in any of the following ways:

- Carrying the belongings of the tomb owner.
- Depicted as part of the procession but not carrying anything.
- Not including dwarfs / hunchbacks[736]/ young boys.

When these men are shown immediately under the carrying-chair, the implication is that they are part of the close attendants or close members of the tomb owner's household/family.

Excluded are the porters of the chair, sunshade carriers, escorts of animals, and supervisors (who were dealt with above) and the tomb owner (who will be dealt with soon).

---

[730] In Ipy, Kagemni, and Sabw - the supervisor is wearing a pointed kilt, while in Nikauisesi he wears a flapped kilt.

[731] Bissing, Die Mastaba des Gem-ni-kai, vol. 1, pl. 22.

[732] Vandier, Manuel d'archéologie égyptienne, vol. IV, 346.

[733] Verner, Abusir-I: The Mastaba of Ptahshepses, 99."Look well forward. You quiet down, you favoured one».

[734] Boreux, Études de nautique égyptienne, 413.

[735] In the tombs of : Khnumhotep (pl. 43), Niankhkhnum (pl. 42 and 58), Hesi, Khuwer, Inisnfrw-ishtef, Ipy, Itisen, Iymery*, Kagemni*, Mereruka* (pl. 53b), Meryteti (pl. 47), Nikauisesi*, Ptahshepses*, Seankhuiptah*, Ty, and Seshemnefer-Tjetti*.
* An asterisk indicates a rope sling is present, whereas all the others have only sticks/rods as markers of authority.

[736] Personal communication: A. M. Roth, (New York University), 2010.

These subsidiary persons present a problem.

If one accepts that a depiction of the whole procession in a profile view would take up many walls, then one must also accept that parts of the procession may be shown in different registers. Additionally the total number of people, who are shown catering to the needs of the tomb owner, would be an indication of his status and power and the community's social duties towards him.

In terms of this logic, all these other persons would then have to be ranked and then added together to indicate any emerging patterns, taking into account all available ranking indications and their position in front, behind or underneath the tomb owner or in the various sub-registers. However the weight given to each of these items would have to be different, precisely because of the observed differences in status and rank that they may portray, e.g. title, family relationship, appearance, etc. Herein lies the difficulty, because this is something, which is difficult to measure objectively: what for example is the difference between two overseers - one of the house and one of linen? How is one to rate the different relationships of the tomb owner towards his parents, wife, eldest son, other sons and daughters, closest colleagues, etc? A good example of this difficulty is the carrying-chair representation in the tomb of Iymery.[737] The person in the carrying-chair is not the tomb owner but his father identified as Shepseskafankh. The register is divided such that the procession train appears below the carrying-chair as well as on a sub register behind, under, and in front of Shepseskafankh.

The others carrying the various belongings appear behind (a man carrying a curved rod and sack across his shoulders) and below the carrying-chair (two men, one carrying a flywhisk, a bucket and ladle, the other carrying a basket and a pair of sandals); both these men wear a flapped short kilt and are identified as Ny-ankh-Re and Ny-ptah respectively).

His three sons are depicted facing the carrying-chair in differing scale - beginning with the eldest described as "his eldest son, his beloved, Acquaintance [of the king Iymery]", his other son, described as "the scribe Shepeskaf-ankh the younger", and presumably his youngest son described as "the scribe". They are followed by a man described as his brother identified as Neb-meny. All of them wear pointed kilts and have short "wigs", except for the eldest son (who happens to be Iymery and is drawn in large scale) and is shown wearing a shoulder length wig and a broad collar. Additionally, they all make formal gestures of reverence, which "probably had social significance" and the one made by the brother has been stated to be a rare occurrence.[738]

Ranking therefore is impossible and all one can say is that the nearness to Shepseskafankh and scale of drawing would favour Iymery. However this cannot be followed for the other persons described who are all drawn on the same smaller scale. Are we to rank the sandal carrier ahead of the one carrying the flywhisk? Again if a person is identified more than once in the tomb, is he more important than someone who is only mentioned once but has a higher title? These problems cannot be solved; therefore a possible solution is to treat all persons carrying the tomb owner's belongings irrespective of their being identified or not, on an equal footing. Persons drawn on a larger scale and wearing status goods will be accorded differential treatment.

From the iconography it appears that the carriage of the belongings of the tomb owner and freestanding personnel evidencing a variety of gestures are a standard depiction of the carrying-chair motif and is found in the majority of the scenes.[739]

It is assumed that the items being carried were required for the comfort of the tomb owner. These include the ewer and basin (Sawtj - which constituted the equipment for everyday hand washing during the Old Kingdom),[740] a wood chest/box/casket (commonly used for the storage of linen, jewellery, cosmetics and other similar items),[741] a sack for his clothes, a rod, throw stick, and sandals. Junker points out that attendants carrying sandals, staff of authority, basket plus brush and sack for clothes is a distinctive feature of the carrying-chair motif, and that men carrying the tomb owner's belongings are never followed by men bearing food and meat, which has an altogether different connotation.[742]

Only 8 tombs depict specific sandal bearers as part of the carriage of goods sub-motif[743] and indeed the sandals can be displayed even where the tomb owner is depicted wearing sandals,[744] as in the tomb of Niankhkhnum and Khnumhotep. Evidence of their use is found as early as Dynasty 1 at Saqqara.[745] The only fact with relative certainty is that there is no scene, which only depicts a lone sandal carrier as part of the carrying-chair procession, and that carriage of goods judging by its frequency, is a definite part of the carrying-chair motif.

The positioning of those that are both freestanding and making gestures of reverence towards the tomb owner will now be considered.

---

[737] Weeks, *Mastabas of Cemetry G 6000*, ed. P. Der Manuelian and W. K. Simpson, vol. 5, fig. 32.

[738] Ibid. 39.

[739] In the tombs of: Ankhmare, Ankhmahor, Khnumhotep (fig. 43), Hetepniptah, Hesi, Inisnfrw-ishtef, Ipy, Itisen, Iymery, Kagemni, Kaemnofret, Khuwer, Khnumenti, Mereruka (fig. 14 and 158), Meryteti (fig. 47), Nefer-Khuwi, Nikauisesi, Niankhkhnum (fig. 42 and 60), Nimaatre, Ptahshepses, Qar, Sabw, Seankhuiptah, Seneb, Senedjemib-inti, Seshemnefer-Tjeti, Ty, and Waatetkhethor.

[740] Arnold, "Reinigungsgefässe", in *LÄ,* vol. 5, 213-30.

[741] Altenmüller, *Die Wanddarstellungen im Grab des Mehu in Saqqara, AV,* (42), pl. 98.2.

[742] Junker, *Giza,* vol. 5, 84.

[743] In the tombs of: Ankhmare, Khnumhotep (pl. 43), Hesi, Iymery, Khnumenti, Niankhkhnum (pl. 42), Ptahshepses and Ty.

[744] Sandal bearers are depicted as symbols of royal authority as far back as the Narmer Palette, where one is labelled a "servant of the ruler". The implication is both a religious and a symbolic one as evidenced from the stela erected by Khaskehmwi at Hierakonpolis. He describes himself as an "effective sandal against the hill-countries". Since then, they feature prominently as part of the depiction of a pharaoh. Archaeological evidence pointing to the take up by the elite of this custom, is then of little surprise.

[745] Emery, *Archaic Egypt,* 233, fig. 138.

Gestures of reverence could be offering thanks, or a public display of goodwill towards the tomb owner. In Nimaatre's tomb in front of his palanquin, are three men, all wearing pointed kilts, one is in the act of handing something (a scroll?) to the tomb owner and behind the tomb owner is another man in a pointed kilt. All the others are in a posture of a gesture, which Roth suggests is an act, which confirmed the payment, the tomb owner made to the craftsmen[746] for work done on his tomb.

The positioning of these 'other persons' does not follow any strict pattern; they are always represented such that they appear to surround the carrying-chair in front, behind or below the palanquin procession but never above. A modern analogy would be the security services surrounding politicians and celebrities. By analogy therefore, the appearance of these other persons around the central figure of the tomb owner, could be a symbol, which provides information about the tomb owner in socio-cultural terms. This also reinforces the view that all these other persons carrying the tomb owner's belongings, irrespective of where they occur in relation to the carrying-chair, should not be treated separately but as part of the carrying-chair motif. Accordingly it has been decided to include all those men, irrespective of their particular placement in the context of the carrying-chair motif. The justification being that a motif in a tomb is an expression of varied processes, which are seldom transparent but which in the end result in an autonomous depiction - one which contains everything necessary for it to be recognized as a specific motif and a repository of information of cultural value.

Moreover, one way of defining the status of the tomb owner is by depicting subsidiary figures having various attributes of stable well-known identities, which then serve as a marker against which the tomb owner's own status can be defined – a kind of comparing of socially significant yet hierarchically based elite cultural vocabulary.[747] Further any particular pattern in the placement of these subsidiary figures will also influence both their position and that of the tomb owner. From the data[748] it became clear that they appear equally both behind and in front of the carrying-chair and in a minority of cases they appear below it too. However they never appear above the occupant of the carrying-chair. It is best to consider these other persons as appearing in all areas surrounding the tomb owner because they are part of the carrying-chair processional train, the very existence of which serves to exhibit the discretionary power and control which the tomb owner had over a certain number of persons in his household, reflecting his social position.

Chart 13 summarizes the data.

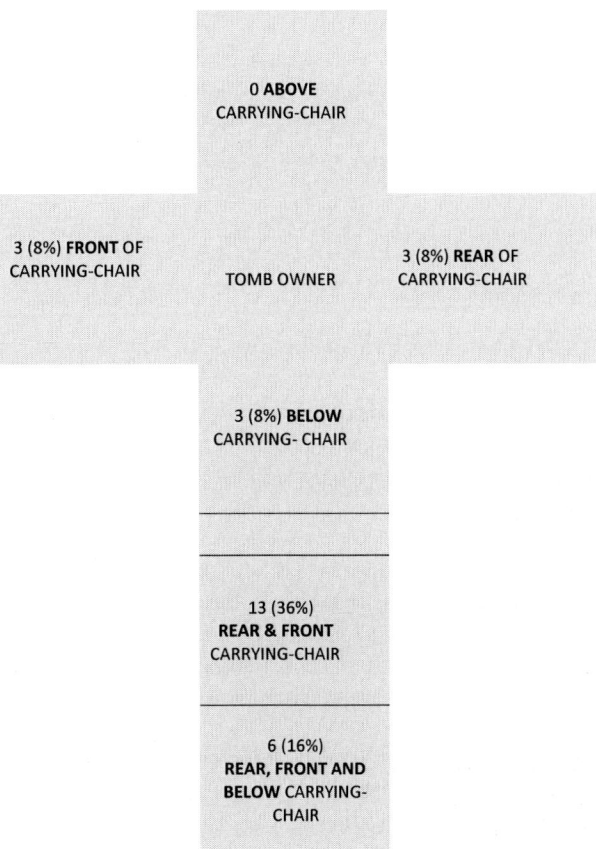

CHART 13: ATTENDANT PLACEMENT BY TOMBS

0 **ABOVE** CARRYING-CHAIR

3 (8%) **FRONT** OF CARRYING-CHAIR

TOMB OWNER

3 (8%) **REAR** OF CARRYING-CHAIR

3 (8%) **BELOW** CARRYING-CHAIR

13 (36%) **REAR & FRONT** CARRYING-CHAIR

6 (16%) **REAR, FRONT AND BELOW** CARRYING-CHAIR

THE NUMBERS REFER TO THE NUMBER OF TOMBS, WHERE THE ATTENDANTS HAVE A SPECIFIC POSITION RELATIVE TO THE TOMB OWNER BUT NOT TO THE NUMBER OF ACTUAL ATTENDANTS IN EACH TOMB. DWARFS ARE EXCLUDED.
CHART 13 SHOWS ATTENDANT PLACEMENT FROM 28 TOMBS (I.E. IN 76% OF THE TOTAL 37 TOMBS EXAMINED).

Attendants' Clothing

The clothing too of these predominantly male persons (females in the case of Waatetkhethor) and any other relevant markers, is certainly a pointer of their status. In all cases they are shown either wearing a pointed kilt or a short kilt and apart from 2 exceptions (in the tomb of Seshemnefer.Tjetti and Khnumenti) they are never depicted wearing a loincloth. These two exceptions need an explanation.

In the tomb of Seshemnefer.Tjetti, a man in a loincloth is represented in a sub-register. He holds a staff curved at the end and the other hand is holding what looks very much like a rope sling used by the supervisors. The position of the supervisor in a separate sub-register would

---

[746] Roth, "The practical economies of tomb building in the Old Kingdom," 230.
[747] Walsem seems to imply that the individual's position in society is also measured against a pre-existing cultural vocabulary, his ability to communicate with the living, the parameters of funerary culture and decorum. See Walsem, *Iconography of Old Kingdom elite tombs*, 11-12.
[748] In the tombs of: Ankhmahor (B), Ankhmare (RF), Khnumhotep (fig. 43- RF), Niankhkhnum (pl. 42 and 60- RF), Hesi (RF), Khuwer (RF), Inisnfrw-ishtef (F), Ipy (RF), Itisen (RFB), Iymery (RF), Kagemni (RF), Kaemnofret (R), Khnumenti (RF), Mereruka (pl. 158- RFB), Meryteti (pl. 47 and 48- RF), Nefer-Khuwi (RF), Nikauisesi (F), Nimaatre (RF), Hetepniptah (B), Ptahshepses (R), Qar (RFB), Sabw (RFB), Seankhuiptah (F), Seneb (B), Senedjemib-inti (RF), Seshemnefer-tjetti (R), Ty (RFB) and Waatetkhethor (RFB).
Meanings (Quantity): R = Rear of carrying-chair = (3); F = Front = (3); B = Below = (3); RF = (13) and RFB = (6).

be incompatible with his function of co-coordinating the train of porters. Perhaps the compressed nature of the scene required him to be depicted in a sub-register, which in actual terms should be with the porters and so should not be recognized as an 'other escort'.

In the tomb of Khnumenti, 7 men in 3 separate sub-registers are shown behind the palanquin. Six of them wear a loincloth and only one wears a pointed kilt but they are all carrying articles, which appear to be the belongings of the tomb owner, e.g. sandals, head-rests, walking stick, etc. already encountered in the other tombs. In addition there is a nude dwarf carrying a box on his head and a basket in his right hand.

Appearing in front of the tomb owner is part of a man wearing a pointed kilt and presenting him with a scroll and a person presenting him with a lapwing (maybe his son).

The deliberate nature of the attire of only one of the attendants, points to a distinction being made in the composition of the processional train, but it is difficult to justify why the other carriers are wearing loincloths, when in all the other tombs the pointed kilts dominate the scene and are the preferred clothing as in Chart 14.

Apart from identifying the predominant type of clothing and position of the attendants, another way of establishing a pattern would be to equate the tombs, to the type of attendant - mainly by initially ranking them into family and non-family and equating the clothes they wear.

Twenty-eight tombs depict attendants.[749] In 7 of these tombs, 'his son' is identified. Where sons and attendants appear together, both categories are always shown wearing a pointed kilt, with two exceptions in the tombs of Kagemni and Ty, where short kilts are shown being worn.

Of the 28 tombs where clothing was identified, there were:

17 with attendants wearing pointed kilts,
12 with of attendants wearing short kilts,
1 with females wearing sheath dresses.[750]

A clear majority seems to favour the pointed kilt; see Chart 14 which provides a detailed breakdown.

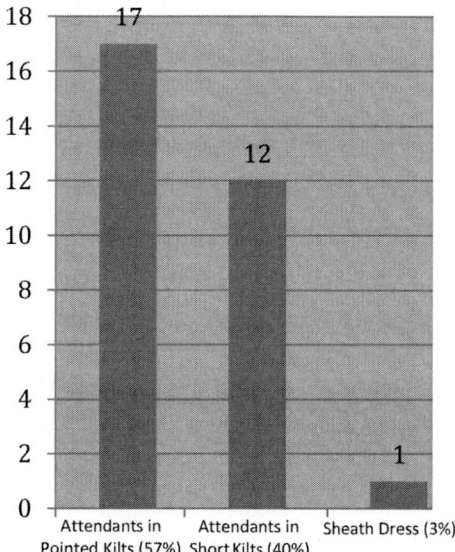

CHART 14: MAIN CLOTHING OF ATTENDANTS

* CHART 14 RELATES TO 28 TOMBS WITH ATTENDANTS (76% OF THE TOTAL 37 TOMBS EXAMINED). NINE TOMBS (I.E. 24%) DEPICT NO ATTENDANTS. THE NUMBERS REFER TO THE NUMBER OF CASES IN WHICH ATTENDANTS WEAR A PARTICULAR TYPE OF CLOTHING BUT NOT TO THE NUMBER OF ACTUAL ATTENDANTS IN EACH TOMB. THESE NUMBERS SHOULD NOT BE ADDED BECAUSE OF DUPLICATION IN CLOTHING ACROSS THE TOMBS.

7.5 Tomb-Owner

The central focus in Egyptian funerary art is always on the tomb owner and this is not different in the carrying-chair motif, where certain of his attributes are highlighted in various ways, e.g. by:

- Occupancy (number of occupants of the carrying-chair)
- Posture (way he sits in the carrying-chair)
- His attire
- His body adornments
- Objects he displays in his hands
- Objects handed to him

These attributes will now be discussed.

Occupancy

The tomb owner the focus of attention always occupies the carrying-chair, and therefore in keeping with his social position he is generally the sole occupant.

There are however 3 exceptions:

1. In the complex of Mereruka he is shown together with his son Meryteti in ONE carrying-chair.[751]

---

[749] In the tombs of: Ankhmare*, Ankhmahor, Khnumhotep (pl. 43), Hetepniptah, Hesi, Inisnfrw-ishtef, Ipy, Itisen, Iymery*, Kagemni*, Kaemnofret, Khuwer, Khnumenti, Mereruka (pls. 14 and 158*), Meryteti (pl. 47), Nefer-Khuwi*, Nikauisesi, Niankhkhnum (pls. 42 and 60), Nimaatre, Ptahshepses*, Qar, Sabw, Seankhuiptah, Seneb, Senedjemib-inti, Seshemnefer-Tjeti, Ty,* and Waatetkhethor.
* Asterisks indicate the 7 tombs, which also depict a son as an attendant.
[750] Attendants in Pointed Kilts in 17 tombs: Ankhmare, Hetepniptah, Insneferweshtef, Ipy, Itisen, Kagemni, Khnumenti, Mereruka (pl. 158), Meryteti (pl. 47), Nefer-Khuwi, Niankhkhnum, Nimaatre, Ptahshepses (pl. 60), Qar, Sabw, Senedjemib-Inti, and Seankhuiptah. Attendants in Short Kilts in 12 tombs of: Khnumhotep (pl. 43), Hesi, Ipy, Kagemni, Kaemnofret, Khuwer, Niankhkhnum (pl. 42), Nikauisesi, Qar, Seneb, Ty, and Waatetkhethor. Attendants in Sheath Dresses in 1 tomb of: Waatetkhethor.
[751] Wreszinski, *Atlas zur ägyptischen Kulturgeschichte* . He titles the

Kanawati regards the double occupancy as "an attempt to indicate Mereruka's wish to assign the chapel to Meryteti" which would explain why on the adjoining North wall, Meryteti is depicted as a child with the side lock of youth in a carrying-chair, with his mother Waatetkhethor. Another explanation may lie in the individuality of the scene. This scene is never found anywhere else. It may be that the occupants are trying to relay a message that their eldest beloved son is their undisputed heir - a sort of a testament much like the presentation of the heir by medieval European aristocracy.

2. Also in the same complex, Mereruka's, son Meryteti is shown with his mother Waatetkhethor in the SAME carrying-chair..[752]

3. In the tomb of Iymery, the tomb owner's father (Shepseskafankh) is depicted in the carrying chair. This may relate to filial affection similar to that seen in the rock tomb of Djau, where Djau asserts that although he could have built a tomb for himself he desired to be buried near his father in the same tomb, so that he could "see him everyday".[753] Possible explanations are that two massive tombs would have been very costly or that this could be the expression of individuality by these tomb owners wishing to consolidate their position as the heir.[754] In both tombs the sons are depicted modestly, while the father is given pride of place and adornments. In Iymery the eldest son is shown standing in a slightly bowed posture facing his father, who is being carried in a palanquin; while in Djau, the son depicting a lector priest band is shown behind his father, who is adorned in a panther skin, even though the father did not or could not provide a tomb for himself.[755]

Because the centre of focus is always the tomb owner, all these instances are quite unusual and never appear in any other carrying-chair scene.

Posture

The posture of the tomb owner reveals that the majority (58%) favoured the squatting position;[756] as can be seen in Chart 15.

CHART 15: TOMB OWNER'S POSTURE

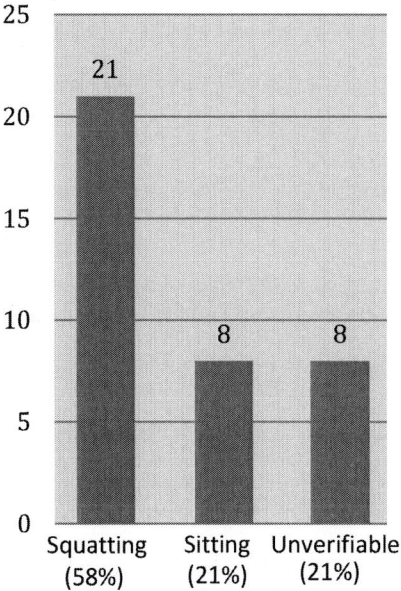

The squatting position is one in which the buttock and the soles of the feet are at the same level. At least from Dynasty 5 onwards, the form of chair evolves to a type, which has high back and arms and a low platform, but without legs: the high back and arms providing an anchor for holding onto during locomotion. The low platform which is in fact the floor of the carrying-chair also provides stability to the occupant, who has to 'sit' either with legs drawn up or in a kneeling position, both of which postures are part of the squatting position.[757]

Indeed it makes sense to be in the squatting posture because when one is being carried in a procession, it would not be in keeping with the status, rank or decorum to be transported other than in an pre-ordained and accepted manner. The squatting position may have been the equivalent of a valuable object of display.

May be one is witnessing artistic influence here because it is easier and more effective to display one compact unit rather than a not so compact one, which would be the case of a sitting display. The sitting position is that seen in the Nefermaat type of chair, the oldest example of its kind. Nefermaat[758] is depicted sitting in an upright position, with his buttock higher than the soles of his feet and with his legs touching the bottom of the chair frame. Significantly, he is shown being carried at hip level to reduce the risk of top heaviness. The squatting position is a refinement of this position because it enables a smoother carrying movement.

---

scene as "Der Herr und die Frau in der Sänfte" but Kanawati seems to think that it is Mereruka with his son Meryteti because of the remains of the kilts (see Kanawati, *Mereruka and his family: the tomb of Meryteti*, 28. Probably Kanawati is correct because there are no known carrying-chair scenes depicting the tomb owner and his wife.

[752] Ibid. pl. 11. Meryteti is shown wearing an amulet, a youth lock of hair and holds a lettuce in his right hand and a flying bird (toy) in the other hand. What is also unusual is that although he is depicted as a boy, he is shown wearing the full long kilt.

[753] Davies, *The rock tombs of Deir el Gebrâwi*, vol. II, pl. 7.

[754] It would appear that burial of a parent by the eldest son was a precondition of recognition as rightful heir. See Helck, *Wirtschaftsgeschichte des Alten Ägypten im 3. und 2. Jahrtausend vor Chr*, 76-77.

[755] Davies, *The rock tombs of Deir el Gebrâwi*, vol. ll, 35-38.

[756] Squatting in 21 tombs of: Ankhmahor, Ankhmare, Khnumhotep (pl. 43), Idu, Itisen, Kagemni, Khuwer, Mereruka (pl. 158), Meryteti (pls. 47 and 48), Methethi, Nefer-Khuwi, Niankhkhnum (pls. 42 and 60), Nikauisesi, Nimaatre, Perneb, Ptahhotep II, Ptahshepses, Qar, Seneb, Seshemnefer-Tjetti, and Ty.

Sitting in 8 tombs of: Ipy, Kaemnofret, Khnumenti, Nefermaat, Sabw, Senedjemib-inti, Seshemnefer, and Waatetkhethor

Unverifiable in 8 tombs of: Hetepniptah, Hesi, Insneferishtef, Iymery, Merwtetiseneb, Pepydjedi, Rashepses, and Seankhuiptah.

[757] Lepsius, *Denkmäler aus Ägypten und Äthiopien*, pls. 42, 47, 52, 56, 57, 61 and 74 (c).

[758] Petrie, *Medum*, pl. 21. Also see Harpur and Scremin, *The tombs of Nefermaat and Rahotep at Maidum*, 55-76.

A

FIG. 7: CLEARLY DEPICTS THE SHEATH DRESS AS WELL AS THE SHORTENED VERSION OF THE POINTED KILT. FROM THE STELA OF HETEPNEB (PRIVATE COLLECTION BASLE)

B

C

FIG. 8: SHOWS TWO MEN, AN ELITE AND AN OFFERING BEARER IN SHORT KILTS. THE ELITE (AKHETHETEP) WITH SCEPTER, AND STAFF IN SHORT KILT IS FROM COLLECTION KOFLER-TRUNIGER, LUZERN. THE OFFERING BEARER IN SHORT KILT IS FROM COLLECTION DR. E. BOROWSKI, BASLE. (*CATALOGUE DES STÈLES, PEINTURE ET RELIEFS ÉGYPTIENS DE L'ANCIEN EMPIRE ET DE LA PREMIÈRE PÉRIODE INTERMÉDIAIRE*, PARIS 1990)

be heavy enough to weigh down his kilt and as such it could have been either of wood, copper or stone. While its depiction may be artistic license it could also indicate individuality in having access to a privileged object whose use was associated with another status object, i.e. the long kilt.

Attire

Apart from any other considerations of the generics, both the sitting and the squatting postures could have an effect on the attire of the occupant. Where the rear and feet of the occupant are at the same level as the platform of the chair, practical reasons would dictate the long skirt as a preferred mode of dress. However in the case of the sitting position, where the feet are below that of the seat, the pointed kilt or short kilt could also come into question.[760]

The common clothing of the Egyptian male was the short kilt, a rectangular piece of fabric held up by cords or a cloth belt and wrapped tightly around the waist. The front of the kilt was loose enough to permit the legs to move freely.

A version of this short kilt was a stiffly starched front that stood out in the form as an inverted "v", which would have made any sort of physical labour impossible, which is referred to as the pointed kilt. Perhaps its main function-was to distinguish the wearer with enhanced and exaggerated masculinity or as one who did not have to do physical labour.

A similar aspiration may have led to the adoption of the long skirt style, which came down below the knee but was otherwise similar to the pointed kilt and was even more impractical for manual work. I will refer to this as the long kilt.

FIG. 9: IS FROM A FALSE DOOR DEPICTING THE TWO VERSIONS OF THE POINTED KILT: THE ONE ENDING JUST ABOVE THE KNEE AND THE OTHER BELOW THE KNEE FROM JUNKER, *GIZA*. VOL. 8, FIG. 104

As far as females were concerned, the common attire was a sheath held up by shoulder straps. It enveloped the body rising to just under the breasts. In some cases wider straps that cover the breasts completely replace this.

Representations of the various types of clothing are amply demonstrated in the iconography. The five pictures (A-E) shown are examples from actual finds in the Old Kingdom, which depict the attire mentioned above,[761] and so can be taken as evidence of their use. Just because these are depicted in the funerary context does not mean that these were not worn on other ceremonial occasions during the life of the tomb-owner.

All of the above range of attire can be seen worn by the occupants of the carrying-chair. Apart from the primary utilitarian purpose, one would expect the Egyptian craftsman to produce something in which there would be some relationship between the need for display, the need for practicality and the need for accuracy and realism.

Additionally the squatting mode of transportation would not only imply order and social position but would also make the desired impact of a dignified pose and authority on all concerned. The majority of squatting scenes depict the tomb owner with both feet flat on the base of the extension.

However in the tombs of Inisnfrw-ishtef, Itisen, Kagemni, and Nikauisesi, the nearer foot is shown flat while the farther foot rests on its heel on the extension. In between these feet is a round cylindrical object, clearly seen in the tomb of Kagemni, which Harpur explains as an object that was used to weigh the kilt down to prevent it from billowing, especially when the occupant's hands were occupied in holding on to the carrying chair and to any ther objects of status display.[759] We do not know what this object was made of but in any case it would have to

---

[759] Harpur and Scremin, *The Chapel of Kagemni*, pl. 278, p. 174.

[760] Staehelin, *Untersuchungen zur ägyptischen Tracht im Alten Reich*, 253-57.
[761] Schlögl, ed., *Le Don du Nil: Art Égyptien dans les Collections Suisses*.

E

Fig. 10: Methethi in ceremonial attire, (note the side pleats): Photograph by author at the Brooklyn Museum, No. 11, New York (see also Kaplony, *Studien zum Grab des Methethi*, 60-61).

CHART 16: CORRELATION BETWEEN POSTURE AND DRESS

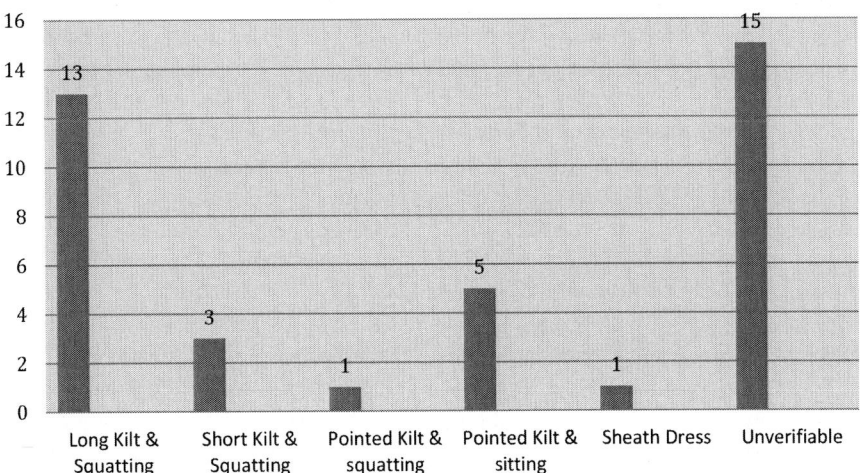

DUPLICATION OCCURS BECAUSE THE TOMB OF NIANKHKHNUM, PL. 42 DEPICTS A SHORT KILT AND SQUATTING POSTURE AND ON PL. 60 HE IS SHOWN IN A POINTED KILT AND SITTING POSTURE.
THE NUMBERS ABOVE REFER TO THE TOMBS IN WHICH THESE POSTURES AND DRESS-TYPES OCCUR.

However as Schäfer points out while the Egyptians were capable "of producing true portraits, the tendency to the typical and idealizing is dominant".[762]

If this is correct, then one would expect that the squatting pose would demand a long kilt and a sitting upright pose would be satisfied with a short or a pointed kilt. Females would be expected to wear a sheath type dress, indeed there is one example of a female in a carrying-chair, and she wears the sheath dress with straps that cover her breasts.[763] It is of interest that her son who is also in the same palanquin and who is in a squatting pose is clearly wearing a long kilt.

The results tabulated in the Chart 16 reveal that a certain correlation exists between posture and dress.

Chart 16's analysis of posture and type of attire reveals that the squatting posture together with the long kilt as well as the pointed kilt with an inverted "v" flap was the predominant mode of attire when using a carrying-chair carted by humans.[764] Importantly in this chart both spatial posture, and the attire of the occupant have been combined

to project a result enabling one to identify more than one aspect, quantify it, and see how these act together.

The results from the verifiable tombs are quite telling and produce a better understanding of the degree to which the elite were enmeshed in the social network emphasizing clothes and display; consolidating the fact that the pointed kilt with a prominent inverted "v" projection and the long kilt are markers of elevated status clothing.[765] In NO tombs is a squatting posture shown with other than a long kilt, the only exception being in the tomb of Perneb.

This could be explained away as part of a presenting a document scene, where the carrying-chair is no longer held aloft but on the ground; if so, then allowance for adjustment of the kilt may have to be provided for.

In the three tombs where the tomb owner is riding in a carrying chair on the backs of donkeys he wears a short kilt, even though he is in the squatting position.[766] This may be explained by the necessity of wearing tight fitting attire much like that worn by present day sport enthusiasts and if this is correct then it is not an exception.

A similar co-relationship exists between the pointed kilt and the sitting posture. A single exception is that in the tomb of Ptahhotep II, where the panther hide is given prominence being depicted worn over a kilt (not shown) in a carrying-chair. Appearing as it does on a false door and the fact of the tomb owner's priestly titles obviates the need for any further underpinning of rank.

---

[762] Schäfer, *Principles of Egyptian Art,* 18.
[763] Wreszinski, *Atlas zur ägyptischen Kulturgeschichte,* pl. 11.
[764] Long kilt and Squatting in13 tombs of: Ankhmahor, Ankhmare, Idu, Itisen, Kagemni, Mereruka (pl. 158), Meryteti (pls. 47, 48), Nikauisesi, Nimaatre, Patahshepses, Qar, Seshemnefer-Tjeti, and Ty.
Short kilt and Squatting in 3 tombs of: Khnumhotep (pl. 43), Niankhkhnum (pl. 42), and Khuwer.
Pointed Kilt and Squatting in the tomb of: Perneb.
Pointed kilt and Sitting in 5 tombs of: Ipy, Khnumenti, Niankhkhnum (pl. 60), Sabwi, and Seshemnefer.
Sheath dress in the tomb of: Waatetkhethor.
Unverifiable in 15 tombs of: Hetepniptah, Hesi, Insnferwishtef, Iymery, Kaemnofret, Mejetji, Merwtetiseneb, Nefer-Khuwi, Nefermaat, Pepydjedi, Ptahhotep II, Rashepses, Seankhuiptah, Seneb, and Senedjemib-Inti.

[765] Staehelin, *Untersuchungen zur ägyptischen Tracht im Alten Reich,* 10 and 20.
[766] In the 3 tombs of: Khnumhotep, Niankhkhnum, and Khuwer.

Body Adornments

When the body is understood as an object, then the imagery produced by its adornment, serves in the creation of meaning in this world and the hereafter. It is known that both men and women adorned their heads with "wigs", their faces with cosmetics, and their bodies with jewellery; the differences in style probably broadcast differences in social status. Generally the reliefs today are so weathered that any trace of cosmetic paint is seldom visible in the carrying-chair scenes. However other archaeological remains do attest to the fact that both sexes used either green or black paint around the eye.[767] The composition of both colours is well known: ground malachite for green and ground galena for black, which became more common in the New Kingdom. These were mixed into a paste with fat and stored in kohl jars for personal use and are well attested in the archaeological finds.[768] As far as the face is concerned almost all men have no facial hair in relation to the carrying-chair motif, with one exception that from the tomb of Khuwer.[769] While few men are depicted with mustaches in Dynasty 4 and 5 of the Old Kingdom they are seldom seen after this period.[770] Pharaohs wore "false beards" on ceremonial occasions, some gods are depicted with "false beards", and evidence exists that beards were in vogue since the earliest times.[771] However, whether it was "false" has never been proven, and so must remain an open question.

As far as items of adornment are concerned, there is evidence of the 'wig' and jewellery, plus other regalia, which the tomb owners display, and to these I will now turn.

'Wigs'

Hair is one element, which occurs, in all the selected motifs. The comments below are therefore general in nature and can be applied to the headdress found on all wearers; this will also avoid unnecessary repetition in the other parts where the headdress is discussed.

A headdress is a manner of arranging or styling real or artificial hair and the name 'wig' is now strongly associated with a style of artificial headdress. This book uses the word 'wig' to denote a style of headdress. However, the use of this name should not be thought of as supporting the claim that false hair, or wigs were actually worn in the Old Kingdom.

In a hierarchically ordered society as will now have become evident, identity and its creation become extremely important requisites in projecting the social standing of an individual. The means employed can be verbal or non-verbal as in visible outer appearance. Examples of the first method are the type of speech and language inscribed, and the emphasis on kinship relationships as indicated by the words his father, his mother, his eldest son, my lord, etc. occurring numerously in a variety of motifs. Examples of the latter method are varied and can be indicated by the manner of attire, style of hair and facial appearance, etc.

The way the 'wig' is depicted can convey different significances ranging from erotic, magical, and religious[772] to encoding information about gender, age, social status,.[773] Hair in many societies is charged with meaning. In the way it is worn, it also encodes and broadcasts information. Just as the human body is, as Barkan puts it - "simultaneously abstract and concrete, general, and specific the 'wig' too is both of the body and not of it, natural product, and a work of art, a culturally dynamic abstract concept and a material artifact subject to time".[774] It thus possesses powerful symbolic and ideological values.

Considering the warm climate of Egypt, it seems strange that one would resort to some form of head covering. A closer look at the functional structure of the 'wig' reveals the reason. It helped to dissipate the heat from the shaven head as well as provide protection against the sun. However if this were the only reason, one would expect to find this as the normal style of all people in that period. However this is not the case and one must look to the symbolic significance of the 'wig', the social position of its wearers, and the occasion when it was worn.

What we witness in the motifs in the elite tombs is the compulsion of all members of society, to try to construct an identity, which because it changes over time in accordance with the individual's station in life, also becomes a pointer to the generics.

All elite males NEVER appear without a 'wig'. The most prestigious is the shoulder length 'wig'; with hair that can be arranged in strands or curls while the commoner form is that of the short round 'wig'. Robins suggests, "the intricate styling of the wigs … shows that their wearers had the resources to acquire and maintain them".[775] While this is true in certain tomb scenes, it may not always be the case because the full range of hairstyles is not depicted in the mortuary art. Economic reasons alone could dictate a differentiation in status, "wigs" being visible signs of being able to wear the hair of others as well as being able to hide the visible signs of ageing and baldness, an exception

---

[767] For a description of the use of various colours in a Dynasty 5 tomb, see Fischer, "A Scribe of the Army of the Fifth Dynasty", *JNES,* (18), 240-241. For general details on colour conventions in the Old Kingdom, see Smith, *A History of Egyptian Sculpture and Painting in the Old Kingdom,* 257-63.

[768] Lucas and Harris, *Ancient Egyptian Materials and Industries,* 83, also see Nicholoson and Shaw, *Ancient Egyptian Materials and Technology,* 104-116

[769] Lepsius, *Denkmäler aus Ägypten und Äthiopien,* pl. 17.

[770] Staehelin, *Untersuchungen zur ägyptischen Tracht im Alten Reich,* 93.

[771] Ibid. 92.

[772] Derchain, "La perruque et le cristal", *SAK,* (2), 55-57.

[773] Robins, "Hair and the Construction of Identity in Ancient Egypt", *JARCE,* (XXXVI), 55.

[774] Barkan, *Nature's work of art: the human body as image of the world,* 3.

[775] Robins, "Hair and the Construction of Identity in Ancient Egypt", *JARCE,* (XXXVI), 63.

being that seen in the bust of Ankhaf.[776] The comparison with the balding, unkempt hair of the ordinary worker in mortuary art is self-evident.

Both sexes adorned the head by the use of a 'wig'. While there is evidence of a variety of "wigs", the ones that we see in these motifs, are restricted to the short curly, the tight fitting, "the shoulder length, and the tri-partite 'wig'. The tomb owners 'wigs' and their type, and development in the OK were as follows:

1. Short tightly fitting wigs are depicted with the topmost curls higher than the rest, in finely divided vertical lines, fitting like a skullcap, which by early Dynasty 5 are less pronounced than they were during Dynasty 3 and 4.[777] While in the beginning and right until early Dynasty 4 it is the predominant headdress of the elite, it begins to be shown on the non-elite after this period.[778]

2. Shoulder length wigs are depicted as usually covering the ears and are exclusively worn by the elite, their family, and the lector priest. While it is often depicted as composed of strands it can also appear smooth. Non-elite servants NEVER wear it. This shoulder length wig is rarely depicted in the early Old Kingdom, being altogether absent at Maidum; nevertheless it appears frequently by Dynasty 5, when it is the predominant and preferred type of wig especially in the elite tombs at Saqqara.[779] However, the short tight fitting wig is never fully displaced. It continues to be depicted in the Old Kingdom mastabas.

3. Short tight fitting wig with a headband, which tapers into mostly two filets - a long and a short one and which is held by a papyrus shaped buckle or as a stiff ribbon knot, both types being attested in Dynasty 5 and 6.[780]

4. Tripartite wigs usually are depicted with the hair divided into three distinct lappets - falling on either side of the breasts and on to the back. The hair can appear smooth, twisted, or braided in strands. The only indication of one's natural hair is a strip of hair, which is sometimes visible under the wig on the forehead. Examples of this type of wig are frequent among the female population. While the evidence is from elite females like Meresankh III, Nebet, and Khamerernebti, (in non-carrying-chair motifs), plus Waatetkhethor, nevertheless unlike their male

counterparts these wigs are also to be seen on their servants and villagers.[781]

If one accepts that the carrying-chair motif when shown is the depiction of a ceremonial occasion, then the fact that "wigs" would be obligatory on such occasions, is self-explanatory. The tomb owner in a majority of the carrying-chair scenes from the Memphite region, sports a 'wig'. Admittedly "wigs" are not only associated with ceremonious occasions, yet they seem to be omnipresent both on the tomb owner as well as the other people including porters, much like the costume of the lord of the manor and his coach bearers in medieval aristocracy.[782]

In the period under study, 24 carrying-chair motifs may be construed as showing "wigs" of which 7 are of the striated shoulder length type.[783] The only exception is in the tomb of Niankhkhnum (pl. 60), where he is claimed to be without a 'wig'.[784] In 13 tombs[785] the "wigs" were unverifiable, primarily because of the time-damaged nature of the scene; the headgear if there was one, has suffered at the hands of time. It has been suggested that in the latter part of the Old Kingdom, a new style evolved in that the ears were always shown as exposed on persons wearing shoulder length wigs.[786] In the carrying-chair scenes the only example showing an ear when wearing a shoulder length 'wig', is that in the tomb of Ipy – ALL OTHERS with similar headgear never show an exposed ear. Further when the tomb owner is wearing a shoulder length 'wig', all other subsidiary attendants are NEVER shown wearing this form of 'wig'.[787]

Harpur states, "out of a total of forty-five extant carrying-chair scenes seventeen show the major figure without a 'wig'.[788] It is unknown how she derives this but she probably included all scenes with a carrying-chair, whether or not these are occupied, are fragments, and possibly a few provincial scenes.

The earlier discussion about porter's headgear, mentions the difficulty of deciding unambiguously whether a real 'wig' is present or not, and so it would have been helpful if Harpur had given a set of criteria. Harpur's assertion that

---

[776]   Smith, *A History of Egyptian Sculpture and Painting in the Old Kingdom*, pls. 14 and 15.

[777]   Cherpion, *Mastabas et hypogées d'Ancien Empire,* 55-56.

[778]   Smith, *A History of Egyptian Sculpture and Painting in the Old Kingdom*, pls. 40 (a), 42 (c) and 49. These Dynasty 4 examples show villagers and servants with a short curled hairstyle. Seen in the 10 tombs of: Kanefer, Meryib, Nefer, Nefer and Kahay, Perneb, Rashepses, Seneb, Tjenti, Ty (pl. 56), and Whemka.

[779]   Cherpion, *Mastabas et hypogées d'Ancien Empire,* 57-58. Seen in the tombs of: Iymery, Iynefert, Kahif, Kaniniswt, Kaemnofret, Khafkhufu I, Khafre-ankh, Khnumenti, Neferbauptah, Nisutnefer, Niankhkhnum and Khnumhotep (pl. 13), Sekhemka, Senedjemib. Mehi, and Seshathotep.

[780]   Ibid. 58-59. Seen in the tombs of: Kagemni, Nebet (Female), Ptahhotep II, and Shetwy.

[781]   Smith, *A History of Egyptian Sculpture and Painting in the Old Kingdom*, pl. 4, and 13 (a). For its depiction on villagers, see Steindorff, *Das Grab des Ti*, pl.112.

[782]   Livery "arose because medieval nobles provided matching clothes to distinguish their servants from others". See also *The Oxford Dictionary of Current English*.

[783]   In the 24 tombs of: Ankhmahor, Ankhmare, Khnumhotep (pl. 43)*, Idu*, Ipy*, Itisen, Iymery, Khuwer, Kagemni, Kaemnofret*, Khnumenti*, Methethi, Merwtetiseneb, Nefer-Khuwi, Niankhkhnum (pl. 42)*, Nimaatre, Perneb, Ptahhotep ll, Ptahshepses, Sabw, Seneb, Senedjemib-inti, Seshemnefer* and Waatetkhethor.

* An asterisk denotes a shoulder-length wig, while all others wear a short wig.

[784]   Altenmüller and Moussa, *Das Grab des Nianchchnum und Chnumhotep*, 129.

[785]   In the 13 tombs of: Hesi, Inisnfrw-ishtef, Mereruka, Meryteti, Nikauisesi, Nefermaat, Hetepniptah, Qar, Sabw, Seankuiptah, Seshemnefer-tjetti, Pepydjedi, and Ty.

[786]   Brovarsky, "A Second Style in Egyptian Relief of the Old Kingdom", in *Egypt and Beyond*, 56.

[787]   In the 3 tombs of: Ipy, Seshemnefer and Seshemnefer-Tjeti.

[788]   Harpur and Scremin, *The Chapel of Kagemni*, 424.

Kagemni does not wear a 'wig' and that it shows the owner in a relaxed image "rather like a man discarding a tie for a less formal occasion" is questionable. A way of getting around the problem is to consider the 'wig' as a 'coiffure' in which case the question becomes one of style, rather than distinguishing between real hair, and 'artificial' hair.

In a recent review researchers at Manchester University analyzing mummies at Dhakla, found that fatty material was used to preserve hairstyle. This fatty material was different in chemical composition to that used in preserving the body. Accordingly they assert that this is an indicator emphasizing the importance of hair in ancient Egypt (both in life and death), and the identity and the individuality of the tomb owner.[789]

Jewellery

Invariably present around the tomb owner's necks is jewellery. It is known from the material record that a variety of neckwear was worn, e.g. chokers especially by women, single, and multiple strand necklaces plus broad collars, which could be up to 260 mm wide, hence the name. The broad collar also known as the *wsḥ* is also present in the majority (57%) of depictions[790] but there is no way of distinguishing from the reliefs, the various types of material used in their production. This could have been one useful tool in deciding on the levels of eliteness. In most of the examples there are depictions of multiple strands of beads, tubes or maybe amuletic figures, which terminate in solid endings, which serve to anchor the many strands. Most of these have lost their original colour. Possibly the original broad collars were covered with precious metals in keeping with the status of the tomb owner like the one now in Vienna but this is no longer apparent.[791]

In the tomb of Kagemni, he is shown wearing both a collar as well as a chain with an amulet shaped like a heart, which supposedly gave the wearer protection (mkt) and divine intervention,[792] should he require it. This small amulet is crafted with tiny holes so that it could be hung on a necklace.

Amulets were made of a variety of materials (precious stones, metals, wood and faience) and were produced according to strict convention, as seen from the MacGregor Papyrus,[793] which has an unusual list of seventy-five amulets with their names and religious functions presented in a grid. Alas the bottom part of the amulet worn by Kagemni is partly visible, one can just detect the curved part of the top of the heart, but as the rest is hidden by the hand of the tomb owner one cannot tell its exact nature, and therefore one is unable to comment on its precise protective significance.[794] Indeed this is the only time that we see an amulet being worn in a carrying-chair motif and this could probably have something to do with individuality.

In most scenes where there is a 'wig' (24 cases), there is a collar present (21 cases). In the few scenes where this is not, these are either damaged, or the upper part is missing and so unverifiable. A relational link between the collar and the 'wig' is thus well established.

The Egyptians also adorned their arms and legs with ornaments like the bracelet and anklet.[795] In the Old Kingdom the most common form of material used was ivory,[796] bone,[797] tortoiseshell,[798] horn,[799] and gold.[800] The carrying-chair scenes show a kind that consisted of flexible strings of beads or other brightly coloured stone like carnelian, as well as those made of pure bands of gold with inlays of stone. However, the bracelets actually recovered in this period are made from faience having strands of ring shaped beads divided by bead spacers at regular intervals. This separation of the rows of beads would have provided additional strength to the bracelet, as well as being a possible fashion statement if both the bracelet and the broad collar were made of matching material.[801] However this explanation cannot be backed up with actual numbers.

It might be expected that both the limbs and the head would be adorned to the same extent, but this cannot be proved conclusively. Erosion and grave robbery have played havoc here and therefore it may be wrong to assume that bracelets/anklets were not worn to the same extent as the 'wig' and the collar, just because they do not appear so in the archaeological record. Similarly the "false beard," if it indeed was an elite option, could be expected to be prominent on ceremonial occasions but there is limited evidence for this. This is especially relevant when one is confronted with a scene whose very nature calls for elaborate personal pomp and display of which all six items (bracelet, anklet, 'wig', broad collar, amulet, and may be 'false beard') are an integral part. There is only one

---

[789] McCreesh, Gize, and David, "Ancient Egyptian Hair gel: New insight into ancient Egyptian mummification procedures", *JOAS*, doi: 10.1016/j.jas.2011.08.004. The general consensus that hair was coated with beeswax may need to be examined further in the light of this research.

[790] Collars present in the tombs of: Ankhmahor, Ankhmare, Khnumhotep (pl. 43), Idu, Ipy, Itisen, Kagemni, Khnumenti, Khuwer, Meryteti (pl. 47), Methethi, Nefer-Khuwi, Niankhkhnum (pls. 42 and 60), Perneb, Ptahhotep II, Ptahshepses, Sabw, Seneb, Senedjemib.Inti, Seshemnefer and Waatetkhethor. For more details, also see E. Haslauer, „Bestattungsschmuck aus Giza," in *Jahrbuch der kunsthistorischen Sammlungen in Wien 87* (1991).

[791] See the example now in the Kunsthistorisches Museum, Vienna, ÄS 9072, of a broad collar dated between Dynasty 5 and early Dynasty 6, made of faience and gold leaf.

[792] Faulkner, *A concise dictionary of Middle Egyptian,* 119.

[793] Capart, «Une liste d'amulettes,» *ZÄS,* (45), 14-21. It is admitted that this is a New Kingdom papyrus and that all it can evidence is the continuing protective nature of amulets and its connection with changing New Kingdom funerary practices.

[794] Harpur and Scremin, *The Chapel of Kagemni,* pl. 278. See also Bonnet, *Reallexikon,* 26-31, for the magical functions attributed to amulets. For a general survey see Andrews, *Jewellery,* 44-45.

[795] Bracelets in the 6 tombs of: Ankhmahor, Idu, Kagemni, Mereruka (pl. 158), Meryteti (pl. 47) and Waatetkhethor.
Anklets in the tomb of: Waatetkhethor.
Amulet in the tomb of: Kagemni.

[796] Brunton, *Matmar,* tombs 800 and 17.

[797] Ibid. tomb 865.

[798] Petrie, *Diospolis Parva,* tomb N 19.

[799] Brunton, *Mostagedda and the Tasian Culture,* tombs 243 and 677.

[800] Ghoneim, *Horus Sekhemkhet,* vol. I, 13-14.

[801] Haslauer, „Bestattungsschmuck aus Giza," 9-21.

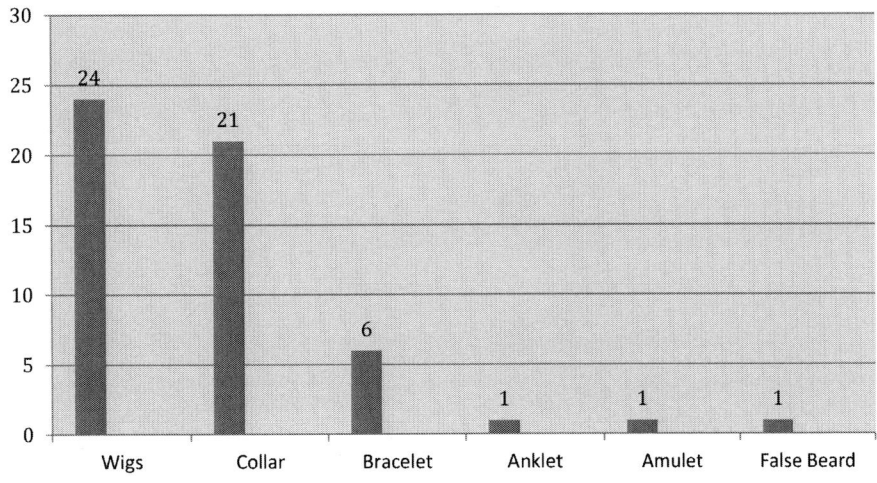

CHART 17: BODY ADORNMENTS OF TOMB OWNER

*DUPLICATION OF ADORNMENTS IN 17 TOMBS. THE NUMBERS ABOVE REFER TO THE NUMBER OF CASES WITH ADORNMENTS BUT NOT TO THE NUMBER OF ADORNMENTS.

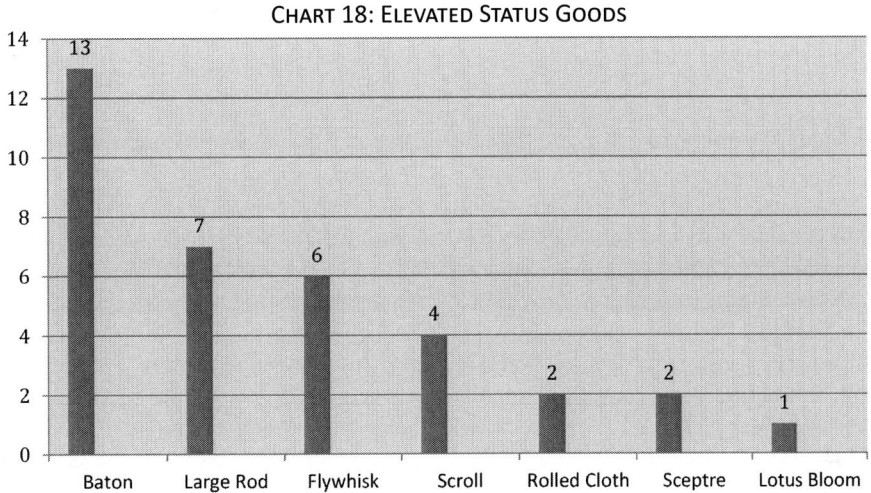

CHART 18: ELEVATED STATUS GOODS

DUPLICATION OCCURS IN ELEVEN TOMBS OF WHICH THERE ARE TWO TOMBS WITH MORE THAN ONE PLATE AND NINE TOMBS WITH MORE THAN ONE STATUS GOOD; THEREFORE THESE SHOULD NOT BE ADDED. THE NUMBERS SHOW NUMBERS OF CASES IN WHICH THE STATUS GOODS OCCUR BUT NOT THE NUMBERS OF GOODS THEMSELVES. IN THREE TOMBS NO STATUS GOODS ARE PRESENT AND IN TEN TOMBS THESE WERE UNVERIFIABLE.

example in this motif of a 'false beard', which is in the tomb of Khuwer (LD ll, pl. 43(a)).

These objects contributed to the survival of the deceased in the memory of their social surroundings because they were a means of eliciting eliteness, without having to spell it out.

Chart 17 summarizes these findings.

Ceremonial Objects

The occupant of the carrying-chair is also shown with objects, which may be either a symbol of office or a ceremonial object. These objects include the baton, large rod, sceptre (sxm),[802] flywhisk,[803] (usually made from

foxtails) rolled cloth, papyrus scroll, and the lotus bud. Various combinations of these appear in the carrying-chair motif; the only certainty being that these objects are depicted in one or both hands of the tomb owner. Fischer suggests that the baton substituted for the unwieldy sceptre as a symbol of authority and may be the reason why it is found in thirteen of the carrying-chair motifs.[804]

One would expect these to occur in all similar scenes in keeping with its objective (display of wealth plus status, to consolidate his status plus identity and to depict the transport of the tomb owner) and this is indeed so.[805] See Chart 18.

---

[802] Gardiner, *Egyptian Grammar*. Usually this is the *sḫm* scepter also known as ʿbȝ. Also see Faulkner, *A concise dictionary of Middle Egyptian*, 241 and 40 respectively.
[803] Gardiner, *Egyptian Grammar.* 510. He terms this a flagellum. The

flail was used for encouraging/restraining cattle and it could similarly imply the coercive encouraging/restraining power of the king, whose symbolism was adopted by the elite.
[804] Fischer, "Notes on Sticks and Staves in ancient Egypt", *MMJ*, (13), 18-19.
[805] Batons in 13 tombs of: Ankhmahor, Ankhmare, Niankhkhnum (pl.

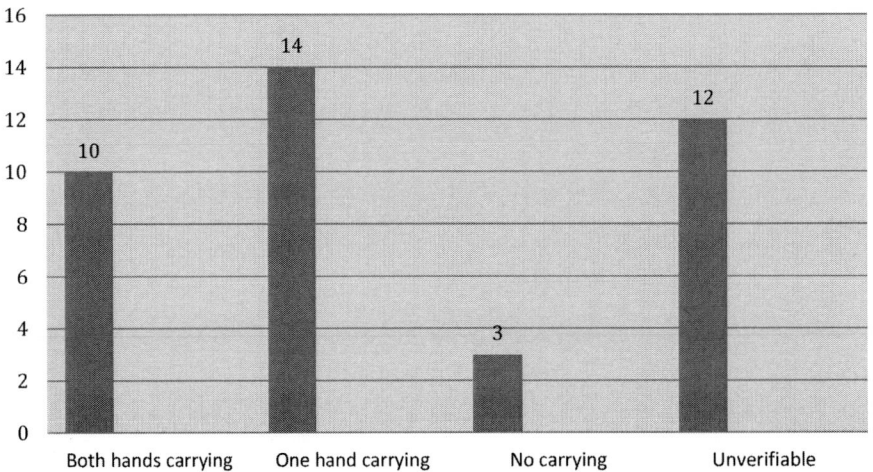

CHART 19: CARRYING STATUS GOODS

DUPLICATION OCCURS BETWEEN THE FIRST AND SECOND COLUMNS BECAUSE THERE ARE TWO TOMBS WITH CARRYING SHOWN ON MORE THAN ONE PLATE. THE ABOVE NUMBERS SHOW HOW MANY TOMBS THERE ARE IN WHICH THE STATUS GOODS OCCUR BUT NOT THE NUMBERS OF GOODS THEMSELVES.

Three tomb owners Seneb, Mereruka (pl. 158), and Perneb are not depicted carrying any status goods. An explanation may be that the first two persons did not need to show attributes of eliteness because both were married to the king's daughter (Seneb is also depicted on the southern side panel of his tomb wearing a long animal skin robe, a style which is normally associated with royalty as observed on the Giza slab stelae e.g. Wepem-neferet, Khufunakht, Kaemah, Kainefer, Neferiabet, Setjihenket, Ini, Seshatsehentyu, Meretites, and Iuenu). It may be that an aesthetic reason also came into play here; his dwarfishness would be accentuated if objects were depicted (but then why do others who are similarly placed, insist on showing these attributes?). The better reasoning would be to explain these deviances (the non-carrying of status goods) as instances of individuality.

Perneb seems to be concentrating his attention on the receiving of a papyrus but a comparison with a similar motif in the tomb of Qar, would not preclude him from carrying a status good and so this too can be explained as a probable case of individuality.

The obvious thing about these ceremonial objects is that they are depicted in such a way as to give more prominence to the arm carrying them. However in those cases where only one object is carried, it is interesting that this is shown at all times in the hand which is furthest away from the viewer. This is in keeping with the basic principle of Egyptian art, which was to display reality in relief, to present the human form in a perfect way (in the carrying-chair motif this would be the hand on the armrest). At the same time the artist took great care not to detract from the unambiguous nature of the scene, which would be the portrayal of how an elite was to be depicted holding an object while in a carrying-chair.[806] The presentation then of the tomb owner, such that both arms could be seen as part of an ideal body and the portrayal of ceremonial objects in a manner that these are not obstructed, makes obvious sense. Further by displaying the object in this way, the object's reality and worth was enhanced because it, and not the arms became the focus of attention, pointing to the object's social/cultural significance. Whether or not there is any correlation between the hand carrying an object and the direction of movement of the carrying-chair is uncertain. In any case, any correlation has extremely limited value because it is of no use in indicating the direction of travel, nor is it in any way essential to the focus of this study as stated in the 'Introductory Remarks'.

Considering that the requirements of decorum would be satisfied if both arms hold status objects, then it is surprising that only 10 tombs depict carrying of these goods in both hands.[807] In contrast, there are 40% tombs (14 tombs) showing the tomb owner carrying an object

60), Idu, Ipy, Itisen, Kagemni, Kaemnofret, Khnumenti, Meryteti (pl. 47), Merwtetiseneb, Ptahshepses, and Sabw.
Large rods in 7 tombs of: Khnumhotep (pl. 43), Khuwer, Nefermaat, Niankhkhnum (pl. 42), Ptahhotep ll, Seshemnefer, and Seshemnefer-Tjeti.
Scepters in 2 tombs of: Ptahhotep ll, and Seshemnefer.
Flywhisks in 6 tombs of: Ipy, Iymery, Qar, Merwtetiseneb, Meryteti (pl. 47), and Senedjemib-Inti.
Rolled Cloth in 2 tombs of: Khnumenti, and Khuwer.
Papyrus scrolls being handed over in 4 tombs of: Qar, Methethi, Nimaatre, and Perneb.
Lotus bud in the tomb of: Waatetkhethor.
No objects in the 3 tombs of: Seneb, Mereruka (pl. 158), and Perneb.
Unverifiable in 13 tombs of: Hesi, Hetepniptah, Inisnfrw-ishtef, Meryteti (pl. 48), Nefer-Khuwi, Nikauisessi, Pepydjedi, Rashepses, Seankhuiptah, and Ty.

[806] Fechheimer, *Die Plastik der Ägypter*, 48-57 for examples.
[807] In the tombs of: Khuwer, Ipy, Khnumenti, Merwtetiseneb, Niankhkhnum (pl. 42), Khnumhotep (pl. 43), Ptahhotep II, Qar, Senedjemib-inti, and Seshemnefer.

in one hand only.[808] Included among these are 4 tombs, which have one arm missing and therefore all one can say is that there are 10 tombs showing a complete body and arms but which definitely depict the holding of the status object by one arm only. In 12 tombs this depiction was not verifiable.[809]

The three exceptions as already explained are the tombs of Seneb and Mereruka (pl. 158), and Perneb which are the only Old Kingdom carrying-chair motifs in which the occupants do not carry any status goods (8% of the total population out of 37 tombs examined).

Chart 19 summarizes these findings and shows that ca. 70% of the total population display some form of status goods being carried in one or both hands of the tomb owner. As to which of the hands was preferred the evidence is too sparse to come to any conclusion. The unverifiable tombs represent some 30% of the total population and even if all of these were definitely found to have no such depiction it still would not be a statistically fatal.

7. 6 Captions and Titles

Old Kingdom captions/titles reveal scant information about the elite's lives, society, or economic organization. Titles include both those held by the tomb owner and those of his attendants and they will be treated separately.

Using captions and titles to elicit such information, presents the following difficulties:

- The material record's poor preservation making parts illegible is particularly troublesome, because for the Old Kingdom to have existed as long as it did, it must have had an adequate bureaucracy with many attendant records, which would have been useful for Egyptology. This difficulty applies to all historic studies but is particularly vexing in the context of smaller illegible inscriptions.
- Documents preserved especially of the period prior to and including the Old Kingdom, are extremely limited. Even when inscriptions are to hand, they are seldom narrative as evidenced by the Dynasty 5 Abusir papyri, which is really an archive of the local pyramid temples and a number of legal texts mainly related to endowments.[810] From Dynasty 5 onwards, personal details in the autobiographies begin to develop but these are more in the nature of self-presentation, and comments on the society of that period are never directly portrayed.

- Captions on representations in elite tombs were probably subject to the individual whim of the tomb owner (subject of course to the provisions of decorum), and one can never be certain of the extent to which, individuality influenced the depiction of certain captions in the representations.

Captions

There are few captions and these relate to:

- Tomb owner's self-eulology/inspection visit (for the work done on his tomb[811])
- Porter's Songs[812]
- Porter's Remarks to Supervisor[813]
- Tomb owner's business/objectives

In all of these, one can detect the concentration of the ideas, which were necessary to promote those concepts, which are termed generic as regards the tomb owner, as well as ethical ideas of conduct regarded as conducive to societal welfare. These ideas seem to be shared by the members of the group, as seen in the captions below.

Tomb owner's Inspection Visit

In the tomb of Ankhmare, just above the carrying-chair motif, the caption reads:

"Proceeding in peace homewards after viewing the work which was done in his tomb of the necropolis, the administrator of the granary Ankhmare".

(sḏȝt m ḥtp r ẖnw m-ḫt mȝ [kȝ] t
irt m [is]=f [n] ẖrt-nṯr ẖry-tp
šnwt ꜥnḫmꜥrꜥ)

In the tomb of Nefer-Khuwi, it reads:

"Proceeding in peace to the residence after seeing the work that was done in his tomb of the necropolis. This tomb was made for him because he was well venerated before god. As for his tomb, every craftsman who made it, he gave them a very great payment, so that they praised all the gods on behalf of him, the overseer Nefer-Khuwi".

(š [ḏ]ȝt m[ḥtp r ẖnw]
m ḫt mȝ[ȝ] kȝt ir [.ti]
m [is] f n ẖrt.nṯr)
[ir n.f is] f [pn]
[m šw i] mȝḥ.f [nfr ḥr nṯr]
[ir is] f ḥmwt nb
ir sw rdi.n.f n.sn. ḏbȝ
ꜥȝ wrt dwȝ.n.sn n. f nṯrw n
[imi]-r…[Nfr-ḫw-w(i)]

808 In the tombs of: Ankhmahor, Ankhmare, Itisen, Iymery, Kagemni, Kaemnofret, Methethi, Niankhkhnum (fig. 60), Nefermaat, Ptahshepses, Sabw, Senedjemib-inti, Seshemnefer-Tjetti, and Waatetkhethor.
809 In the 12 tombs of: Hesi, Hetepniptah, Inisnfrw-ishtef, Mereruka (pl. 158), Meryteti (pl. 47). Nefer-Khuwi, Nikauisesi, Nimaatre, Pepydjedi, Rashepses, Seankhuiptah, and Ty.
810 Posener-Kriéger and Cenival, *Hieratic Papyri in the British Museum. Fifth Series. The Abu Sir Papyri.* For private Old Kingdom documents see Goedicke, *Die privaten Rechtsinschriften aus dem Alten Reich.*

811 In the tombs of: Ankhmare, Nefer-Khuwi, and Nimaatre.
812 In the tombs of: Ipy, Itisen, and Mereruka.
813 In the tomb of: Ptahshepses.

Nimaatre's carrying-chair captions are much damaged but parts of the above phraseology are there too.

Relevantly in all the three carrying-chair scenes where thanksgiving is depicted, the tomb owners (Ankhmare, Nefer-Khuwi, and Nimaatre) are shown being carried from the inside of the tomb to the outside door of the tomb, and thus correspond with the captions pertaining to the purpose of the visit.

Examples of thanksgiving captions for the building of a tomb are also evidenced in other motifs,[814] sometimes in detail. It would also appear from these inscriptions that exchange of labour for material benefits, was a common practice since at least Dynasty 4; thus pointing to the growing societal complexity these organized relationships must have.

In the tomb of Hetepherakhti, it reads:

"I have made this tomb from my rightful means, and I never took the property of anyone".[815]

(ir. n (.i) is pw m išt (.i) m3ꜥ, n sp iṯy (.i) ḫt nt rmṯ nb)

The details of payments are inscribed on the left doorjamb.

Similarly in the tomb of Remenu-ka[816] it reads:

"As for this tomb, I made it because I was venerated before god. Never was a block of stone belonging to any man brought to me for this tomb, for one remembered the judgement in the West. I made this tomb on bread and beer which I gave to all the craftsmen who made this tomb, I having given them also very great payments in great quantity of linen of all kinds for which they asked and they praised god for it".

(ir is pn n(i) ḏt.(i)
ir.n.(i) sw m- šwt im3ḫ.(i) nfr ḫr nṯr
ni ḥm sp in.t (y) n.(i) inr n(i) rmṯw nb(w) (i)r is.(i) pn n sḫ3.t(i) wḏꜥ-mdw m imntt
ir.n.(i) is pn ḥr t ḥnḳt rḏi.n.(i) n ḥmwt nb(w)t ir(w)t is pn
sk igr rḏi.n.(i) n.sn ḏb3w (r ꜥ3t wrt m sšr nb dbḥ.n.sn dw3.n sn nṯr ḥr.s)

In the tomb of Inti it reads:[817]

"As to every craftsman - it was after they had built this (tomb) [that I satisfied them], so that they praised god for it. (It) was pleasant for them to make. They never

really suffered from working too much, with the result that they might thank praise god for it".

(ir ḥmwt nb(w)t [sḥtp.n.(i) sn] ir.n.sn nw dw3.sn n nṯr ḥr.s mry n.sn irt [ni] šn.n.sn[is] irt ꜥ3 wrt m-mrwt dw3. sn n. nṯr im)

Porter's Song

This song appears in 4 Memphite representations.[818] The porters sing the carrying-chair song, which may have the triple purpose of - revealing the burden of their occupation, the joy in having the honour to carry the tomb owner and the implicit well wishes for his life in the here and possibly in the hereafter.[819]

From the material record, it would appear that although there are variations of the porter's song, their basic sentiment is quite clear. Although carrying the chair, might be a burden, nevertheless to carry their lord on it, is the porters' highest joy! A full version[820] reads:

"Go down in order to protect the prosperous
Go down in order to protect the healthy
O Sokar, who is on the sand come and protect N
Act verily as [I] wish it full more than when it is empty".

In the tomb of Ipy where this song appears, it can be related to the wish of reaching the hereafter by travel overland in a carrying-chair to:

"attain the mountain heights of the necropolis".

Abbreviated versions of the song are present in the tomb of Mereruka:

"I like it filled, more than it is empty".[821]

Altenmüller suggests that this could also refer to the consolidation of the social identity and ideology of the elite.[822] Hieroglyphs referring to *wr* and *mḥnk* are evident in the song: the former meaning great/mighty and the

---

[814] Edel, "Inschriften des Alten Reichs", *MIO,* (1), 328-329. The caption in the tomb of Mehuakhti reads: "Concerning this tomb of mine, it was for bread and beer that it was made for me, and all the craftsmen who built it thanked me, after I had given them garments, oil, barley in great quantity, saying: O all the gods of the necropolis, we are satisfied, our hearts being satisfied with the bread and beer that Mehuakhti, the venerated one, has given to us".

[815] Sethe, *Urkunden des Alten Reiches,* 50. l, 1-2.

[816] Hassan, *Excavations at Giza,* fig. 206.

[817] Sethe, *Urkunden des Alten Reiches,* 70, l. 5-10.

[818] In the Memphite tombs of: Ipy, Mereruka (pl. 158), Sabw, and Senedjemib. Inti, and in the provincial tombs of: Djau (*Deir-el-Gebrawi,* vol. II, pl.8), Pepyankh (*Meir,* vol. 5, pl. 31) and Shepsi-Pu-Min/Kheni (*el-Hawawish,* vol. II, fig. 21, and p. 26). For a detailed analysis of the Porters' Song, see Walsem, "Sense and Sensibility. On the Analysis and Interpretation of the Iconography Programmes of Four Old Kingdom Elite Tombs," in *Dekorierte Grabanlagen im Alten Reich,* eds. M. Fitzenreiter and M. Herb, 302-03.

[819] Erman, *Reden, Rufe, und Lieder auf Gräberbildern des Alten Reiches,* 52-53.

[820] This translation of the Porters' Song in the tomb of Ipy is by Heerma Van Voss, in *Phoenix,* (14), 131.

[821] Duell, *The Mastaba of Mereruka,* vol. I, pl. 53 (b).

[822] Altenmüller, "Das Sänftenlied des Alten Reiches", *BSEG,* (9/10), 28. The idea of setting up a certain social position by the tomb owner in terms of a cultural vocabulary including attire, headgear, elevated status objects, etc. can be understood by all. Nevertheless to postulate that these culturally significant terms can be established by a combination of hieroglyphs, can surely be of limited effect, especially when the target audience (the elite) is literate and presumably already aware of these subtle connotations.

latter refer to persons who worked either for the king or another lord and who could be 'leased' by others, i.e. not so great. Accordingly he suggests that their juxtaposition is comparable to the words "empty" and "full" ; when the carrying-chair is full the tomb owner's status is established but not so when it is empty.

Another variation in the tomb of Senedjemib-inti immediately before the sole sunshade carrier, reads:

"Go in your [carrying-chair] satisfied one".

Porters' Remarks to Supervisor

In the tomb of Ptahshepses[823] a conversation is inscribed relating to remarks between a supervisor and porters. It points to the hierarchical nature of society, and the nature of the consideration for the occupant of the carrying-chair.

This interpretation is a translation result from incomplete ideas, and therefore meaning is derived by analogy with the tomb of Kagemni. The supervisor has reminded one of the porters:

"behave yourself, do [his] task properly my companion and look at your order very (well /careful)"

(*ir rk nfr t(w)t Ihr nty ḥnꜥ. M33 n=k n tpt-rd=k wrt*)

The porters' reply that the supervisor should rather look forward and fulfill his duties as the leader of the palanquin procession.

"Look well forward! Quiet down, you favoured one".

(*ḥr=k m ḥ3t nfr, ihr ḥr(y)–ḥs(w) t pw*)

Tomb owner's Other Objectives

In the tomb of Niankhkhnum and Khnumhotep (pl. 42 and 43), the journey in a carrying-chair slung between two donkeys, is characterized by the caption:

"Proceeding to the beautiful West"

(*sd3t r imnt nfrt*)

 The purpose of the journey can relate to the inspection of his tomb, which was being built in the west.

In pl. 60 of the same joint tomb, Niankhkhnum is depicted in a carrying-chair and the objective following his name and titles, is given as

"Proceeding to the fields to view all work of the fields"

(*h3it r sḫt r m33 k3t nbt nt sḫt*)

The importance of the porter's song, and the other captions illustrating the tomb owner's objectives, is the manner in which matters of respect and moral certitude are being shown by all the participants: the tomb owner by paying the craftsmen, the craftsmen at being happy that they are so appreciated, and the porters in their refrain.

The porter's song should be understood in the wider context, to include the official journeys, the recreational ones, plus the final one to the beautiful West and are secular in concept. One cannot read more into the song based on the evidence,[824] and their objective is neatly summed up in the scene, which appears on the false door of Ptahhotep II.[825] Inscribed on the left jamb, where the hieroglyphs translate as follows:

"entering the house of eternity in most excellent peace, he being in a state of worthiness before Anubis at the head after he has received the funerary offerings at the top of the pit, after the tour, after the service of making him a revered one by the lectors by reasons of his exceedingly great favour before the king and Osiris".

This translation expresses the purposes of the journey and the respect shown towards the tomb owner. These inscriptions were debatably written by the tomb owner and as such have questionable veracity. If building and decorating a tomb was a joint effort (no matter how small), then it is highly unlikely that in a well-knit small community, such continued baseless assertions would have been tolerated, and propagated successively. That this expression of mutual respect, persisted through successive pharaonic generations with little alteration to its fundamental character, proves the point of a connectivity based on levels of hierarchy, and again a pointer to the cultural generics.

Tomb owner's Titles

The following discussion will not consider the philology of titles. In this study, titles are used as a means of illustrating the social position of the tomb owner and any agency relationships with the subsidiary figures that are found in the iconography.

Titles usually followed the career path of the official, as demonstrated in the Dynasty 4 tombs of *Phrnfr* and *Mtn*.[826] Instructive of the general situation regarding titles, are the titles of Pehernefer; he had two of the highest titles *ḥ3ty-ꜥ* and *ḥry-tp* as well as overseer of the treasury (*imy-r3 pr-ḥḏ*) and overseer of the royal granaries (*imy-r3 šnwt nbt*

---

[823] Verner, *Abusir-I: The Mastaba of Ptahshepses*, 99. He remarks that the inscriptions here "are not easy to interpret".

[824] Walsem, "Sense and Sensibility," 303. He correctly states that the Porters' Song has "no deeper metaphorical implications" compared to the conjecture by Strudwick that the song is "an allusion to the desire to be brought back to earth after death" see Strudwick, *Texts from the Pyramid Age,* 418.

[825] Murray, *Saqqara Mastabas,* vol. I, pl. 8.

[826] Junker, "*Phrnfr*", *ZÄS,* (75), 63-72. For Metjen see Lepsius, *Denkmäler aus Ägypten und Äthiopien,* pls. 4, 5, 6 and 7. Also see Strudwick, *The Administration of Egypt in the Old Kingdom.* 85. A similar conglomeration of titles is that of Nefermaat, ibid: 110.

nt nswt) yet he had forty other rank and administrative titles. Presumably these were required at that time for the fulfillment of his duties, and were based on what was the trend at the time.[827] As this is the case for most of the elite persons, one can sense in the string of titles, an attempt to portray the order in which these were accumulated, the increase in the order of social prestige and something akin to a type of Old Kingdom curriculum vitae.

There is a difference in titles in the administration of Lower and Upper Egypt in that each of these areas did not have the same official titles; the meanings of titles used by the elite tomb owner thus follow a certain set pattern which is outside the scope of this study.

Accordingly the tomb owner holds those titles, which are typical of the period and place, identifying him as a person who is in the upper echelons of society in terms of social identity.[828] Significantly the carrying-chair motif makes a clear division between the statuses of the tomb-

owner, his family, and the remaining subsidiary figures. These relationships then are more informative about the structure of Egyptian society than the string of titles of the tomb owner. The strings of titles generally appear in a long series of columns above the representation of the tomb owner; the most important titles tend to be displayed on the false door and grouped as near as possible to his name.[829] Accordingly this would imply that the titles which one finds in the carrying-chair motifs are not the most important ones he possessed, but this cannot be proven.

In the earliest example of a carrying-chair motif in the tomb of Nefermaat, are the following titles:

Above the carrying-chair:

> "Hereditary Prince, Count, Guardian of Nekhen, Chief Justice and Vizier, Stolist of the God Min, Priest of the Goddess Bastet, Priest of the Goddess Shezmetet, Priest of the Ram of Mendes, Nefermaat".

On the offering panel on the false door are:

> "Hereditary Prince, Count, Guardian of Nekhen, Seal bearer of the King of Lower Egypt, King's eldest son. Nefermaat".

On the drum there appears:

> "Hereditary Prince Nefermaat".

Running in vertical columns on the extreme sides of the offering panel, is a repetition of the titles already encountered in the offering panel.[830]

Rather than trying to rank these titles (which are outside the scope of this study), it is suggested that one other way of looking at all these various titles is to accept that the more titles that are displayed in motifs other than the false door, the more important these are as an indicator of status. One goal of this exercise is to illustrate the concept of the tomb owner's status. Of course a further indicator can be a title that is so exalted as to be self-contained, because a single title in itself can denote an established designation of an area of responsibility, which because it depended initially on the authorization by the king, comes to have residual value, and indicates eliteness. Consequently the eliteness of Nefermaat is immediately made plain by the title 'hereditary prince', even though he has other important string of titles. Likewise a survey of the tomb owners in the carrying-chair motif reveals that these are elite persons of varying degrees - not all are of the highest order of hereditary prince, yet most belong to the highest officials in the administration and it is not intended to enumerate each of these because ranking titles is of little relevance to this study.[831]

Titles of the Other Attendants

More illuminating than the titles of the tomb owner, are those associated with the attendants including certain members of his family, who are in the vicinity of the carrying-chair, because these could point to duty relationships, which in turn could relate to the social position of the tomb owner.

Generally in the Memphite tombs under study, the identified subsidiary figures are not divided into separate groups but are part of the larger motif. They frequently form part of the mortuary cult and are attached to all types of scenes, e.g. banqueting, carrying-chair, etc. with other, non-identified figures. However, in all cases the image of the tomb owner is evident nearby, thus they all fit into the design of the motif. Most significantly in the Memphite region, these subsidiary figures are never shown with members of their own or the tomb owner's family but separately.

The very existence and identification of these attendants and their role in the mortuary cult, sets them apart from all others, and points to the interdependencies which must have existed between the tomb owner and his attendants. The term mortuary cult is used broadly as follows:

- To enable an understanding in the larger context of the monumental tomb.
- To differentiate between the relationship connecting the tomb owner and other things and people, as compared to his relationship with his immediate family.

On the one hand there are those subsidiary figures that are necessary for the composition of

[827] Baer, *Rank and title in the Old Kingdom*, 5.

[828] Ibid. 234-39.

[829] Helck, "Titel und Titularen", *LÄ*, vol. 6, 599.

[830] Harpur and Scremin, *The tombs of Nefermaat and Rahotep at Maidum*, 68-70.

[831] For details on the development of administrative titles see: Endesfelder, *"Formierung der Klassengesellschaft"*, ed. J. Hallof, 40-43.

the motif, e.g. the porters - without whom there would be no carrying-chair motif. Then there are the officials and family members who may be specifically attired, and wigged, described by title, or identified by name. The officials show only a few titles; therefore it is not possible to give a precise picture of their standing in the community. But if their commonly depicted titles are anything to go by, then some of these indicate that they had jobs connected to the running of a large elite household, e.g. the titles of overseer of the estate, *imy-r pr* or follower/elder of the domain, *šmsw* / S*msw pr*. These officials worked for the tomb owner but also had other underlings beneath them. Other titles suggest that they also had outside duties, e.g. overseer of the gang of workmen, *imy-r iswt* and director of the gang of workmen, *ḥrp ist*. The officials' titles suggest responsibility both during the tomb owner's life as well as in his mortuary cult but do not reveal a specific function in the household. Those titles which belong to the family members e.g. his son/s is/are general; the eldest son is usually the 'testamentary' and rightful heir of the tomb owner while the combination of family members represented, probably points to the collective grief of the family/clan.

The critical factor is that these were not just ordinary persons but officials who had a certain standing in the local community, which tended to set them apart both in life and in the tomb art. They were charcaterised sometimes by name, by title, and shown having access to the tomb owner's belongings. This personal commitment between the tomb owner and attendants consolidates and maintains the identity of the tomb owner and points to the nature of Egyptian society during this period. Accepting this line of argument also implies that the tomb owner's sphere of influence over the community of dependants (especially the funerary priests), was maintained by including these in his tomb decoration.

Another way by which the tomb owner gained posthumous control over his household and funerary priest is analogous to the royal mortuary cult. The king's influence over the priesthood was greatly increased because of their continuous rotation and dependency on the reversionary offerings and because the mortuary cult was staffed by a group of continually part-time rotating officials, one month out of every ten.[832] Priests and other higher status officials were also given priesthoods in the royal mortuary cult and thus had even more status and rewards.

A somewhat similar arrangement and functioning may have applied to the elite mortuary cult, but it must be stressed that information about the structure of private mortuary cults is less known than that about royal mortuary cults.[833] In any case the rotational arrangement of the number of people, who had a dependency relationship to the tomb owner, greatly increased his influence over a certain section of the community. This meant that the tomb owner was guaranteed loyalty/dependency/service during his lifetime and for his funerary cult, while the funerary priests received status and reward during the lifetime of the tomb owner and after his death. Implicitly by being included in his cult and in his iconography, any particular identified subsidiary figure comes to have higher status than others not so included – a most suitable arrangement for all concerned. Additionally, the identification of specific subsidiary individuals and their titles could indicate that like the eldest son, but at a different level, they too were legitimated as the rightful heirs and benefactors of his mortuary cult - a kind of 'will'.

Therefore it is suggested, that these subsidiary figures should be understood as occupying a midway position between that of the tomb owner and the rest of the population, underpinning their mutual interdependency.

The identity of the tomb owner is thus entrenched in "the firm belief in a post-mortem existence, not as an anonymous shadow, but in complete preservation of personal identity as it has developed during the lifetime of an individual".[834]

Concomitantly it must be assumed that because there were higher levels of priesthood who belonged to phyles in the Old Kingdom,[835] this must have imposed a greater burden on the posthumous assets of the tomb owner, which in due course probably was one of the many reasons, which contributed to the eventual breakdown of the Old Kingdom.

Accordingly while the titles of the tomb owner's attendants provide certain links to the items of generics, the underlying idea of this study, yet their statistical analysis poses problems.

At the outset it became apparent that associating the number of people holding certain titles as an attribute of the social identity of the tomb owner, would lead to problems. The nature of the material record is such that it is impossible to say with any certainty, that a tomb owner, who for example only depicts 2 of his four attendants with titles, had less social significance than one that thanks to preservation shows all 4 attendants with similar titles.

It became also clear that ranking these titles would be an equally futile exercise, because of the uncertainty involved

[832] Roth, "The Organization and Functioning of the Royal Mortuary Cults of the Old Kingdom in Egypt", in *The Organization of Power: Aspects of Bureaucracy in the Ancient Near East*, ed. M. Gibson and R. D. Biggs, 133-40. I am assuming that the elite mortuary cult had some similarities to the royal mortuary cult because of the basic desire to emulate the king by rituals, e.g. the transformation of the deceased into a venerated one in the hereafter.

[833] Roth, *Egyptian phyles in the Old Kingdom, SAOC,* (48).
[834] Assmann, "Preservation and Presentation of Self in Ancient Egyptian Portraiture", vol. I, 80.
[835] Roth, *Egyptian phyles in the Old Kingdom, SAOC,* (48), 3.

TABLE 2 GROUPED TITLES AND OCCURRENCES

Occurrences	Titles	
11	Overseer	Overseer[a4, a7, a12]
		Overseer of the house[a2, a14]
		Overseer of linen[a4, a8, a12, a16, a17, a19]
		Overseer of scribes[a15]
		Overseer of the gate of Nesuhora[11]
7	Priests	Funerary priest[a9, a10, a13, a17, a18]
		Inspector of funerary priests[a3, a6, a10]
		Funerary priest and Elder of the dockyard[a17]
		Lector priest[a3]
7	Scribes	Scribe[a1, a3, a5, a6, a10, a11, a14]
5	Family Members	His eldest son, his beloved[a3, a6]
		His son[a3, a4, a6, a12, a13]
		His brother[a6, a12]
4	Seal Bearers	Seal bearer[a4, a13]
		Sear bearer in monthly service[a13]
		Inspector of seal bearers[a2, a4, a13, a17]
4	Archivist	Archivist[a2, a5, a6, a14]
2	Director	Director of the gang of workmen[a7]
		Director of followers[a8]
1	Court Councilor	Court councilor, Sole councilor, Servant of the throne[a3]
	Others denoting a particular activity:	Physician[a1]
		Barber[a9, a13]
		Manicurist[a9]
		Carpenter[a9]
		Follower[a4]
		Inspector of the fowling pond[a13]
		Inspector of hairdressers of the Great House[a1]

in any method of ranking depending on meanings based on modern understanding of hierarchy, but which cannot be linked into the actual understandings which the ancient Egyptians may have had. While some of the titles are clear-cut in the context of hierarchical implications, others are difficult to position, e.g. the difference between an inspector and an overseer (*sḥḏ/imy-r*) is obvious, however that between an overseer and a director (*ḥrp/imy-r*) is less so. These problems while not totally defeated lead to the following alternative suggestion; namely to consider the frequency of a certain type of official or family member with a title using the method below:

1. All the various attendants' and family members title's were collated.
2. Only one genre of any title was counted, e.g. 7 seal bearers in a tomb would have the same weighting as 1 seal bearer in another tomb. All similar titles were grouped under the main function, e.g. "sealer", would include "sealer in the monthly service" etc. Titles with two functions would be treated as 2 separate functions, e.g. "scribe and sealer" would then appear as 1 scribe and 1 sealer for that tomb.
3. Steps (1) and (2) were then repeated for all the titles within the tombs known to have a carrying-chair. A survey of all the titles appearing in the

carrying-chair representation using the above method resulted in 19 tombs, which displayed titles relating to the subsidiary persons, and these were then segregated in accordance with the suggested method into 8 major genres of titles Table 2 - "Grouped Titles and Occurrences".[836]

---

[836] In order to determine the frequency of title appearance in the carrying-chair scene, the tombs in which they appear have been designated with a superscript as follows:
a1 Nefer-Khuwi, see Roth, "*A Cemetery of Palace Attendants*", fig. 191.
a2 Perneb, see Hayes, "*The Sceptre of Egypt*", vol. 1, fig. 51.
a3 Ptahshepses, see Verner, "*Abusir-1, The Mastaba of Ptahshepses*", pls. 53-55.
a4 Kagemni, see Harpur and Scremin, "*The Chapel of Kagemni*", fig. 278.
a5 Methethi, see Kaplony, "*Studien zum Grab des Methethi*", fig. 2.
a6 Iymery, see Weeks, "*Mastabas of Cemetery G 6000*", fig. 32.
a7 Nikauisesi, see Kanawati, "*The Teti Cemetery at Saqqara*", 6, fig. 55.
a8 Hesi, see Kanawati, "*The Teti Cemetery at Saqqara*", 5, pl. 55.
a9 Niankhkhnum, see Altenmüller and Moussa, "*Das Grab des Nianchchnum und Chnumhotep*", figs. 42 and 60.
a10 Khnumhotep, see Altenmüller and Moussa, "*Das Grab des Nianchchnum und Chnumhotep*", fig. 43.
a11 Qar, see Simpson, "*The Mastabas of Qar and Idu*", pl. XI (b).
a12 Mereruka, see Duell, "*The Mastaba of Mereruka*", vol. 1 and 2, pl. 14 and 158. (Mereruka is known to have 7 sons: Meryteti, Pepyankh, Memy, Khenty, Apref, Khenu, and Nefer but the scene only identifies 9 brothers and 2 sons).
a13 Ty, see Épron, "*Le Tombeau de Ti*", pl.16/17.
a14 Itisen, see Hassan, "*Excavations at Giza*", vol. 5, fig. 123.
a15 Senedjemib. Inti, see Brovarski, "*The Senedjemib Complex*", part 1, fig. 40-41.

Their attested titles, their transliteration, and their tomb(s) [superscripted], also appear in Appendix F.

An attempt was made in Table 3 to correlate the above-mentioned titles with the dating of the tombs.

This revealed that no specific titles could be attributed to either Dynasties 5 or 6 because the titles appear in both periods.

TABLE 3 GROUPED TITLE OCCURRENCE BY DYNASTY

Tomb owner	Dynasty	Overseer	Priests	Scribes	Relatives	Seal Bearers	Archivists	Director	Court Councillor	Others
Titles→		A	B	C	D	E	F	G	H	I
a6 Iymery	V.3L		√	√	√		√			
a9 Niankhkhnum										
a10 Khnumhotep	V.6L-7		√ √	√						√
a3 Ptahshepses	V.6-8?	√	√	√ √	√		√		√	
a14 Itisen										
a15 Senedjemib.Inti	V.8M-L	√								
a1 Nefer-Khuwi	V.8-9	√	√	√	√	√ √	√			√ √
a13 Ty										
a2 Perneb										
a7 Nikauisesi	VI.1	√ √ √ √ √	√ √		√	√		√		√
a18 Meryteti										
a12 Mereruka										
a17 Sabw										
a19 Waatetkhethor										
a16 Seshemnefer.Tjetti										
a4 Kagemni	VI.2	√		√	√	√	√			
a5 Methethi										
a8 Hesi	VI.3	√						√		
a11 Qar	VI.4	√		√						
Occurences →		11	7	7	5	4	4	2	1	4

NOTE: WHERE THERE IS NO DISTINCT SEPARATION BETWEEN DYNASTY PERIODS, E.G. BETWEEN V. 8M-L AND V. 8-9, THEY APPEAR CLUSTERED TOGETHER. WHERE THIS IS NOT THE CASE, E.G. VI.3 AND VI.4, THE TICKS APPEAR IN THE MIDDLE OF THE TABLE.

a16 Seshemnefer,Tjetti, see Junker, "*Giza*", vol. 11, fig. 100.
a17 Sabw, see Borchardt, "*Denkmäler Des Alten Reiches*", vol. 1, pl. 1419.
a18 Meryteti, see Knanwati, "*Mereruka and his Family*", part 1, fig. 47.
a19 Waatetkhethor, see Kanawati, "*Mereruka and his Family*", part 2, fig. 69.

CHART 20: TITLES OF SUBSIDIARY FIGURES

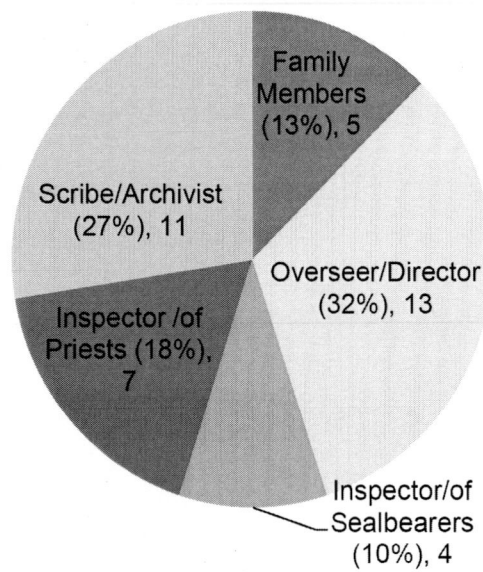

THE ABOVE PIE CHART IS INTENDED TO GIVE AN IDEA OF THE MAIN TITLES USED BY SUBSIDIARY FIGURES BUT NOT OF THE NUMBER OF TOMBS IN WHICH THESE OCCUR. FOR DATA SEE TABLE 2.

Also instructive is Pie Chart 20. It indicates the frequency of main titles of the subsidiary figures in the 19 tombs (52% of the total population of 37 tombs) that result in keeping with established conceptions of mortuary art in that a preponderance of overseers, scribes, and priests are present. Additionally it indicates a conspicuous constant public reminder of power by the Old Kingdom elite, the status of the tomb owner, which is maintained and enhanced by his being surrounded by a cross section of elite members of society, and thus a pointer to the generics.

7.7 Implications of Language Games

Part 1 referred to Wittgenstein and his theory of language games, which among other things, considers that some problems and their solutions are related to the way language, is used to formulate questions. Wittgenstein's use of language games to explain certain philosophical problems or ambiguities might assist in clarifying how the ancient Egyptians felt about certain things, i.e. the ancient Egyptians' probable mindset. By considering a number of language games, it is hoped that one (or more) will coincide with the Egyptians' original language game(s) of the "emic" type. The modern "etic"

type language game one that is most consistently relevant to the evidence is likely to be the one most similar to the original language game. It's associated attitudes are also more likely than not, to be the ones most similar to those of the ancient Egyptians, because of the reliance on consistent relevant evidence. Thus a shift from the initial etic starting point to an end-point of varying emic degree/s) may be possible. Consider the following:

Language Game 1: Social and Economic Value

At the elementary level, the carrying-chair consists of pieces of joined wood. Its value depends entirely upon the people who use it (initially royalty), the material out of which it is made and the functionality of the product. The modern response depends on which of these element(s) is required for proving a certain issue and all or any of these will be influenced by the particular cultural embeddedness of the analyst. People who live in places where there is abundance of hard wood and of animals used for transport, would probably pay very little attention to these elements. Again others could pay more attention to these because these elements of utility and transport are scarce, yet are an essential element of their own culture. Different cultural environments could thus produce different approaches as to the system of government. Functionality of certain products, in our example the carrying-chair and the material used to produce it will vary, and this is why the responses to the carrying-chair scene in its most elementary form will be different.

Objects, which belong to the dead elite, e.g. the carrying-chair, can also be perceived with the same essential social significances as perceived by previous elite owners. The object's social value and the values associated by the elite tomb owner become synonymous, because the object have past prestige. The object thus comes to have some power to influence other people's minds,[837] which in turn serves to reinforce and maintain the generics.

Language Game 2: Role and Societal Analysis

At yet another level, one can use the carrying-chair's role in the analysis of a society at a particular point in time. It then becomes necessary to examine such diverse factors as:

Who carries it?
How is it carried?
How many persons are involved in the process?
What do these carriers wear?
Who is the occupant?
What attributes does he try to show?

These issues then become part of the current language game responses, and because these can be evidenced and related to common ideas and beliefs prevalent at a particular time can expand on the understanding of that society.

Language Game 3: Societal Change

At the third level, enquiry into change as an aspect of cultural development another language game was played by asking such questions as:

Why do habits/mores change?
Are there any general triggers of change?

What are the changes in the carrying-chair motif such as its different material forms, usage by the elite and differences

---

[837] Mills and Walker, eds., *Memory Work,* 81.

in subsidiary attributes, e.g. number of porters, attire, etc. that are apparent?

In answering these questions some changes (part of the answer) were attributed to the aberrations of individual behaviour and be widespread, but this could not be pursued because of the limited nature of the time frame of this study (however where possible, references to other periods were made).

Another answer can be found in the concept of entropy already discussed in Part1; that because every more or less closed system ultimately degrades toward a state of maximum entropy, this situation will result in automatic non-deliberate change, so change is not something pre-ordained by the individual tomb owner? Societies are seldom completely closed systems, because these are composed of a combination of varied internal and external sub-systems. By responding to societal pressures differences are introduced. Societies generally tend to evolve rather than completely die off; even modern day Egypt can be considered as a transformation following the displacement of the original pharaonic culture by (amongst others) the present day Islamic Society.

As regards the carrying-chair this is a symbol of Egyptian elite society evidenced early in the history of Egypt. By Dynasty 5 and 6, it presents a new, fresh and an energetic view of the elite, one, which depicts boldness, and unlimited promise of potential upward movement. There is change in its usage, character, and depiction, as evidenced from the pre-dynastic to the late period.

From a chair used for royal ceremonial religious purposes such as the heb sed festival, as in Narmer mace head (found at the Hierakonpolis Main deposit, now in the Ashmolean Museum, Oxford, E3631), through usurpation by the elite for transport in the Old Kingdom, and eventually used mainly for the processional carrying of gods' statues in the New Kingdom. Further, from the late Middle Kingdom onwards, the use of the carrying-chair starts to diminish and finally becomes obsolete during the Hyksos period. Thus what appears as change or even decay, nevertheless appears in another form in another time zone, e.g. the horse and wagon during the early 18th Dynasty, replace the carrying-chair as an elite attribute, comparable to the nineteenth and the twentieth century's exchange of the horse carriage for automobiles by the elite. This then is an example of change and evolution because of the interaction of the elite, who ensure that change is entrenched, and that entropy as meaning a progression towards a dead culture does not develop, or takes longer. In due course of time, differences in the way social and religious issues were addressed in the context of the carrying-chair motif, also become noticeable, e.g. differences in the number of porters, the type of canopies, attire, etc.

Language Game 4: Generic Involvement

The language game extended for the carrying-chair motif was identified from the start as one in which aspects of

identity, individuality, and ideology, would be explored in the context of Dynasty 5 and 6 Old Kingdom elite tombs. This demanded that the search for the clues to these issues, employ a wide variety of approaches/disciplines to illustrate the relationship between the tomb owner and his subsidiary attendants depicted in this motif. Elimination of one's own cultural baggage, especially in relation to the levels of hierarchy was made possible using statistical tools. One is fully aware that cold mathematics can never fully explain human systems; however mathematical quantification enables one to draw useful analogies, which are shown in the 29 charts and 9 tables presented in this book.

The crucial point to observe is that in all the four language games that are being used to elicit different responses, none encapsulates an answer suitable for all occasions. This substantiates the hypothesis by Wittgenstein, that there can be no one single and final meaning and it all depends on which language game is being employed, which theory has been applied to Egyptian Art as illustrated by: Frankfort (multiplicity of approaches),[838] Hornung (Quantum Theory), and more recently refined by Van Walsem (in explaining how things can exist in an either/or situation).[839]

This analysis of the carrying-chair has resulted in a foray into many multifaceted and competing worlds and perhaps this complexity is best summed up in the words of Williams, he writes:

"Every human society has its own shape, its own purposes, and its own meanings. Every human society expresses these, in institutions, and in arts and learning. The making of a society is the finding of common meanings and directions, and its growth is an active debate and amendment under the pressures of experience, contact, and discovery, writing themselves into the land. The growing society is there, yet it is also made and remade in every individual mind. The making of a mind is, first, the slow learning of shapes, purposes, and meanings, so that work, observation, and communication are possible. Then, second, but equal in importance, is the testing of these in experience, the making of new observations, comparisons, and meanings. A culture has two aspects: the known meanings and directions, which its members are trained to, the new observations and meanings, which are offered and tested.

These are the ordinary processes of human societies and human minds, and we see through them the nature of a culture: that it is always both traditional and creative; that it is both the most ordinary common meanings and the finest individual meanings".[840]

[838] Frankfort, *Ancient Egyptian Religion*.
[839] Hornung, *Conceptions of God in ancient Egypt*, 241. See the refined version by Walsem in "The Struggle Against Chaos as a "Strange Attractor" in Ancient Egyptian Culture", 321-23 and 333-34.
[840] Williams, *Resources of hope: culture, democracy, socialism*, 4.

Chapter 8: Officials' Records and Taking Account

This chapter sketches the relations between the living and the dead especially with regard to the dialogue that is conducted in presenting records of presumably the tomb owner's property. The 'Taking Account' motif has been purposely chosen because it directly relates to a particular cultural aspect of society's members in the way they communicate with each other, and because communication is an indispensable element of all existence, namely the accumulation of the avenues of information. The salient point is that there is a change in the modes of human interaction, from primary oral to written and that this change becomes embedded in different forms of communication and display, of which the Taking Account motif is one such example.

At its most basic level communication can be of an oral nature but with increasing societal complexity, this process is supplemented by other forms. Writing becomes a crucial part of this social process and eventually forms an essential component of the organization and administrative elements of a culture. Organization and administration together with communication then play a role in the stability and unity of a society, which is essential for its ordered and secure existence.

Communication and display of document records also reflect the broader concerns of the elite, one of which must have had to do with material possessions, since their well thought-out display in some form is omnipresent in all the tomb depictions. It would also satisfy the tomb owner's posthumous needs plus reinforce the social structure that his heir would inherit. In order for these actions to have maximum societal impact, they are made to become part of the monumental culture and related ceremony. In the private elite tombs of the Old Kingdom, communication, display, material possessions, and ceremony are combined to form part of the Taking Account motif, based on a continuing belief in the religious concepts of the time and ultimately reflect the cultural generics in the specific case.

8.1 Confronting the Tomb owner with Written Records

This motif will consider the inspection and transfer of the officials' records. It will be called the 'Taking Account' motif because this term understood as a verb (not to be confused with the financial procedures of the accountancy profession) covers all that is depicted in this motif, e.g.

- Reflects the interaction of both protagonists.
- Demonstrates the relative status of the protagonists.
- Deals with the idea of the tomb owner's property transfer, and related cultural aspects.
- Illustrates possibly simultaneous oral and written communication, i.e. information.

  In the literature this motif has been referred to as "Presenting the Scroll"[841] but this highlights only one aspect of the obvious activity - that of the presenter, and takes the focus away from the tomb owner, which the terminology in this book does not. Further even if all the presenting individuals were officials who were in some form directly or indirectly connected with the king and so of high standing, Egyptian art does not usually allow any diminution of the focal point of view i.e. the tomb owner. Accordingly one cannot demote these scenes simply to that of presenting the scroll, just highlighting one function of the presenter. Baines's assertion is nearer the mark when he stresses that "complex cultural topics could only be communicated in writing through visual arrangements" and that "its formal character is probably its most significant aspect".[842]

There is no commonly accepted alternative terminology for this motif and some authors may prefer other words if they want to emphasize a particular component factor.

- Taking account refers to an act within a particular context in which assent and deliberation are required. In the Old Kingdom context both of these are apparent from the depictions themselves. This contrasts with those communicative articulations, which are so general as to be applicable in any context, and where no assent or deliberation is required.

This motif's development can be traced tentatively to the time when the principal requirement was the provisioning of the deceased with food. From actual food to written offering lists, to depictions and models of food, to prayers and the biographical inscriptions in Dynasty 5; the strongest support that the dead need provisioning is found in the Pyramid Texts, where it is the primary requirement for the king.[843] These ideas of what was essentially a provisioning requirement are depicted in the:

- Banqueting motif, where offerings are presented to the passively watching but non-eating tomb owner.
- Taking Account motif, where the proffered papyrus document(s) suffice.

Whether this development as stated above actually took place, is debatable.[844]

[843] Faulkner, *The Ancient Egyptian Pyramid Texts*, § 474. "... the corpse is bound for the earth, and what men receive when they are buried is its thousand of bread and its thousand of beer".

[844] Lichtheim, *Ancient Egyptian Literature*, vol. I, 3-8. Also see Junker, *Giza*, vol. 3, 58-59.

[841] Manuelian, "Presenting the Scroll", 561-88.

[842] Baines, *Visual and Written Culture in Ancient Egypt*, 149-52.

The Taking-Account motif and the form in which it is depicted in elite tombs of the Old Kingdom provide a non-verbal language. Both the tomb itself and the tomb owner, function to unite the members of his group of people (as evidenced in the funerary rituals), and to make permanent those property rights, which the tomb owner had prior to his death. The endowing of permanence (through display) to property rights across generations was a factor in the claims of lineal descent and must therefore be regarded as significant.[845]

A prominent feature during the pharaonic period was the administration and written recording in the archives of wills, title deeds, taxes, etc.[846] The word 'administration' is to be understood as including the state's apparatus in its entirety and the means employed for its effective functioning – communication and recording are two facets of this intricate web.

The nature of the source material is patchy and numerous studies have focused on certain specific aspects,[847] e.g. seal impressions and their related offices, the phyle system, aspects of the administrative system of the Memphite region and legal inscriptions relating to the Old Kingdom.

The Taking-Account motif allows for a more specialized approach by highlighting certain relevant aspects of the early administrative system, especially those related to communication and documentation, which existed from Dynasty 1 into the Old Kingdom.[848] These aspects ensured the elite's effective economic control derived during the recording of products from their estates, official gifts from the king, and taxes on surplus of produced goods.[849]

Eventually, this was not only an elite concern and it must have filtered down to all people for their specific needs, i.e. how information given, recorded and shared becomes an integral part of society at all levels. This is why this motif has been chosen, because it is expressed in different forms of communication throughout all levels of society.

In the elite mastaba decoration repertoire of the Old Kingdom, there occurs a motif in which an official 'presents' the tomb owner with a document possibly concerning some aspect of his *pr ḏt* (goods of his funerary endowment).[850] The presentation of this document is depicted in a wide variety of ways, but in all cases the presenter(s) always faces the tomb owner. In keeping with the objects of this study (see Introductory Remarks) those sub-motifs which are mainly concerned with practices that characterize the Egyptian's interaction with the divine sphere, shall be excluded, namely:

- Offering rituals with priests reciting formulae from a papyrus scroll held in front of them.[851]
- Officials inscribing papyri generally and reciting invocations or other cultic recitations in front of the tomb owner.

This part will therefore be limited to document offerers and the tomb owner and the word *m33* shall have no overriding meaning, i.e. the motif can still be that of Taking-Account even if the word *m33* is present, provided the viewing is that of general items and not specific ones. How then does one explain the presence of a person holding a document in front of the tomb owner with varied captions? There is no definite answer to this question and the following solutions have been proposed:

- Accept all such motifs as nonspecific presenting motifs- however this is probably incorrect because this fails to explain why there is no reference to the document at all.
- Der Manuelian's method is to de-emphasize the captions; he writes "The presence or absence of a specific hieroglyphic caption is unrelated to the presence or absence of a more general, overall scene description relating directly to the large scale figure of the tomb owner".[852]

However this too is imprecise, because in such cases textual evidence is being relegated to something of no import. In addition, the scene could describe a document, which is being inspected by the scribe, in order to ensure that the items and goods depicted are correctly accounted for. The document then is just for the scribe's benefit and

---

[845] N. de G. Davies, *The Tomb of Rekh-mi-Re at Thebes*, vol.I, 18, 25 and 33. Theban tomb TT 100 is a New Kingdom tomb, however it clearly indicates this process of organization and communication, i.e. the tomb owner says that he was responsible for the maintenance of the archives, appointment, and supervision of officials and exercise of law. Also see G. P. F. van den Boorn, *The duties of the Vizier: civil administration in the early New Kingdom.*

[846] Posener-Kriéger and Cenival, *Hieratic Papyri in the British Museum. Fifth Series. The Abu Sir Papyri,* pl. XXXIV.

[847] For seal impressions, see Kaplony, *Die Inschriften der ägyptischen Frühzeit,* vol. II, and III. Also see Roth, *Egyptian phyles in the Old Kingdom,* and Strudwick, *The Administration of Egypt in the Old Kingdom,* and Goedicke, *Die privaten Rechtsinschriften aus dem Alten Reich.*

[848] Emery, *The tomb of Hemaka,* 14. Although there is evidence for the existence of papyrus as a writing material, no examples of written papyrus have survived from the earliest dynasties.

[849] Trigger, *Early Civilizations,* 45-46. His analysis of early civilizations, found that elites in every analyzed state, were able to expropriate economic surpluses from the poorer classes and use them to their advantage.

[850] Seidl, *Einführung in die ägyptische Rechtsgeschichte bis zum Ende des Neuen Reiches,* 44. The hieroglyphic symbol for house is attested since Dynasty 1. By Dynasty 4, it comes to have an extended meaning as evidenced in the tomb of Metjen - "von dem aus ein im Lande verstreutes, umfangreiches, grundherrschaftliches Vermögen für alle Zeit verwaltet werden soll - durch die dereinst im Haus befindlichen Nachfolger des Meten", see Urk. 1. 4, 10 [C7]. This is evidence for the multi-faceted meaning of this common symbol relating to a host of concepts, e.g. house, house owner, estate, his family, his heir and in all probability to the goods of his funerary endowment (*pr ḏt*). For a more subtle distinction and interpretation, see Fitzenreiter, *Zum Toteneigentum im Alten Reich,* 57-64 and 89-91. Also see Manuelian, "Presenting the Scroll", 582 and 585. He mentions (*pr ḏt*) only three times relating it to offerings both invocation and reversionary. However, in view of its possible extended meanings, the nuanced approach of Fitzenreiter is certainly more revealing.

[851] Badawy, *The Tomb of Nyhetep-ptah at Giza and the Tomb of Ankhmahor at Saqqara,* pl. 17.

[852] Manuelian, "Presenting the Scroll", 563.

has nothing to do with the tomb owner. In the tomb of Nebet,[853] the inspection or receipt by the tomb owner of the proffered document from as many as twelve proffering scribes is nowhere captioned. Instead all the focus is on the items that are seen and described as such by the tomb owner. The frequent captions specify what she is viewing, despite men each with a document being present. The captions are specific in nature, e.g.

"Bringing wine to you my lady"
"Viewing the wine"
"Viewing the wine brought from the palace"
"Viewing the gifts that are brought"
"Viewing the agricultural labour"
"Viewing all the hoofed animals".

If the scribes are seen with a document but are only 'counting' the goods in the tomb owner's presence, this cannot be a 'taking-account' motif because this is a passive act of seeing by the tomb owner. However if this is a presentation of the document itself, then it could be a Taking Account motif. Accordingly, in distinguishing if a document is being presented or not, the absence of any supportive caption makes certainty of interpretation very difficult.

In a largely pre-literate society, the artist is probably more accurate when he portrays the actual objects rather than texts of the object. A modern analogy where people are conditioned to accept symbols as substitutes for reality is seen when we accept pieces of printed-paper as money, instead of gold. Similarly in Old Kingdom Egypt, the proffering of a document has to be differentiated from all the other viewing motifs because it represents a very precise signal, one that is not casual but causal in effect.

The determination of taking account motifs will be based on the following guidelines.

Definite Proof if both:

1. Presence of a tomb owner, a presenter and a document AND
2. Sufficient proof of taking-account in the form of :

   a) Caption(s) stating the handing over, extending, proffering, etc. of the document to the tomb owner and/or
   b) Depiction of the tomb owner's obvious acceptance of the document.

Insufficient proof (even when the tomb owner, a presenter, and a document are depicted) if:

1. No supportive captions are present.
2. Scribes with a document in their hands, described or shown as counting goods, which are viewed by

the tomb owner in a passive manner requiring little or no conscious effort or deliberation.
3. No obvious receipt by the tomb owner.

An example from the tomb of Idut makes this clear. It meets the definite proof guidelines.

1. All persons and a document are present and
2. The caption reads:

"inspecting or viewing the gifts and all good offerings of the year which are brought for her from the estates and the towns".[854]

(*m33 nḏt-ḥr rnpt nbt nfrt innt*
n=s m ḥwwt ni nwt)

The depiction shows a document being presented. Therefore this scene would fall into the category of a Taking Account motif.

A contrasting example is that from the tomb of Seshathetep. heti that does not meet the guidelines above, and is therefore not to be considered a taking account motif.[855]

It must be stressed that even with the above scheme difficulties persist, one good example being that in the tomb of Meryib.[856] In Meryib's entrance thicknesses, the Taking-Account motif can be said to be composed such that if one were to put the Southern entrance thickness (with its indefinite caption) behind the Northern one (with its definitive caption), the combined depiction would be a fully detailed Taking-Account motif.

In the Northern entrance thickness, the tomb owner is depicted with his son Meryib junior, and the seal bearer of the festival ointment Isi presents a specific document, followed by the supervisor of linen. The caption reads:

"Presenting the list by the seal bearer of the festival and the supervisor of linen".

Above these two figures another caption reads:

"Viewing the invocation offerings brought from the house of the king"

and presumably, this is what the list being presented contained.

On the Southern entrance thickness, the tomb owner in shoulder length striated 'wig'; panther skin outer garment with 'false beard', bracelets and a rod of authority is seen with his three children (two daughters Sedjenet and

---

[853] Munro, *Der Unas-Friedhof Nord-West: Das Doppelgrab der Königinnen Nebet und Khenut*, vol. 1, 66 and pl. 3/38.

[854] Kanawati, *The Unis Cemetery at Saqqara: the tombs of Iynefert and Ihy (reused by Idut)*, vol. 2, fig. 71.
[855] Kanawati, *Tombs at Giza*, vol. 2, pl. 45. Here it is clear from the captions that the son/scribe is counting all the property.
[856] Junker, *Giza*, vol. 2, 127-30.

Nesdjerkai and a son Meryneteru-khufu). The caption reads:

> "Viewing the valuable ($htmt$)[857] offerings brought from the house of the king".

In contrast to the previous caption, this caption probably refers to general valuables but there is no specific document or a presenter and so this southern part would not meet the above guidelines (although the combined northern and southern parts would meet the guidelines). This is a good example of the difficulties of classifying the taking-account motif.

A further confusion is in the use of the verb $m33$ for viewing and presentation in the captions, which cannot be easily resolved. Because there are different verbs, which exist, and were used to describe such actions, it is incredulous that the ancient Egyptians were unaware of the subtle differences. The same verb may have slightly different meanings, which might only be detected in the context of their usage, and as such it is exceedingly difficult to draw a line between the multiple meanings of such a verb, e.g. $m33$. Similar problems exist in the Taking-Account motif in the tombs of Meresankh III, and Kahfkhufu I.[858] This is why I have chosen to differentiate these apparently similar motifs as far as is possible.

Admittedly my guidelines might be regarded as arbitrary, but it is necessary to distinguish between two types of different yet ostensibly similar scenes. Many of the viewing scenes come under the general rubric of $m33$ scenes. These include actions such as 'viewing', and/or, 'in order to view', and sometimes the recitation of glorifications indicated by the words $m33/r.m33/\check{s}dt$.

Contrasting with these, are those scenes in which a specific reference is made to the acts of handing, proffering, giving, extending, and spreading of a document, indicated by the words $di/r\underline{d}i/rdit/di.t/si\text{'}/\exists wt$. In distinguishing these scenes it is hoped to make transparent the fine distinction between seeing and inspecting/taking-account. 'Seeing' is an act of little interpretative cultural value, while 'inspecting', i.e. Taking Account, imposes a certain discipline on the giver and the receiver and emphasizes a significant cultural habit, which is being communicated and documented. It is the defining and main parameter of this motif and contrasts with any incidental activity. While the Taking Account motif's title incorporates most of the notions associated with reporting, this nomenclature does no justice to all the different ways the scene is represented, and captioned, and grey areas exist when applying the guidelines proposed.

Some of the motifs clearly point to the ceremonial transfer of a document and its contents, indicated by the tomb owner extending his hand to receive the document.[859] At other times this can be understood from the use of the verb $r\underline{d}it$ but this has similar problems as already indicated when discussing the verb $m33$. The point of focus is distributed between the tomb owner and his sub-ordinate and the various depictions show the subordinate in a wide variety of poses, which could be accidental or deliberate but this cannot be established.[860]

The meaning of this motif can best be understood if one contrasts this ceremonial function (formal occasion where careful attention is paid to form and detail) with that of a liturgical one as in the Pyramid Texts or an aesthetic recreational one as in the Banqueting scenes but there are overlapping grey areas. Indeed the motif indicates the tomb owner's relative power over other people, which would not be demonstrated if he was depicted alone. The tomb owner is seen actively exercising control over his $pr \underline{d}t$ (goods of his funerary endowment), official business, recreational goals, etc. previously partly seen in the royal iconography of Senefru the first king of Dynasty 4,[861] which now becomes part of private elite tombs. This control is shown when the tomb owner is presented with the list/accounts and he inspects and accepts them. Accordingly this scene may have a variety of cultural meanings including the generic, all of which are related to the social position of the tomb owner, e.g.

- Communicating with other elite.
- Documenting of his endowment goods by scribes.
- Implementing what is described or presented permanently.
- Honoring the deceased.
- Legitimizing the presenter(s).
- Legitimizing and showing control of inheritance.

The last mentioned 'acts' are problematic because of a lack of evidence and have to be reconciled with the way property was known to be transferred and inherited, and can be ascertained only from texts.[862] In the Old Kingdom the normal way property was transferred and inherited, is well defined. If you wanted to buy property for use during your life only, you had to have a sales document known as an $swnt$. However if you wanted to pass this property to your heirs, you would also need an $imyt\text{-}pr$ document. Since the eldest son was normally present at the funeral, could this be the depicted handover of the inheritance? Whether the Taking-Account motif has any relation to this, is unclear.

The interest here is to demonstrate that in Taking-Account of his worldly goods, the tomb owner is in fact demonstrating that although he is dead, he still can ask the

---

[857] Hannig, *Grosses Handwörterbuch*, 627. (List of?) valuables

[858] Dunham et al., *The Mastaba of Queen Mersyankh III*, fig. 3 (b) and 12. Also see Simpson, Chapman, and Reisner, *The mastabas of Kawab, Khafkhufu I and II*, fig. 28 and 29.

[859] In the 5 tombs of: Kahif, Kaninisut, Nefer and Kahay, Qar, and Senedjemib-Mehi

[860] For details of the various poses by the presenter, see Manuelian, "Presenting the Scroll", 570-574.

[861] Fakhry, *The Monuments of Senefru at Dashur II*, fig. 16; redrawn by B. Garfi.

[862] Logan, "The *Imyt-pr* Document: Form, Function, and Significance", *JARCE*, (XXXVll), 71.

CHART 21: TOMB OWNERS' POSTURE AND GENDER

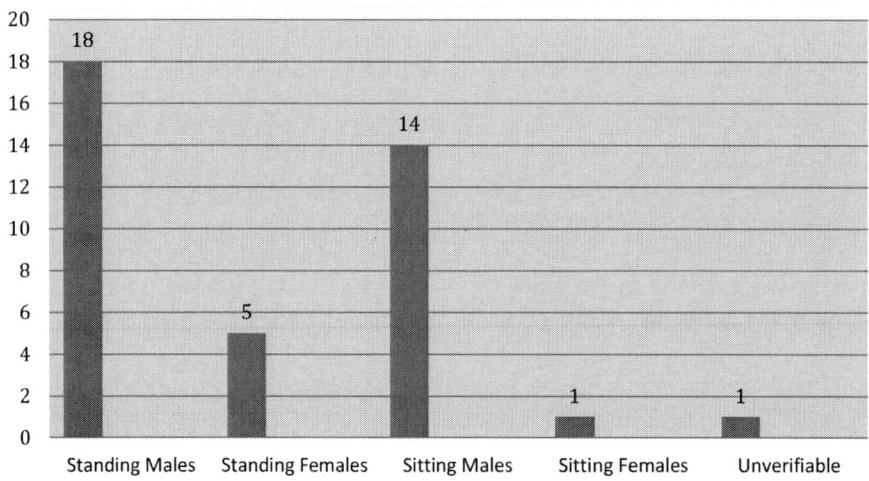

DUPLICATION OCCURS BECAUSE THERE ARE TWO DIFFERENT PLATES (TY PL. 56 AND 128) IN ONE TOMB. THE ABOVE NUMBERS SHOW HOW MANY TOMBS THERE ARE INDICATING POSTURE AND GENDER. FOR THE DETAILS OF THESE TOMBS, PLEASE REFER TO 'APPENDIX C'.

living to be accountable as per his wishes when he was alive, something which carries significant meaning with regard to his identity and his desire to be remembered posthumously.

The four main elements of the Taking-Account motif subject to the rules proposed (see page 124) would then be as follows:

1. Presence of a document as the central focus of the motif around which the tomb owner is shown Taking-Account, which can include viewing, inspecting, accepting, reading, or hearing the proffered document.
2. Person(s) is/are shown bringing, reading, giving, or reporting the document in the immediate presence of the tomb owner. A hallmark of this scene is that the presenter is always shown facing the tomb owner with his back to the offerings.
3. The document shown is usually a papyrus scroll as the vehicle by and through which information is being organized and delivered to the tomb owner.[863] The document has no one form and can be open, rolled up and sometimes appears in a stiffened form, which gives it the appearance of a stiff board.
4. The appropriate captions relating to what is being done are sometimes informative but not always so. Indeed one has to be careful not to mix up the two types of scenes (i.e. Taking Account and accompanying activity) and as already indicated; the essential attribute of all Taking Account motifs is the implied element of assent and deliberation based on its context of usage.

Similar to the methodology followed in the previous (Carrying-Chair Motif) chapter, the rest of the present chapter will deconstruct the Taking-Account motif in its context.

8.2 Tomb Owner's (Recipient's) Posture

Generally the male tomb owner's relatively formal posture and dress with the maximum display of rank and wealth, indicates he is attending an important ceremony. The majority of the tomb owners in this Taking-Account motif are male, there being only six females,[864] who have this motif in their tomb.

In Dynasties 4 to 6 the tomb owner is either standing or sitting with no significant preference for either position. Further both postures and genders occur in the dynasties mentioned and there appears to be no specific pattern,[865] illustrated in Chart 21.

8.3 Elevated Status Goods

Rod, Sceptre and Rolled Cloth

The rod, the sceptre and the rolled cloth were used to form a concept of the prevailing social relations, which were the hallmark of the lifestyle of the elite that clearly distinguished

---

[863] Černý, *Paper and Books in Ancient Egypt*, 21-29. He gives a useful history of papyrus and its use in writing in ancient Egypt.

[864] In the 6 tombs of: Hemetra, Idut, Khentkawes, Khenut, Meresankh III, and Nebet.
[865] Standing males in 18 tombs of: Ankhmahor, Fetekty, Iymery, Iynefert, Kagemni, Kairer, Kaniniswt, Kaemnofret, Khafre-ankh, Meryib, Neferbauptah, Niankhkhnum and Khnumhotep, Ptahhotep II, Sekhemka, Shetwi, Tjenti, Ty (fig. 128), and Whemka.
Standing females in 5 tombs of: Hemetra, Khentkawes, Khenut, Meresankh III, and Nebet
Sitting male in 14 tombs of: Kahif, Kanefer, Khafkhufu I, Khnumenti, Nefer, Nefer and Kahay, Nisutnefer, Perneb, Qar, Rashepses, Seneb, Senedjemib-Mehi, Seshathotep, and Ty (fig.56).
Sitting female in the tomb of: Idut.
Unverifiable in the tomb of: Mereruka (fig. 51).

them. While these status symbols were originally part of the sphere of royal religion, their depiction in private tombs is evidence for the way how certain symbols were chosen by the elite in order to disseminate the social meaning of the term 'elite', which in time became a widely understood concept expressed graphically. They also provide a pointer to the way certain items of perceived value become co-opted, and are indicative of the complex additions and omissions which in due time form the basis of the generics and the reason why Egyptian Art cannot be fully understood if the generics are ignored.

The constituent of the elite lifestyle, expressed in commemorative art in these status symbols in the Taking-

Account motif, probably was a reflection of the reality of elite life.

Significant majorities in the Taking-Account motif display a combination of rod, sceptre, and rolled cloth.

The hieroglyphs, which describe the word rod and the different names for rods, are numerous.[866] Rods have an ancient lineage, and are evidenced as grave goods as far back as the early Dynasty 1 graves at Tarkhan.[867] The majority of the tomb owners (seventeen (74%)) are shown with a rod of which the rounded-knobbed end is on top, while five tomb owners hold a simple straight rod.[868] The only exception is that in the tomb of Kaninswt, where he is depicted holding a rod with the rounded-knobbed end at the bottom. This is surprising as rods with knobbed end downwards (typifying the hieroglyph for *mdw*) are depicted only up to the time of Khufu. From his reign, rods with knobbed end on top are depicted in the hands of the officials as confirmed by the 74% majority in the Taking-Account motif.[869]

These objects of prominent power and display, maintain, reinforce, and consolidate the sphere of the elite's authority, especially in a society in which inequality was an accepted fact, and where rank was expressed in terms of lifestyle and display.[870]

The hierarchical nature of Egyptian society meant that different people ranging from the old man in the village, the official, the elite to the king, used rods. While the overlap between uses in most of these categories, makes

delineating precise rank (excepting the king) impossible, nevertheless it enables one to understand how the ancient Egyptians might have understood the words/concepts relating to power, office and dignity. Since the rod's use as an instrument of coercive physical power is outside this study, the concentration shall be on the rod as a visible symbol of:

- Individual's passive social position.
- Holder's active position in the state administrative role.

Both the above categories fuse into each other in the representations of the elite. The rod then is more than just a fancy adornment because of its link with certain official positions and occupations. The rod's ubiquitous appearance in grave decoration and goods, demonstrates its symbolic function was thus understood by society as can be seen even in Egypt today (carrying a stick is a common feature of the village headman), albeit in a less exaggerated form. Indeed the overseer or an official without a rod of authority was an unthinkable proposition in ancient Egypt. Its presence materializes social identity as well as the ideology of fulfillment of a duty towards society, because only then could one be in a position to carry such a symbol.

The degree of dignity symbolized in the act of being represented holding a rod/sceptre/rolled cloth, would probably vary with the different levels of social position, and can be usefully examined by the use of levels of the language game. In this language game the different facets (levels) of the tomb owner shall be considered.

1. At the level of the general elite, it probably denoted a certain minimum of religious and cultural knowledge, which in turn symbolized that the individual carrying a rod/sceptre/rolled cloth led a type of life and actions accepted as fundamental values by society.
2. At the level of the highest official, it probably meant that the office holder in the fulfillment of his duties used his position and his character in following the principles of *Mȝʿt*. Although the vizier (chief official) is present in the Old Kingdom elite tombs, yet in his depiction with the staff and sceptre, he is not differentiated from other officials. The earliest ordination of a vizier of which we have textual evidence, is that from the biography of the vizier Rekhmire, in which he states that the king gave him the staff of experience (metaphor for the attainment of an official rank).[871]
3. At the level of seniority by virtue of age and experience, which would also imply that being old was by itself a symbol of one who was worthy of carrying this emblem, and thereby of being treated accordingly.

---

[866] Hassan, *Stöcke und Stäbe im pharaonischen Ägypten bis zum Ende des Neuen Reiches, MÄS*, (33), 6-9. He has collected 74 such names.
[867] Petrie, Wainwright, and Gardiner, *Tarkhan 1 and Memphis V*, pl. 8. Three rods were found measuring 107, 117, and 124cm., which now are all in the Petrie Museum under catalogue numbers 8466, 8467, and 8468.
[868] Rounded Knobbed end on top in the tombs of: Iymery, Iynefert, Kagemni, Kanefer, Kaemnofret, Khafre-ankh, Khafkhufu I, Meryib, Nefer, Neferbauptah, Niankhkhnum/Khnumhotep, Rashepses, Sekhemka, Seshathotep, Shetwi, Tjenti, and Ty.
Straight rods in the tombs of: Ankhmahor*, Fetekty*, Nisutnefer, Seneb and Whemka.
* Tombs marked with an asterisk, are ambiguous because of their damaged nature.
[869] Fischer, "Stöcke und Stäbe", *LÄ*, vol. 6, 49-57.
[870] Trigger, "Monumental Architecture: A Thermodynamic Explanation of Symbolic Behaviour", *WA*, (22), 119-132.

[871] Sethe, *Urkunden der 18. Dynastie*, IV, 1076, l. 4. "The king gave me a rod of experience".

CHART 22: STANDING WITH ATTRIBUTES OF AUTHORITY

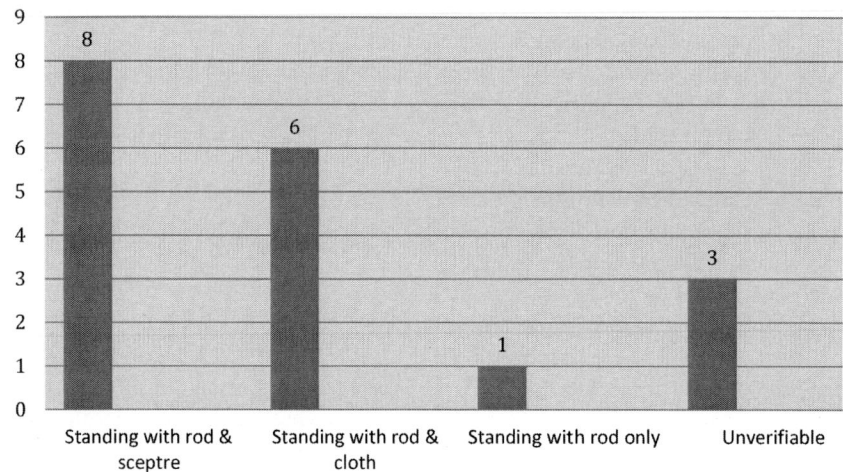

It is not clear how far these different levels of language game were connected to reality and it is correct to assume that "… there are exaggerations on both sides, the picture of the ideal rule of justice was never one of attainment, and the corruption of the ruling class differed from age to age and from individual to individual. Egypt was never wholly noble or wholly corrupt".[872]

STANDING plus Attributes of Authority

The elite in the majority of the Taking Account motifs hold emblems of power in their hands, which are the rod of authority and either a sceptre or a rolled cloth.

The same attributes of authority are combined in many different ways in this motif. Therefore whilst these attributes are accurately numbered in the following text and charts, one must be careful when using these numbers because simple addition of them can involve duplication errors.

Depictions of rods in any combination of sitting or standing are found in twenty-three tombs, i.e. 61% of all examined tombs.[873]

There are 18 depictions of standing tomb owners of which 15[874] hold a rod of authority, and 3 (Fetekta, Kairer, and Ptahhotep II) are unverifiable.

The earliest sceptre comes from a grave in Helwan and points to the earthly dignity that this must have represented[875] because in all probability, it was a royal attribute as evidenced in the Pyramid texts, which in time was usurped by the elite. Its appearance in grave decoration would be expected in places where the tomb owner is the main centre of cultic attention, especially on false doors and entrance thicknesses, and in motifs in which the purpose is to depict the tomb owner in his official capacity, where he is also shown in full ceremonial regalia.

Of the 15 instances depicting a standing male tomb owner holding a rod of authority, there are eight instances[876] where the tomb owner is depicted with a rod in one hand and the sceptre in the other and six instances[877] where the tomb owner is depicted holding a rod in one hand and a rolled cloth in the other. There is one instance (Ty fig. 128) where the tomb owner is standing with a rod only but with no other attributes (sceptre/rolled cloth) of authority.

A summary is provided in Chart 22.

The rolled piece of cloth probably had a utilitarian function used much like a handkerchief but it could also have ideological functions because it is being shown in a ceremonial occasion. This then results in a statistically significant percentage of nearly 83% (in chart 21- 15 out of 18 standing male tomb owners are depicted with a symbol of authority).

The three exceptions are in the tombs of Fetekta, Kairer, and Ptahhotep II. While Fetekta and Kairer are now damaged and fragmented, judging by what is left, they probably had in their pristine state some sort of symbol of authority; that of Ptahhotep II can be explained in terms of individuality. Ptahhotep II holds no symbols of authority whatsoever and a comparison with the tombs of Kagemni

---

[872] Frankfort et al., *The intellectual adventure of ancient man*, 87.

[873] 23 combinations of Sitting or Standing tomb owner with rod in the tombs of: Ankhmahor, Fetekty, Iymery, Iynefert, Kaninisut, Kaemnofret, Kagemni, Kanefer, Khafkhufu I, Khafre-ankh, Meryib, Nefer, Neferbauptah, Nisutnefer, Niankhkhnum/Khnumhotep, Rashepses, Sekhemka, Seneb, Seshathotep, Shetwi, Tjenti, Ty (fig. 128 and fig.56), and Whemka.

[874] Standing tomb owner with rod in the 15 tombs of: Ankhmahor, Iymery, Iynefert, Kaniniswt, Kaemnofret, Kagemni, Meryib, Neferbauptah, Niankkhnum/Khnumhotep, Sekhemka, Shetwi, Tjenti, Whemka, Khafre-ankh, and Ty (fig. 128)

[875] Junker, *Giza*, vol. 12, 8.

[876] Standing and carrying a rod and a sceptre in different hands in the 8 tombs of: Ankhmahor, Kagemni, Kaninisut, Meryib, Sekhemka, Shetwi, Tjenti, and Whemka.

[877] Standing and carrying a rod and piece of rolled cloth in different hands in the 6 tombs of: Iymery, Iynefert, Kaemnofret, Khafre-ankh, Neferbauptah, and Niankhkhnum/Khnumhotep.

and Shetwi is instructive. In both these cases the tomb owners are similarly attired and presented but each also holds a rod and sceptre as well. Another explanation lies in the depiction of all the farmwomen bringing in the varied detailed produce and animals, which being symbols of extreme wealth and authority, might have been thought to be enough in themselves.

Although the rod is frequently depicted in the standing position, it is not restricted to this posture and is seen in the sitting position but not with the same frequency.

Standing with Lotus Bloom

There are 6 female tomb owners in the Taking Account motif.[878] Five of these are in the standing posture of whom 3 (Khenut, Meresankh III, and Nebet) are holding a lotus bloom, which has other connotations including attributes of authority. When they are shown with a lotus bloom to their nose, the other free hand hangs down the side. During the various periods of Egyptian history, the lotus bloom came to symbolize a wide variety of meanings:[879] continual life and regeneration, feminine beauty, hypnotic effect, erotic connotations, pleasing perfume and connection to love poetry,[880] most of which may have something to do with vanity but not authority. The motif of the lotus being sniffed originated in Dynasty 4 with women, and in the second half of Dynasty 6 came to be also used by men[881] as a symbol of rejuvenation.

In the Taking-Account motif, only Khenut, Meresankh III, and Nebet clearly hold a lotus bloom. In the case of Khnetkawes it is unclear whether she holds a lotus bloom because the upper part is missing, but it is possible she too held a lotus bloom based on their similarities to the composition of Meresankh III. The exception is in the case of Hemetra, who is shown holding nothing.

The sitting posture is illustrated in the tomb of Idut.

SITTING plus Attributes of Authority

Sitting in any **combination of attributes** occurs in 19 cases of which 4 are duplications resulting in 15 tombs involving sitting with attributes of authority.[882]

Carved Chair: In five cases the tomb owner is depicted in a sitting posture on a carved chair, with the left hand holding only a rod at an angle in front of him, with the other empty

arm resting on his lap[883] uncannily similar in their display of both intent and relaxation, as in the standing position. In two cases the tomb owner holds in addition to the rod, a piece of rolled cloth[884] and in two other cases he holds only a flywhisk.[885]

The tomb owner sits in a carved chair with feline or bulls' legs[886] and in three cases that of Qar, Perneb, and Khnumenti, he is depicted being sat in a carrying-chair, while being presented with a scroll.[887]

Chairs are part of the early offering lists and the hieroglyph for the chair is an unassuming sort of legless seat. However, chairs are used in the word *špss* which depicts a man seated on a chair with animal legs, meaning 'to be noble and/or wealthy' and sometimes even a chair by itself is understood to denote this concept.[888] Thus the chair's importance can be seen from the hieroglyph for noble/wealthy. Interestingly, the association of the type of carving on the chair's legs with attributes of divine and royal power (bulls and feline) is another indication of their importance. While bovine legs appear earlier on and continue right into the New Kingdom, the preference from Dynasty 5 onwards is for feline legs.[889] It would seem that making of furniture legs was an important craft as indicated by the title - *imy-rꜣ wꜥrt n irw wḥmt* "Overseer of the guild of makers of furniture legs".[890] This also supports in some respects Cherpion's method of dating, at least as far as the type of socle is concerned,[891] because those depictions with feline carved legs in this motif are all dated to between late Dynasty 5 and 6, while those with bulls' legs are all dated to an earlier period.

In 10 instances the carved chairs have a small cushion, further reinforcing the attributes of eliteness. There are only 4 instances of carved chairs with no cushions.

Lotus Bloom

There is only one tomb showing a female with a lotus bloom (Idut), where she is shown holding it in the typical fashion to her nose

---

878 In the 6 tombs of: Hemetra, Idut, Khenut, Khentkawes, Meresankh III, and Nebet.

879 Pieke, "Der Grabherr und die Lotosblume", in *The Old Kingdom Art and Archaeology* ed. M. Barta, 259-80.

880 Manniche, "Reflections on the Banquet Scene", in *La Peinture Egyptienne Ancienne*, ed. R.Tefnin, 34.

881 Dittmar, *Blumen und Blumensträusse als Opfergabe im alten Ägypten*, *MÄS*, (43), 132-33.

882 Various attributes of authority in the 15 tombs of: Kahif, Sendjemib. Mehi, Perneb*, Rashepses*, Khnumenti*, Qar*, Idut, Kanefer, Khafkhufu I, Nefer, Nefer and Kahay, Nisutnefer, Seneb, Seshathotep, and Ty (pl. 56).
*Tombs marked with an asterisk contain duplications.

883 In the 5 tombs of: Kanefer, Khafkhufu I, Nefer, Nisutnefer, and Seshathotep.

884 Sitting with rod and rolled cloth in the 2 tombs of: Rashepses, and Ty (pl. 56).

885 In the tombs of: Nefer and Kahay, and Qar.

886 Feline legs in the tombs of: Idut, Kahif, Rashepses, Seneb, Ty, and Sendjemib.Mehi.
Bull's legs in the tombs of: Kanefer, Khafkhufu I, Nefer, Nefer and Kahay, Nisutnefer, and Seshathotep.
Carrying-chair in the tombs of: Qar, Perneb, and Khnumenti.

887 Simpson, *The Mastabas of Qar and Idu*, fig. 27. Also see Hayes, *The scepter of Egypt*, vol. I, fig. 51. Also see Brovarski, Manuelian, and Simpson, *The Senedjemib Complex. Part 1*, fig. 86.

888 Newberry, Beni Hasan, vol. I, pl. 26, col. 206. Also see Hannig, Ägyptisches Wörterbuch I: Altes Reich und Erste Zwischenzeit, 1293.

889 Fischer, "Stuhl", *LÄ*, vol. 6, 91-99. Also see Killen, *Egyptian Furniture*, fig. 30.

890 Ward, *Index of Egyptian Administrative and Religious Titles*, 67.

891 Cherpion, *Mastabas et hypogées d'Ancien Empire*, 25-41.

CHART 23: SITTING WITH ATTRIBUTES OF AUTHORITY

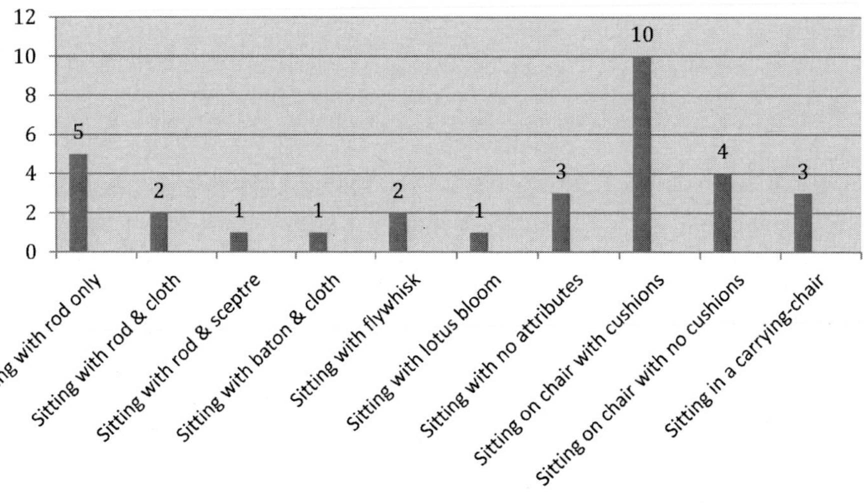

IN 15 (I.E. IN 40%) OF THE 38 TOMBS, HE/SHE IS SITTING, AND CARRIES VARIOUS COMBINATIONS OF THE ABOVE-MENTIONED ELEVATED STATUS GOODS. DUPLICATION OCCURS IN THE ABOVE COLUMNS BECAUSE MULTIPLE ATTRIBUTES OF AUTHORITY CAN OCCUR IN THE SAME TOMB.

Flywhisk and Rolled Cloth

The flywhisk is depicted in the two tombs of Nefer and Kahay and Qar. Its relation to a symbol of rank and dignity can only be inferred indirectly from the fact that in the Old Kingdom, it is never carried by any other than the elite. Additional supporting evidence, that it was not an ordinary item comes from its depiction on the architrave of the false door in the late Dynasty 5 tomb of Sekhemka, where the tomb owner is twice portrayed sitting on a carved chair with feline legs and holding a flywhisk.[892]

The above frequencies confirm the fact that the rod, sceptre, and rolled cloth were part of the ceremonial habitat. However there are three exceptions (Perneb, Kahif, and Senedjemib-Mehi).

The tombs of Perneb and Kahif which do not depict any of the authoritarian attributes (rod, sceptre, or rolled cloth) need to be explained. In the case of Perneb the possession of a carrying-chair is a statement in itself much like the modern day possession of a private jet plane. The case of Kahif is difficult to explain because the sitting posture does not preclude the holding of a rod of authority - and this could then be another case of individual behaviour. Certainly the combination of the huge space occupied by the figure of the sitting tomb owner on a chair with carved feline legs, which occupies as Junker puts it "bis zur Höhe der dritten Gabenreihe"[893] plus the elaborately painted wall carpet of plant fibres and papyrus, broadcasts an assemblage of value and wealth and needs no further comment. In the tomb of Senedjemib.Mehi the tomb owner is shown extending his hand to receive the scroll and therefore it would be impossible to show him also

holding another attribute of authority. In any event if any such was essential, it is seen in his elaborately carved chair with high back and feline claws.

The frequency of authoritarian attributes in the sitting position is illustrated in Chart 23 and the rod's combination with other items would appear to augment the status of the tomb owner in the Taking Account motif.[894] A comparison with Chart 22 is equally instructive in that it exposes the dominant position of the rod also as an eminent symbol of authority in these ceremonial motifs.

Taken together all these symbols of authority (rod, sceptre, flywhisk and carved chair/cushion) and hope (lotus bloom), demonstrate the important significance of these items for the elite especially in the manner of their conventional depiction.

Age, experience, authority, and beliefs of the afterlife are combined with the dominant figure of the tomb owner holding these elevated status goods, to produce a non-verbal statement, which needs little elaboration. Indeed this can be seen as a composite symbol of the male elite, their power, and control. Even if there are no texts extolling

---

[892] Murray, Saqqara Mastabas, vol. 1, pl. 8.
[893] Junker, Giza, vol. 6, 114.

[894] Sitting with rod only in the 5 tombs of: Kanefer, Khafkhufu I, Nefer, Nisutnefer, and Seshathotep.
Sitting with rod and rolled cloth in the 2 tombs of: Rashepses and Ty, (fig. 56 only).
Sitting with rod and scepter in the tomb of: Seneb.
Sitting with baton and rolled cloth in the tomb of: Khnumenti.
Sitting with flywhisk in the 2 tombs of: Nefer and Kahay, and Qar.
Sitting with lotus bloom in the tomb of: Idut.
Sitting on a chair with cushions in the 10 tombs of: Idut, Kahif, Khafkhufu I, Khnumenti, Nefer and Kahay, Nefer, Nisutnefer, Seneb, Seshathotep, and Ty (fig. 56 only).
Sitting with no cushions in the 4 tombs of: Senedjemib-Mehi, Qar, Perneb, and Rashepses.
Sitting with no attributes (rod/sceptre/rolled cloth) in the 3 tombs of: Kahif, Perneb, and Senedjemib-Mehi.

CHART 24: JEWELLERY AND SANDALS

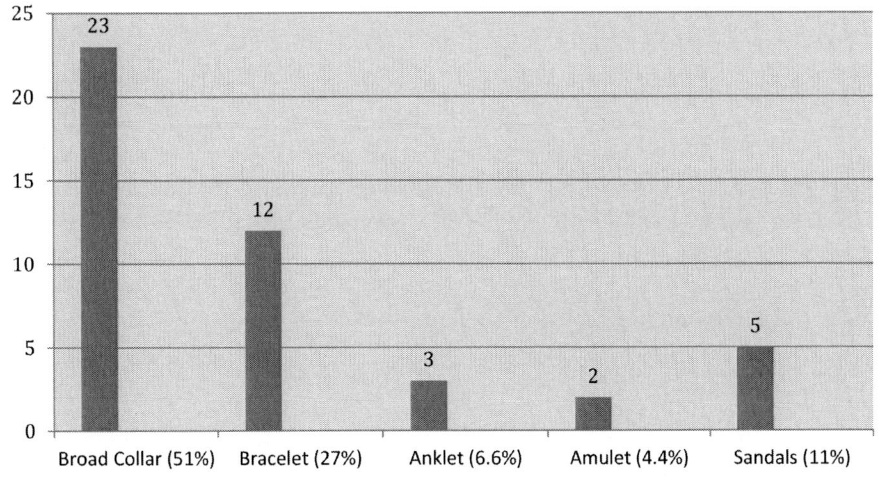

DATA IS FROM 29 TOMBS FROM A TOTAL POPULATION OF 38 TOMBS EXAMINED. DUPLICATION OF ADORNMENTS/SANDALS IN TOMBS RESULTS IN THE ABOVE TOTAL (45), AND THE PERCENTAGES ARE BASED ON THIS FIGURE AND NOT THE TOTAL NUMBER OF TOMBS NOR THE AMOUNT OF JEWELLERY OR SANDALS.

their status similar to that, which is so predominant in the biographies, nevertheless these examples illustrate the fact that symbols do not have to be described. Compositions, which include norms/beliefs, encompass (in this case what it was to be an elite) and which are widely known and understood, then have the tendency to become self-fulfilling icons, such that their ideology is accepted without doubt. Once this dominant ideology is widely accepted, the aspirations of the common people become totally submerged in the quest for a better life, just like the elite, and this motivation combined with acquiescence to the current value systems, then result in an ordered society – supporting collective harmony and struggle.

Jewellery and Sandals

Jewellery and sandals are well known hallmarks of elevated status goods since pre-dynastic times, and their depiction reminds one of the detailed work that must have been required to produce them. The tomb owners are depicted with evidence of various types of jewellery including the bracelet, anklet, chokers, broad collar, and chains with an amulet. It was thus thought that jewellery and sandals would fit together in an exposition of status symbols worn on the person of the tomb owner in the Taking Account motif. It is outside the scope of this study to go into the physical nature of the jewellery or sandals, the interest being to elicit only that type of information that could be of assistance in supporting the hypothesis in this book; of the widespread existence in funerary art of the generics.

Jewellery and/or sandals appear in 29 tombs (76% of the total population of 38 tombs). In the majority of the tombs (23 cases) the protagonists are seen wearing a broad collar (*wsḫ*). In those 6 cases where there was no collar depicted nor can now be seen, there was always another adornment

present; the bracelet is depicted in 3 cases (Kaniniswt, Nesutnefer, and Qar); two depict the tomb owner wearing sandals (Shetwi and Ty- fig. 56), and one with both bracelet and sandals (Ankhmahor). While the bracelet and collar are seen being worn together in the majority of tombs, the evidence where this is not the case, points to only 6 such tombs, and thus is not a statistically significant number. However taken together with the damaged and fragmentary nature of much of the evidence, it is perhaps wise not to be categorical about this correlation. The only certainty is that all of the 29 tombs depicting jewellery or sandals, depict the tomb owner with external evidence of adornments, and they show at least one component which may be any or a combination of the following elevated status goods:[895] bracelets, anklets, broad collars, amulets or sandals as shown in Chart 24.

Headdress and 'False Beard'

In the Taking-Account motif both a short curly 'wig' ending at the cape of the neck, and the full 'wig' falling beyond the shoulder, occur. It would seem that right from the earliest times, these were regular items of dress for the elite; the vizier on the reverse side of the Narmer palette, is shown wearing a full 'wig' and the sandal carrier on the front side is shown wearing a short 'wig'.[896]

---

[895] Broad collars in the 23 tombs of: Hemetre, Idut, Iymery, Iyenfert, Kagemni, Kahif, Kanefer, Khafkhufu I, Khnumenti, Meresankh III, Nebet, Nefer, Niankhkhnum and Khnumhotep, Ptahhotep II, Rashepses, Sekhemka, Seneb, Shetwi, Whemka, Perneb, Senedjemib-Mehi, Nefer and Kahay, and Ty (fig. 128).
  Bracelets in the 12 tombs of: Ankhmahor, Hemetre, Idut, Iymery, Kaniniswt, Khafkhufu I, Khenut, Nebet, Nefer, Nisutnefer, Qar, and Seshathotep.
Sandals in the 4 tombs of: Ankhmahor, Kagemni, Shetwi, and Ty (figs..56 and 128).
Amulets in the 2 tombs of: Kagemni, and Ptahhotep II.
Anklets in the 3 tombs of: Hemetre, Idut, and Nebet.
[896] Quibell, "Slate palette from Hieraconpolis", *ZÄS,* (36), 81-84.

CHART 25: MALE HEADDRESS

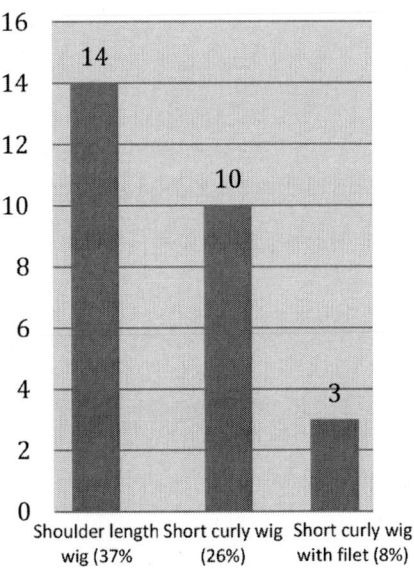

THE NUMBERS REPRESENT TOMBS IN WHICH THE PARTICULAR HEADDRESS WAS WORN. THE PERCENTAGES ARE BASED ON THE TOTAL NUMBER (38) OF TOMBS EXAMINED AND NOT ON THE TOTAL OF THE FIGURES.

All the females shown with intact upper bodies in this motif,[897] wear a full tripartite 'wig', apart from Idut. The headband with a filet tied in a buckle usually in the shape of a papyrus bud, is also present in a few motifs, and where it is present, it is always in conjunction with a short 'wig' indicating the elevation of this part of the tomb owner's body as a focusing element.[898]

It is not surprising that the elite marked their status by preference for a certain style of headdress, and this is all the more apparent when the occasion is a ceremonial one, which may have posthumous generic connotations.

Of the 38 tombs analyzed, 6 belonged to female tomb owners, and 5 were unverifiable due to their current damaged state. The resulting 27 male tomb owners depict the following headdress:

Long striated 'wig' (37%)
Short curled 'wig' (26%)
Headband with the filet (8%)

However, considering that the short curled 'wig' with filet and buckle is essentially a sort of ornamental headband worn as a crown, it would not be too radical to include this with the figure for the long striated 'wig', which was only worn by the elite. The result then becomes 45% as against 37%, and is statistically more significant. It shows that there is a good probability of the long striated 'wig' being a dominant feature of the Taking-Account motif as an important occasion.

Of the 6 female tomb owners in the Taking-Account motif, the upper part is damaged in 2 (Khenut and Khnetkawes) and in the tomb of Idut the female tomb owner is shown with the lock of youth pointing to her adolescent status. Three females (Hemetra, Meresankh III, and Nebet) are shown with the tripartite 'wig' and it can be assumed that this too was the case with the damaged motifs. Fuller details about headdress implications are discussed in Chapter 7: Carrying Chair's Tomb Owner's section on 'Wigs'.

Chart 25 summarizes the findings for the male tomb owners'.

'False Beard'

There are significant arguments[899] that the ancient Egyptians did not wear "false beards". Apparently there was a fashion to grow hair on their chins linked by narrow strips of hair to their scalp hair and this narrow strip of hair looked liked a string holding a false beard in place. Because of this visual effect, most Egyptologists find it convenient to continue to refer to this custom as a 'false beard' even when there is no definite evidence to this effect. One would also expect the 'false beard' to be part of every presentation scene because of its royal precedents depicted as far back as the time of the Narmer palette[900] but this is not the case. While the 'false beard' is depicted on Narmer, it would not seem to be far stretched to assume that this style also came to be adopted first by the other male members of the royal family, and finally by the elite due to its royal precedent and associations of higher status. The 'false beard' appears on men as early as the pre-dynastic period[901] and continues into early Dynasty 2[902] as well as being sporadically evidenced at Giza in the Dynasty 4 elite tombs of Wepemnefret and Iwnw.[903]

However, just because it appears infrequently does not mean that it was a 'false beard'. It may be that due to the nature of some damaged cases; this is not verifiable now, but in all clear motifs where the 'false beard' is present, it is clearly distinguished. Its appearance in certain scenes then may reflect a personal choice, which may be an indicator of individuality.

Interestingly, it is frequently represented in the Taking-Account motif in Dynasties 5 and 6; fifteen tomb owners are shown with a 'false beard' of which six appear together with the shoulder length 'wig' and eight appear together with the short curled variety.[904] Considering that the 'false

---

[897] In the 2 tombs of: Hemetra, and Meresankh III.
[898] In the 5 tombs of: Kagemni, Nebet, Ptahhotep ll, Shetwi, and Whemka.

[899] Kunst, "De Baard in de koningsikonografie van het Oude Rijk en het Middenrijk (The Beard in royal Iconography in the Old and Middle Kingdom)", unpublished M.A. thesis, 1995.
[900] Quibell, "Slate palette from Hieraconpolis", 36, Taf. XII-XIII.
[901] Petrie and Griffith, *The Royal Tombs of The First Dynasty, Part I*, pl. XIV (9).
[902] Köhler and Jones, *Helwan II*, 140-41.
[903] Reisner, *A History of the Giza Necropolis,* vol. 1, pl. 17. For *Iwnw* see Junker, *Giza,* vol. 1, fig. 31.
[904] 'False beard' in the tombs of: Kagemni, Kahif, Khafkhufu I, Khnumenti, Meryib, Nefer, Nefer and Kahay, Nisutnefer, Ptahhotep II, Rashepses, Sekhemka, Senedjemib, Mehi, and Seshathotep (Note that Junker, *Giza,* vol. 2, fig. 29 does not display a 'false beard' on

beard', the *ḥry-ḥb* lector priest sash, the rod, the sceptre, and the long striated 'wig' are all depicted in the standing figure of a predynastic king Den-Setui (Wedymuw), it is probably correct to categorise the appearance of these as elements on the body of elite tomb owners, as a display of high status.

As to why in certain periods or cemeteries, the 'false beard' was not depicted, the evidence does not permit one to draw any definite conclusions.

Attire

Attire as a visual expression is culturally comprehensible. In continuation with the book's object of exposing the generics, this book will focus on the use of the word attire in its symbolic functions, as a means of identification and decoration. However, this does not mean that it may not have had any other functions, e.g. protective, which in this context is irrelevant but which of course was its original function.

If one accepts that the Taking-Account motif had its progenitor in the basic desire of all deceased, irrespective of their social status, that they be adequately provisioned in the hereafter; then the early representations of the funerary goods categorize this as a formal occasion. Being a formal occasion demanded that its representations also contain elements of formality.

In addition, the type of attire worn in which the ideology of kingship was promoted[905] (e.g. in votive ceremonial palettes, when founding temples, at the *heb sed* festival, when smiting of the enemy, etc.), are also pointers to occasions when attire played an important role, which to the extent feasible, was copied by the elite. In the New Kingdom the 'gold of honour' and the 'tribute presenting' motif displays the elite in a specific situation from which elements of ceremonial accoutrements can be seen. However, in the Old Kingdom there are very few such occasions, (rewarding scenes are restricted to weavers, and even then they are "relatively unusual in private tombs, being currently confined to a few at Giza and Saqqara"[906]).

In the few rewarding scenes in the Old Kingdom, the weavers are depicted with either a short 'wig' and a headband or a tripartite 'wig' and a sheath dress but they are too few to make any definite conclusions.[907]

The textual evidence from the biographies of Sabni and Nekhebu while relating to being rewarded, are unhelpful, because of the absence of any description as regards the manner of dress or headdress.[908]

Kilts

The Taking-Account motif depicts the majority of the male tomb owners wearing the formal kilt which can include a ceremonial long kilt ending below their knees, a pointed kilt with a flared trapezoidal front, an elaborately side pleated short kilt or a normal short kilt. The actual variations in the details, e.g. cloth material, dating criteria, etc. of these types of attire have been examined elsewhere[909] and are outside the scope of this study.

These kilts either depict a knot or an elaborate belt with a buckle, a panther skin outer garment with shoulder knot or half-oval tags (similar in concept to the aiguillettes (an ornamental braided cord worn on uniforms/academic dress, where it denotes an honour)). In two cases (Khafkhufu I and Meryib), they are also depicted with the sash of a lector priest. All the above-mentioned items and type of clothing are symbols of a certain perceived status because they appear in some combination in all the royal and elite tombs.[910] Their frequency of occurrence and possible background shall now be examined.

The connection to ceremonial occasions and type of kilt has already been referred to previously. The short kilt however, because it was also worn by the common man calls for an explanation, as this would not be the sort of kilt, which one would expect to be worn on a ceremonial occasion. In six tombs the owner is depicted with a short kilt in a sitting position sometimes with an outer garment of panther skin. The frequencies and the tombs in which these occur are shown in Table 4.

TABLE 4 ATTIRE AND POSITION

Tomb owner	Short Kilt	Sitting Position	Panther Skin Garment
Kahif	✓	✓	✓
Kanefer	✓	✓	✗
Nefer	✓	✓	✗
Nefer and Kahay	✓	✓	✓
Nesutnefer	✓	✓	✓

Seshathotep, whereas Kanawati, *Tombs at Giza* II, fig. 47 does), Tjenti, and Whemka.

[905] Altenmüller, "Feste", *LÄ,* (2), 182-184.

[906] Harpur and Scremin, *Decoration in Egyptian tombs of the Old Kingdom,* 114. She cites six examples, four being from the tombs of Seneb and Nebemakhet at Giza plus Ptahhotep, and Akhethetep at Saqqara. It is unclear why gold was given to weavers. This could mean that the product (linen) created, was of high value, that the weavers were of a high social status similar to officials, or that gold was a symbolic item for high value reward goods.

[907] For a general description of these rewarding scenes see Junker, *Giza,* vol. 5, 41-60.

[908] For Sabni, see Breasted, *Ancient Records of Egypt,* vol. 1, § 372. For Nekhebu, see Dunham, "The Biographical Inscriptions of Nekhebu in Boston and Cairo", *JEA,* (24), 2.

[909] Staehelin, *Untersuchungen zur ägyptischen Tracht im Alten Reich.* Also see Bonnet, *Die ägyptische Tracht bis zum Ende des Neuen Reiches.*

[910] In Utterance 263 it is stated, "… my panther-skin is on me, my sceptre is in my arm, my baton is in my hand, and I [rule] for myself those who have gone to it". See Faulkner, *The Ancient Egyptian Pyramid Texts,* § 338.

CHART 26: TYPES AND FREQUENCIES OF KILTS

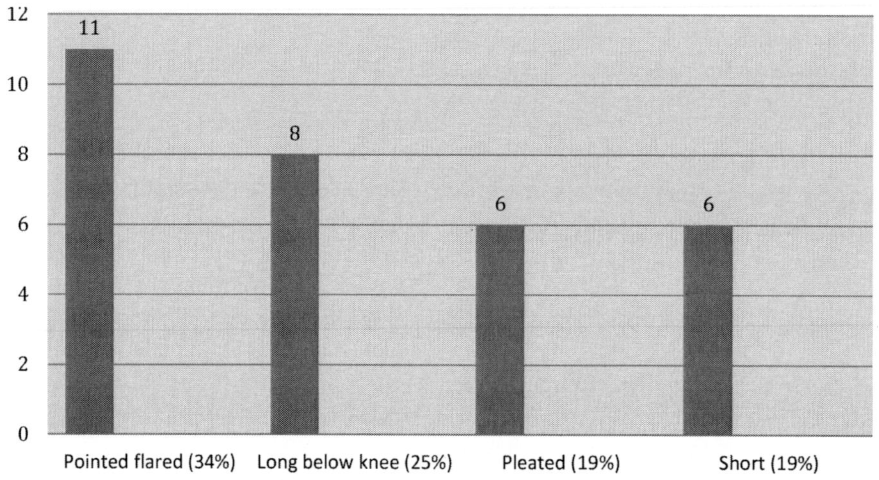

*THE NUMBERS REFER TO THE TOMBS WITH THE TYPES OF MALE DRESS. 1 UNVERIFIABLE
(I.E. 3%) AS WELL AS THE FEMALE TOMBS ARE NOT SHOWN IN THE CHART.

The sitting position does not allow for the depiction in profile of a ceremonial kilt and the distortion is evident when one observes how the flared kilt is depicted in the tomb of Rashepses.[911] Further in three of the instances (Kahif, Nesutnefer, and Nefer and Kahay), the tomb owner is wearing an enveloping panther skin outer garment, which distorts the image even further. The tomb owner is however depicted in all six cases being attended to by men, in five instances wearing the long knee-length kilt and in 1 instance a pointed flared kilt. In these circumstances it is hardly likely that the main protagonist would be wearing anything less than his juniors, and it is probably due to the way in which the sitting tomb owner is depicted in profile, that adequate portrayal of the kilt becomes exceedingly difficult. Accordingly the short kilt can be explained away.

Another item of adornment the ceremonial pleated kilt, in the six instances where it occurs always displays a belt and a buckle

Analysis of the male tomb owners in the thirty-two tombs examined revealed the following:

- The pointed kilt with a flared trapezoidal front extending away from the body, accounted for 34%.
- The below knee length long kilt, accounted for 25%.
- The side pleated short kilt, accounted for 19%.
- The normal short kilt, also accounted for 19%.

One unverifiable example amounting to 3%.[912]

The frequency of occurrence of all the kilts depicted in the Taking-Account motif is given in Chart 26.

Panther Skin Outer Garment, Shoulder Knot, and Lector Sash

The panther skin garment with tags is a rare occurrence and is seen in the Dynasty 4 tomb of prince Nefermaat at Maidum. Another example is the undated seated figure of anx at the Leiden Museum, who has the title of a smw priest. These high ranked individuals are attested from the Old Kingdom into the New Kingdom.[913] They were originally connected with the Opening of the Mouth and Eyes ritual, where they performed the role of son for father in the funeral ceremonies, and were initially the sole wearers of this distinctive item of priestly dress, the panther skin outer garment sometimes with the shoulder tags.[914] Thereafter these tags disappear and then occur in the early Dynasty 5 tomb of Kaninswt, who has among other titles – 'son of the king, living son of the king and sem priest' and who is depicted with such tags in all of his tomb representations including that in the Taking-

Account motif.[915] While the reason for this is unclear, it may be connected with a desire to show his individuality because he had all the relevant titles – twenty in all.

Contrary to Kaninswt, who is standing and a sem priest, a latter example is in the early Dynasty 6 tomb of Kahif, where although he is shown in a sitting posture the tags are clearly seen (Junker incorrectly describes this as some sort of a clasp "Umhang aus Pantherfell, der auf der linken Schulter mit einer Schliesse zusammengehalten wird"[916]).

---

[911] Lepsius, *Denkmäler aus Ägypten und Äthiopien,* pl. 64 (a).
[912] Pointed Flared Kilts in the 11 tombs of: Ankhmahor, Iynefert, Kagemni, Khnumenti, Niankhkhnum/Khnumhotep, Perneb, Ptahhotep II, Rashepses, Senedjemib-Mehi, Seshathotep and Ty (figs. 56 and 128). Long below knee-length Kilts in the 8 tombs of: Fetekta, Iymery, Kaemnofret, Kairer, Khafre-ankh, Neferbauptah, Qar, and Shetwi. Pleated Kilts in the 6 tombs of: Kaninisut, Khafkhufu I, Meryib, Sekhemka, Tjenti, and Whemka. Short Kilts in the 6 tombs of: Kahif, Kanefer, Nefer, Nefer and Kahay, Nisutnefer, and Seneb.

Unverifiable Kilt in the tomb of: Mereruka (fig. 51).

[913] Doxey, "Priesthood", *OEAE,* vol. 3, 69.
[914] Staehelin, *Untersuchungen zur ägyptischen Tracht im Alten Reich,* 57-60.
[915] Junker, *Giza,* vol. 2, fig. 15, 16, 18,19 and p. 159.
[916] Junker, *Giza,* vol. 6, 114.

In contrast the shoulder knot[917] is a more regular occurrence, generally encountered especially where the tomb owner is involved in a ceremony, e.g. banqueting, Taking Account, scenes in which he is viewing his estate, etc. However there are wide variations here too. In the tomb of Kahif, the Taking Account motif displays as indicated both a panther skin outer garment and shoulder tags, while in the same tomb the banqueting motif on the South Wall depicts him in a short kilt – the only insignia of eliteness being a short beard.

The panther skin with shoulder tags appears in two tombs, while that with shoulder knot appears in six tombs (from early Dynasty 5 and well into Dynasty 6), with one tomb that of Ankhmahor being unverifiable, since the relevant upper part of the panther skin garment is missing.[918] Of the 38 tombs analyzed, two that of Ankhmahor and Kairer were unverifiable, and of the remaining 36, six are of females who usually do not wear a panther skin (although there are examples of females in another context- sitting before an offering table and wearing a panther skin garment (e.g. Neferiabet[919]) or standing (e.g. Atet in Maidum[920]). The eight instances of males wearing a panther skin outer garment in this motif, thus represent only 26% of the analyzed tombs and based on this percentage no conclusion is possible.

Interestingly in six of these examples, the tomb owners are shown wearing an ordinary short kilt and in the majority (four cases) wear this under a panther skin; thus partly obscuring it as well as emphasizing their functions as a sem priest.[921]

In three instances the tomb owner is depicted with the sash of a lector priest, implying his role and knowledge with that of the lector priest.[922] These priests were primarily concerned with reciting the spells in the funerary rituals, and belonged to a distinct group of priests, who had the specialized understanding necessary for the conduct of funerary rites. They are usually depicted with a pointed kilt and wide sash worn diagonally across the chest or draped on one shoulder and are identified as the *ẖry-ḥbt* (the one who literally carries the sacred texts). They were well versed in the hieroglyphic signs of the ritual texts and ensured that the ceremonies were performed in accordance

with the written tradition. The earliest members of this group of priests were members of the royal family, but by the Middle Kingdom, this title could be held by any literate official.[923] Accordingly the depiction of the sash on the tomb owner can be related both to secret knowledge, and the implication that he was someone who devoted his life to its maintenance, which generates a related respect in society and in time becomes a direct pointer to social identity.

8.4 Presenter

Presenter's Attributes

All the Taking-Account motifs depict a male presenter, who 'holds' a document, mostly in the direction of the tomb owner. No female presenter is depicted although there are at least six instances of a female tomb owner with the Taking-Account motif in her tomb. This is indeed surprising when it is known that females did act as funerary priestesses (from the reign of Khufu right through to Dynasty 6, thirty female priestesses are evidenced in the necropolises of Giza and Saqqara[924]).

Since the presenter is usually depicted as a scribe, one must conclude that the presenter was an 'educated' person of some status, and if one includes those presenter(s) who are identified as the son(s) of the tomb owner, the implication that the presenter was not of low socio-economic class, is reinforced.

Of the 38 tombs examined there are:

- 22 tombs (58%) in which presenters are overseers.[925]
- Seven tombs (18%) in which the presenters are sons and where other relatives are depicted viewing the Taking Account occasion.[926]
- Nine tombs (24%) in which the presenter's title is unverifiable.[927]

However, even if this is not an accident of preservation their literacy qualifies them as important members of the community. The relationship between the tomb owner and the presenters' titles follows on page 142. The Taking-Account motif demonstrates the tomb owner's eliteness, which is again a pointer in the direction of the generics.

The presenter is usually the first person in the procession to face the tomb owner because the attention of the tomb

[917] Staehelin, *Untersuchungen zur ägyptischen Tracht im Alten Reich*, 54-57.

[918] Shoulder tags in the 2 tombs of: Kahif, and Kaninisut.
Shoulder knot in the 5 tombs of: Kaemnofret, Nefer and Kahay, Nisutnefer, Shetwi, and Tjenti.
Unverifiable in the tomb of: Ankhmahor (because the relevant upper part is damaged).

[919] Manuelian, *Slab Stelae of the Giza Necropolis*, 58-61.

[920] Petrie, *Medum,* pl. 18.

[921] In Kahif, Nefer and Kahay, Nisutnefer, and Tjenti's tombs, the panther skin covering is shown; while in two cases that of Seneb and Nefer, this is not so. Seneb can be explained by the fact that the artist was at pains to hide the dwarfism of the deceased, while Nefer is shown sitting on a carved chair with bulls legs and cushion, wearing wristlets, a broad collar and 'false beard', while holding a large rod of authority and thus the emphasis shifts away from the short kilt.

[922] Wearing a sash across chest: in the tombs of = Khafre-ankh, Meryib, and Sekhemka.

[923] Doxey, "Priesthood", *OEAE*, vol. III, 69.

[924] Lemke, Die nichtköniglichen Priesterinnen des Alten Reiches (4.-6. Dynastie), Ph.D. Dissertation, Universität Würzburg, 2008, 193-94.

[925] Overseer of the house in the tombs of: Fetekta, Hemetra, Idut, Iymery, Kagemni, Kairer, Kaniniswt, Kaemnofret, Khentkawes, Khenut, Mereruka (pl. 51), Meresankh lll (fig. 12), Meryib, Nebet, Niankhkhnum/Khnumhotep (fig. 13), Perneb, Rashepses, Seneb, Senedjemib-mehi, Seshathotep, Tjenti, and Ty (figs. 56 and 128).

[926] In the tombs of: Khafkhufu I, Khafre-ankh, Nefer, Nisutnefer, Ptahhotep II, Qar, and Sekhemka.

[927] In the tombs of: Ankhmahor, Iynefert, Kahif, Kanefer, Khnumenti, Nefer and Kahay, Neferbauptah, Shetwi, and Whemka.

owner is a requirement of these motifs.[928] This position is maintained even when there are multiple presenters depicted, there being ten such instances,[929] accounting for about 25% of the tombs. They range from mid-Dynasty 4 to early Dynasty 6 but no correlation between time frame and changed depiction can be established. Is this exceptional behaviour, in view of the fact that all the other 28-tomb owners depicting this motif show only one presenter? Possibly these ten cases are examples of individuality by which the tomb owner is trying to emphasize his own status by bolstering this with more than one presenter, i.e. he had so many possessions that more than one scribe was required. The seemingly excessive displays of status in this motif and in those showing convoys of offering bearers and extravagant banqueting common in tombs from Dynasty 5 onwards may reflect modern attitudes being imposed on the past.

Presenter's Attire

Being one of the main officiants in this ceremony, an appropriate form of dress would be perceptible and this is indeed the case in all these motifs. The analysis showed that there are 17 presenters with the long, below knee length kilt and 20 with the pointed flared kilt. Therefore no preference for one or the other can be established. There are only 2 instances of the presenters wearing an elaborately pleated kilt and one only with a short kilt[930] as shown in Chart 27.

Presenter's Headdress

The headdress presents the same problem as was referred to in the carrying-chair analysis, i.e. that of distinguishing between wigged and non-wigged heads. In an important ceremony as depicted in this motif, some form of head covering would be an essential requirement, especially when the majority of the presenters are high officials. Accordingly unless there is a definite depiction of the long striated 'wig', one shall assume that the presenters have a short curly 'wig'. This does not solve the stylistic problem in the depiction of the headdress, but as it is outside the scope of this study, it cannot be taken any further.[931] The iconography reveals that the majority of the presenters

CHART 27: PRESENTERS' ATTIRE

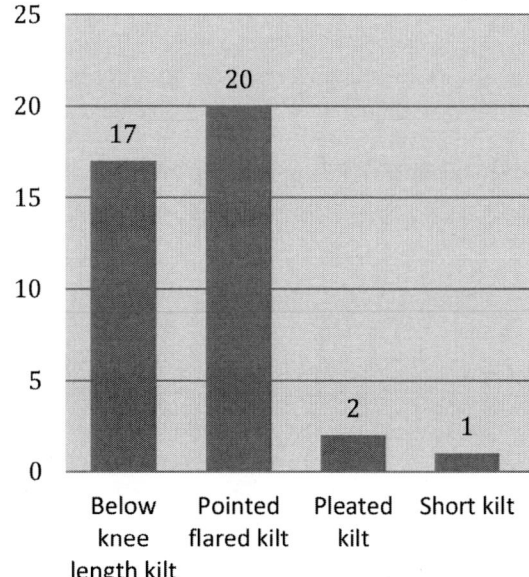

DUPLICATION OCCURS BECAUSE THE TOMB OF TY DEPICTS THE SAME TYPE OF KILT ON TWO PLATES (FIGS. 56 AND 128) BUT WAS IN ONE TOMB; IN THE TOMB OF NEFER TWO DIFFERENT TYPES OF KILTS ARE SHOWN ON THE SAME MOTIF, THEREFORE THE TOTAL EXCEEDS THE NUMBER OF TOMBS.

have as their headdress, some form of the short curly 'wig' falling to the nape of the neck and covering part of the forehead. In two instances in the tombs of Qar and Khnumenti, the damaged nature prevents any assumption.

One definite exception is that in the tomb of Khafkhufu. The two presenters here are very elaborately attired with striated shoulder length full wigs, wear a pleated short kilt, a 'false beard', and the sash of the lector priest in a manner similar to that of the tomb owner. The explanation may lie in the fact that they are the two sons of the tomb owner, identified as Wetka and Iunka; the caption reads:

"Presenting the document by the king's son Wetka ... and Iunka".[932]

In the tomb of Khafre-ankh, the son is depicted doing the presenting and he also wears the same attire as his father but has only a short 'wig'. In all other instances where sons are present and not doing the actual presenting but follow the presenter, e.g. in the tombs of Kahif and Meryib, no such correlation was found.

Two instances (abut 5%) distinctly show the presenter wearing a collar and a further two depict the presenter with a 'false beard'.[933]

---

[928] Manuelian, 'Presenting the Scroll', 193-94.

[929] In the tombs of: Iynefert, Kagemni, Kairer, Khafkhufu I, Kaninisut, Khenut, Nebet, Nefer, Rashepses, and Tjenti.

[930] Below knee length kilts in the 17 tombs of: Hemetra, Iymery, Kanefer, Kaninisut, Kaemnofret, Khafre-ankh, Meresankh III, Nefer and Kahay, Nefer*, Neferbauptah, Nisutnefer, Qar, Sekhemka, Seneb, Senedjemib-Mehi, Seshathotep, and Whemka.
Pointed flared kilts in the 20 tombs of: Ankhmahor, Fetekta, Idut, Iynefert, Kagemni, Kahif, Kairer, Khentkawes, Khenut, Khnumenti, Mereruka, Nebet, Nefer*, Niankhkhnum/Khnumhotep, Perneb, Ptahhotep II, Rashepses, Shetwi, and Ty (figs. 56 and 128).
Pleated kilts in the 2 tombs of: Khafkhufu I, and Meryib.
Short kilt in the tomb of: Tjenti.* Duplication because both 'below knee length' and 'pointed flared' kilts are depicted in the tomb of Nefer.

[931] Staehelin, *Untersuchungen zur ägyptischen Tracht im Alten Reich*, 84-91 and 178-82. She gives details of masculine and feminine wig types and their occurence .

[932] Simpson, Chapman, and Reisner, *The mastabas of Kawab, Khafkhufu I and II*, 12-13.

[933] 'False beard' in the tombs of: Khafkhufu I, and Meresankh III. Collar in the tombs of: Nefer and Kahay, and Ptahhotep II.

CHART 28: PRESENTERS' HEADDRESS

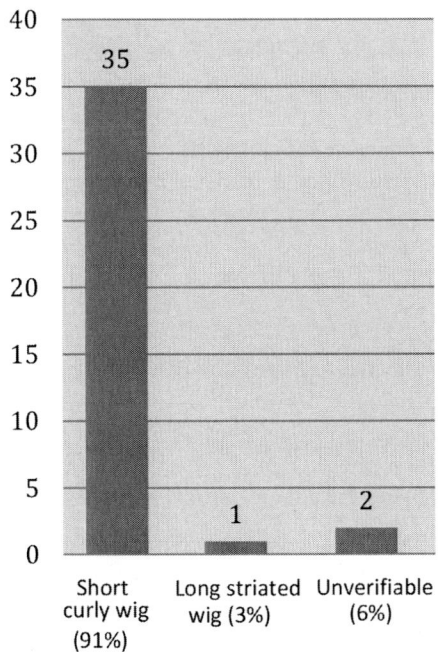

THE NUMBERS REFER TO TOMBS DEPICTING THE SPECIFIC TYPE OF HEADDRESS, BUT NOT THE NUMBER OF PRESENTERS WEARING IT. THE FIRST COLUMN CONSISTS OF ALL OF APPENDIX C APART FROM THE THREE TOMBS OF KHAFKHUFU I, KHNUMENTI, AND QAR, WHICH ARE INCLUDED IN THE SECOND AND THIRD COLUMNS.

If the objective was to enhance the status aspect of the tomb owner, then it may well be that these few instances may be considered as individualistic behaviour. One can also blame the nature of the preserved archaeological remains but it is highly doubtful that the tomb owner would have wanted the presenter to be depicted in an equivalent manner.

The dominance of the presenters' short curly 'wig' is indicated in Chart 28.

As is apparent from the above chart that the presenter in all cases is appropriately attired and wigged, however it would appear from the depictions that were it not for his size, he would appear to have a partial similarity to the main protagonist – the tomb owner.

In line with the research assumptions (2) and (3),[934] humans have a strong tendency to want to inter-relate with others who are perceived as superior status individuals. Attitude adoption or herd instinct is associated with wanting to belong to something bigger than oneself. This wanting is based on the appeal to some values regarded as being of elemental and higher value involving concepts about social justice, religious beliefs, and natural law. Many animals have this instinct too.

With humans, there are varied types of association. Some people settle for the easiest, closest, and most convenient

herd, others for a group at their maximum extreme of acceptability, e.g. exclusive clubs/ideological associations. The individual's decision to appear as part of a particular group is often the only significant decision in his life because after this decision has been made, he is loyal to all of the group's attitudes, rather than be a heretic. Sometimes the individual does not even decide to join a particular group but just follows the rest of his peers. The amount of adjustment/compromise varies with the individual and the available groups. Its importance with respect to presenters is as follows.

Identification with the norms of the powerful is possibly the biggest factor for servants. In a stable society, its elite would dominate the 'Zeitgeist' of their society and by adopting elite norms the servant would feel part of society. By adopting these norms, the servant can even partly predict his master's whims, which eases the servant's burden. The elite domination of the servant and of his society was so great that the servant had little choice. In considering themselves from the same point of view, they become to identify themselves with their lord's attitudes and in the case of the Taking-Account motifs, would appear to go so far as to become his accessory. In this way the presenter is detached from himself, aligns himself totally with that of his lord, and finally ends up by creating a similar appearance for himself like his master. A similar analogy can be seen in present times: the majority of USA citizens, who although they are working class, vote for rich candidates (who do little for the poor), apparently because the voters can delude themselves that they are closer to success in the American dream. Another extreme modern example is the Stockholm syndrome, where the kidnapped absorb the ideology of their captors and retain that ideology long after their release.[935]

In a hierarchical society based upon religious beliefs as in Old Kingdom Egypt where authority was assigned to the king, one might expect that society tends to become immobile and people come to accept their static lot but this is not quite so.

When the mind-set of the elite changes servants adopt the attitude of their masters, because there is a consequential change in their attitude, which results in socio-economic shifts.[936] These shifts can be related to some aspects of the generics, which would come to be depicted on the wall paintings.

The adoption by the servants of the outwardly appearing norms of the elite, results in a propagation and preservation of the elite status, primarily for the tomb owner but secondarily also for the presenter, whose position is confirmed and maybe this facilitated change in the structure

---

[934] See Chapter 2: page 14.

[935] Graebner, *Patty's got a Gun: Patricia Hearst in 1970s America.*
[936] Converse, 'The Nature of Belief Systems in Mass Publics', In *Ideology and Discontent*, ed. D. Apter, 206-261.

of ancient Egyptian society. This is in direct contrast with the idea of a static hierarchical society in which there can be no change.

Presenter's 'Gifts'

- There are 3 problems when considering 'gifts' as part of the Taking-Account motif and in its analysis:
- Impossibility of defining the essential differences between categories, e.g. of various staple food items like bread and beer[937] increases the difficulty of categorization.
- The exaggerated numerical nature of the provisions described in many instances makes any comparison between the thousands of bread, beer, alabaster vessels and linen, statistical or otherwise, a near impossibility.

  In any event the document itself supposedly contained a list of what was being shown or presented, and as such, it would seem superfluous to have depictions of the listed gifts, or maybe this is another example of abundant caution on the part of the elite.

The gifts can be the document itself or as in the majority of instances, depictions of desert animals, cattle and fowl being led behind the presenter. While the document is always prima facie the first element of the gift, there is no special pattern recognizable in the order of the other gifts and several combinations are observable.[938] Of the 38 tombs examined, twenty-four (63%) had some combination of desert animals, cattle, fowl and other food as the main gifts.[939] These are usually shown being led or brought to the tomb owner following the presenter, or may appear in a register below. Five tombs (13%) had no verifiable depictions of any gifts although the captions indicate otherwise and this could well be due to the problem of preservation,[940] most of them being severely damaged. The remaining nine tombs (24%) present difficulties;[941] while the majority of these can be explained in terms of reading the motif in conjunction with a representation of

provisioning appearing nearby, on an adjoining wall or entrance thickness, two tombs defy such an explanation.

In the tomb of Khafkhufu I, the Taking-Account motif appears ostensibly on the inner Northern entrance thickness. Here the tomb owner's sons are presenting him with a document, each which has hieroglyphic characters on it. These characters read:

> "a thousand of young bulls, antelopes, young goats, gazelles, *sr*-geese, *trp* geese, *st*-ducks and *mnwt* pigeons"

This presumably dispenses with the need to depict the gifts themselves. The caption on the Northern entrance thickness set in vertical lines facing the tomb owner reads:

> "Viewing the invocation offerings which are brought from the king's house (and) from his towns of the funerary estate …"

Underneath this are characters, which again depict the thousand sign together with the head of the type of animal meant.

Similarly on the Southern entrance thickness opposite is a caption, which reads, "Viewing the sealed deliveries which are brought from the house of the king …" Underneath this are the characters indicating a thousand together with sealed jars, and linen. However, there is no person presenting a document. This suggests that both these jambs should be read together, which would then indicate that the gifts are recorded on the documents being presented by his sons (Wetka and Iunka).

The other difficulty is from the tomb of Senedjemib-Mehi. Here a punishment scene immediately follows the presenter, and the following register depicts cattle being offered. Does this mean that food was not important? It is suggested that this would be an incorrect reading of this scene. Indeed this is the clearest possible evidence that while food was important, ignored duties could result in punishment. Normally punishment scenes are a genre in themselves but here it is being combined with a motif, which evokes a connection with power and material wealth, to communicate control over people belonging to his community. While this is the only punishment scene in conjunction with a Taking-Account motif, nevertheless its importance is in the individuality shown.

Another issue in connection with gifts is as follows: if the reference point is only taken to be the offerings following the presenter, there would be no need for a separate document listing for what was already depicted. The fact that a document is illustrated in a prominent manner in every Taking-account motif, and the main actors are in ceremonial attire and adornments, is an affirmation of the socio-economic embeddedness of communication and display, which are its hallmarks. Altenmüller belittles this issue and describes all such motifs as merely an extension

[937] Lepsius, *Denkmäler aus Ägypten und Äthiopien,* pl. 35. Also see Barta, *Die altägyptische Opferliste,* 47-50. The offering list in the Dynasty 5 tomb of Debehni is typical of the difficulty - with 20 different types of 'bread' and 7 types of 'drinks', etc.

[938] C D F in the tomb of: Iymery
D F C in the tomb of: Senedjemib-Mehi
F C D in the tomb of: Nefer
D C F in the tombs of: Kahif, Kagemni, and Niankhkhnum/Khnumhotep
F C in the tomb of: Meresankh III
D C in the tombs of: Kaemnofret, Kanefer, and Ptahhotep II
C F (fig. 13) and C D C D (fig. 17) in the tomb of: Nebet
* C = Cattle, D = Desert Animals, and F = Fowl.

[939] Cattle, Desert Animals, Fowl, and Food in the tombs of: = Idut, Iymery, Iynefert, Kagemni, Kahif, Kanefer, Kaemnofret, Khafre-ankh, Khentkawes, Mereruka (fig. 51), Nebet, Nefer, Nefer and Kahay, Nisutnefer, Niankhkhnum/Khnumhotep, Perneb, Pathhotep II, Sekhemka, Seneb, Seshathotep, Shetwi, Tjenti, Ty (fig. 128), and Whemka.

[940] No depiction in the tombs of: Fetekta, Kairer, Qar, Rashepses, and Khnumenti.

[941] In the tombs of: Ankhmahor, Hemetra, Kaninisut, Khafkhufu I, Khenut, Meresankh III, Meryib, Neferbauptah, and Senedjemib-Mehi.

of the offering scene: a variety of long and short narrative by stressing the gifts only.[942] Considering that both of these are compulsive acts, essential in elite human behaviour right throughout the pharaonic times if not earlier, and have their basis in the importance, which they attached to these modes in their civilization, they are well understood. However, just because something is important, does not mean that it is useful, usual or has to have similar meaning, wherever depicted. Offerings abound in all tombs because they are the central preoccupation of one basic element: provisioning for the deceased depicted in the early slab stelae and the motif of the tomb owner before a table of food. Accordingly when patterns of offerings, which resemble each other, closely appear in other places and motifs, the duplication must involve a refinement of the original meaning, implying that the tomb owner chose to use the same situation but to handle it in terms different to the dominant purpose.

Undoubtedly the Taking-Account motif is about material possessions. The context of its usage (e.g. a presenter of a document associated with individuals of high social rank and the stress on the resources collected and expended by the tomb owner for his posthumous benefit) has to be understood in terms of the elevating the social status. Understood in this way, the gifts themselves when depicted become subsidiary to the main issue of Taking-Account.

8.5 Document Material and Type

Document Material

Most of the presenters seem to be holding some sort of rectangular piece of material, which one assumes to be papyrus, because paper was not invented at this time in Egypt. Closer examination reveals that in the majority of cases, it indeed was papyrus, because there is not a single motif in which the presenter does not use both hands to present the document (papyrus being pliable). However, even then one has to be careful to ascertain that it is actually a document and a Taking-Account motif.

A case in point is that in the tomb of Akhethetep.[943] The southern entrance thickness shows two men holding a large piece of rectangular material right in front of the tomb owner, who is seen in the act of accepting it, which on a cursory examination may be taken to be a document of some sort. In fact based on a similar scene in the tomb of Werirni at Sheikh Said,[944] the depiction is that of a piece of cloth being presented and not a document.

Most of the presenting motifs do not have anything written on the documents, at least nothing that is legible today.[945]

The ancient Egyptians probably knew what this scene meant, and it could be, that this was a symbolic form of showing the reality of presenting in a two dimensional way. If this is correct, then anything that was being presented, whether it had writing or not, would allude to the variety of meanings, which are lost to us today. What the documents in these motifs contain is not clear but following on from the inscriptions, it probably pertains to material possessions, either of the tomb owner (e.g. the offerings and gifts which are being brought from the estates once owned by the tomb owner) or gifts from the king (see Documents and Captions page 140 for the actual textual description).

Document Type

Der Manuelian has collated the various inscriptions[946] according to the way the document is being held. While this might be of use in stylistic examinations, it is of limited use in studies where the symbolic meaning of what is being done is far more significant, than how it is being done. The motifs are not very clear as to 'what is being done' and indeed it is easy to switch between showing, causing it to be shown, reading, proffering, etc. if one were to rely entirely on the depictions alone. Accordingly one must also rely on the captions. The problem then becomes one of relating the philological meaning of the various inscriptions and this presents us with a dilemma: the same word in Old Egyptian can have a variety of very similar yet distinctive meanings. However if one analyses the captions, we find that most of these start with infinitive verbs like *di*[*di.w*], *di.t*, *rdi*[*rdi.w*], *rdi.t*, *siꜥ.t*, *ꜣw.t*, *šd.t*, and like all infinitives, these describe an action as such, which in Egyptian can only be recognized by the way it is used grammatically, and not only by its form.[947] The captions contain the verbs frequently encountered in presenting motifs and they all relate to action of some sort: seeing, presenting, extending, reciting, inspecting, or proffering. Because the motif in question mainly involves two persons: the recipient (tomb owner) and the one doing the presenting (presenter), it is obvious that in order to be clear both the depiction and caption should correlate. If this is not the case then identifying its precise meaning becomes an exceedingly difficult task. An example of this difficulty can be seen in the tomb of Meresankh III, where the caption and the motif contradict each other. While the motif is clear, the caption reads "viewing the writing [by] the overseer of the funerary priests" which would mean that the overseer is doing the viewing or it can be broken down to mean "viewing the writing" by Meresankh III, the presentation being done "by the overseer of funerary priests".[948]

---

[942] Altenmüller, 'Presenting the *nḏt-ḥr* offerings to the tomb owner', in *The Old Kingdom Art and Archaeology*, ed. M. Barta, 25-35.

[943] Ziegler, *Le Mastaba d'Akhethetep*, fig. 35 (loose plate).

[944] Manuelian, 'Presenting the Scroll', 566.

[945] The exceptions are those in the tombs of: Fetekta, Khafkhufu I, and Meryib. Each of these three exceptions contains writing. It has been conjectured that these persons are giving accounts concerning the tomb equipment, and that the papyrus roll records the individual items. See

Helck, *Altägyptische Aktenkunde des 3. und 2. Jahrtausends v. Chr.*, *MÄS*, (31), 5-6.

[946] Manuelian, 'Presenting the Scroll', 561-88.

[947] Ockinga and Brunner, *A concise grammar of Middle Egyptian*, 53-55. Infinitives, which do not end in a 't', should end with a 'w'; which in many cases is omitted. These are to be treated as nominal infinitives based on the syntax, where these appear.

[948] Dunham et al., *The Mastaba of Queen Mersyankh III*, 20 and fig. 12.

TABLE 5 DOCUMENT TYPE

nḏt-ḥr
   (Offerings)[1]
wḏb-rd/pḥrt
(Reversionary offerings)[2]
sš n niwt n pr ḏt
   (Document of towns of the funerary estate[3])
sš n iḫt bnrt
   (Document of sweet things)[4]
mḏ3t sš n ꜥwt, n iw3 imy mḏt, n wnḏw[5]
... nḏt [ḥr] innt m niwt=f [6]
m ḥwt niwwt=s n pr ḏt[7]
   Document of sheep and goats, oxen in stall and short horned cattle respectively, offerings which are brought from his village from her villages and estates.
INSPECTING
sš r m33 prt ḥrw
   (Document for Inspection (of the) invocation offerings)[8]
rdit r m33
   (Presenting for inspection)[9]
rdit sš n ḥmw-k3
   (Presenting the document [of/by]? the funerary priests)[10]
rdi[t] sš r m33 <...> pr ḏt
   (Presenting the document for inspection [of] the funerary estate.)[11]
rdit sš
   (Presenting the document)[12]
rdit sš n nḏt ḥr
   (Presenting the document of offerings)[13]
dit sš n pr-ḏ
   (Presenting the document of the Funerary estate)[14]
rdit sš r m33 prt ḥrw
   (Presenting the document for inspecting invocation offerings)[15]
rdit sš r m33
(Presenting the document for inspection)[16]
di[t] sš in ḫtmw sṭi-ḥb ḥry-tp sšr
   (Presenting the document by the sealer of the festival ointment and the supervisor of linen)[17]
di.t sš in s3 nswt wtk3
   (Presenting the document by the king's son Wetka)[18]

rdit sš n nḏt-ḥr
   (Presenting the document of offerings)[19]
rdit sš nḏt-ḥr imy-r ḥm-k3 K3nfr
   (Presenting the list [of] offerings by the overseer of the funerary priests Kanefer)[20]
rdit sš niwwt n...sš ip rmṯ
   (Presenting the document of villages of and ... the document of the census of the people)[21]
VIEWING
m33 sš
   (Viewing the document / See the document)[22]
m33 sš n pḥrt..
   (Viewing the document of reversionary offerings)[23]
m33 nḏt-ḥr innt r prt ḥrw ...
   (Viewing the gifts which were brought as funerary offerings ...)[24]
m33 pr[t]-ḥrw int m pr-nswt m niwwt=f pr ḏt
   (Viewing the invocation offerings which are brought from the king's house [and] from his villages of the funerary estate)[25]
m33 nḏt-ḥr rnpw.t nb.t nfrt innt n=s m ḥwwt niwwt
   (Viewing gifts and all good offerings of the year which are brought for her from the estates and the towns)[26]
m33 sš n nḏt ḥr nt in prt-ḥrw
   (Viewing the list of his funerary gifts brought as funerary offerings)[27]
m33 ḥsb ḥk3.w ḥwwt.t niww.t=f mḥw šmꜥw
   (Viewing the account of the governors of his villages of Lower and Upper Egypt)[28]
m33 ḥtmt innt pr-nswt
   (Viewing the xtmt offerings, those that have been brought from the house of the king)[29]
m33 nḏt-ḥr innt m niwwt=f nbt ṯzt iḫt bnrt r pr ḏsr
   (Viewing the gifts brought from all his villages and the accumulation of sweet things to the 'red house')[30]
PROFFERING
siꜥ mḏ3t n ...
   (Proffering the document of ...)[31]
[m3]3 siꜥ mḏ3t n
   (Overseeing the proffering of the document of ...)[32]
siꜥ mḏ3t n
   (Proffering the document of lists of ...)[33]
BRINGING
int nḏt-ḥr in niwwt nt pr-ḏt nt šmꜥw
   (Bringing the offerings by the villages of the funerary estate of Upper Egypt)[34]
EXTENDING
3w.t sš
   (Extending or spreading the document)[35]
READING/HEARING
šd.t n=f sš n krst=f dyt n=f m ḥtp di nswt imy-r k3t sši
   (Reading to him the document for his burial equipment which was given to him as an "offering which the king gives", the overseer of works Seshi)[36]

---

[1] In Khentkawes, Ptahhotep II, and Sekhemka. Also see Altenmüller, "Presenting the nDt-Hr offerings to the tomb owner," 32. He infers that *nḏt-ḥr* were offerings, which were presented as in an act of worship during a ceremony.
[2] In Meryib, Nisutnefer, and Seshathotep. (Kanawati, *Giza* vol. 2, p. 28, describes this as *pḥr.t* contrary to Manuelian "Presenting the Scroll", 580. Because there is no leg determinative, Kanawati's translation is to be preferred). The word *wḏb-rd* is not to be confused with *int-rd* the "removing the foot" ritual and for its meaning in the sense of "returning from the cult-chamber in order to carry the offerings elsewhere", see Gardiner, "The Mansion of Life and Master of King's Largess," *JEA,* (24), 87-88.
[3] In the tomb of: Kaninisut. See Perepelkin, *Privateigentum in der Vorstellung der Ägypter des Alten Reichs*, 109. For the purposes of this study *pr-ḏt* shall be understood to include not only the personal house of the official but all his privately earned income. Altenmüller stresses that the word has a nuanced judicial and technical use, and in common with other words that indicate possession and property, a 'streng terminolologischen Stellenwert' is not detectable. See Altenmüller, „Besitz und Eigentum," in *LÄ*, vol. I, 733.
[4] Niankhkhnum and Khnumhotep
[5] Kagemni
[6] Fetekta
[7] Khenut
[8] Shetwi
[9] Ty (fig. 128)
[10] Meresankh lll
[11] Tjenti, Ty, and Neferbauptah
[12] Kaemnofret
[13] Khentkawes, and Ptahhotep II
[14] Seneb
[15] Shetwi
[16] Neferbauptah, and Ty (pl. 56)
[17] Meryib
[18] Khaf-khufu I

[19] Sekhemka, and Ptahhotep II
[20] Kanefer
[21] Kaninisut
[22] Whemka, Meresankh lll, Seshathotep, Nisutnefer, and Kaemnofret
[23] Nisutnefer, and Seshathotep
[24] Iymery
[25] Khaf-khufu I
[26] Idut
[27] Kaemnofret
[28] Rashepses
[29] Meryib
[30] Niankhkhnum/Khnumhotep
[31] Kagemni
[32] Kagemni
[33] Kagemni
[34] Ptahhotep II
[35] Mereruka
[36] Ankhmahor

Rare examples where the meanings are clearer are in the tomb of Kaemnofret and Khafkhufu I. Here the presenter is described as 'presenting the document' and the tomb owner is described as 'viewing the list of funerary gifts brought as funerary offerings' and 'viewing the invocation offerings' respectively.[949]

In most other instances, one has to fall back on decorum and assume that the tomb owner was literate as well, that seeing and inspecting were continuing prerogatives of the deceased, while all other actions are being done by the 'presenter', who is the subordinate in this drama. It is constructive to contrast this use of language with that of the Old Kingdom biography. In this genre, the tomb owner broadcasts what he has done for others, so that his status is improved.[950] By contrast, in the Taking Account motif, it is the presenter, who is doing the action, but it is clear from the motif that he is the subordinate. This act is then just one part in the enhancement of the status of the tomb owner; the central driver of status must however be seen in the fact that he broadcasts his access to resources, from which he could receive, even when deceased. Thus we must draw on the greater scale of depiction, of the tomb owner's unique symbols of office, the evident respect showed by the presenter and the implied system of rank and identity. The captions used in the presentation motifs are then used to look at wall paintings and reliefs, to elucidate meaningful affirmations and cultural comparisons. How far these are true is another matter and one way of avoiding this debate, which one can never solve, is to look at them as Assmann does, i.e. "this truth is subject to changes with every new identity and every new present. It lies in the story, not as it happened but as it lives on and unfolds in collective memory"[951] what he terms 'memohistory'.

Indirectly all these instances are pointers to the hierarchical position/status of the two protagonists and the underlying fact that wealth and status during the Old Kingdom, came mainly from participation in the government: one requirement of which was the ability to administer and communicate. Texts and inscriptions should be regarded as one part of a range of practices, which by providing information produce culture and again point to the generics.

With a view to exposing the different meanings, their nuances and perhaps the way the Egyptians themselves may have perceived the different categories of meaning, I summarize the captions in their context below.

Documents and Captions

The use of different words by the ancient Egyptians when describing similar things/actions must have been a differentiating use of the meaning itself and this presents a difficulty in being categorical about a particular meaning. Consider the word for an offering. We have evidence of 6 different words ($n\underline{d}t$-$\underline{h}r$, $w\underline{d}b$-$r\underline{d}$, $p\underline{h}rt$, prt-$\underline{h}rw$, $m\underline{d}3t$, $s\check{s}$) used to convey some meaning of an offering in the Taking-Account motif, but expressed in different ways. This was how the Egyptians probably understood and used them with different subtleties of meaning. This may relate to the document/list itself, to mortuary offerings in general, as well as to a combination of these two.

While the philological debate is outside the scope of this study, similar limitations/extensions probably apply to the captions in Table 5 (tombs are indicated by names of tomb owners full references to which appear in Appendix I).

8.6 Presenter's Relationships to the Tomb owner

An aspect, which may be of assistance in understanding cultural implications, is to seek the filial relationships of the presenters, i.e. whether family is shown as part of the line of the procession following the presenter and is present in this motif. The three main types of subordinate participants in the motif are scribes, officials, and/or sons. Ideally the main cult officiate was the son of the owner probably reflecting the myth of Horus in which Horus performs the funerary offices for his dead father.[952] This mythical connection between death and lasting beneficial effects (vindication by the divine tribunal) had an equivalent meaning relating to the life of the elite or for that matter all Egyptians. This connection is never directly shown on the depictions of the Old Kingdom but indirectly, probably due to the interconnection between burial and inheritance. An inscription from the door architrave of Tjenti reads:

> "I am her (Bebi, his mother's) eldest son and heir, I am the one who buried her in the necropolis".[953]

However, as Klebs observes this could include others. "Das Verzeichnis aller dieser Dinge ist auf eine große Papyrusrolle geschrieben und wird dem Herrn von einem Schreiber oder Beamten oder auch von einem seiner Söhneüberreicht oder zum Lesen vorgehalten ..."[954] If the eldest son was the presenter, then it could be that this motif was part of establishing inheritance rights.

---

[949] Lepsius, *Denkmäler aus Ägypten und Äthiopien*, 91 c. For Khafkhufu I, see Simpson, Chapman, and Reisner, *The mastabas of Kawab, Khafkhufu I and II*, fig. 29.

[950] Edel, 'Untersuchungen zur Phraseologie der ägyptischen Inschriften des Alten Reiches', in *MDAIK*, 31-56.

[951] Assmann, *Moses the Egyptian*, 14.

[952] Blackman, *Gods, Priests, and Men*, 266-72. It is accepted that this evidence points to an annual play being performed in later times, when the victory of Horus was commemorated in addition to securing a prosperous reign for the future king. However the reliance on Horus of Behdet would imply a much earlier connection in Egyptian history. Also see Kemp, *Ancient Egypt: Anatomy of a Civilization*, 98, who writes that "the myth of the state ... was a clever transformation of an earlier, more generalized statement of an ideal world ... created as part of the great codification of court culture ... in effect a process of internal colonization at an intellectual level".

[953] Sethe, *Urkunden des Alten Reiches*, 164, l. 2-3. Also see Janssen and Pestman, "Burial and Inheritance in the Community of the Necropolis Workmen at Thebes," *JESHO*, (11), 140. This 'rule' of inheritance by the eldest son, is accepted right into the New Kingdom (since it was the eldest son who buried his parents). The authors in footnote 3 on p. 164 write as follows "so far as we know these principles also apply to the law of inheritance at other periods". Textual evidence is from papyrus Bulaq X (recto) which states "let the possessions be given to him who buries".

[954] Klebs, *Die Reliefs des Alten Reiches*, 23.

TABLE 6 PRESENTERS' TITLES

Title	Translation	Tomb owner
ḥtmy sṯi-ḥb	Sealer of the Festival Perfume	Meryib
ḥry-ḥb smsw	Eldest Lector Priest	Qar
sš	Scribe	Meresankh III
sš nswt sȝ=f	Royal Scribe, his son	Nisutnefer
sš ḥm(w)-kȝ pr ʿȝ	Scribe of the Funerary Priests of the Palace	Idut
sš ḥm(w)-kȝ	Scribe of the Funerary Priests	Iymery
sȝ nswt	King's son	Khaf-khufu I
sȝb sš	Magistrate and Scribe	Ptahhotep II
sȝb sḥd sš	Magistrate and Inspector of Scribes	Nefer
sȝb imy-r sš	Magistrate and Overseer of Scribes	Kagemni and Senedjemib-Mehi
sḥd sš	Inspector of Scribes S	ekhemka
sḥd sš ʿ(w)nswt (sš) ʿprw imy-r ḥm(w)-kȝ	Inspector of Scribes of Royal Documents, Scribe of the Work-gangs and Overseer of Funerary Priests	Ty
imy-r ḥmw-kȝ	Overseer of the funerary priests	Iymery, Khentkawes and Meresankh III
imy-r pr	Overseer of the house	Fetekta, Hemetra, Idut, Iymery, Kagemni, Kairer, Kaniniswt, Kaemnofret, Khentkawes, Khenut, Mereruka (fig. 51), Meresankh III (fig. 12), Meryib, Nebet, Niankhkhnum/Khnumhotep (pl. 13), Perneb, Rashepses, Seneb, Senedjemib-mehi, Seshathotep, Tjenti, and Ty (figs. 56 and 128).

1. The tomb owner had two primary obsessions:
2. Provisioning for the afterlife (in which the rise of specialist priests and the developments in religion must have played a significant role).

Being remembered (i.e. what was displayed had to be permanent).

Obsessions lead to among other things the construction of social goals of which the perpetuation of memory and the resulting components of generics are an integral part. One of the ways to achieve these goals was to accumulate and display as many titles as possible, because success in this life was a precursor to owning a mastaba or appropriate rock-cut tomb. By the time of his death, the tomb owner was usually mature enough to realize that his continued afterlife could only be maintained by the next generation of family and high officials. Therefore he chose among other things to depict in his tomb these persons, especially in ceremonial scenes; scenes which he probably realized were constructive in the maintenance and furtherance of his 'obsessions' and which would influence later generations, and most importantly, those which emphasized his social reality.

If this theory about the Taking-Account motif being a primarily ceremonial event with cultural significance for the community is correct, the major and minor participants can be seen as confirming the social goals of the tomb owner, in the way they are described and depicted therein.

Titles of Presenters

- Of the total number of 38 tombs examined:
- 22 tombs, (58%) have 'overseer' as one title of the presenter.[955]
- Seven tombs, (18%) presenter exhibits titles other than 'overseer', but equally prestigious.[956]
- Nine tombs, where the presenter's title is unverifiable.[957]

If one combines the cases where the presenters have other titles with those where they have the title of overseer, the percentage shoots up to a significant 76% (58% + 18%), testifying to among other things the importance of the Taking Account occasion.

---

[955] Overseer of the house in the tombs of: Fetekta, Hemetra, Idut, Iymery, Kagemni, Kairer, Kaniniswt, Kaemnofret, Khentkawes, Khenut, Mereruka (fig. 51), Meresankh III (fig. 12), Meryib, Nebet, Niankhkhnum/Khnumhotep (fig. 13), Perneb, Rashepses, Seneb, Senedjemib-mehi, Seshathotep, Tjenti, and Ty (figs. 56 and 128).

[956] In the tombs of: Khafkhufu I, Khafre-ankh, Nefer, Nisutnefer, Ptahhotep II, Qar, and Sekhemka, e.g. eldest lector priest (Qar), magistrate and inspector of scribes (Nefer), etc.

[957] In the tombs of: Ankhmahor, Iynefert, Kahif, Kanefer, Khnumenti, Nefer and Kahay, Neferbauptah, Shetwi, and Whemka.

The presenter has other titles across a wide range of tombs and Der Manuelian has appropriately collated these.[958]

As already observed the majority of presenters have titles. That these are depicted and identified, demonstrates the social and functional relationship and the connection to the tomb owner during his lifetime. Hidden behind the titles is the network in which an alliance of reciprocal duties was formed between superior and subordinate. A good parallel to similar depictions is in the royal temples, where the king is shown with high officials, who too had a social and functional relationship to the king.[959] Because the king provided his officials and favoured employees with priesthoods and offices in pyramid and sun temples, so the official's personnel received k^c priesthoods in his tomb and cult, which gave them rights to land and income in return for agreed duties.[960]

A note of caution is required when examining the titles: while the titles may be self-explanatory, they only provide a glimpse at a specific point in time (death), at a specific place (tomb in the necropolis), and only information that the elite want to show. As such they are heavily biased towards an un-changing view of society. Of course it will have become apparent by now that this book vehemently disagrees with such a stylized viewpoint, and demands that change be accepted as a dominating pivot point.

A sample list of the titles and their varied occurrences in the tombs are shown in Table 6.

Family and Non-Family Relationships

- Of the 38 tombs examined, twenty cases depict a combination of the family,[961] which can include the following:
- Son(s) presenting.
- High official presenter followed by son(s).
- Other relatives 'viewing'.

The family members identified consist of 6 cases of sons actually doing the presenting. However, there are numerous instances where other family members, e.g. wives, daughters, other sons, a brother and one instance of the tomb owner's parents being present during the Taking Account ceremony. Since the active part of this motif entails presenting a document and taking account of it, the active and passive participants should be separated. There are 8 cases of sons presenting or sons following the presenter, and 28 cases of relatives viewing passively in 20 tombs.[962] There is no filial relationship depicted in the six female tomb owners in this motif. While it is probably best to delineate the presenting act by the sons from other passive acts of the family, nevertheless the combination of family members in this motif yields both a historical and a comparative perspective. This in turn provides a key to the one of the central themes of this book, which is to examine social relationships to the dead and may tell us something about the business of living itself.

The details of the type of relationships in the Taking Account motif are as follows:

- Son[963]
- Wife[964]
- Daughter[965]
- Brother[966]
- Parents[967]

Chart 29 identifies all cases in which a son is present irrespective of his capacity and that of the other relatives. Their presence together, points to the importance of the formal occasion, which would not be out of place in a motif, which depicts material possessions. These were of course once the property of the tomb owner but now have been passed to the eldest son.

The details of their occurrence are given in Chart 29.

The least that can be said is that the family members' roles in acting as presenters and taking part in the proceedings complement the status of the tomb owner.

The titles and relationships found in the Taking Account motif are especially telling of the fact that mutual gains were expected from long-term contact and interdependence. The high numbers of senior officials and close family members as well as other subordinates, are probably present to witness the correctness of the Taking Account scene, and to affirm and accept this state of

[958] Manuelian, 'Presenting the Scroll', 564.

[959] Posener-Kriéger, *Les archives du temple funéraire de Néferirkarê-Kakaï*, 384-91. The numerous and differently titled officials who were involved in various functions related to the mortuary temple of Neferirkare, are depicted here.

[960] Junker, ' Die gesellschaftliche Stellung der ägyptischen Künstler im Alten Reich', *SÖAW*, (233/1), 50-69.

[961] The combination consists of Sons presenting in the tombs of: Khafkhufu I, Khafre-ankh, Nefer, Nisutnefer, Niankhkhnum/ Khnumhotep, and Ptahhotep II. (Not included is the tomb of Khnumenti, where it is uncertain whether the presenter is the son).
Sons following the presenter in the tombs of: = Iymery, Kahif, and Khafre-ankh.
Viewing by Tomb Owner and Family members in the tombs of: Ankhmahor, Iymery, Iynefert, Kaninisut, Kaemnofret, Khafkhufu I, Meryib, Nefer and Kahay, Nisutnefer, Niankkhnum/Khnumhotep, Rashepses, Sekhmeka, Senedjeib-mehi, Seshathotep, Ty (fig. 128), and Whemka.

[962] In the tombs of: Ankhmahor, Iymery, Iynefert, Kahif, Kaninisut, Kaemnofret, Khafkhufu I, Khafre-ankh, Meryib, Nefer, Nefer and Kahay, Nisutnefer, Niankhkhnum/Khnumhotep, Ptahhotep II, Rashepses, Sekhemka, Senedjemib-Mehi, Seshathotep, Ty, and Whemka.

[963] Sons depicted presenting or following presenter or viewing Taking Account with relatives in the tombs of: Iymery (PV), Iynefert (V), Kahif (P), Kaninisut (V), Kaemnofret (V), Khafkhufu I (PV), Khafre-ankh (P), Meryib (V), Nefer (P), Nefer and Kahay (V), Nisutnefer (PV), Niankhkhnum/Khnumhotep (PV), Ptahhotep II (P), Rashepses (V), Sekhemka (V), Seshathotep (V), Senedjemib-Mehi (V), Ty (fig. 128) (V), and Whemka (V)
* P = Presenting , V = Viewing with other sons and relatives. Duplication exists.

[964] Wives present in the 7 tombs of: Iynefert, Kaemnofret, Nefer and Kahay, Nisutnefer, Seshathotep, Ty, and Whemka.

[965] Daughter/s present in the 4 tombs of: Khafkhufu I, Meryib, Senedjemib-mehi, and Whemka.

[966] Brother present in the tomb of: Ankhmahor.

[967] Both parents present in the tomb of: Whemka.

CHART 29: RELATIONSHIP DISTRIBUTION

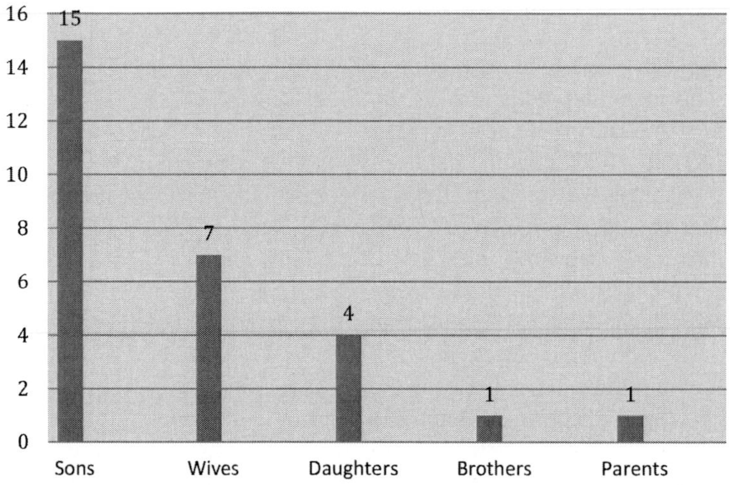

SONS ARE INVOLVED IN DIFFERENT CAPACITIES (E.G. PRESENTING, FOLLOWING THE PRESENTER, AND VIEWING WITH OTHER RELATIVES); TO AVOID DUPLICATION PROBLEMS, THIS CHART'S FIRST COLUMN INDICATES TOMBS WITH ANY SON SHOWN, NOT THE ACTUAL NUMBER OF SONS SHOWN. THE OTHER COLUMNS OF RELATIVES ARE INDICATED IN THE SAME MANNER TO AVOID ANY DISTORTION IN THE RELATIONSHIP PATTERN.
NOTE: SINCE A NUMBER OF THE ABOVE TOMBS SIMULTANEOUSLY SHOW A MIXTURE OF THE RELATIVES PRESENT, THE SAME TOMB MAY BE INDICATED IN MORE THAN ONE OF THE ABOVE COLUMNS.

institutionalized communication and formalized display. The focus here is on the interaction of the tomb owner, a document, and another person within a specific social context, i.e. of Taking Account.

This would support the initial hypothesis that the Taking Account motif is a formal occasion. The presence of this motif in his tomb ensured among other things, the construction of his social memory through inscribing practices, which included depiction and writing. These practices also reveal the way the tomb owner controlled his material world during his lifetime. In the manner of its depiction, the motif then represents both a tool used by the tomb owner for his posthumous purposes, and manifests what was probably an important part of actual elite social/ family life in the Old Kingdom.

The Taking Account motif therefore provides useful material for the study of ancient cultural forms and processes: the analysis helps to differentiate the specific actions of the Old Kingdom tomb owner and to understand the important role of culturally conditioned behaviour and thus the importance of the generics.

Further this motif among others (e.g. the banqueting motif) is a prime example of the evolving independent nature of the tomb owner's identity. Whether he appears in a long striated 'wig' or headband with buckle, standing or sitting in carved wooden chairs or carrying-chairs, ceremonially attired and wigged, or even inflicting punishment (the ultimate Taking Account); the tendency is to validate his

encroachment of power and show his grasp on authority. Finally the tomb owner's assent and deliberative response as regards the document, results in mutual understanding, mutual trust, shared knowledge, the ideology of continuing order and the maintenance of institutional inequalities, all of which point to the generics.

While initially this extension of his powers consolidates the supremacy of the king, ultimately it is this very instrument of widening and intruding bureaucracy, which will result in the demise of the Old Kingdom; because in a closed system everyone had a pre-determined place, bound together by a network of households and obligations, which in time were not maintained and ultimately succumbed to entropy. For now though, the seemingly ordered world of the elite as seen in the Taking Account motif, is secure.

Chapter 9: Mourning Motif

In all human societies, the death of people with whom one is familiar is a constant, and because we are human, we experience grief. The literature on death and grief is wide ranging and the interest in this chapter is limited to aspects of death as follows:

> *To identify the immediate cultural responses to the problems that death creates.*
> *To get a perspective on how the ancient Egyptians tried to solve the problem of giving up the emotional and internal attachment to a love/object, e.g. like another human being.*
> *To analyze how mourning following death was depicted in elite Old Kingdom tombs.*

Every death of a known one is the death of so many shared memories, as well as the realization that every death is a step forward towards one's own dying. At the moment of death, both the disintegration of the body and the cleavage of the social bonds that existed, had to be reconciled with the customary views on mortality and immortality: the former by 'denying death's effective power' and the latter by religious rituals.

This chapter deals with one theme of an ancient society's response to death, i.e. mourning, because mourning is as much about the individual's and the community's past as it is about its future. It is this aspect of mourning - a relationship of reciprocity and obligation, which has the ability to communicate precisely to the community left behind what will in time, become vast amounts of cultural information. With the growth in collective memory it can then also be seen as a means whereby the implications for power, and the maintenance and development of hierarchy are encoded.

Ethnographic studies show that there is 'no society, in which the emotions[968] of bereavement are not shaped and controlled, for the sake of the deceased, the bereaved person, or others'.[969] However, it is stressed that death, grief, and mourning are interconnected.

Additionally ancient ceremonies, especially those surrounding elite funerals of which mourning must have been an integral part, must have had a powerful impression on those left behind. Because this is based on and perceived by the senses, one should integrate this into the theoretical foundations of the ideas about the culture of that period. This sensory perception then requires one to make use of other disciplines, e.g. psychology and biology, which are outside, mainstream Egyptology. Involving other disciplines may allow for more insights into the culture and society of the Old Kingdom, even though there are only three tombs representing members of the bureaucratic elite. All the three with mourning as a motif are from Dynasty 6 (Idu, Ankhmahor, and Mereruka – 'the three tombs').

9.1 Death, Grief, and Mourning

This analysis is partly based on previous work by Binford[970] as elaborated by Saxe[971] and Tainter[972] and draws on some of his conclusions, which are listed below, together with the implications for a mourning scene.

1. All humans die and the host society makes some funeral arrangements.
2. The organization and nature of the society relate with what funeral arrangements are allowed, and discard those, which are forbidden.
3. The more prolific the funeral arrangements, the higher the status of the deceased.

It is outside the scope of this work to go into the debate between processual and postprocessual archaeology. However, when analyzing the mourning motif reliance is mainly on a processual approach, because this eliminates allocating beliefs, which can never be fully ascertained.[973] However, this does not mean that the postprocessual approach has been totally ignored.

Because three interconnected words, death, grief, and mourning are so interlinked one needs to clarify their boundaries at the outset.

---

[968] Cognitive processes give rise to emotion(s) which refer(s) to any turmoil in feeling, which may manifest itself in facial and vocal expressions as a result of fear, anger, disgust, grief, joy, or surprise. See Ellsworth and Scherer, 'Appraisal Processes in Emotion', in *Handbook of Affective Sciences*, eds. R. J. Davidson, H. Goldsmith, and K. R. Scherer, 572-595.

[969] 969 Rosenblatt, 'Grief in small societies', in *Death and Bereavement Across Cultures*, ed. C. Parkes, P. Laungani, and B. Young, 37.

[970] Binford, 'Mortuary practices', 6-21. "Differentiation in burial practice bears a relationship to the 'total' status of the deceased; the social persons, the sum of all the roles and statuses held by an individual in his/her lifetime, carrying rights, duties, and obligations; the differentiation in burial practice also reflects the composition and size of the social unit recognizing obligation to the deceased". I am aware that the Binford-Saxe hypothesis of mortuary process, has been subjected to various criticisms based on statistics, archaeological survivability of material deposited and reuse of burial facility, see Polz, *Excavation and Recording of a Theban Tomb: Some Remarks on Recording Methods,* 119-140. Problems arise from the conflicting demand of reconstruction in archaeology and the tracing of cultural change in anthropology.
However two analytical principles survive these criticisms, namely:
1) The economic scale and political complexity of a society affects the scale and complexity of its mortuary ritual. 2) Any funeral involves an unavoidable amount of time, effort, and resources.
Therefore these principles' contribution to understanding certain aspects of social organization are significant, despite methodological shortfalls.

[971] Saxe, *Social dimensions of mortuary practices,* Ph.D. Dissertation, University of Michigan, 1970, 4-7.

[972] Tainter, 'Mortuary practices and the study of prehistoric social systems,' in *Advances in Archaeological Method and Theory*, ed. M. B. Schiffer, 105-41.

---

[973] The processualists (Binford, Saxe, Tainter, and O'Shea) believe that mortuary differentiation is patterned and these patterns can be linked to aspects of the socio-cultural system. The post-processualists (Hodder and Parker Pearson) argue that mortuary evidence may be distorted or misunderstood without an understanding of the concept of beliefs, which are prior to the exhibited symbolic behaviour.

9.2 Death

Death has been described in various ways in the egyptologoical literature. Attested in the Pyramid Texts are many roundabout ways of expressing it, e.g. the transitive verb *mni* (to land), *šm* (to go), *ḫpi* (to travel). While this chapter is not only about death itself, yet its links with consequential actions following death, require clarification about how death was conceived in the vast literature on this subject and indeed by the ancient Egyptians themselves.

The ideas and the authors cited below, represent a wide cross section of ideas:

Sander-Hansen describes death in six ways:[974]

> (1) Destroyer of body and soul.
> (2) Sleep weariness and night.
> (3) Silence.
> (4) Sickness and suffering.
> (5) Thief and a prison.
> (6) A journey.

Assmann has described death as the ultimate culture generator (his is by far the most wide-ranging treatment on this subject), which in regard to ancient Egypt, he spells out in eight main ways[975] as follows, i.e. death as:

1. Conflict
2. Social isolation
3. Enemy
4. Disassociation
5. Separation
6. Transition
7. Coming home
8. A secret

Gardiner understood death as an ultimate solution.[976] He contrasted the fear of the dead with that of fear of death. While he concluded that the ancient Egyptians did not fear the former, they (the elite) did have a fear of not being able to live as they had done on earth. The excessive expenditure on their tombs is a pointer to this fear, which in any event was 'truly pathetic' as they knew with "certainty that these (their tombs) would soon fall a prey to the plunderer".[977]

Zandee provides a useful compendium of annotated terms used by the Egyptians in dealing with death.[978] He views death negatively based on the natural fear of death in humans.

All the intricate ideas related above, point to the fact that "Das heiligste Weltgeheimnis ist der Tod".[979] The ancient Egyptians were also aware of death's vagaries and the refrain from a later period text 'The Instructions of Any,' correctly refers to this inviolable of all humankind's secret, as the ultimate reality, it reads, "Do not say, "I am young to be taken," For you do not know your death. When death comes he steals the infant who is in his mother's arms, just like him who reached old age."[980] Death though feared and unloved was never ignored for it was not accepted as the end, and in this thought process indicates, "that in the mind of the Egyptian death was in fact the beginning of life".[981]

The funeral was one of the most important elements in the life and death of the ancient Egyptian, yet in the Old Kingdom, the Egyptian attitude towards death, is rarely depicted. This is strange, when the funeral is well evidenced in both representations and texts from the earliest periods to the Late Period, and when it is said to be composed of sixteen different ritual elements.[982] However, there are always parts of the funeral process that are left out, which brings us again to that age-old issue of fathoming intention from the archaeological record. If one accepts, that depictions no matter how scanty they might be are a vital communicative aid to an understanding of the culture of that period, then one's task becomes the teasing out of these cultural values and the role these played in the society of that time. Gardiner in this connection sums up this problem when he writes that although there are reliefs depicting Old Kingdom burials on a papyrus:

> "… these contain, apart from the inevitable posturing of grief, no hint whatsoever of the elaborate goings on revealed, in however a fragmentary form, by this unique papyrus" the substance of which is dated by him to the Third Dynasty.[983]

In any event, representing death is a problem in all societies because philosophically speaking death cannot be adequately represented mentally, because no society's members like to think of their own complete oblivion without contradictions, and because one's own death does not allow total participatory observation.[984]

What one sees are manifestations or instances of coming to terms with the concepts of continuation in the hereafter and mortality in the living world.

An Old Kingdom text: the 'Instruction of 'Merikare' is instructive about the Egyptian's changed thoughts on death. While the preoccupation to build a fitting and

[974] Sander-Hansen, *Der Begriff des Todes bei den Ägyptern*, 9-18.

[975] Assmann, *Death and Salvation in Ancient Egypt*, 23-200.

[976] Gardiner, *The Admonitions of an Egyptian Sage*, 37. "Forsooth great and small <say>: I wish I might die. Little children say (??): he ought never to have caused me to live (??)".

[977] Gardiner, *The attitude of the ancient Egyptians to death and the dead*, 34.

[978] Zandee, *Death as an enemy, according to ancient Egyptian conceptions*, 1-44.

[979] Assmann and Macho, *Der Tod als Thema der Kulturtheorie*, 47.

[980] Lichtheim, *Ancient Egyptian Literature*, vol. II, 138.

[981] Tobin, *Theological Principles of Egyptian Religion*, 130.

[982] Altenmüller, 'Bestattungsritual', *LÄ*, vol. 1, 745-65.

[983] Gardiner, 'A Unique Funerary Liturgy', *JEA*, (41), 16-17. Also see Helck, 'Papyrus Ramesseum E', *SAK*, (9), 166, where he goes even further back to Dynasties 1 and 2.

[984] Hahn, 'Unendliches Ende', in *Das Ende*, eds. K. Stierle and R. Warning, 155-56. In this connection, see Ions, *Egyptian mythology*, pl. 40., where a representation of how death was perceived albeit in the TIP, is illustrated.

eternal resting place is similar to that in the Instructions of Hardedef, what is now new, is the stress on the doing of *M3ʿt* in one's life, which results in social recognition of having been an upright individual.

> "Enrich your mansion of the West,
> Embellish your dwelling of the necropolis
> With uprightness and with the observance of *M3ʿt*,
> For in this (men's) hearts are confident".[985] (Merikare)

This text is based on two parameters, which contain in them the ideas of how, both continuation in the hereafter, and immortality in the living world, can be achieved. Leading an ethical life, and leaving a visible symbol of the tomb and its decorations meant leaving behind a memory of his righteousness: this was the only way memory in eternity could be vouchsafed. The tomb owner has died and as a result the private and the social structure of which the tomb owner was a part, is affected because "when a man dies, society loses in him much more than a unit, it is stricken in the very principle of its life, in the faith it has in itself".[986] The study of these anthropological aspects becomes the study of the symbolic and sociological contexts in relation to the corpse, which can provide an understanding of what life and death meant to a particular community and indeed is the underlying basis for many of the funerary compositions in the Old Kingdom.

From a religious/economic standpoint, this meant an awareness that the time spent on this earth (*tp-t3*) is so miniscule compared to that which will be spent in the netherworld (*ḥrt-nṯr*) exemplified by the term (*ḏt*) meaning infinity; that one can only be remembered, if one has lived according to the principles of (*M3ʿt*) without which life is worthless.[987] This theme runs like a golden thread through all funerary depictions. The worst that could happen to any Egyptian was that he would be forgotten, he would have no past worth remembering, the corollary being that the ideal man was one who had a past which would be remembered.[988]

9.3 Grief and Mourning

The other two interconnected words (grief and mourning) if understood as internal states of the human being cannot

be adequately depicted (yet they can be expressed by conventional gestures, e.g. the grimace of the face etc.), nor do we have any OK non-royal texts relating to these phenomena, and so the psychological viewpoint must be called in to aid. At first glance both these words might appear similar yet they have distinct meanings as follows:

Grief

Grief means the emotions that are caused by death, and can include sorrow, mental distress, fear of being left alone, of being unable to have ones needs satisfied (that which the deceased person had satisfied), etc.

Mourning

Mourning refers to specific 'ritual' behaviour by individuals or groups of persons who mourn the dead. The English verb 'to mourn' and its derivatives occasionally have uses outside of death contexts[989] but in the particular context of the mourning motif, one can argue for a limited use of this term as demarcated above.[990] It is not meant to include all behavior, such as reactions felt by humiliated persons, shamed armies who come back after a lost war, loss of a job or a home, etc.

In the three Old Kingdom tombs with this motif it is a conscious choice, and unfortunately limited by the material record available. These depictions do no justice to what actually transpired since they are just a snap shot of the essentials, the fulfillment of tradition. It is only during the NK that the funeral process and actual conduct is reified, and so we turn to a NK stela of Tehuti for a description of events likely to have transpired and feelings generated:

> "The beautiful burial, may it come in peace after your seventy days are completed in your embalming hall.
> May you be laid on a bier in the house of rest … until your arrival at the entrance to your tomb.
> May the children of your children all be assembled and wail with loving heart".[991]

Mourning is thus grief externalized. This is partly channeled and facilitated by custom, thus represents what is socially expected and significant, and therefore is a culturally defined act. These externalized emotional responses and culturally designated rituals have a mutually influential relationship[992] and "serve a variety of social purposes, including marking out social and hierarchical relationships at times, dissolving them at others, inviting or demanding specific social relationships, or marking/ protesting the abrogation of social or moral contracts".[993] Thus, mourning acts in two ways.

1. It reinforces the pre-existing social relationships.
2. By allowing for change in the new relationship that is created by death, (because mourning the dead

---

[985] Simpson, ed., *The Literature of Ancient Egypt,* 164, l. 128. Recent research on the Instructions of Merikare, indicate a FIP origin, Ibid. 152-153.

[986] Hertz, *Death and the Right Hand*, 78.

[987] Assmann, *Death and Salvation in Ancient Egypt*, 374.

[988] See the Dynasty 12 text: *The Tale of the Eloquent Peasant, Reading Ancient Egyptian Poetry*, comments by Parkinson (p. 54-63), and translation (p. 309, lines 338-341).

[989] Freud, *Mourning and Melancholia*, 214. Compare his extensive use of the word 'mourning', he writes, "mourning is regularly the reaction to loss of a loved person, or to the loss of some abstraction which has taken the place of one, such as one's country, liberty, an ideal, and so on".

[990] *Webster's New Third International Dictionary: Unabridged*, 1478.

[991] N. de G. Davies, 'Tehuti, Owner of Tomb 110 at Thebes', in *Studies Presented to F. LL. Griffiths,* ed., S. R. K. Glanville, 288.

[992] Huntington and Metcalf, *Celebrations of death,* 2-5. For the cross-cultural basis of their studies, see 33-37, 79-107.

[993] Ebersole, 'The Function of Ritual Weeping Revisited: Affective Expression and Moral Discourse', in *History of Religions,* (39), 214.

was never a solitary state of affairs), the ancient Egyptians were always with the dead.

These may be over-neat classifications but are helpful if one accepts that grief is a noun which includes the gamut of private negative emotions; whereas to mourn generally is an external aspect of grief which is influenced by culture. This distinction is made clear when one realizes that personal loss produces grief (emotions of various sorts) and this grief has to be mourned (acted out in some socially acceptable way to both simultaneously forget and remember). A way one can share in the experience of death is by mourning. As already indicated, mourning is not to be confused with grief. Grief is an emotion common to humans and some non-human primates and it generally concerns the closest blood relatives. Mourning is the expression of grief, and is a social activity which can include persons other than blood relatives, and is only practiced by humans. By this rationalization mourning then is commonplace experienced by everyone at some time, whenever we encounter a serious problem in our lives involving loss of someone whoever he/she may be. In the majority of known societies and ancient Egypt was no different, bereavement (the objective state of having lost someone) resulted in grief and mourning, which would have affected a whole range of circumstances concerning the individual such as inheritance, and shifting social status, all of which were part of that cultural milieu.

9.4 Social Dynamics of Death, Grief, and Mourning

Following death, the deceased is a corpse going through the process of putrefaction and this raises three related issues, which in the manner they are addressed, are pointers to the social dynamics of a particular society. In ancient Egypt they may have been as follows:

1. How does one depict the appearance at death?
2. How does one relate visual biological change to the supposed permanent transformation in the hereafter?
3. How does one understand the symbolisms used by the living relatives, friends, and society in general, and relate these to the dead tomb owner?

While the first issue can be of a purely aesthetic nature and incidental to mourning, one shall consider the second and third questions in detail.

Death's Depiction

The moment of death is never depicted in the Old Kingdom. Death and representations of dead persons as inert bodies are therefore rare.[994] Could it be that the strong belief in the hereafter made it impossible to depict sorrow and pain (the negative sides of death) which happen to be the very aspects of death, which the Old Kingdom Egyptians did

not eulogize? Precisely these aspects become predominant in the New Kingdom especially in the post-Amarna period, and question the value of preparation for death, the sureness of life after death, and not expressing sorrow.[995] It would also seem that the Egyptians had a loathing for depicting certain emotions artistically, because one does not find scenes depicting sickness, stupidity, anger, or injustice – "Ästetische Gesichtspunkte bleiben bei seiner Entstehung völlig aus dem Spiel".[996]

Visualizing Biological Change

Egyptians countered the appearance of decomposition initially by by wrapping the body in linen soaked in resin and finally by specific mummification techniques.[997]

The cadaver has always been a symbol of mortality. The embalming of the body had as its prime object, the preservation of this symbol of mortality. By 'preventing' the physical corruption of the body, it followed that self-identity was not lost in the mummy. In Egypt this meant accepting as a fact that the individual although biologically dead, was socially alive. Socially alive meant that he had to be transformed into a state that would enable him to live among those who like him, had made a 'home in the West'.

Transformation of the dead individual into someone, who could exist in the hereafter, was the sphere of the religious ritual, the essence of which was his transformation to a state of becoming an *3ḫ* which quality could only be attained after death. "The man shall be transformed into any god the man may wish to be transformed to".[998] This transformation ensured that the deceased was both in a state in which he could communicate with the living (although he was outside the society of the living), as well as secure his existence in the hereafter. This is why in their inscriptions the elite never call themselves 'the dead'.

Mortality however was socially stratified. The elite, although excluded from direct immortality like the king, could through mummification and transformation rituals, achieve a kind of immortality. The immortality that they aspired to had nothing to do with the biological fact of death of which they were well aware, but was tied up with continuity, "that which has gone on before and that which will continue after," and the imaginative form of transcending death.[999] The ancient Egyptians knew that everything on earth was brief, and this wish for permanence and eternal continuance could only be achieved in the

---

[994] Vandersleyen and Altenmüller, *Das alte Ägypten*, pl. 266. Illustrates a very rare example of the idealized appearance of the mummified dead? (Tomb of Djar, no. 366 at Deir-el-Bahari, Dynasty 11).

[995] Lüddeckens, üntersuchungenüber religiösen Gehalt, MDAIK,(11), 109-110 and pl. 24: Theban Tomb 49 "O you who loved to talk with me, you are silent, you do not speak", etc.
[996] Müller, 'Studien zur Ägyptischen Kunstgeschichte', in *HÄB*, (29), 39-56, esp. 43.
[997] Jones, 'Towards mummification: new evidence for early developments', *EA*, (21), 5-7. Also see Nicholson and Shaw, *Ancient Egyptian Materials and Technology*, 372-85.
[998] Faulkner, *The Ancient Egyptian Coffin Texts*, vol. 1, Spell 290. Transformation rituals are also common in the Pyramid Texts, e.g. § 1011-1019, where of course the reference to a resurrection is that of the king.
[999] Litton, *The Future of Immortality*, 12-27.

context of having a tomb made of 'righteous' deeds, which would last forever. This becomes clear from the Instructions of Ptahhotep:

"That man will endure who is meticulous in uprightness
… He will make a testament thereby;
But for the greedy there will be no tomb".[1000]

Moreover from the Judgment of the Dead as depicted in the 'books of the dead', it is clear that the *B3* of the deceased once he had been transfigured, had complete freedom to enter the world of the living and the gods, and thus his continuance was guaranteed.[1001]

We have no knowledge of how the unknown others looked on the period of their afterlives. While the verb 'to die' *mwt* with its determinative of a prostate man holding his head, and the various euphemisms for death such as *mni, šm, ḫpi* (to land, to go, to travel resp.) have been extensively studied, yet their anthropological aspects as regards funerary practices raises crucial questions which need to be addressed, especially as regards the others. It is incredulous to surmise that these others had no hope for some sort of after-life, especially when they were instrumental in constructing monuments to the dead, just because we do not find adequate evidence in the material records.

Survivors' Symbolic Reactions

The emotions generated following death, are hinted at by artistic representation in the way they depict certain aspects of mourning behaviour such as tearing their garments, tearing their hair, weeping, sitting on the ground with their heads upon their knees, and lying on the ground. These are all signaling devices and in the context of the funeral they signal to us a sense of loss, separation, and a release.

While the Egyptian attitude towards death in general is imprecise, ranging across the negative and positive spectrum as already described previously; where it does appear specifically as in the mortuary texts, it deals with standard practical consequences of death, and is of little help in understanding how the Egyptians understood mourning.

Because death is associated with a wide variety of emotions this presents a problem, because the inner feelings of individuals are like intention, not prone to objective analysis and accordingly one has to rely on inference. Accordingly the emotions of mourning that are depicted in this motif are only useful to the extent that they refer to collective negative emotions for public display. This show of public grief in the mourning context thus may be useful in revealing a part of the thinking behind which bonds linking individuals and groups were affirmed, re-negotiated, or terminated. Also the time frame and

consequences over which the collective emotion is enacted/felt, means that it is liable to be culturally transmitted and of being maintained over a longer time frame, eventually to become a part of the collective memory, e.g. the death of Mohandas Karamchand Gandhi, Martin Luther King, etc.

Radcliffe-Brown has asserted that collective participation strengthens the social bonds in a community.[1002] While generally true, the universal and automatic translation of collective expression into collective solidarity is questionable because there are instances in society when this is not realized, e.g. the collective barracking for a particular football club or behaviour during a pop-concert.

However, in the context of a funeral of prominent individuals it seems to have validity. Social pressures evoke behaviour, which is in harmony with that of other members of society, even if one does not directly feel the sorrow, and that is why there is extremely limited behavioral individuality in the funerary context. Consider the modern day custom of bringing flowers for shared display, as evident at the death of the Princess of Wales, and Michael Jackson. This act is nothing other than the expression of social intention – the joining in is part of affirming the common bonds that exists in the identity of being an Englishman/American. To the extent that this sorrow is demonstrably felt by other nationalities, this may demonstrate a particular biological aspect of universal sorrow, as being part of the human race. There are no instances where loss is greeted with emotional indifference, i.e. "grief is universal … but its manifestations in different cultures are extremely varied".[1003] The depiction of collective mourning then goes beyond that of an expressed personal act and becomes a symbol, whose meaning can be discovered in the social context of the corpse. While this statement is generally true it does not mean that in all cultures sentiments of loss will always result in a feeling of collective social bonding.

The phenomenon of the changed situation (loss) appears in scanty form in the Old Kingdom judging by the appearance of the mourning motif in only three tombs. However, where it appears, the Egyptians made sure through the visual depiction of mourning that it also became an enabling method for all who wished to understand and remember (this assertion is based on the few motifs in the Old Kingdom and the many such which are continued into the Middle and New Kingdoms). In the context of the Old Kingdom this means that mourning,

---

[1002] Radcliffe-Brown, *The Andaman Islanders*, 240. Durkheim who investigated the nature of collectively held beliefs heavily influenced Radcliffe-Brown and how these affect social bonds, even when the protagonists had separate identities. However unlike Durkheim, he did not separate between joyous rituals and funerary rites that are exemplified by feelings of pain.
[1003] Stroebe and Stroebe, *Bereavement and Health*, 54. In contrast, cf. Bowlby (Ibid. 60) and in his trilogy *Attachment and Loss* (1971, 1975, 1981.), where he emphasizes the biological rather than the psychological function. Mourning by seeking reunion with the deceased, is nature's way of enhancing the individual's chances of surviving depression and distress because of the loss of a loved one. This would then view mourning as a way of enhancing survival, i.e. a product of natural selection.

[1000] Simpson, ed., *The Literature of Ancient Egypt,* 138, l. 10.5
[1001] Hornung, *Das Totenbuch der Ägypter,* 198-199.

when depicted, becomes vital to the reproduction and transformation of social memory for the living as well as the dead. The changed situation demands that the mourners (assuming that the majority were family and members of his household) have to rethink the ideas about their identity. The concept of identity is only intelligible with reference to a definite layer of categories; if one is no longer a wife, no longer a mother, no longer has a lord etc. then the mourners identity has to be reworked and adapted to the new situation. Unfortunately while loss is implicit, the working of a new identity can only be conjectured, since this is not depicted in any way in the mourning motif. All one can say is that the way the mourners are depicted, shows how their communities handle separation, and conceptualize institutional and personal sorrow in the cultural sphere.

As regards the tomb owner the depiction of emotions on the part of the mourners points to his social identity and the tomb owner's position in the group when alive. It also affirms and maintains the new identity of the dead tomb owner once all the rituals had been performed. More importantly, this affirmation of social identity reflects communal beliefs about death as a separation with respect to the people left behind, the way this separation had to be externalized and the value system of that society in the way in which cultural memory is processed (remembered).

The proof for this is seen in the visual arts: tomb decoration, the process of mummification, and the textual evidence of celebrating the dead on festival days; which have been used from the earliest times to provide a kind of *memento mori* to sustain the memory and the affiliation of the deceased to his community.

In his discussion on the rites of passage, Van Gennep advocates a tripartite division of separation, transformation, and reincorporation into a new status, as frequently appearing during the lifetime and death of the individual.[1004] In the context of death ceremonies, they are particularly relevant in ancient Egypt, where the funeral process can be seen as divided into various stages - which include an initial separation, a liminal period, and the incorporation into a new status and role. However, before the dead can become 'ritually' dead, they continue to "constitute a special group between the world of the living and the world of the dead",[1005] and thus must be mourned. By emphasizing the concepts of loss (separation), change (transformation), and progression (reincorporation), he points a way of understanding funeral symbolism, which ultimately results in remembrance.

The issue as to what kinds of memories were given a permanent material form (became understood and accepted symbols) and indeed why a particular version

had precedence is open-ended. Another open issue is why only parts of the funerary process are depicted? The Old Kingdom provides very limited answers.

A possible understanding of this issue is that the depiction of a particular part of the funerary process was a way of stressing just one single aspect/function, e.g. tradition, cultic, instructional, aesthetic, individuality etc. This answer has the danger that it ignores issues that may be an amalgam of those just mentioned, and possibly lead to imbalanced, incomplete answers.

Relationship to the Dead

In so far mourners identify themselves in some manner with the dead[1006] mourning acquires a communicative dimension in addition to the purely private emotional dimension of the next of kin. In the three Old Kingdom tombs:

The mourner is separated visually, which then acts to broadcast the special status of the mourner.

This motif then becomes a collective symbol of mourning by the community, broadcasting an array of information.

What one observes from the depictions are actions, which are the result of the disruption of existing social relationships, which now must be reworked.[1007] Though one cannot be sure, it is possible that the symbolic link between the acts of showing respect for the dead through mourning was intended to establish new, mutually beneficial relationships between the mourner and the dead (as seen for instance in the letters to the dead in Old Kingdom Egypt).[1008] It is therefore best to relate this to some motivation, which is ultimately internal to the executants but which one can perceive (but not fully comprehend) if exhibited collectively. In specific circumstances e.g. mourning it can be regarded as a normal outcome of regularly occurring human senses, which as humans, one knows in the context of culturally expected modes of behaviour, to which I shall now turn.

9.5 Mourning as a Psychological Process and a Contradiction

Psychological Process

From a psychological viewpoint, the starting point for the analysis of grief and mourning will be based on the works of Sigmund Freud. His approach to grief arose from a psychoanalytical framework for grief before the

---

[1004] Gennep, *The Rites of Passage*, fig. 1. While his model does enhance our understanding, it must be stressed that the model must be continually subject to modification in the light of any new data concerning the model's population and societies that becomes available.
[1005] Ibid. 148.

[1006] Hertz, *Death and the Right Hand*, 81. "... the image of the recently deceased is still part of the system of things of this world ...".
[1007] Turner, *The forest of symbols: aspects of Ndembu ritual*, 8-9. "In all life-crisis rituals changes take place in the relationships of all those people connected with the subject of the ritual. When a person dies, all these ties are snapped, as it were…Now a new pattern of social relationships must be established ...and everyone who stood in a particular relationship with him must know where they stand…".
[1008] Wente and Meltzer, *Letters from ancient Egypt*, 54-68.

time when empirical evidence was available, and was too extended a definition (being also applicable to objects). Freud saw grief as something, which would free the ego from attachment to the deceased and in so doing, allow new attachments to be formed. In his view this was an effective way of resolving the psychological dilemma due to death. In other words mourning was of great assistance in surviving psychologically, i.e. a way of forgetting and getting on with life. Specifically he said:

> "Each one of the memories and situations of expectancy which demonstrate the libido's attachment to the lost object is met by a verdict of reality that the object no longer exists. The ego is persuaded by the sum total of narcissistic satisfactions it derives from being alive to sever its attachment to the object".[1009]

Freud's views have been the subject of critique. However it would seem that we have to approach Freud using his language games, i.e. 'reality' and 'loss' in his language of psychoanalysis. Therefore criticism in this context is somewhat unjustified.

Bowlby's modern empirical studies led him to introduce a more detailed concept of the four stages of grief, Disbelief, Searching, Despair, and Reorganization.[1010] These phases are not clear cut and an individual may move back and forth between any two of them; nevertheless, even this can take us only part of the way because mourning involves a rich array of thoughts and feelings, which it is impossible to work out fully.

The ancient Egyptians were humans like us and in this context Van Walsem writes:

> "*Nowhere* does there exist a *fundamental* difference between the Egyptian way of thinking and ours".[1011]

If the ancient Egyptian's cognitive brain processes are considered similar to our own, then their behaviour in a universal dilemma can be analyzed using the same scientific principles (e.g. from modern psychoanalysis) that are applied to study mourning in modern humans and could therefore extend our knowledge of their culture.

Contradiction

As already stated mourning as used in this book has a restricted meaning being applied to human loss only because while experiences with 'things' change when we are alive, no experience is as definitive and unchanging as death of a loved/valued 'person'. Cultures have ways of sharing in the experience of death. One should therefore view mourning as the initial stage of an adaptive solution, to the dilemma of retaining and ending a relationship with the deceased, and at the same time mitigating the suffering

of those left behind. In this way the successful completion of the mourning process, results in a memorial of the ideas of the cultural generic, which were embedded in the mourning process? The contradiction is seen in the way that the permanent absence of the deceased from community life coexists with the permanent presence of the deceased, but now in the hereafter, part of him has vanished to another world and another part exists in this world of our memory, the 'consciousness of the survivors'.[1012] Mourning is thus a part of both loss and memory. It is "the painful experience of collective loss, mourning, or the healing response to the pain of that loss; and the building of monuments or the construction of cultural symbols to re-present the loss over time and render it memorable, meaningful, and thereby bearable".[1013] Because it involves a contradiction which must be reconciled it results in cultural input of some sort. It may be that the ancient Egyptians were aware of this contradiction and resolved it through the institution of the depiction of mourning in their tombs, which impliedly includes the stages advocated by Bowlby.

9.6 Mourning Distinguished as a Ritual from a Collective Physiological Act

This book is only concerned with the social significance of mourning because including the religious significance would lead to a concentration on ritual transformative processes of aiding the deceased, through appropriate acts and ceremonies; these are outside its scope. However for completeness's sake the act of mourning as part of a ritual, and the collective physiological act of mourning by those left behind, a brief *discussion* is necessary.

The mythical story of Isis and Nephthys mourning the death of their brother Osiris[1014] is paralleled in the mourning for the deceased, which became an integral part of the rituals associated with the funerary processes. However this is not to be confused with the socio-physical process of mourning by the relatives and friends of the deceased. This act of mourning is at one level the product of what society expects, has little if anything to do with the myth of Isis or with what religion expects and is depicted in only three Old Kingdom tombs.[1015] Assmann explains the original ritual ideas clearly such that any further attempts, would add little to his full explanation. It is worthwhile to quote him fully:

> "The mythic prototype of the widow's lament was the mourning of Isis over the corpse of Osiris. Her songs speak the same language as the widow's laments in the tomb inscriptions. These laments belong to the

---

[1009] Freud, *Mourning and Melancholia,* 255.
[1010] Bowlby, *Attachment and Loss,* vol. 3, 85.
[1011] Walsem, 'The Struggle Against Chaos as a 'Strange Attractor' in Ancient Egyptian Culture', 322-23.

[1012] Hertz, *Death and the Right Hand,* 82.
[1013] Homans, *Symbolic loss,* preface (IX).
[1014] Münster, *Untersuchungen zur Göttin Isis; vom Alten Reich bis zum Ende des Neuen Reiches, MÄS,* (11), 23. Both are also mentioned as goddesses in the Pyramid Texts § 1254a, 1255c, and 1280a, present at either side of the dead Osiris, whom they have found. They appear in depictions of the funeral since Dynasty 5, and in the MK they are differentiated into a larger (*drt wrt*), and a smaller (*drt ndst*), but by Ramessid times they are no longer depicted.
[1015] In the tombs of: Idu, Ankhmahor, and Mereruka.

female, to Isis-Nephthys, aspect of bestowing life on the deceased, and thus to the physical side of the efforts to restore life and personhood. Horus does not mourn: his words describe the restoration of honour, the punishment of the enemy, the elevation and enthronement of Osiris, but never longing, love, or grief. Mourning occurs in the intimate space of the physical constellation of spouses, not in the social space of honour, sovereignty, and vindication, for which the son is responsible. Lyric, the language of emotions is a sensuous, feminine language, and its earliest expression - at least, in the texts preserved to us - is to be found in the laments of Isis and Nephthys. In the organization of the life endowing and renewing activities by means of which ritual endeavoured to treat and to heal death, there was a strict differentiation of the sexes. Even a deceased woman played the role of Osiris, and in the rituals, Isis, Nephthys, and Horus acted on her behalf, as well. Grief, and specifically *female* grief, was an unconditional form of handling death by bestowing life".[1016]

Women referred to as *ḏrt* 'kites' are routinely depicted playing the part of these two goddesses.[1017] The mourning by these goddesses was vital to the reawakening of the deceased Osiris in the afterlife but played a different role than the personal sorrow of the son, Horus. Isis and Nephthys mourned for their lost brother and husband and as far as Isis is concerned; their sorrow brought him to life. This display of sorrow took on a distinctly ritualistic character with the presence of the two 'kites' within the funeral process. Depictions of the kites as two women at the head and the feet of the coffin show them accompanying the body to the tomb, but they do not display similar actions associated with mourning as shown by family and the collective. They just stand or sit silently by the body and mourn the dead in form and ritual only. They are characteristically each dressed in a long sheath dress. Their headdress is known as a *khat,* and resembles a tight fitting cap of white cloth around which is a filet. This sort of headdress is generally seen in goddesses.

The suggestion has been made that the depiction of kites with this headdress could be an indication of a shifting of the woman's role from a secular to a religious identity,[1018] in the same way when the tomb owner's identity shifts from that of addressee to that of the venerated one in the tomb chapel. However it seems that this suggestion is misguided because the social construction of identity cannot be merely based on a relationship to past mythical entities.

Trigger, in connection with the problem of shifting social identity is correct when he writes, "such efforts are similar in that they treat society as 'social culture' rather than a system of social relations". By linking the various criteria,

e.g. artifact type, social organization, language etc., one can examine these "on their own terms rather than within a rigid framework of arbitrarily defined culture".[1019] Accordingly all human identities should not be examined in isolation but be viewed within the framework of a social system because they are the product of multiple influences.[1020] This is again a pointer to the social and cultural dynamics.

The rituals associated with death, the Old Kingdom depiction of mourners as exemplified in the three tombs to be discussed, can be classified as 'Trauerriten', i.e. mourning concerned with the bereaved, which would place them outside of the official rituals for the dead. These can be contrasted with the 'Totenriten', in which mourning by the kites is concerned with the transformation of the dead himself.[1021] An instructive insight is provided by Podella[1022] who writes:

> *"Totenriten und Trauerrituale reagieren in jeweils spezifischer Weise auf den eintretenden und eingetretenen Tod. Totenriten beziehen sich auf den Verstorbenen selbst: sie umfassen die Bestattung und ihre Vorbreitung. Trauerrituale thematisieren den Verstorbenen ... als Verlust ... der sozialen Gestalt der Hinterbliebenen. Obgleich Totenriten und Trauer ... ineinanderübergehen, ... empfielt sich hier eine differenzierende Darstellung."*

It appears therefore that private scenes of mourning did not serve a ritual function within the funeral process itself, but this distinction should not be stretched too far because often there is a merging of the religious and the profane. They are an expression of on the one hand, the personal private and very real emotions of the members of the household, and on the other hand, the collective grief felt by members of his community, left behind by the death of the tomb owner.

Sorrow when displayed collectively, becomes a culturally embedded process which maintains/re-negotiates social bonds and denies death's effective power by using mourning for both remembering (changing death's remembrance into a cult) and forgetting (celebrating the spirit of the deceased).

- Both of the above beliefs were very much a part of Egyptian culture of that time;[1023] the Old Kingdom was in many ways an elaboration on early Dynastic cultural themes, and the issue why mourning then does not appear explicitly in many more Old Kingdom tomb representations becomes all the

[1016] Assmann, *Death and Salvation in Ancient Egypt,* 115.

[1017] Kucharek, 'Isis und Nephthys als *ḏrt* - Vögel', *GM,* (218), 57-61.

[1018] Robins, 'Hair and the Construction of Identity in Ancient Egypt', 67-68.

[1019] Trigger, *Beyond history,* 18-23.

[1020] Díaz-Andreu et al., *The Archaeology of Identity,* 2.

[1021] Assmann and Macho, *Der Tod als Thema der Kulturtheorie,* 19. "Was dieses Behandeln des Todes angeht, unterscheidet man Trauerriten und Totenriten. Die einen konzentrieren sich auf die Hinterbliebenen, die anderen auf den Toten oder die Tote selbst."

[1022] Podella, 'Totenrituale und Jenseitsbeschreibungen', in *Tod, Jenseits und Identität,* eds. J. Assmann and R.Trauzettel, 532-33.

[1023] Taylor, *Death and the afterlife in Ancient Egypt,* 41-45.

more relevant. If the texts and the representations are our only source, then it would follow that until Dynasty 4, personal private mourning was not a motif in the repertoire of elite tomb decoration and when it first appears as in the tomb of Debehen, it is not too explicit.[1024] However in three tombs it appears as a fully developed personal mourning motif. Possible explanations for this scarce depiction of mourning might be as follows:

- Mourning motifs were too realistic, too painful for most 'tomb owners' and thus did not fit within the ideological framework of that time, which was to present the deceased in as favourable a situation as possible.[1025]
- Again unfavourable representations of death might cause evil influences to be directed at the individual from the iconography, and it was best to describe only those circumstances, which would be favourable to the deceased.[1026] Further the Egyptian generally chose (at least in the Old Kingdom) to depict only those aspects, which had favourable connotations of life in the hereafter. Mourning as meaning dismal death, was therefore virtually outside of what was acceptable, as belonging within the official genre of tomb decoration. Although this might have been the case in the early part of the Old Kingdom; from the FIP onwards, mourning scenes reappear and continue right through the pharaonic period.

Could this imply that the idiom of decorum was limited to the earthly and the now with all its problems? Concepts of transition and reincorporation were far more relevant to a successful afterlife in ancient Egypt, than mere mourning. As Van Gennep observes "On first considering funeral ceremonies, one expects rites of separation to be the most prominent component, in contrast to rites of transition and rites of incorporation, which should be only slightly elaborated. A study of the data, however, reveals that the rites of separation are few in number and very simple, while the transition rites have a duration and complexity sometimes so great that they must be granted a sort of autonomy".[1027]

One would expect the idea of mourning to be depicted widely in the Old Kingdom tombs, because it was something that every person would wish for, in the sense of detailing the superior nature of connectedness as compared with death's disconnectedness. Precisely because it does not appear generally in the Old Kingdom, it takes on added significance, and calls for an explanation (especially when there are 108 registers depicting the funerary processes in

35 tombs (main theme 'funeral') and 53 registers of a sub-theme, 'dragging the statue' appearing in 28 tombs).[1028]

Periods of mourning for the elite were most likely public events with family members loudly expressing their grief outside the private confines of the home and this is even seen in present day Egypt. Generally the women are seen in utter despair watching the funeral procession as it leaves; they can only show their loss and leave it to the observer as to what it entailed, sociologically speaking. The issue is not primarily what we as moderns, understand by mourning, but more to the point what the ancient Egyptians understood and how they experienced mourning. In order to do so, one has to observe the motif not as an outsider but imagine oneself as a participant, because certain occurrences, e.g. mourning resist linguistic appropriation and are better understood in a visual way.

Let us follow this argument by considering an elite Old Kingdom funeral in the tomb of Ankhmahor.

For the sake of argument, let us consider a scene, which is part of a funeral process but relates to the acts done by others (excluding offering bearers) following death.

On the Northern and Southern entrance thicknesses (pls. 52 and 53 going from room III to V), are depicted identified and named funerary priests (only on pl. 53 reg. 1 and 2), each wearing the short kilt and the short curled 'wig', carrying: seven different types of oils, cloth, bags, vases, collars, pendants and straps.[1029] They carry these as if in a ceremonial procession in a dignified manner and one can well imagine the scene with all its pomp and pageantry being played out.

Now let us add to these two scenes the mourning motif on pl. 56 and imagine this procession of dignified carriers of personal/funeral goods being led by mourners with its train of people tearing their hair, swooning and wailing women, cacophony of music and dancing, clouds of incense and you have what is an intense experience.

Mourning can therefore be used as a metonym for a theoretical understanding of mourning as a composite emotion, which includes physical and emotional aspects of mourning, i.e. the necessity of appropriate provisions required for the dead.

These expressions of emotions become important particularly when one investigates general issues about the psychological nature of physiological actions, such as the pain and suffering of separation. One is then forced to concede that these are some areas, which cannot be fully comprehended by the application of purely hard cold logic only, i.e. the scenes with carriers of grave goods and nothing else would not do justice to the underlying emotion of the scene.

[1024] Hassan, *Excavations at Gîza*, (IV), fig. 122.

[1025] Simpson, ed., *The Literature of Ancient Egypt*, 128. In the Instruction of Hardedef (First Part), it reads "Accept for death is bitter for us. Accept for life is exalted for us".

[1026] Zandee, *Death as an enemy, according to ancient Egyptian conceptions*, 5.

[1027] Gennep, *The Rites of Passage*, 146.

[1028] Data is from Leiden University's LMP MastaBase.

[1029] Kanawati, *The Teti Cemetery at Saqqara: the Tomb of Ankhmahor*, vol. II, 47-48, pl. 52-53 and 56.

All humans eventually die. The physical nature of emotional reactions following death (mourning) is common to all societies, where verification is possible. There is no reason why the Old Kingdom Egyptians should have a different psychology towards mourning, despite the lack of archaeological evidence. This is based on a series of ethnographic studies, which show that there is enough similarity in emotionality across cultures, that in virtually any society, death typically produces emotional distress and all societies have 'rules' on how the emotion of grief is to be displayed.[1030] The interest here is to tease out any extended entrenched meaning, which may lie hidden behind this physical action, which is not amenable to be recovered from the archaeological record, either because it is scant or just does not exist. Therefore there is justification in using such disciplines as modern psychology, to make statements about the virtual certainty of these Egyptians' emotions and the social significance of their mourning.

Another argument for expanding the boundaries of this analysis is the fact that we use our senses just as much as our ability to reason logically in any analysis, albeit with different degrees of priority. So why not give the sensual part more priority when, as is the case with mourning motifs in the Old Kingdom, no other avenue is available, particularly when emotional reactions to loss and death are so universal. It is important to emphasize that the mourning motif is a depiction of mourning in only three tombs, and that dependency on depiction means that one cannot access actual practice in a direct way, e.g. through detailed and descriptive texts. The depictions may therefore reflect idealization or hyperbole, and could have served a mix of different ideological aims of the tomb owner. Nonetheless, because depictions in funerary art are not generated in a vacuum, it seems reasonable in light of the cross-cultural research (see page 161) that they suggest something about mourning as it was practiced then.

This book follows the hypothesis that both practical and theoretical reasoning are different but related activities;[1031] because purely personal actions and choices are the result of biological and psychological impulses, whereas behaviour is the result of a mixture of personal desires and demands imposed by society. Mourning's analysis thus calls for a combination of approaches. Collective mourning is exactly such an instant of human behaviour, which can benefit from the inclusion of some 'non-objective' analysis. Being immediate in its effects, the individual participants feel the intense power of involvement (active or passive) in the mourning experience and not as something abstract, but something which they can retain, carry forward and broadcast socially. In so doing, they in time unwittingly become a part of the method by which symbolic systems are transmitted and culture maintained. It is difficult to establish the difference related to categories such as collective mourning and religious rituals. The

transmission of culture cannot be explained in terms of a single determining factor and motivation may come from several directions. An explanation of the mechanism of how physiological action, (i.e. mourning) can produce a change in culture (abstract action) has been given by Turner and is a helpful starting point although he does not expand on why change takes place.[1032]

9.7 Fundamentals of the Mourning Motif

As the mourning motif appears in only three Old Kingdom tombs, these three tomb owners are among the first known elite to depict the mourning motif.

Should these therefore be considered individualistic as the start of a new type of representation, although death and related loss and sorrow are a known universal in all societies? Schäfer disagrees that they show individuality. He observes[1033] when discussing the mourning gestures in the tombs of Ankhmahor and Mereruka, that mourning as depicted there should be understood as a composite picture, with deeply grieving participants. In any event without further evidence, the matter is still open.

The Mourning motif has three well-defined fundamentals as follows:

1. It is related to a time frame, not part of the tomb ritual. The mourners who are depicted convey a sense of communal ceremonial undertaking prior to burial and can be partly related to research assumption 2 (see page 14), that the higher the status of the tomb owner the more prolific the funeral treatment. Even if we accept Strudwick's caveat that not all individuals of equal means placed equal emphasis on mortuary expenditure,[1034] we must accept the fact that expenditure connected with artistic depiction must have had some links to the amount of depiction, which in turn would depend upon space, meaning a bigger mastaba and consequently more expenditure. Bigger space alone can be used as one indicator of social rank and higher status, and the mourning motifs therein are explicit indicators of the culturally acceptable ways of showing grief as far as society is concerned.

2. This is the only motif in which the tomb owner does not play a dominant role (contrasting with the previously discussed case of the Carrying-Chair and the Taking Account motifs in which this

---

[1030] Davies, *Death, Ritual, and Belief,* 44-48.

[1031] Velleman, *Practical Reflection,* 15.

[1032] Turner, 'Encounter with Freud: The making of a comparative symbologist', in *The making of psychological anthropology,* ed. G. D. Spindler and J. W. M. Whiting, 574-76. Turner describes two 'clusters' of cultural symbols, which he terms the 'physiological' and the 'normative', each being at the opposite ends of the spectrum. The physiological cluster produces an immediate effect; and culture is created and sustained when this effect, later becomes part of the normative cluster. This seems to me an apt way of coming to grips with the cultural effects of mourning or indeed any physiological action, which can only be felt or perceived by the senses.

[1033] Schäfer, 'Eine unerkannte Trauergebärde und ein angeblicher 'Plötzlicher Tod' in Reliefs des Alten Reiches', *ZÄS,* (73), 106.

[1034] Strudwick, *The Administration of Egypt in the Old Kingdom,* 5.

is physically the case). The difference lies in the emphasis on the functions; because mourning has as a prime purpose, the mitigation of the suffering of those left behind, whereas the prime purpose of a funeral as a whole is to pay respects to the deceased, thus emphasizing the tomb owner. Although it is highly likely that he may have given instructions on how his funeral was to be carried out, nevertheless the actual performance of it, is left to his progeny. His influence now is not that of an authoritative patriarc, but that of an apprehensive supplicant, desiring certain rituals to be executed in order to live an equally 'rich' life in the hereafter, the fulfillment of which wish becomes one indication of the esteem in which he was held.

3. Because of its predominantly emotional content, it is one motif that is amenable to some serious psychological/biological explanations in the course of which one can get as close as possible to the ancient Egyptian's intention.

The mourning motif does not distinguish clearly between institutional mourning – that of a compulsory nature, culturally imposed on the deceased's kin group to deal with the loss to the community as a whole, and that of mourning as an example of the grief felt by the participating individuals. It is highly likely that both types of mourning that by the individual as part of the collective (loss of a guiding hand), and that experienced by the individual himself (the new status of a widow, and the fact of physical separation) were part of the socio-cultural system, and in so far as they relate to the existence and maintenance of prior social bonds, they can be considered identical in effect. Both types of mourning may be read in the three Old Kingdom depictions to be discussed but again the main concern is with the type of (collective) mourning, which alone is suggestive of creating social meaning.

In the Memphite region, the three Old Kingdom tombs of Idu, Ankhmahor, and Mereruka all dated to Dynasty 6, are the only ones that have a mourning motif in this sense. While these may be considered as isolated examples, the mourning genre is continued right throughout albeit in changed form in the FIP, Middle, and the New Kingdoms.[1035] The result being, that when change impinges on activities considered useful and desirable, e.g. mourning which among other things was fundamental to the integration of the deceased into the survivor's ongoing life; there is inevitably the high probability that these changes would become part of the blend and continue into other times. Change is mirrored in the methods and approaches as seen in the latter period representations, which although they vary considerably in detail, are not unique because the problem of alleviating loss through death and reintegration into the community of family, friends, superiors, and subordinates plus the netherworld of gods, was timeless.

9.8 Developmental Evidence of the Mourning Motif in the Old Kingdom

Funerary scenes were introduced as a topic during Dynasty 4 at Giza, yet in the first documented attempt in the tomb of Debehen, mourning and ritual are so intertwined that it is impossible to separate the two.[1036] Indeed if one compares the scene in Debehen to the gestures in the three Old Kingdom scenes it will be apparent that there is a complete absence of any form of mourning gestures, and one is left to search for mourning in an apparent funeral process.

A textual description from the stela of *d3g*[1037] dated to between the FIP and the Middle Kingdom, is more informative about the details of mourning, and reads:

> "I went out of my house and I descended to my tomb in a beautiful burial equipment that I had acquired with my own strong arms, (and while) my house was weeping and my city (following after me) (in the funerary procession) (and my) children were greeting for me without her missing (anybody)".
> (*pr.n.(i) m. pr.(i) h3.n.(i) r is.(i) m ḳrst nfrt irt.n.(i) m ḫpšwy.(i) pr.(i) ḥr rmt niwt.(i) m-s3.(i) mswt.(i) ḥr nini m-s3.(i) nn nḥ.s*).

Unfortunately only one of the Old Kingdom mourning motifs has any captions describing the real visible act of mourning[1038] and assistance must be sought from other sources: funerary texts, which are either royal in nature or are from a different period.

The hieroglyphic words, which accompany the mourning motif, describe and identify mourners, and acts/gestures of farewell. Only one tomb (Idu) refers to the actual act of mourning, e.g. weeping. Accordingly the texts are of little help. Although one is restricted to three tombs, parallels with similar motifs in other periods may eventually assist in supporting the assumption, that all collective mourning scenes have similar cultural components.

The hieroglyphs for mourners, mourning, wailing, lamenting, and grief are well documented.[1039]

However, what strikes one in these texts, are the different words for determining grief, which appear during the Dynastic periods. While the words themselves are different (as one would expect of developing nuances in a

---

[1035] Settgast, *Untersuchungen zu Altägyptischen Bestattungs- darstellungen*, 112-14. Also see the comprehensive review by Lüddeckens, 'Untersuchungen über religiösen Gehalt, Sprache und Form der Ägyptischen Totenklagen', *MDAIK*, (11).

[1036] Wilson, 'Funeral Services of the Egyptian Old Kingdom', *JNES*, (3), pl. 18. This is also apparent in the egyptological literature, where mourning seems to have been discussed as an afterthought, whereas it is one of the richest sources for understanding social organization, because it is a well-experienced situation.

[1037] Lange and Schäfer, *Grab-und Denksteine des Mittleren Reichs*, vol. 1, pl. 20007, 6. In this connection, see Settgast, *Untersuchungen zu Altägyptischen Bestattungsdarstellungen*, 7, (his footnote 5). "Meine Stadt war hinter mir, meine Kinder machten *nini* hinter mir, es fehlte nicht eines".

[1038] In the tomb of Idu, the caption reads *prt in mrt=f ḥr rmt* (coming forth by his meret-serfs weeping).

[1039] Lüddeckens, 'Untersuchungen über religiösen Gehalt', *MDAIK* (11),16-28. Also see Table 7 in this book.

TABLE 7 HIEROGLYPHIC MEANINGS AND DETERMINATIVES

Word	Meaning	Determinative	Reference
iȝkb	Beklagen	Mourning man is shown with one hand in front of his face, the other hangs on the side.	Hannig, *Ägyptisches Wörterbuch* I: 33
iww	Wehgeschrei	Mourning man/woman is shown with one upturned hand held in front of his/her face, the other arm rests by his/her side.	Hannig, *Ägyptisches Wörterbuch* I: 50
imw and *irty.w*	Weheklagen and Jammern	Mourning man is shown with one upturned hand against his face, the other arm hangs at the side.	Hannig, *Ägyptisches Wörterbuch* I: 70 and 198 resp.
ik (transitive verb)	Beklagen	Mourning man is shown with one hand outstretched in front of his face; the other arm is by his side (Gardiner list number D77).	Hannig, *Ägyptisches Wörterbuch* I: 226
ḥȝ(i)	Klagen, Beklagen, Beweinen	Mourning man is shown with both arms raised above his head (It can also mean joy; therefore context is crucial in determining meaning).	Hannig, *Ägyptisches Wörterbuch* I: 754
ḥȝytjw	Trauernden	Sparrow is shown with a rounded tail indicating something bad.	Hannig, *Ägyptisches Wörterbuch* I: 754

language), it is the determinatives that are more revealing in the context of their usage, because these embody gestures.[1040] This would also indicate that the Egyptians had an extensive vocabulary, and that they tried to use appropriate words in scenes to show what they really wanted to depict, i.e. linguistic development and attendant refinements proceed in parallel to cultural development and ultimately go through the process of refinement and eventual obsolescence.

Words meaning 'Mourning'

The following is a review of hieroglyphic words and determinatives, which refer to negative emotions, which are useful in describing mourning.

While they mainly appear in the Coffin Texts, the determinatives are very similar to the hand gestures seen in the Old Kingdom mourning motif, and therefore are useful aids to developing meaning. These hand gestures continue as a symbol of mourning and form an important part of the funerary scenes in both the Middle and New Kingdoms.[1041]

Hands and the way they are used and depicted are therefore an important part of the mourning scene as will be observed from the hieroglyphic words and determinatives given in Table 7.

Texts describing 'Mourning'

- As already stated there are not many texts available and the oldest continuous texts from the Old Kingdom are those relating to the king. These frequently describe mourning as the lamentation of Isis and Nephthys at the destruction of Osiris.
- In a Pyramid text[1042] mourning is described as, Isis sitting with her hands on her head, Nephthys clutching her breast and both of them weeping for their brother.
- In another similar royal text describing how mourning was performed for a dead king,[1043] the souls of Pe are said to "smite their flesh for you (probably refers to smiting the chest), they clap their hands for you, they tug their side-locks for you", (probably means pull out their hair). In the non-royal tomb of Idu, the caption reads "coming forth by his meret- serfs weeping" (*prt m mrt=f ḥr rmṯ*).
- In the Middle Kingdom tale of Sinuhe, one reads that the people mourn for their dead king, by

---

[1040] 'Gesture' means a conscious or sub-conscious movement of the body, especially of the hands, arms, and face, which can convey a state of mind. Since this definition cannot apply with certainty to all movements, this discussion is restricted to those that are actually depicted in the OK mourning motif.

[1041] Werbrouck, *Les Pleureuses dans l'Égypte ancienne*. Also see Radwan, 'Der Trauergestus als Datierungsmittel', *MDAIK*, (30). While both are helpful in tracing the continuity and development of mourning gestures especially in the New Kingdom, they do not distinguish between institutionalized (state funerals) and private mourning. It may be that the concept of state funerals for the elite was not an established practice. However, in light of the strong kinship bonds that existed, elite funerals may represent an amalgam of the two forms (private and state), something

that in light of the current level of knowledge cannot be distinguished.

[1042] Faulkner, *The Ancient Egyptian Pyramid Texts,* § 1281f.

[1043] Ibid. § 1005.

TABLE 8 LANGUAGE GAMES

Religious	Relating to the course of one's eternal destiny and in the formal/informal religious rites of remembrance.
Psychological	How to confront loss (the past is dead) and simultaneously continue an on-going engagement with loss and its remains, whereby the past remains alive in the present.
Biological	Severance of biologically significant social connections results in grief, and is evidenced in behaviour, seeking to regain attachment to the departed person. Grief being a universal feature of being human.
Individual	The deceased and the mourner join in a symbolic way to become the writers of the very last episode: that of accepting loss and creating subsequent memory.

holding their heads down on to their legs drawn up to their chest.[1044]

- In "The Tale of the Two Brothers" from the New Kingdom, it is said: "He wept when (he) saw (his) young brother lying in death ..."[1045]

Mourning Gestures Depicted in the three Old Kingdom Tombs

Reference to hand gestures seem to be the common denominator as a permanent fixture of the mourning process and is also present in the three Old Kingdom motifs under reference. The variety of gestures indicate different shades of meaning and as already observed (see Table 7), there is no one word with a definite meaning, but a sort of fluid continuum reflecting the development of understanding, which is the consequence of the impact of the continuing process of change.

These gestures from the depictions in the three tombs under reference give an idea of their extensive range associated with a collective display of public grief. Because of the different gestures, one may conclude that these are not related to an isolated identity but may be the result of variations in the drama of mourning, which the Egyptians applied as they saw fit. Therefore it is possible that mourning as a social practice which while drawing on pre-established norms, also permitted some improvisations. This could then produce certain effects, including an intellectual exchange of ideas, which could give rise to innovation and change.

Gestures are crucial for an understanding of mourning because they are visible and structured parts of all human communication. However, this is not a mechanical automatic understanding, because even similar gestures can have a wide variety of hierarchical meaning, depending on the context of their usage, as in the case of the practice of bowing in Japan.

Part of the problem with regard to the mourning motifs, lies as already averred to, in the scant nature of the captions, such that some gestures depicted, e.g. both arms raised above the head, could mean jubilation or sorrow depending on the context of usage.

A crucial issue raised by Van Walsem in his review of a dissertation on gestures, clearly exposes the issue in Egyptian Art, when he writes:

"Here we touch upon the central problem for an artist who has to make a fixed two-dimensional representation of a two/three-dimensional movement in a specific situation ... Which gesture, or rather which *phase* in gesture should be chosen for its unequivocal interpretation by an observer".[1046]

Because of the sample number of tombs, the gestures are not to be considered as being a typology. However, it is of interest to note, that nearly all the gestures that appear in the three tombs are also mentioned in countless biblical passages[1047] such as: weeping and lamentation, following the coffin in procession, hand on head as a mourning gesture, putting ashes/dust on head, tearing garments/hair, etc. Keeping in mind the problems posed by Van Walsem, gestures are best understood as merged symbols, which the ancient Egyptians understood to convey emotions and because they appear associated within a funerary setting at death, these refer to emotions connected with mourning.

A coherent understanding of some aspects of these symbols can be achieved by the use of the various levels of the covering language game of mourning in funerals. These may be any of the following encompassed in Table 8.

The details of the gestures in the three tombs of Ankhmahor, Idu, and Mereruka do not need illustrating, because this is not a book on gestures as such. These can be found in other studies.[1048] Gestures, which appear in the three Old Kingdom tombs, are detailed in Table 9. It is admitted that certainty of unambiguous interpretation is problematic in the absence of texts. However, in the context of a particular motif, bearing in mind universal psychological primate reactions, one can relate gestures with motifs in order to gain a better understanding.

In the 21 gestures enumerated therein, the emphasis in them demonstrates a show of 'support' by both genders in the grieving process, and a commitment to the tomb owner and the members of his family and the community, which is

---

[1044] Lichtheim, *Ancient Egyptian Literature*, vol. I, 224.
[1045] Simpson, ed., *The Literature of Ancient Egypt*, 87, l. 13.4.

[1046] Walsem, 'Boekbesprekingen - Faraonisch Egypte', *Bibliotheca Orientalis*, (55), 125.
[1047] *The Holy Bible*, 2 Sam. 13:19, 15:30, and 3 Sam. 31-37.
[1048] Dominicus, *Gesten und Gebärden in Darstellungen des Alten und Mittleren Reiches*, 58-75.

paralleled in the emotions, which the depicted gestures evoke. Additionally it reinforces the individuality of these three tomb owners because in each of their tombs the total ratio of male to female mourners is 1:1, 1:2, and 1:3 in total 5:8.

The detail of each of the mourning motifs in the three OK tombs of Idu, Ankhmahor, and Mereruka will now be addressed.

9.9 Tomb of Idu[1049]

Mourning motif's Location

The mourning motif is on the North wall at the sides of the entrance (the eastern part) is a group of six registers of which four depict the mourning scene. It is not certain whether this is taking just outside Idu's home, as there are no identifying texts in contrast to the text in the tomb of Ankhmahor where the entrance is defined as *pr n ḏt*.

Mourners

Two groups are shown with the females below the males; this scheme is seen in all the three tombs under discussion.

There are alternative ways of reading this motif. One can start from the bottom register, if one accepts that the door from which the women have exited is indeed the deceased's house. However, if one relies on the tradition in ancient Egypt of male dominance as well as the way papyri are read, one can then equally start from the top and work downwards.

Female Mourners

In this register we have the first group of six females, who are each identically dressed in a long sheath dress with two straps. This type of dress being common from the Old Kingdom to the New Kingdom is seen in all the three mourning motifs. Because the tight fitting, ankle length dress depicted is very difficult to walk in, it may have something to do with emphasizing the female body.[1050]

The usual headdress is that of a tripartite 'wig' but there are exceptions. In the tomb of Idu all except two, wear a tripartite 'wig'. One of the women with a tripartite 'wig' is also seen with a shaved forehead, a depiction that is mainly seen among royal mourners.[1051] The others are shown wearing a short 'wig' but this may be due to the artist not wishing to hide the prostrate nature of one and the bowing nature of the arm of the other. No adornments are worn.

One woman is tearing her hair, two are being helped off the ground where they are sitting prostrate, and in the consoling nature of the embraces by the others, shows mourning.

The caption reads *prt in mrt=f ḥr rmt* (coming forth by his meret-serfs weeping), one of the tomb owner's titles was overseer of the scribe of meret-serfs (*imy-r sš mrt*).

This is the only actual 'description' of what constitutes mourning from an Old Kingdom tomb.

In no other Old Kingdom mourning motif is the act of mourning described (admittedly we have only two such other motifs). In the next register, a group of five women is shown; two with a hand on their head and the other three are trying to console each other. The caption reads, *i. nb=i n mrwt* (oh my beloved lord) an exhortation, which in the context of mourning could refer to the feeling of loss and sadness resulting from the departure of their lord. The hieroglyph for the interjection '*i*' never appears in any other part of the funeral processes, its appearance in the mourning motif thus is to be construed as a symbol of expressing pain. Similar to the register below, they all wear a sheath dress with two straps and shoulder length wigs (only one wears a short wig) and no adornments of any kind.

Male Mourners

The next register shows a group of 5 males. One of them is on the ground tearing his hair and is shown being helped off the ground. Another two are consoling each other by friendly gestures of arm entwining and the holding of hands. Another holds his clenched hand in front of his face. They all wear a short kilt and a short 'wig' with no adornments. The caption reads:

i nb=i it n=k w(i)
(Oh my lord take me to you)

The fifth register following shows a group of five males. Three are standing and two are in a bent position. They are all tearing their hair.

Again they are all similarly dressed in short kilts as in the previous register wearing 'wigs' with no adornments with the exception of 2 men who have long hair. The caption reads:

i it= [i] n mrwt
(Oh my beloved father)

There are no titles describing any of these five men.

The last (sixth) register shows the entrance to 'the embalming place/mortuary workshop' but this is only a tentative interpretation, as it could equally be the other gate of the house.[1052]

[1049] Simpson, *The Mastabas of Qar and Idu*, pl. 35.
[1050] Brewer and Teeter, *Egypt and the Egyptians*, 116.
[1051] Kaplony, *Kleine Beiträge zu den Inschriften der ägyptischen Frühzeit*, ÄA, (15), 68. Shaving the forehead is attested since Dynasty 3, for an illustration see Smith, *A History of Egyptian Sculpture and Painting in the Old Kingdom*, fig. 48. Another illustration from Dynasty 4 is to be seen in Junker, *Giza*, vol. 12, fig. 11. The line drawing in Simpson, *The Mastabas of Qar and Idu*, does not depict this, and reliance is therefore on the older line drawing in Werbrouck, *Les Pleureuses dans l'Égypte ancienne*, fig.1.

[1052] Wilson, 'Funeral Services of the Egyptian Old Kingdom', 202.

9.10 Tomb of Ankhmahor[1053]

The caption on the eastern part just above the doorway, reads:

prt m pr n ḏt r imnt nfrt
(Going forth from the estate to the beautiful West).

It would seem that the mourners are part of the funeral procession. The mourners are divided into two main groups, one composed of 15 females and another with 11 males. Each group will be described separately.

Female Mourners

The females are shown in small groups (three groups of three each and two groups of two). There are no titles shown in the female group and the only indication of any close relationship is the inscription above two women who mourn, it reads:

i it=(i) nb=(i) imȝy
(O my father, (O) my lord, the kind one).

Following this is the depiction of two women, who appear to have been overpowered by their emotions and are depicted sitting with knees drawn up and being helped off the ground. Another woman is shown tearing her dress (also seen in the tomb of Mereruka pls. 130-131). The next group is shown helping to lift a fellow mourner off the ground (who may have fainted). The foremost group is seen with their arms entwined around each other's waists, probably a way of showing physical support, should it be needed. There are two females who appear pregnant (or could this just be the realistic depiction of sagging stomachs of older women depicting fatness -the eighth from the left and the second from the right), similar to the male figure who is being helped off the ground and who appears to have a sagging belly in the register above.

The hand gestures are varied, but where they are depicted they show one hand either lifted up in front of or to the side of their faces, a hand placed on top of the head, both hands raised as if in despair or both hands in front of their face.

All the women wear a long sheath dress with two straps and a tripartite wig. No other adornments are shown. The focus is on their gestures and their faces. If one considers the latter, one cannot but notice from the different facial expressions, the solemnity of the occasion.

Male Mourners

In the male group, two persons are identified and described 1) inspector of the seal bearers named Ptahshepses (*sḥḏ sḏȝwt[yw] Ptḥšpss*) and the person behind him as 2) funerary priest named Senbeshi (*ḥm kȝ snbši*).[1054] It has been suggested by Wilson that the seal bearer had special significance, because he was one who was responsible for official travel by boat basing it on the determinative of a boat after the title.[1055] The boat can be understood as either 'in' or 'of' the boat. Sometimes two boats are shown as the determinative, therefore the preference is for the 'of' meaning (because you cannot be in two boats at the same time, the determinative probably relates to some type of authority, like a modern day harbour master). Since the funeral procession had to cross the Nile (especially where the necropolis was situated in the West); the inspector of seal bearers may be considered as an indicator of status in the funerary procession of the elite; equivalent to a modern motorcycle escort!

Like their female counterparts, they do not have any adornments, a short curly wig covers their head, and they all wear a short kilt.

The gestures of mourning are equally vivid, with the most poignant being the person being supported off the ground and that of the person with his head upon his knees. The consoling nature of a supportive arm around the waist is also depicted. Other gestures include both hands on top of head, both hands in front of face, both hands outstretched as in gesture of 'praise', one hand held high above the face and one hand in front of the face.

These are all supportive of the connectivity and solidarity that must have existed generally among the mourning household.

The importance of this scene is emphasized in conjunction with the preceding group consisting of the overseer of the seal bearer of the gods, an embalming priest of 'Anubis' and a lector priest preceded by a kite, plus a caption giving the name of the tomb owner (Ankhmahor whose beautiful name is - *šsi*).

All the priests are shown in their official uniforms with full regalia: (shoulder length wigs and false beards for the lector priest and the embalming priest, who are led by the overseer of the seal bearer of the gods, carrying a sceptre and staff.

The caption on the mourning motif, describes the nature of the journey and some of the people, but surprisingly does not describe the mourning as such. It reads:

pr m pr n ḏt r imntt nfrt
(Going forth from the estate to the beautiful West).

[1053] Kanawati, *The Teti Cemetery at Saqqara: the Tomb of Ankhmahor*, pl. 56.
[1054] Wilson, 'Funeral Services of the Egyptian Old Kingdom', 204.
[1055] Ibid.: 205. Also see Junker, *Giza*, vol. 2, 132 and Jones, *A glossary of Ancient Egyptian Nautical Titles and Terms*, 104-05.

TABLE 9 MOURNING GESTURES

Male		Ankhmahor		Idu		Mereruka		Total	
		Female	Male	Female	Male	Female	Male	Female	
1	Single hand with palm facing inward held in front of face with free arm hanging on side		✓						1
2	Single hand with palm facing inward held in front of face with free arm held across body				✓				1
3	Single hand with palm facing outward held in front of face with free arm hanging on side				✓				1
4	Single hand with balled fist held in front of face or side with other arm hanging to side			✓				1	
5	Single arm held aloft over head with palm facing inwards, the other arm hanging by side				✓				1
6	Single arm aloft over head with palm facing outward, the other held in front of face with palm facing inwards	✓						1	
7	Single arm held aloft over head, the other held above knee with palms facing outward		✓						1
8	Both hands held aloft on side of body		✓		✓				2
9	Both hands held in front of face with palms facing outwards	✓			✓		✓	1	2
10	Both hands held in front of face with palm facing inward	✓	✓					1	1
11	Both hands held on head forming an equilateral parallelogram	✓						1	
12	Both hands and arms of mourners entwined		✓	✓				1	1
13	One arm around waist of another mourner	✓			✓		✓	1	2
14	One arm around shoulder of another mourner				✓				1
15	Head upon drawn up knees	✓						1	
16	Hands tearing hair			✓				1	
17	Hands clutching breast				✓				1
18	Hands tearing clothes		✓				✓		2
19	Smearing dirt on hair and clothes						✓		1
20	Prostate mourner on ground	✓	✓	✓	✓	✓	✓	3	3
21	Lifting mourner from ground	✓	✓	✓	✓	✓	✓	3	3
	Total Gestures	8	8	5	10	2	6	15	24

9.11 Tomb of Mereruka[1056]

The mourning motif is only partly preserved and again there are two groups of figures - the males at the top and the females at the bottom. Unfortunately we can only describe the female as the male group apart from the legs of one man and a part of a figure on the ground is much damaged. Nevertheless based on the parallels in Idu and Akhmahor we can suppose that these too would have been quite similar and possibly depict a prostate mourner being helped off the ground by another person.

The female group is composed of a group of 13 women. The whole group gives one an impression of sadness and mourning. There is a woman shown tearing her hair, another 'whispers' words of 'commiseration', a small group of five and another group of three women have their arms entwined and are giving each other comfort, while one female who may have fainted, is supported by another woman. The women all wear similar clothes, which we saw in both Idu and Ankhmahor, consisting of a long sheath dress with two straps and have no adornments. While they all wear wigs, three of them have the tripartite 'wig', while the rest have a short wig. The caption reads:

i mry nb=(i) imȝḫw sȝḥ tw'Inpw.
(Oh Mery (my) revered lord may Anubis transfigure you)

9.12 Commonalities between the Old Kingdom Mourning Motifs

1. They all are dated to Dynasty 6.
2. They only appear on the North or South walls[1057] (A minor observation is that an ornamental element, the kheker freeze, is present in the tomb of Idu which continues to be used in the Theban tombs of the New Kingdom - and might have a meaning of a sacred place).
3. The ancient Egyptians spent much of their time in preparing for that time, when they would be dead and this importance of the afterlife is reflected in the elaborate iconography of the elite tombs one such motif being mourning.[1058]
4. The males appear on the top part of the motif with the females occupying the bottom in all the three tombs.
5. All the mourned tomb owners titles,[1059] indicate very high officials. Important titles include:
   a. *imy-r sšw mrt* (overseer of scribes of the meret serfs)
   b. *sš nswt ḫft ḥr* (king's scribe in the presence) frequently used by Idu

c. *tȝy sȝb tȝti* (he of the curtain, judge and vizier) used by Akhmahor
   d. *tȝti* (vizier) used by Mereruka, who as the son-in-law of king Teti needs no further elaboration.
6. Their collective negative emotions acts/gestures (e.g. weeping, hurting one self and one's belongings) relate to the expected social behaviour at a specific period and thus are culturally significant.
7. These collective acts/gestures are restricted to the loss of a prominent individual, whose rank and reputation is well known through his belonging to a specific group of higher-class individuals. Mourning over poor individuals is not documented but it is assumed that the social dynamics of each are similar because death always creates expected emotional responses in individuals, irrespective of status.
8. Mourning participants are not restricted to kin and include other members of society, who may not have had any intimate connection with the deceased. This is based on the assumption, that the number of mourners depicted is only a part of the close-knit circle of the tomb owner, rather than the actual number of mourners that would have been present. The development of a 'social persona' (bundle of identities) of the tomb owner can only be explained by this assumption.
9. The interjections of grief referred to are very similar in their show of respect towards the departed and their sense of loss. The only difference is the fact that in the tomb of Idu, both male and female mourners make these, whereas in the other two tombs of Ankhmahor and Mereruka, they are restricted to the females (Admittedly the depiction of the male mourners of Mereruka is fragmentary). In this respect two passages are enlightening which show the cross-cultural universality of pain but also reflect what we read in the captions in the three Egyptian mourning motifs. Time seems stationary and the grief is virtually identical to the captions, when expressed in the following cross-cultural words of mourning: (By a South American Tribe) "O my dear husband … separated us! O, dear what will become of me.[1060]" (By a South African Tribe) "I have remained alone in the lonely plain … Where did you go? You have left me … my mother! O my mother! You have left me, where did you go.[1061]" The above cross-cultural ethnographic studies show how the similarities in emotional responses which exist across time, are indicative of a type of similarity throughout the world, although there are wide variations in the nature, extent and duration of emotional reactions in different cultures.[1062] These

[1056] Duell, *The Mastaba of Mereruka*, vol. 2, pl. 130.
[1057] The mourning motifs in the tombs of Ankhmahor and Idu appear on the Southern Wall, while that in Mereruka is found on the Northern Wall.
[1058] Meskell, 'The Egyptian Ways of Death', in *Social Memory: Identity and Death,* ed. M. S. Chesson, 32.
[1059] For the various titles see Kanawati, *The Teti Cemetery at Saqqara: the Tomb of Ankhmahor,* 11-12; Simpson, *The Mastabas of Qar and Idu,* 30-31, and Duell, *The Mastaba of Mereruka,* vol. 2, pl. 130.

[1060] Karsten, *The head-hunters of Western Amazonas,* 457.
[1061] Junod, *The life of a South African Tribe,* vol. 1, 143.
[1062] Assmann, in *Der Abschied von den Toten: Trauerrituale im Kulturvergleich,* eds. J. Assmann, F. Maciejewski, and A. Michaels. This useful work describes cross-cultural mourning in Asia (37-181), in

are related to the differences in cultural beliefs about life and death, and about the expression of emotions.

10. No adornments of any kind are shown on either gender.
11. Clothes are a vehicle for the public display of wealth and status, and can be used on special occasions, e.g. death to assist in the deeply rooted need for a proper burial.[1063] In the Old Kingdom the above statement is partly true because of the repetitive nature of certain types of attire, which are not limited to ritual functions only. As we do not have any written evidence for the reasons behind wearing a particular type of attire and are entirely dependent upon the iconography, one cannot be categorical about the connection between rank, wealth, and attire in the mourning motif. What is striking in the mourning motif are the similarities in the colour (white seems to be the preferred colour) and style of the dress (for females the sheath dress with straps and for males the short kilt). A modern day analogy would be a parallel with modern day conventions of black skirt/suit and tie at funerals in the European cultural tradition.

While the indicated captions are of limited help, they do indicate that from at least Dynasty 6, maybe sorrow could be depicted and/or that these tomb owners' were individualists. The mourner's social position is only indicated in the tomb of Ankhmahor; where these are identified as 'Inspector of the seal-bearers, Ptahshepses' and the 'funerary priest Senbeshi', i.e. not low class individuals. However, just because Idu's and Mereruka's tombs do not have identified people in the mourning motif, does not imply that they had no higher officials present. The social custom of those times was the participation of mourners in the farewell of the departed and while the gravity of the ceremony may differ, one can suppose that this type of emotional reaction was indeed the case across all classes.

9.13 Mourning Motifs' Differences

Indeed the differences are minor, because of the conventions of decorum. However, they are there. One would expect more differences because when people are experimenting initial wide variation is an essential creative step before becoming standardized over time but maybe this is a modern gloss.[1064] If differences are to be seen, then these are to be seen in the persons immediately preceding and following the mourners. Admittedly the

influences of these 'non-mourners' can only aid through indirect inference.

Indeed I have omitted until now, the other persons who precede/follow the mourners, because strictly speaking they do not form part of the mourning motif, but of the totality of the funeral instead. However they are significant because they are an element of the approaching funerary rituals, their presence reinforces the nature of the social hierarchy and its demands of show and splendour precisely at a moment of loss, as a way of reinforcing the memory of someone about to become an 'absent one'. Finally, because they point to subtle differences in composition, differences that may help expand on the cultural significance of the mourning motif, they assist in more understanding.

Some readers may well be skeptical of my use of inferences. I would argue that even a biologist like Darwin routinely inferred assumptions of past behaviour to support his examples: he related the variation in beak morphology of Galapagos finches to different diets and feeding behaviour.[1065] In any event anything that we claim to know about the distant past, in the absence of evidence can only be deduced by inference. To study behaviour requires inferring it, there are no direct avenues.

A consideration of the presence of 'non-mourners' in each of the three motifs is as follows:

Thirteen mourning women are preceded by a lector priest (*ḥry-ḥbt*) in the tomb of Mereruka who is holding a roll, and wears a pointed kilt. The lector priest is usually depicted with a scroll in one hand, a sash across his chest and wearing a pointed kilt, but due to the damaged nature of the representation this is not visible here. His task was the performance of the beatification rituals. The earliest holders of the title of lector priest *ḥry-ḥbt* were members of the royal family.[1066]

An embalming priest[1067] (*wt*) is also present, carrying a rod and a scepter and wearing only a short kilt with probably a scarf thrown on his left shoulder but again this is not visible. A woman described as *ḏrt* 'kite' in a long sheath dress.

In front of her are three men, all in pointed kilts and holding on to the extended pole of the coffin. Six men in short kilts are probably the coffin bearers. Preceding them is another group of three men, all in pointed kilts. From their attire we can say that they are important officials of a higher social order than the pallbearers. The fact that they are holding only the extended pole would suggest a function

Europe and the USA (235-294) and in Ancient Egypt (307-359).

[1063] Taylor, *Mourning dress: a costume and social history*, 19. Whilst her survey is restricted to the European custom from 1600 to 1900 AD, her examples are quite revealing as to the reason behind the wearing of particular types of dress. The reason(s) may have been different in ancient Egypt and no automatic inference is suggested.

[1064] Only holds true if these were indeed the only three tombs to depict the mournng motif, and these are regarded as the first acts of individuality.

[1065] Schiffer, 'Some Relationships between Behavioral and Evolutionary Archaeologies' *American Antiquity*, (61), 643-662.

[1066] Doxey, 'Priesthood', *OEAE*, vol. 3, 69.

[1067] The word '*wt*' means to wrap (*Wörterbuch*. I, 379:13). It is a usual title but its significance lies in the fact that the embalming priest was given free access to temples and was an associate of the priests. His role in the performance of a sacerdotal function, meant that he was not tainted with ritual impurity, unlike those whose job it was to perform incisions.

other than carrying and it has already been suggested that these were honorary pallbearers.[1068]

The motifs of Ankhmahor and Idu differ from the motif in Mereruka because they do not depict honorary pallbearers in their pointed kilts. Admittedly in the tomb of Ankhmahor, there are three persons shown holding the extended arm of the coffin but they are dressed in the same manner as the coffin carriers - all in short kilts! Considering that the embalming priest is always shown in a short kilt, perhaps one should not read too much into this minor difference. Further while all scenes have the usual depiction of funerary goods, these are shown already deposited[1069] in the tombs of Mereruka, and Idu but are being carried ceremoniously[1070] in the tomb of Ankhmahor.

In the tomb of Idu there is a complete absence of the accompanying lector and embalming priests, who precede and follow the coffin. Only the kite is depicted on the journey across the river. The lector priest is NOT shown at the entrance to the tomb, following the coffin being dragged by a pair of oxen, ready to perform the Opening of the Mouth and Eyes ritual, as one would expect. Indeed there is no evidence of any tomb (usually represented by palm type pillars).

The above differences are small, because increasing number of lector and embalming priests by itself would have little significance, as they could be just an indication of individuality, but in the context of mourning, points to elements of power and rank and thus to the generics. Both the lector and the embalming priests are seen in their full regalia in the funeral procession and the very fact that they are there, stresses the rank of the tomb owner as well as the manifestation of the ideology of the social order. Not only is the tomb owner being mourned, but also his departure entails the performance and depiction of certain traditional ways, which were thought to be symptomatic of an ordered society, again a pointer to the generics.

Because mourners are seldom described and/or identified, one has to assume that these would be part of the household or extended kin, and that the kite is the ritual representation of sorrow, but she (the kite) should not be confused with the wife of the tomb owner. Neither the wife nor the children are ever shown in these three Old Kingdom mourning scenes. In view of the fact that these persons would be involved in the immediate aftermath of death, this lacuna is even more surprising. In both the tombs of Idu and Ankhmahor, the kite is shown wearing a headband with a single filet and is never in the presence of the other mourners but is always accompanied by priests (while the motif in Mereruka is damaged, a parallelism might be accepted).

These again are minor differences; what is important is that in time they become part of a constant repertoire of funerary scenes that extend to the end of the New Kingdom.[1071]

The show of sorrow in the mourning motifs, by means of visible practices such as tearing garments, tearing hair, and sitting on the ground, lying on the ground or smearing the head with dust/ashes, is made even more real by the participation of the various members of society. The aspect of social connectivity to the departed is complemented by the gestures of support shown by the mourners to each other, and results in the formation of a new social association of those left behind. At the same time the bundle of social identities of the tomb owner is enhanced by the public display of mourning, which because it appears prolific, also serves to reinforce accepted hierarchical society. It is through these means the 'others' are made to understand and the image of the ideal elite is embedded across the community.

After the funeral, the tomb owner goes on to 'live' a venerated life in the company of his fellow peers, $M3^ct$ is reinforced and maintained, order rules once more and the tomb owner is relegated to posterity.

Perhaps it is opportune to end with a more modern quotation from Shakespeare's *Macbeth* that sums up the complexity and continuity of this most intricate of emotions. Malcolm tells Mac-duff, whose wife and children have been killed by Macbeth that he should mourn so that he can overcome his loss:

> "Give sorrow words: the grief that does not speak
> Whispers the o'er-fraught heart, and bids it break"[1072]

.

[1068] Wilson, 'Funeral Services of the Egyptian Old Kingdom', 203.
[1069] Duell, *The Mastaba of Mereruka*, vol. 2, pl. 130. Also see Simpson, *The Mastabas of Qar and Idu,* pl. 35.
[1070] Kanawati, *The Teti Cemetery at Saqqara: the Tomb of Ankhmahor*, pls. 53 and 54.

[1071] Settgast, *Untersuchungen zu Altägyptischen Bestattungs-darstellungen,* 114. "Man macht dir die Prozession wie den Vorfahren".
[1072] Shakespeare, *Macbeth*, 1623a, IV, iii, 209.

Chapter 10: Final Observations

The **Part I** introductory section first describes past methodologies used to analyze reliefs and the resulting problems. It then describes the author's research methodology used to analyze the material that was used to transmit the ideas associated with the Egyptian elite. The challenge was to understand the individuals behind the reliefs, their web of diverse communal connections, and their society, and to discover any widespread underlying concepts, which would be valid for funerary cultures in general.

Any funerary culture in any society based on ideas of remembrance will need as an essential element the creation of the means of understandable transmission, because of the predominance of the non-literate element in ancient society. The various transmission methods can include the following: oral, philological (e.g. papyri and inscriptions) and material (e.g. architecture, grave goods and tomb decoration). As ancient Egyptian society had only a small number of literate people, this resulted in the creation of signs/symbols with inherent meanings understandable by the majority of the community. These signs/symbols did not exist in a vacuum. Consideration of the ideological facets of the recovered material in the contexts of the tomb decoration indicates that these signs eventually matured into well-known symbols, representative of the ideology of the elite. The difficulty in understanding these symbols is the fact that they are 'entrée, plat de résistance, fromage, desert et digestif', all rolled into one, which realization is as essential as the analysis of the selected motifs.

Previous analysis of the iconography of the Old Kingdom was based on an inadequate selection criterion of what should be observed and how, because the focus primarily

was on describing and conjecturing about the decoration and philological context, rather than looking for any underlying concept. Accordingly this previous line of enquiry missed out on the crucial fact that there are layers of understanding; that the variegated patterns of social roles are as much the product of the individual as well as those conferred by other members of society. The consideration of these layers of influences enables one to conceptualize how social identities were created in funerary cultures based on the concept of memory. This involves analyzing both vertical as well as any discernible horizontal structural differences in society.

It is clear there were different investments in the amount and type of tomb decoration because of variations in the tomb owners' social abilities and their unequal access to goods. The resultant effect was to confer real economic power and legitimatize the differences in social structure (status) - the Saxe-Binford approach. Inscriptions carved above a representation of a male figure answer the basic questions of who what and where, evidenced in the usual form, e.g. "I am the vizier of Upper and Lower Egypt dearly loved by his lord and my name is NN". If performance were to be measured only by these few metrics, a nuanced and long-term outlook would be actively discouraged in the population at large, leading to instability. However in view of the fact that Egypt was a stable society for some 500 years during the Old Kingdom this would appear not to be so. In fact for the analysis to proceed, it has to try to address all other significant social factors that affect this inscription, and take into account other known statements and depictions of NN and the contexts in which these are found. It is only by connecting material objects with human behaviour that one can appreciate that all objects are used as a means of individual or group communication, and manifestations of social order.

However this does not explain why and how social identities were created in the first place, nor the buildup and/or disposal of accumulated social identities. For this we need to extend the analysis further to include the concepts of ideology (domination as ideological manipulation and physical coercion, as well as shared fundamental values) and individuality (forerunner of possible change).

1. Ideological factors are a component of a matrix of intertwining influences. These are:
2. The royal ideology of domination, (where the myth of the king's unique role as intermediary between the world of the living and the world of the gods), is perpetuated via the elite.

The ideology of shared fundamental values, (in which the elite express their paternalistic responsibility for the well-being of their local community as an expression of $M3^ct$), as seen in their tomb biographies.

The motives behind such utterances are ambiguous because of the complexity of the elite's actual behaviour, which may be the result of a constant interplay between the forces of self-interest and those innate ones of being human. The general belief was that the practice of the fundamental virtues of kindness, justice, and self-control resulted in an ordered society. However any effective discourse on the coercive element which must have existed is lacking, because the institutionalized order (read ideology) cannot tolerate any deviation from the mindset of cardinal values, which it has worked to create, a deviation which would undermine the status quo. With increasing

---

[1073] Gardiner, 'Hymns to Sobk in a Ramesseum Papyrus', *RdE,* (11), 56.

societal complexity the ancient Egyptians must have also realized (at least by Dynasty 5) that they had to allow/have practices, which could increase resiliency among the population, the tomb biography, and the development of the self-being such avenue. This liberating of the freedom of thought/expression, coupled with respect for the old ways of doing things, allowed the people of the Old Kingdom to engage in self-interested adaptations to their world.

The balancing of these forces enabled the Old Kingdom to last as long as it did, and inspires a positive picture of the elite. Viewed in this light *M3ˁt* (perceived as the most important aspect of human relations) fostered a sense of social consciousness, and a concern for the future in the ancient Egyptians. Perhaps the contemporary world needs a similar call to moral action.

Ideology thus played a central role because it represented the efforts undertaken by individuals to create, maintain, and transform power relationships. In order to understand ideological connotations, we must separate what is actually being said and depicted, from the packaging it comes in. This packaging (read the belief that the mighty religious and moral traditions could control any dangerous situation) plays an important role in determining both what is being related and how it is to be understood. Hornung, referring to the above phenomena writes "Im Alten Orient sind ideologische Geschichtsbilder noch stärker als heute treibende Kräfte im Weltgeschehen".[1074] Indeed in order to cement and maintain the ideology of the times, ideology demands an understanding of it as something, which is recurrent and typical, and this can be observed in the texts (mostly royal) and the iconography (royal/non royal) of the Old Kingdom.

It is also clear that ideology cannot be based purely on coercion since it requires some sort of cooperation between the governing and governed. The elite's successful claim to say the surplus of agricultural produce (if the taking account scenes are taken at face value) is itself a pointer to the ideology of the elite in positing the alleged acquiescence of all parties.

- The full extent of the elite's power is not known (either in the form of visible coercive power, or persuasive power of the softer variety which is reminiscent of past behaviour). Therefore one cannot build up a checklist of factors, which differentiate the ways in which ideology influenced the development of status or social rank. Doing so would tend to exacerbate the tension between the constancy of observed values and those that cause variations. Indeed in the extreme case one would rely predominantly on factors of material wealth (read economic) at the expense of equally important factors such as:

- Shifts and changes within both the vertical and horizontal layers of society, both of which ultimately determine the social classes.

Ideological factors, which go towards the legitimization and maintenance of the social classes.

1. As far as individuality is concerned, it is present in various forms in all cultures because:
2. It is the conditio sine qua non of the first step towards change.

It explains the almost universal embeddedness of the idea of competition in humans.

The degree of this drive may vary within a group and within the people of a society who constitute it. If culture however is to thrive, by which I mean undergo periods of renewal and renegotiation, then individuality becomes an essential element of the generics in the sense of a precursor of change. Hornung, in the context of the structure and the development of graves in the Valley of the Kings indirectly refers to this phenomenon (reading it a bit circuitously) what he terms the "Erweiterung des Bestehenden"[1075] because for the expansion of the existing to occur, some form of change is inevitable which is an indirect pointer to individuality. It also points indirectly to the other components of cultural generics, e.g. identity and ideology.

In this connection the idea of change based on 'chaos theory' has been used. In its common usage, the word 'chaos' has a negative connotation and is synonymous with disorder and confusion. However in its original Greek and its equivalent in the ancient Egyptian cosmologies, 'chaos' is to be understood as a universal primordial state from which the divine will, generated order. If the divine aspects are removed, what remains mirrors the theories of contemporary astrophysicists for whom chaos means a positive and powerful state, which holds the potential for new order and forms. Indeed in certain circumstances, chaos becomes a prerequisite for all that is new and meaningful and the precondition for cultural change. This use of the term chaos explains change in action and how trends in iconography are born, mature, and die to begin the cycle all over again. This is to be contrasted with 'entropy', which explains why change occurs (localization or dissipation of energy). In other words change is part of existence and part of every culture, whose progress once begun becomes a system, which tends to be self-perpetuating, until circumstances change and the process starts all over again, or is transformed.

The process of cultural translation is further assisted by the use of the approach formulated by Wittgenstein. It requires the use of language games, crucial for the understanding and translation of cultures. This approach gives modern

---

[1074] Hornung, *Geschichte als Fest: zwei Vorträge zum Geschichtsbild der frühen Menschheit*, 10.

[1075] Hornung, 'Struktur und Entwicklung der Gräber im Tal der Könige', *ZÄS*, (105), 64. Although his article concerns the New Kingdom royal tombs, the underlying principle seems equally valid for the non-royal OK elite tombs, and indeed for the whole of ancient Egyptian culture.

people a means by which to understand other cultures and translate their phenomena into their own categories and concepts, which they can relate to. Language games thus have implications for the problem of relativity between cultures and the translation of cultures. As Wittgenstein observes in Philosophical Investigations - a language game is "meant to bring into prominence that the speaking of a language is part of an activity, or a form of life".[1076]

This books approach is in direct opposition to mere description plus a smattering of function added as a disguise to support some concept of objectivity. By characterizing the ideas of identity, individuality, ideology, and change as the complex building blocks for the transmission and maintenance of collective memory, access is gained to concepts, which can be used for a multi-dimensional approach. Indeed these culturally conceptualized generics occupy a central role in (Part 2). The proposition relating to their importance can be stated as follows: all funerary iconography can be understood and analyzed by the use of these concepts alone, because there is not one single surviving tomb, nor any main theme in the Memphite tombs in the Old Kingdom, which does not display elements of these generics. Even in the different motifs selected, there is evidence of the generics **in all of these without exception.**

Part 2 consisted of case studies of three types of motifs from the iconography of the Old Kingdom tombs in the Memphite region. It seeks to demonstrate how the elite tomb owners and their communities expressed differentiation within itself, and within a specific period in clear personalities, which can be made visible using the generics. The traditional approach was that cultural similarities were the product of interaction within, and differences were the product of social or physical differences from without[1077] - another mainly descriptive approach. The approach taken seeks to reconcile the previous descriptive approach with the view that because culture is a social process, it is subject to the 'laws' of chaos and entropy theory which are valid for both 'within' and 'without' and therefore never static - always in a sort of flux. The iconography itself reveals this dynamism because no two reliefs are the same and patterns start to emerge, which if traced diachronically into other time frames do show certain continuity coupled with change. To copy any artifacts 100% by hand (only modern industry can do this with the aid of machinery) because of the irreversibility of time (which points to the future only), is intrinsically impossible. To exactly recreate the position of the chisel and/or the hit of the hammer of the earlier sculpting processes is in principle impossible. Therefore change is not only certain but always with us. In considering the iconography of the elite tombs an initial caveat must be introduced.

- The funerary iconographic world must have related in some way to the actual lived world, because it

was the latter, which provided the vocabulary and context for constructing the world represented on funerary monuments. Insofar as this view is the worldview of the elite, it presents the problem of bias. Unfortunately this investigation can only be of those things that are represented. In exposing the view of the elite, it is hoped to offer a glimpse into the world of the non-elite too, because as contemporaries, they would have been of a more or less common psychological makeup. An examination of the iconographic motifs selected reveals various forms of cultural generics within all of them, and these can be subsumed under the following headings (see Appendix H):

- Iconography understood as a sign/symbol of possible levels of meaning.
- Iconography understood as a sign/symbol of hierarchical status.
- Iconography understood as a sign/symbol of group cohesion.

Iconography understood as a sign/symbol of individuality.

Statistical analysis has indicated a clear difference among the tombs with regards to the visualization of the generics as would be expected by the extant social hierarchy at that time. What is interesting is that there is no one single 'identity kit' that exists for the elite. This suggests that there are other identifying factors at work, and that wealth may be only one such factor, e.g. these may be the idealized images of the elite involving competing claims of wealth, craft or ritual specialization, made by those organizing the funeral.

The key concepts of the generics can be understood as an inviolable framework around the central construct of memory. It is because of the need to be remembered that we need something to remember us by which then calls for the creation of identities, whose basis is the individual interaction with the prevailing ideology of the time.

However, because of the existence of the change paradigm, chaos is omnipresent and intrinsically no ideology can survive the collision with the changing reality perfectly intact. General principles have to bend to accommodate the complexities of history. For example the survival of a particular ideology is better served by compromise than by zealous intellectual consistency resulting in the differentiation of visual and textual display. Again access to cultural goods and the increasing participation of those previously excluded from high culture can itself be an index of progressive change. While the evidence is difficult to quantify because the exact social structure of the elite is not certain, nevertheless the very proliferation of tomb/tomb art and with it the effects this must have had on the economic system, is an important indication of the continuing unintended reform of the social system. The consequences of this differentiation are mostly available if seen from a distant perspective when these are expressed as visual representational and intrinsic cultural change. In

---

[1076] Wittgenstein, *Philosophical Investigations,* § 23.
[1077] Jones, *The Archaeology of Ethnicity,* 25.

this light the generics reveal both the past as it was, and an understanding of why the present is what it is.

- Furthermore the generics can be applied within any time frame because they can be used to explain things at any particular point in time, i.e. they are universal in applicability. The universality claimed in culturally valid generalizations is a specific one, related to the field of funerary art only. They open a way by which we can analyze and understand diverse data provided they all belong to the realm of funerary culture, which then enables us to get an insight into the culture of a period or a people. In this context language games play a very important role in making one realize that getting the answer to what one wants, is dependent on asking the relevant questions. Just like the visual representation of a complex molecule, e.g. the DNA helix, is used by scientists to understand the structure of the molecule, the deconstruction of the motifs in the elite tombs of the Old Kingdom will yield an understanding of:
- The significance of their elements.
- An understanding of what causes these elements to be there in the first place.

Why are, in some cases, changes evidenced?

This is where the generics become paramount. Understood in the above way, the concept of, say, social identity takes on added meaning. High-ranking individuals often have inherited or ascribed status (titles) and are shown with distinctive attire (garments, headdresses, body adornments and elevated status goods). These act as instruments (along with other artifacts of material culture) through which the elite could express their own (or their family's) status within an existing social hierarchy, including their wider cultural affiliation with others. Possibly the elite wished their society to conform to their ideal of eliteness, and they fulfilled this desire with the symbolic forms with which the realities of the elite were displayed. This is because cultural systems are dominated in the main by all the actions and projections of the individuals who have the power and authority, to constitute the system. What is especially compelling is the notion that body adornments and hence the 'dead bodies' play an active role in marking and reinforcing social group affinities, while at the same time promoting an individual image of relative strength and power. In this way both vertical and horizontal difference in social identity may be distinguished.

Similarly in the mourning motif, since the dead cannot bury themselves, the others who are involved indicate not only their individual status but also reinforce that of the deceased, which may assist in our understanding of social organization and prevalent religious beliefs. This can then be used to demonstrate how material remains can be analyzed beyond mere description, to explain facts with which at first glance, only a very remote connection is discernible.

Different academic disciplines, e.g. archeology, anthropology, sociology, psychology, physics, economics, quantum mechanics, and 'chaos theory' have been called in aid. The essential feature of this approach has been to embrace and use these wherever possible.[1078] For example, the use of charts and tables are based on elementary statistics, in some of these percentages are given, while in others this is not the case. Percentages enable one to see the variation in the scenes in the total population of tombs examined, and in other cases a percentage is not based on the total population of tombs but on the number of cases of a particular type found, irrespective of the total number of tombs. This is a mathematical necessity and an essential quantitative tool that can be usefully employed, especially when there is a difference between the number of tombs, the number of representations that these tombs have, and the number of places in the tomb's iconography, where these depictions occur - something which is common in all ancient Egyptian iconography.

In any event it is suggested that the use of the generics is a way of looking at, and this should not be dismissed as an exercise in pedantic terminology. The cultural generics are to be thought of as a mode of thinking which may provide a possible solution to the problems of iconographical interpretation. In their application to funerary iconography they are also a reflective mode in that they force one to compare what was and what is, and so expand our understanding.

In addition they explain why general principles govern human behaviour which after all is what the accumulated material culture is evidence of, something which is complex and uncertain, and which can be further analyzed by the use of quantum mechanics, chaos theory, and the theory of evolution. They also open the way for getting away from only looking at things analytically, and to delve into fields, which far too often have been unjustly termed 'fuzzy' precisely because they are uncertain and not mathematically solvable. If Physics is now turning away from mechanistic Newtonian linearity to the recognition of black holes and dark matter, is it not time that Egyptology undertook a similar journey?

In writing this book my role has been that of exposing an old tradition to fresher winds and currents. The book purposely began with a broad strategic overview of what I considered underpinned the legacy of Egypt. In doing so I gradually became aware of certain principal reference points which seemed to run right across the ceaseless nature of the challenges facing the elite tomb owner. What is certain is that his participation in the intermingling of the religious and social ideas, with its many gods, and his location in the semi-closed system where each person

---

[1078] The dangers of incorporating frameworks developed in the natural sciences with social science are known. This book takes the view that social systems are complex, non-linear and shaped by multiple factors, which arise from them being part of the human beings' interactions. Precisely because these social systems cannot be studied using scientific cause and effect methodology, a multi-disciplinary approach is essential.

had his predetermined place, must have contributed to his adaptation to the complexity around him. These adaptations would ultimately lead to a certain freedom of thought, which realization then enabled the ancient Egyptians both "to admit internal contradictions and to see them as compatible",[1079] i.e. interminable existential challenges.

It was in figuring out how he mastered these challenges (especially in his tomb iconography), that I realized the importance of the cultural generics.

Of course I realize that this book is a combination of history and philosophy, and if you my reader, feel that I have been selective in my evidence; then this is entirely due to the fact that it is impossible to be both a historian and a philosopher, because the former is circumscribed by facts while the latter looks for the interpretation of the relevant facts which accord with his value system.

The very last word will be dedicated to the ancient Egyptians because by making me think about their tombs and decoration, they made me better understand their world and remember them, although they were long gone, and indirectly once again revealed the power of the generics.

> "They shall not grow old as we that are left grow old
> Age shall not wither them nor the years condemn
> At the going down of the sun and in the morning
> We shall remember them".

(Lawrence Binyon in 'For the Fallen'. This verse is now known as the 'Ode of Remembrance' and is read out at Dawn Services and other ANZAC tributes in Australia, Remembrance Day in Canada, and Remembrance Sunday services in the United Kingdom. It first appeared in 'The Times' on 21 September 1914).

[1079] Tobin, *Theological Principles of Egyptian Religion,* 6.

Appendix A   Carrying-Chair Motif   Total Population = N = 37

Tomb Owner	SV/LMP No.	Tomb No.	Dating Harpur
Ankhmahor	1 /190	T65	VI.1-3
Ankhmare	2 / 94	G7837	V.9
Hesi	3 /184a	T59a	VI.3
Hetepniptah	4 /227	G2430/LG25	VI.1
Idu	5/230	G7102	VI.3-4E
Inisnfrw-ishtef	6 /258	CG 1769	VI.1?
Ipy	7 /221	CG 1536	VI.2-7
Itisen	8/104	T28	V.6-8?
Iymery	9/113	G6020/LG16	V.3L
Kagemni	10/183	T58	VI.2
Kaemnofret	11/ 44	D23	V.8-9?
Niankhkhnum	12/ 48	T13	V.6L-7
Khnumenti	13/228a	G2374	VI.1
Khuwer	14/117	LG95	V.8-9
Mereruka	15/182a	T57A	VI.1M-L
Merwtetiseneb	16/186	T61	VI.2E-M?
Meryteti	17/182c	T57A	VI.2M-L
Methethi	18/184	T59	VI.2?
Nefermaat	19/002a	M16	IV
Nefer-Khuwi	20/131D	G2098	V.8-9
Niankhkhnum and Khnumhotep	21/ 48	T13	V.6L-7
Nikauisesi	22/184b	T59b	VI.M ?
Nimaatre	23/120	G2097	V.9
Pepydjedi	24/215	MM E9	VI.2-7
Perneb	25/ 67	QS913	V.8-9
Ptahshepses	26/ 36a	T7	V.6-8E
Ptahhotep II	27/ 62	LS 31	VI.2
Qar	28/229	G7101	VI.4
Rashepses	29/ 59	QS902/LS	VI.8M
Sabw	30/181a	MM E 1and	VI.1M?
Seankhuiptah	31/183a	G5520/LG28	V.9-VI.1E
Seneb	32/ 27a	T1a	VI.5-7
Senedjemib.Inti	33/114	G2370/LG27	V.8M-L
Seshemnefer.Tjetti	34/247	LG53	VI.1?
Seshemnefer	35/257	T113	VI.1
Ty	36/ 49	MM D 22	V.8-9
Waatetkhethor	37/182b	T57B	VI.1

The LMP number is that allocated by the Leiden MastaBase (University of Leiden) to their database of decorated and known Old Kingdom tombs. Since these are not allocated sequentially a sequential number, the SV number precedes the LMP number.
Niankhkhnum/Khnumhotep is a joint tomb and counted as two in this motif.
Publication details about the tomb of Remni (VI.2?) came at a time when the book was nearly complete and thus has not been included, but this does not alter any conclusions.

Appendix B Empty Chairs** and Carrying-Chair Fragments*

Tomb Owner	SV/LMP No.	Tomb No.	Location
Mereruka**	38/182	T57	Saqqara
Ptahshepses**	39/36a	T7	Abusir
Ty**	40/49	D22	Saqqara
Seshathetep.heti**	41/89	G5150/LG36	Giza
Waatetkhethor**	42/182	T57	Saqqara
Unknown*	43/008a	G4260	Giza

Appendix C   Taking-Account   Total Population = N = 38

Tomb Owner	SV/LMP No.	Tomb No.	Dating/Harpur
Ankhmahor	44/190	T65	VI.1-3
Fetekty	45/132	LS1	V.6-VI
Hemetra	46/	n/a	IV.6-V?
Idut	47/218	T86	VI.1
Iyenefert	48/217	T85	V.9
Iymery	49/113	G6020-LG16	V.3L
Kagemni	50/183	T58	VI.2
Kahif	51/232	G2136	VI.2
Kairer	52/133	T40	VI.2
Kanefer	53/086	G2150	V.1-3
Kaninisut	54/087	G2155-4870	V.1-3
Kaemnofret	55/44	D23	V.8-9?
Khafkhufu I	56/008	G7130-7140	IV.4
Khafreankh	57/	n/a	
Khentkawes	58/242	T100	VI
Khenut	59/063b	T17b	V.9
Nebet	60/063a	T17a	V
Khnumenti	61/228a	G2374	VI.I
Mereruka	62/182a	T57A	VI.1M-L
Meresankh III	63/013	G7530	IV.6
Meryib	64/029	G2100=LG24	IV.6-V.1
Nefer	65/149	G4761	V.8-VI
Neferbauptah	66/100	G6010	V.6
Nefer and Kahay	67/053	T14	V.6
Nesutnefer	68/091	G4970	V.1-2
Niankhkhnum and Khnumhotep	69/ 48	T13	V.6L-7
Perneb	70/ 67	QS913	V.8-9
Ptahhotep II	71/ 62	LS 31	VI.2
Qar	72/229	G7101	VI.4
Rashepses	73/ 59	QS902/LS16	VI.8M
Seneb	74/ 27a	T1a	VI.5-7
Sekhemka	75/099	G4411/LG51	V.6-9
Senedjemib.Mehi	76/116	G2378/LG26	V.9
Seshathetep.Heti	77/089	G5150/LG36	V.1-2
Shetwi	78/147	T45	V.9-VI
Tjenti	79/092	G4920/LG47	V.1-5
Ty	80/ 49	MM D 22	V.8-9
Whemka	81/088	MM D 117	V.1-3

Appendix D   Mourning Motif   Total Population = N = 3

Tomb Owner	SV/LMP No.	Tomb No.	Dating/Harpur
Ankhmahor	82/190	T65	VI.1-3
Idu	83/230	G7102	VI.34E
Mereruka	84/182a	T57A	VI.1M-L

Appendix E   Lists of Charts, Tables and Figures

Carrying-Chair

Chart Number	Page	Description
1	82	Canopy Type
2	84	Porter Attire
3	85	Total Porter Count
4	87	Distribution of Porters
5	88	Carrying Method
6	90	Accuracy of Depiction of Carrying by Porters
7	91	Use of Porters' Hands
8	93	Fan and Sunshade Carriers
9	93	Sunshade and Fan Carrier Placement
10	95	Dwarfs and Other Escorts
11	97	Animal Placement
12 (I)	98	Dog Placement
12 (II)	98	Monkey Placement
13	101	Attendant Placement by Tombs
14	102	Main Clothing of Attendants
15	103	Tomb Owners' Posture
16	107	Correlation between Posture and Dress
17	111	Body Adornments of Tomb Owner
18	111	Elevated Status Goods
19	112	Carrying Status Goods
20	120	Titles of Subsidiary Figures

Taking Account

21	126	Tomb Owners' Posture by Gender
22	128	Standing plus Attributes of Authority
23	130	Sitting plus Attributes of Authority
24	131	Jewellery and Sandals
25	132	Male Head Dress
26	134	Types and Frequencies of Kilts
27	136	Presenters' Attire
28	137	Presenters' Head Dress
29	144	Relationship Distribution
30	177	Individuality - Carrying-Chair Motif by Dynasty
31	177	Individuality - Taking Account Motif by Dynasty

Table Number	Page	Description
1	40	Semiotic Components
2	118	Grouped Titles and Occurrences
3	119	Grouped Titles by Dynasty
4	133	Attire and Position
5	140	Document Type
6	142	Presenters' Titles
7	156	Hieroglyphic Meanings and Determinatives
8	157	Language Games
9	160	Mourning Gestures

Figure Number	Page	Description
1	21	Sheikh el-Beled, Egyptian Museum, Cairo, CG 34
2	81	Carrying-chair of Queen Hetepheres
3	83	Head of Menkaure. Museum of Fine Arts Boston 09.203
4	83	Snefru-nefer. Kunsthistorisches Museum, Vienna ÄS 7506
5	90	Overlapping effect
6	92	Tomb of Nimaatre
7	104	Stela of Hetepneb (picture A)
8	104	Akhethetep (picture B)
9	105	False door of Senedjemib.inti (picture C)
10	106	Methethi in ceremonial attire (picture D)

Appendix F   Attendants' Titles (andTombs*)

*References to named tombs as superscripted below are to be found on page 118.

Transliteration	Title tomb in superscript
swnw ḥȝif	Physician Hayef [a1]
ḫnty š pr ꜥȝ	Palace attendant of the great house [a1]
stp sȝ pr n Kȝ(i)	Inspector of the retainers of the residence and court councilor Perenka(i) [a3]
sḥd ḥtmy.w	Inspector of seal bearers [a4, a2, a13, a17]
sḥd ḥm kȝ	Inspector of funerary priest [sa3]
šmsw	Follower [a4]
ḥtm.w	Seal bearer [a4, a13]
ḥtm.yw imy ȝbd	Seal bearer who is in his monthly service [a13]
iry mdȝt	Archivist [a5, a2, a6, a14,]
sdȝwti	Archivist [a5]
sš	Scribe [a1, a11, a14,]
sš snwt	Scribe of the granary [a5]
sš mdȝ.wt stp sȝ	Scribe of the documents of the Court [a3]
sš pr ḥd sḥd ḥmw kȝ	Scribe of the treasury (and) Inspector of the funerary priests [a10, a3]
sš sḥd ḥm kȝ	Scribe, Inspector of the funerary priests [a6, a10]
ḥrp ist	Director of the gang of workmen [a7]
ḥm kȝ smsw wḫr [t]	Funerary priest and Elder of the dockyard [a17]
imy-r	Overseer [a7, a12,]
imy-r pr	Overseer of the house [a2, a14]
imy-r šsr	Overseer of linen [a4, a8, a12, a16, a17, a19]
ꜣmy-r iswt	Overseer of the gangs of workmen [a7]
ꜣmy r pr n rwt Nsw. ḥr	Overseer of the gate of Nesuhor [a11]
ꜣmy-r ḫȝ	Overseer of… [a4]
sȝb imy-r sšw	Dignitary (and) Overseer of scribe [sa15]
ḥrp šms(w)	Director of followers [a8]
ḥry.ḥbt	Lector priest [a3]
ḥm kȝ	Funerary priest [a9, a13, a9, a10, a17, a18,]
ḥm kȝ ḥry sštȝ	Funerary priest well versed in the secrets
ḥm kȝ mdḥ	Funerary priest and carpenter [a9]
ḥm kȝ iry ꜥnwt	Funerary priest and manicurist [a9]
ḥꜥkw ḥm kȝ…	Barber and funerary priest [a9]
ḥꜥkw	Barber [a13]
nḫt ḫrw	He of the strong voice
sȝ=f	His son [a12, a3, a6, a4,]
sȝ=f sš	His son the scribe [a6]
sȝ=f sš…..šry	His son the junior scribe [a6]
sȝ=f imy-r zš	His son inspector of the fowling pond [a13]
sȝ=f sḥd ir [y] šn pr ꜥȝ	His son inspector of hairdressers of the Great House [a13]
sȝ=f smsw mry=f rḫ nswt	His eldest son his beloved the acquaintance of the king [a6]
sȝ=f šmsw mry=f smrwꜥty ḥry-ḥbt ḥm ist …	His eldest son, his beloved, sole councilor, Lector priest, the servant of the throne [a3]
sn=f	His brother [a6, a12,]

Appendix G   Dating Convention Used

Explanation of the dating reference used in this book with respect to the Pre dynastic period (1) and to the early, middle and late period dating of the Old Kingdom (2) tombs as appearing in appendices 'A', 'C', and 'D' is as follows:

1. Where reference to the relative chronological framework for the Predynastic period has been made it is to be understood as being revised notably by Kaiser, who while confirming the three major phases of the Naqada period, refined these by subdividing them into 11 *Stufen* from 1 a to III b.
2. Regarding the Old Kingdom the chronology is that used by Strudwick.[1080] The explanation for indicating early, middle, and late is as follows and is adapted for all the periods of the Old Kingdom.

It is accepted widely that Dynasty V lasted 157 years. Accordingly it can be divided into three almost equal periods called EARLY, MID and LATE as follows:

EARLY = 2504-2452
MID   = 2452-2400
LATE = 2400-2347

By slightly revising the above periods, these will coincide with the reigns of three groups of kings as follows:

EARLY = 2504-2456 (Userkaf, Sahure, Neferirkare and Shepeskare)
MID   = 2456-2405 (Neferefre, Niuserre and Menkauhor)
LATE = 2405-2347 (Djedkare and Unas)

If an item can only be identified as 'Dynasty V' but for some reason has to be given a more precise date, then it should be classed with the average date, i.e. in MID.

The biggest problem is the dating of some item that straddles two periods (e.g. early to middle Dynasty V), and (e.g. between Dynasty V and Dynasty VI).

The following solutions have been adopted:

- If Dynasty V is divided into three almost equal periods, then the centre of the straddle points for these three periods would be at the 2452 and 2400 boundaries (see above), however the period boundaries were then slightly revised to coincide with the kings' reigns (see above). An 'early to middle' item would straddle the original 2452 boundary, which falls within the revised MID period of 2456-2405. Similarly for a 'middle to late' straddle item, the original similar sized MID and LATE periods would meet at 2400, which now falls within the revised LATE period.
- Dynasty V lasts 157 years and Dynasty VI lasts 131 years. Therefore all other things being equal, something is more likely to be in Dynasty V than VI.

Here is a summary of related assumptions as adopted:

'Mid-Dynasty V' items would be grouped in MID.
'Dynasty V' in MID
'Early to mid' in MID
'Mid to late' in LATE
'Dynasty V to Dynasty VI' in LATE (Dynasty V).

[1080] Strudwick, *Texts from the Pyramid Age.*

Appendix H

Evidence of Individuality in the Carrying-Chair Motif	Tomb owner(s)
Non-exclusive occupation	Mereruka, Meryteti, and Waatetkhethor
Object to weigh down kilt	Kagemni
Chair strapped between 2 donkeys	Niankhkhnum/Khnumhotep, and Khuwer
Depicted with 'false beard'	Khuwer
Depicted with amulet	Kagemni
Not carrying any status goods	Seneb, Perneb, and Mereruka (pl. 158)
Squatting with pointed kilt	Peneb
Porter's Song in only 4 depictions	Ipy, Mereruka (pl. 158), Sabw, and Sendjemib.Inti.
Method of carrying at hip level	First in D4. Nefermaat then D6. Mereruka (pl.158), Meryteti (pl.48), and Waatetkhethor (pl.69).
Porters carry a rolled cloth in one hand	Meryteti (pl.48)
5 Sunshade carriers	Ipy
Porters carry palm frond type fan	Khuwer, and Hesi
1 Baboon under carrying-chair including 2 dogs and a monkey	Itisen
Monkey shown nearer to tomb owner	Hetepnitah
Supervisors wearing loincloth	Mereruka, Seshemnefer.Tjetti, and Ptahshepses
Sandal bearers depicted although tomb owner shown wearing sandals	Niankhkhnum/Khnumhotep, and Khuwer
Shoulder length wig with exposed ear	Ipy
Trapezoidal and decorated canopy	Ipy, Meryteti

Evidence of Individuality in the Taking Account Motif	Tomb owner(s)
Not carrying any symbols of authority while standing	Ptahhotep II
Holding rod with knobbed end at bottom	Kaninswt
Holding no lotus bloom	Hemetra
Taking account while sitting in a carrying-chair	Perneb, Qar, and Khnumenti
Holding flywhisk	Nefer & Kahay, and Qar
Not carrying any status goods while sitting	Perneb, and Kahif
Wearing a youth lock although depicted as adult female	Idut
Wig with headband with two tapering filets held by a papyrus buckle	Kagemni, and Ptahhotep II
Shoulder tags	First in D4 Nefermaat, in D5 Kaninswt, and on D6 Kahif
Female tomb owners have male presenters only	Hemetra, Idut, Khenut, Khentkawes, Meresankh III, and Nebet
As many as 12 presenters	Nebet
Presenter wearing a short kilt	Tjenti
Presenters with shoulder length wig, pleated kilt, 'false beard' and sash of lector priest	Khafkhufu I
Presenter with broad collar	Nefer & Kahay, and Ptahhotep II
Punishment scene in connection with Taking Account	Senedjemib.Mehi
Document contains visible writing	Fetekty, Khafkhufu I, and Meryib
Caption of motif contradictory-who is doing the viewing, the tomb owner or presenter?	Meresankh III
Tomb owner's deceased parents present	Whemka
Tomb owner's brother present	Akhmahor
Evidence of Individuality in the Mourning Motif	Tomb Owner(s)
Only mourning motif in the Old Kingdom	Akhmahor, Idu, and Mereruka
Description of mourning	Idu
Ratio of male to female mourners equal	Ankhmahor
Female mourner with shaved forehead	Idu
Pregnant women plus fat man	Akhmahor
Honorary pallbearers	Mereruka
Funerary goods being ceremoniously carried	Ankhmahor
No accompanying lector or embalming priest	Idu

*ALL THE GENERICS WITH THE EXCEPTION OF INDIVIDUALITY TEND TO OVERLAP, WHEREAS INDIVIDUALITY CAN BE UNIQUELY IDENTIFIED AS IN THE ABOVE TABLE. THE ABOVE EVIDENCE INDICATES THE PERIODS WHEN IT WAS MOST LIKELY THAT THE INDIVIDUALITY OF THE TOMB OWNER BECOMES APPARENT IN HIS BEHAVIOUR, I.E. ACTIONS, WHICH ARE REFLECTED IN THE CHARTS BELOW WITH THE CAVEAT WE MUST NOT BE OVERLY EAGER TO INFER INDIVIDUALITY, WITHOUT CONSIDERING ALL THE OTHER POSSIBILITIES.

CHART 30: INDIVIDUALITY IN THE CARRYING-CHAIR MOTIF BY DYNASTY

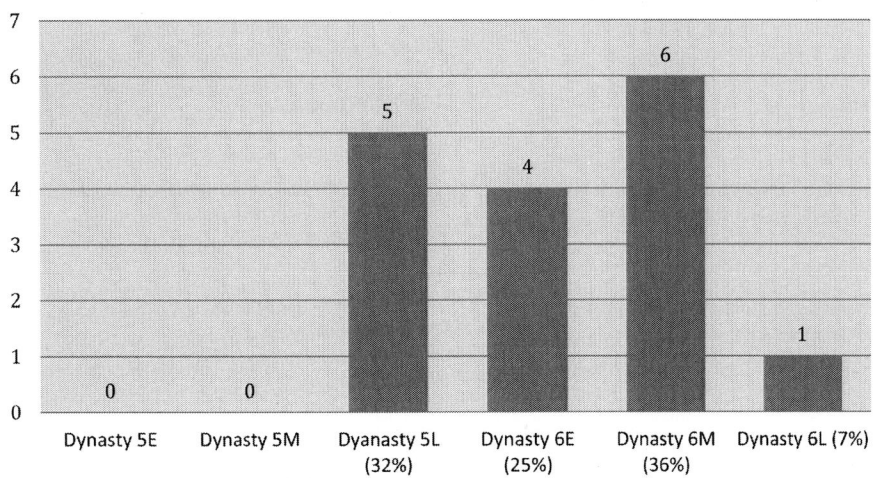

CHART 31: INDIVIDUALITY IN THE TAKING ACCOUNT MOTIF BY DYNASTY

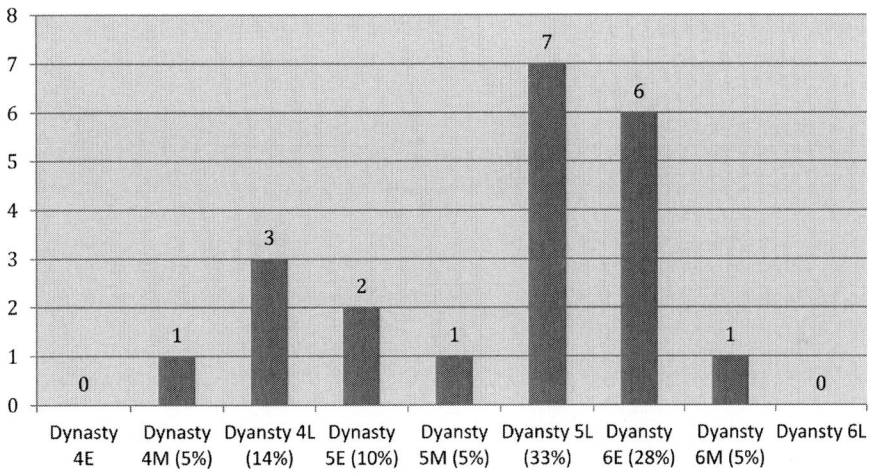

Appendix I

SV Number 1   **LMP Number** 190

Tomb Owner   Ankhmahor

Literature ref.   Kanawati, *The Teti Cemetery at Saqqara: the Tomb of Ankhmahor.* Vol. 2, fig. 71.

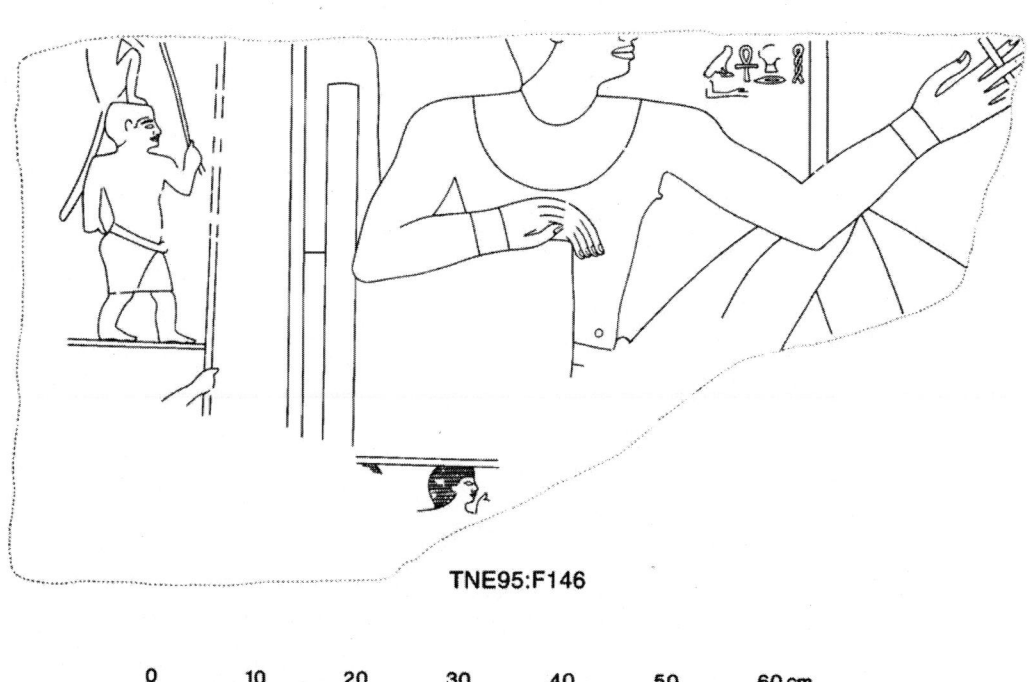

TNE95:F146

Plan

Fragment TNE95:F146 not attributable to a definite wall.

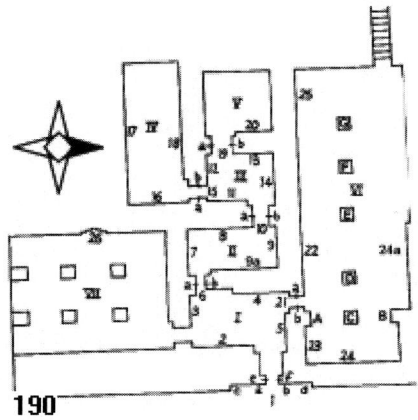

190

SV Number	2	**LMP Number**	94

Tomb Owner   Ankhmare

Literature ref.   Simpson, "Topographical Notes on Giza Mastabas" in *Festschrift for Elmar Edel*: 499.

Plan

P M XXI. Eastern wall, north of entrance.

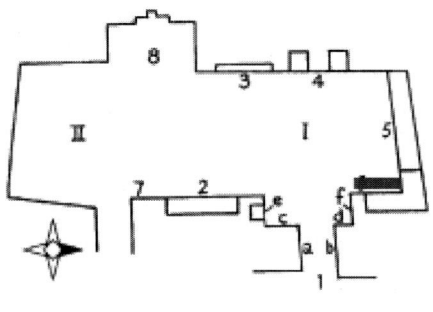

094

SV Number	3	**LMP Number**	184a
Tomb Owner	Hesi		
Literature ref.	Kanawati, *The Teti Cemetery at Saqqara*: *the tomb of Hesi.* Vol. V, plate. 55.		

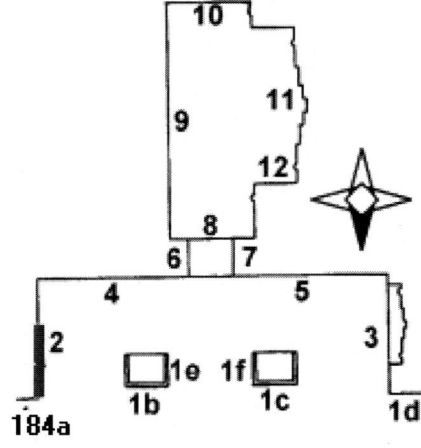

Plan

The Teti Cemetery at Saqara. Vol. V, plate 47. Eastern wall.

SV Number	4	**LMP Number**	227
Tomb Owner	Hetepniptah		
Literature ref.	Altenmueller, *SAK,* (9), fig. 2.		

Plan

P & M XXVI. Southern wall of chapel.

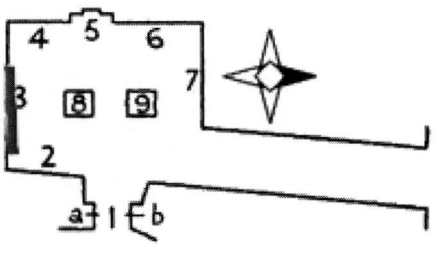

227

SV Number	5	**LMP Number**	230
Tomb Owner	Idu		
Literature ref.	Simpson, *The Mastabas of Qar and Idu.* Fig. 38.		

Plan

P & M XXX. Southern wall.

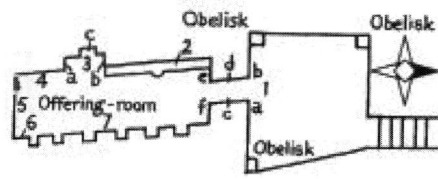

230

SV Number   7   **LMP Number**   221

Tomb Owner   Ipy

Literature ref.   Borchardt, *Denkmäler des Alten Reiches.* Vol. I, pl. 1536 a.

Plan   **NO PLAN AVAILABLE**

SV Number 8   **LMP Number** 104

Tomb Owner Itisen

Literature ref. Hassan, *Excavations at Giza*. Vol. 5, fig. 122.

Plan

P & M XXXII. Northern part of east wall .

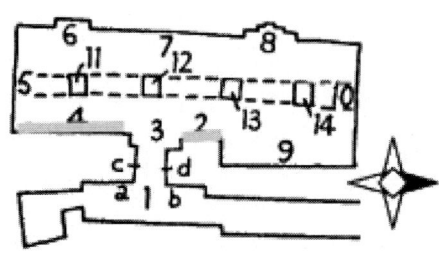

104

SV Number	9	**LMP Number**	113
Tomb Owner	Iymery		
Literature ref.	Weeks, *Mastabas of Cemetery G6000*. Fig. 32.		

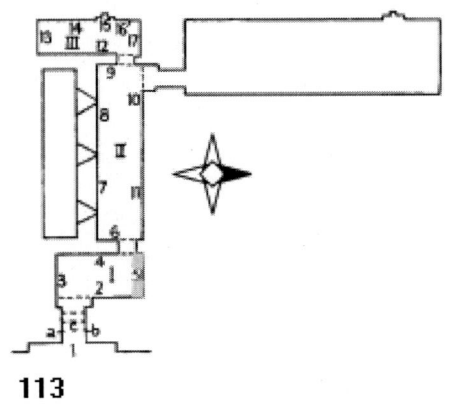

Plan

P &M XXIX. Northern wall in room 1.

113

SV Number	10	**LMP Number**	183
Tomb Owner	Kagemni		
Literature ref.	Harpur and Scremin., *The Chapel of Kagemni*. Fig. 17.		

Plan

P & M LV. Northern wall in room 4.

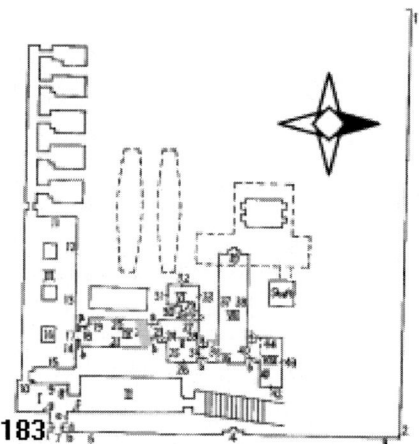

183

SV Number   11   **LMP Number**   44

Tomb Owner   Kaemnofret

Literature ref.   Simpson et al., *The offering chapel of Kayemnofret.* Plate. 17 (b).

Plan

P & M XLVII. Southern wall of cult chapel.

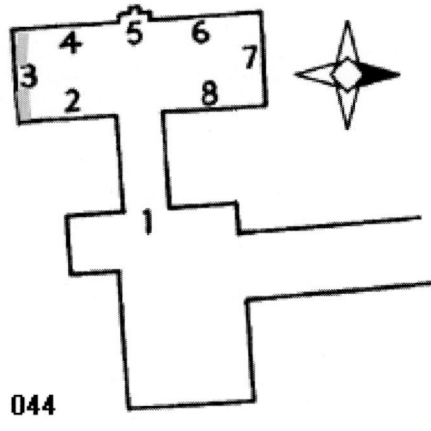

044

187

SV Number	12	**LMP Number**	48
Tomb Owner	Niankhkhnum		
Literature ref.	Altenmüller and Moussa, *Das Grab des Nianchchnum und Chnumhotep*. Fig. 60.		

Plan

P & M LXVI and Altenmüller. Entrance to rock cut part on western pillar.

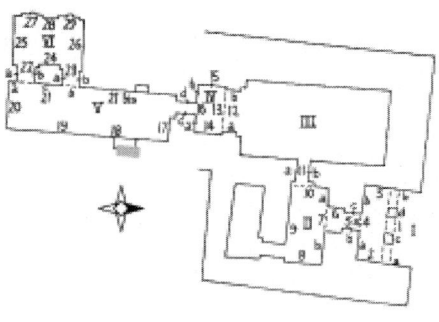

048

SV Number	13	**LMP Number**	228a
Tomb Owner	Khnumenti (A)		
Literature ref.	Brovarski, *The Senedjemib Complex,* Part 1, plate 86.		

Plan

Plan from *Jacquet-Gordon fig. 94 and Brovarski fig. 3.* Eastern wall.

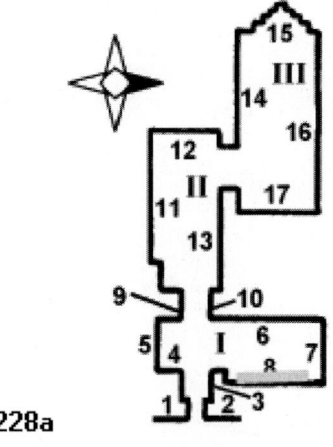

228a

SV Number	14	**LMP Number**	117
Tomb Owner	Khuwer		
Literature ref.	Hassan, *Excavations at Giza.* Vol. 5, fig. 104.		

Plan

P & M XXXV. Eastern wall room 2.

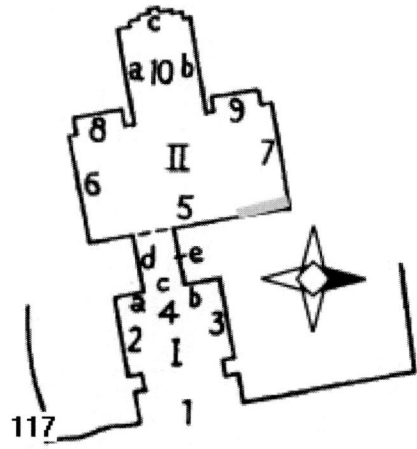

SV Number	15A	**LMP Number**	182a
Tomb Owner	Mereruka		
Literature ref.	Duell et al., *The Mastaba of Mereruka.* Vol. II, plate 158.		

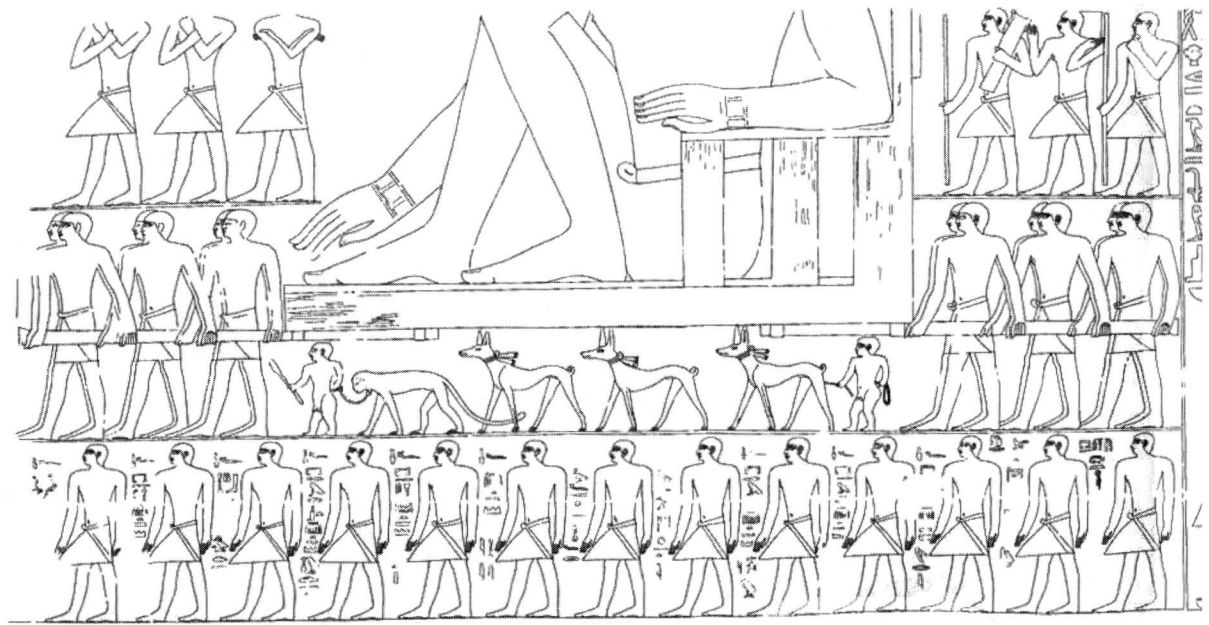

Plan

P & M LVI. Northern wall.

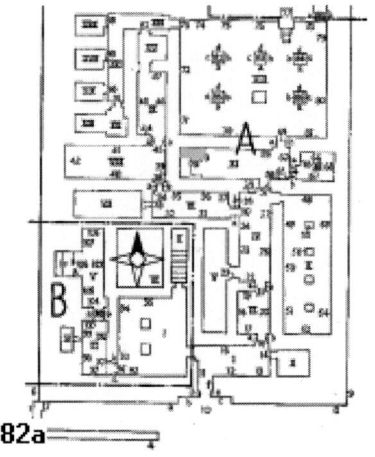

182a

SV Number	15B	**LMP Number**	182a
Tomb Owner	Mereruka		
Literature ref.	Duell et al., *The Mastaba of Mereruka.* Vol II, plate 53 (b).		

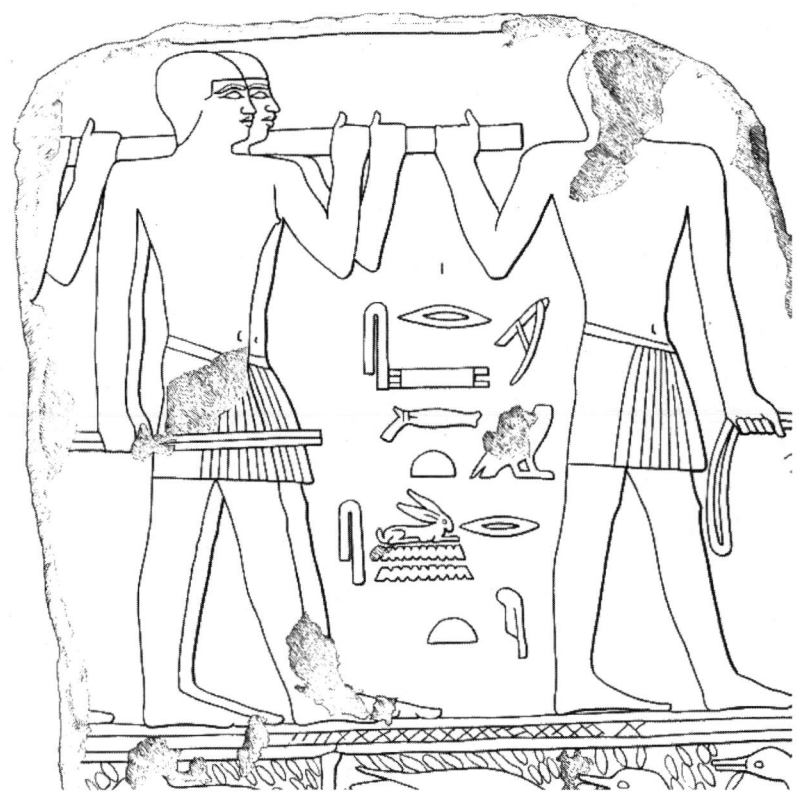

Plan

P & M. LVI West wall (seems incorrect reconstruction of fragment block)?

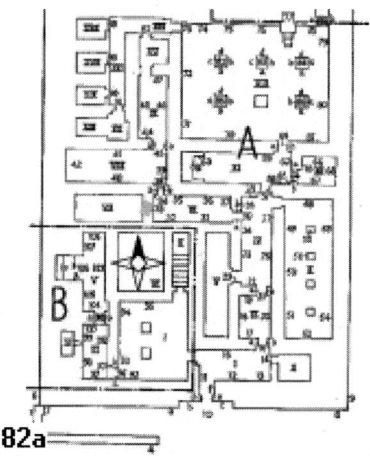

182a

SV Number	16	**LMP Number**	186
Tomb Owner	Merwtetiseneb		
Literature ref.	Lloyd et al., *Saqqara Tombs II: the Mastabas of Meru, Semdenti, Khui and Others.* Plate 7.		

Plan

P & M LV. Northern wall of room 1.

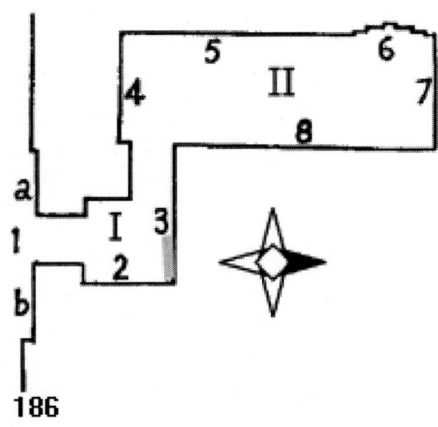

SV Number	17A	**LMP Number**	182c
Tomb Owner	Meryteti		
Literature ref.	Kanawati, *Mereruka and his family: the tomb of Meryteti*. Part I, fig. 47.		

Plan

P & M LVI with addn. LMP numbering. North wall above doorway from C1 to C3.

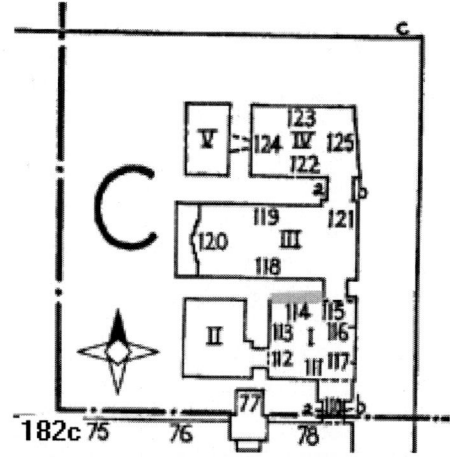

SV Number	17B	**LMP Number**	182c
Tomb Owner	Meryteti		
Literature ref.	Kanawati, *Mereruka and his family: the tomb of Meryteti*. Part. I, fig. 48.		

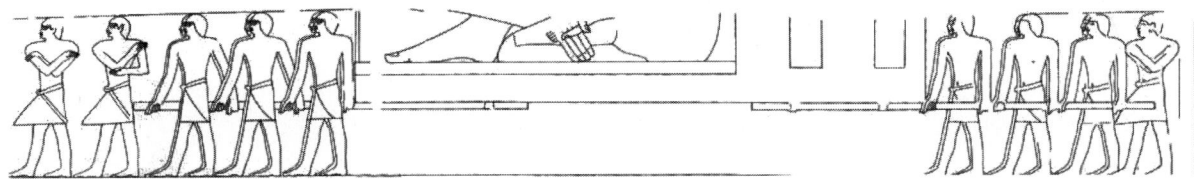

Plan   *P & M LVI* with addn. LMP numbering. Eastern wall.

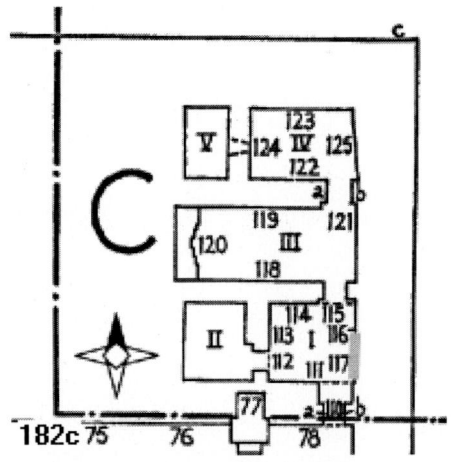

SV Number   18   **LMP Number**   184

Tomb Owner   Methethi

Literature ref.   Kaplony, *Studien zum Grab des Methethi.* Fig. 2.

Plan   No plans exist. Parts of decoration in various museums.

SV Number 19   **LMP Number** 002a

Tomb Owner Nefermaat

Literature ref. Harpur & Scremin, *The Tombs of Nefermaat and Rahotep at Maidum.* Fig. 77.

Plan

Petrie, *Medum.* Plate lll, Northern wall.

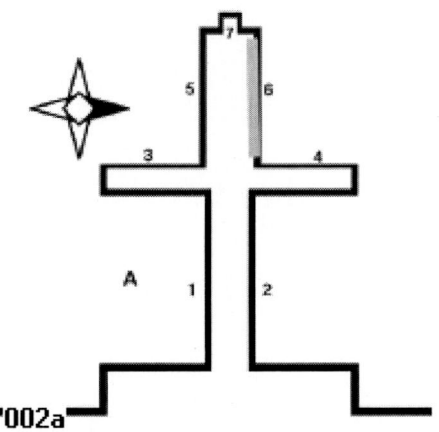

SV Number	20	LMP Number	131d

Tomb Owner   Nefer-Khuwi

Literature ref.   Roth, *A Cemetry of Palace Attendants*. Vol. 6, fig. 191.

Plan

Roth, *A Cemetry of Palace Attendants*. Fig. 79, Northern wall.

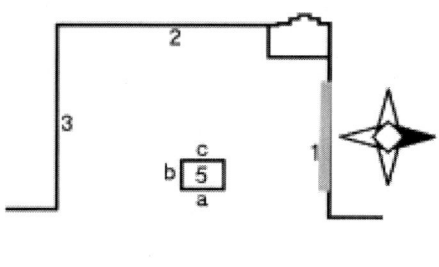

131d

SV Number	21A	**LMP Number**	48
Tomb Owner	Niankhkhnum		
Literature ref.	Altenmüller and Moussa, *Das Grab des Nianchchnum und Chnumhotep*. Fig. 42		

Plan

P & M LXVI and Altenmueller. Southern entrance to room 3

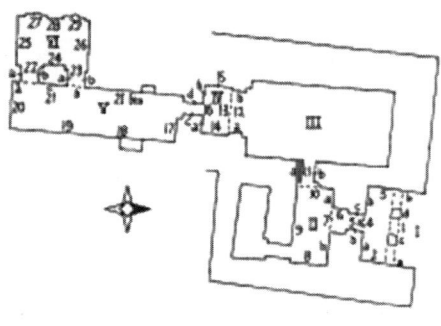

048

SV Number	21B	LMP Number	48

Tomb Owner   Khnumhotep

Literature ref.   Altenmüller and Moussa, *Das Grab des Nianchchnum und Chnumhotep*. Fig. 43.

Plan

P & M LXVI and Altenmüller. Northern entrance to room 3

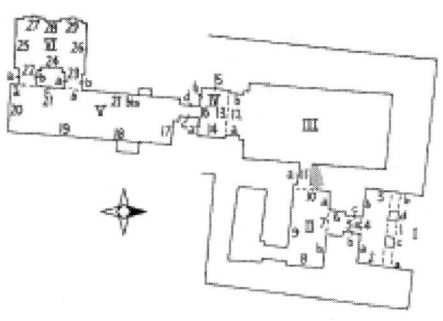

048

200

SV Number   22   **LMP Number**   184b

Tomb Owner   Nikauisesi

Literature ref.   Kanawati, *The Teti Cemetery at Saqqara: the Tomb of Nikauisesi.* Vol. 6, fig. 55.

Plan

Kanawati, *The Tomb of Nikauisesi. Plate 39,* Northern wall room 2, with addn. LMP

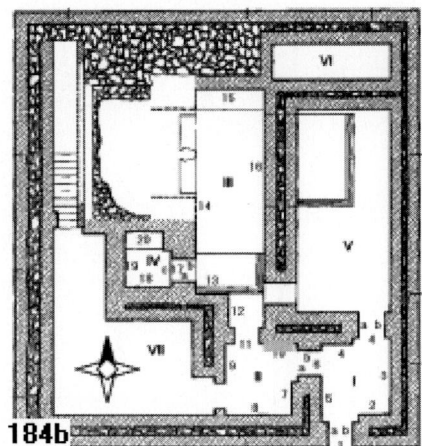

SV Number	23	**LMP Number**	120
Tomb Owner	Nimaatre		
Literature ref.	Hassan, *Excavations at Giza.* Vol. II, fig. 240.		

Plan

P & M XXXIII. Lower part eastern wall in entrance direction(room 1/ wall 2).

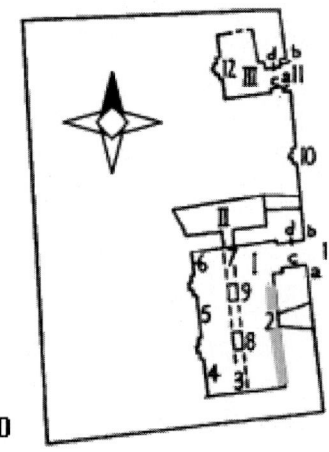

120

SV Number   24   **LMP Number**   215

Tomb Owner   Pepydjedi

Literature ref.   Mariette, *Les Mastabas de l'Ancien Empire.* **Textual description only. No available relief.**

Plan

Mariette, *Les Mastabas de l'Ancien Empire.* p. 401. Eastern wall.

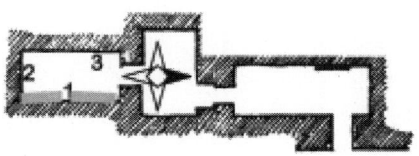

215

SV Number	25	**LMP Number**	67
Tomb Owner	Perneb		
Literature ref.	Hayes, *The Sceptre of Egypt*. Vol. I, fig. 51.		

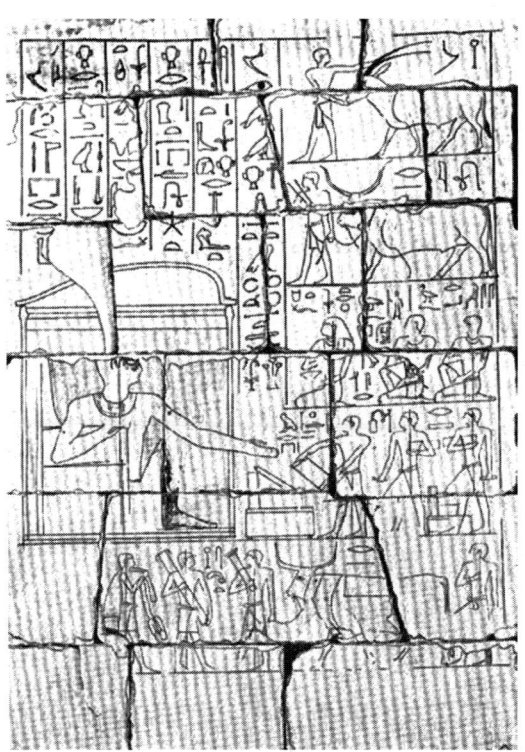

Plan

P & M L. Western wall of vestibule.

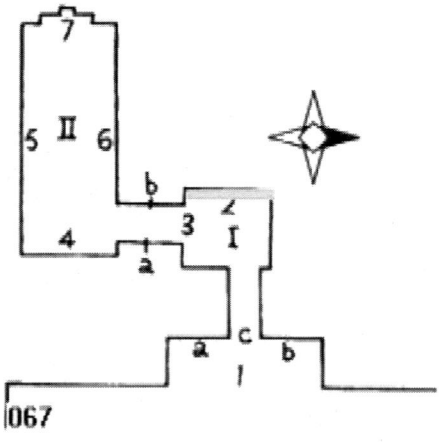

SV Number	26	**LMP Number**	36a
Tomb Owner	Ptahshepses		
Literature ref.	Verner, *Abusir-I. The Mastaba of Ptahshepses*. Plates 53-55.		

Plan

Verner, *Abusir-I: The Mastaba of Ptahshepses. Plan XXXVII*. Northern wall room 3.

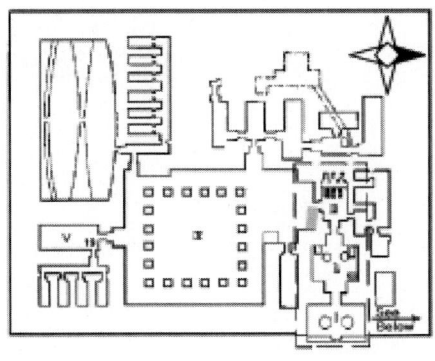

036a

SV Number	27	**LMP Number**	62b
Tomb Owner	Ptahhotep ll		
Literature ref.	Quibell et al., *The Ramesseum and the Tomb of Ptah-Hetep.* Plate 39 (part from false door).		

Plan

P & M LX . Southern false door in the western wall.

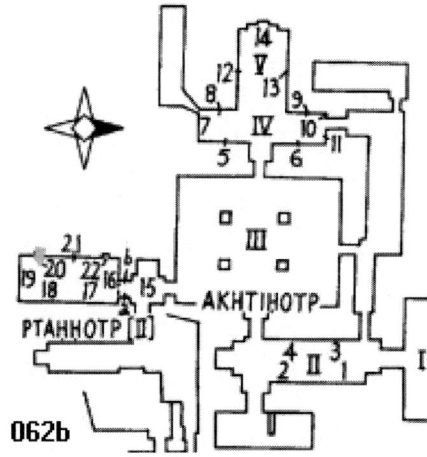

SV Number 28   **LMP Number** 229

Tomb Owner Qar

Literature ref. Simpson, *The Mastabas of Qar and Idu.* Fig. 27.

Plan

P & M XXX with upper staircase added and addn. LMP numbering. Room 3 Eastern wall

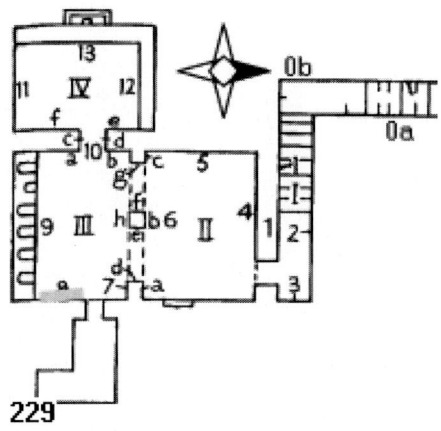

SV Number	29	**LMP Number**	59
Tomb Owner	Rashepses		
Literature ref.	Porter & Moss, *Topographical Bibliography - Memphis,* Vol. III: 496; and Quibell, *Excavations at Saqara,* 23/4. Partial textual description only.		

No picture available

Plan

P & M XLIX. West wall of corridor to room VII. This context is not verifiable.

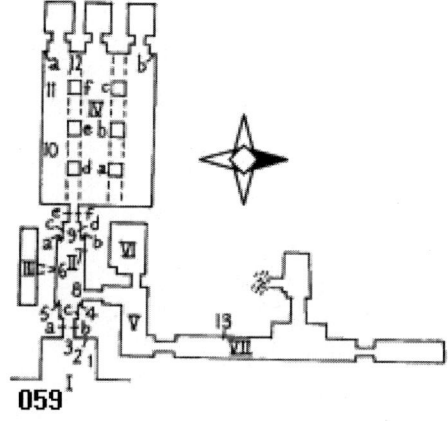

SV Number	30	**LMP Number**	181a
Tomb Owner	Sabw		
Literature ref.	Borchardt, *Denkmäler des Alten Reiches*. Vol. I, plate 1419. 96. Line drawing below from Mariette, *Mastabas*, 183.		

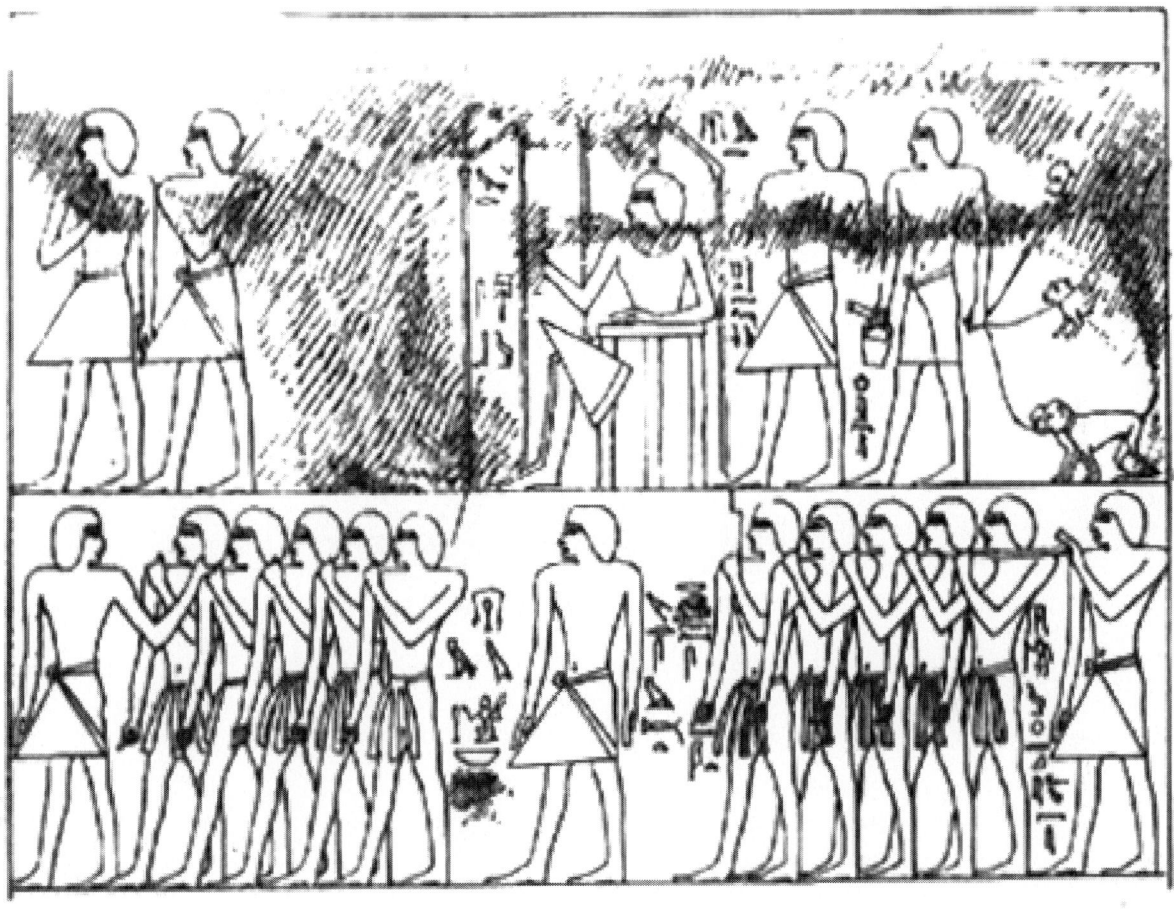

Plan

P & M XLVII. Northern wall of cult chapel.

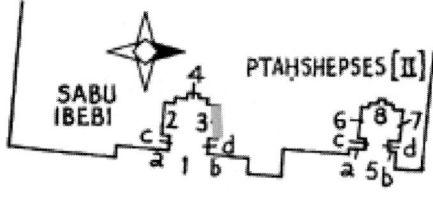

181a

SV Number	31	LMP Number	183a
Tomb Owner	Seankhuiptah		
Literature ref.	Kanawati, *The Teti Cemetery at Saqqara.* Vol. 3, plate 69.		

Plan

Kanawati, *The Teti Cemetery at Saqqara.* Vol. 3, plate 61. Eastern wall.

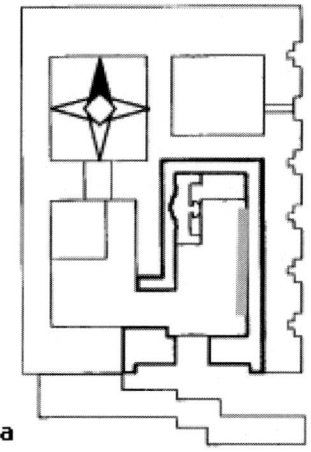

183a

SV Number   32   **LMP Number**   27a

Tomb Owner   Seneb

Literature ref.   Junker, *Giza,* Vol. 5, fig. 20.

Plan

P & M XXVII. Western wall-inner jamb of false door.

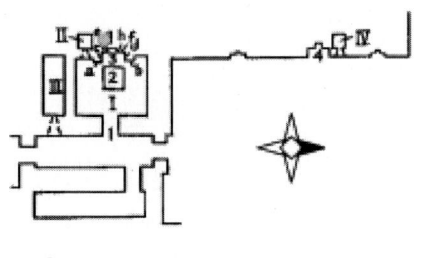

027a

211

SV Number   33   **LMP Number**   114

Tomb Owner   Senedjemib. Inti

Literature ref.   Brovarski, *The Senedjemib Complex,* part I. Fig. 40 .

Plan   *P & M XXVI*. Southern wall in room 2.

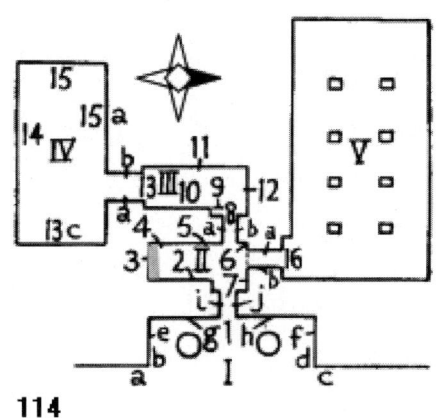

114

SV Number   34   **LMP Number**   247

Tomb Owner   Seshemnefer.Tjetti

Literature ref.   Junker, *Giza*, Vol. XI, fig. 100.

Plan

P & M XXXII. LMP numbering only. Southern wall in question?

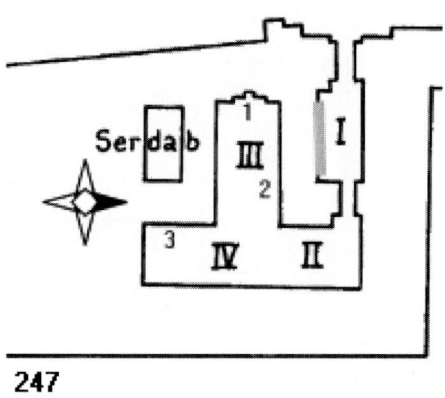

247

213

SV Number	35	**LMP Number**	257
Tomb Owner	Seshemnefer		
Literature ref.	Morgan, *Fouilles à Dahchour,* Vol. 2, fig. 3.		

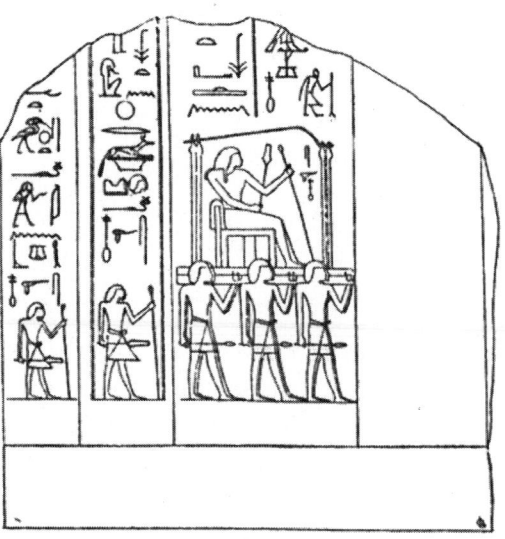

Plan

P & M XLVII. Fragment of false door. Morgan indicates this is in a northern room ?

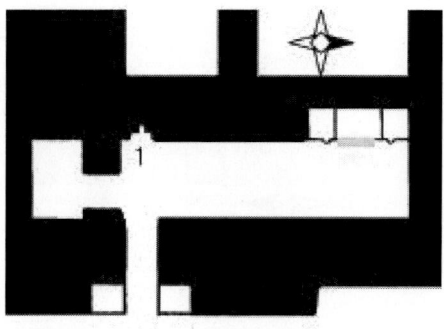

257

SV Number	36	**LMP Number**	49
Tomb Owner	Ty (B)		
Literature ref.	Epron et. al., *Le Tombeau de Ti: La Chapelle.* Vol. I, plate XVI.		

Plan

P & M XLVIII. Eastern wall in room 2 (MastaBase numbering).

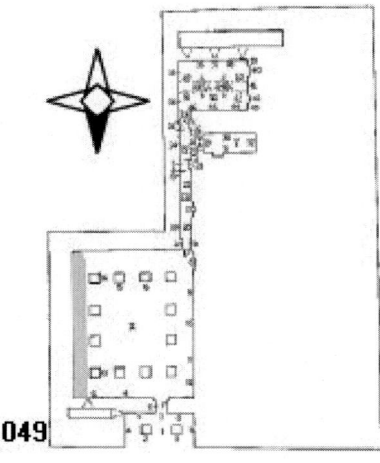

SV Number	37	**LMP Number**	182b
Tomb Owner	Waatetkhethor		
Literature ref.	Kanawati, *Mereruka and his family: the tomb of Waatetkhethor.* Part II, plate 69.		

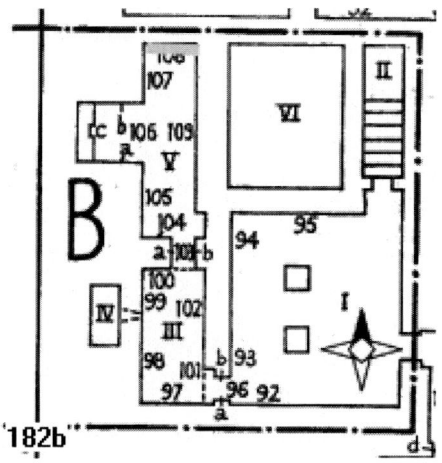

Plan   *P & M LVI.* Northern wall in room V, wall number 108.

SV Number	38	**LMP Number**	182a
Tomb Owner	Mereruka (A)		
Literature ref.	Duell et al., *The Mastaba of Mereruka.* Vol. I, plate 14.		

Plan

P & M. LVI. Eastern wall in room 1. Empty chair.

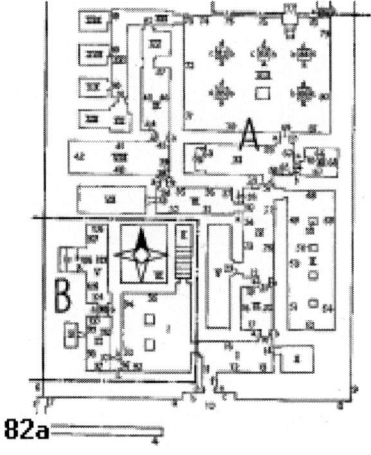

182a

SV Number   39   **LMP Number**   36a

Tomb Owner   Ptahshepses (A)

Literature ref.   Verner, *Abusir-I, The Mastaba of Ptahshepses*, pl. 10

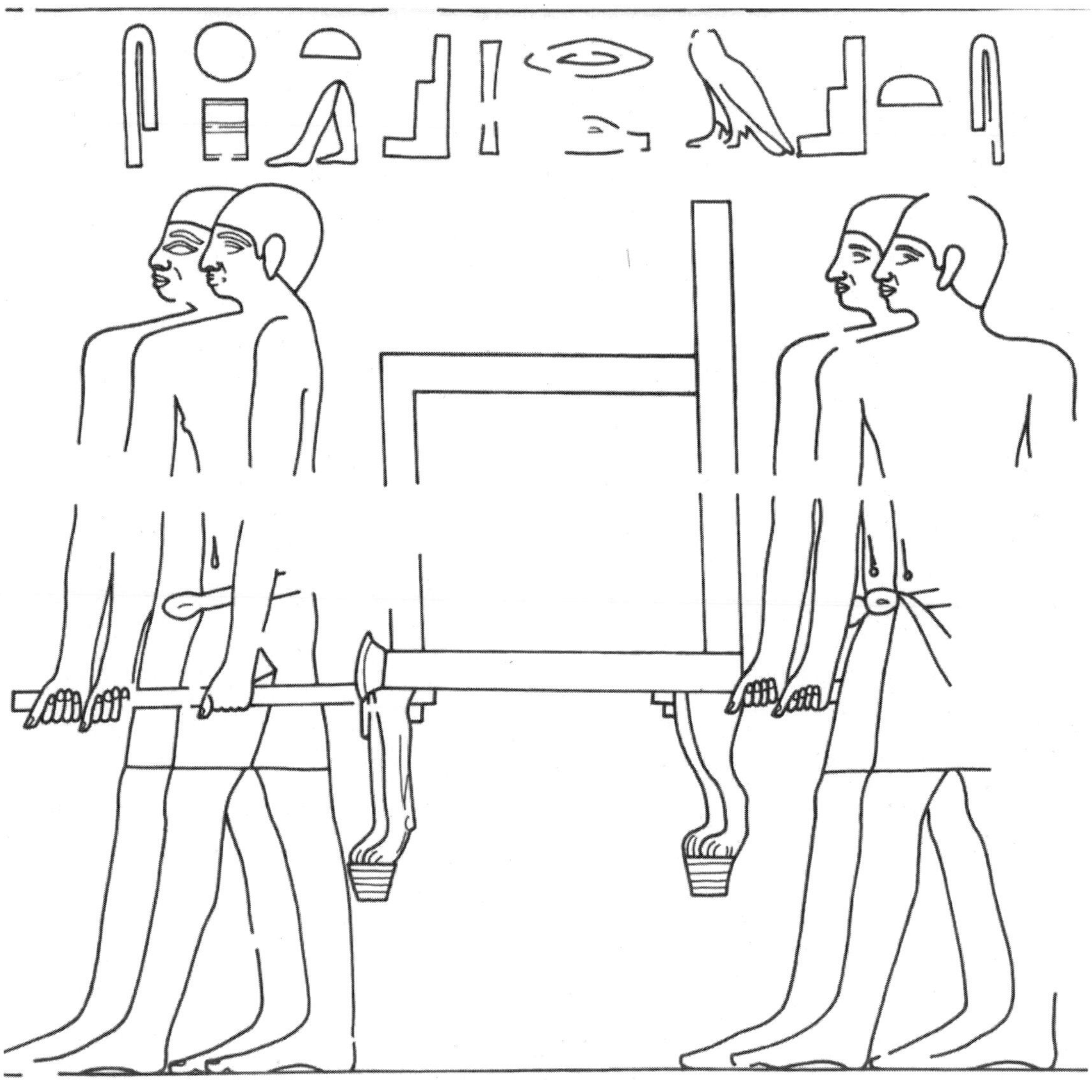

Plan

Plan XXXVII. Western wall of room 3 (southern section).

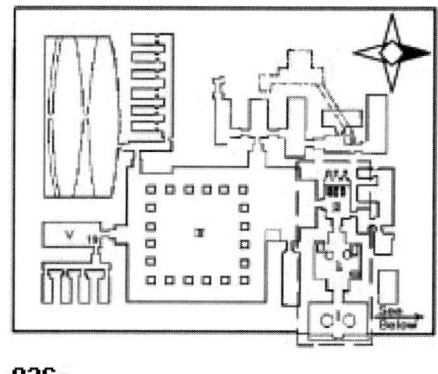

036a

SV Number   40   **LMP Number**   49

Tomb Owner   Ty (A)

Literature ref.   Epron et al., *Le Tombeau de Ti: La Chapelle.* Vol. I, plate XVII.

Plan

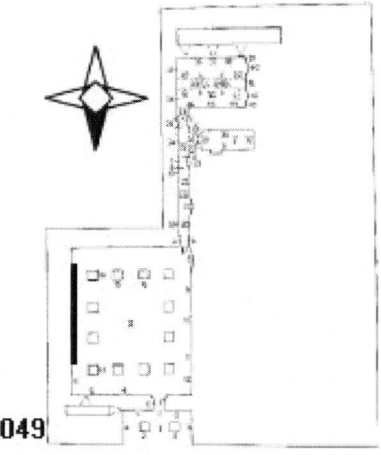

SV Number	41	**LMP Number**	89
Tomb Owner	Seshathetep . Heti		
Literature ref.	Junker, *Giza.* Vol. 2, fig. 31		

Plan

P & M XXVIII. Eastern wall (southern part).

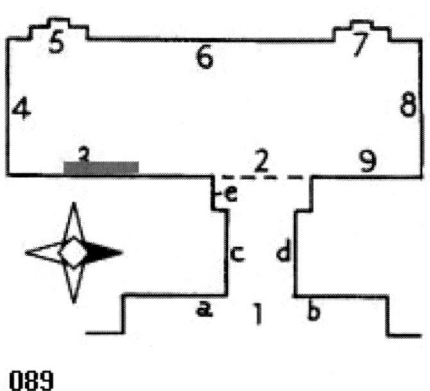

089

SV Number   42   **LMP Number**   182b

Tomb Owner   Waatetkhethor

Literature ref.   Kanawati, *Mereruka and his family: the tomb of Waatetkhethor*. Part 2, pl. 57 A.

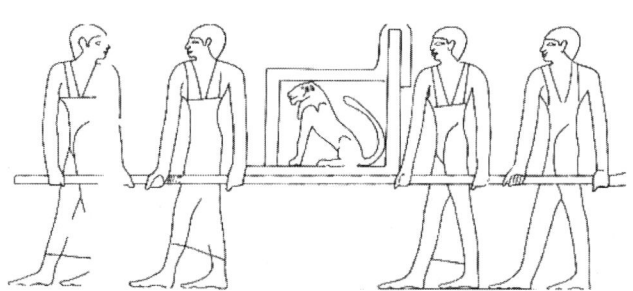

Plan

P & M LVI. Northern wall in room V, wall number 108.

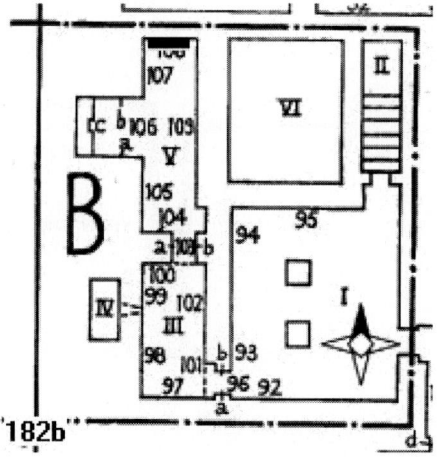

221

SV Number	43		LMP Number	008a
Tomb Owner	Unknown			
Literature ref.	Junker, *Giza*. Vol. 1, fig. 37(3). Possible remains of a fragment of a palanquin scene.			

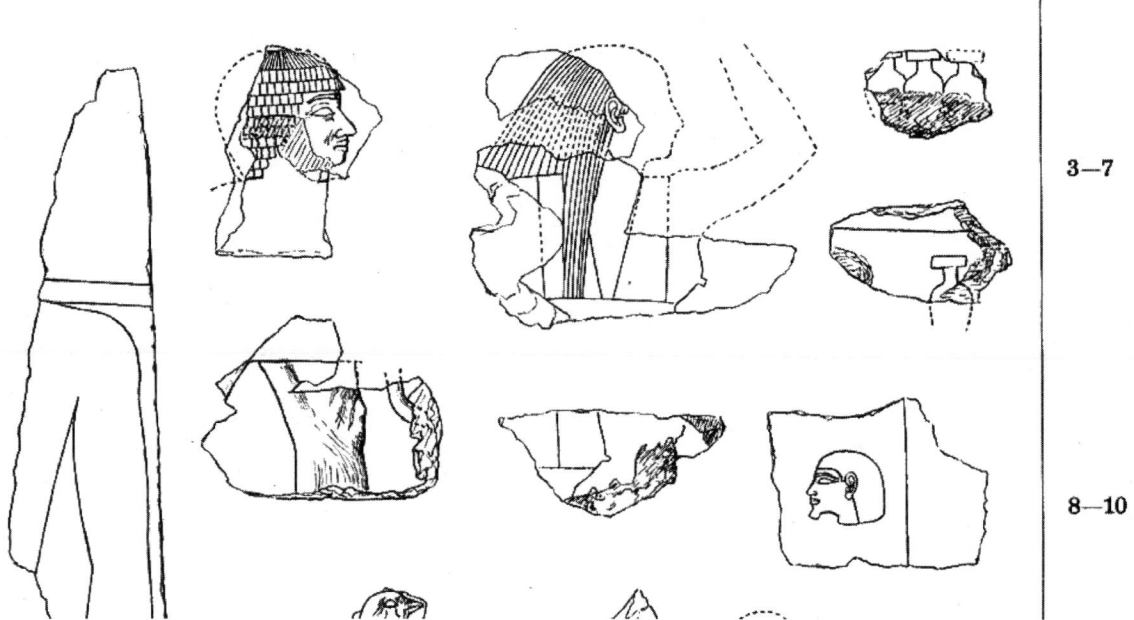

Plan

Junker, *Giza*. Vol. I, fig. 35, reconstruction of outbuilding. Wall not clearly marked.

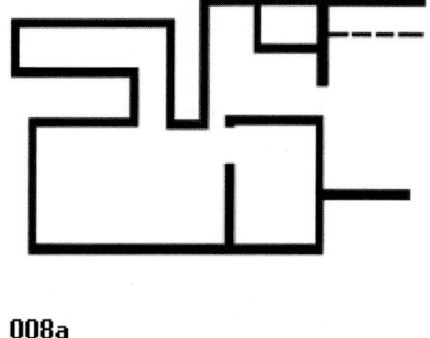

008a

| SV Number | 44 | LMP Number | 190 |

Tomb Owner Ankhmahor

Literature ref. Kanawati, *The Teti Cemetery at Saqqara: the Tomb of Ankhmahor*. Vol. 2, plate 45.

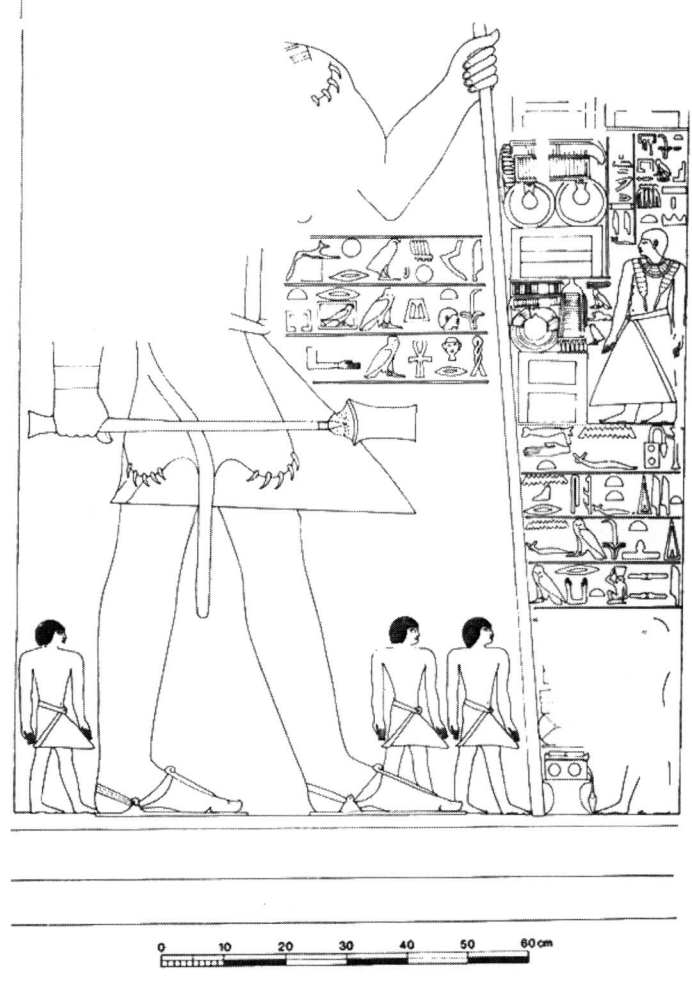

Plan

P & M. L. Southern wall, room 3, wall 12.

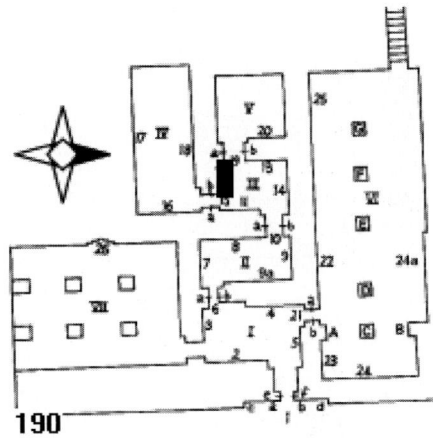

223

SV Number	45	**LMP Number** 132
Tomb Owner	Fetekty	
Literature ref.	Lepsius, *Denkmäler aus Ägypten und Äthiopien.* LDII, plate 96.	

Plan

P & M XL. Eastern wall of room I (as modified by Barta, in *Abusir V*, fig. 3.13).

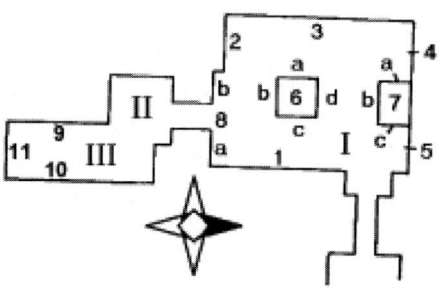

132

SV Number   46   **LMP Number**   n/a

Tomb Owner   Hemetra

Literature ref.   Hassan, *Excavations at Giza.* Vol. 6 (3), fig. 40.

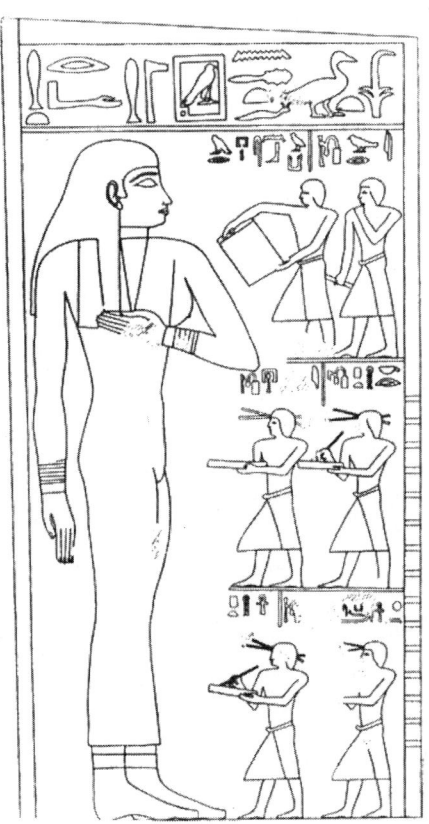

Plan

NO PLANS AVAILABLE For more details see Hassan vol. 6 (3), page 45.

SV Number	47	**LMP Number**	218
Tomb Owner	Idut		

Literature ref.   Kanawati, *The Unis Cemetry at Saqqara: the Tombs of Iynefert and Ihy (reused by Idut)*. Vol. 2, fig. 71.

Plan

P & M LXIII. Room V, Eastern wall 24.

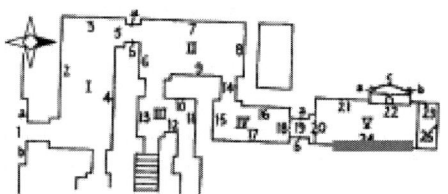

218

SV Number   48   **LMP Number**   217

Tomb Owner   Iynefert

Literature ref.   Kanawati, *The Unis Cemetry at Saqqara: the tombs of Iynefert and Ihy (reused by Idut)*. Vol. 2, fig. 42.

Plan

P & M LXIII. Eastern wall 9, in room 2.

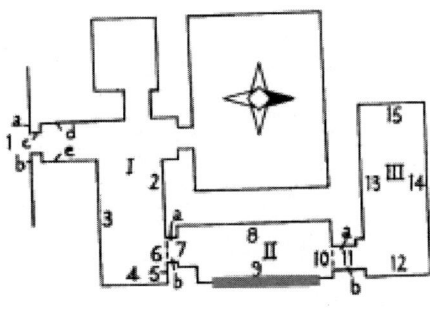

217

SV Number	49	**LMP Number**	113
Tomb Owner	Iymery		
Literature ref.	Weeks, *Mastabas of Cemetery G6000.* Fig. 26 and 27.		

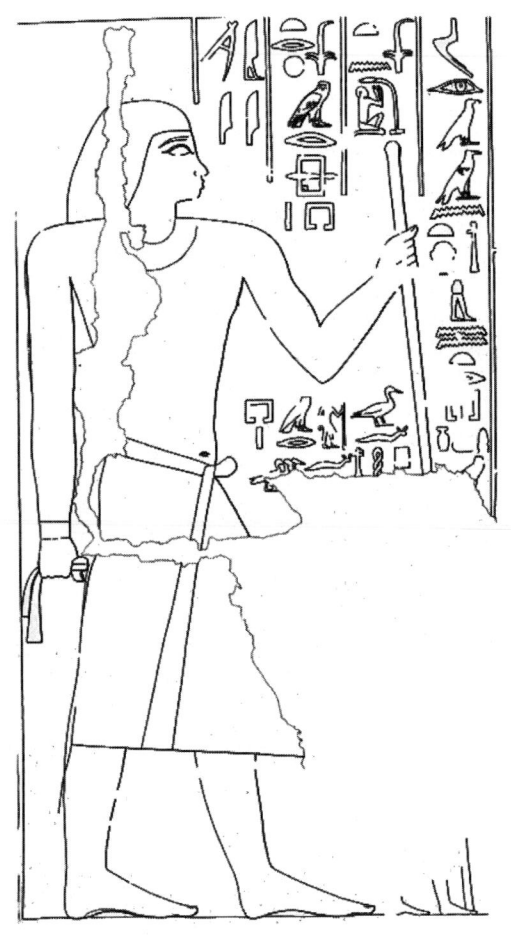

Plan　　*P & M XXIX.* Eastern wall 2, room I.

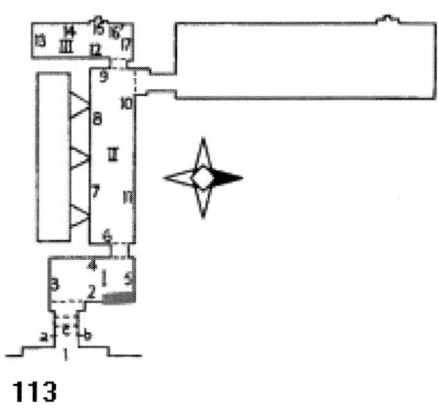

113

SV Number	50	**LMP Number**	183
Tomb Owner	Kagemni		
Literature ref.	Harpur and Scremin, *The Chapel of Kagemni.* Plate 13.		

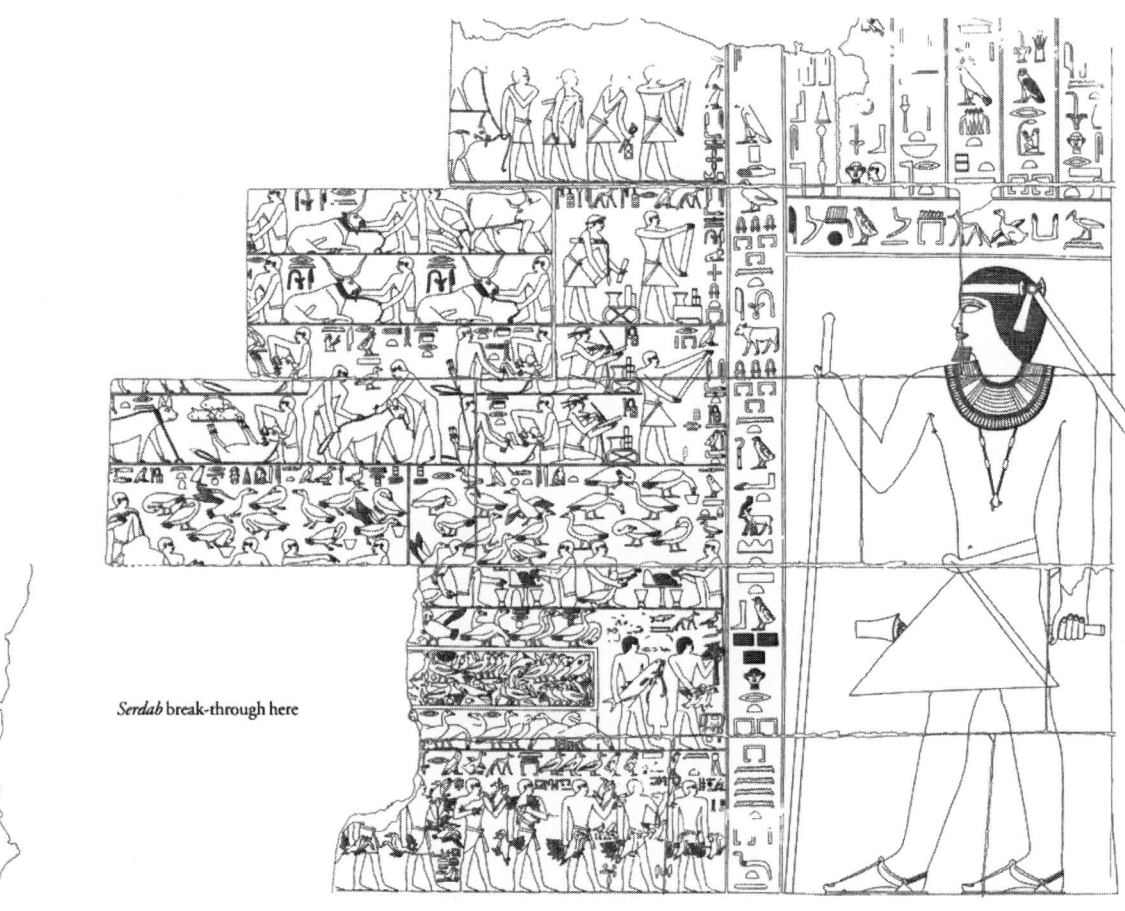

Serdab break-through here

Plan

P & M LV. Western wall 20 in room IV.

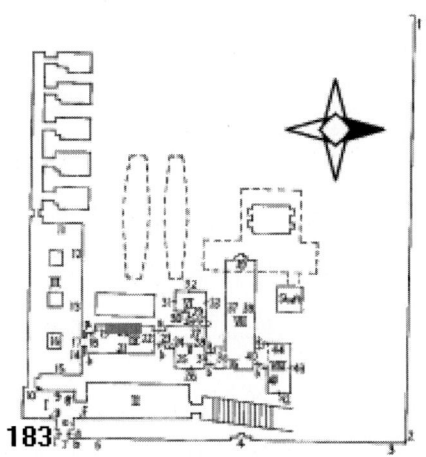

183

SV Number	51	LMP Number	232
Tomb Owner	Kahif		
Literature ref.	Junker, *Giza.* Vol. 6, fig. 34.		

Plan

P & M XXV. , Western wall 6, in room I.

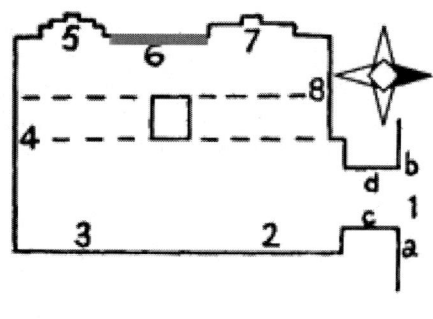

232

SV Number   52   **LMP Number**   133

Tomb Owner   Kairer

Literature ref.   Lauer, *Saqqara: The Royal Cemetery of Memphis.* Plate 68.

Plan

P & M LXV. Northern wall in room 1.

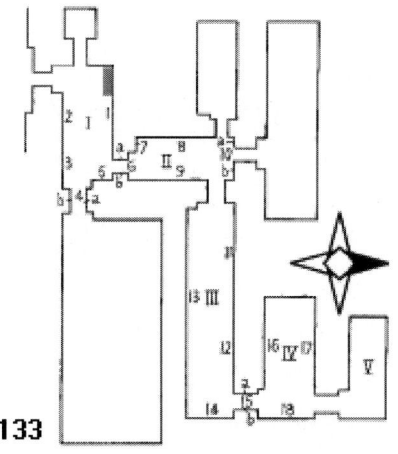

133

231

SV Number	53	**LMP Number**	086
Tomb Owner	Kanefer		
Literature ref.	Reisner, *A History of the Giza Necropolis.* Vol. I, fig. 262.		

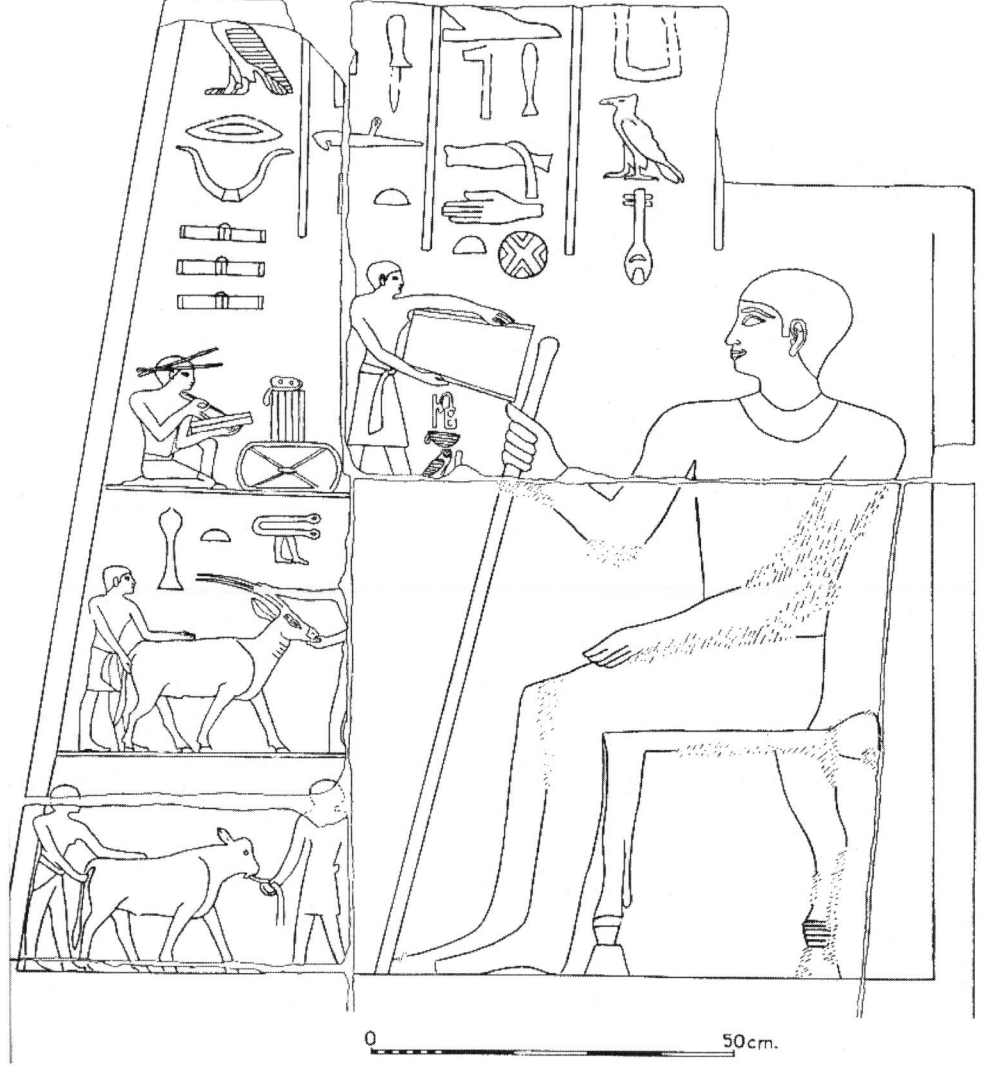

Plan

P & M XXV. Southern entrance thickness.

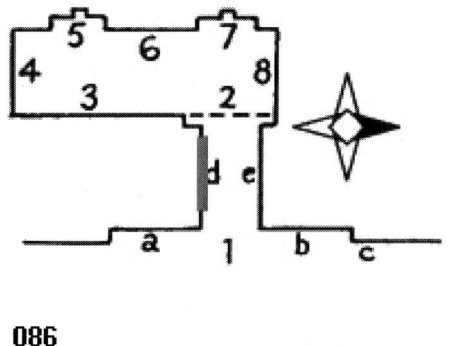

086

SV Number	54	**LMP Number**	087
Tomb Owner	Kaninisut		
Literature ref.	Junker, *Giza,* Vol. 2, fig. 19.		

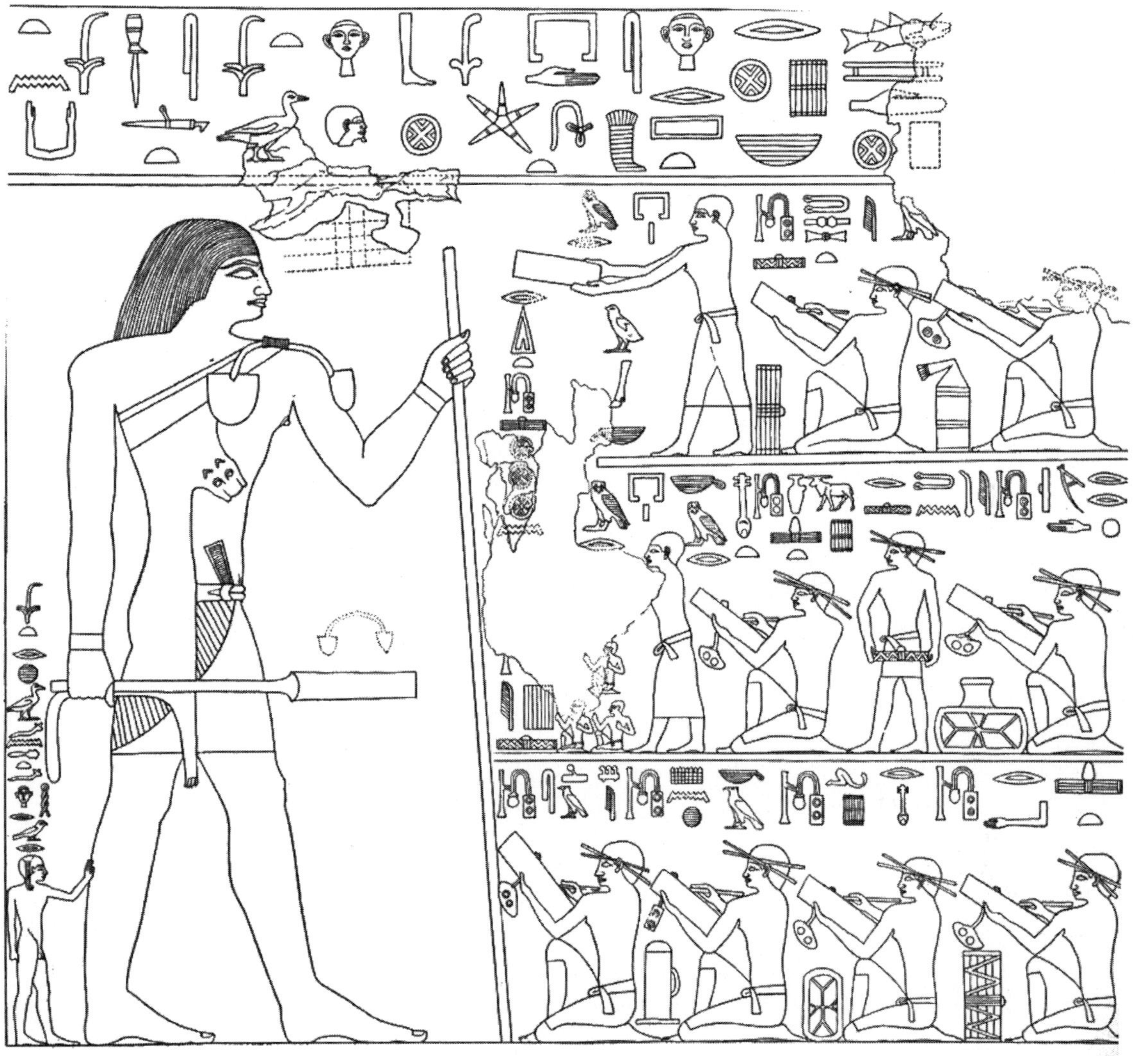

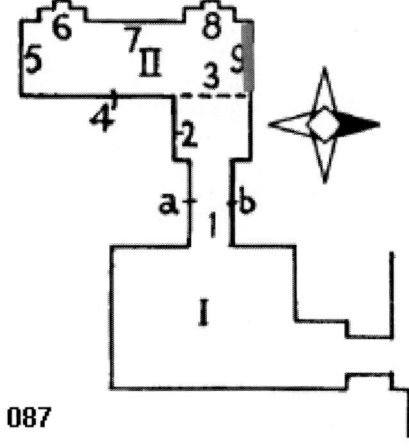

Plan   *P & M XXV*. Northern wall 9, in room 2.

087

SV Number 55	**LMP Number** 172

Tomb Owner Kaemnofret

Literature ref. Badawy, *The Tombs of Iteti, Sekhemankhptah, and Kaemnofret at Giza.* Fig. 29.

Plan *P & M XXXI.* Southern wall 3.

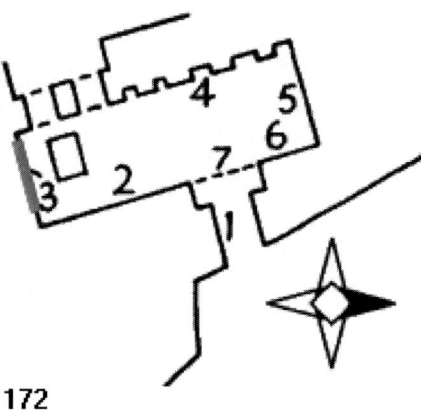

172

SV Number	56	**LMP Number**	008
Tomb Owner	Khafkhufu I		
Literature ref.	Simpson et al., *The mastabas of Kawab, Khafkhufu I and II.* Fig. 29.		

Plan

P & M XXX. Northern entrance thickness, wall 4c.

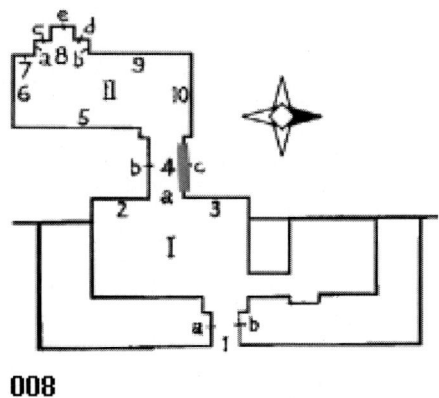

008

SV Number	57	**LMP Number**	n/a
Tomb Owner	Khafreankh		
Literature ref.	Lepsius, *Denkmäler aus Ägypten und Äthiopien.* LDII, plate BI 9.		

Plan   **Not available**

SV Number   58   **LMP Number**   242

Tomb Owner   Khentkawes

Literature ref.   Junker, *Giza.* Vol. 7, fig. 31.

Plan   *P & M XXXIV.* Western wall 2, in room II in the eastern chamber, NOT chapel.

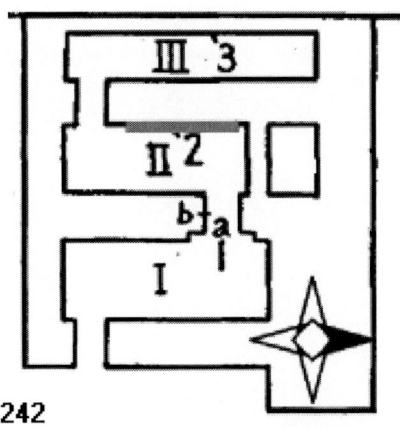

242

SV Number	59	**LMP Number**	063b
Tomb Owner	Khenut		

Literature ref. Munro, *Der Unas-Friedhof Nord-West: Das Doppelgrab der Königinnen Nebet und Khenut.* Vol. I, fig. 38.

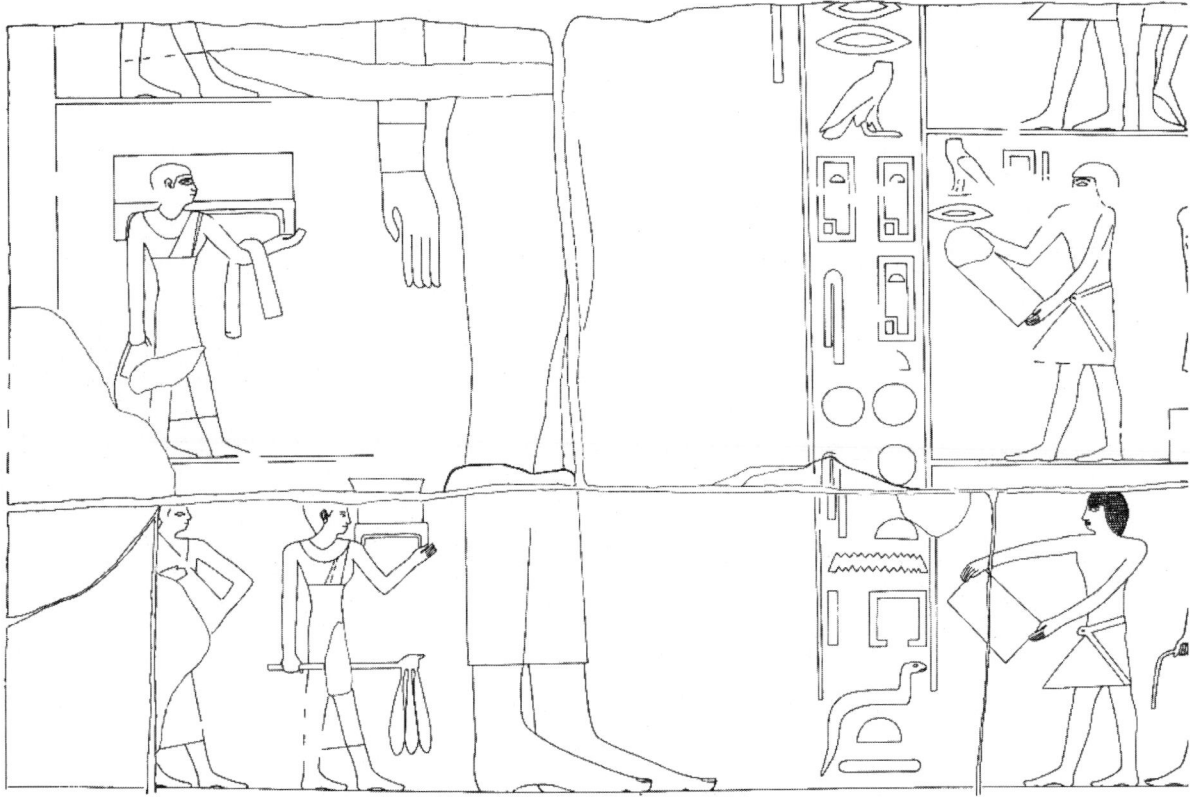

Plan

P & M LXIV. Eastern wall 6, in room II.

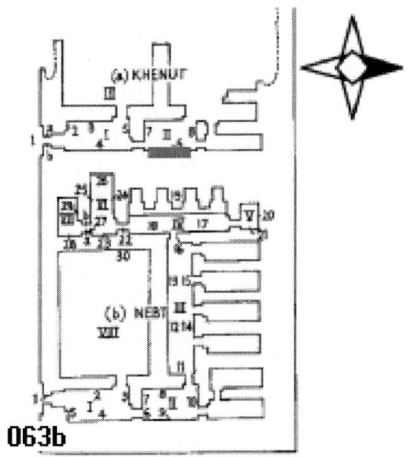

SV Number	6	LMP Number	258

Tomb Owner Inisnfrw-ishtef

Literature ref. Borchardt, *Denkmäler des Alten Reiches.* Vol. II, pl. 102 (fragment 1769).

Plan De Morgan, *Dahchour II.* Fig. 8. Orientation of fragment ?

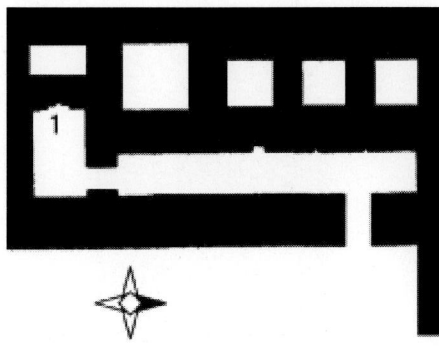

258

SV Number   60A   **LMP Number**   063a

Tomb Owner   Nebet

Literature ref.   Munro, *Der Unas-Friedhof Nord-West: Das Doppelgrab der Königinnen Nebet und Khenut.* Vol. 1, fig. 13.

Plan

P & M LXIV. Eastern walls 13.

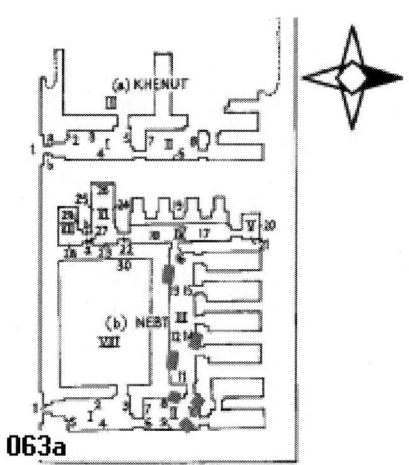

SV Number	60B	**LMP Number**	063a
Tomb Owner	Nebet		

Literature ref. Munro, *Der Unas-Friedhof Nord-West: Das Doppelgrab der Königinnen Nebet und Khenut*. Vol. 1, fig. 14.

Plan *P & M LXIV*. Western walls 14.

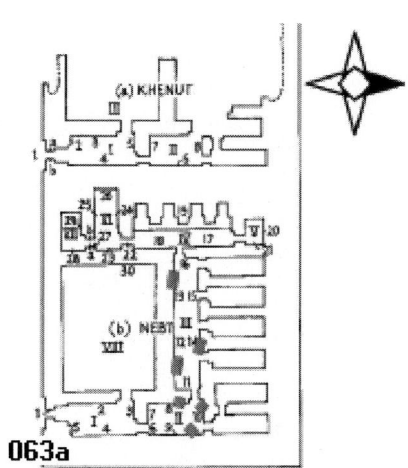

SV Number	60C		LMP Number	063a
Tomb Owner	Nebet			

Literature ref. Munro, *Der Unas-Friedhof Nord-West: Das Doppelgrab der Königinnen Nebet und Khenut.* Vol. 1, fig. 17.

Plan

P & M LXIV. Northern walls 17.

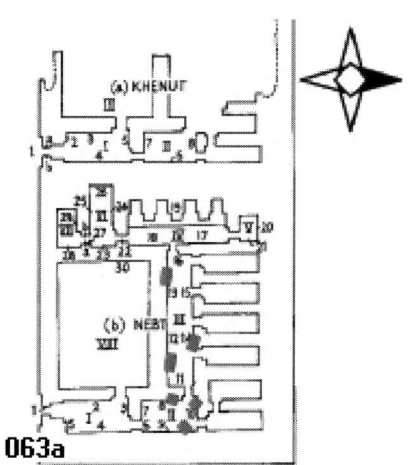

063a

SV Number	60D	**LMP Number**	063a
Tomb Owner	Nebet		

Literature ref. Munro, *Der Unas-Friedhof Nord-West: Das Doppelgrab der Königinnen Nebet und Khenut.* Vol. 1, fig. 19.

Plan *P & M LXIV*. Southern walls 19.

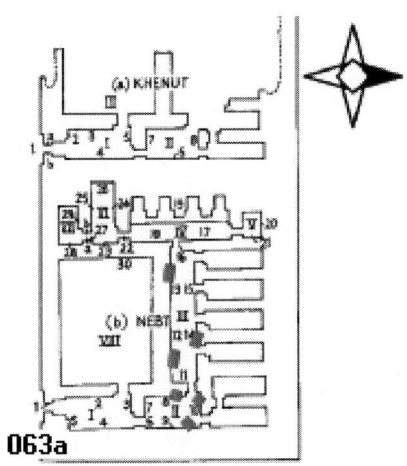

063a

SV Number	61	LMP Number	228a
Tomb Owner	Khnumenti (B) refers to taking account.		
Literature ref.	Brovarski, *The Senedjemib Complex.* Part 1, plate 86.		

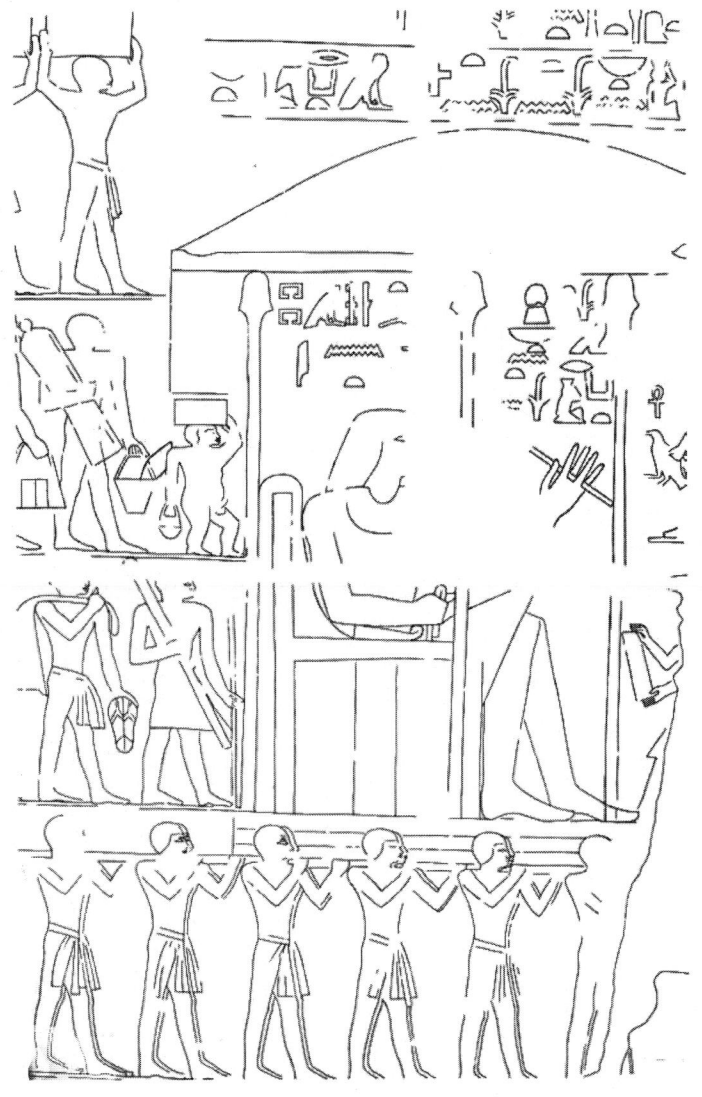

Plan Plan from Jacquet-Gordon fig. 94 and Brovarski fig. 3.

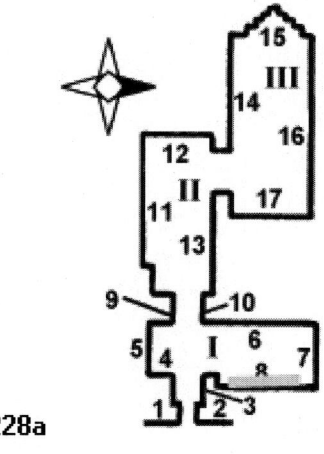

228a

SV Number	62	**LMP Number**	182a
Tomb Owner	Mereruka (D) refers to 'taking account' part.		
Literature ref.	Duell et al., *The Mastaba of Mereruka*. Vol. 1, plate 51.		

Plan

P & M LVI. Room VI, Soutehrn wall 31 & 32.

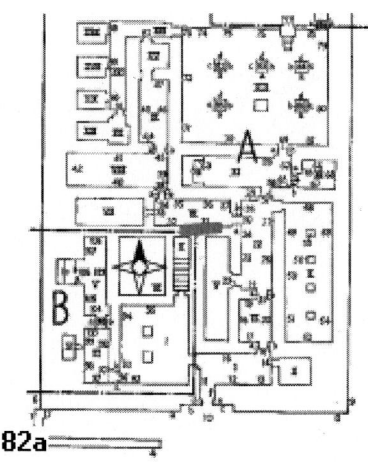

SV Number	63	**LMP Number**	013
Tomb Owner	Meresankh III		
Literature ref.	Dunham et al., *The Mastaba of Queen Merysankh III*. Fig. 3b.		

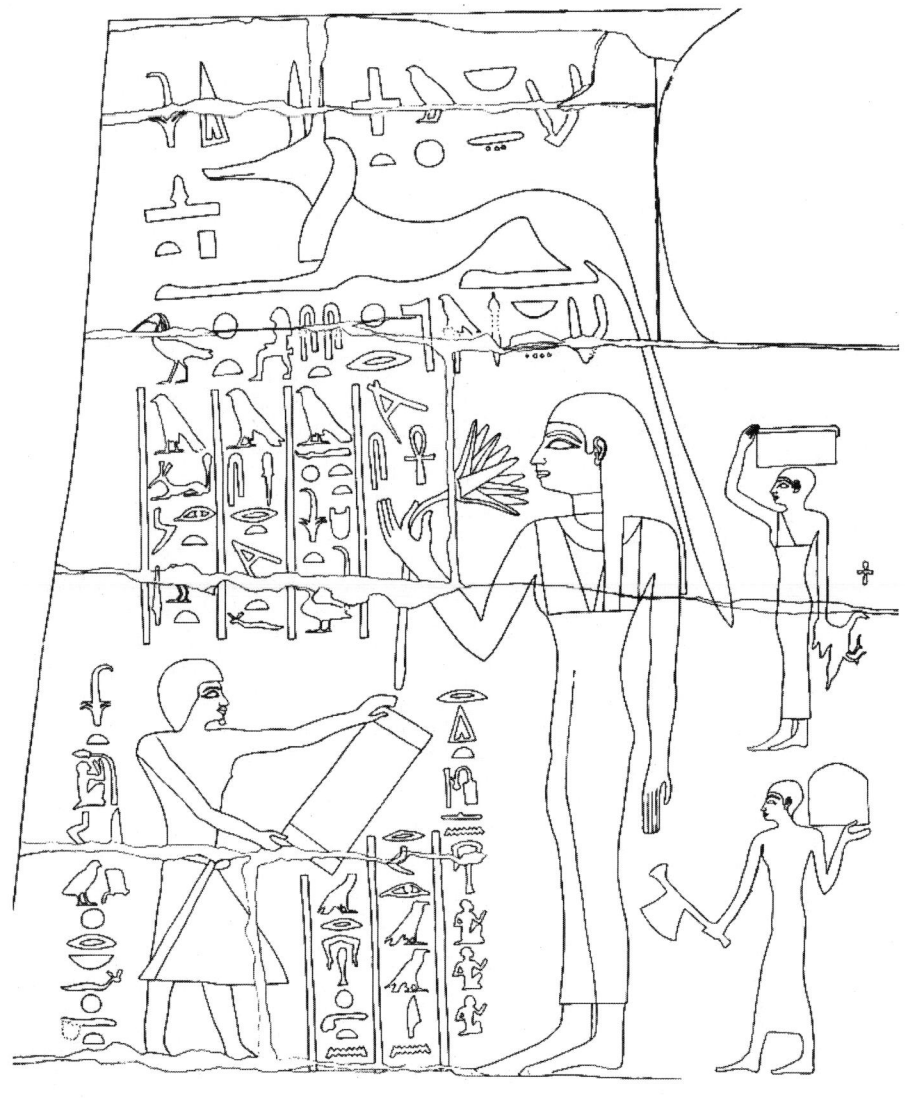

Plan

P & M XXX. Southern Entrance jamb of wall 5.

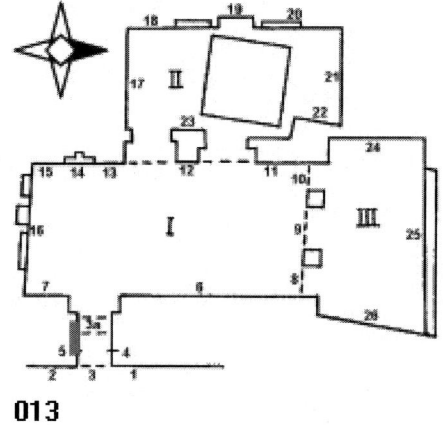

013

SV Number	64	**LMP Number**	029
Tomb Owner	Meryib		
Literature ref.	Junker, *Giza*. Vol. 2, fig. 11.		

Plan

P & M XXIV. Northern entrance thickness. (See also Southern thickness)

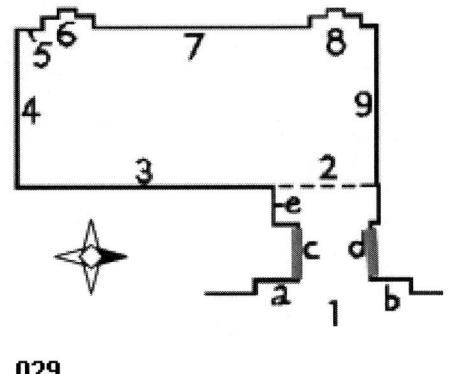

029

SV Number	65	**LMP Number**	149
Tomb Owner	Nefer		
Literature ref.	Junker, *Giza.* Vol. 6, fig. 5.		

Plan   *P & M XXVIII*. Eastern and Western entrance thickness.

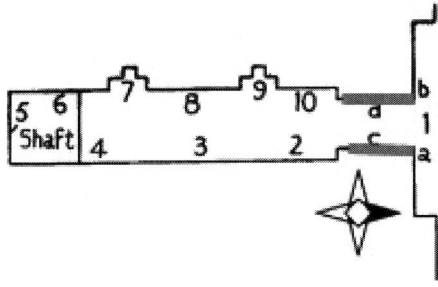

149

SV Number 66 **LMP Number** 100

Tomb Owner Neferbauptah

Literature ref. Weeks, *Mastabas of Cemetry G 6000*. Fig. 9.

Plan *P & M XXIX*. Northern half of Eastern wall of chapel, in room I.

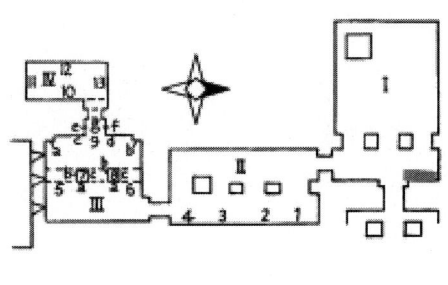

100

SV Number	67	**LMP Number**	053
Tomb Owner	Nefer & Kahay		
Literature ref.	Altenmüller and Moussa, *The Tomb of Nefer and Kahay*. Fig. 24a.		

Plan

P & M LXV. Southern walls 4 & 5.

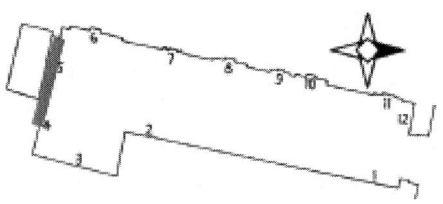

053

SV Number	68	**LMP Number**	091
Tomb Owner	Nesutnefer		
Literature ref.	Kanawati, *Tombs at Giza.* Vol. 2, fig. 57.		

Plan

P & M XXVIII. Northern wall 8, in room I.

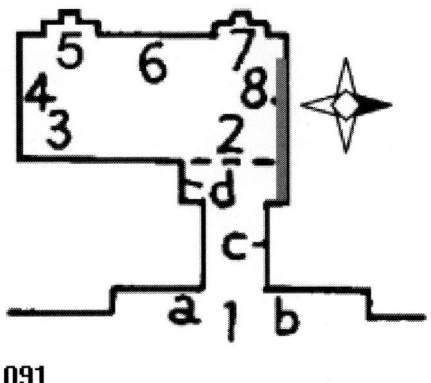

091

SV Number	69	**LMP Number**	48
Tomb Owner	Niankhkhnum & Khnumhotep		
Literature ref.	Altenmüller and Moussa, *Das Grab des Nianchchnum und Chnumhotep*. Fig. 13.		

Plan

P & M LXVI. Southern wall 9, in room 2.

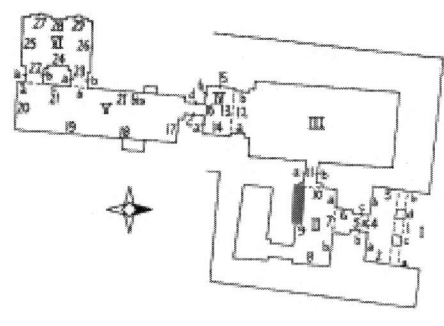

048

SV Number   70   **LMP Number**   67

Tomb Owner   Perneb (A) refers to taking account.

Literature ref.   Hayes, *The Sceptre of Egypt*. Vol. 1, fig. 51.

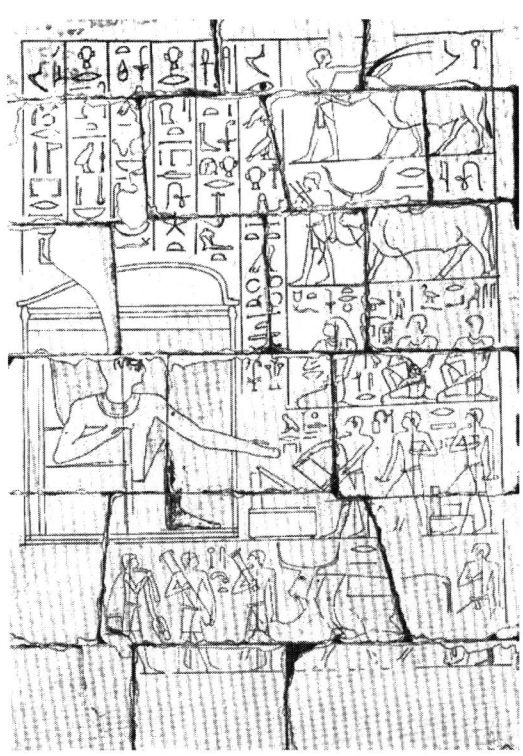

Plan   Possibly North Wall of recessed chapel?

SV Number	71	LMP Number	60
Tomb Owner	Ptahhotep II		
Literature ref.	Murray, *Saqqara Mastabas*, part I. Plate IX.		

Plan

P & M LX. Southern wall 16, in room IX.

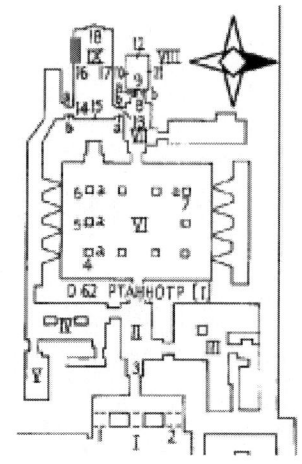

254

SV Number   72   **LMP Number**   229

Tomb Owner   Qar (A) refers to taking account part only.

Literature ref.   Simpson, *The Mastabas of Qar and Idu.* Fig. 27.

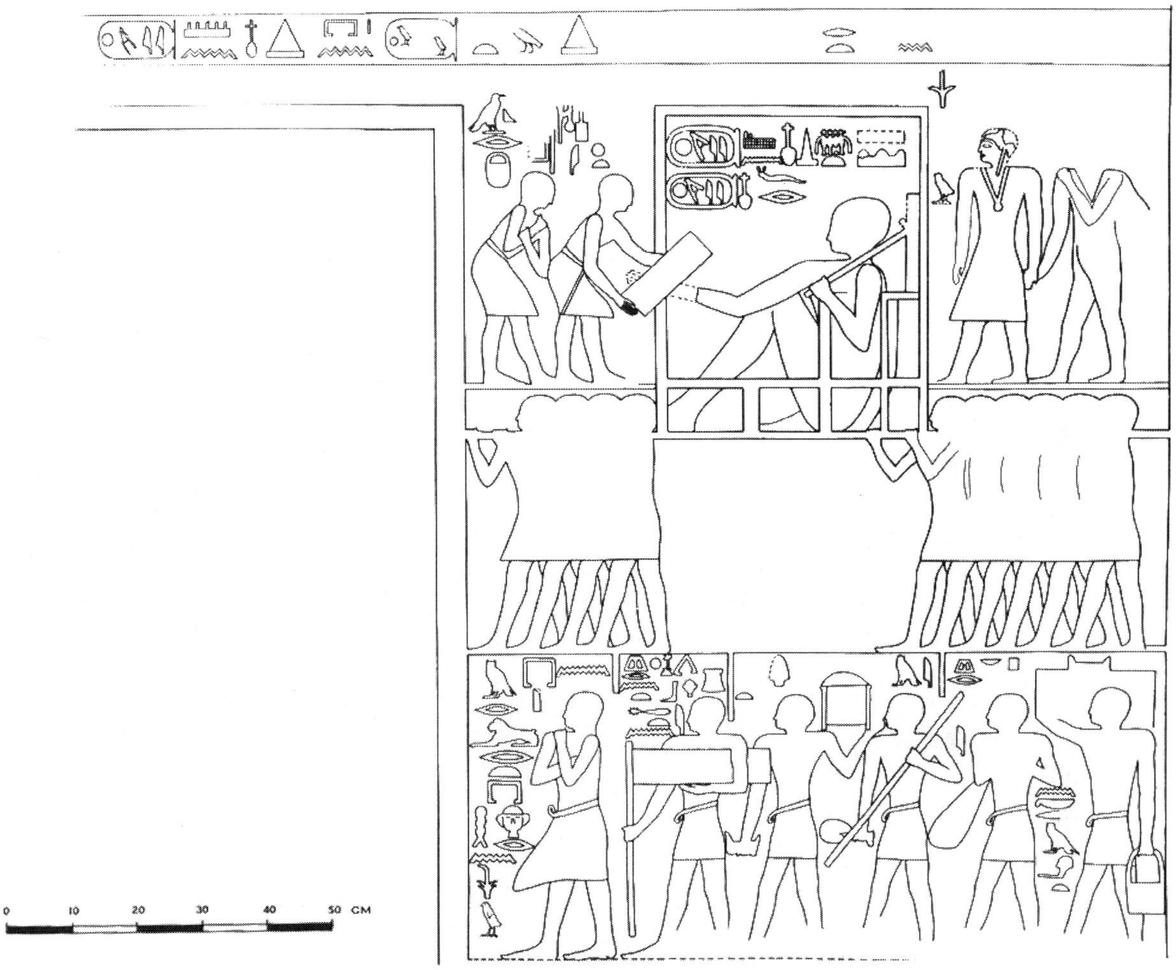

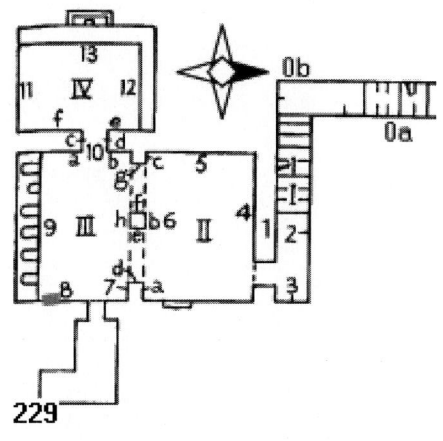

Plan

P & M XXX. Upper Staircase added. Eastern wall 8, in room III .

SV Number	73	**LMP Number**	59
Tomb Owner	Rashepses		
Literature ref.	Lepsius, *Denkmäler aus Ägypten und Äthiopien.* LDII, plate 64 (a).		

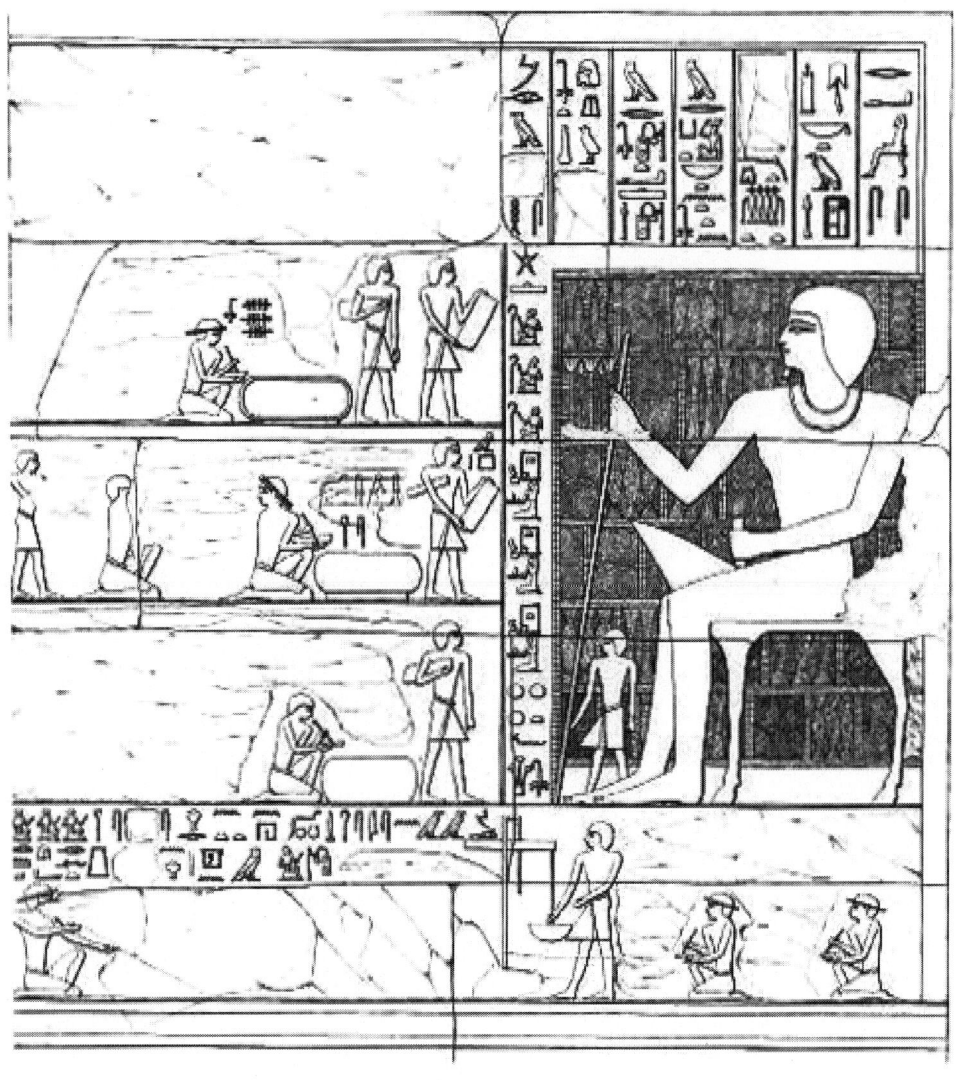

Plan

P & M XLIX., Southern wall 10-11, in room IV.

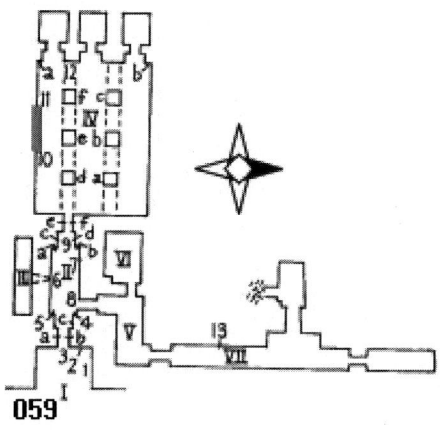

059

SV Number	74	**LMP Number**	027a
Tomb Owner	Seneb		
Literature ref.	Junker, *Giza.* Vol. 5, fig. 22.		

Plan

P & M XXVII. West. Topmost part of Northern Inner Jamb of false door.

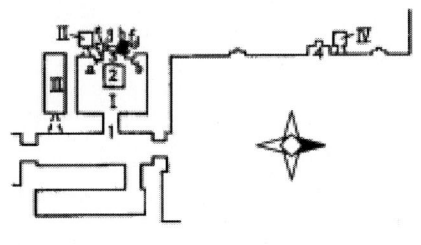

027a

SV Number   75   **LMP Number**   099

Tomb Owner   Sekhemka

Literature ref.   Steindorff, *Die Kunst der Ägypter*. Plate 196.

Plan

Lepsius, *Denkmäler II*. Northern wall 1c, in room I (entrance to chapel).

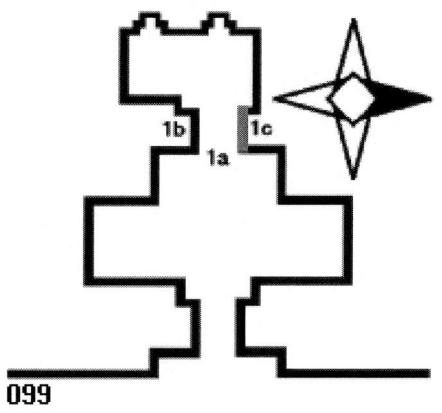

SV Number	76	**LMP Number**	116
Tomb Owner	Senedjemib. Mehi		
Literature ref.	Brovarski, *The Senedjemib Complex.* part I. Fig. 118b.		

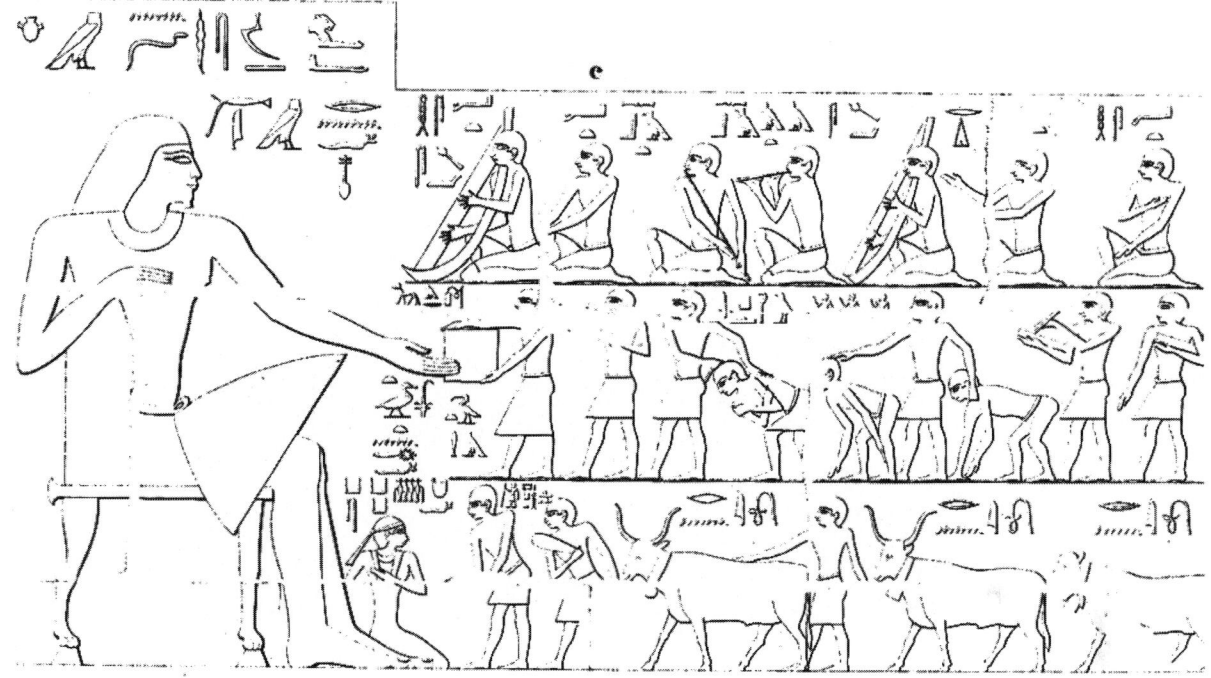

Plan   *P & M XXVI*. Southern wall, in room I.

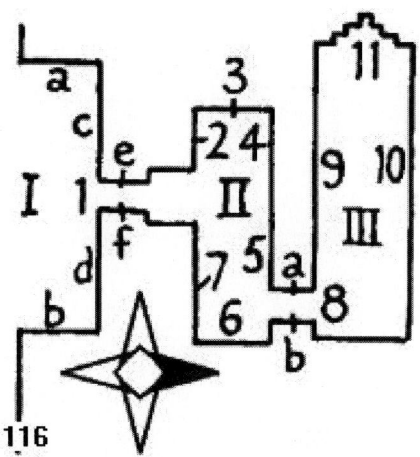

SV Number	77	**LMP Number**	089
Tomb Owner	Seshathetep. Heti		
Literature ref.	Junker, *Giza.* Vol. 2, fig. 29.		

Plan

P & M XXVIII. Northern wall 8, in room I.

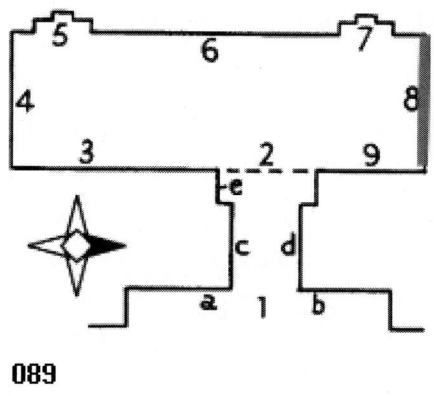

089

SV Number	78	LMP Number	147
Tomb Owner	Shetwi		
Literature ref.	Junker, *Giza.* Vol. 9, fig. 86.		

Plan *P & M XXXIV*. Fragment of Eastern wall 2.

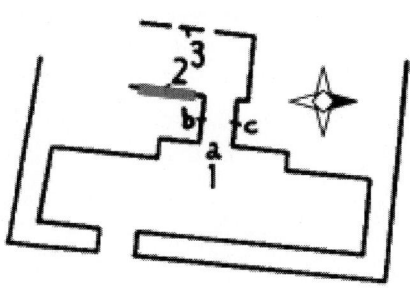

147

SV Number	79	**LMP Number** 092
Tomb Owner	Tjenti	
Literature ref.	Lepsius, *Denkmäler aus Ägypten und Äthiopien.* LDII, plate 30.	

Plan

P & M XXVIII. West. Between the false doors.

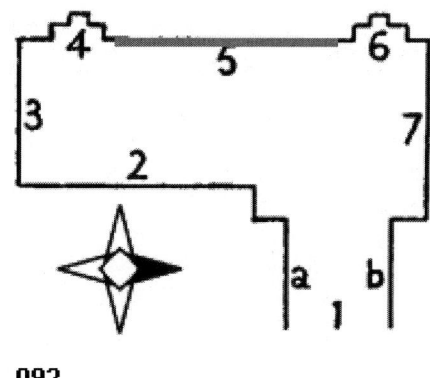

092

SV Number	80A	**LMP Number**	49
Tomb Owner	Ty		
Literature ref.	Wild et. al., *Le Tombeau de Ti: La Chapelle.* Vol. 3, fig. CLXVll.		

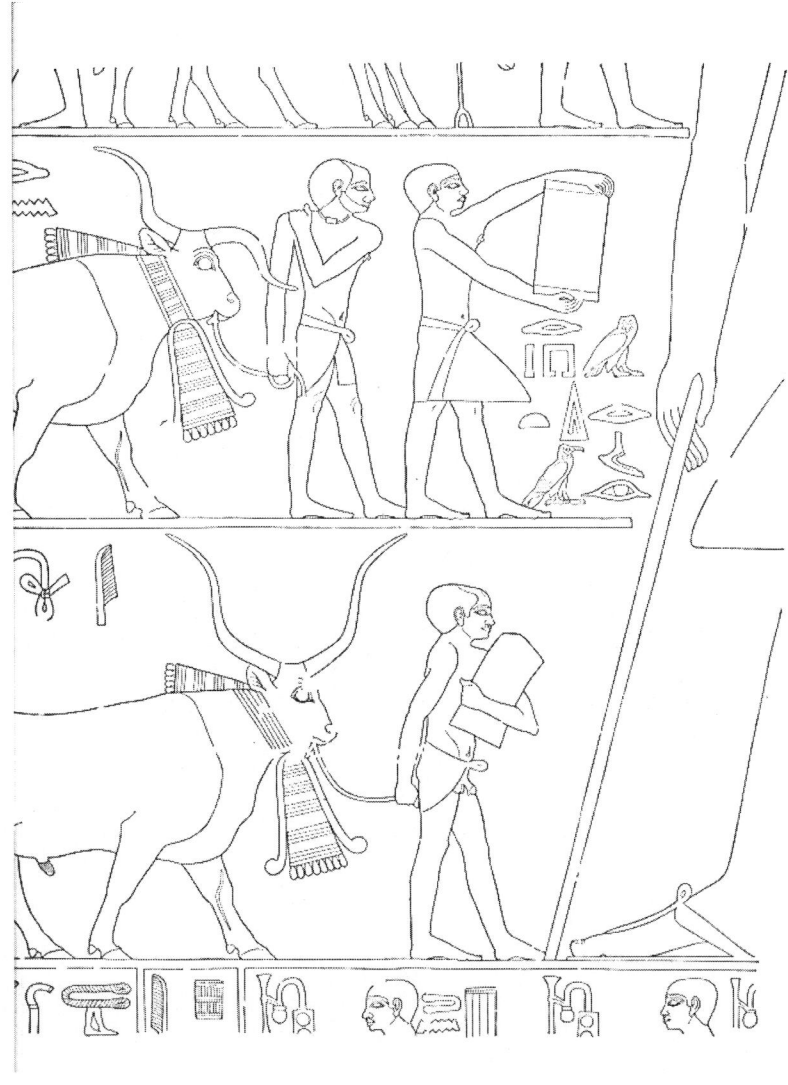

Plan

P & M XLVIII. Southern wall 36-38 of offering chapel, in room Vl.

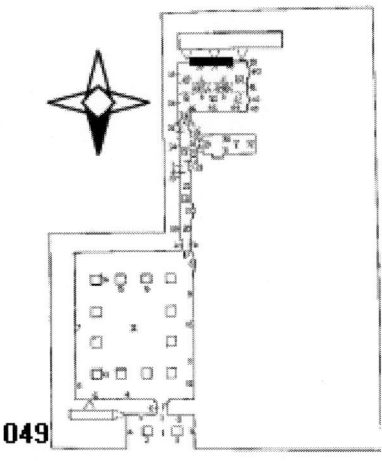

049

SV Number	80B	**LMP Number**	49
Tomb Owner	Ty		
Literature ref.	Steindorff, *Das Grab des Ti.* Fig. 56.		

Plan

P & M XLVIII. Southern wall 23a, (entrance to Room IV).

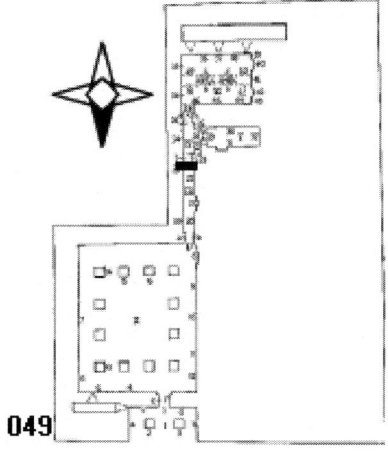

049

264

SV Number 81 **LMP Number** 088

Tomb Owner Whemka

Literature ref. Kayser, *Die Mastaba des Uhemka*, 36-37. (No figure numbering)

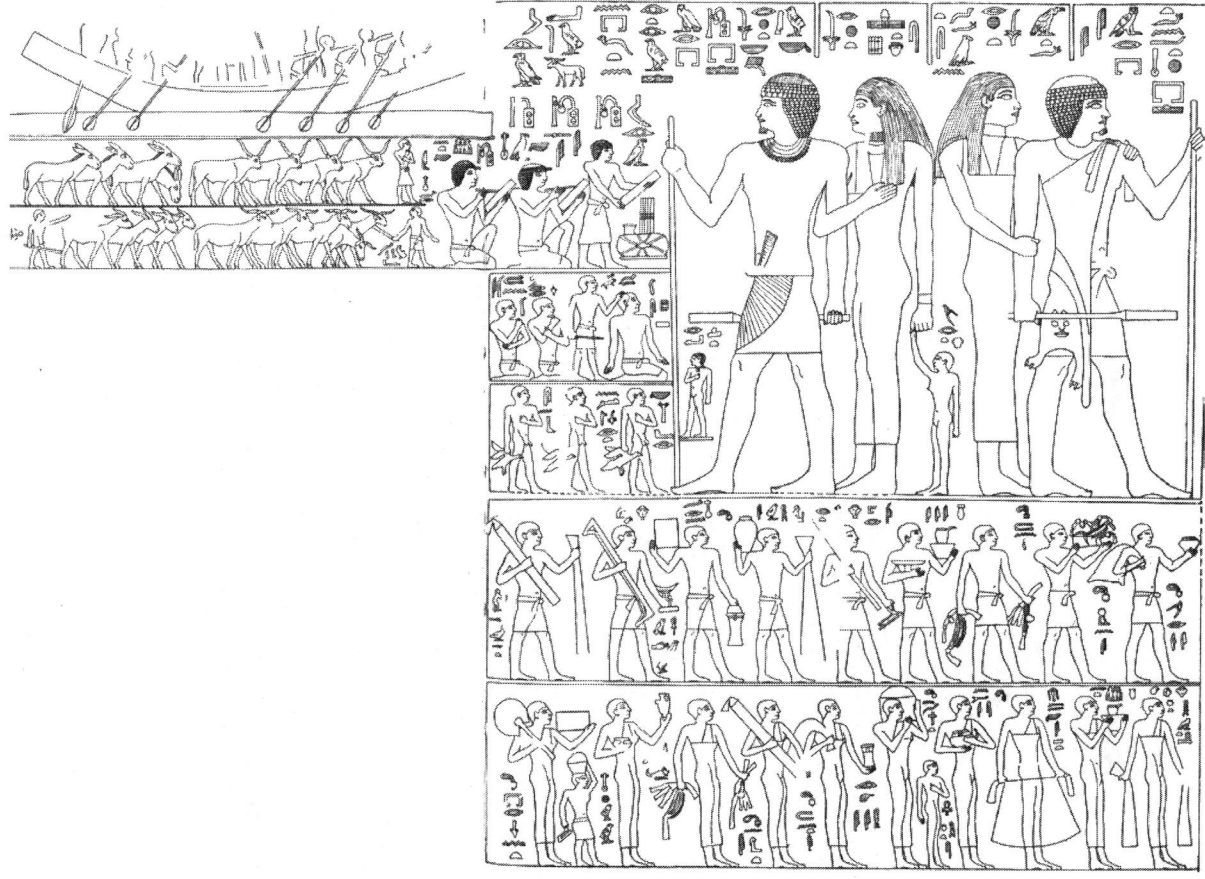

Plan *P & M XXVII*. Eastern wall 3.

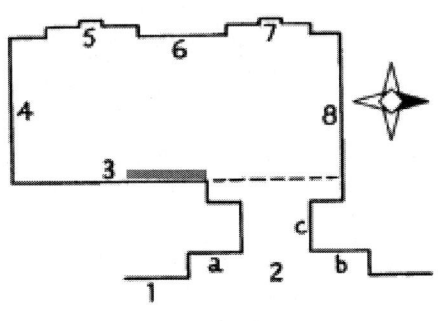

088

SV Number	82	**LMP Number**	190
Tomb Owner	Ankhmahor		
Literature ref.	Kanawati, *The Teti Cemetery at Saqqara: the Tomb of Ankhmahor*. Vol. 2, plate 56.		

Plan

P & M. L. Southern wall, in room VI.

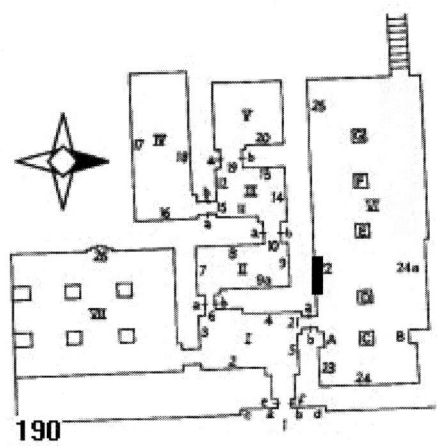

190

SV Number   83   **LMP Number**   230

Tomb Owner   Idu (A)

Literature ref.   Simpson, *The Mastabas of Qar and Idu*. Part of fig. 35.

Plan   *P & M XXX*. North wall of right entrance.

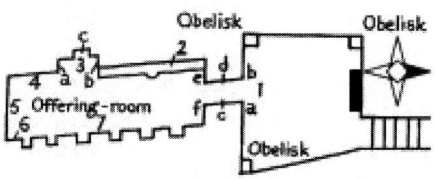

230

SV Number	84	**LMP Number**	182a
Tomb Owner	Mereruka (E)		
Literature ref.	Duell et al., *The Mastaba of Mereruka.* Vol. 1, part of plate 130.		

Plan

P & M. LVI. Southern wall in room XIII.

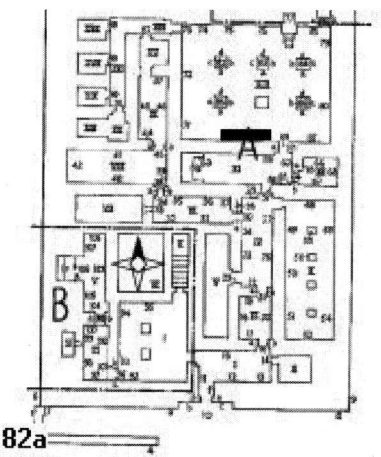

182a

Glossary

A

Abydos	Cult centre for Osiris, a town located ca. 100 kilometers from modern Luxor in Upper Egypt
Amun	Principal god of the Theban triad, dominant through much of the NK
Anubis	Jackal god of the dead and guardian o the netherworld
Apotropaic	Able to ward off evil
Archaism	A term used to describe incidents, where a previously established artistic model including an intangible cultural artifact, is re-introduced at a later time without a tradition; comparable to the word 'renaissance' used by French Egyptologists (for a more nuanced approach see Neureiter, *SAK*, 21 (1994): 219-254)

B

BA	A component of the human self often depicted as a bird with a human head that was free to leave the tomb to seek earthly pleasures

C

Caption	A descriptive title to an illustration
Ceremony	An act conducted elaborately in accordance with prescribed religious or social procedures, which serves to reinforce and renew the event
Chaos Theory	The study of unpredictable behaviour in simple systems, which are sensitive dependence on initial conditions
Civilization	To achieve or impart refined manners and improvements especially with regard to the process of social development in a society. From the Latin 'civitas', civilization was a Renaissance formulation in French derived from the verb 'civiliser'
Cognition	Relates to all aspects of conscious and unconscious mental functions
Communication	Refers to the exchange of knowledge, ideas, thoughts, concepts, and emotions among people
Complexity	Refers to phenomena and concepts which defy calculation because they are inherently full of randomness and uncertainty
Corvée	Relates to a conscripted labour force, generally meaning payment of service for benefits obtained
Cosmological	Refers to that branch of philosophy that deals with the character, composition, and workings of the universe
Craftsman	A person skilled in a vocational trade, having mastery over a particular technique or craft, e.g. carpenter, but as opposed to an artist lacking artistry
Cult	Reverential homage rendered to a supernatural being or beings in the belief of some divine or transcendental power. It is therefore holy action requiring sacred space for its performance. The difference between service to the dead and worship of the gods must be distinguished even though cult is generally used in both senses
Culture	The word originally applied to working of the land. After 1700 A.D. it was applied innovatively to society, and, history with its meaning similar to civilization. Definitions abound, and in the context of this study Matsumoto's definition in 'Culture and Psychology' is followed: "a dynamic system of rules, explicit and implicit, established by groups in order to ensure their survival, involving attitude, values, beliefs, norms, and behaviors, shared by a group but harbored differently by each specific unit within the group, communicated across generations, relatively stable but with a potential change across time"

D

Decorum	A set of rules and practices defining in which context and in what form something may be represented pictorially with captions, displayed, and possibly written down. See Baines, *JARCE,* 27 (1990): 1-23.) Extended now to what Baines terms 'lived practice', thus not only implying strict rules. (Baines, *Visual, and Written Culture in Ancient Egypt*: Oxford University Press, 2007.)
Demography	The study of population
Domain	A foundation established to provide income for the mortuary cult
Didactic T	exts that share several characteristics: repetition of certain texts, stock phraseology, and marked reference to student-teacher relationships

E

Early Dynastic	A term applied to the first two dynasties in Egyptian history

Emic	A process of acquiring knowledge by considering what the subjects think and say about their beliefs and intentions: their culture is judged by their own and not our standards. Emic thus refers to the study of a system from within (Lee-Pike 1967, 37)
Emotion	Agitated feelings arising from love, hate, desire, or fear
Entropy	Inevitable, and steady deterioration of a system in society; a mathematical measure of disorderliness
Epithet	A general statement about a person
Etic	A process of acquiring knowledge through observation, which seeks understanding by using categories that are outside of the belief systems and ideologies of the subjects under investigation. Etic thus refers to the study of a system from the outside
Extra-somatic	Deposited outside the physical bodies of individual organisms in the sense of psyche, soul, and mind

F

Funerary Rites	The rites of funeral and burial

G

Generic	Those characteristics which can be applied to a whole group

H

Historiography	The study of the techniques of historical research
Heliopolis	A town, which was the cult centre for the sun god
Horus	Falcon headed god embodiment of living kingship and the reigning king

I

Iconography	A system of symbols and motifs used in a consistent way, expressing notions of religion and ideology
Iconology	A study of the 'logos' (science) of 'icons' (images)
Ideology	A system of values and ideas that promote social behaviour benefitting some classes or interest groups more than others and thus legitimizes the sectional interests of hegemonic groups Idiom Constitutional linguistic unit, which is not predictable simply by knowing the rules of grammar, and the vocabulary of language. Accordingly, these have to be learned as a whole, and are non-compositional
Individualism	A belief in the value of individuals in opposition to the community, thus valuing it at a higher level
Individuality	A form of intelligent self-assertion
Isis	Mother of Horus and consort to Osiris encompassing maternal love

K

K3	An Egyptian term denoting the life force, which survived the death of a person/gods, and required sustenance in the afterlife. It was seldom depicted and rarely personalized in the Old Kingdom
Khnum	Ram headed creator god

L

Lector priest	Priestly title associated with the recitation of ritual texts
Lower Egypt	The area of Egypt from the Fayum entrance in the south to the Mediterranean Sea; it includes the Memphite region

M

M3ˁt	An Egyptian term denoting truth, justice and good order entailing "the equilibrium of the whole universe, the harmonious co-existence of its elements, and the essential cohesion, indispensable for maintaining the created forms". Poesener, *Dictionary,* (1962), and often personified as the goddess of truth
Mastaba	A term meaning 'bench' in Arabic and the name given to an Old Kingdom tomb with a rectangular superstructure with inwardly sloping walls

Memphite	The capital of Egypt from the beginning of the First Dynasty ca. 20 kilometers upstream of Cairo; used as an adjective, it means that which belongs to the region of Memphis
Mnemonic	Helping or meant to help the memory, as in a mnemonic device
Metonymy	A figure of speech in which the name of one thing is used in place of associated with it, e.g. 'be careful, the ham sandwich has wandering hands'
Mortuary Rites	Reserved for rituals and activities that involve the dead, including the funeral but extending indefinitely beyond it
Motif	By motif in the context of the ancient Egyptian artifact is meant a part of a visually comprehensible reality from an area of daily life, or of abstract ideas
Mourning	Ritual behaviour by individuals or groups of persons, who mourn the dead
Mut	Goddess, consort to Amun at Karnak

N

Nonlinear	Systems in which the variables are not related to one another in strict proportionality
Nome	Indicating a province of Egypt of which there were forty-two. Upper Egypt was divided into 22 nomes, Lower Egypt into 20

O

Objectivism	A concept which has as its basis, the idea that we have access to absolute and undeniable truths about the world
Old Kingdom	Refers to the period between Dynasties 3 to 6 inclusive.
Ontology	Branch of metaphysics dealing with the nature of being and specifically the kinds of abstract entities that can be admitted to a language system
Osiris	God of the dead and king of the netherworld

P

Persona	The outer personality or façade presented to others by an individual
Programme	(Decorative) This is a term which encompasses all motifs and sub-motifs in the iconography
Pluralism	Refers to the coexistence within one society, of a diversity of ideologies, and worldviews
Polysemic	The phenomenon whereby a linguistic unit exhibits multiple and distinct yet related meanings
Pre-dynastic	A term applied to the period of Egyptian prehistory ending with the unification of Egypt ca. 3100 BC

R

Raised relief	A way of decoration whereby the background is cut away, leaving the figures raised above the surrounding surface
Re	The sun god, incorporating the cyclical patterning of the cosmos
Register	In ancient Egyptian art, a series of horizontal strips into which scenes are divided
Relational	The self as defined and experienced through an array of personhood significant relationships with others past and present, living and dead
Ritual	Definitions abound according to the research interest of the scholar. The one given below coincides most with the ideas behind this book:
	"Repetitive acts, performed according to established rules in the accepted belief that they please the higher powers into being benevolent towards the devotee or person on whose behalf these acts are performed" (Turner, *The Great Cultural Traditions*, 1941: 105-107)
	"those conscious and voluntary, repetitious and stylized symbolic bodily actions that are centered on cosmic structures and/or sacred presences". (E. M. Zuesse, 1987:405)
	"rule governed activity of a symbolic character which draws the attention of its participants to objects of thought and feeling which they hold to be of special significance". (S. Lukes, *Political, Ritual and Social Integration*, 1975: 291)

S

Saqqara	OK pyramid area, main non-royal necropolis for Memphis, and principal elite cemetery of the Ramessid period
Sem-priest	A high ranking priestly title linked with Horus, and associated with mortuary rituals

Serdab	An inaccessible room meaning 'cellar' in the superstructure of an elite tomb, where a statu of the tomb-owner was placed so that he could receive the offerings.
Seth	God associated with chaos and disorder; but also positively during the Ramessid period to aspects of royal power
Settlement	A collection of basic living and working structures: their main features being a pooling of shared activities and communal facilities
Sub-motif	Refers to a specific activity in a theme, e.g. the activity of fishing is a theme, whereas the actual type of activity involved in this operation – fishing, e.g. with a hook or a hexagonal net, is a sub-theme
Sui generic	Latin termed meaning of its own accord or spontaneous
Sun-folk	A high status individual with a mythical aspect, associated with Heliopolis
Symbol	"Any structure of signification in which a direct, primary, literal meaning designates, in addition, another meaning which is indirect, secondary, and figurative and which can be apprehended through the first". (Ricoeur, *The Conflict of Interpretations: essays in Hermeneutics*, 1974: 12-13)

T

Thebes	Main city of Upper Egypt (present day Luxor)
Title	An appellation given to a person or family, indicating a specific office, function, or dignity
Two Lands	Designation of Egypt, expressing the dual nature of Upper and Lower Egypt

U

Upper Egypt	The area of Egypt from the Fayum entrance in the north to Elephantine in the south

V

Venerated	Signifies a deceased person who has received a mortuary cult
Vizier	The title given to the head of the administration: the full title is 'vizier, dignitary, he of the curtain'

W

Wab priest	Lower order priest meaning the 'pure one'
Was-sceptre	A scepter with a rounded head which symbolized divine/royal power and dominion
Wepwawet	Jackal god of the desert whose name means 'one who opens the ways'
West	Signifies the necropolis and the next world

Bibliography

Aldred, C. ‚Bild‘ (‚Lebendigkeit‘ eines Bildes). In *Lexikon der Ägyptologie*, vol. 1, edited by W. Helck, E. Otto and W. Westendorf, 793-95. Wiesbaden: Otto Harrassowitz, 1975.

Alexanian, N. Social Dimensions of Old Kingdom Mastaba Architecture. In *Eighth International Congress of Egyptologists*, vol. 2, edited by Z. Hawass and L. P. Brock, 88-96. Cairo, 2003.

———— 'Tomb and Social Status.' In *The Old Kingdom Art and Archaeology*, edited by M. Barta, 1-8. Prague, 2004.

Allen, J. P. *Middle Egyptian. An Introduction to the Language and Culture of Hieroglyphs.* Cambridge: Cambridge University Press, 2000.

Altenmüller, H. ‚Besitz und Eigentum.‘ In *Lexikon der Ägyptologie*, vol. I, edited by W. Helck, E. Otto and W. Westendorf, 732-43. Wiesbaden Otto Harrassowitz, 1975.

———— ‚Bestattungsritual.‘ In *Lexikon der Ägyptologie*, vol. 1, edited by W. Helck, E. Otto and W. Westendorf, 746-65. Wiesbaden: Otto Harrasowitz, 1975.

———— ‚Das Sänftenlied des Alten Reiches.‘ *Bulletin Société d'Égyptologie, Genève*, no. 9-10 (1984-1985): 15-30.

———— *Die Wanddarstellungen im Grab des Mehu in Saqqara, Archäologische Veröffentlichungen 42*. Mainz, 1998.

———— ‚Feste.‘ In *Lexikon der Ägyptologie*, vol. 2, edited by W. Helck, E. Otto and W. Westendorf, 171-91. Wiesbaden: Otto Harrassowitz, 1977.

———— ‚Lebenszeit und Unsterblichkeit in den Darstellungen der Gräber des Alten Reiches.‘ In *5000 Jahre Ägypten: Genese und Permanenz pharaonischer Kunst*, edited by J. Assmann and G. Burkhard, 75-87. Nussloch: IS-Edition, 1983.

———— 'Old Kingdom: Fifth Dynasty.' In *Oxford Encyclopedia of Ancient Egypt*, vol. 2, edited by D. B. Redford, 597-601. Oxford: Oxford University Press, 2001.

———— 'Presenting the *nḏt-ḥr* offerings to the tomb owner.' In *The Old Kingdom Art and Archaeology*, edited by M. Barta, 25-35. Prague: Czech Institute of Egyptology, 2006.

Altenmüller, H., and A. M. Moussa. *Das Grab des Nianchchnum und Chnumhotep, Archäologische Veröffentlichungen 21*. Mainz am Rhein: Philip von Zabern, 1977.

Andrews, C. *Jewellery, 1: From the Earliest Times to the Seventeenth Dynasty*. London: British Museum Publications, 1981.

Andrews, C. A. R. 'Amulets.' In *Oxford Encyclopedia of Ancient Egypt*, vol. 1, edited by D. B. Redford, 75-82. Oxford: Oxford University Press, 2001.

Arnold, D. 'Reinigungsgefässe.' In *Lexikon der Ägyptologie*, vol. 5, edited by W. Helck, E. Otto and W. Westendorf, 213-20. Wiesbaden: Otto Harrassowitz, 1984.

Aruz, J., ed. *Art of the First Cities, The Metropolitan Museum of Art, New York*. New Haven: Yale University Press, 2003.

Assmann, A., J. Assmann, and C. Hardmeier, eds. *Schrift, Tod und Identität: Das Grab als Vorschule der Literatur im Alten Ägypten, Schrift und Gedächtnis: Beiträge zur Archäologie der literarischen Kommunikation*. Munich, 1983.

Assmann, J. In *Der Abschied von den Toten: Trauerrituale im Kulturvergleich*, edited by J. Assmann, F. Maciejewski and A. Michaels, 307-25. Göttingen: Wallstein Verlag, 2005.

———— ‚Denkformen des Endes der Altägyptischen Welt.‘ In *Das Ende: Figuren einer Denkform*, edited by K. Stierle and R. Warning, 1-31. München: Wilhelm Funk Verlag, 1996.

_____ ‚Die Inschrift auf dem äusseren Sarkophagdeckel des Merenptah.‘ *Mitteilungen des Deutschen Archäologischen Instituts Abteilung Kairo*, 28 (1972): 47-73.

———— *Ma'at: Gerechtigkeit und Unsterblichkeit im Alten Ägypten*. Munich: Verlag C. H. Beck, 1990.

_____ *Theologie und Frömmigkeit einer frühen Hochkultur.* Stuttgart: Verlag W. Kohlhammer, 1984.

_____ *Das kulturelle Gedächtnis.* Verlag C. H. Beck München, 1992.

———— *Moses the Egyptian: The Memory of Egypt in Western Monotheism*. Cambridge: Harvard University Press, 1997.

———— ‚Persönlichkeitsbegriff und -bewusstsein.‘ In *Lexikon der Ägyptologie*, vol. 4, edited by W. Helck, E. Otto and W. Westendorf, 963-78. Wiesbaden: Otto Harrassowitz, 1982.

————. 'Preservation and Presentation of Self in Ancient Egyptian Portraiture.' In *Studies in Honor of W. K. Simpson*, edited by Peter Der Manuelian, 55-81. Massachusetts: Henry N. Sawer Company, Charlestown, 1996.

———— *Religion and Cultural memory*. Translated by R. Livingstone. Stanford: Stanford University Press, 2006.

———— *The Search for God in Ancient Egypt*. Translated by D. Lorton. Ithaca: Cornell University Press, 2001.

———— ‚Sepulkrale Selbstthematisierung im Alten Ägypten.‘ In *Selbstthematisierung und Selbstzeugnis: Bekenntnis und Geständnis*, edited by A. Hahn and V. Kapp, 208-32. Frankfurt: Suhrkamp, 1987.

———— 'State and Religion in the New Kingdom.' In *Religion and philosophy in ancient Egypt*, edited by

W. K. Simpson, 55-88. New Haven: Yale University, 1989.

——— *Stein und Zeit: Mensch und Gesellschaft im alten Ägypten*. Munich: Wilhelm Fink Verlag, 1991.

——— *Tod und Jenseits im Alten Ägypten*. München: C. H. Beck, 2001.

_____ *Death and Salvation in Ancient Egypt*. Translated by D. Lorton. Ithaca: Cornell University Press, 2005.

——— ,Todesbefallenheit im Alten Ägypten.' In *Tod, Jenseits und Identität*, edited by J. Assmann and R. Trauzettel, 230-51. Freiburg: Verlag Karl Alber, 2002.

_____ *Theologie und Weisheit im alten Ägypten*. München: Wilhelm Funk Verlag, 2005.

——— 'When Justice fails: Jurisdiction and Imprecation in Ancient Egypt and the Near East.' *Journal of Egyptian Archaeology* 78 (1992): 149-62.

_____ Assmann, J., and T. H. Macho. *Der Tod als Thema der Kulturtheorie: Todesbilder und Totenriten im alten Ägypten*. 1. Aufl., Erstausg. ed, *Erbschaft unserer Zeit Bd. 7*. Frankfurt am Main: Suhrkamp, 2000.

Averill, J. R. 'Grief: its nature and significance.' In *Psychological Bulletin* 70 (1968): 721-48.

Badawy, A. *The Tomb of Nyhetep-ptah at Giza and the Tomb of Ankhmahor at Saqqara*. Berkeley: University of California Press, 1978.

Baer, K. *Rank and title in the Old Kingdom; the structure of the Egyptian administration in the fifth and sixth dynasties*. Chicago: University of Chicago Press, 1960.

_____ ' The Low Price of Land in Ancient Egypt.' In *Journal for the American Research Centre in Egypt* 1 (1962) : 25-45.

_____ ' An Eleventh Dynasty Farmer's Letters to His Family.' In *Journal of the American Oriental Society* 83 (1963) : 1-19.

Baines, J. 'Ancient Egyptian Concepts and uses of the past: 3rd to 2nd millennium B.C. evidence.' In *Who needs the past? Indigenous Values and Archaeology*, edited by R. Layton, 131-149. London: Unwin Hyman, 1989.

——— 'Communication and Display: the integration of early Egyptian art and writing.' *Antiquity* 63 (1989): 471- 82.

_____ 'Practical Religion and Piety.' In *Journal of Egyptian Archaeology* 73 (1987): 79-98.

——— *Fecundity figures: Egyptian personification and the iconology of a genre*. Warminster: Aris and Phillips, 1985.

_____ 'Literacy, Social Organization, and the Archeological records: the Case of Early Egypt.' In *State and Society. The Development of Social Hierarchy and Political Centralization,* edited by J. Gledhill, B. Bender, and M. T. Larson, 192-214. London: Unwin Hyman, 1988.

——— 'Forerunners of Narrative Biographies.' In *Studies on Ancient Egypt in Honour of H. S. Smith*, edited by A. Leahy and J. Tait, 23-37. London: The Egypt Exploration Society, 1999.

——— 'Interpretations of religion: logic, discourse, rationality.' *Göttinger Miszellen* 76 (1984): 25-54.

——— 'Modelling Sources, Processes, and Locations of Early Mortuary Texts.' In *Textes des Pyramides et Textes des Sarcophages (Bibliothéque d'étude 139)*, edited by S. Bickel and B. Matthieu, 15-41. Cairo: Institut Français d'Archéologie Orientale, 2004.

_____ 'Restricted knowledge, hierarchy, and decorum: modern perceptions and ancient Institutions.' *Journal of the American Research Center in Egypt* 27 (1990): 1-23.

——— 'Society, Morality, and Religious practice.' In *Religion in Ancient Egypt*, edited by B. E. Shafer, 123-200. London: Routledge, 1991.

_____ 'Egyptian Myth and Discourse: Myth, Gods, and the Early Written and Iconological Record.' *Journal of Near Eastern Studies* 50 (1991): 81-105.

——— 'Symbolic roles of canine figures on early monuments.' *Archeo-Nil*, no. 3 (1993): 57-74.

——— 'Temple Symbolism.' *Royal Anthropological Institute Newsletter*, no. 15 (1976): 10-15.

——— 'Temples as symbols, guarantors, and participants in Egyptian civilization.' In *The Temple in Ancient Egypt*, edited by S. Quirke, 216-41. London: British Museum Press, 1997.

——— *Visual and written culture in ancient Egypt*: Oxford University Press, 2007.

Baines, J., and C. J. Eyre. 'Four Notes on Literacy.' *Göttinger Miszellen* 61 (1983): 65-96.

Baines, J., and P. Lacovara. 'Burial and the dead in ancient Egyptian society: respect, formalism, neglect.' *Journal of Social Archeology* (2) (2002): 5- 36.

——— 'Death, the Dead and Burial in Ancient Egyptian Society.' Paper presented at the American Reserach Center in Egypt Meetings, New York 1996.

Baines, J., and N. Yoffee. 'Order, legitimacy and wealth in ancient Egypt and Mesopotamia.' In *The Archaic State: A Comparative Perspective*, edited by G. M. Feinman and J. Marcus, 199-260. Santa Fe: School of American Research Press, 1998.

——— 'Order, legitimacy, and wealth: setting the terms.' In *Order, legitimacy and wealth in ancient states*, edited by J. Richards and M. van Buren, 13-17. Cambridge: Cambridge University Press, 2000.

Bard, K. 'An Analysis of the Predynastic Cemeteries of Nagada and Armant in Terms of Social Differentiation. The Origin of the State in Predynastic Egypt.', Ph.D. Dissertation, University of Toronto, 1987.

——— 'The Egyptian Predynastic: A Review of the Evidence.' *Journal of Field Archaeology*, no. 21/3 (1994): 265-88.

——— *An introduction to the archaeology of ancient Egypt*. Oxford: Blackwell Publishing Ltd., 2008.

Barkan, L. *Nature's work of art: the human body as image of the world*. New Haven: Yale University Press, 1975.

Barocas, C. 'La Décoration des chapelles funéraires égyptiennes.' In *La mort, les morts dans les sociétés anciennes*, edited by G. Gnoli and J. P. Vernant, 429-40. Cambridge, 1982.

Barta, M. *Abusir V: The Cemeteries at Abusir South I*: Czech Institute of Egyptology, 2001.

_____'The Transitional Type of Tomb at Saqqara North and Abusir South.' In *Texte und Denkmäler des Ägyptischen Alten Reiches*, edited by S. J. Seidlmayer, 69-87. Berlin: Achet Verlag, 2005.

Barta, W. *Das Selbsterzeugnis eines altägyptischen Künstlers, Münchner Ägyptologische Studien* (22). Berlin: Verlag Bruno Hessling, 1970.

———— *Die altägyptische Opferliste, Münchner Ägyptologische Studien* (3). Berlin: Verlag Bruno Hessling, 1963.

Barthes, R. 'Theory of the Text.' In *Untying the text: a post-structuralist reader*, edited by R. Young, 31-47. London, 1981.

Barthes, R., and Honoré de Balzac. *S/Z*. 1st American ed. New York: Hill and Wang, 1974.

Baud, M. 'The birth of Biography in Ancient Egypt: Text format and content in the lVth Dynasty.' In *Texte und Denkmäler des Ägyptischen Alten Reiches*, edited by S. J. Seidlmayer, 91-124. Berlin: Achet Verlag, 2005.

_____'La date d'apparition des xnti-s', *Institut Francais d'Archeologie Orientale, Cairo* 96 (1996): 13-49.

Bell, C. *Ritual Theory, Ritual Practice*. Oxford: Oxford University Press., 1992.

Benedict, R. *Patterns of culture*. Boston: Houghton Mifflin, 1989.

Binford, L. 'Mortuary practices: Their Study and Potential.' In *Approaches to the social dimensions of mortuary practices*, edited by J. A. Brown, 6-21, 1971.

Blackman, A. M. *Gods, Priests, and Men: Studies in the Religion of Pharaonic Egypt, Studies in Egyptology*. London: Kegan Paul International, 1998.

_____*The Story of King Kheops and the Magicians: Transcribed from Papyrus Westcar (Berlin Papyrus 3033)*. Kent: J. V. Books, 1988.

Blackman, A. M., and M. R. Apted. *The rock tombs of Meir*. vol. 5. Oxford: The University Press, 1953.

Bloch, M. 'Property and the end of affinity.' In *African Studies Association Studies: 2*, edited by M. Bloch, 5-28. London: Malaby Press, 1975.

Boessneck, J. *Die Tierwelt des alten Ägypten*. Munich: C. H. Beck, 1988.

Bolshakov, A. O. 'The Ideology of the Old Kingdom Portrait.' *Göttinger Miszellen,* 117/118 (1990): 89-142.

———— 'The Old Kingdom Representations of Funeral Procession.' *Göttinger Miszellen*, 121 (1991): 31-54.

Bommas, M. 'The mechanics of social connections between the living and the dead in ancient Egypt'. In *Living through the Dead: Burial and Communication in the Classical World,* edited by M. Carroll and J. Remple, 159-182: Oxford: Oxbow Books, 2011.

Bonhême, M. 'Kingship.' In *Oxford Encyclopedia of Ancient Egypt,* vol. 2, edited by D. B. Redford, 238-44. Oxford: Oxford University Press, 2001.

Bonnet, H. *Die ägyptische Tracht bis zum Ende des Neuen Reiches, Untersuchungen zur Geschichte und Altertumskunde Ägyptens* (2) Leipzig: J. C. Hinrichs, 1917.

———— *Reallexikon der Ägyptischen Religionsgeschichte*. Berlin: Walter de Gruyter and Co., 1952.

Boochs, W. ,Religiöse Strafen.' In *Religion und Philosophie im Alten Ägypten. Festgabe für Philippe Derchain zu seinem 65. Geburtstag am 24. Juli 1991*, edited by U. Verhoeven and E. Graefe., 57-64. Louvain: Peeters, 1991.

Boochs., W. ,Religiöse Strafen.' In *Religion und Philosophie in Alten Ägypten. Festgabe für Philippe Derchain zu seinem 65. Geburtstag am 24. Juli 1991*, edited by U. Verhoeven and E. Graefe., 57-64. Louvain: Peeters, 1991.

Boorn, G. P. F. van den. *The duties of the Vizier: civil administration in the early New Kingdom*. London: Keagan Paul, 1988.

Borchardt, L. *Das Grabdenkmal des Königs Sáhu-re*. Leipzig, 1913.

———— *Denkmäler des Alten Reiches*. Berlin: Reichsdruckerei, 1937.

Boreux, C. Études de nautique égyptienne. Le Caire: Institut Français d'archéologie orientale du Caire, 1925.

Borghouts, J. *Egyptian: An Introduction to the Writing and Language of the Middle Kingdom*. 2 vols. Leiden: Nederlands Instituut voor het Nabije Oosten, 2010.

Borioni, G. C. *Das Ka aus religionswissenschaftlicher Sicht*. Wien: AFRO-PUB, 2005.

Bowlby, J. *Attachment and Loss*. London: The Hogarth Press and Institute of Psychoanalysis, 1980.

Boyd, R., and Richerson, P. J. *Culture and the Evolutionary Process*. Chicago: Chicago University Press, 1985.

Bratman, M. E. *Intention, plans, and practical reason*. Cambridge: Cambridge University Press, 1999.

Breasted, J. H. *Ancient Records of Egypt: Historical Documents*. vol. 1: University of Chicago Press, 1906.

———— *Development of Religion and Thought in Ancient Egypt*. New York: Charles Scribner's Sons, 1912.

_____ *The Dawn of Conscience*. New York: Charles Scribner's Sons, 1934.

Brewer, D. J., and E. Teeter. *Egypt and the Egyptians*. 2nd ed. Cambridge: Cambridge University Press, 2007.

Brinks, J. *Die Entwicklung der königlichen Grabanlagen des Alten Reiches: eine strukturelle und historische Analyse altägyptischer Architektur, Hildesheimer Ägyptologische Beiträge* (10). Hildesheim: Gerstenberg, 1979.

———— ,Mastaba.' In *Lexikon der Ägyptologie,* vol. 3, edited by W. Helck, E. Otto and W. Westendorf, 1214-31. Wiesbaden: Otto Harrassowitz, 1980.

Brovarski, E. *Senedjemib Inti - G2370: Text, Part I, The Senedjemib Complex*: Museum of Fine Arts, Boston, 2001.

———— 'Serdab.' In *Lexikon der Ägyptologie,* vol. 5, edited by W. Helck, E. Otto and W. Westendorf, 874-79. Wiesbaden: Otto Harrassowitz, 1984.

Brovarski, E., P. Der Manuelian, and W. K. Simpson. *The Senedjemib Complex. Part 1, The mastabas of Senedjemib Inti (G2370), Khnumenti (G2374), and Senedjemib Mehi (G2378), Giza mastabas*. Boston, 2001.

Brovarsky, E. 'A Second Style in Egyptian Relief of the Old Kingdom.' In *Egypt and Beyond; Essays presented to Leonard H. Lesko*, edited by S. E. Thompson and P. Der Manuelian, 49-89: Brown University, 2008.

Brunner-Traut, E. ,Die Weisheitslehre des Djedef-Hor.' *Zeitschrift für Ägyptische Sprache und Altertumskunde*, LXXVl (1940): 3-9.

———— ,Lieblingstier.' In *Lexikon der Ägyptologie,* vol. 3, edited by W. Helck, E. Otto and W. Westendorf, cols. 1054-56. Wiesbaden: Otto Harrassowitz, 1980.

Brunner, H. *Die Anlagen der Ägyptischen Felsengräber bis zum Mittleren Reich.* Hamburg: Verlag Augustin, 1936.

—————— *Hieroglyphische Chrestomathie.* Wiesbaden: Harrasowitz, 1965.

Brunton, G. *Matmar: British Museum Expedition to Middle Egypt, 1929-1931.* London: Egypt Exploration Fund, 1948.

————. *Mostagedda and the Tasian Culture, British Expedition to Middle Egypt, First and Second Years, 1928, 1929.* London: Egypt Exploration Fund, 1937.

Bryan, B. M. 'The Disjunction of Text and Image in Egyptian Art.' In *Studies in Honor of William Kelly Simpson*, edited by P. der Manuelian, 161-68. Boston: Museum of Fine Arts, 1996.

Byers, W. *The Blind Spot: Science and the Crisis of Uncertainty*, Princeton University Press, 2011.

Campagno, M. 'Kinship and the emergence of the ancient Egyptian State.' *Bulletin of the Australian Centre for Egyptology* 11 (2000): 35-47.

Capart, P. J. ,Une liste d'amulettes.' *Zeitschrift Ägyptische Sprache und Altertumskunde*, (45) (1908): 14-21.

Carlton, E. *Ideology and Social Order.* London: Routledge and Kegan Paul, 1977.

Case, H., and J. C. Payne. 'Tomb 100: The Decorated Tomb at Hierakonpolis.' *Journal of Egyptian Archaeology* 48 (1962): 10-11.

Cerný, J. *Paper and Books in Ancient Egypt.* London, 1952.

Cherpion, N. *Mastabas et hypogées d'Ancien Empire: la problème de la datation.* Bruxelles, 1989.

Converse, P. The Nature of Belief Systems in Mass Publics. In *Ideology and Discontent*, ed. D. Apter, 206-261. New York: Free Press, 1964.

Crehan, K. *Gramsci, Culture and Anthropology.* London: Pluto Press, 2002.

D'Auria, S. H., P. Lacaovara, and C. H. Roehrig. *Mummies and Magic: the funerary arts of ancient Egypt.* Boston: Museum of Fine Arts, 1988.

Darwin, C. *The Descent of Man,* vol. 1, London: John – Murray, 1871.

Dasen, V. *Dwarfs in Ancient Egypt and Greece*: Clarendon Press, Oxford, 1993.

David, A. R. 'Mummification.' In *The Oxford Encyclopedia of Ancient Egypt,* vol. 2, edited by D. B. Redford, 439-44. Oxford: Oxford University Press, 2001.

David, B. 'Intentionality, Agency and an Archaeology of Choice.' *Cambridge Archaeological Journal* 14, no. 1 (2004): 67-71.

Davies, D. J. *Death, Ritual, and Belief: the rhetoric of funerary rites.* London: Cassell, 1997.

Davies, N. de G. *The rock tombs of Deir el Gebrâwi.* 2 vols. London: Egypt Exploration Fund, 1902.

———— *The Tomb of Rekh-mi-Re at Thebes.* 2 vols. New York: PMMA, 1943.

———— 'Tehuti, Owner of Tomb 110, at Thebes', in *Studies Prsented to F. LL. Griffiths,* edited by S. R. K. Glanville, London: Oxford University Press, 1932.

Davis, W. 'The Earliest Art in the Nile Valley.' In *Origin and Early Development of Food-Producing Cultures in North-Eastern Africa*, edited by L. Krzyzaniak and M. Kobusiewicz, 81-94. Poznan: Polish Academy of Sciences, 1984.

Deetz, J. *In small things forgotten: an archaeology of early American life.* Expanded and rev. Anchor Books ed. New York, 1996.

Derchain, P. 'La perruque et le cristal.' *Studien zur Altägyptischen Kultur*, 2 (1975): 55-74.

Díaz-Andreu, M., S. Lucy, S. Babic, and D. N. Edwards. *The Archaeology of Identity: approaches to gender, age, status, ethnicity and religion.* London Routledge, 2005.

Diodorus. *Diodorus 'On Egypt'.* Translated by E. Murphy. Jefferson: McFarland, 1985.

Dittmar, J. *Blumen und Blumensträusse als Opfergabe im alten Ägypten.* vol. 43, *Münchner Ägyptologische Studien.* Berlin: Verlag Bruno Hessling, 1986.

Dodson, A. *Egyptian Rock-Cut Tombs.* Princes Risborough: Shire, 1991.

Dominicus, B. *Gesten und Gebärden in Darstellungen des Alten und Mittleren Reiches, Studien zur Archäologie und Geschichte Altägyptens.* Heidelberg: Heidelberger Orientverlag, 1994.

Doxey, D. M. 'Names.' In *The Oxford Encyclopedia of Ancient Egypt,* vol. 2, edited by D. B. Redford, 490-92. Oxford: Oxford University Press, 2001.

———— 'Priesthood.' In *The Oxford Encyclopedia of Ancient Egypt,* vol. 3, edited by D. B. Redford, 68-73. Oxford: Oxford University Press, 2001.

Duell, P. *The Mastaba of Mereruka.* 2 vols. Chicago: The University of Chicago Press, 1938.

Duke, J. T. *Issues in Sociological Theory: Another look at the 'Old Masters'.* Lanham, MD: University Press of America, 1983.

Dumont, L. *Homo Hierarchicus: The caste system and its implications.* Translated by M. Sainsbury: Nature of Human Society. London: Weidenfeld and Nicolson, 1970.

Dunand, F, and C. Zivie-Coche. *Gods and Men in Egypt*: *3000 BCE to 395 CE.* Translated by D. Lorton: Ithaca: Cornell University Press, 2004.

Dunham, D. 'The Biographical Inscriptions of Nekhebu in Boston and Cairo.' *Journal of Egyptian Archaeology* 24 (1938): 1-8.

Dunham, D., W. K. Simpson, G. A. Reisner, and W. S. Smith. *The mastaba of Queen Mersyankh III: G7530-7540.* Boston: Museum of Fine Arts, 1974.

DuQuesne, T. *The Jackal Divinities of Egypt: From the Archaic Period to Dynasty X*. London: Darengo Publications, 2005.

Earle, T. *How Chiefs come to Power. The Political Economy in Prehistory*: Stanford University Press, 1997.

Eaton-Krauss, M. 'Fragment of Egyptian Jar Lid.' In *Ebla to Damascus: Art and Archaeology of Ancient Syria*, edited by H. Weiss, 170. Washington: Smithsonian Institution, 1985.

Ebersole, G. L. 'The Function of Ritual Weeping Revisited: Affective Expression and Moral Discourse.' In *History of Religions, 39*, 211-46. New York, 2000.

Eco, U. 'Social Life as a sign system.' In *Structuralism: the Wolfson Lectures 1972*, edited by D. Robey, 57-72. Oxford: Clarendon Press, 1973.

———— *A theory of semiotics*. Bloomington: Indiana University Press, 1975.

Edel, E. *Die Felsengräber der Qubbet el Hawa bei Assuan, 2 Abt: Die althieratischen Topfaufschriften. 1.Bd. Die Topfaufschriften aus den Grabungsjahren 1960-1963 und 1965. 2.Teil: Text*. Wiesbaden: Harrassowitz, 1970.

———— ,Inschriften des Alten Reichs , *Mitteilungen des Instituts für Orientforschung Berlin*, no. I (1953): 327-36.

———— ,Untersuchungen zur Phraseologie der ägyptischen Inschriften des Alten Reiches.' In *Mitteilungen des Deutschen Instituts für Ägyptische Altertumskunde in Kairo*, 31-56. Berlin, 1944.

Eggebrecht, A. *Schlachtungsbräuche im Alten Ägypten und ihre Wiedergabe im Flachbild bis zum Ende des Mittleren Reiches*. Munich: Ludwig-Maximilians Universität, Munich, 1973.

El-Metwally, E. *Entwicklung der Grabdekoration in den Altägyptischen Privatgräbern*. Edited by F. Junge and W. Westendorf. vol. 24, *Göttinger Orientforschung*. Wiesbaden: Otto Harrassowitz, 1992.

Ellsworth, P. C., and K. R. Scherer. 'Appraisal Processes in Emotion.' In Handbook of Affective Sciences, edited by R. J. Davidson, H. Goldsmith, and K. R. Scherer. Oxford: OUP, 2003.

Emberling, G. 'Ethnicity in complex societies.' *Journal of Archaeological Research* 5 (4) (1997): 295-340.

Emery, W. B. *Archaic Egypt*. Harmondsworth, Middlesex: Penguin Books, 1961.

———— *Excavations at Saqqara: Great Tombs of the First Dynasty*. vol. I. Cairo: Government Press, 1949.

———— *A funerary repast in an Egyptian tomb of the Archaic period*. Leiden: Nederlands Instituut voor het Nabije Oosten, 1962.

———— *The tomb of Hemaka, Service des Antiquités de l'Egypté: Excavations at Saqqara*. Cairo: Government Press, Bulâq, 1938.

Emery, W. B., T. G. H. James, and A. Klasens. *Excavations at Saqqara: Great Tombs of the First Dynasty*. Vol. III. London: Egypt Exploration Society, 1958.

Endesfelder, E. ,Formierung der Klassengesellschaft.' In *Probleme der frühen Gesellschafsentwicklung im Alten Ägypten*, edited by J. Hallof, 5-59. Berlin: Humboldt - Universität zu Berlin, 1991.

Englund, G. *Akh, une notion religieuse dans l'Égypte pharaonique*. Uppsala: Boreas 11, 1978.

Épron, L., F. Daumas, G. Goyon, and P. Montet. *Le Tombeau de Ti*. vol. I. Le Caire: L'Institut français d'archéologie orientale, 1939.

Erman, A. *Reden, Rufe, und Lieder auf Gräberbildern des Alten Reiches*. Berlin: Verlag der Akademie der Wissenschaften, 1919.

Erman, A. E. *Life in Ancient Egypt*. Translated by H. M. Tirard. 1971 ed. New York: Dover Publications, Inc., 1971.

Erman, A., H. Grapow, and W. F. Reineke. *Wörterbuch der ägyptischen Sprache*. Unveränderter Nachdruck. ed. 7 vols. Berlin: Academie-Verlag, 1971.

Evans, V. *A glossary of cognitive linguistics*. Edinburgh: Edinburgh University Press, 2007.

Evers, H. G. *Staat aus dem Stein*, vol. 2. Munich: Verlag Bruckmann A.G., 1929.

Eyre, C. J. 'Work and the Organization of Work in the Old Kingdom.' In *Labor in the Ancient Near East*, edited by M. A. Powell, 5-47. New Haven: American Oriental Society, 1987.

F. W. von Bissing. *Die Mastaba des Gem-ni-kai*. vol. 1. Berlin: Verlag von Alexander Duncker, 1905.

Fakhry, A. *The Monuments of Senefru at Dashur II*. Cairo, 1963.

Faulkner, R. O. *The Ancient Egyptian Pyramid Texts*. Oxford: Clarendon Press, 1969.

————*The Ancient Egyptian Coffin Texts*. vol. 1. Warminster: Aris and Phillips Ltd., 1973.

———— 'The Bremner-Rhind Papyrus-IV.' *Journal of Egyptian Archaeology* 24 (1938): 41-53.

———— *A concise dictionary of Middle Egyptian*. Oxford: University Press, 1962.

———— *Ancient Egyptian Book of the Dead*. New York: Barnes and Noble Publishing Inc., 2005.

Fechheimer, H. *Die Plastik der Ägypter*. Berlin: Bruno Cassirer Verlag, 1918.

Fentress, J, and C. Wickham. *Social Memory*. Oxford: Blackwell Publishers, 1992.

Firth, C. M., and B Gunn. *Teti Pyramid Cemetries 1*. Cairo, 1926.

Firth, C. M., J. E. Quibell, and J. P. Lauer. *Excavations at Saqqara: The Step Pyramid*. 2 vols. Le Caire: L'Institut français d'archéologie orientale, 1935.

Fischer, H. 'Notes on Sticks and Staves in ancient Egypt.' *The Metropolitan Museum Journal, New York*, no. 13 (1978): 5-32.

Fischer, H. G. 'A fragment of Late Predynastic Egyptian relief from the Eastern Delta.' *Artibus Asiae* 21 (1958): 67-73.

———— 'A Scribe of the Army of the Fifth Dynasty.' *Journal of Near Eastern Studies* 18 (1959): 233-72.

———— ,Stöcke und Stäbe.' In *Lexikon der Ägyptologie*, vol. 6, edited by W. Helck, E. Otto and W. Westendorf, 49-57. Wiesbaden: O. Harrassowitz, 1986.

———— ,Stuhl.' In *Lexikon der Ägyptologie*, vol. 6, edited by W. Helck, E. Otto and W. Westendorf, 92-99. Wiesbaden: O. Harrassowitz, 1986.

Fitzenreiter, M. ,Grabdekoration und die Interpretation Funerärer Rituale im Alten Reich.' In *Social Aspects of Funerary Culture in the Egyptian Old and Middle Kingdoms*, edited by H. Willems, 67-140. Leuven: Uitgevrij Peeters and Departement Oosterse Studies, 2001.

——— ,Raumkonzept und Bildprogrammen in dekorierten Grabanlagen im Alten Reich.' In *Dekorierte Grabanlagen im Alten Reich*, edited by M. Fitzenreiter and M. Herb., 61-109. London: Golden House Publications, 2006.

_____ *Zum Toteneigentum im Alten Reich*, Berlin: Achet Verlag, 2004.

——— ,Zum Ahnenkult in Ägypten.' *Göttinger Miszellen*, 143 (1994): 51-72.

Fletcher, J. 'Hair.' In *Ancient Egyptian Materials and Technology*, edited by P. T. Nicholson and I. Shaw, 495-501. Cambridge: Cambridge University Press, 2000.

——— 'A Tale of Hair, Wigs and Lice.' *Egyptian Archaeology*, no. 5 (1994): 32-34.

Franke, D. ,Arme und Geringe im Alten Reich Altägyptens.' *Zeitschrift für Ägyptische Sprache und Altertumskunde*, 133 (2006): 104-20.

Frankfort, H. *Ancient Egyptian Religion*: Harper and Row, 1961.

Frankfort, H. A. *Arrest and movement; an essay on space and time in the representational art of the ancient Near East*. New York,: Hacker Art Books, 1972.

Frankfort, H., W. A. Irwin, T. Jacobsen, J. A. Wilson, and H. A. G. Frankfort. *The intellectual adventure of ancient man; an essay on speculative thought in the ancient Near East*. Chicago: The University of Chicago Press, 1946.

Freud, S. *Mourning and Melancholia*. Translated by J. Strachey, *Standard Edition 14*. London: Hogarth Press and the Institute of Psycho-Analysis, 1917.

——— *The standard edition of the complete psychological works of Sigmund Freud*. Edited by J. Strachey. vol. 14. London: Hogarth Press, 1953.

Fritz, U. *Typologie der Mastabagräber des Alten Reiches: strukturelle Analyse eines altägyptischen Grabtyps*. Berlin: Achet, 2004.

Gardiner, A. H. *The Admonitions of an Egyptian Sage: From a Hieratic Papyrus in Leiden*. Leipzig: J. C. Hinrichs'sche Buchhandlung, 1909.

——— *The attitude of the ancient Egyptians to death and the dead*. Cambridge: Cambridge University Press, 1935.

——— *Egyptian Grammar*. 3rd. ed. Oxford: Oxford University Press 1957.

——— 'Hymns to Sobk in a Ramesseum Papyrus.' *Revue d'égyptologie, Paris* 11 (1957): 43-56.

——— 'The Mansion of Life and Master of King's Largess.' *Journal of Egyptian Archaeology* 24 (1938): 83-91.

_____ ' A New Letter to the Dead.' *Journal of Egyptian Archaeology* 16 (1930): 19-22.

——— 'A Unique Funerary Liturgy.' *Journal of Egyptian Archaeology*, 41 (1955): 9-17.

Gardiner, A. H., and K. Sethe. *Egyptian letters to the dead*. London: The Egypt Exploration Society, 1928.

Garnot, J. Sainte Fare. *L'appel aux vivants dans les textes funéraires égyptiens des origines à la fin de l'Ancien Empire*. Le Caire: Impr. de l'Institut français d'archéologie orientale, 1938.

Garstang, J. *Mahâsna and Bêt Khallâf, Egyptian Research Account*. London, 1901.

Gennep, A. van. *The Rites of Passage*. Translated by M. Vicedom and S. Kimball. Chicago: University of Chicago Press, 1960.

Germer, R. 'Problems of Science in Egyptology.' In *Science in Egyptology,* edited by A. R. David, 521-525. Manchester : Manchester University Press, 1986.

Ghoneim, Z. *Horus Sekhemkhet: The Unfinished Step Pyramid at Saqqara*. Vol. 1. Cairo, 1957.

Giddens, A. *Central Problems in Social Theory: Action, Structure and Contradiction in Social Analysis*. London: Macmillan, 1979.

——— *The Constitution of Society: Outline of the Theory of Structuration*. Berkeley: University of California Press, 1984.

——— *Modernity and Self-identity: Self and Society in the Late Modern Age*. Stanford: Stanford University Press, 1991.

Giedion, S. *The Eternal Present: the beginnings of architecture*. Oxford: Oxford University Press, 1964.

Gleick, J. *Chaos: The amazing science of the unpredictable*, London: Minerva, 1996.

Gluckman, M. 'Les Rites de Passage.' In *Essays on the ritual of social relations*, edited by M. Gluckman and C. D. Forde, 1-53. Manchester: Manchester University Press, 1962.

Gnirs, A. 'Die ägyptische Autobiographie.' In *Ancient Egyptian Literature: History and Forms*, edited by A. Loprieno, 191-234. Leiden: E. J. Brill, 1996.

Goebs, K. ,The Cannibal Spell: Continuity and Change in the Pyramid Text and Cofin Text Versions.' In *Textes des Pyramides versus Textes des Sarcophages,* edited by S. Bickel et B. Mathieu, 143-173. *Institut Francais d'Archéologie Orientale* 139 (2004): 143-173.

Goedicke, H. *Die privaten Rechtsinschriften aus dem Alten Reich*. Vienna: Verlag Notring, 1970.

——— ,Ein Verehrer des Weisen Djedefhor aus dem späten Alten Reich.' *Annales du Service des Antiquités de l'Égypte* 55 (1958): 35-55.

——— ,A Fragment of a Biographical Inscription of the Old Kingdom.' *Journal of Egyptian Archaeology* 45 (1959): 8-11.

——— *Königliche Dokumente aus dem Alten Reich*, Ägyptologische Abhandlungen (14). Wiesbaden: Harrassowitz, 1967.

Goldwasser, O. *From Icon to Metaphor: Studies in the Semiotics of the Hieroglyphs, Orbis Biblicus et Orientalis* 142. Fribourg/Switzerland: Universitätspress, 1995.

Gombrich, E. H. *Symbolic Images*. London: Phaidon, 1972.

Goodman, N. *Languages of art: an approach to a theory of symbols*. 2nd ed. Indianapolis: Hackett, 1976.

Goody, J. *Representations and contradictions: ambivalence towards images, theatre, fiction, relics and sexuality*. Oxford: Blackwell Publishers, 1997.

Gordon, A. H. 'The ka as an animating force.' *Journal of the American Research Center in Egypt* 32 (1996): 185-96.

Graebner, W. *Patty's got a gun: Patricia Hearst in 1970s America*. Chicago: University of Chicago Press, 2008.

Habachi, L. *Elephantine IV. The Sanctuary of Heqaib*. 2 vols, *Archäologische Veröffentlichungen (33)*. Mainz am Rhein: Philip von Zabern, 1985.

Hafemann, I. ,Feinde und Ahnen-Briefe an Tote als Mittel der Feindbekämpfung.' In *Feinde und Aufrührer*, edited by H. Felber, 161-72. Leipzig, 2005.

Hahn, A. ,Unendliches Ende.' In *Das Ende: Figuren einer Denkform*, edited by K. Stierle and R. Warning, 155-82. München: Wilhelm Funk Verlag, 1996.

Halbwachs, M. *The Collective Memory*. Translated by F. J and V. Ditter. New York: Harper and Row, 1980.

Hannig, R. *Ägyptisches Wörterbuch I: Altes Reich und Erste Zwischenzeit*. Mainz am Rhein: Philipp von Zabern, 2003.

———— *Die Sprache der Pharaonen: Grosses Handwörterbuch*. vol. 1. Mainz: Philipp von Zabern, 2001.

Harpur, Y., and P. Scremin. *The Chapel of Kagemni*. Reading: Oxford Expedition to Egypt, 2006.

———— *The Chapel of Ptahotep*. Oxford: Oxford Expedition to Egypt, 2008.

Harpur, Y., and P. J. Scremin. *Decoration in Egyptian tombs of the Old Kingdom: studies in orientation and scene content*. London: KPI Ltd., 1987.

———— *The tombs of Nefermaat and Rahotep at Maidum: Discovery, Destruction and Reconstruction*. Cheltenham: Oxford Expedition to Egypt, 2001.

Hart, G. *The Routledge dictionary of Egyptian gods and goddesses*. 2nd ed, *Routledge dictionaries*. London: Routledge, 2005.

Haslauer, E. 'Bestattungsschmuck aus Giza.' In *Jahrbuch der kunsthistorischen Sammlungen in Wien* 87, 9-21, 1991.

Hassan, A. *Stöcke und Stäbe im pharaonischen Ägypten bis zum Ende des Neuen Reiches*, *Münchner Ägyptologische Studien* (33). München Deutscher Kunstverlag, 1976.

Hassan, F. A. 'Primeval Goddess to Divine King: The Mythogenesis of Power in the Early Egyptian State.' In *The Followers of Horus: Studies Dedicated to Michael Allen Hoffman*, edited by R. Friedman and B. Adams, 307-21. Oxford: Oxbow Books, 1992.

Hassan, S. *Excavations at Giza*. vol. IX. Cairo: Government Press Bulâq, 1944.

———— *Excavations at Giza 1930-1931*. vol. II. Cairo: Government Press, Bulâq, 1936.

———— *Excavations at Giza 1933-1934*. vol. V. Cairo: Government Press, Bulâq, 1944.

———— *Excavations at Gîza 1932-1933*. vol. IV. Cairo: Government Press, Bulâq, 1943.

Hawass, Z. 'The Statue of the dwarf Perniakhw, recently discovered at Giza.' *Mitteilungen des Deutsche Archäologischen Instituts Abteilung Kairo*, 47 (1991): 157-62.

Hayes, W. C. *The scepter of Egypt: a background for the study of the Egyptian antiquities in the Metropolitan Museum of Art*. 2 vols. vol. 1. New York: Harper, 1953.

Helck, W. *Altägyptische Aktenkunde des 3. und 2. Jahrtausends v. Chr.*, *Münchner Ägyptologische Studien* (31). Berlin, 1974.

———— ,Die soziale Schichtung des ägyptischen Volkes im 3. und 2. Jahrtausend v. Christus.' *Journal of the Economic and Social History of the Orient*. 2 (1959): 1-36.

———— *Geschichte des Alten Ägypten*. Leiden: E. J. Brill, 1968.

———— ,Ma'at.' In *Lexikon der Ägyptologie*, vol. 3, edited by W. Helck, E. Otto and W. Westendorf, 1110-19. Wiesbaden: Otto Harrasowitz, 1980.

———— ,Papyrus Ramesseum E.' *Studien zur Altägyptischen Kultur*, (9) (1981): 151-66.

———— ,Titel und Titularen.' In *Lexikon der Ägyptologie*, vol. 6, edited by W. Helck, E. Otto and W. Westendorf, 596-601. Wiesbaden: Otto Harrassowitz, 1986.

———— *Untersuchungen zu den Beamtentiteln des Ägyptischen Alten Reiches*, *Ägyptologische Forschungen* (18). Glückstadt: J. J. Augustin, 1954.

———— *Wirtschaftsgeschichte des Alten Ägypten im 3. und 2. Jahrtausend vor Chr.* Leiden/Köln: E. J. Brill, 1975.

———— ,Zur Frage der Entstehung der ägyptischen Literatur.' *Wiener Zeitschrift für die Kunde des Morgenlandes, Wien*, no. 63/64 (1972): 6-26.

Hendrickx, S., and P. Vermeersch. ,Prehistory: From the Paleolithic to the Badarian Culture.' In *The Oxford History of Ancient Egypt*, edited by I. Shaw, 17-44. Oxford: Oxford University Press, 2000.

Hermann, A. ,Zur Anonymität der ägyptischen Kunst.' *Mitteilungen des Deutschen Instituts für Ägyptische Altertumskunde in Kairo* (6) (1936): 150-57.

Herodotus. *The Histories*. Translated by A. de. Selincourt. Edited by J. M. Marincola. London: Penguin Classics, 1954.

Hertz, R. *Death and the Right Hand*. Translated by R. and C. Needham. London: Cohen and West, 1960 (originally published in Année sociologique, 10 [1907].

Hobbes, T. *Leviathan*. Edited by M. Oakeshott. New York: Touchstone, 1997.

Hodder, I. *Reading the past: current approaches to interpretation in archaeology*. 2nd ed. Cambridge: Cambridge University Press, 1991.

Holland, J. H. *Hidden Order: How Adaptation Builds Complexity*, Addison-Wesley Publishing Co., 1995.

The Holy Bible. 21st Century King James Version ed: Deuel Enterprises Inc., 1994.

Homans, P. *Symbolic loss: the ambiguity of mourning and memory at century's end*. Charlottesville: University Press of Virginia, 2000.

Hornung, E. *Conceptions of God in ancient Egypt: the one and the many*. London: Routledge, 1982.

———— *Geschichte als Fest: zwei Vorträge zum Geschichtsbild der frühen Menschheit*. Darmstadt: Wissenschaftliche Buchgesellschaft, 1966.

———— *Ideas into Image*. New York: Timken Publishers, 1992.

———— ,Struktur und Entwicklung der Gräber im Tal der Könige.' *Zeitschrift für Ägyptische Sprache und Altertumskunde* 105 (1978): 59-66.

———— , *Das Totenbuch der Ägypter,* Zurich: Artemis and Winkler Verlag, 1979.

Houlihan, P. F. *The Animal World of the Pharaohs*. London, 1996.

Huntington, R., and P Metcalf. *Celebrations of death: the anthropology of mortuary ritual*. Cambridge: Cambridge University Press, 1979.

I. Shaw, and P. Nicholson. *The British Museum Dictionary of Ancient Egypt*. London: The British Museum Press, 2008.

Ikram, S. *Choice Cuts: Meat Production in Ancient Egypt*. Cambridge: Cambridge University Press, 1995.

———— 'Portions of an Old Kingdom offering list reified.' In *The Old Kingdom Art and Archaeology*, 167-73. Prague: Czech Institute of Egyptology, 2004.

Ions, V. *Egyptian mythology*. Rushden: Newnes Books, 1983.

Iversen, E. 'The Canonical Tradition.' In *The Legacy of Egypt*, edited by J. R. Harris, 55-82. Oxford: Clarendon Press, 1971.

Jakobson, R., and P. Bogatrev. 'Le folklore, forme spécifique de la création.' In *Questions de poétique*, edited by R. Jakobson, 59-72. Paris, 1973.

James, T. G. H. *Pharaoh's people: scenes from life in Imperial Egypt*. London: Bodley Head, 1984.

James, T. G. H., and M. R. Apted. *The Mastaba of Khentika called Ikhekhi*. London: Egypt Exploration Society, 1953.

James, T. G. H., and B. G. Gunn. *The Hekanakhte papers: and other early Middle Kingdom documents*. New York: Metropolitan Museum of Art, 1962.

James, W. *The ceremonial animal: a new portrait of anthropology*. New York: Oxford University Press, 2003.

Jánosi, P. *Die Gräberwelt der Pyramidenzeit*. Mainz am Rhein: Philipp von Zabern, 2006.

———— *Giza in der vierten Dynastie. Die Baugeschichte und Belegung einer Nekropole des Alten Reiches Band I: Die Mastabas der Kernfriedhöfe und die Felsgräber*. Wien: Österreichischen Akademie der Wissenschaften, 2005.

———— ,The tomb of officials: Houses of Eternity.' In *Egyptian Art in the Age of the Pyramids*, edited by J. P. O'Neill, 27-39. New York: Metropolitan Museum of Art, 1999.

Janssen, J. J. 'The Early State in Egypt.' In *The Early State*, edited by H. Claessen and P. Skalnik, 213-14. The Hague, 1978.

Janssen, J.J., and P. W. Pestman. 'Burial and Inheritance in the Community of the Necropolis Workmen at Thebes.' *Journal of the Economic and Social History of the Orient.* 11 (1968): 137-70.

Jéquier, G. *Le monument funéraire de Pepi II*. vol. 2, *Fouilles à Saqqarah*. Le Caire: L'institute Français d'archéologie Orientale, 1936.

Johnson, J. H. 'What's in a Name.' *Lingua Aegyptica* 9 (2001): 143-52.

Jones, D. *A glossary of Ancient Egyptian Nautical Titles and Terms*. London Kegan Paul International 1988.

———— *An Index of Ancient Egyptian Titles, Epithets and Phrases of the Old Kingdom, B A R International Series*. Oxford: Archaeopress, 2000.

Jones, J. 'Towards mummification: new evidence for early developments.' *Egyptian Archaeology* 21 (2002): 5-7.

Jones, S. *The Archaeology of Ethnicity*. London: Routledge, 1997.

Junge, F. ,Versuch zu einer Ästhetik der ägyptischen Kunst.' In *Studien zur ägyptischen Kunstgeschichte*, edited by M. Eaton-Krause and E. Graefe, 1-26. Hildesheim: Gerstenberg Verlag, 1990.

———— ,Vom Sinn der ägyptischen Kunst.' In *5000 Jahre Ägypten : Genese und Permanenz pharaonischer Kunst.*, edited by J. Assmann and G. Burkhard., 43-74. Nussloch: IS-Edition, 1983.

Junker, H. ,Das Lebenswahre Bildnis in der Rundplastik des Alten Reiches.' *Anzeiger der Österreichischen Akademie der Wissenschaften in Wien*, no. 19 (1951): 401-06.

———— ,Die gesellschaftliche Stellung der ägyptischen Künstler im Alten Reich.' *Sitzungsberichte der Akademie der Wissenschaften in Wien*, no. 233/1 (1959): 50-69.

———— *Giza*. vol. 1. Wien: Hölder-Pichler-Tempsky A.G., 1929.

———— *Giza*. vol. 2. Wien: Hölder-Pichler-Tempsky A.G., 1934.

———— *Giza*. vol. 3. Wien: Hölder-Pichler-Tempsky A.G., 1938.

———— *Giza*. vol. 5. Wien: Hölder-Pichler-Tempsky A.G., 1941.

———— *Giza*. vol. 6. Wien: Hölder-Pichler-Tempsky A.G., 1943.

———— *Giza*. vol. 7. Wien: Hölder-Pichler-Tempsky A.G., 1944.

———— *Giza*. vol. 11. Wien: Hölder-Pichler-Tempsky A.G., 1953.

———— *Giza*. vol. 12. Wien: Hölder-Pichler-Tempsky A.G., 1955.

———— ,Phrnfr.' *Zeitschrift für ägyptische Sprache und Altertumskunde* no. 75 (1939): 63-84.

Junod, H. A. *The life of a South African Tribe*. London: Macmillan, 1927.

Jürgens, P., *Grundlinien einer√berlieferungsgeschichte der altägyptischen Sargtexte.* Wiesbaden: O. Harrassowitz, 1995

Kahl, J. *Das System der ägyptischen Hieroglyphenschrift in der 0 - 3. Dynastie, Göttinger Orientforschungen. IV. Reihe.* Wiesbaden: Harrassowitz, 1994.

——— ,*nsw und bit*: Die Anfänge.' In *Zeichen aus dem Sand: Streiflichter aus Ägyptens Geschichte zu Ehren von Günter Dreyer*, edited by E. M. Engel, V. Müller and U. Hartung, 307-51. Wiesbaden: Otto Harrasowitz, 2008.

Kaiser, W. ,Trial and Error.' *Göttinger Miszellen,* 149 (1995): 5-14.

Kampp-Seyfried, F. 'The Theban Necropolis: An Overview of Topography and Tomb Development from the Middle Kingdom to the Ramessid Period.' In *The Theban Necropoils: Past, Prsent and Future*, edited by N. Strudwick and J. H. Taylor, 2-10. London: British Museum Press, 2003.

Kanawati, N. *Governmental Reforms in the Old Kingdom.* Warminster: Aris and Phillips Ltd., 1980.

——— 'The Living and the Dead in Old Kingdom Tomb Scenes.' *Studien zur Altägyptischen Kultur*, 9 (1981): 213-25.

——— *The Rock Tombs of El-Hawawish: the cemetery of Akhmin.* 9 vols. Sydney: The Macquarie Ancient History Association, 1980-1989.

_____ *Deshahsa: The Tombs of Inti, Shedu and Others.* Sydney: The Australian Centre for Egyptology, 1993.

——— *The Teti Cemetery at Saqqara: the Tomb of Ankhmahor.* vol. 2, *The Australian Centre for Egyptology: Reports 9.* Warminster: Aris and Phillips Ltd., 1997.

——— *The Teti Cemetery at Saqqara: the tomb of Hesi.* vol. 5, *The Australian Centre for Egyptology: Reports 14.* Warminster: Aris and Phillips Ltd., 1999.

——— *The Teti Cemetery at Saqqara: The Tomb of Nikauisesi.* vol. 6, *The Australian Centre for Egyptology: Reports 14.* Warminster: Aris and Phillips., 2000.

——— *Tombs at Giza.* vol. 2, *The Australian Centre for Egyptology: Reports 18.* Warminster: Aris and Phillips Ltd., 2002.

——— *The Unis Cemetery at Saqqara: the tombs of Iynefert and Ihy (reused by Idut), The Australian Centre for Egyptology: Reports 19.* Oxford: Aris and Phillips, 2003.

Kaplony, P. *Die Inschriften der ägyptischen Frühzeit.* vol. I, Ägyptologische Abhandlungen. Wiesbaden: O. Harrassowitz, 1963.

——— *Die Inschriften der ägyptischen Frühzeit.* vol. III, Ägyptologische Abhandlungen. Wiesbaden: O. Harrassowitz, 1963.

——— ,Eine neue Weisheitslehre aus dem Alten Reich (*) Zusätze und Nachträge.' *Orientalia* 37 (1968): 339-45.

——— ,Ka.' In *Lexikon der Ägyptologie,* vol. 3, edited by W. Helck, E. Otto and W. Westendorf, 275-82. Wiesbaden: Otto Harrassowitz, 1980.

——— *Kleine Beiträge zu den Inschriften der ägyptischen Frühzeit*, Ägyptologische Abhandlungen (15). Wiesbaden: Harrassowitz, 1966.

——— *Studien zum Grab des Methethi, Monographien der Abegg-Stiftung* (8). Bern: Abegg-Stiftung, 1976.

Karsten, R. *The head-hunters of Western Amazonas: the life and culture of the Jibaro Indians of eastern Ecuador and Peru.* 1st AMS ed. New York: AMS Press, 1979.

Katary, S. L. D. *Land Tenure in the Ramesside Period.* London: Kegan Paul, 1989.

Kees, H. *Totenglauben und Jenseitsvorstellungen der alten Ägypter.* 5th unaltered ed. Berlin: Akademie-Verlag, 1956.

Kemp, B. J. *Ancient Egypt: Anatomy of a Civilization.* 2nd ed. London: Routledge, 2006.

——— 'Photographs of the Decorated Tomb at Hierakonpolis.' *Journal of Egyptian Archaeology* 59 (1973): 36-43.

_____ 'How Religious Were the Ancient Egyptians?' *Cambridge Archaeological Journal* 5, no. 1 (1995): 25-54.

_____ 'Old Kingdom, Middle Kingdom and Second Intermediate Period'. *In Ancient Egypt – A Social History,* Cambridge: Cambridge University Press, 1983.

Kendall, T. 'An unusual Rock-Cut Tomb at Giza.' In *Studies in Ancient Egypt, the Aegean and the Sudan*, edited by W. K. Simpson and W. M. Davis, 104-14. Boston: Metropolitan Museum of Fine Arts 1981.

Keynes, J. M. *The General Theory of Employement, Interest and Money,* Cambridge: Macmillan, 1936.

Kiel, L. D. *Chaos Theory in the Social Sciences.* Ann Arbor: University of Michigan Press, 1996.

Killen, G. *Egyptian Furniture.* Warminster: Aris and Phillips Ltd, 1980.

Kitchen, K. A. *Ramesside Inscriptions: Translated and Annotated Translations.* vol. 3. Oxford: Blackwell Publishers, 2000.

Klebs, L. *Die Reliefs des Alten Reiches.* Heidelberg: Carl Winters 1915.

Kloth, N. ,Beobachtungen zu den biographischen Inschriften des Alten Reiches.' *Studien zur Altägyptischen Kultur*, no. 25 (1998): 189-205.

——— *Die Autobiographischen Inschriften des ägyptischen Alten Reiches.* Hamburg: Helmut Buske Verlag, 2002.

Köhler, E. C. 'Seven Years of Excavations at Helwan in Egypt.' *The Bulletin of the Australian Centre for Egyptology* 15 (2004): 79-88.

——— ,Ursprung einer langen Tradition: Grab und Totenkult in der Frühzeit.' In *Grab und Totenkult im Alten Ägypten.*, edited by H. Guksch, E. Hoffmann and M. Bommas, 11-26. Munich: C. H. Beck, 2003.

Köhler, E. C., and J. Jones. *Helwan II: The Early Dynastic and Old Kingdom Funerary Relief Slabs.* Rahden: Verlag Marie Leidorf GMBH, 2009.

Kripke, S. A. *Naming and Necessity.* Oxford.: Basil Balckwell, 1980.

Kucharek, A. ‚Isis und Nephthys als *drt* - Vögel.‘ *Göttinger Miszellen*, 218 (2008): 57-61.

Kuhlmann, K. P., and W. Schenkel. *Das Grab des Ibi, Obergutsverwalters der Gottesgemahlin des Amun (Thebanisches Grab Nr. 36), Archäologische Veröffentlichungen (15)*. Mainz am Rhein: Philipp von Zabern, 1983.

Kunst, J. ‚De Baard in de koningsikonografie van het Oude Rijk en het Middenrijk (The Beard in royal Iconography in the Old and Middle Kingdom).‘ M. A. thesis, 1995.

Lacau, P., and H. Chevrier. *Une chapelle d'Hatshepsout à Karnak*. vol. I. Le Caire: L'Institut français d'archéologie orientale du Caire, 1977.

Lakoff, G. *Women, Fire and Dangerous Things: What categories reveal about the Mind*. Chicago: University of Chicago Press, 1987.

Lakoff, G., and M. Johnson. *Metaphors we live by*. Chicago: University of Chicago Press, 1980.

Lange, H. O., and H. Schäfer. *Grab-und Denksteine des Mittleren Reichs*. Berlin: Reichsdruckerei, 1902.

Langner, U. *Forschungsarbeiten zur frühen Kultur der Menschheit: Das Alte Ägypten*. Frankfurt am Main: Peter Lang GmbH, 2007.

Lapp, G. *Die Opferformel des Alten Reiches*. Mainz: Philipp von Zabern, 1986.

Latin Dictionary. Edited by C. T. Lewis. Oxford: Clarendon Press, 1980.

Leach, E. *Culture and Communication: the logic by which symbols are connected*. Cambridge: Cambridge University Press, 1976.

Lee-Pike, K. *Language in relation to a unified theory of the structure of human behavior*. 2d, rev. ed, *Janua linguarum. Series maior*. The Hague: Mouton, 1967.

Lefebvre, G. *Historie des grands prêtres d'Amon de Karnak*. Paris, 1929.

Lehner, M. ‚Fractal House of Pharaoh: Ancient Egypt as a Complex Adaptive System, a Trial Formulation.’ In *Dynamics in Human and Primate Societies*, edited by T. A. Kohler and G. J.Gumerman., 275-353. Oxford: Oxford University Press, 2000.

Leitz, C. ‚Die Schlangensprüche in den Pyramidtexten.‘ *Orientalia* 65 (1996): 381-427.

Lemke, Y. G. ‚Die nichtköniglichen Priesterinnen des Alten Reiches (4.-6. Dynastie).‘ Ph.D dissertation, Julius Maximilians Universität Würzburg, 2008.

Lepsius, C. R. *Denkmäler aus Ägypten und Äthiopien*. vol. lll,Tafelwerke Abteilung 02. Berlin: Nicholaische Buchhandlung, 1897.

Lesko, L. ‘Literacy.’ In *Oxford Encyclopedia of Ancient Egypt*, vol. 2, edited by D. B. Redford, 297-99. Oxford: Oxford University Press, 2001.

Lichtheim, M. *Ancient Egyptian Autobiographies Chiefly of the Middle Kingdom: a Study and an Anthology, Orbis Biblicus et Orientalis 84*. Fribourg/Switzerland: Universitätsverlag, 1988.

——— *Ancient Egyptian Literature*. vol. 1: The Old and Middle Kingdoms. Berkeley: University of California Press, 1973.

——— *Ancient Egyptian Literature*. vol. 2: The New Kingdom. Berkeley: University of California Press, 1976.

——— *Ancient Egyptian Literature: A Book of Readings*. vol. 1: The Old and Middle Kingdoms. Berkley: University of California Press, 1975.

Lifton, R. J. *The Future of Immortality and Other Essays for a Nuclear Age*. New York: Basic Books, 1987.

Lloyd, A. B. 'Psychology and Society in the Ancient Egyptian Cult of the Dead.’ In *Religion and Philosophy in Ancient Egypt*, edited by W. K. Simpson, 117-33. New Haven: Yale University, 1989.

Locke, J., G. Berkeley, and D. Hume. *A letter concerning toleration; The second treatise of government; An essay concerning human understanding*. Franklin Center, Pa: Franklin Library, 1984.

Logan, T. 'The Imyt-pr Document: Form, Function, and Significance.’ *Journal of the American Research Center in Egypt*, no. XXXVll (2000): 49-73.

Loprieno, A. *Ancient Egyptian literature: history and forms*. Leiden: E. J. Brill, 1996.

——— ‚Drei Leben nach dem Tod: Wieviele Seelen hatten die alten Ägypter.‘ In *Grab und Totenkult im Alten Ägypten*, edited by H. Guksch, E. Hoffmann and M. Bommas., 200-25. Munich: C. H. Beck, 2003.

——— La Pensée et L'Ècriture, Pour une Analyse Sémiotique de la Culture Ègyptiene. Paris: Cybele, 2001.

——— *Topos und Mimesis, zum Ausländer in der Ägyptischen Literatur*. Wiesbaden: Otto. Harrassowitz, 1988

Lucas, A., and J. R. Harris. *Ancient Egyptian Materials and Industries*. London, 1989.

Lüddeckens, L. ‚Untersuchungen√ber religiösen Gehalt, Sprache und Form der Ägyptischen Totenklagen.‘ *Mitteilungen des Deutschen Instituts für Ägyptische Altertumskunde in Kairo*, 11 (1943): 1-187.

Lukes, S. ‚Political Ritual and Social Integration.‘ *Sociology*, no. 9 (1975): 289-308.

Malek, J., and W. Foreman. *In the Shadow of the Pyramids*. London: Orbis Book, 1986.

Mandal, M. K., and T. Dutta. 'Left handedness: Facts and Figures across Cultures.’ *Psychology and Developing Societies* 13 (2) (2001): 173-91.

Mann, M. *The Sources of Social Power*. Cambridge: Cambridge University Press., 1986.

Manniche, L. 'Reflections on the Banquet Scene.’ In *La Peinture Egyptienne Ancienne: Un Monde de Signes á Préserver*, edited by R.Tefnin, 29-36. Bruxelles: Fondation Égyptologique Reine Élisabeth, 1997.

Manuelian, P. Der. 'Presenting the Scroll.’ In *Studies in Honor of W. K. Simpson*, edited by P. Der Manuelian, 561-88. Boston: Museum of Fine Arts, Boston, 1996.

——— 'The Problem of the Giza Slab Stelae.’ In *Stationen: Beiträge zur Kulturgeschichte Ägyptens, Rainer Stadelmann Gewidmet*, edited by H. Guksch and D. Polz, 115-34. Mainz: Philipp von Zabern, 1998.

——— *Slab Stelae of the Giza Necropolis*. New Haven: Pennsylvania-Yale Expedition to Egypt, 2003.

Marcia, J. E. 'The ego identity status approach to ego identity.' In *Ego Identity: A Handbook for psychological research*, edited by J. E. Marcia, 3-21. New York: Springer, 1993.

Mariette, A., and G. Maspero. *Les mastabas de l'ancien empire*. Hildesheim: G. Olms (Reprint of 1898 ed. published by F. Vieweg, Paris), 1898.

Marrais, E. de, L. J. Castillo, and T. Earle. 'Ideology, materialisation and power strategies.' *Current Anthropology* 37 (1) (1996): 15-31.

Martin-Pardey, E. ‚Das ‚Haus des Königs' pr-nijswt.' In *Gedenkschrift für Winfried Barta*, edited by D. Kessler and R. Schulz, 269-85. Frankfurt-am-Main: Peter Lang, 1995.

Matsumoto, D. R. *Culture and psychology: people around the world*. 2nd ed. Australia: Wadsworth Thomson Learning, 2000.

Mauss, M. *Sociology and Psychology*. Translated by B. Brewster. London: Routledge and Keagan, 1979.

McCreesh, N. C., Gize, A. P. and David, A. R. 'Ancient Egyptian Hair gel: New insight into ancient Egyptian mummification procedures'. In *Journal of Archaeological Science*, internet ref. doi:10.1016/j.jas.2011.08.004

Melas, E. M. 'Etics, emics and empathy in archaeological theory.' In *The Meaning of Things: material culture and symbolic expression*, edited by I. Hodder, 138-42. London: Unwin Hyman Ltd, 1989.

Mendelsohn, E. *The English Auden*. London: Faber, 1977.

Merquior, J. G. *The Veil and the Mask: Essays on Culture and Ideology*. London: Routledge and Kegan Paul, 1979.

Meskell, L. 'The Egyptian Ways of Death.' In *Social Memory: Identity and Death: Anthropological Perspectives on Mortuary Rituals* edited by M. S. Chesson, 27-40. New Haven, 2001.

Mesoudi, A. *CulturalEvolution: How Darwinian Theory Can Explain Human Culture and Synthesize the Social Sciences*. Chicago: University of Chicago Press, 2011.

Midant-Reynes, B. *The Prehistory of Egypt: From the First Egyptians to the First Pharaohs*. Translated by I. Shaw. Oxford: Blackwell 1992.

Mills, B. J. , and W. H. Walker, eds. *Memory Work: Archaeologies of Material Practices*. Santa Fe: School for Advanced Research Press, 2008.

Mitchell, W. J. T. *Iconology: image, text, ideology*. Chicago: University of Chicago Press, 1986.

Mohr, H. T. *The Mastaba of Hetep-Her-Akhti: Study of an Egyptian tomb chapel*. Leiden: E. J. Brill, 1943.

Mond, R., and O. H. Myers. *Cemeteries of Armant I*. London: The Egypt Exploration Society 1937.

Montet, P. *Eternal Egypt*. New York: New American Library, 1964.

———— *Les scènes de la vie privée dans les tombeaux égyptiens de l'Ancien Empire*. Strasbourg Librairie Istra, 1925.

Morschauser, S. *Threat Formulae in Ancient Egypt*. Halgo Inc, 1991.

Morenz, L. *Sinn und Spiel der Zeichen*. Böhlau Verlag, 2008.

Morenz, S. Ägyptische Religion. Stuttgart: W. Kohlhammer Verlag, 1960.

———— *Egyptian Religion*. Translated by A. E. Keep. Ithaca: Cornell University Press, 1973.

Mrsich, T. Q. ‚Ein Beitrag zum Hieroglyphischen Denken.' *Studien zur Altägyptischen Kultur*, no. 6 (1978): 107-29.

Mueller, J. R., K. D. Sakenfeld, and M. J. Suggs. *The Oxford study Bible: revised English Bible with the Apocrypha*. New York: Oxford University Press, 1992.

Müller-Wollermann, R. *Krisenfaktoren im Ägyptischen Staat des ausgehenden Alten Reichs Eberhard-Karls Universität Tübingen (Thesis)*. Tübingen, 1986.

Müller, M. ‚Studien zur Ägyptischen Kunstgeschichte.' In *Hildesheimer Ägyptologische Beiträge* (29). edited by M. Eaton-Krauss and E. Graefe, 39-56, 1990.

Munro, P. *Der Unas-Friedhof Nord-West: Das Doppelgrab der Königinnen Nebet und Khenut*. vol. 1. Mainz am Rhein: Philipp von Zabern, 1993.

Münster, M. *Untersuchungen zur Göttin Isis; vom Alten Reich bis zum Ende des Neuen Reiches. Mit hieroglyphischem Textanhang, Münchener Ägyptologische Studien* (11). Berlin: Verlag Bruno Hessling, 1968.

Murray, M. A. *Saqqara Mastabas*. 2 vols. vol. 1, *Egyptian Research Account: Tenth Year 1904*. London, 1989.

Myśliwiec, K., and K. Kuraszkiewicz. *Saqqara 1: The Tomb of Merefnebef*. Warsaw: Editions Neriton, 2004.

Newberry, P. E. *Beni Hasan*. vol. I. London: K. Paul, Trench, Trübner and Co., 1893.

Newberry, P. E., G. W. Fraser, and F. L. Griffith. *El Bersheh*. vol. 1. London: Egypt Exploration Fund, 1893.

Nicholson, P. T., and I. Shaw. *Ancient Egyptian Materials and Technology*. Cambridge: Cambridge University Press, 2000.

Nielson, A. E. In *Memory Work: Archaeologies of Material Practices*, edited by B. J. Mills and W. H. Walker, 207-31: Santa Fe: School for Advanced Research, 2008.

Nordh, K. *Aspects of Ancient Egyptian Curses and Blessings*. Uppsala: Acta Universitatis Upsaliensis, 1996.

Nunberg, G. 'The non-uniqueness of semantic solutions: Polysemy.' *Linguistics and Philosophy* 3 (1979): 143-84.

Nuzzolo, M. 'The 'Reserve Heads': some remarks on their function and meaning. ' In *Old Kingdom New Perspectives,* edited by N. and H. Strudwick, 200-215. Oxford: Oxbow Books, 2011.

O'Connor, D., and D. P. Silverman. *Ancient Egyptian kingship, Probleme der Ägyptologie* (9). Leiden: E. J. Brill, 1995.

O'Donoghue, M. 'The 'Letters to the Dead' and Ancient Egyptian Religion.' *Bulletin of the Australian Centre for Egyptology* 10 (1999): 87-104.

O'Shea, J. M. *Mortuary Variability*. Florida: Academic Press, Inc., 1984.

Obsomer, C. *Les Campagnes de Sésostris dans Hérodote: Essai d'interprétation du texte grec a la lumière des réalités égyptiennes*. Bruxelles: Connaissance de l'Egypte ancienne, 1989.

Ockinga, B. G., and H. Brunner. *A concise grammar of Middle Egyptian: an outline of Middle Egyptian grammar*. Mainz Philipp von Zabern, 2005.

Otto, E. *Das ägyptische Mundöffnungsritual*. vol. 2, Ägyptologische Abhandlungen 3. Wiesbaden: Otto Harrassowitz, 1960.

——— *Die biographischen Inschriften der ägyptischen Spätzeit, Probleme der Ägyptologie (2)*. Leiden: E. J. Brill, 1954.

The Oxford Pocket Dictionary of Current English. Oxford: Oxford University Press, 2009.

Palmenatz, J. *Ideology*. London: Macmillan, 1971.

Park, T. K. 'Early Trends toward Class Stratification: Chaos, Common Property and Flood Recession Agriculture.' *American Anthropologist* 94 (1992): 90-117.

Parkinson, R. B. *Poetry and Culture in the Middle Kingdom: A Dark Side to Perfection*. London: Continuum, 2002.

——— *Reading Ancient Egyptian Poetry*. Oxford: Wiley-Blackwell, 2009.

——— 'The Teaching of Khety.' In *The Tale of Sinuhe and other Ancient Egyptian Poems*, 275-79. Oxford: Clarendon Press, 1997.

——— *Voices from Ancient Egypt: An Anthology of Middle Kingdom Writings*. London: British Museum Press, 1991.

Payne, J. C. *Catalogue of the Predynastic Egyptian collection in the Ashmolean Museum*. Oxford: Oxford University Press, 1993.

Peden, A. J. *The Reign of Ramses IV*. Warminster: Aris and Phillips Ltd, 1994.

———. *Egyptian Historical Inscriptions of the Twentieth Dynasty*. Jonsered: Paul Åströms förlag, 1994.

Peirce, C. S *Collected Papers*. Cambridge: Harvard University Press, 1931.

Perepelkin, J. J. *Privateigentum in der Vorstellung der Ägypter des Alten Reichs*. Translated by R. Müller-Wollermann. Tübingen: Dissertations Druck Darmstadt, 1986.

Petrie, W. M. F. *Diospolis Parva: The Cemeteries of Abadiyeh and Hu*. London: Egypt Exploration Fund 24, 1901.

——— *Medum*. London: David Nutt, Strand., 1892.

——— *Tarkhan II*. London: Bernard Quaritch, 1914.

Petrie, W. M. F., and F. Ll. Griffith. *The Royal Tombs of the Earliest Dynasties, Part II*. London: Kegan Paul 1901.

——— *The Royal Tombs of The First Dynasty, Part I*. London: Kegan Paul, 1900.

Petrie, W. M. F., and J. E. Quibell. *Naqada and Ballas*. London: British School of Egyptian Archaeology Publications, 1896.

Petrie, W. M. F., G. A. Wainwright, and A. H. Gardiner. *Tarkhan 1 and Memphis V*. London: British School of Archaeology in Egypt and Egyptian Research Account, Publication 33., 1913.

Piacentini, P. 'Scribes.' In *Oxford Encyclopedia of Ancient Egypt*, vol. 3, edited by D. B. Redford, 187-91. Oxford: Oxford University Press, 2001.

Pieke, G. ,Der Grabherr und die Lotosblume.' In *The Old Kingdom Art and Archaeology* edited by M. Barta, 259-80. Prague: Czech Institute of Egyptology, 2006.

Peirce, C. S. 'The icon, index, and symbol.' In *Collected Papers of Charles Sanders Peirce*, edited by C. Hartshorne and P. Weiss, 156-73. Cambridge: Harvard University Press, 1960.

Platvoet, J. G., and K. van der Toorn. *Pluralism and Identity: studies in ritual behaviour*. Leiden: E. J. Brill, 1995.

Podella, T. ,Totenrituale und Jenseitsbeschreibungen.' In *Tod, Jenseits und Identität*, edited by J. Assmann and R.Trauzettel, 530-61. München: K. Alber, 2002.

Posener-Kriéger, P. *Les archives du temple funéraire de Néferirkarê-Kakaï (Les papyrus d'Abousir): traduction et commentaire*. Le Caire: Institut français d'archéologie orientale du Caire, 1976.

Posener-Kriéger, P., and J. L. de Cenival. *Hieratic Papyri in the British Museum. Fifth Series. The Abu Sir Papyri*. London: Trustees of the British Museum, 1968.

Preucel, W. R., and A. Bauer. 'Archaeological Pragmatics.' In *Norwegian Archeological Review* (34), 85-96. Oslo: Universitetsforlaget, 2001.

Prigogine, I., and Stengers, I. *La Nouvelle Alliance,* Paris: Gallimard, 1979.

——— *Order Out of Chaos: Man's New Dialogue with Nature,* New York: Bantam Books, 1984.

Quibell, J. E. *Excavations at Saqqara (1912-1914): archaic mastabas*. Le Caire: L'Institut français d'archéologie orientale, 1923.

——— 'Slate palette from Hieraconpolis.' *Zeitschrift für ägyptische Sprache und Altertumskunde*, no. 36 (1898): 81-84.

Quibell, J. E., and F. W. Green. *Hierakonpolis*. vol. 2. London: Egyptian Research Account, Memoir 5, 1902.

Quibell, J. E., F. W. Green, and W. M. F. Petrie. *Hierakonpolis*. vol. 1. London: Egyptian Research Account, Memoir 4, 1900.

Quibell, J. E., W. Spiegelberg, F. Ll Griffith, A. A. Pirie, and R. F. E. Paget. *The Ramesseum and The Tomb of Ptah-hetep*. London: Histories and Mysteries of Man Ltd., 1989.

Quirke, S. *Egyptian Literatue, questions and readings*. London: Golden House Publications, 2004.

Radcliffe-Brown, A. R. *The Andaman Islanders*: Cambridge University Press, 1948.

Radwan, A. ,Der Trauergestus als Datierungsmittel.' *Mitteilungen des Deutschen Archäologischen Instituts Abteilung Kairo*, 30 (1974): 115-29.

Ranke, H. *Die ägyptischen Personennamen*. Vol. I. Glückstadt: J. J. Augustin, 1935.

Rappaport, R. A. 'Ritual, Sanctity and Cybernetics.' *American Anthropologist* (73) (1971): 59-76.

Reisner, G. A. *The development of the Egyptian tomb down to the accession of Cheops*. London: Oxford University Press, 1936.

———— 'The Dog which was honored by the King of Upper and Lower Egypt'. *The Brooklyn Museum Annual, Brooklyn* XXXIV, no. 204 (1936): 96-99.

———— *A History of the Giza Necropolis*. vol. 1. London: Oxford University Press 1942.

Reisner, G. A., A. C. Mace, A. M. Lythgoe, and D. Dunham. *The early dynastic cemeteries of Naga-ed-Dêr*. Leipzig: J. C. Hinrichs, 1908.

Renfrew, C. 'Beyond a subsistence economy.' In *Reconstructing Complex Societies*, edited by C. B. Moore, 69-96. Cambridge, MA., 1974.

Richards, J. E., and M. van Buren. *Order, legitimacy, and wealth in ancient states, New directions in archaeology*. Cambridge: Cambridge University Press, 2000.

Rickal, E. *'Les épithètes dans les autobiographies de particuliers du Nouvel Empire égyptien'*, Ph.D. dissertation, 3 vols. Université de Paris IV-Sorbonne, 2005.

Ricoeur, P. *The Conflict of Interpretations: essays in Hermeneutics.* Edited by D. Ihde. Evanston: North Western University Press, 1974.

Ritner, R. K. 'Magic in the afterlife.' In *Oxford Encyclopedia of Ancient Egypt,* vol. 2, edited by D. B. Redford, 333-36. Oxford: Oxford University Press, 2001.

Robins, G. 'Hair and the Construction of Identity in Ancient Egypt ' *Journal of the American Research Center in Egypt* XXXVI (1999): 55-69.

———— 'Problems in interpreting Egyptian art.' *Discussions in Egyptology* 17 (1990): 45-58.

———— *Proportion and Style in Ancient Egyptian Art.* Austin: University of Texas Press, 1994.

———— *Women in Ancient Egypt*. London: British Museum Press, 1993.

Roe, M. J. 'Chaos and Evolution in Law and Economics', Harvard Law Review 109 (1996): 641-48.

Rosenblatt, P. 'Grief in small societies.' In *Death and Bereavement Across Cultures*, edited by C. Parkes, P. Laungani and B. Young., 27-51. London: Routledge, 1997.

Rössler-Köhler, U. 'Sänfte.' In *Lexikon der Ägyptologie,* vol. 5, edited by W. Helck, E. Otto and W. Westendorf, cols. 334-39. Wiesbaden: Otto Harrassowitz, 1984.

Roth, A. M. *Egyptian phyles in the Old Kingdom: The Evolution of a System of Social Organization, Studies in Ancient Oriental Civilization (48)*. Chicago: The Oriental Institute 1991.

———— 'The Organization and Functioning of the Royal Mortuary Cults of the Old Kingdom in Egypt.' In *The Organization of Power: Aspects of Bureaucracy in the Ancient Near East*, edited by M. Gibson and R. D. Biggs, 133-40. Chicago: University of Chicago, 1987.

———— 'The Organization of Royal Cemeteries at Saqqara.' *Journal of the American Research Center in Egypt* 25 (1988): 203-14.

———— 'The practical economies of tomb building in the Old Kingdom: A visit to the Necropolis in a Carrying Chair.' In *For his Ka: Essays offered in memory of*

Klaus Baer, edited by D. P. Silverman, 227-40. Illinois: The Oriental Institute, 1994.

Russel, L. 'Can Archaeology Recover Past Intentions?' *Cambridge Archaeological Journal* 14, no. 1 (2004): 63-80.

Russell, B. *Authority and the Individual*. New York: Simon and Schuster, 1949.

Russmann, E. R. 'Aspects of Egyptian Art: Archaism.' In *Eternal Egypt: masterworks of ancient art from the British Museum*, 28-45. London: British Museum Press, 2001.

———— 'Aspects of Egyptian Art: Two-dimensional Representation.' In *Eternal Egypt: masterworks of ancient art from the British Museum*, 28-45. London: British Museum Press, 2001.

———— 'The State of Egyptology at the end of the second Millennium: Art ' In *Egyptology at the dawn of the twenty-first century: proceedings of the Eighth International Congress of Egyptologists (2)*, edited by Z. A. Hawass and L. P. Brock, 23-26. Cairo: American University in Cairo Press 2002.

———— *Egyptian Sculpture: Cairo*. First ed. London: British Museum Press, 1989.

Sainte Fare Garnot, J. *L'appel Aux Vivants dans les Textes Funéraires Égyptiens des Origines À la Fin de l'Ancien Empire*. Le Caire: Impr. de l'Institut français d'archéologie orientale, 1938.

Saleh, M., and H. Sourouzian. *The Egyptian Museum Cairo: Official Catalogue*. Mainz, 1987.

Sander-Hansen, C. E. *Der Begriff des Todes bei den Ägyptern*. Copenhagen: Bianco Lunos Bogtrykkeri A/S, 1942.

Saussure, F. de, A Riedlinger, A Sechehaye, and C. Bally. *Course in general linguistics*. LaSalle: Open Court, 1986.

Saxe, A. *Social dimensions of mortuary practices (Dissertation)*: University of Michigan, 1970.

Schäfer, H. ‚Eine unerkannte Trauergebärde und ein angeblicher, Plötzlicher Tod' in Reliefs des Alten Reiches.' *Zeitschrift für ägyptische Sprache und Altertumskunde* 73 (1937): 102-06.

———— *Principles of Egyptian Art*. Translated by J. Baines. Oxford: Clarendon Press, 1974.

Schenkel, W. *Memphis, Herakleopolis, Theben. Die epigraphischen Zeugnisse der 7.-11. Dynastie Ägyptens*. Wiesbaden: Harrassowitz, 1965.

———— *Tübinger Einführung in die klassisch-ägyptische Sprache und Schrift*. Tübingen: Universität Tübingen, 2005.

Schiffer, M. B. ‚Some Relationships between Behavioral and Evolutiponary Archaeologies.' In *American Antiquity* 61, no. 4 (1996): 643-662.

Schlögl, H. A. *Das Alte Ägypten: Geschichte und Kultur von der Frühzeit bis zu Kleopatra*. München: C. H. Beck, 2006.

———— ed. *Le Don du Nil: Art Égyptien dans les Collections Suisses*. Basle, 1978.

Schneider, T. ‚Zur Etymologie der Bezeichnung König von Ober- und Unterägypten.' *Zeitschrift für ägyptische Sprache und Altertumskunde*, no. 120 (1993): 166-81.

Schönpflug, U., and L. Bilz. ‚Introduction to Cultrural Transmission.' In *Cultural Transmission,* edited by U. Schönpflug, 1-8. Cambridge: Cambridge University Press, 2009.

Schulz, R., and M. Seidel, eds. *Egypt: The World of the Pharaohs*. Munich: Könemann, 1998.

Seidl, E. *Einführung in die ägyptische Rechtsgeschichte bis zum Ende des Neuen Reiches*. Glückstadt: J. J. Augustin, 1951.

Seidlmayer, S. J. ‚Die Ikonographie des Todes.' In *Social Aspects of Funerary Culture in the Egyptian Old and Middle Kingdoms*, edited by H. Willems, 203-52. Leuven: Uitgeverij Peeters, 2001.

——— ‚Funerärer Aufwand und soziale Ungleichheit.' *Göttinger Miszellen,* 104 (1988): 25-51.

——— ‚Vom Sterben der Kleinen Leute.' In *Grab und Totenkult im Alten Ägypten*, edited by H. Guksch, E. Hoffmann and M. Bommas, 60-74. Munich: C. H. Beck, 2003.

Sethe, K. *Dramatische Texte zu altägyptischen Mysterienspielen*. Leipzig: J. C. Hinrichs'sche Buchhandlung, 1928.

——— *Urkunden der 18. Dynastie: historische-biographische Urkunden*. Leipzig: J. C. Hinrichs'sche Buchhandlung, 1909.

——— *Urkunden des Alten Reiches*. vol. I. Leipzig: J. C. Hinrichs'sche Buchhandlung, 1933.

Settgast, J. *Untersuchungen zu Altägyptischen Bestattungsdarstellungen*. Hamburg, 1963.

Shakespeare, W. *Macbeth*. edited by A. W. Verity. Cambridge: Cambridge University Press, 1925.

——— *Troilus and Cressida,* edited by D. Bevington, London: Thomson Learning, 2006.

Shotter, J. 'Becoming Someone: Identity and Belonging.' In *Discourse and lifespan identity*, edited by J. F. Nussbaum and N. Coupland, 5-27. London: Sage Publications, 1993.

Silverman, D. P. 'Textual Criticism in the Coffin Texts.' In *Religion and Philosophy in Ancient Egypt*, edited by W. K. Simpson, 29-53. New Haven: Yale University, 1989.

Silverman, D. P. 'The Nature of Egyptian Kingship.' In *Ancient Egyptian Kingship*, edited by D. O'Connor and D. Silverman, 49-92. Leiden: E. J. Brill, 1995.

Simpson, W. K. *The Mastabas of Qar and Idu*. Boston: Museum of Fine Arts, 1976.

——— *Mastabas of the Western Cemetry (Part 1)*. vol. 4, *Giza Mastabas*. Boston: Metropolitan Museum of Fine Arts, Boston., 1980.

——— *The Terrace of the great God at Abydos: the offering chapels of dynasties 12 and 13*. New Haven: Yale University 1974.

——— 'Topographical Notes on Giza Mastabas.' In *Festschrift Elmar Edel*, edited by M. Görg and E. Pusch, 489-96, 1979.

——— ed. *The Literature of Ancient Egypt*. Cairo: American University in Cairo Press, 2003.

Simpson, W. K., and S. E. Chapman. *The offering chapel of Kayemnofret* Boston: Museum of Fine Arts, 1992.

Simpson, W. K., S. E. Chapman, and G. A. Reisner. *The mastabas of Kawab, Khafkhufu I and II: G7110-20, 7130-40, and 7150, and subsidiary mastabas of Street G7100*. Boston: Museum of Fine Arts, 1978.

Smith, M. 'Democratization of the Afterlife.' In *UCLA Encyclopedia of Egyptology*, edited by W. Wendrich, J. Dieleman, E. Frood and J. Baines. Los Angeles, 2009.

Smith, W. S. *A History of Egyptian Sculpture and Painting in the Old Kingdom*. New York: Hacker Art Books, 1978.

Sørenson, J. P. 'Divine Access: The so-called democratization of Egyptian funerary literature as a socio-cultural process.' In *The Religion of the Ancient Egyptians: Cognitive structure and popular expression*, edited by G. Englund, 112-13. Uppsala: Acta Universitatis Upsaliensis BOREAS 20, 1989.

Spalinger, A. 'The Limitations of Formal Ancient Egyptian Religion.' *Journal of Near Eastern Studies* 57 (1998): 241-60.

Sperber, D. *Rethinking Symbolism*. Translated by A. L. Morton. Cambridge: Cambridge University Press, 1974.

Spiegelberg, W. ‚Eine Formel der Grabsteine.' *Zeitschrift fuer ägyptische Sprache und Altertumskunde*, no. 45 (1908): 67-71.

Stadelmann, R. ‚Die Wiedererlebung religiösen Gedankenguts des Alten Reiches in der Architektur des Totentempels Sethos' I. in Qurna.' In *Structure and Significance*, edited by P. Jánosi, 485-91. Vienna: Verlag der Österreichischen Akademie der Wissenschaften, 2005.

Staehelin, E. *Untersuchungen zur ägyptischen Tracht im Alten Reich, Münchner Ägyptologische Studien* (8). Berlin: Verlag Bruno Hessling, 1966.

Steindorff, G. *Das Grab des Ti*. Leipzig: J.C. Hinrichs'sche Buchhandlung, 1913.

Steindorff, G. *Die Kunst der Ägypter*: Im Insel-Verlag zu Leipzig, 1928.

Stevenson-Smith, W. *A History of Egyptian Sculpture and Painting in the Old Kingdom*. London: Oxford University Press, 1946.

Stroebe, W., and M. Stroebe. *Bereavement and Health*. Cambridge: Cambridge University Press, 1987.

Strudwick, N. *The Administration of Egypt in the Old Kingdom. The Highest Titles and their Holders*. London: KPI Limited, 1985.

——— *Texts from the Pyramid Age*. Edited by R. J. Leprohon, *Writings from the Ancient World*. Leiden: Brill, 2005.

Suaad, A. *Space Kinship and Gender* University of Edinburgh, 1987 (Ph. D. Dissertation).

Taifel, H. 'Social Categorization, Social Identity and Social Comparison.' In *Differentiation between Social Groups*, edited by H. Taifel, 61-76. London: Academic Press, 1978.

Tainter, J. A. *The Collapse of Complex Societies*. Cambridge: Cambridge University Press 1998.

——— 'Mortuary practices and the study of prehistoric social systems.' In *Advances in Archaeological Method and Theory*, edited by M. B. Schiffer, 105-41. New York: Academic Press, 1978.

Taylor, J. H. *Death and the afterlife in Ancient Egypt*. London: British Museum Press, 2001.

Taylor, L. *Mourning dress: a costume and social history*. London Allen and Unwin, 1983.

Thompson, J. B. *Studies in the Theory of Ideology*. Berkley: University of California Press, 1984.

Thompson, J. W. *Economic and Social History of the Middle Ages*. New York: Frederick Ungar Publishing Co., 1966.

Thucydides, *History of the Peloponnesian War.* Translated by C. F. Smith. London: W. Heinemann Ltd. 1962.

Tobin, V. A. *Theological Principles of Egyptian Religion*. New York: Peter Lang, 1989.

Traunecker, C. *The gods of Egypt*. Translated by D. Lorton. Ithaca Cornell University Press, 2001.

Trigger, B. G. *Beyond history: the methods of prehistory*. New York: Holt, 1968.

——— *Early Civilizations: Ancient Egypt in Context*. Cairo, 1993.

——— 'Monumental Architecture: A Thermodynamic Explanation of Symbolic Behaviour.' *World Archaeology* 22 (1990): 119-32.

Trigger, B. J. et al., *Ancient Egypt: A Social History*. Cambridge: Cambridge University Press, 1983.

Turner, J. C., K. J. Reynolds, S. A. Halsam, and K. E. Veenstra. 'Expressing and Experiencing Individuality and the Group.' In *Individuality and the Group*, edited by T. Postmes and J. Jetten. London: Sage Publications, 2006.

Turner, V. 'Encounter with Freud: The making of a comparative symbologist.' In *The making of psychological anthropology*, edited by G. D. Spindler and J. W. M. Whiting, 558-83. Berkeley: University of California Press, 1978.

Turner, V. W. *The forest of symbols: aspects of Ndembu ritual*. Ithaca: Cornell University Press, 1967.

Tyldesley, J. A. *Hatchepsut: the female pharaoh*. London: Penguin, 1996.

Valbelle, D. 'Craftsmen.' In *The Egyptians*, edited by S. Donadoni, 31-59. Chicago: The University of Chicago Press, 1997.

Vandersleyen, C., and H. Altenmüller. *Das alte Ägypten*. Berlin: Propyläen Verlag, 1975.

Vandier, J. *Manuel d'archéologie égyptienne*. vol. 6. Paris: A. et J. Picard, 1978.

——— *Manuel d'archéologie égyptienne*. vol. 4. Paris: A. et J. Picard, 1964.

Velde, H. Te. 'Scribes and literacy in ancient Egypt.' In *Scripta Signa Vocis*, edited by H. l. J. Vastiphout, K. Jongeling, F. Leemhuis and G. J. Reinink, 253-64. Groningen: Egbert Forsten, 1986.

Velleman, J. D. *Practical Reflection*. Princeton: Princeton University Press, 1989.

Verhoeven, U. 'The Mortuary Cult in Ancient Egypt.' In *The World of the Pharaohs*, edited by R. Schulz and M. Seidel, 481-90. Cologne: Könemann, 1998.

Verner, M. *Abusir-I: The Mastaba of Ptahshepses*. Prague: Charles University-Prague, 1977.

Vernus, P. 'La formule 'Le souffle de la bouche' au Moyen Empire.' *Revue d'Égyptologie, Le Caire* 28 (1976): 142-42.

——— 'Name.' In *Lexikon der Ägyptologie,* vol. 4, edited by W. Helck, E. Otto and W. Westendorf, cols. 320-23. Wiesbaden: Otto Harrasowitz, 1980.

Vogelsang-Eastwood, G. *Pharaonic Egyptian Clothing*. Leiden: Brill, 1993.

Waldrop. M. M. *The Emerging Science at the Edge of Order and Chaos*. New York : Simon and Shuster

Walsem, R. Van. Bookreview : Dominicus, B.'Gesten und Gebärden in Darstellungen des Alten und Mittleren Reiches' 1994, *Bibliotheca Orientalis* 55 (1998): 125-29.

——— *Iconography of Old Kingdom elite tombs: analysis and interpretation, theoretical and methodological aspects*. Leiden and Leuven: Peeters, 2005.

——— *Leiden MastaBase*: Peeters/Leuven, 2008.

——— 'Sense and Sensibility. On the Analysis and Interpretaion of the Iconography Programmes of Four Old Kingdom Elite Tombs.' In *Dekorierte Grabanlagen im Alten Reich*, edited by M. Fitzenreiter and M. Herb, 277-332. London: Golden House, 2006.

——— 'The Struggle Against Chaos as a 'Strange Attractor' in Ancient Egyptian Culture.' In *Essays on Ancient Egypt in Honour of Herman Te Velde*, edited by J. van Dijk, 317-42. Groningen: STYX Publications, 1997.

Walthall, A. ed. *Servants of the Dynasty:Palace Women in World History*, Berkeley: University of Californiua Press, 2008.

Warburton, D. A. *Macroeconomics from the Beginning, Civilisations du Proche-Orient*. Neuchatel: Recherches et Publications, 2003.

Ward, W. A. ‚Lexicographical miscellanies.' *Studien zur Altägyptischen Kultur*, 5 (1977): 265-69.

——— Index *of Egyptian Administrative and Religious Titles of the Middle Kingdom*. Beirut: American University of Beirut, 1982.

Weber, M. *Beiträge zur Kenntnis des Schrift- und Buchwesens der alten Ägypter*. Köln: 1969.

Webster's New Third International Dictionary:Unabridged. Chicago: G. and C. Merriam Co., 2002.

Weeks, K. 'Art , Word, and the Egyptian World View.' In *Egyptology and the Social Sciences*, edited by K. Weeks, 59-81: The American University in Cairo Press, 1979.

——— *Mastabas of Cemetry G 6000*. Edited by P. Der Manuelian and W. K. Simpson. vol. 5, *Giza Mastabas*. Boston: Museum of Fine Arts, Boston, 1994.

Weeks, K. R. 'Preliminary report on the first two seasons at Hierkonpolis. Part II: the Early Dynastic palace.' *Journal of the American Research Center in Egypt*, no. 9 (1971-2): 29-33.

Wengrow, D. *The archaeology of early Egypt: social transformations in North-East Africa, 10,000 to 2,650 B.C.* Cambridge: Cambridge University Press, 2006.

Wente, E. F., and S. E. Meltzer. *Letters from Ancient Egypt.* Atlanta: Scholars Press, 1990.

Werbrouck, M. *Les Pleureuses dans l'Égypte ancienne.* Bruxelles: Fondation Reine Élisabeth, 1938.

Westendorf, W. ‚Die Anfänge der altägyptischen Hieroglyphen.‘ In *Frühe Schriftzeugnisse der Menschheit,* 56-87. Göttingen: Vandenhoeck u. Ruprecht, 1969.

Whitehead, A. N. *Religion in the Making.* New York: Fordham University Press, Reprinted 1996.

Wiebach, S. *Die ägyptische Scheintür, morphologische Studien zur Entwicklung und Bedeutung der Hauptkultstelle in den Privat-Gräbern des Alten Reiches.* Hamburg: Verlag Borg GmbH, 1981.

——— 'False Door.' In *Oxford Encyclopedia of Ancient Egypt,* vol. 1, edited by D. B. Redford, 498-501. Oxford: Oxford University Press, 2001.

Wild, H. *Le Tombeau de Ti: La Chapelle.* vol. III. Le Caire: L'Institut français d'archéologie orientale, 1966.

——— *Le Tombeau de Ti: La Chapelle.* vol. II. Le Caire: L'Institut français d'archéologie orientale, 1953.

Wildung, D. ‚Besucherinschriften.‘ In *Lexikon der Ägyptologie,* vol. 1, edited by W. Helck, E. Otto and W. Westendorf, 766-67. Wiesbaden: Otto Harrassowitz, 1975.

——— ‚Erschlagen der Feinde.‘ In *Lexikon der Ägyptologie,* vol. 2, edited by W. Helck, E. Otto and W. Westendorf, 14-15. Wiesbaden: Otto Harrassowitz, 1977.

Wilkinson, R. H. *The complete temples of ancient Egypt.* New York: Thames and Hudson, 2000.

Wilkinson, T. A. H. *Early Dynastic Egypt.* London: Routledge, 1999.

——— 'Social Stratification.' In *Oxford Encyclopedia of Ancient Egypt,* vol. 3, edited by D. B. Redford, 301-05. Oxford: Oxford University Press, 2001.

——— *State formation in Egypt: chronology and society.* Oxford: Tempus Reparatum, 1996.

Willcocks, W. 'Egyptian Irrigation'. London: Spon Ltd.

Willems, H. O. 'Food for the dead.' In *Pap Uit Lemen Potten,* edited by W. H. van Soldt, 98-108. Leiden: Schap Publications XI, 1991.

Williams, R. *Resources of hope: culture, democracy, socialism.* New York: Verso, 1989.

Williamson, J. *Decoding Advertisements: ideology and meaning in advertising.* London: Marion Boyars, 1978.

Wilson, J. A. 'The Artist of the Egyptian Old Kingdom.' *Journal of Near Eastern Studies* 6 (1947): 231-49.

——— *The Burden of Egypt: an Interpretation of Ancient Egyptian Culture.* Chicago: University of Chicago Press, 1956.

——— 'Funeral Services of the Egyptian Old Kingdom.' *Journal of Near Eastern Studies* 3 (1944): 201-18.

Windus-Staginsky, E. *Der ägyptische König im Alten Reich, Marburger altertumskundliche Abhandlungen* 14. Wiesbaden: Harrassowitz Verlag, 2006.

Wittgenstein, L. J. *Philosophical Investigations.* Edited by G. E. M. Anscombe and R. Rhees. Oxford: Blackwell Publishers, 2001.

Wreszinski, W. *Atlas zur ägyptischen Kulturgeschichte.* Leipzig: J. C. Hinrichs, 1914.

Žabkar, L. V. *A Study of the Ba Concept in Ancient Egyptian Texts. Studies in Ancient Oriental Civilization* (34). Chicago: The Oriental Institute 1968.

Zandee, J. *Death as an enemy, according to ancient Egyptian conceptions.* Leiden: E. J. Brill, 1960.

Ziegler, C. *Le Mastaba d'Akhethetep, Musée du Louvre Éditions.* Louvain: Peeters, 2007.

Zijlmans, K., and K. R. van Kooij. *Site-seeing: places in culture, time and space.* Leiden: CNWS Publications, 2006.